The Natural Gas Industry
in Appalachia

SECOND EDITION

The Natural Gas Industry in Appalachia

*A History from the First Discovery to the
Tapping of the Marcellus Shale*

Second Edition

David A. Waples

McFarland & Company, Inc., Publishers
Jefferson, North Carolina, and London

LIBRARY OF CONGRESS CATALOGUING-IN-PUBLICATION DATA

Waples, David A., 1958–
The natural gas industry in Appalachia : a history from the first
discovery to the tapping of the Marcellus Shale / David A. Waples. — 2nd ed.
p.   cm.
Includes bibliographical references and index.

ISBN 978-0-7864-7000-6
softcover : acid free paper ♾

1. Gas industry — Appalachian Region — History — 20th century.
I. Title.
HD9581.U53A8668 2012   338.2'72850974 — dc23   2012010698

BRITISH LIBRARY CATALOGUING DATA ARE AVAILABLE

On the cover (*left to right*): 1959 Oil Well Shooting Demonstration
(*courtesy National Fuel Gas Company*); Marcellus Drilling Rig
(*courtesy Seneca Resources Corporation*); gas production units
or "separators" at a Marcellus gas well (*author's collection*)

Manufactured in the United States of America

McFarland & Company, Inc., Publishers
Box 611, Jefferson, North Carolina 28640
www.mcfarlandpub.com

To the memory of my parents,
and the dreams of my children.
And to Nathan, who taught me that
everything old can be new again.

Acknowledgments

I am not a professional historian. I'm just a writer. Writing history is not an exact science, and undeniably it is a subjective experience even among the best intentioned. Telling of a past where one was not present reminds me of the allegory of Plato's Cave in which prisoners in the cave are held captive with their backs to a fire providing the only light. Unable to turn their heads, they must define the real world based upon only the shadows cast upon the wall in front of them. This definition of reality based upon silhouettes is fraught with assumptions and potential errors in judgment. Despite the investigation of the past by the most industrious researchers, perhaps nothing could ever replace experiencing history more than living through it. I keep this in mind as I write about the activity of thousands of people whose lives and contributions to the natural gas industry — though well documented — can never be completely or accurately measured. Though different historical accounts cited in this volume sometimes contain conflicting information, any inaccuracies in fact or in judgment contained within are solely the responsibility of the author.

As all authors know, and most people should know, any significant accomplishment is never reached without the help of others. And I had plenty. I would like to thank the employees, retirees, and management of National Fuel Gas Company, who have given me a career and interest in the industry, as well as the initial push into researching the early natural gas business and access to many historical documents and photographs. I am also indebted to Susan Beates, curator of the Drake Well Museum in Titusville, Pa., for helping me wade through the great volume of published and unpublished material written on the natural gas industry. Thanks go as well to Fred Previts of the Youngstown Center for Labor and Industry in Youngstown, Ohio, and Ed Reis of the George Westinghouse Museum in Wilmerding, Pa. All are wonderful museums that Americans should visit to better understand how the energy and manufacturing industries created the power and wealth of the industrial age. I am especially grateful to Carl Carlotti of National Fuel Gas Company in Erie, Pa., Marc Gura of Equitable Resources in Pittsburgh, Pa., Elmore Lockley of Peoples in Pittsburgh, Pa., Terry Bishop of Dominion East Ohio in Cleveland, Ohio, Robert Fulton, of Dominion Hope in Clarksburg, W.Va., and the late C. Hax McCullough for their assistance in obtaining information and industry photographs. Thanks also go to Patrick Jarrell of Universal Well Services, Meadville, Pa., for arranging for additional photographs for the second edition and Doug Hartle for an extensive tour of Marcellus well sites. Also, special thanks to those who reviewed drafts of the chapter on the Marcellus Shale, especially William Brice, Matt Cabell, Art Coon, and Helene C. Maichle, Esq. Their friendship and expertise is invaluable. An eternal appreciation to the late John Comet, past president of United Natural Gas Company in Oil City, Pa., who provided much inspiration. And, most important, completion of this book could never be achieved without the love and support of my wife Barbara, who, with her inexhaustible patience, helped me to keep my eye on the prize.

This book is built on the vast work of numerous historians and writers who documented the early natural gas industry in illustrious fashion, making my effort a joy. It is my pleasure to attempt to tell it all again on their behalf. And this effort is also dedicated to the thousands of devoted individuals—plutocrats and pipe fitters, meter readers and marketers, roughnecks and rascals—who built a vast new industry up from a hole in the ground.

Contents

Preface to the First Edition

A Well of One's Own

When northwestern Pennsylvania gave birth to the commercial petroleum industry in 1859, the great oil rush that followed christened the black gold as the newborn prince of energy. Nearly a century and a half later, oil rules the energy world, and the United States imports more than one-half of its domestic consumption.[1] Producing countries' governments reign by its value. Consuming countries' economies are subject to its price. Wars are fought over the liquid carbon prize that once was only a greasy nuisance in Appalachian creeks. But while oil remains the critical lifeblood of the industrial world, petroleum's invisible twin, natural gas, delivered from the same earth mother, became the oft-ignored stepchild of the American energy industry. By strict definition, natural gas is often mislabeled as petroleum's byproduct. Long desired to be recognized as a full-fledged member of the hydrocarbon family, natural gas has been mostly a footnote in oil's history. Not until the early twenty-first century, with the development of ample supplies of domestic shale supplies, has natural gas found a room of one's own in America's energy home.

Living in the shadow of the oil industry, few know that after several accidental discoveries, natural gas was first commercially used in the United States in Fredonia, N.Y., in 1821, nearly four decades before oil was first drilled, less than seventy miles south in Titusville, Pa. The great boom and bust oil rush brought all eyes to western Pennsylvania, including the likes of future petroleum tycoon John D. Rockefeller. The lust for oil also resulted — neither intended nor desired — in the discovery of enormous supplies of petroleum's transparent partner. Although the next half-century was the epoch of oil exploration in the Appalachian basin, the great oil fields were quickly drained. The coming of the twentieth century turned the reins of discovery over to natural gas, even in oil's birthplace. Amazingly, according to the U.S. Geological Survey, by the end of 1906, the value of Pennsylvania's natural gas was greater than the worth of the Keystone State's petroleum.[2] Natural gas as an American energy source was born and bred in Appalachia, and until a century after its first useful discovery, the product was largely considered a local resource, of little use in far off municipalities, and appallingly wasted.

Like Romulus and Remus, the twin fossil fuels of oil and natural gas founded energy's Rome from the Appalachian wells that gave suckle to the nascent industries. However, one sibling proved victorious in getting most of the press. Even today, nat-

1

ural gas stands both literally and figuratively as oil's doppelgänger, though the nation's gas supply is produced almost entirely in North America and provides the United States with 25 percent of its energy needs, heating six out of ten homes.[3] The world's original "oil region," however, quietly enjoyed the benefits of its ghostly double long before the rest of the nation.

Though many well-researched volumes document the development of the petroleum industry, this work is the chronicle of a vital American enterprise that began as a significant force of its own in the Appalachian states in the mid-nineteenth century. Because the natural gas business was largely a regional affair prior to World War II and took a supporting role to oil, there has been little attention paid to its individual development. The natural gas industry spread through various finds, most accidental, and those who were able to harness the specter fuel without peril used the product in a limited fashion. Before proper utilization techniques and sufficient consumer demand were developed, an incalculable amount of efficient energy was obscenely squandered in the search for oil, as billions, if not trillions, of cubic feet of natural gas were blown off into the atmosphere or carelessly flared—a fact not widely appreciated until massive shortages affected the nation's industrial production in times of war, and, eventually, damaged our own personal pocketbooks.

The natural gas industry evolved in three main segments: exploration (drilling and producing natural gas wells), transportation (moving the product through long-distance pipelines), and distribution (dispensing the fuel through local utility networks). For that reason, this work does not approach the history of the Appalachian natural gas industry in a purely chronological fashion. Chapter One, "Burning Springs," discusses the first natural gas discoveries in the 1800s and how innovative entrepreneurs used the fuel. Chapter Two, "The Gas Light Era," depicts the artificial gas industry which arrived first on the scene, providing lighting. The artificial gas was produced in the midst of natural gas discoveries in the Appalachian region, but ultimately eclipsed by the natural product. Chapter Three, "Pew, Westinghouse, and the Iron City," outlines the first major manufacturing uses of natural gas. The discoveries and innovations by gas industry pioneers provided the clean-burning product that supplanted Pittsburgh's thirst for industrial fuel previously dominated by more expensive and pollution-generating coal. Chapter Four, "The House That John D. Built," details the expansion of an Appalachian natural gas network, largely initiated by Standard Oil interests, that transformed the spotty, isolated usage of the new fuel into major regional markets. Chapters Five, "From the Ground Down," Six, "Hidden Highway," and Seven, "The Gas House Gang," illustrate the development of the three major industry segments respectively: the exploration and production of natural gas in the Appalachian province; creation of a long-distance interstate pipeline network, innovation of gas transportation compression, and invention and expansion of natural gas storage; and maturation of industrial, commercial, and residential gas markets through utility distribution in the region. Chapter Eight, "Expansion, Crisis, and Recovery," describes the evolvement—growth, regulation, shortage, and deregulation—of the Appalachian natural gas industry since its major source of supply shifted from local wells in the 1950s to new discoveries of natural gas in the southwestern United States and Gulf of Mexico in the latter twentieth century. Finally, Chapter Nine, "Back to the Future," is a comprehensive description of the new Appalachian natural gas industry, beginning with the development of the first unconventional Marcellus gas well and the rapid growth of shale gas that is transforming the domestic fossil fuel industry, including all the controversy of hydraulic fracturing and promise of ample clean energy supplies.

Natural gas is now prevalent in most populated markets in the United States and is in public favor for its environmentally benign characteristics over its rival energies. It provides not only residential space heating, water heating, cooking, clothes drying, and fuel for thousands of industrial processes, but also is increasingly desired for clean-burning electrical generation, filling the void left by the lack of new coal, oil, and nuclear power facilities. The natural gas industry has survived opposition from rival fuels, control by major energy monopolies, severe shortages, shortsighted federal price controls, awkward steps toward deregulation, and is now spinning in a whirlwind of environmental protest. As natural gas is perceived as an attractive bridge fuel in the twenty-first century until new, perhaps unconventional, energy technologies are developed, the innovative inventions of energy pioneers, shrewd entrepreneurial ventures of Gilded Age titans, and lessons of a wasteful past loom in our minds. The history of the natural gas industry in Appalachia is a portrait of the American spirit itself—bold, fearless, dangerous, adventurous, and occasionally reckless. It was a quest for discovery of new frontiers, opportunity for building unprecedented wealth, and, in the end, a chance to better the human condition.

Preface to the Second Edition

When the first edition of *The Natural Gas Industry in Appalachia* was published in 2005, it closed with an understatement that geologists thought that the amount of natural gas still undiscovered in the mountainous basin was "vast." Most of this fuel, however, was located in geologic formations scientists knew about for years, but the enormous quantities were considered "unconventional" reserves because traditional drilling methods were unable to easily extract these fossil-fuel treasures locked away far beneath the surface of the earth. Thanks to drilling technology employed in the early twenty-first century, these unconventional supplies unveiled one of the greatest natural gas plays in the world in the backyard where the industry was born nearly two centuries before.

The first commercial natural gas well was sunk less than 20 feet in surface slate in a creek in Fredonia, N.Y., in 1821 and lit a few gaslights and cooked some meals. Now, a similar shale, in a formation 6,000 to 10,000 feet below the depth of that original well, may play a major role in achieving the goal of a relatively clean, domestic energy for the United States for the next generation and beyond. The natural gas industry primarily reached its first foothold in the Appalachian region, fueled major cities that helped transform late nineteenth-century America into a major world industrial power, and forever altered how many Americans heated their homes, cooked their food, and heated their water. After a half-century of production, the region's supplies dwindled and the oil and gas industry left its crib of development for the Southwest and Gulf region that made states like Texas synonymous with oil and gas. Now America's stepchild energy source is resurging in its birthplace, due to its environmentally benign qualities, ample supply, and proximity to major energy markets. The history of natural gas is one of wonder, waste, and eventually, worthiness. Its immediate future is one of promise, profit, but also, some protest. Natural gas grew to be the favored member of the fossil fuel family, but this new energy powerhouse's extraction from the earth is not as easy as placing a wooden washtub over a shallow gas spring as it was at its inauguration in 1821. Today's extraction is novel, expensive, and complicated. The effort to harvest potential domestic, clean, and affordable energy involves potential environmental consequences that are hotly debated among experts.

The hope for the natural gas industry is an incredible reservoir of domestic fuel whose extraction can result in cleaner air, reduced carbon emissions, energy security, massive job creation, and unexpected economic gains for business, job seekers, landowners, and governments. The fear emanates largely from the legacy of earth, water, and air environmental nightmares from previous clumsy efforts to extract resources from the earth, including oil spill disasters and coal mining degradation. The environmental argument is still raging. This once quiet stepchild fuel raised in the hills of Appalachia now must reconcile the hopes and fears of a nation.

ONE

Burning Springs
The Cradle of the Industry

"Give me ae spark o' Nature's fire, That's a' the learning I desire."
— Robert Burns, First Epistle to J. Lapraik, 1786

"Mom always liked you best."
— Tommy Smothers, famous words to his brother, Dick

Sibling Rivalry

Early settlers in North America initially used wood gleaned from the bountiful forests of the New World to heat their homes, cook their food, and power their businesses. The thick woods in the Appalachians also provided plentiful construction materials for the pioneers, but much of the pristine forest was cleared to make room for development. Before fossil fuels, the lumber industry was the region's claim to fame with ample supplies of softwood pines along with hardwoods such as cherry and walnut. But the mineral richness below the land held the key to America's future growth as an industrial powerhouse. Coal was discovered in Ohio in 1755, and much of it was later mined throughout Pennsylvania, West Virginia, and Kentucky. Coal became king of energy, displacing wood as an energy source around 1890. Coal was widely used for residential and commercial heating, as well as the primary fuel for industrial processes. The solid black fuel was also tapped to produce light through manufactured gas (see Chapter Two). However, after the discovery of oil in northwestern Pennsylvania and West Virginia in the mid-nineteenth century that led to the production of kerosene, and later, the invention of the electric light, gaslights became a quaint memory of the past. Still, coal provided 80 percent of the nation's energy needs until World War I. However, coal's dominance declined to only 52 percent by 1933, due to competition by oil, gas, and hydroelectric power.[1] Coal remained the largest single energy source in most of the United States until the 1950s, and then oil became the major fossil fuel for the nation, truly transforming the industrial age.[2]

Meanwhile, natural gas, often found with oil as its "right bower," fought fiercely for its role in the energy spotlight. With methane, a compound of one carbon atom and four hydrogen atoms (CH_4) as its chief ingredient, natural gas is the ideal fossil fuel — clean, efficient, economical, and available in generous supply in North America.

Natural gas has significant environmental advantages compared to coal and oil. As a fuel, it was described in the late nineteenth century as the "brightest, cleanest, steadiest, hottest on earth."[3] When natural gas is ignited, it produces mostly carbon dioxide and water, with only trace amounts of pollutant gases. And the vaporous fuel possesses domestic security benefits over imported foreign energy. However, despite the endearing qualities of this "miracle fuel," the expansion of the stepchild natural gas industry was slow, often filled with challenges and obstacles. For a century natural gas was found primarily in rural Appalachia, searching for its place in the fossil fuels hierarchy.

God's Breath

Natural gas in its purest form is odorless and colorless, an invisible force that puzzled mankind for thousands of years. The gaseous compound is believed among many to have formed a billion years ago by thermal decomposition of buried organic matter (e.g., dead plants and marine organisms) covered with rock and mud. The theory, mentioned by J. S. Newberry in 1859, maintains that over the ages the organisms converted into a gaseous fossil fuel under intense pressure, along with coal and oil. Another possible theoretical origin of gas is inorganic. First advanced in 1834 by Virlet d'Aoust and Rozetl, the theory states that fossil fuels are part of deep crustal processes formed during the creation of the Earth. Whatever its origin, natural gas (initially given the names of carbureted hydrogen gas, natural petroleum gas, rock gas, earth gas, or the sobriquet god's or Apollo's breath) is found in porous rock formations, usually consisting of limestone or sandstone, holding gas like a sponge holds water. Non-porous rock traps the gas beneath it, securing it in underground reservoirs of stone.[4]

Natural gas was observed emitting from the earth for thousands of years waiting to be harnessed. In fact, gas and oil seeped from the ground in many places from faults and fissures, but was never put to much commercial use until the nineteenth century in the United States. Greeks, Persians, Romans, and American Indians all noted these flaming "burning springs." These "eternal fires," perhaps ignited by lightning strikes, drew worshiping pilgrims, mesmerized by the miracle flame.[5] Upon Mount Parnassus about 1000 B.C., the Greeks believed the mysterious fire to be the presence of a supernatural force. They built a temple where the priestess, the Oracle of Delphi, spoke of prophecies inspired by the fire of the gods.[6] The ruins of an old Parsee temple remain at a burning spring noted around A.D. 967 on the Caspian Sea near Baku, Russia.[7] The ancient structure was dedicated to the deity of fire. Stories of flaming rocks are mentioned in Biblical references and legends.

About 500 B.C., the Chinese found some use for these burning springs. The gas was, as in many early cases, accidentally discovered while digging for saltwater (brine) and thought to be an evil spirit. In some instances, the unexpected find ignited, with flames shooting from the boreholes, perhaps causing a massive explosion that could kill an entire crew of well diggers. By 68 B.C., two particular burning springs, one in Sichuan, China, and one in neighboring Shaanxi, became infamous where the evil spirit emerged.[8] However, the ancient energy entrepreneurs tamed some of the flaming wells, placing cooking pots over the flames. The innovative Chinese also built large carburetors that mixed the gas, and they carried the vaporous fuel away in leather bags that were used as "methane ovens."[9] By A.D. 100, the diggers were well aware of the invisible substance. Some funneled the gas from their "fire wells" through short bamboo pipes and ignited it to heat brine until the water evaporated to extract the salt crystals.[10] By A.D. 200, the bamboo tubes, also used to move fresh water in elaborate above-ground labyrinths resembling modern-day roller coasters, were insulated with mud and used to funnel the invisible gas to boiling houses where the pots of brine cooked.[11]

In Europe, the noted "Fontaine Ardente" (burning fountain), near Grenoble, France, was said to be the source for natural gas lights in the first century A.D. Also in ancient times, gas fires lighted the city of Genoa, Italy.[12] In western Asia, eternal fires in the area of present day Iraq were cited in ancient writings by Plutarch between A.D. 100 and 125.[13] Gas wells were also known in Japan in A.D. 615. Despite all these observations of natural gas, the western world would not discover the potential of the mysterious fuel until the 1820s in western New York.

Hail Fredonia — Gas Born in the USA

The first hint of natural gas in North America came from French missionaries who recorded that the Indians ignited gases in the shallows of Lake Erie and in streams flowing into the lake. Joseph de la Roche Dallion, a Franciscan missionary traveling with the Huron Indians, may have been the first to note a "fontaine de bitume" (oil and gas spring) in North America in 1627 near Cuba, N.Y.[14] In 1669, M. de La Salle, a French explorer, and M. de Galinee, a French missionary, noticed a gas spring (perhaps a sink hole filled with water with the gas bubbling upward) in the area later known as Bristol Center in Ontario County, N.Y., which they torched at the suggestion of an Indian guide — it "took fire and blazed like brandy."[15] Yale University chemist and geologist Benjamin Silliman noted in the *American Journal of Science* in 1833 that saline springs emitted "large volumes of inflammable gases ... south of Lake Erie."[16] Written documents from 1794 in Canada mention that a burning spring two miles above Niagara Falls along the Niagara River would "boil a tea kettle in 15 minutes."[17] *The West Virginia Encyclopedia* cites an incident where a traveler in the 1700s discovered gas seeping from the ground that he ignited with a flash from his rifle.[18] Both George Washington and Thomas Jefferson noted gas springs during their pre–Revolutionary War travels. During one expedition during the French and Indian War, Washington observed a site near Pomeroy, Ohio, which "the Indians said is always a fire."[19] Scouts near Macksburg, Ohio, reported seeing oil springs in 1787. On the Kanawha River near present day Charleston, W.Va., General Washington observed water that looked like it was boiling because of natural gas escaping. The ebullient burning spring was located on a 123-acre site that he found so impressive, he wanted to dedicate the land as a national park in 1775, deeding the property to the public in his will. He described the burning spring as "of so inflammable a nature as to burst forth as freely as spirits, and is nearly as difficult to extinguish."[20] Jesse Hughes, a wilderness scout, discovered another site in a sulfur spring just east of Parkersburg on the Little Kanawha River, forty-one miles above the larger river's mouth, naming it "Burning Springs Run."[21] Thomas Jefferson recorded in his *Notes on the State of Virginia* in 1781 that thrusting a lighted candle at the site produced a flame.[22] Oil and natural gas ignited at the location burned for months.

Early settlers in Ohio, Kentucky, and what would later become West Virginia, provoked unwanted natural gas and oil from shallow wells drilled for brine. Salt was a desirable product for the early Americans as it was used for tanning leather, food preservation, and livestock agriculture. In 1814, Ohio's first accidental oil discovery occurred in Noble County on Duck Creek near the Muskingum River, thirty miles north of Marietta, by a brine well driller named Robert McKee, who drilled a hole 475 feet deep.[23] Natural gas was also seeping from other brine wells in the region. A brine well drilled near the south bank of the Ohio River near Pittsburgh hit gas in 1820, caught fire to the salt works, and destroyed all the buildings.[24] Dr. S. P. Hildreth, who rode a horse from New England to Ohio making a comprehensive description of the geology of the Ohio Valley, documented the numerous petroleum sites. He noted in the *American Journal of Science* of 1826 that the oleaginous substance — "vulgarly called snake oil" — was being produced in a well in the Muskingum Valley along with "tremendous explosions of gas." Hildreth also later claimed the petroleum was used for medicinal, light, and lubricant purposes as early as 1830.[25]

Spring Pole Drilling — Many early natural gas discoveries were conducted by a process comparable to this "spring pole" method, often in an effort to find salt water. The unintentional finding of the explosive gas instead of brine occasionally led to disastrous outcomes (courtesy Drake Well Museum, Pennsylvania Historical and Museum Commission).

The first saltwater well in the Kanawha Valley in present day West Virginia was dug by hand in 1779. In 1806, both oil and gas were discovered in a brine well by brothers David and Joseph Ruffner in the Great Kanawha valley near Washington's Burning Springs site. Unsatisfied with the results, the brothers decided to bore a hole similar in size to those drilled for powder blasting.[26] The Ruffners drilled with a "spring pole" device, and were among the first to develop hard rock drilling tools, including a long iron drill with a two-and-a-half-inch chisel, drilling jars, and well casing (first made out of a hollowed-out sycamore log).[27] Near Charleston, W.Va., Captain James Wilson reportedly discovered natural gas in 1815, looking for brine. One story goes that he claimed to drill "clear to hell" to get good brine, but hit a gas gusher instead.[28] The area was described as "a tract of several rods in extent, near the river bank, so charged with it [gas] that on making shallow cavities in the sand, and applying a firebrand, it immediately becomes ignited, and burns with a steady flame for an indefinite period, or until extinguished by covering it with sand."[29] Women used the gas to boil their water when washing clothes, and boatman cooked their food with it. Salt makers diverted undesirable oil from the spring to the nearby Kanawha River, and it became known as "Old Greasy" to the boatmen.[30] Oil historian J. T. Henry wrote:

> The boatmen, a rude but jolly race, often amuse themselves by tracing a circle in the sand around some one of the company unacquainted with the mystery, and applying fire, a flame immediately springs up as if by magic around the astonished wight, which being entirely confined to the circle traced, adds much to his terror, and increases the delight of his boisterous companions.[31]

Likewise, Kentucky's oil and gas industry also began mistakenly in 1818 when drillers found oil and gas while initially searching for brine.[32] In 1819, a saltwater well digger named Martin Beatty of Virginia drilled in southeast Kentucky on the South Fork of the Cumberland River in what is now McCreary County. He struck oil instead of brine, and the unwanted oleaginous substance ruined the salt well, leaked into the river, and caught fire.[33] It was plugged and forgotten until 1873, when the well then produced commercial quantities of oil.[34] A decade after his first well, Beatty was drilling on March 11, 1829, on a farm on Rennox Creek near Burkesville, vowing, "I will strike salt or strike hell." He hit neither when he drilled through a limestone layer into a pool of oil and gas that is known as the "Great American" well, Kentucky's first gusher. The stream of black ooze and gas rose at least fifteen feet high, the oil igniting on the nearby Cumberland River, burning for miles.[35] According to a story in the *Burkesville Herald*, Beatty supposedly proclaimed: "I've struck it; I've struck it; I've struck hell itself. May God have mercy on me."[36] The oil flow lasted three weeks, and eventually oil was bailed or pumped from the well until 1860, and shipped in wooden barrels by barge on the Cumberland River. The product was bottled and sold for fifty cents under name "American Oil," as the "sovereign remedy for all the ills that flesh is heir to."[37]

In the 1820s, gas springs observed by settlers near the shores of the Lake Erie halfway between Erie, Pa., and Buffalo, N.Y., gave birth to a new use for the ancient wonder. Fredonia, N.Y., known for its verdant vineyards near the shores of the Great Lake, became the mother of an industry. Gas escaping from the shallow slate in Canadaway Creek that flowed through the western New York town was noticed for years. Popular lore of the recognition of gas on the creek includes various versions ranging from a traveler igniting the gas with his tobacco pipe to young boys throwing burning embers from a family picnic across the creek and seeing flames erupt. Despite the dubious verisimilitude of the yarns, the gas bubbles from Canadaway Creek soon produced more than curiosity.

In 1821, William Aaron Hart (1797–1865), an enterprising gunsmith, decided to convert this legend into a useful product. After noticing gas bubbles from a failed water well, Hart drilled a seventeen-foot hole in the shale of the creek, seeking natural gas. After two earlier attempts failed, Hart's third try to "kick in" the well succeeded. He then drilled an inch-and-a-half bore another ten feet and capped the gas in a cistern-like hole with sheet metal, used as a rude gasometer (gasholder), collecting eighty-eight cubic feet of gas in twelve hours.[38] Hart, a Connecticut native who moved to Fredonia in 1819, provided gas service through three-quarter-inch lead pipe to some local stores and buildings around 1825, including Abell House, an inn at Fredonia, which used the gas not only for lighting, but also to cook food.[39] Lead pipes supplied gas to tin tubes crimped into a "fishtail" shape for about 100 crude gaslights, costing about $1.50 a year, half the cost of tallow candles, which along with Sperm Whale oil, previously provided artificial lighting.[40] In a few major cities on the East Coast, the fuel for lighting some urban area streets was provided by the burgeoning manufactured gas industry, which generated an illuminating, though sooty gas from heated coal. Published after the Fredonia experiment, Chautauqua County's oldest newspaper, the *Fredonia Censor*, boasted on August 31, 1825: "What Village can compare with Fredonia? There are now in this village, two stores (one a grocery), two shops and one mill, that are every evening lighted up with brilliant gas lights as are to be found in any city in this or any other country." The newspaper added, "What adds to the value of this gas above that manufactured [gas], is, that it is entirely void of any offensive smell when burning."[41] This environmentally benign character of natural gas remains a positive attribute of the fuel today. The article's editor hoped that Fredonia's gas well would last for ages. It did not.

Ruffner Well — The cable tool method of drilling is traced to a brine well by brothers David and Joseph Ruffner at Great Kanawha Valley begun between 1806 and 1808 near George Washington's Burning Springs site in West Virginia. This roadside marker is located near the Kanawha River (courtesy Drake Well Museum, Pennsylvania Historical and Museum Commission).

According to local legend, the effort did not go unnoticed. The word spread across the scientific world. Baron Alexander von Humboldt, a European geologist, called the discovery and use of natural gas in the area "the eighth wonder of the world."[42] Fredonia was on the stagecoach line between Buffalo and the West, and travelers passing through became aware of this community lighted by natural gas. In 1825, French General Marquis de Lafayette, who fought in the Revolutionary War with George Washington, arrived in Fredonia at 2 A.M. on June 4, 1825. According to an account by one resident, Lafayette was en route to Dunkirk, where an American sloop of war awaited to bring him to Buffalo. On his second and final visit to the United States, the French general was brought to a reception held in his honor despite the early hour. "A great throng had gathered to greet his arrival at Fredonia, including the military company of the village.... Refreshments were served, even at this untimely hour, by the light of natural gas."[43] Although tradition has it that Lafayette was in awe by the gaslights, other historians suggest that if he saw gaslights, he probably did not know what they were since natural gaslights were unknown at the time.[44]

Still, though gas was found accidentally in other places, most consider Fredonia as the site for the first commercial use of natural gas and the birthplace of the American natural gas industry. And in 1858, the state of New York authorized the Fredonia Gas Light & Water Company as the first natural gas corporation in the United States. The company operated both the original well and others that were subsequently discovered beginning in 1850, extending the life of the gas another thirty-five years.

Beacon of Gas— The Barcelona Lighthouse

A few years after Hart's first well, the gas entrepreneur had a hand in the second milestone of the natural gas industry — the world's first natural gas navigational beacon. Hart continued his quest by supplying natural gas from another section of a bubbling creek to a lighthouse owned by the U.S. government in Barcelona, N.Y., outside of Westfield, about twenty miles west of Fredonia. At that time, Barcelona was a thriving

Fredonia Well — The Daughters of the American Revolution placed a boulder and bronze tablet near the site of the first commercial natural gas well on the east bank of the Canadaway Creek on West Main Street in Fredonia, New York, during a centennial celebration in 1925 (courtesy National Fuel Gas Company).

Lake Erie port with a great volume of ships coming in and out of Portland Harbor. Whale oil was the standard illuminant for lighthouses for some time, and oil lamps were specified and installed in the Barcelona beacon. Natural gas seeped from Tupper Creek about three-quarters of a mile away (known as Ottaway Park) for years—the petroleum-like smell often making visitors to the area sick—but there seemed no practical use for the gas.[45] Hart and a few other entrepreneurs, including an influential Chautauqua County judge, placed a fish barrel, then a cone-shaped masonry structure over the gas spring, which served as a gasometer.

The group hollowed out pine logs, and extended a wooden pipeline one-half mile to the lighthouse. One scribe predicted in 1830 that the experiment would be a failure, assuming that gas, being lighter than air, would not flow downhill to where the lighthouse was located. A previous attempt to fuel a Dunkirk, N.Y., lighthouse through one-half inch lead pipe from the Maddern gas spring reportedly had failed because the gas supply was 150 feet higher than the lakeshore.[46] However, on the night of July 5, 1830, the Barcelona Lighthouse began using natural gas as its illuminant. The gas spring provided enough fuel for 144 gas burners installed in two tiers and arranged in a semi-circle so as to appear as one bright, unwavering light.[47]

The Barcelona Lighthouse on Lake Erie in New York—lighted by natural gas between 1830 and 1859—is listed on the National Register of Historic Places. The beacon was relit by natural gas in 1962, during special ceremonies celebrating National Gaslight Day (courtesy National Fuel Gas Company).

Natural gas as a lighthouse illuminant was a success, but in 1852, a railroad routed along the lakeshore hit

Barcelona's shipping hard. The lighthouse was discontinued in 1859 when the harbor was no longer active, though the stone structure stands to this day.[48]

After his natural gas breakthroughs, Hart — who also secured the first patent for a percussion lock of a gun in 1827 — was a nurseryman until 1838, and then moved to Buffalo in 1843 and set up a business. He would accumulate a "large fortune from petroleum activities" until his death in 1865.[49]

The Family Fight for Energy Superiority

The fossil fuel sisters of coal, oil, and natural gas sought industrial, commercial, and residential markets in the nineteenth century, and the pecking order left natural gas as the black sheep of the family. The natural gas uses at Fredonia and Barcelona were anomalies. Those areas without a local supply of natural gas had no alternative but to use coal-generated manufactured gas (a.k.a. "town gas" or "city gas") that had a lower heating value, making it unsuitable for much use other than street lighting. Still, energy pioneers attempted to put the new "nature gas" to use where it was found. Natural gas was discovered in a 627-foot well, most likely by accident, in Saw Mill Run in the Pittsburgh area as early as 1830.[50] Besides gas lighting, other novel uses of the fuel were introduced. West Virginia historians assert that natural gas was moved in wooden pipes and used as a heat source by salt manufacturers at the Kanawha Salines as early as 1831.[51] Initially, brine was boiled by burning wood, and then coal when it was discovered there around 1817.[52] According to historian J. P. Hale of Charleston, "The saltwater and gas from this well were partially collected and conveyed through wooden pipes, to the nearest furnace, where they were used for making salt. For many years this natural flow of gas lifted the saltwater 1,000 feet from the bottom of the well, forced it a mile or more through pipes, to a salt furnace."[53]

Natural gas discoveries popped up all over the region, but the industry remained in an embryonic stage. Ohio's first use of natural gas was traced to an unexpected find when drilling a water well near the Muskingum River in 1836. The gas was fed from a wooden pipe to a farm nearly Findlay, Ohio, south of the western edge of Lake Erie, and ignited off the end of a gun barrel.[54] The farmer, David Foster, boiled water, roasted coffee, and illuminated his house with the invisible fuel from the earth.[55] Nearly a half-century later, another Findlay find set off a historic gas boom in 1884 based on the vast Trenton limestone gas field that stretched over fourteen counties in northwestern Ohio and twenty-one counties in eastern Indiana. In 1886, Indiana drillers sunk numerous gas wells, where much gas was wasted as the wells were ignited by their owners "lighting up the sky in vast panorama."[56] Though some oil was recovered as well, samples revealed that the petroleum had a high sulfur content, becoming known as "skunk oil." Malodorous "sour gas" wells laced with sulfur were also a plague. One of the first operators drilling for saltwater in McConnelsville, Ohio, struck a vein of natural gas laced with acrid sulfur that caused the driller Rufus Stone to exclaim, "We have drilled through into hell."[57]

In Pennsylvania, a saltwater well near Centerville, Butler County, struck gas at 700 feet in 1840. Driller John Criswell of nearby New Castle used the fuel to evaporate brine from his other wells to produce salt, much like the ancient Chinese did.[58] The following year, not far from George Washington's burning spring, gas was used for the same purpose by West Virginia saltmaker William Thompkins, who replaced coal grates under his evaporating kettles and replaced them with homemade gas burners, resulting in considerable savings in fuel costs.[59]

According to an 1872 industry publication *The Petroleum Monthly*, the first deep —1,200 feet—commercial natural gas well, first bored for oil, was drilled near Erie, Pa., in 1854, five years before the first oil well in Titusville. Though no oil was obtained, it produced brackish water and an abundant supply of gas, which was used to light a few homes.[60] In 1860, the Erie gas pool (production field) was the first such recorded in Pennsylvania.[61] That same year, the first recorded dry hole (nonproducing well) was drilled, a 500-foot well on a farm in West Millcreek Township on the shore of Lake Erie.[62] Later in 1868, H. Jarecki and Company Petroleum Brass Works— an oil well supply firm in Erie — became the first industrial user of natural gas in the nation fueled from an area well.[63] A second Jarecki well was bored in March 1871 to the depth of 700 feet and used to light the shop and heat the boilers, supplanting eight to ten tons of coal per month.[64] By 1870, natural gas light illuminated Erie, and the lakeshore city had twenty-five wells (between 500 and 700 feet) drilled specifically for gas.[65] Boilers at the Erie Water Works were heated by natural gas from an area well drilled 510 feet deep that cost $1,500. However, the savings over coal amounted to $8 to $10 a day. Other wells fueled a soap factory, a brewery, a seminary, and various homes. Proponents of the new fuel proclaimed: "There is no smoke, no dust, no ashes, and nothing to

Lighting of Findlay Well — The discovery of vast amounts of natural gas in Findlay, Ohio, in the 1880s ignited a short-lived historic gas boom in northwestern Ohio and eastern Indiana. Depicted here is the lighting of one of the massive wells, a practice later recognized as appallingly wasteful (courtesy Drake Well Museum, Pennsylvania Historical and Museum Commission).

do except turn a faucet to either shut off all heat or put on full force, in a twin-kling."[66]

In 1873, Peter Neff also began the manufacture of lampblack from natural gas—formed by the deposition of carbon resulting from the imperfect combustion of the gas—at Gambier, in Knox County, Ohio. The first two wells were drilled in June 1866, a few miles east in the Kokosing Valley, as a source of illumination and fuel. According to one account, "water was ejected with such violence as to form inter-mittent fountains over one hundred feet in height," and in the winter "the water thrown out soon covered the derrick with ice, forming a kind of chimney sixty feet in height." The gas was frequently ignited, and "the effect, especially at night, of this fountain of mingled fire and water shooting up to the height of 120 feet, through a great transparent and illuminated chimney, is said to have been indescribably mag-nificent."[67] Also around the same time, gas was being piped to Dexter City, Ohio, near Macksburg.

In a limited extent beginning in 1865, gas was also used for the manufacture of lampblack near McCoy's Station, Pa.[68] Since the 1830s, natural gas was used at New Cumberland, W.Va., above Wheeling in Hancock County, the northern most county adjacent to Pennsylvania, for forming lampblack and burning firebrick.[69] Natural gas was utilized for home heating, lighting, and powering oil pumping engines at the West Virginia Burning Springs oil fields in the mid–1860s, providing enough power for about ninety steam engines.[70] Gas was subsequently found and applied in Wellsburg, W.Va., in 1869, and also used for lighting streets in the Mountain State oil boomtown of Volcano.[71] A few years later, some oil producers piped waste gas from oil wells in Bradford, Pa., to area homes for heat and cooking when that region south of the New York State line became one of the largest oilfields in the mid–1870s.

Soldiers who had campaigned in Kentucky during the Civil War observed oil and gas seepages in the region. Gas and saltwater discoveries inaugurated a thriving salt industry in the state.[72] The first commercial gas wells in Kentucky were drilled between 1863–64 in Meade County in the north-central part of the state. Like other first experiences with natural gas, the fuel was burned to evaporate brine for salt and was later delivered by pipeline to Louisville for lighting and domestic heat.[73]

Despite numerous natural gas discoveries, only those communities near a natural gas well benefited from the high-heating value of the seemingly unlimited quantity of the invisible fuel. Though natural gas was commonly used for lighting and cooking in towns and villages in the immediate vicinity of the wells, utilization on a wider scale did not occur until after the production of large quantities of oil in western Pennsylvania.[74]

The Queen City Delivers a Prince

The search for natural gas was placed on the backburner in 1859, when the drive to find a competing fossil fuel took center stage. In the very same region where the fledgling natural gas industry began, entrepreneurs were looking for a new prod-uct — petroleum — that could be used for lighting and other aims. American Indians, as early as 1460, had utilized rock oil that bubbled up near Oil Creek in northwestern

Pennsylvania for medicinal purposes.[75] A legend of the first discovery of petroleum in western New York involved an Indian woman's effort to help her wounded husband. According to the tale, the woman found oil in a creek known as the Seneca oil spring about a mile and a half southwest of the village of Arcade in Cattaraugus County, and applied it to her husband's wounds as a balm.[76] Much later, local residents also collected oil on the banks of Marsh Run in Erie County, Pa., and in small pools among quarrying stone.[77]

Capitalizing on the ample natural availability of the "medicinal" substance, in the early 1850s, Samuel Kier, a Pittsburgh druggist, collected the "carbon" oil from saltwater wells and marketed it as "Pennsylvania Rock Oil."[78] Kier, whose first experience with oil around 1848 occurred about twenty miles north of Pittsburgh at Tarentum, Pa., put the substance in eight-ounce bottles that sold for $0.50 each, and peddled it from highly decorated wagons.[79] But, when it was discovered that oil products could be made into an illuminant and lubricant, petroleum was skimmed from area springs where New York attorney George H. Bissell helped form the Pennsylvania Rock Oil Company in 1854.[80] Bissell also claimed to use the rock oil to help cure a cold.[81] The first oil investors sent a former railroad conductor from Connecticut, "Colonel" Edwin L. Drake (1819–1880) to Titusville, and renamed the firm the Seneca Oil Company in 1858.[82] Titusville, a small logging hamlet named in 1847 after its first settler Jonathan Titus in 1796, was surrounded by forest, and only had mail communication to nearby Franklin and Meadville twice a week.[83] Though never a military man, Drake was given the title of "Colonel" to impress the backwoods population of the small community.

Nearly sixty years earlier, Nathaniel Carey skimmed crude from oil springs near Titusville in small kegs, and carried them by horse making deliveries to customers.[84] After several unsuccessful attempts to dig and mine oil, Drake, born in Greenville, N.Y., decided to bore in an oil spring — similar to how the Ruffner brothers in West Virginia drilled their salt wells—hoping for the production of the liquid black substance that could be refined for kerosene lighting. Drake partnered with a blacksmith named William A. "Uncle Billy" Smith of Tarentum, Pa., who was experienced with salt well drilling. The duo's handmade drilling equipment weighed a little more than 100 pounds and cost $76.50.[85] Many thought him "crazy," but after a year of no success, oil finally bubbled up on August 28, 1859, at the same time investors planned to shut the operation down and relieve Drake of his job.[86] Suddenly, many people became infected with "oil on the brain" (a popular tune in 1865) on the news of the event.[87] The population of Titusville (dubbed the "Queen City") shot up almost overnight to approximately 10,000 people, and land prices skyrocketed from oil pandemonium in the new "Oildorado." Oil became a synonym for gold, as writer Alex Winchell wrote in *The Petroleum Monthly* in 1871: "The very word has wrought like magic. The smell of the article has turned men crazy."[88] The creation of the oil age was not welcomed by one local preacher in Crawford County who berated Drake for taking oil from the ground, supposedly saying, "God put that oil in the bowels of the earth to burn up the world on the last day, and you, poor worm of dust, are trying to upset his plans."[89] But nothing would stop the incipient industry. A small town south of Titusville known as "Cornplanter," named after a Seneca Indian chief, was re-titled "Oil City," and refineries spread to produce kerosene.[90] In large urban areas, the kerosene refined from oil practically eliminated the use of tallow candles and eventually competed with the "town" or "city" gas extracted from coal.

Simultaneously, oil fever spread south in western Virginia (what would become West Virginia during the Civil War), where some researchers claim that a commercial oil industry was in process as early as 1819. Around the same time of Drake's effort, Dr. Robert W. Hazlett, a physician, may have drilled some of the first major oil wells early in 1859. Later, oil wells were sunk at a town aptly named Petroleum, and in Burning Springs, outside of Parkersburg.[91] According to researchers David McKain and Bernard Allen, before Drake's historic discovery, western Virginians were

Titusville Well — Colonel Edwin Drake (at right in foreground, wearing a top hat) at his first successful oil well in Titusville, Pennsylvania, along with Peter Wilson, a local druggist. Drake, a railroad conductor from Connecticut, was given the title "Colonel" to impress the local residents. The frantic search for oil led to many unexpected natural gas discoveries, many wasted due to the lack of markets and the inability to transport the product safely (courtesy Drake Well Museum, Pennsylvania Historical and Museum Commission).

operating a commercial oil well drilled by water power; were manufacturing or refining coal oil (kerosene); were selling oil in quantity as a lubricant ... had invented some of the most crucial drilling tools and methods ... were casing, piping and burning natural gas as a fuel for manufacturing, and, most importantly, had already prospected, developed and drilled the first well or wells, solely for the purpose of finding oil.[92]

Further west, late the following year after Drake's find in 1860, the first commercial production of oil in Ohio was discovered at fifty feet using the Chinese spring pole method, approximately one-half mile south of Macksburg, in Washington County in the southeastern corner of the state.[93]

The early oil business was boom or bust, and market vicissitudes drove prices up and down erratically. A town known as Pithole, located fifteen miles from Drake's well in Titusville, transformed from a farm to a thriving community of 15,000 after the discovery of oil. A drilling "wildcatter" named Thomas H. Brown, with his "mysterious witch hazel twig," doodled the rod and selected the precise spot for the famous "United States" well, and set off the Pithole boom in 1864.[94] The discovery attracted numerous investors, including southern actor John Wilkes Booth, one of the partners of the Dramatic Oil Company in Franklin.[95] Booth made no profit from drilling, but claimed infamy the following year by assassinating President Abraham Lincoln in April 1865. Six weeks after Booth's capture and killing, the well the assassin invested in produced oil.[96]

Pithole was full of wild speculation, where "gamblers plied their trade by the wayside, crying their business to the multitude, after the manner of barkers at a county fair."[97] Despite its reputation as a classic case of ephemeral "oil fever," Pithole may have been the first oil town to be illuminated by natural gas.[98] Because virtually all oil wells produce gas in some amount, the excess gas was found useful in some ways. An oil pipe was inserted near the bottom of the barrel or "hogshead," to funnel the oil either into barrels or directly into a storage tank. Meanwhile, another pipe inserted near the top flowed the gas either into the air, or it was flared. According to author William Darrah, "The flame illuminated the derrick space at night and provided a little warmth for workmen in cold weather. Thousands of lights in the oil region at night created an impressive sight."[99] The gas lighted a local Pithole hotel, Morey House, in September 1865, most likely from wells on the Morey Farm, on the slope just below the hotel, a distance of not more than 250 feet. Gas was also available to fuel two well engines on the Rooker Farm in 1866. Gas use for oil pumps was made practical by the invention of the "casing head" by L. H. Smith in Pithole. Also in 1866, the local water company changed its name to the Pithole City Water and Gas Company, advertising a "large stock of lamps, jets and cooking and heating stoves."[100]

Despite the oil gushers and the innovative use of former "waste gasses," Pithole, which had no incorporation or legal status but was just a "private development isolated in near wilderness," converted into a ghost town worthy of its name once the oil production halted almost as quickly as it started.[101] Whiskey barrels transporting oil were suddenly worth twice as much as the oil inside.[102] The people fled and a parcel of land that sold for $200 in 1865 was later dumped for $4.37 in 1878.[103] Oil was indeed a speculative commodity in northwestern Pennsylvania and oil was traded on the Titusville Oil Exchange, which opened in 1871. In 1875, the Appalachian region's greatest oil field — Bradford — was opened after a former Oil Creek driller named David Beaty moved to Warren and drilled for natural gas to supply fuel for his "impressive brick mansion" on Conewango Creek.[104] Beaty hit oil instead, and by the 1880s, the Bradford oil field supplied 77 percent of the world's oil supply. The Warren Oil Exchange was organized in 1882 to traffic the speculative product. Despite the price volatility, developers rushed to produce — often at severe cost to the surrounding environment — using the "rule of capture" to drain oil that perhaps pooled under lands leased to others. Pipelines were also created to avoid the high rates of the teamsters.[105] Until 1875, Pennsylvania produced practically all the petroleum in the United States and 88 percent of oil produced in the world.[106]

The Birth of a Stepchild Industry

Ironically, the lust for oil resulted in finding massive amounts of a sister fossil fuel — natural gas. Though often produced during the oil drilling process, natural gas was largely ignored and "shockingly wasted."[107] The first oil lease to mention gas was noted in April 1860 from B. W. Lacy to the Warren Oil Company which said, "should no oil be found in profitable quantities, but other minerals or gas be found ... they are to have ... one-fourth of the gas or other mineral."[108] But most oil prospectors found natural gas useful only because it provided the pressurization necessary to push the oil flow to the surface. In fact, natural gas is the energy that moves the oil through the rock to the borehole. Oil in the reservoir rock lies motionless if there is no natural gas in it to push it. However, the gas itself was commonly allowed to escape into the atmosphere, or flared, as it was considered a "waste product." Not until the 1930s, however, would the oil industry discover how to efficiently use gas pressure to increase the output of oil wells. Natural gas wells were often abandoned when oil was not discovered, left to blow freely. If ignited purposely or accidentally by friction, lightning, or careless open flames, they would burn for months or years, wasting much of their production capability.

Still, some oil entrepreneurs found a use for the invisible substance. The product was reportedly used on Oil Creek and Petroleum Center in Venango County, Pa., in 1862, rudely and dangerously collected in gun barrels.[109] In July 1866, a Buffalo "capitalist" intended to pipe natural gas from Garrettsville, about twelve miles from Oil City, Pa., where a promising gas strike was made the year previous while drilling for oil.[110] The following year D. G. Stilwell, a.k.a. "Buffalo Joe," drilled a gas well in Oil City near the north end of the Relief Street Bridge and piped the product into a dozen houses.[111] However, the danger from changes in gas pressures resulted in the abandonment of the project. In addition to pressure problems, the primary stumbling block to widespread use of natural gas was the lack of a safe and efficient pipeline system to move gas from the wellhead (the assembly of fittings and valves at the well) to the burner tip (a customer's appliance). But in 1870, a harbinger pipeline project became another pioneering event in the region — this time in western New York, south of the Lake Ontario shoreline city of Rochester.

Operators of a West Bloomfield, N.Y., well sought oil and deserted the drilling project in 1865 when they hit only gas at 480 feet. The Bloomfield and Rochester Natural Gas Light Company later purchased the well and built a long distance wooden pipeline to transport the gas twenty-five miles to the city. The line, constructed out of hollowed-out Canadian white pine logs, was turned on in 1872. However, consumers in Rochester found that the hotter burning natural gas did not produce as much light as their manufactured gaslight burners. In addition, the lines developed serious leaks and were later abandoned.[112] However, that groundbreaking event foretold the future of the natural gas pipeline industry (see Chapter Six).

Still, the use of natural gas as an ideal fuel grew, if languidly. Powerful gas wells were discovered in Ohio in 1871.[113] In Pennsylvania, where most of the petroleum

Wooden Pipeline — Oil drillers abandoned a well in West Bloomfield, New York, around 1865 when they found only natural gas. Innovative entrepreneurs attempted to pipe the natural gas through hollowed-out Canadian white pine logs to Rochester, twenty-five miles away. This section of wooden pipe was later unearthed in the 1930s. Though the project was largely unsuccessful, it was the foundation for future natural gas transmission (courtesy National Fuel Gas Company).

activity was centered, the Newton Well — drilled in 1872 on the A. H. Nelson farm about five miles north of Titusville in Crawford County, by a firm organized by Henry Hinckley and A. R. Williams — was estimated to have had an open flow (unrestricted volume of gas) of 4 million cubic feet daily at a pressure at seventy-five pounds per square inch (psi). Thinking the description of the "monster" well exaggerated, local scribes traveled to the site to hear noise like "a huge steam-boiler blowing off." The escaping gas through the well pipe caused an "impression upon the ears [that] became painful, and compelled us to resort to filling the orifice with a handkerchief, in order to prevent injury to the tympanum." The howling gas caused area cattle to disperse and dismissal of a school three-quarters of a mile away.[114] Later, a three and one-quarter-inch line, traveling five and one-half miles to Titusville, served approximately 250 domestic and industrial consumers.[115] In 1872, natural gas was also used in furnaces in Leechburg and Apollo in Armstrong County, Pa., and a cutlery works in Beaver

The Newton Well discovery in the so-called Dotyville Oil Pool led to the first successful transmission of natural gas — waste gas from the oil wells — through a two-inch wrought iron line, capable of carrying 80 pounds pressure per square inch (courtesy Drake Well Museum, Pennsylvania Historical and Museum Commission).

Falls, northwest of Pittsburgh, in 1876.[116] In addition, in 1878, citizens in Harmony, Pa., near Zelienople in Butler County — a community settled by fervently religious German immigrants—fueled most industry in the town with the new miracle fuel.[117]

Organized gas interests assembled in western Pennsylvania around the time of the nation's centennial. In 1874, natural gas was first used in iron making, and the next year, the Natural Gas Company, Ltd., bankrolled by future Standard Oil pipeliners Jacob J. Vandergrift and John Pitcairn, Jr., laid one of the first pipelines in Pittsburgh. It supplied natural gas to an iron mill in the northern suburb of Etna.[118] Vandergrift's United Pipelines, purchased by Standard Oil in 1884, was one of the key components of the John D. Rockefeller natural gas pipeline network operated by its behemoth oil and natural gas pipeline firm, National Transit Company (see Chapter Four).[119]

In urban areas in northwestern Pennsylvania, the primary gaseous fuel used for lighting was coal gas and the natural product was ignored. But natural gas use expanded as it flowed from oil wells to nearby homes. Some residents living near gas wells used the gas for heating and cooking purposes, "taking no concern as to the hazard — possibly because they did not realize there was any."[120] In 1885, a six-inch line from wells on the Speechley farm at McPherson's Corners, east of Oil City in Venango County, supplied enough gas for the communities of Oil City, Franklin, and Titusville (see Chapter Five).[121] The Manufacturers Gas Company then laid lines in Oil City, offering competition for the manufactured product. This formed a rate war that lasted two years, and the *Oil City Derrick* newspaper wrote: "When it was at its height consumers were informed they could burn all [the natural gas] they wanted — there were no meters—for 50 cents a month."[122] Though coal-produced gas was costly, the natural gas supply was inexpensive and plentiful. The two firms later merged and were acquired by Standard Oil interests.

Since gas was prevalent in the oil fields, innovators used the "right bower" of oil to run oil-pumping engines. Gas-powered oil pumps were first used by Chambers Green at the Mead and Baillet well, in Tidioute, Pa., in 1860.[123] In 1873, two Venango County, Pa., gas wells supplied all the boilers on the Columbia farm on Oil Creek that were used for drilling and pumping oil, saving the owners $60,000 compared to the money previous spent for coal.[124] Later, Justin Bassett Bradley (1826–1904), an oil explorer who searched for the black gold from Canada to Ohio, was attracted to the Pennsylvania oil boom and went into business with his brother Edwin Colton Bradley (1833–1913) in the Oil Creek area. The brothers were one of the early entrepreneurs who sensed the potential of natural gas. Born in Meadville in Crawford County, Pa., Justin Bradley, after drilling early oil wells in Canada, sold natural gas produced from oil wells in the Allegany Oil Field in New York, and then formed the Empire Gas Company in 1881 to sell gas to household consumers.[125] Likewise, future Pittsburgh natural gas developers Joseph N. Pew and Edward O. Emerson sold the initially worthless and discarded natural gas to oil fields as a fuel.[126] Previously, the fuel of preference to drive oil-pumping steam engines was bituminous coal, but it was expensive, causing drillers to "resort" to using gas that escaped from the wells.[127]

Gas replaced steam for oil-pumps in New York State oil fields in 1897, providing cheaper fuel ($0.15 worth of fuel for ten hours) to produce the crude. The first gas cylinder used in New York was designed by Dr. E. J. Fithian and built by the Bessemer Gas Engine Company of Grove City, Pa. Other engines were later built in Wellsville, N.Y. Compared to an individual engine for each oil well, by 1904 a single natural gas engine could power at least twenty area oil well engines, reducing drilling costs from seven to eight cents per foot with coal-powered steam to a penny per foot with natural gas.[128]

Several western Pennsylvania wells introduced natural gas for industrial establishments as a substitute for coal, principally for the iron, glass, and pottery industries. Gas was discovered again in the Pittsburgh area at Murrysville, near Monroeville, Westmoreland County, in 1878. Five years later, Pew's Penn Fuel Gas Company opened a pipeline to 16th Street in Pittsburgh from Murrysville, the first business group to supply a major city as a substitute for manufactured gas.[129] Pew and Emerson then formed the Peoples Natural Gas Company in 1885, the first officially chartered natural gas firm in the state (see Chapter Three).[130]

In 1886, Pennsylvania became an exporter of natural gas. That year, Wheeling, W.Va., factories received natural gas from the Hickory gas fields from the Manufacturers Gas Company, in Washington County, Pa., about six miles from Canonsburg.[131] Also that year, the new Wheeling Natural Gas Company laid gas pipes.[132] Additionally, the Columbia Gas Light and Fuel Company, which formed in Franklin, Pa., and received its supply from small wells in the area, built pipelines to the Ohio state line, and Standard Oil interests in the United Natural Gas Company constructed the nation's first long-distance metal pipeline eighty-seven miles from the northern Pennsylvania gas fields in McKean County to Buffalo, N.Y. (see Chapter Six).

Still, natural gas had limited applications, and outside Appalachia, it was virtually unknown. In some cases, natural gas was only an oddity. In 1887, natural gas was used for inflating a balloon in Erie, Pa., much like an oil-produced manufactured gas-filled balloon once used as a "public relations" stunt in England.[133] Gas-filled balloons were previously used during the Civil War to make observations on Confederate batteries in Virginia.[134] A coal-gas balloon trip in 1859 of 1,150 miles flew from St Louis, Missouri to Adams, N.Y., a new world record. Natural gas had the potential to attend the energy ball as an innocent, vibrant, and attractive Cinderella, but it first had to move out of the shadow of its bold stepsisters—unctuous oil and dirty coal. Petroleum author John J. McLaurin wrote towards the end of the nineteenth century the words of a gas fairy godmother: "Natural-gas, a gift worthy of poets and historians, the agent of progress and saver of labor, is not a trifle to be brushed off like a fly or dismissed with a contemptuous sneer."[135]

But long before the natural gas industry would make significant inroads in the United States, the only gas that most people knew was its romantic, but smoky, "artificial" gaseous relative that radiated a charming glow on nighttime urban streets. In many areas of Appalachia, the two vaporous cousins would be wed.

Two

The Gas Light Era
Manufacturing "Unnatural" Gas

"My tea is nearly ready and the sun has left the sky;
It's time to take the window to see Leerie going by;
For every night at tea time and before you take your seat,
With lantern and with ladder he comes posting up the street."
— Robert Louis Stevenson, *The Lamplighter*

Let There Be Gaslight

Despite the innovations in Fredonia and Barcelona in the 1820s, the natural gas industry was not an overnight success. Natural gas was neither widely available nor used. It would be half a century before the new product found a wider market. In fact, the gas industry developed both in Europe and the United States in reverse. Unlike many products that are first produced naturally and later duplicated synthetically, the manufactured gas industry preceded the natural gas industry as a going energy concern.

The route to manufactured gas, once referred to as the "soul of coal," began when Belgian physician and alchemist, Jean Baptiste van Helmont (1577–1644), became the first scientist to identify the differences between gases and air.[1] He experimented with heated charcoal that released gas in 1609 proclaiming, "I call this Spirit, unknown hitherto, by the new name of geest"—a Flemish word meaning ghost or spirit.[2] The English word "gaz," later gas, may have been suggested from the Greek word khaos (chaos).[3] A Yorkshire minister named Dr. John Clayton conducted gas experiments about 1688 by distilling "shelly coal" in animal bladders and lighting the invisible substance with a candle. Later, in 1781, a French chemist named Antoine Laurent Lovoisier discovered the principles of the gasholder, resembling a collapsible drinking cup turned upside down that rose as gas entered the bottom, as a way to capture the produced gas. He later invented the first portable gaslight by filling bags of leather, bladders, and vessels with gas.[4]

Unlike the many natural gas heating and industrial processes used today, manufactured gas was primarily used for lighting. Like a candle, which produces its own "gas" for illumination from the melted wax transforming by heat from a solid to a liquid, and eventually to gaseous form, coal would substitute for tallow. Jean Pierre Minckelen, a philosophy professor from the University of Louvain in France, invented gas lighting in 1785, illuminating his classroom with light from a gas flame.[5] A short time later, Scottish mechanic and engineer William Murdock developed a portable gaslight system for use as headlights on a steam-powered carriage. In 1792, he adapted the method for his home in Cornwall, England, and later equipped a business with gaslights in 1798, piping the gas through old gun barrels.[6] Murdock built a coal-gas works in Soho in 1802, and is considered by many as the "father of the manufactured gas industry."[7] But coal was not the only source for gas lighting. As early as 1789, French engineer Philippe Le Bon talked of making gas by distilling wood, eventually receiving a patent for the process—called a thermolamp—in 1799.[8] Le Bon then experimented with compressing an air-gas mixture before ignition, forming a kind of internal combustion engine.[9]

Gas lighting first found commercial use in British cotton mills. It was inexpensive, bright, and safer in many ways than oil lamps that could spill and spread a fire. A German national, Friedrich Albrecht Winzer (later Winsor) promoted commercial gas lighting first in Germany, then later in Britain over much "public prejudice."[10] He also proposed gas as a heating fuel. Winsor succeeded in the first public street lighting in Pall Mall in London in 1807 through sheet lead pipes. Parliament later allowed him to incorporate the National Light and Heat Company—renamed London and Westminster Gas Light and Coke Company in 1812. Westminster Bridge was lighted with gas in 1813, and, by 1815, the company had twenty-six miles of main gas lines.[11] But there were critics. Scottish writer Sir Walter Scott, considered the inventor of the historical novel, ridiculed the proponents of creating light from smoke.[12] And like Sir Scott, when France's Napoleon viewed LeBon's wood-gas lit home and gardens in Paris in 1801, he described it as a "grand folly."[13] However, Paris would have gaslights by 1820.[14] Berlin, Germany, followed in 1827.[15]

Gas Emigrates to America

In the United States, early demonstrations of gaslights took root in the early 1800s, and Pennsylvania hosted one of the first experiences in the industry. Forty years after Benjamin Franklin promoted oil lamps for street lighting in 1756, the first American gas lighting experiments were conducted by M. Ambroise & Co., an immigrant Italian fireworks maker in Philadelphia. A few years later, the first public demonstration of gaslight occurred in Baltimore by Benjamin Henfrey in 1802, and the following year he lit a huge gas lamp on a forty-foot tower in Richmond, Virginia.[16] Next, Newport, Rhode Island merchant David Melville lighted his house with coal gas in 1806, and later illuminated a lighthouse in the state at Beaver Tail, with the manufactured product. Melville also received a patent in 1813 for gas-making machinery and introduced lights at a cotton mill at Watertown, Massachusetts, and near Providence, R.I.[17] Philadelphia's James McMurtie proposed gas lighting in that city in 1815, and the following year gas lighting was installed in the Philadelphia New Theatre.[18] Despite the second Philadelphia exhibition, the city did not get its first gas works for another twenty years.

Gas lighting got off the ground again in Baltimore in 1813, when Charles Wilson

Peale, probably best known as a portrait painter of leading American Revolution figures, helped develop a pine tar or "pitch"-based gas manufacturing process producing what was known as "carbureted hydrogen gas" that was set up in a city museum promoting "Gas Lights without Oil, Tallow, Wick or Smoke."[19] Peale's museum was the first major American museum — later imitated by others such as P. T. Barnum's American Museum in New York City. However, at that time, gas lighting was still considered a novelty.

The first commercial manufactured gasworks in the United States was established in Baltimore on June 17, 1816, founded by Peale's son from Bucks County, Pa., Rembrandt Peale, also a museum owner and portrait painter.[20] The younger Peale, remembered for his portrait masterpiece of Thomas Jefferson and others of George Washington, drew upon a process to produce gas from coal, rather than pine tar, but it got off to a slow start, serving only seventy-three customers five years later.[21] Coal was expensive, but the coke by-product (a contraction of "coal-cake") was sold for heating to offset fuel costs.

At that time, there was no way to measure consumption of the invisible product, so customers were charged by estimating the number of burners they operated. By

Coke Trucks, 1930 — Coke, a byproduct of roasting coal to produce manufactured gas primarily for lighting, was also sold for more than a century for heating by companies that produced the artificial gas (courtesy National Fuel Gas Company).

1833, the Gas Light Company of Baltimore owned two miles of gas mains for 3,000 private and 100 public lamps, and began metering gas sales. The first so-called "wet meters" were imported from England and were simple, but accurate.

Over the next century, there were three principal raw materials used in manufactured gas. Coke-oven gas, used initially in the early nineteenth century, was produced by roasting bituminous coal creating gas and coke. The gas was produced often in a series of brick ovens, extracting the sulfur and phosphorus that exist in soft coals. Second, carbureted water gas was made from coke, air, steam, and oil, first patented in the United States by John and Thomas Kirkman in 1854.[22] In 1873, Professor Thaddeus S. C. Lowe perfected his carbureted water-gas set that produced superior heating and illuminating qualities.[23] The first water-gas plant was built in Phoenixville, Pa., near Philadelphia, in 1874.[24] In the water-gas process, extensively utilized by the 1880s due to its lower cost than coke-oven gas, hard coal was heated and exposed to a blast of steam, producing a combustible gas.[25] It produced two kinds of gas: "blue" or "water" gas; and oil gas that enriched the blue gas. The process used much oil, but produced twice the candlepower (a measure of light) of coal gas.[26] The United Gas and Improvement Company in southeastern Pennsylvania later bought Lowe's water-gas patents, and used much of John D. Rockefeller's oil supplies from western Pennsylvania to produce it.[27] Third, oil gas was also produced. Oil gas was first used in 1870 in Saratoga, N.Y., using naphtha or light oils to produce a better grade of gas for lighting.[28] It burned with a white flame, and when purified it was supposedly odorless.[29] The manufacture of "Pintsch gas" from oil for illumination was often supplied to railroad cars, and, in Buffalo, N.Y., in the late nineteenth century, to light the buoys that were placed in the Lake Erie harbor. All manufactured gas, however, had only about one-half the heating content of natural gas.

Not everyone embraced the creation of the "Gas Light Era" that lit streets and businesses with a charming glow from the artificial product. In the early 1800s, a New England newspaper claimed gaslights interfered with "God's divine plan of the world separating light from darkness," and would increase colds, drunkenness and depravity, embolden thieves, and frighten horses.[30] But after the initiation of the domestic manufactured gas industry in Baltimore, other cities quickly followed. Though opposed by the whale oil and tallow candle interests who obviously saw a threat to their market, New York City first used manufactured gas in 1825 funneled through tin pipes, and, in 1828, Broadway's "Great White Way"—between Grand Street and Battery—was illuminated by gaslights.[31] When manufactured gas service came to New York City, one woman refused to have the vaporous product installed in her house because she claimed it was the "breath of the devil."[32] However, by 1852, gaslights outnumbered oil lamps in the city.[33] Gaslight migrated to Boston in 1828, Louisville in 1832, and New Orleans in 1835. Philadelphia started up a gasworks at 22nd and Market streets in 1836. Philadelphia Gas Works, the current descendant of the city's first manufactured gas operations, became a city-owned institution in 1841, the first such municipal firm in the nation. PGW now provides natural, rather than manufactured gas, and is the largest municipal gas company in the United States, serving more than a half-million consumers.

By 1859, the United States had 297 manufactured gas companies that served an estimated 4,857,000 customers.[34] Multiple companies sprang up in major cities (e.g., by 1863, New York City had four gaslight firms). By 1887, *Brown's Directory of American Gas Companies* listed 130 manufactured gas companies in New York, 111 in Pennsylvania, seventy-eight in Ohio, twenty-one in Kentucky, and seven in West Virginia.[35]

Dance by the Light of the Moon

During the second half of the nineteenth century, the gas lamplighter became an indelible figure all over the country. A familiar sight in the "Gas Light Era" was a boy who ran along urban streets, lighting gas lamps. One Erie, Pa., historian wrote, "When a boy was skilled, he could do it on his bicycle without slowing down."[36] Other lamplighters used a special high-wheel cart. In the 1800s, the first coal gas used for lighting was expensive. Therefore, the so-called "town gas" was primarily used for street lamps and for middle- and upper-class homes, since only wealthier individuals could afford it.[37] Gaslights' nostalgic appeal is carried over in outdoor lamp design today, though most of the fixtures are electric.

Pittsburgh's first recorded use of gaslights was in the Lambdin's Museum in 1829.[38] Sperm Whale oil lamps first lighted the streets. After several false starts, the Pittsburgh Select and Common Council authorized the first gasworks in the city to the Pittsburgh Gas Light Company and gaslights brightened streets, hotels, and stores by 1837, the seventh American city to obtain gaslight. Competing interests ensued. By the 1880s, Pittsburgh had the unique advantage of possessing both manufactured and natural gas supplies. Inventor and electric and natural gas industrialist George Westinghouse formed the Fuel Gas and Electric Engineering Company in 1887 to manufacture gas in case his natural gas supply would run out.[39] In 1894, Westinghouse's firm bought Brunot Island on the Ohio River near McKees Rocks on which to erect a manufactured fuel gas plant, but it was never constructed.[40] Still, as many as nine former manufactured gas plants existed in hilly Pittsburgh, where the "topographic irregularity of terrain" possibly required numerous sites.[41] The firms included the East End Gas Company, Pittsburgh Gas Company, South Side Gas Light Company, and West Pittsburgh Gas Light Company.[42] In 1897, five of the largest manufacturing firms in the city merged in a new company called the Pittsburgh "Consolidated" Gas Company (incorporated in 1871), first owned by Dr. David Hostetter, and the firm constructed a new $800,000 plant on Second Avenue.[43]

Manufactured gas service spread in larger western Pennsylvania towns and various urban centers in western New York in the second half of the nineteenth century, paying good returns to its investors. The gasworks in Pittsburgh and Buffalo reportedly paid "liberal" dividends.[44] In some cases, natural gas and the "town gas" interests intersected, as they did in Pittsburgh.

The eastern Pennsylvania community of Reading followed the Commonwealth's two largest cities' experience with gaslight in 1848, and western towns like Meadville had the product by 1854.[45] Around the same time, two gas firms, the Erie Fuel Gas Company and the Erie Gas Company, initially served Erie in the northwest corner of the state. The Erie Gas Company was chartered on March 5, 1852, and the Lake Erie shore city provided gaslight on August 22, 1853, for thirty-two customers. The firm built a gasholder with a capacity of 30,000 cubic feet, laid three and one-half miles of pipe, and increased its customer load to 150 by end of the year. By 1883, the company owned twenty miles of mains, lit 425 street lamps, and signed up 800 customers.[46] Soon after that firm began service, the City Gas Company, formed in Erie in 1860, provided manufactured and later a mix of manufactured and natural gas. Other franchises operating for a time included the Erie Mining and Natural Gas Company and Pennsylvania Fuel Gas Company, both formed in 1884, and South Erie Gas Company, formed in 1890.[47] In Titusville, Pa., gas produced from benzene fueled pneumatic gaslights in 1867. The Titusville Gas Company formed between 1864 and 1865 initially to produce coal gas.[48] Natural gaslights would not illuminate city streets until 1885.[49] In 1876, the Oil City Gas Company was organized to supply that city with coal gas, filtered through lime. "Limelight," invented in 1801, produced a brilliant incandescence used for stage lighting at the time, and thus the source for the well-worn expression. Oil City was piped, the mains were laid for street lighting, and a gasholder known as the "Roundhouse" was built in 1878.[50] The natural gas firm Oil City Fuel Supply Company bought out the manufactured gas operations in 1881, though the coal plant operated until 1890. Other firms in municipalities in western Pennsylvania included companies in Allegheny, Beaver Falls, Corry, Chambersburg, Greenville, Kittanning, Indiana, Latrobe, McKeesport, Mount Pleasant, Lawrence, Sewickly, Sharpsburg, Etna, Tidioute, Warren, Waynesboro, and New Castle.[51]

Cleveland's first experience with manufactured gas began on February 6, 1846, with the organization of the Cleveland Gas Light & Coke Company. The first streetlights shined on the east side of the city on December 8 of that year, from Superior Street at the river to Erie Street, the Public Square, and Water, Merwin, and Bank streets. Cleveland's streetlights burned gas until midnight, except when moonbeams were considered adequate.[52] The Cleveland newspaper, *True Democrat*, wrote in 1849: "Our city now looks like a living place in the night.... The new gas lights give everywhere a social air, and people move about as if there was no more trouble from darkness and the evils thereof."[53] By 1850, gaslight was introduced in public buildings. When St. Paul's Church in the city was illuminated, it was suggested that it was what "all places of worship ought to be."[54]

A poem circulated to commend the experience:

> The glory of the stars and moon,
> And comets, too, may pass;
> Then let 'em go—however soon,
> For Cleveland's burning gas.[55]

The coal-gas firm applied to the city to spread gaslight to the west side in 1856. A decade later on December 28, 1866, a second coal-gas operation, the People's Gas Light Company, purchased pipes and meters of the Cleveland Gas Light & Coke Company on the west side of Cleveland's Cuyahoga River, and provided service there. The two firms served the city without direct competition until natural gas was introduced in 1903. "Bitter struggles" followed between the artificial gas companies and natural gas interests, with spurious claims that natural gas "dried out" furniture so it would fall apart.[56] But in the end, the manufactured firms selling gas for $0.75 per thousand cubic feet could not compete with lower-priced natural gas at $0.30.[57] The coal-gas firms later consolidated with the natural gas-providing East Ohio Gas

Small Gas Holder — Manufactured gas was often held in small gas holders such as this "roundhouse" brick structure built in Oil City, Pennsylvania, in 1878. This holder was 141 feet in circumference and nineteen feet high, and enclosed an inverted metal tank that sat on a bed of oil that acted as a seal. Gas was pumped into the structure during the daytime so there would be enough supply to light the streets at night. It was torn down in 1963 (courtesy National Fuel Gas Company).

Company on February 24, 1910. A Cleveland lakeshore site that contained several of the conventional water seal type of gasholders was used as a gas plant for many years, and the firm's current headquarters is located in the area.

In southern Ohio, Cincinnati also began manufacturing gas in 1846. When manufactured gas was introduced in Dayton, in 1848, it was produced from refuse grease obtained from slaughterhouses.[58] Manufactured firms also existed in various areas in northeastern Ohio, including the Ashtabula Gas Light Company, incorporated in 1873, with an original gas works that produced artificial gas from crude oil.[59] Manufactured gas also lit streets beginning in the 1860s in Canton, Youngstown, Painesville, and Akron until natural gas came on the scene toward the end of the nineteenth century. Other communities lit by gaslight included Zanesville, Steubenville, Toledo, Sandusky, Painesville, Lancaster, Dayton, East Liverpool, Findlay, and Columbus. New natural gas supplies eventually weaned the region from the coal-gas supplies.

Though efforts to introduce manufactured gas in western New York date back to 1836, the Buffalo Gas Light Company officially incorporated in 1848, the first manufactured gas firm in the Niagara Frontier region.[60] It was one of the first organized in New York under the general Act for the formation of "Gas Light" companies. Previously, other gaslight firms were organized under special acts of the legislature. Ground was broken near the Erie Canal that year, and soon the gasworks burned coal to produce manufactured gas.

Gaslights illuminated the streets of Buffalo for the first time on election night, Tuesday, November 7, 1848, when President Zachary Taylor and Vice President Milliard Fillmore proved victorious. The gas lamp district covered various downtown streets with a total of 179 gaslights.[61] According to the *Buffalo Commercial Advertiser*, the unveiling of gaslights created some "public relations" problems. The paper reported, "Several persons were detected last evening climbing the Gas Light Lamp Posts, and turning or detaching the 'Gas Cocks,' thus measurably frustrating the effort."[62] In the spring of 1859, the new company built the turret and gable frontage of the Gas Works on Jackson Street in downtown Buffalo. The ornate building was described at the time as "architecturally handsome, and ... creditable to the officers of the Gas Company."[63]

The first lighting by gas was unique and innovative. A row of five gas lamps lighted the Academy of Music, Buffalo's first theater building, and was considered "a great novelty as it was the first gas made in Buffalo."[64] The Henry Huntington Sizer Mansion, built in 1827 at the corner of Niagara Square and Delaware Avenue in Buffalo, was one of the first homes in the city lighted with manufactured gas. A newspaper account reported that at a family wedding "the young people got such a kick out of dancing by gas light that they pulled down all the shades, thus reversing the old song of the Bufaflo [*sic*] girls who came out at night to dance by the light of the moon."[65]

It was only a matter of time however, that firms like the Buffalo Gas Light Company were not the only flame in town. In December 1876, two companies for supplying gas obtained grants from Common Council. The Buffalo Mutual Gas Light Company formed in 1870, and the Buffalo Oxygen and Hydrogen Gas Company, organized in 1871 to make gas under a French patent called the Tessie du Motay "water gas" process, similar to the Lowe process. The firm "made great claims for its superiority, quality and cheapness." After a while, this project fizzled, and the company continued to make hydrogen gas carbureted with naphtha, a derivative of oil. This high candle-power illuminating gas from oil supplied railroad cars entering the city with light. Later, after that failed, a new company called the Citizens Gas Company organized to utilize some of its assets.[66]

Toward the end of the nineteenth century, there were as many as five companies serving Buffalo, causing much confusion among consumers. As competing gas works vied for business, the argument erupted against multiple gas companies serving the same area. Many claimed that a "natural monopoly" system was the best way to serve customers, contending that two sets of pipelines down the same street did not make sense. An industry document asserted: "If one company can supply the whole city, no advantage can be derived from any number of parallel lines, which must be injurious in any respect it may be viewed.... The larger the making and distribution of Gas by one set of works and supply mains, the cheaper it can be supplied to consumers...."[67]

Buffalo Gas Works — Though the natural gas industry was not an overnight success, the United States manufactured gas industry expanded rapidly. The Buffalo Gas Light Company's Jackson Street Gas Works, constructed in 1848, produced gas by roasting coal. The Norman-style architecture caused the gas plant to be later mistakenly identified as a "city armory" or a "jail." The facade of the structure still stands today and is listed on the National Register of Historic Places (courtesy National Fuel Gas Company).

The hazards of multiple pipeline networks included the fact that leaks were hard to identify and multiple companies often resulted in higher, rather than lower costs.[68] By 1899, gas was compressed to 200 psi and piped through two-inch extra heavy wrought iron pipe enclosed in concrete.[69] Leaking gas at such pressure was obviously hazardous.

Like similar consolidation in Pittsburgh, and larger and more numerous operations in Chicago and New York City, the Buffalo Gas Company incorporated in 1899 to acquire certain assets from some of the companies manufacturing gas in the city. Illustrating some critical public sentiment that naturally favored cutthroat competition, critics raised objections about the consolidation fearing the "Gas Trust" monopoly would result in higher prices.

Elsewhere in western New York, Rochester also inaugurated manufactured gas lighting in 1848, followed by Utica and Syracuse in central New York in 1849.[70] The Rochester Gas Light Company organized with capital stock of $700,000 and opened

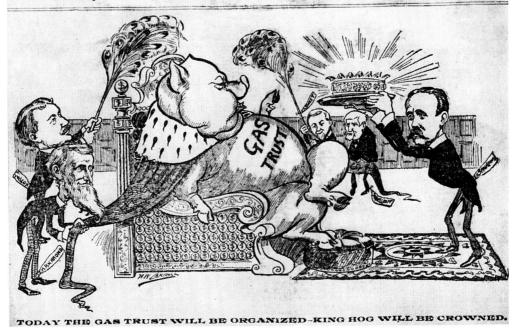

`ALO ENQUIRER` 5 O'CLOCK EDITION

Y. SATURDAY, MAY 29, 1897.   NUMBER 246

Other---They Get the Same News Service---Our Service is Exclusive

TODAY THE GAS TRUST WILL BE ORGANIZED-KING HOG WILL BE CROWNED.

Editorial cartoonists raised objections about the consolidation of manufactured gas light firms, fearing the "Gas Trust" monopoly would result in higher prices (courtesy National Fuel Gas Company).

an office and gasworks at the corner of Mumford Street and Genesee River. Later, Rochester's Citizens Gas Company incorporated in 1872, with capital stock of $500,000, along with the Municipal Gas Light Company.[71]

Auburn, west of Syracuse, built its first gasworks in 1850 and laid gas mains built out of hollowed-out logs. The community first made gas from "whale's foot," a product from a whaling fleet in Connecticut that was rapidly fading due to the exhaustion of whales, and later, produced gas from lower-priced resin from North Carolina pine trees, similar to Peale's Baltimore method.[72] The western New York town of Lockport also produced gas that way with their operations constructed in 1851, but soon converted to soft coal.[73] Other plants followed in the Finger Lakes Region including Ithaca and Geneva in 1852, Palymyra in 1856, and Penn Yan, Cortland, Homer, and Norwich, south of Syracuse, in 1860.[74]

North of Buffalo, the Niagara Falls Gas Company formed in 1859. The firm completed a coal-gas works at the foot of Niagara Street in the city the following year.[75] The *Niagara Falls Gazette* announced in May 1860, "The (gas) works were ready for operation last week and several residences, stores and hotels, where the fixtures were in readiness, were lighted Monday evening. The gas was of good quality and gave great satisfaction."[76] Later, the Niagara Light, Heat and Power Company operated a company office in the early twentieth century on Young Street with an all-glass penthouse on the roof. Gas arc lights illuminated the company's name at night.

Elsewhere in Appalachia, manufactured gas was used for lighting streets in the West Virginia communities of Charleston, Clarksburg, Grafton, Martinsburgh, Parkersburg, and Wheeling, and the Kentucky cities of Richmond, Louisville, Danville, Bowling Green, and Covington.

Manufactured gas and natural gas competitors often were at odds with one another. By 1881, natural gas from nearby wells found inroads into the markets of manufactured gas in Erie, Oil City, Sharon, Meadville, Franklin, and Warren in Pennsylvania, and in Jamestown, Salamanca, and in parts of Buffalo in New York. About 1885, experts noted that natural gas was a "serious menace" to the manufactured gas industry.[77] In response to the competitive threat, Pittsburgh manufactured gas firms attempted to keep the higher-pressure natural gas lines out of city limits. Concern over the "explosive" nature of natural gas was used in arguments in preventing the encroachment of new firms into the service territory of the manufactured companies. For example, a minor accident at George Westinghouse's pioneer natural gas well in Pittsburgh that burned two of his drillers was fodder for those who wanted to keep the new product out of the market. As author Francis Leupp recorded, "it did not prevent the wide circulation of a rumor that some laborers had been killed by gas on the Westinghouse place, and within an hour the yard was swarming with citizens and newspaper emissaries."[78] Manufactured gas was not immune from disasters either — in 1868, a manufactured gas main exploded under the U.S. Capitol building in Washington, D.C., and caused extensive damage, but no injuries.[79] Still, an additional warning put forth by the manufactured interests of The Fuel Gas Company included whether the natural gas supply would hold out considering the huge demand for the fuel if the Pittsburgh steel mills converted to natural gas from coal. Still, the production of natural gas in Pennsylvania exceeded manufactured gas by 1884.

Another obstacle for home use was the different heating values between natural gas and manufactured gas. An attempt to use natural gas for lighting in Rochester, N.Y., in the early 1870s was a fiasco due to the incompatibility of manufactured gas light burners with the hotter-burning natural gas (see Chapter Six). But eventually, many gas competitors in the Appalachian region cooperated and consolidated.

As natural gas supplies became tight in the beginning of the twentieth century, the initially natural gas-rich Erie lakeshore communities in New York built coal-gas plants. The Citizens Gas and Fuel Company evolved from the E. C. Perry & Co. in Dunkirk in 1900 to manufacture and supply gas heat in Dunkirk and Pomfret. The Dunkirk Gas and Fuel Company also incorporated that year to manufacture and sell gas. Even in Fredonia, the birthplace of natural gas and the first natural gas company, the Fredonia Gas Company opened a manufactured gas plant in 1901 that included twelve gas retorts of fire clay where coal was intensely heated to produce gas.[80]

Although manufactured gas works sprouted abundantly where there was a demand for gas lighting, along with it came environmental problems. There were pollution concerns about manufactured gas production as far back as the 1830s, with many worried that the deadly dumping of coal tar in London's Thames River would be repeated in the United States.[81] When a gas works opened in Elmira, N.Y., in 1852, citizens complained of noxious fumes from the plant.[82] A newspaper editorial from Ithaca's *Daily Republican* in December 1852, however, claimed that impurities from the coal-gas operation were "obviated" by carrying them off into the riverbed.[83] In the early 1900s, a Westfield, N.Y., church filed suit against the Westfield Gas Works for permitting a tarry fluid to escape from the facility to the lands of the adjacent property.[84] The entire plant, however, burned in 1904, leading to more drilling of natural gas wells in the area.[85]

The chemicals used in the manufactured gas process did have one unusual use in Buffalo. According to one account: "Around the first week of March people living in the immediate neighborhood of the plant would bring white blossoms to the employees of the plant who took them into the purification room and after exposure to the ammonia fumes the blossoms would turn green, a delight for the Irish on St. Patrick's Day."[86] But more prevalent, the legacy of the artificial gas plants was an environmental scar, and active clean-up efforts at various manufactured gas sites would not begin for another century. An estimated 3,000 former manufactured gas plants exist in the United States, and the federal Environmental Protection Agency stated that coal tar wastes include high concentrations of benzene, toluene, sulfur, and cyanide compounds.[87] Some experts claim there may be as many as 52,000 coal tar waste sites with impurities such as ammonia, cyanide, sulfur, and heavy metals, particularly arsenic.[88] Contaminated soil resulted in millions of dollars of environmental remediation in numerous locations that continues to the present day. Because many of the tar residuals are resistant to natural degradation in the environment, some claim they continue to be a long-term threat.[89]

Manufactured gas operations were not only dirty, but also difficult. One observer put it:

> It took a good man, and a tough man, to throw a heavy scoop-shovel full of coal into a retort without missing the door and scattering it on the gas house floor — particularly when the coal was frozen. And in the summer, the heat would become almost unbearable. Always there were smells from chemicals driven off the coal, naphthalene, familiar to most of us as moth balls, sulfur and coal tar.[90]

Though clean-burning natural gas was obviously a threat to the less environmentally desirable coal-gas operations, the real threat to manufactured gas was new energy technologies. Around the end of the Civil War in 1865, the kerosene lamp, fueled by new oil discoveries, was welcomed for economy and improved light, providing illuminating competition to gas. Carbon arc lights were first demonstrated during the U.S. Centennial Exposition of 1876, but they were no threat to the manufactured gas monopolies that depended on lighting as their primary market (e.g., when Consolidated Gas Company of New York organized in 1884, 95 percent of its market was from lighting).[91] But after Ohio inventor Thomas Edison patented the incandescent light in 1879 (the bulb for his invention was blown at Corning, N.Y., Glass Works), gas and kerosene soon lost the bulk of the lighting market to electricity. The novel electric lights would appeal to consumers as cleaner, since gaslight residue blackened the glass globe enclosures, as well as the surrounding walls and ceiling.

Coal gas—what Edison called "vile poison"—generated small quantities of ammonia and sulfur, as well as carbon monoxide, and when used indoors, made some people sick.[92] Edison criticized the gas distribution system of "sewer pipes," and devised a plan to replace gas light systems with electric lights (though one idea was to lay wires right through the present gas pipes).[93] Edison felt gas represented the dark ages, and he promoted the safety advantages of electricity, claiming manufactured gas was smelly, sooty, dangerous, and caused nearsightedness.[94] Edison said of gaslight "it is a nasty, yellow light, too, and far removed from the color of the lovely natural light."[95] Soon, electric light firms sprouted for street lighting, one of the first in the region in Elmira, N.Y., in 1878. Stocks of manufactured gas firms in New York City plunged.[96] Everyone did not embrace the switch to electric lights, especially gaslight firms. Some gasworks were phased out, such as Parkersburg, W.Va.'s Despard's Gas Works begun in 1864 by the Parkersburg Gas Light Company (later Parkersburg Gas Company) which was converted to generating electricity for lighting the streets in 1888, the first in West Virginia.[97] The gas firm first secured an injunction against the electric interests, but the state's Supreme Court nullified it.[98] The town was without light for a month or so because of the city's slowness in installing electric lights; the gas was turned off before the electricity was turned on.[99] In 1895, some residents in Lockport, N.Y., also objected to converting from gaslights to electric.[100] Still, the new electric competition caused gas companies to stop competing with each other and begin consolidating in the 1890s. For example, the majority of shares of Pennsylvania's Erie Gas Company was absorbed by a consolidated electric concern.[101] In Pittsburgh, George Westinghouse's Philadelphia Company eventually possessed both gas and electric assets. And New York City's Consolidated Gas Company merged with the Edison Illuminating Company in 1899.[102]

Despite the perfection of German Carl Auer's incandescent gas mantle made of a gauzelike cloth that improved the candlepower of gas flames in the 1890s, the gas share of the lighting market continued to decline, slipping to 15 percent by 1925.[103] Later, the charm of gaslights would only be nostalgic attractions such as in the Village of Wyoming in western New York (the town often referred to as "gaslight village") and the borough of Emlenton in western Pennsylvania.

Tanks for the Memories—The "Roaring '20s" and the Manufactured Gas Comeback

Despite the eclipse of gas by electricity in the lighting market by the 1920s, manufactured gas was down, but not out. Due to shortages of natural gas, town gas experienced a small renaissance. Once World War I was over, all of Buffalo's manufactured operations were brought under the umbrella of the Niagara Gas Corporation, officially incorporated in 1920. Despite discoveries in nearby natural gas fields south of Buffalo in North and South Collins from 1918 to 1919 and Bennington between 1918 and 1922, the supply of natural gas available to Buffalo during this period was barely sufficient to meet the demands of its customers on extremely cold days. Francis C. Brown, who first joined the Buffalo Gas Company in 1919, said later the "general opinion at the time was that the gas industry was a dead end enterprise and it was common advice to gas company employees to get out before it was too late."[104] But the manufactured

Large Gas Holder — Gas holders, such as this one constructed in the 1920s, operated on the same principle as a telescope, rising and falling at five distinct levels as it was filled with artificial gas. As gas was piped into the crown, the pressure literally raised the roof of the holder. The holder could store enough gas to heat thirty-two homes for one year, though provide only an eight-hour supply for the entire community (courtesy National Fuel Gas Company).

gas and the natural gas interests in many areas in Appalachia combined for strength and longevity.

In 1921, Iroquois Natural Gas Corporation, which served Buffalo the cleaner, natural product, was ordered by the New York Public Service Commission to augment its supply of gas by the addition of manufactured gas. In the next three decades, several municipalities used the availability of both sources of gas, as well as mixed gas (a combination of manufactured and natural gas) to meet customers' needs. By 1920, there were 966 companies in the United States engaged in supplying manufactured gas to customers, which included ninety-two in New York, eighty-one in Pennsylvania, seventeen in Ohio, nine in Kentucky, and three in West Virginia.[105]

Containing invisible gas was a challenge in the industry's early days, but not as hard as capturing a genie in a bottle. William Hart's first Fredonia well was capped with sheet metal used as a crude gasholder. The first American manufactured gas firm in Baltimore stored its vaporous supplies in large tanks constructed from wooden staves and bound with iron hoops, like giant whiskey barrels.[106] Later, larger capacity iron frame and brick holders appeared, keeping them from being blown down by strong winds. An eight-sided gasometer building constructed of bricks and tin was a Fredonia, N.Y., landmark that reportedly held both manufactured and natural gas during its life span. It eventually collapsed under the weight of winter snow in 1964.[107] Eventually, huge cylindrical steel tanks holding millions of cubic feet of manufactured, and sometimes natural gas, became a common sight in urban areas.

With the "Roaring '20s" industrial demand, the era became the peak of the manufactured gas industry in the United States.[108] In western New York in 1923, an eighty-acre site was built in a rural area outside the city limits of Buffalo to ensure an ample supply of artificial gas, one of the first major mixing natural and manufactured gas stations in the region. The crown of a gasholder spanned 210 feet in diameter. It operated on the same principle as a telescope (the design first used in London in 1861), rising to 200 feet and falling to forty feet at five distinct levels. The first forty feet of the tank contained 8 million gallons of water that acted as a seal. As gas was piped into the crown, the gas literally raised the roof of the holder. Despite the enormous size of the tanks that could store 5 million cubic feet of gas, three Buffalo area holders contained only one day's summertime need and a mere eight-hour supply in winter.[109] The new operations contained 17 million cubic feet production capacity. The Isbell-Porter Company installed the gas-making machines to make coke-oven gas, and, in 1926, a carbureted water gas set was added. According to the February 15, 2008, *Pittsburgh Tribune-Review*, Pittsburgh construction workers building a new casino on the city's north side in 2008 unearthed the foundation of two 200-foot high gasholders, one of which accidentally exploded during repairs on November 14, 1927, killing 26 people and causing massive building damage in downtown Pittsburgh.

Though mixed gas was not entirely common, it had been used before in Pennsylvania, California, Ohio, and Indiana.[110] In fact, the City Gas Company of Erie, Pa., reportedly used mixed gas as far back as 1873, blending a natural source from thirty gas wells in Erie with manufactured supplies.[111] During the first part of the twentieth century, the consolidation of the natural gas industry included takeovers of manufactured gas firms and their distribution networks. The utility companies used the mixture of gases to meet the ever-increasing consumer thirst for gaseous energy. Until the 1920s, the Pennsylvania Gas Company in Erie, Pa., was able to supply customer demands from its own natural gas production and local purchases. But following World War I, PGC also found it difficult to acquire sufficient natural gas to supply rapidly growing communities. In 1925, PGC constructed a manufactured gas purification and storage plant known as the Erie Works on a plot of land bought at Third and Wayne streets immediately south of Perry Iron Works property along the city's Lake Erie shoreline. In 1927, a 5 million cubic feet holder was added. The Lake Shore Gas Company in northeastern Ohio, which used primarily natural gas supplies, also built an additional gasholder in the Ashtabula area in 1925 that spanned 123 feet in diameter with a gas capacity of 1 million cubic feet.[112]

The concoction of natural gas from local fields and the "city gas" achieved a heating value of 900 British Thermal Units (Btu)—one Btu was the amount of heat required to raise a pound of water from 60° to 61° F at a constant pressure of 1 standard atmosphere. This led to distinguishing heat value between lower heat carbureted

Gas House — Despite many new natural gas discoveries in the region, gas shortages occurred during the World War I years. Appalachian natural gas firms added additional manufactured gas capacity to their supply. Pictured here is the inside of a manufactured gas house (courtesy National Fuel Gas Company).

water gas (540 Btu), mixed gas (800–900 Btu), and natural gas from Appalachia (often exceeding 1000 Btu).

Manufactured gas interests in large northeastern urban areas were hurt by the Great Depression and threatened by new natural gas competition. Through the Columbia gas system, mixed gas spread from the gas fields of eastern Kentucky and West Virginia to Washington, D.C., in 1931, through a 460-mile, twenty-inch diameter line built by the Atlantic Seaboard Corporation. Chicago also received all natural gas that year and Minneapolis did as well in 1935.[113] Detroit switched to natural gas about 1936 through a twenty-two-inch line from Columbia.[114] Cincinnati Gas and Electric Company also used mixed gas beginning in the mid–1920s until the late 1940s. After a 1948 Ohio Public Utility Commission Order required a resumption of all natural gas service to customers, CG&E converted its operations at the East Gas Works in the city to produce an oil gas that was interchangeable with natural gas.[115] Still, of the 19 million gas utility customers in the United States in 1945, less than 45 percent used natural gas.[116] Some northeastern manufactured gas operations and coal interests, fuel-oil businesses, and pro-coal state governments like Pennsylvania resisted the introduction of natural gas because the clean-burning newcomer was certain to steal their market. And just as they feared, once southwestern pipeline gas became widely available in the 1950s, the demand for manufactured gas evaporated. Natural gas from Texas reached Cleveland and some parts of western Pennsylvania in 1943, the rest of the Appalachian region shortly after World War II, Philadelphia in 1948, and New York City in 1951.[117] As a result, manufactured gas was slowly phased out, virtually displaced by natural gas by 1965. The huge manufactured gas tanks, symbols of urban energy, were dismantled by the 1970s and '80s, and are now only a memory.

"Artificial gas" would make a brief comeback in the region during the 1970s energy crunch. In addition to Appalachian and Southwest supplies, the regional gas industry once again pursued unnatural sources. In addition to coal gasification projects proposed in the United States in the early 1970s, Buffalo's National Fuel Gas Company entered into a partnership with Ashland Oil Company to produce synthetic pipeline quality gas (SNG) from oil in Buffalo.[118] But the synthetic process was not simple. Sulfur carbons had to be removed from naphtha, a petroleum by-product, from crude oil imported from Canada. Then the fuel was mixed with steam, heated under pressure, and passed over a catalyst of powdered nickel. Passage of gas through a lower temperature reactor increased the proportion of methane, and removal of carbon dioxide and water also increased the Btu rating. Propane was also added to increase the heating content, and in the end SNG was completely interchangeable with natural and mixed gas. The $25 million plant, constructed by Foster Wheeler Corporation and owned by Ashland, was only the third such plant built in the U.S., though there were many similar facilities in Europe. The plant began operation in April 1974 and produced enough gas for 60,000 homes or three industrial factories the size of Bethlehem Steel, NFG's largest customer.[119] Due to high oil prices and new natural gas supplies, the SNG plant was discontinued after a few years.

Though it survived for more than a century in the United States, the days of manufactured gas were first numbered in the late nineteenth century once Appalachian natural gas found a way from the bottom of a rural well to urban area gas appliances. The natural product had a distinct environmental advantage over the sooty town gas. An 1878 issue of *American Gas Light Journal* claimed that natural gas could be breathed like air, without the sickening effects of manufactured gas.[120] Natural gas was not only cleaner, but also considerably less expensive where available. It seemed like an obvious choice. The clean-burning product would make its first major inroad in the dirtiest of cities.

THREE

Pew, Westinghouse, and the Iron City
The New Product

"This is like living in Pittsburgh, if you can call that living."
— Groucho Marx, surrounded in cigar smoke,
A Night at Casablanca, 1946

"All things considered, are you satisfied with the experiment?"
— George Westinghouse (1846–1914) to his wife
after a natural gas well blew up their backyard[1]

Gas Comes to the Smoky City

One appeal of natural gas was that its cost for industrial purposes was lower than other fuels, especially coal.[2] Initially, the rich supplies of soft coal in the mountains and valleys around southwestern Pennsylvania built Pittsburgh into a major industrial center in the second half of the nineteenth century. Coal was also desirable for producing manufactured gas. But the heavy use of coal — in addition to being more expensive than natural gas — made valley communities like Pittsburgh, later proudly referred to as the "Iron City," fraught with air pollution, and the town became known as the "Smoky City."[3] A less flattering description of the city at the time by author James Parton was "Hell with the lid taken off."[4] Day turned into night when the iron and steel mills fired up and a layer of soot covered everything around the confluence of the Allegheny, Monongahela, and Ohio rivers. Prior to 1884, Pittsburgh used 3 million tons of bituminous coal in a year, "the smoke from which hung in a black cloud, like a pall, over the city continually, discharging flakes of soot and fine dust in a steady downfall."[5] Though the pollution was caused by coal, ironically, coal-produced manufactured gaslight illuminated through the smog. In 1875, the local weather bureau noted heavy smoke one morning caused it to "keep gaslights burning to 11 o'clock [in the morning]."[6]

The introduction of natural gas — a much cleaner fossil fuel — spread quickly in the city and it reduced the industrial air pollution problem. The 1889 *History of Allegheny County* recalled, "It [natural gas] has proved a godsend to Pittsburgh in providing heat that needs no handling of materials, makes no dirt, does its work

Darkness at Noon — Pittsburgh was known as the "Smoky City" due to its polluted skies from the burning of coal in the valley's steel mills. Natural gas did much to clean up the smoke in the 1880s, but shortages of gas around World War I again caused increased use of coal. This photograph of downtown Pittsburgh during the business day was taken by Frank E. Bingaman around 1920. Increased natural gas use again helped clean the air after World War II (from the Stefan Lorant Iconography Collection, Carnegie Library of Pittsburgh).

better in every way than coal, and has rendered the city much more tolerable to occasional residents."[7] Another writer penned the results of natural gas use: "Soot and dirt and smoke and cinders disappeared. People washed their faces, men wore 'biled shirts' and girls dressed in white."[8] Some homeowners "celebrated by painting their dwellings white or decorated their homes with bright colors."[9] The dark cloud of dust faded, and the consumption of coal dropped below a million tons a year.[10] An 1885 article in *The New York Times* stated that the "smokeless, odorless fuel" would result in the city losing "its world-renowned title of 'Smoky City.'"[11]

But the clean skies would not last. Gas would not replace all coal consumption in steelmaking as many of the original wells quickly lost pressure, and one resident said, "We are going back to the smoke. We have had four or five years of wonderful cleanliness in Pittsburgh.... We all felt better, we are looked better, we all were better."[12] In 1895, the *Pittsburgh Leader* cynically suggested that a proposed smoke ordinance was "nothing but a smoke screen for a gas franchise monopoly."[13] But despite its beneficial environmental effects, the first motivation for using natural gas in Pittsburgh was economic due to its high and even heat content, critical in manufacturing steel and glass.

Natural gas was first used in the Pittsburgh area at the Great Western Iron Company around 1870.[14] It was then introduced for iron and steel making in 1874 at Rogers & Burchfield's puddling and heating furnaces in Leechburg, Pa., on the Kiskimenitas, a tributary of the Allegheny River.[15] Drilling picked up and an eight-mile line was proposed to fuel the city. In 1875, Jacob J. Vandergrift, a former riverboat captain, along with John Pitcairn, Jr. and Capt. C. W. Batchelor, formed Natural Gas Company, Ltd. The firm installed one of the first natural gas pipelines, a nineteen-mile, six-inch diameter line from gas found in Saxonburg, Pa., in Butler County. Saxonburg was a community founded by the industrious German John A. Roebling, a farmer and wire rope manufacturer turned suspension-bridge builder. He designed many innovative spans including notable projects at Cincinnati, Pittsburgh, a Niagara River crossing north of Buffalo, and the initial plan of the Brooklyn Bridge.[16] The Saxonburg pipeline ran seventeen miles to Graff, Bennett and Company and Chalfant & Company's iron works near Sharpsburg, the first businesses in the area to apply natural gas to manufacturing.[17] A powerful gas well in Etna, Pa., was struck in 1876; however, it was almost abandoned due to the decline of pressure from the wellhead to the furnace.[18]

According to the 1889 *History of Allegheny County*, Vandergrift (1827–1899) "became one of the foremost advocates of it [natural gas] for industrial and fuel purposes, and proceeded in an effective manner to place it conveniently at the disposal of the public."[19] Vandergrift was one of the heaviest investors in the oil boom and bust town Pithole in 1865, where he bought a tract of three acres with wells for $82,500.[20] An organizer of various oil pipeline systems to the railroads, Vandergrift equipped and ran a line of tank cars from

Butler County Gas Well — The Saxonburg pipeline in the 1870s ran seventeen miles from this well in the Butler County oil field to Graff, Bennett and Company and Chalfant & Company's iron works near Sharpsburg, the first businesses in the area to apply natural gas to manufacturing. The roaring initial pressure of the gas blew the drilling tools — weighing 2,000 pounds — out of the well (courtesy Drake Well Museum, Pennsylvania Historical and Museum Commission).

Pithole to Oil City, and laid a four-mile pipeline in Pithole named the "Star Pipeline." Various pipelines in Butler and Venango counties were controlled by Vandergrift, Forman & Co., which consolidated under the name of United Pipelines in 1887. It absorbed competing lines in various parts of the oil region and then formed an alliance with Standard Oil interests. Vandergrift had a hand in developing the Bridgewater Gas Company, Penn Fuel Company, Natural Gas Company of West Virginia, Chartiers Natural Gas Company, United Oil and Gas Trust (of which he was president), Toledo Natural Gas Company, Fort Pitt Natural Gas Company, Apollo Gas Company, and Washington Oil Company.[21]

Pittsburgh was not the only industrial community in the region where the environmental appeal of natural gas was prevalent. By the close of the nineteenth century, the Tri-State Gas Company supplied manufacturers in Pennsylvania, Ohio, and West Virginia from gas provided by Fort Pitt. Tri-State's subsidiary Royal Gas Company (organized in 1898) supplied Steubenville, Ohio, parts of Pittsburgh, and Wheeling, West Virginia. Wheeling, known as the "Nail City," was recognized for its superiority of ample coal supplies used in nail making. But Wheeling also had a "gift of providence" of natural gas discoveries. The *Wheeling Daily Intelligencer* proclaimed: "Wheeling stands on the threshold of a new era…. The smoky, sooty town of the recent past and present will give way to a clear sky, and her inhabitants will breathe the free, fresh air of heaven instead of the sulphur and soot-polluted atmosphere they have been wont to inhale."[22]

Pew and Peoples

The catalyst to widespread use of natural gas in Pittsburgh ignited when the brothers Obediah and Michael Haymaker struck natural gas in 1878 while drilling for oil in Murrysville, Pa., in Westmoreland County. The Haymaker brothers were oil drillers who observed gas escaping along Turtle Creek in Murrysville about eighteen miles east of Pittsburgh. Where there's gas, there's oil, the drillers thought. So they leased the ground and after a slow drilling process with less than ideal drilling equipment, the Haymakers struck gas on November 3, 1878 at 1,400 feet.[23] The gas blew in without warning, and the rig and tools all "whirled around like so much paper in a heavy wind," wrote Michael Haymaker.[24] The blowout was heard as far as fifteen miles away. After some people carried lanterns too close to the well, it ignited in a "blinding flash." Haymaker wrote, "There was an explosion. Flames, it seemed, were everywhere. Then my ears cleared and I heard the familiar roar of the well. Gradually the flame … settled to an even 100 feet straight in the air."[25] The effluent well burned for a year and a half and was finally controlled by the placing a smokestack forty-five feet long over the well. It produced 34 million cubic feet of gas a day and later attracted many tourists, including President and Mrs. Grover Cleveland in the 1880s.[26] The president reportedly commented at the sight of natural gas in the area: "an uncanny picture, a superb spectacle."[27]

Shortly thereafter, a fight about the well's ownership erupted after a Chicago "promoter," a millionaire named Milton Weston, offered to purchase the well for $20,000. The payment was never completed and the Haymakers eventually sold the production to Joseph N. Pew and Edward Octavius Emerson to bring the gas to Pittsburgh. Furious, an armed gang representing Weston arrived at the well site on November 26, 1883, and rioted to control the well. Members of the gang, including Weston, were later arrested and convicted, but the confrontation ended with the death of Obe Haymaker, who was shot once and bayoneted four times.[28] The gas was finally piped to Pittsburgh and more than a hundred wells in the same area would follow. Michael Haymaker later settled in San Antonio, Texas, living into his nineties.

Once the famous, fiery Haymaker well was brought under control, Pew and Emerson's Penn Fuel Gas Company, which commenced operations in 1882, purchased the large natural gas well the following year. Pew (1848–1912), one of ten children and a former Mercer, Pa., teacher and later Titusville real estate investor, entered the natural gas business in Bradford in 1881, forming the Keystone Gas Company to supply Bradford, Pa., and Olean, N.Y.[29]

His partner, Emerson (1834–1912), fourteen years his senior, and a cousin of famed writer-philosopher Ralph Waldo Emerson, was born in York, Maine, where his attorney father was a member of the state legislature. After the Civil War in which he served as a former Lieutenant from the Wisconsin Infantry, he moved to Titusville in 1865, and actively engaged in drilling for oil from Pithole to West Virginia. The

Haymaker Well — This huge monument stands near the site of the famous Haymaker well, which blew in November 18, 1878. The prolific well eventually led to natural gas supplies for Pittsburgh and the formation of the Peoples Natural Gas Company. The Pennsylvania Natural Gas Men's Association dedicated this boulder of Murrysville sandstone with a bronze plaque on one side in 1961 (courtesy Dominion Peoples).

entrepreneurial Presbyterian invested in oil, banking, farming, and ice, and was later elected Mayor of Titusville in 1890, serving three years.[30] He also later engaged in producing oil in Ohio and Indiana.[31]

Pew and Emerson piped gas under its own pressure about fifteen miles from Murrysville to 16th Street in Pittsburgh through a 5⅝-inch line.[32] According to the *Pittsburg Leader*, published around the turn of the century, natural gas was first used domestically in 1883 in the city by a Captain Seeley, who owned a real estate office at Penn and Highland avenues.[33] Another of the first new gas firms, the Chartiers Valley Gas Company, owned by James A. Chambers, also brought natural gas in 1883 from the Murrysville gas field to Pittsburgh mills and glass factories through sixteen- and twenty-inch wrought iron lines, manufactured by J. Pierpont Morgan's National Tube Works.[34] The firm's first line from the Hickory gas field in Pittsburgh also used "telescoping" wrought iron lines— similar to the approach later developed by George Westinghouse — that gradually increased the diameter of the line from the well to reduce the pressure.[35] Gas spread for glass making as the Pittsburgh Plate Glass Company began using the product at its Creighton works and at the Rochester Tumbler Works, in Rochester, Pa.[36] The following year, the Citizens Natural Gas Company was formed in nearby Washington, Pa., providing lower cost natural gas for residents who thought the local manufactured gas prices too high.[37] Gas was introduced into the manufacturing of rolling mills of Wilson, Walker & Co., and Shoenberger & Co. and the flint-glass furnace of the Fort Pitt glass works in 1883.[38] Another firm bringing gas into the area was the Monongahela Natural Gas Company, organized in 1884.[39]

The success of natural gas companies gaining franchises could be traced to the rush of pipelines into Pittsburgh. In 1882, Pew and Emerson's Penn Fuel Company initially was blocked from serving natural gas in the franchise area of a manufactured coal-gas company. The Fuel Gas Company, a manufactured-gas firm organized in Allegheny County in 1874, maintained it had the exclusive right to distribute natural gas in the city as well. After an unsuccessful attempt to purchase the Murrysville Well, the coal-gas company drilled one of its own natural gas wells and delivered it to Pittsburgh's South Side in June 1883. Meanwhile, Pew's natural gas firm, according to the *Romance of American Petroleum and Gas*, "forced its way into Pittsburg[h] over private property and against severe opposition, both political and competitive."[40] Coal miners, fireman, and coal and ash handlers in the manufactured gas plants opposed the introduction of natural gas into the city. After a court challenge by the coal-gas firm, the Pennsylvania Supreme Court ruled in *Emerson v. Commonwealth* that natural gas was a different fuel than coal gas and not subject to manufactured gas charters. As a result, the Pennsylvania legislature passed the Natural Gas Act in 1885, which allowed natural gas companies to compete for business with manufactured firms. The Act also gave natural gas companies the right of eminent domain to lay their lines over public and private property, subject only to local ordinances.[41] Pew's and Emerson's Peoples Natural Gas Company was the first natural gas firm chartered under the Act. Its original incorporators included Pew, Emerson, Theodore Johnson, Robert C. Pew, and R. S. Duffield of Pittsburgh and J. S. Robinson of nearby Allegheny, Pa.[42] By 1885, approximately 500 miles of pipe had been laid in Pittsburgh, some lines with diameters as large as twenty-four inches. Peoples also soon provided gas to nearby Wilkinsburg from area wells and the new firm served 35,000 customers by 1887.[43]

Pittsburgh's manufactured gas interests, however, would not concede to the new upstart natural gas competition lightly. The city's commission on natural gas decreed that "high pressure" gas should not be permitted within city limits.[44] Pittsburghers were concerned about the unpredictable high pressures of natural gas, citing one case where a hostler struck up a match to light a lantern and leaking gas nearby blew the stableman thirty feet through the air, killed a horse, and set a building ablaze.[45] But Peoples won a court case over the matter. Numerous firms then entered the fray. Pittsburgh was soon supplied by the Philadelphia, Manufacturers Light and Heat, Pennsylvania, and Washington gas companies from 107 area wells.[46]

Emerson sold out his gas interests to his partner, Pew, in 1899. As the area wells began to peter out a few years later, Pew sold Peoples to the Standard Oil natural gas interests. Overshadowing Pew's initial natural gas ventures, Pew then founded the Sun Oil Company, acquiring leases in the Southwest and a refinery outside of Philadelphia.[47] Pew's children would later establish the seven Pew Charitable Trusts, a Philadelphia-based foundation with assets of approximately $4 billion.

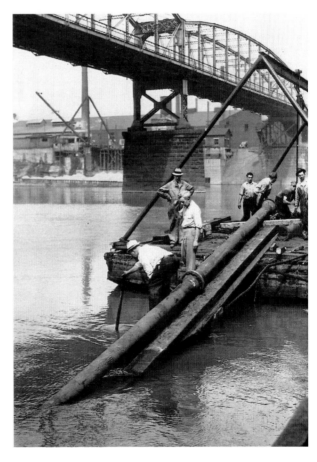

In 1909, Peoples purchased the Lawrence Natural Gas Company, and expanded its lines to Johnstown, Pa., 100 miles east of Pittsburgh. In 1913, the firm extended service further to Altoona, a large railroad center in Blair County, Pa., and acquired the Conemaugh Gas Company in that area.[48] In 1926, Peoples acquired the Columbia Natural Gas Company, initially incorporated in 1891 under the name of Patterson Natural Gas Company, serving customers in five counties in western Pennsylvania, including the areas of Glenshaw, Kittanning, Vandergrift, and Indiana, Pa.[49] Over the years, Peoples continued to expand around Pittsburgh, Greensburg, and Altoona and acquired or merged the following companies in southwestern Pennsylvania:

Allegheny River Line — This Peoples Natural Gas Company eight-inch cast-iron pipeline crossed the Allegheny River in Pittsburgh in 1937 (courtesy Dominion Peoples).

Belle Vernon Light & Heat Company
Cambria & Westmoreland Natural Gas Company
Fayette City Natural Gas Company
Pittsburgh Natural Gas Company
Manufacturers Gas Company of Greensburg
Woodville Gas Company
Rock Run Fuel Gas Company
Altoona Gas Light & Heat Company
Laughner Oil and Gas Company
Tyrone Gas & Heat Company
State Line Gas Company, and
Union Heat & Light Company.[50]

Peoples built a twelve-story headquarters on William Penn Place in Pittsburgh in 1910 and later moved into the Gateway Center on Pittsburgh's Golden Triangle in 1952.[51]

George Westinghouse — Electric and Gas Pioneer

Equitable Gas, a subsidiary of the Philadelphia Company, broke ground in 1888, ten years after the drilling of the Haymaker Well. The firm credits its formation to industrialist and genius inventor George Westinghouse, who, in 1884, found natural gas near his thirty-two room mansion his wife named "Solitude" on Thomas Boulevard in the Homewood section of Pittsburgh. Westinghouse, then a thirty-seven-year-old innovator in electricity, was a six-foot-tall strapping man, with a full head of chestnut-brown hair, bushy sideburns, and a thick, handlebar mustache. The Pittsburgh magnate grew up in the Schenectady area in eastern New York State, worked in a family machine shop as a youth, and during the middle of the Civil War, he enlisted in the Union Army Calvary at age seventeen, and then the Navy. He moved to Pittsburgh in 1868. He was known as a charmer, but also could "be blunt to the point of offense."[52] The second half of the nineteenth century was an industrious age, and it called for assiduous leaders— Westinghouse fit the bill. According to long-time associate Paul D. Cravath, "He was always the same; simple, unassuming, direct, frank, courageous, unfaltering in his faith, and supremely confident in the ultimate triumph of his plans."[53]

After hearing of the excitement about natural gas at the Haymaker Well in Murrysville, Westinghouse built a drilling derrick behind his huge villa and his rig workers first hit a weak supply of gas at about 1,560 feet.[54] It was disparaged by the president of the local manufactured gas company as nice, but small.[55] However, after construction of a larger rig, drillers struck gas at such a volume it blew out the drilling tools and parts of his backyard "with such a roar and racket that nobody could hear … within a block."[56] The well was struck at three A.M., which woke Westinghouse and drew him to the scene. "The lawn and paths were littered with [drilling] debris, and the spewing hole hissed and roared with the infernal violence of a volcano."[57] A visitor recalled, "For days you could not hear your own voice in the Homewood residence … [Westinghouse] alone had a never disappearing smile on his beaming face, while the Fire Department was pumping water over the house to prevent it from catching fire from the burning gas."[58] After futile efforts to plug the well with a heavy piece of coal, a large spruce plank, and a huge rock, Westinghouse devised a stopcock to bring the geyser under control. The stopcock was adjusted one night, the gas lighted with oil-soaked rags, and a 100-foot high torch lit the neighborhood. Author Francis Leupp's romantic account reads:

> The next instant, like a lightning flash connecting heaven and earth, a pillar of fire followed by a steady fountain of flame that was a marvelous study in colors.... The gas lamps of the city dwindled to little points of light, and persons in the street not less than a mile away were able to read distinctly the finest newspaper print by the light of the gigantic natural flambeau on the heights of "Solitude."[59]

Westinghouse became one of the first in the city to light and heat a home with natural gas and soon provided the fuel to his neighbors.[60]

Immediately, the manufactured gas interests in Pittsburgh of the Fuel Gas Company opposed the installation of gas lines by Westinghouse, an "amateur" in the field of gas service, and encouraged their supporters in

George Westinghouse (1846–1914) is primarily known for his pioneering inventions and developments in the field of electricity. However, after he discovered natural gas in the backyard of his Pittsburgh home, he created his own gas company and was granted dozens of patents regarding processes in well drilling, meter measurement, preventing gas leaks, regulating gas pressures, and installing pipelines (George Westinghouse Museum).

city government to oppose the inventor's efforts. However, Westinghouse "took pains at the outset to make it plain that he had no intention of asking a concession from the city without giving something in return, and his first application embraced an offer, if allowed to lay his pipes as indicated, to furnish the fire engine houses and police stations with gas free of cost."[61] Westinghouse claimed he intended "to distribute the benefits of this discovery, receiving merely a fair compensation for my property — nothing more."[62]

The savvy inventor then purchased the inactive Philadelphia Company — a Pennsylvania chartered business granted to several Philadelphia investors but never used — the following year for $35,000 to serve the clean-burning and low-cost natural product to Pittsburgh. According to the firm's charter, it enabled the owner to engage in nearly any business including banking, railroads, water distribution, developing an oil field, or, in Westinghouse's case, beginning a natural gas company. With its raison d'être discovered, Philadelphia commenced operations on October 1, 1884, listing capital stock of $100,000 and the firm's officers as Westinghouse, president; Robert Pitcairn, vice president; John Caldwell, secretary and treasurer; and other board of directors including Westinghouse's younger brother, H. H. Westinghouse, and the inventor's attorney, John Dalzell.[63] The novel business grew rapidly, expanding service to both residential and industrial customers. Westinghouse drilled two or three more wells on his own premises and sought easements on properties in the Murrysville area where much drilling was occurring. He offered $5 million in public stock to help finance the company's expansion. Investors, however, were wary due to the explosive nature of natural gas, so Westinghouse used personal persuasion:

> In blocks ranging from a hundred shares to several thousand, he disposed of as much of the stock of the new corporation as was necessary to enable it to begin business, and before very long the rumors that it was turning out a money-maker caused a lively speculation in its shares. Its first dividends were at the rate of one per cent a month, but later it was thought prudent to reduce this to eight per cent a year.[64]

The remaining shares were soon purchased.

Westinghouse would move forward with moving gas from Murrysville to Pittsburgh, as the 1899 *History of Allegheny County* recalled, Philadelphia "laid pipes from the wells to the city, has traversed all the main streets of the city with them, has absorbed or formed a union with several other companies, and now supplies nearly all the factories using it in the two cities."[65]

Westinghouse, who is better known for revolutionizing the locomotive air brake in 1869 at the age of twenty-two, and later demonstrating practical street lighting by electric alternating current, utilizing hydroelectric power in Niagara Falls, and founding the Westinghouse Electric Company in 1886, also extended his expertise into the production, transportation, and distribution of natural gas. Since the discovery of natural gas had no instruction manual attached, industry pioneers showed no fear in coming up with ways to transport the invisible fuel. Many of his first inventions involved "transmission over distance," including air brakes by compressed air, railroad signals by electricity, and natural gas transmission through pipes.[66] He considered piping gas to gas-engine stations, which in turn would generate power. Westinghouse's patented natural gas inventions—twenty-eight of them in 1884 and 1885 alone—included improved ways of drilling wells, meter measurement, methods to prevent gas leaks, a regulator for controlling air and gas in a steam furnace, and an automatic control which shut off gas when the pressure fell, extinguishing flames.[67] The Westinghouse regulator reduced the gas pressure for private and factory use, and for use in the home, an automatic safety valve cut off the gas supply.[68] In addition to a lack of pipelines, the first gas distributors often could not provide the fuel safely due to irregular pressures, and there was a natural fear among residents about high-pressure gas flowing through pipelines. Westinghouse put his resourceful mind to work and used the pressure of gas wells to move the product to market. After first devising a system of double pipes that would carry any leaking gas from the initial high pressure pipe to vent harmlessly in the atmosphere, he then gradually widened the pipes in stages to reduce the pressure so it could be delivered safely—a concept he later applied to electricity.[69] Westinghouse's patent no. 301,191 was recorded for a "system for conveying and utilizing gas under pressure."[70]

By 1887, the city of Pittsburgh had six natural gas companies competing for business. Philadelphia purchased or controlled about twenty firms by the late 1880s, including Equitable, Pennsylvania Natural Gas Company, Mansfield and Chartiers Gas Company, Low Pressure Gas Company, Valley Gas Company, and Union Gas Company of McKeesport.[71] Equitable built a twenty-one-mile long, thirty-six-inch diameter line — riveted together and caulked to prevent leakage — to increase service to Pittsburgh in 1889.[72] By that year, the company was the largest producer of natural gas in the nation.[73] Philadelphia became a competitor to Pew's Peoples firm, and competition between the descendants of Pittsburgh-area companies exists in some ways to this day where their service territories abut. Philadelphia also purchased the Pittsburgh Consolidated Gas Company, which supplied Pittsburgh and vicinity with manufactured gas for lighting. The Westinghouse-controlled business sought additional gas supplies in Pennsylvania and West Virginia because of increasing demand, eventually purchasing gas interests for $1 million in Lewis County, W.Va., previously owned by the Pittsburgh-based firm of Guffey and Galey, who were backed by the wealthy Mellon family. Philadelphia later purchased the Pittsburgh and West Virginia Gas Company, founded in 1894 after a major gas discovery at the Big Moses well in the Mountain State.[74] As a result, Westinghouse stayed one step ahead of Standard Oil interests in piping this new supply of gas to Pittsburgh by laying a sixteen-inch line from the huge well in Tyler County, W.Va.

Philadelphia later became a combined gas-electric firm when it bought the Allegheny County Light Company in 1899. Philadelphia also purchased the United Traction Company, which provided street railway service in Pittsburgh and surrounding streetcar systems in the early twentieth century.[75]

Westinghouse served as president of Philadelphia until 1899. But the genius inventor's financial troubles after the Panic of 1907 forced him to abandon many of his interests in Philadelphia, Westinghouse Electric & Manufacturing Company, and the Westinghouse Machine Company. In the long run, Westinghouse is known more for his innovations to improve the conditions of humanity rather than his initial wealth or seeking public fanfare for his plethora of inventions. Compared to other titans such as Standard Oil's John D. Rockefeller and U.S. Steel's J. P. Morgan, historian Jill Jonnes portrays Westinghouse in a different light: "At a time when many Americans had come to view the nation's industrialists and financiers as little better than robber barons and 'malefactors of great wealth,' Westinghouse was a notable exception: an honest industrialist who sold the best product for the best price, who relished competition and valued his workers, and who deserved his hard-earned fortune."[76] In the shadow of sundry significant achievements from railway electrification to hydroelectric power, Westinghouse's accomplishments in natural gas are not well known. For example, a mammoth memorial to the great inventor placed in Pittsburgh's Schenley Park contained no mention of his gas achievements.

Still, without Westinghouse, Philadelphia's Equitable grew. By 1901, the firm owned or controlled 1,195 miles of pipelines, and 200,000 acres of mineral rights leases in Pennsylvania and West Virginia.[77] By 1911, the firm controlled about 1,000 oil and natural gas wells, had more than 440,000 acres under lease, owned 3,000 miles of pipeline, and served 110,000 customers.[78] During the first decade of the twentieth century, Philadelphia purchased properties of the Fairmont Grafton Gas Company, including the W. C. Rowland & Company, McGraw Oil and Gas Company, and the Shinnston Gas Company.[79] After securing supplies in West Virginia, the availability of gas continued to be a critical component in Pittsburgh maintaining its industrial strength. Equitable then investigated and later acquired 600,000 acres of gas-leased lands in eastern Kentucky through the Kentucky West Virginia Gas Company, a Philadelphia subsidiary, and soon the first Kentucky gas was delivered to Pittsburgh.[80] Based upon the Bluegrass State success, another 300,000 acres were later secured.

Equitable benefited from the flood of gas-consuming industrial customers producing steel, chemicals, and paint in Pittsburgh. In 1927, Equitable had ten industrial consumers using a regular daily consumption of 9 million cubic feet of gas, which was equal to the load of 30–35,000 residential customers.[81] Despite competition from coal, oil, and electricity, the company steadily accumulated more plants and pipelines and paid reliable dividends to shareholders.

By 1923, the parent firm Philadelphia had merged twenty-three operating gas companies.[82] During the early 1920s, Equitable absorbed six West Virginia gas firms and merged with the Monongahela Natural Gas Company creating a new Equitable company. The firm dedicated a $3.5 million headquarters on Pittsburgh's Sixth Avenue in 1925, and initiated a five-year, $100 million utility improvement program.[83] In the 1930s, the acquisitions of smaller firms continued. As part of the effort of divestiture due to the Public Utility Holding Company Act of 1935 (see Chapter Four), Pittsburgh's Equitable became sole owner of Philadelphia's gas properties in 1947, and in 1950, it received the parent company's holdings in Kentucky and West Virginia.[84] Equitable separated from Philadelphia in 1950 becoming a publicly owned company. The move also resulted in the creation of the Duquesne Light Company after Philadelphia was ordered to dispose of its gas and transportation properties due to the same SEC regulation.[85] In the 1950s, Equitable also acquired the stock of the Pittsburgh and West Virginia Gas Company and added to its utility the smaller firms Newell Gas Company and Hundred Natural Gas Company in West Virginia.[86]

The Mighty Columbia

Numerous natural gas companies sprouted all over the gas region in Pennsylvania in 1885 and the state became the natural gas leader with 150 companies chartered to sell gas. Another of the major new firms in the Pittsburgh area not dominated by Standard Oil (see Chapter Four) was the Manufacturers Natural Gas Company of Pittsburgh, formed in 1885 to serve portions of Allegheny and Washington counties. It later became part of the Columbia Gas System. Manufacturers combined with the Peoples Light and Heat Company of Washington, Pa., and the Bellevue and Glenfield Natural Gas Company to form the Manufacturers Light & Heat Company in 1899. Manufacturers piped Wheeling, W.Va., and moved north at the turn of the century towards Pittsburgh to bring new natural gas supplies from the Mountain State to Pittsburgh industries.[87] Three years later, Manufacturers re-incorporated, consolidating with six smaller companies, some controlled by Pittsburgh's financier, and later Gulf Oil founder, Andrew M. Mellon, including: Fort Pitt Gas Company; Relief Gas Company, Mutual Benefit Gas Company, Citizens Natural Gas Company of Waynesburg, Waynesburg Natural Gas Company, and Canonsburg Light and Fuel Company.[88] By 1902, Manufacturers served 40,474 customers.[89] The firm then merged thirteen affiliated companies, which had previously operated separately in the Pittsburgh area, the northern panhandle of West Virginia, and eastern Ohio around Steubenville and East Liverpool, including the Manufacturers Gas Company of Ellwood City and Franklin-Washington Natural Gas Company.[90] By 1924, Manufacturers served 135 communities in three states.[91]

Although Manufacturers would not become part of Columbia until the 1920s, Columbia's roots can be traced to 1905, when the Columbia Corporation was formed in Huntington, W.Va., to produce natural gas in that state and eastern Kentucky for delivery to Cincinnati, Ohio. Columbia Corporation—formed by Union Gas & Electric of Cincinnati, which in short order changed its name to Columbia Gas & Electric Company—began in 1906 under the laws of West Virginia to develop oil and gas to meet the demands of the large Ohio market. It combined in 1926 with George W. Crawford's Ohio Fuel Supply Company, which was granted a franchise in Cincinnati to serve natural gas. Crawford was one of the early pioneers of Ohio's and West Virginia's natural gas industry, who, with partners, acquired a great deal of acreage from wildcat drillers. In the early 1880s, the Crawfords, along with some wealthy citizens, operated independent companies in Charleston and Huntington, W.Va. The firms included Charleston Natural Gas Company, which later became the nucleus of the United Fuel Gas Company.[92] Charleston laid lines into the city from three area wells in 1893 and was ready to supply its first customer on Broad Street the following year.[93]

George Crawford (1861–1935), a descendant of Scottish immigrants, entered the well supply business in Bolivar, N.Y., in 1886, acquired leases, and operated gathering and transmission oil lines to railroad loading points. His brother Fred (1863–1933) became a roughneck in the oil fields and later worked for the Oil City Fuel Supply Company. George Crawford concentrated on West Virginia, organized the New Martinsville Gas Company, and maintained an interest in the Tri-State Natural Gas Company. Both George and Fred Crawford were involved in several discoveries throughout southern Ohio, and the brothers formed Ohio Fuel in 1902 to centralize operations of four area companies. They began construction and installation of major pipelines that connected smaller systems, including a long-distance line connecting Cincinnati with the West Virginia gas fields.[94]

Both brothers were "rugged entrepreneurs" in the early gas industry. George Crawford believed in "total possession and devotion" to his business that he had "no social connections" and "would not allow himself to get married until his mid-sixties." His brother Fred once claimed, "From the day that I started work until the present I have devoted all my time and efforts to gas."[95] George Crawford, with backing of Standard Oil interests, organized United Fuel (Standard Oil owning 51 percent and Ohio Fuel 49 percent), and acquired other properties in West Virginia, Ohio, and Kentucky.[96] Some of the firms included the Columbia Gas Company, Miami Valley Natural Gas Company in western Ohio, and Logan Natural Gas Company which had built a pipeline from Sugar Grove, Ohio, to Muncie, Indiana.

Another key player in the region was T. N. Barnsdall, a former shoe cobbler and leather dealer around Oil City, Pa., who with many Pennsylvania oil and gas operators had moved south to West Virginia to follow the newest gas discoveries. Barnsdall worked with Standard Oil interests to develop his acreage in Ohio through the River

Gas Company (formed in 1894 serving southeastern Ohio in and around Marietta), and, in West Virginia, through the Reserve Gas Company.[97] Reserve was organized in 1902 and later merged with Hope Natural Gas Company of West Virginia. Barnsdell had in mind the Ohio markets around Columbus, Zanesville, Chillicothe, Dayton, Springfield, and Cincinnati. In 1904, Union Natural Gas Company, the other principal system in Ohio that served the northern half of the state, acquired Barnsdall's interest in Reserve. Union, incorporated in 1902, supplied natural gas to about 95,000 customers in both central and northern Ohio and in northwestern Pennsylvania from gas fields in Ohio, West Virginia, and north-central Pennsylvania.[98] Barnsdall later expanded into the Southwest. Eventually, Standard Oil interests gave up Northwestern Ohio Gas Company, Union Natural Gas Company, and some Sugar Grove, Ohio, companies in a "friendly agreement" with Columbia in 1915.[99] Columbia also exchanged its share of ownership of two manufactured gaslight companies in Cleveland to Standard Oil's East Ohio Gas Company for a controlling interest in United Fuel, which owned 800,000 acres of natural gas production leases in West Virginia, increasing Columbia's control of 1.1 million acres of land in West Virginia and Kentucky.[100]

In 1924, Ohio Fuel acquired ownership of Manufacturers in western Pennsylvania and then combined with Columbia Gas & Electric Company in 1926 to form Columbia Gas & Electric Corporation. The two firms were already located in contiguous areas: Ohio Fuel provided gas to western Pennsylvania, northeastern and central Ohio, and the panhandle of West Virginia; and Columbia served southwestern Ohio, northern and eastern Kentucky, and the western portion of West Virginia. The two firms pooled their gas supply, coordinated their pipeline network, and reduced their drilling expense.[101] Ohio Fuel eventually became part of Columbia's Union Gas & Electric Company, which leased the facilities of manufactured gas and electric operations dating back to 1843 to the creation of the Cincinnati Gas Light & Coke Company.[102]

Manufacturers was the principal firm of one of five major Columbia operating groups, producing and distributing gas in Pittsburgh and New Castle in Pennsylvania, Wheeling, Steubenville, and East Liverpool in Ohio, and other communities in West Virginia, including Wheeling.[103] Further combinations continued with Fayette County Gas Company, Pennsylvania Fuel Supply Company, and Greensboro Gas Company. By the mid–1930s, the Pittsburgh group owned nearly 3,000 gas wells and served 235,000 customers.[104]

In 1930, Columbia, under the leadership of Philip Gossler, who had led the company since 1909, acquired a 50 percent interest in the Panhandle Eastern Pipe Line Company, connecting its lines with natural gas fields in Texas.[105] According to Panhandle's original owners, Columbia reportedly made the purchase to "keep cheap Texas gas out of Columbia's territory."[106] Likewise, American Fuel & Power, a Kentucky gas producer, which intended to construct a pipeline to Toledo and Detroit, was acquired by Columbia in 1930 and the pipeline plans were quickly dropped.[107]

The PUHCA of 1935 forced Columbia to divest its oil operations, along with its interest in Panhandle. After the U.S. Justice Department filed antitrust suits against Columbia beginning in 1938, the company was forced to jettison its electric operations as well in 1946, and the company changed its name to The Columbia Gas System,

Inc.[108] Additional natural gas expansions led Columbia into other parts of New York, Ohio, Pennsylvania, West Virginia, New Jersey, and Maryland. In 1944, the firm began direct service to Warren, Pa., and other towns in north-central Pennsylvania. Columbia also introduced natural gas to Gettysburg, Pa., in 1948. In 1951, Manufacturers bought the Pennsylvania properties of The Natural Gas Company of West Virginia. By 1962, Columbia's holding company eventually included three operating groups: the Columbus Group of Ohio Fuel Gas Company and The Ohio Valley Gas Company; the Pittsburgh Group of Manufacturers, Columbia Gas of Maryland, Columbia Gas of New York, Columbia Gas of Pennsylvania, Cumberland and Allegheny Gas Company, and the Home Gas Company; and the Charleston Group of United Fuel, Columbia Gas of Kentucky, Kentucky Gas Transmission Corporation, and the Virginia Gas Distribution Corporation. At that time, the entire Columbia system served nearly 1.5 million customers in 1,920 communities.[109] Later, the company acquired other south-central Pennsylvania companies including York County Gas Company in the 1960s, and by 1967, evolved into one of the largest natural gas systems in the United States.[110]

Coal's Rival

Gas pioneers Pew, Emerson, Westinghouse, and Crawford indirectly created cleaner air in Pittsburgh and made industrial production in the Steel Valley of eastern Ohio, western Pennsylvania, and West Virginia less expensive. However, the use of natural gas in Appalachia reduced coal consumption significantly, thereby scaling back work for coal miners. For example, steel giant Andrew Carnegie (1835–1919) purchased huge volumes of coke produced by coal extracted from the southwestern Pennsylvania coal fields, much from the so-called "king of coke," Henry Clay Frick. In an effort to control raw materials that went into his finished product, Carnegie eventually owned half of the Frick Coke Company.[111] But the "star-spangled Scotsman" industrialist also quickly utilized even-burning, efficient natural gas in his mills after seeing the impact the fuel had on the local glass industry. Carnegie, one of the first steelmakers who would use gas on a large scale, claimed that the vaporous product supplanted 10,000 tons of coal a day.[112] The manufacturing, and later, philanthropic, giant created his own gas company to fill the need. Carnegie Natural Gas Company (Carnegie) later operated extensively in Pennsylvania and West Virginia, run as part of Carnegie Steel (later U.S. Steel) in Pittsburgh to search for inexpensive gas supplies. Carnegie's first land leases in West Virginia were obtained in 1898 in his quest to explore for clean natural gas for the Pittsburgh area steel mills. The firm drilled numerous wells, installed many miles of pipeline, and built eleven major compressing stations to move the gas to western Pennsylvania.[113]

Gas was cleaner, less expensive, and labor saving over coal. A saw manufacturing company relocated to Pittsburgh from Philadelphia saving itself $60,000 a year, because the cost of natural gas was "practically nothing."[114] *The New York Times* dispatched a reporter to Pittsburgh to periodically chronicle the impact natural gas was having on the city. A *Times* editorial on October 17, 1885, touted: "Still, the inexpensiveness of natural gas as a fuel is not the most important economic item in its favor. The saving of labor by its use is of much greater value. In many of the great works a pound of coal has not been in use for a year."[115] According to the *Pittsburg Leader* published around the turn of the century, natural gas replaced about 7,000 tons of coal in summer, and twice as much in winter.[116] Due to the weakening Pittsburgh wells, half of the gas supply originated from Armstrong and Washington counties in Pennsylvania and the balance from West Virginia. The use of natural gas picked up again in 1902 as a coal miner's strike and subsequent shortage encouraged the demand for gas-burning appliances. The demand for the cleaner-burning and more economical fuel inaugurated a fierce competitive rivalry between the two fossil fuels that continued through the end of World War II, and to some extent, to the present day. As the drilling industry spread, some advocates of wood and coal in the late nineteenth century ominously warned that the drilling of gas wells might cause a fire in the "great gas well in the bowels of the earth" and cause the globe to be "blown to fragments."[117] Needless to say, no one believed them.

By 1929, about twenty natural gas companies served Pittsburgh (some of the heavy gas-using industries operated their own gas divisions), fed from 5 million acres of gas lands and 30,000 miles of pipelines, consuming one-eighth of all natural gas consumption in the United States.[118] Some other smaller firms included the Wise Oil and Gas Company, Indiana Gas and Oil Company, Central Pennsylvania Gas Company, Braden Oil and Gas, Wasco Fuel Company, Beam Natural Gas Company, and many others. Peoples, Equitable, and Columbia later absorbed most of the less significant firms.

Seeing the initial success of natural gas in Pittsburgh in the early 1880s, it was not long before the "Standard Oil crowd," who already dominated the fledgling petroleum market, saw that natural gas had enormous profit potential as well. But the three segments of the natural gas industry — production from the wells, transmission to the major markets, and distribution to individual customers — were largely isolated from one another. It would take the influence of one of the barons of industry to convert the previously worthless invisible fuel from a hole in the ground into a widespread, moneymaking venture.

The House That John D. Built

Gas Corporate Development

"We are not in business for our health, but are out for the dollars."[1]
— Henry Huttleston Rogers, Standard Oil leader (1840–1909)

"God gave me my money. I believe the power to make money is a gift from God."[2]
— John D. Rockefeller (1839–1937)

The Gas Standard

During the Civil War, Cleveland bookkeeper John Davison Rockefeller turned his attention from his bountiful produce business to uncharted ventures in oil refining in his partnership Clark and Rockefeller. Rockefeller quickly became wealthy from the production of kerosene. Rockefeller, who grew up in New York's Southern Tier and Finger Lakes regions, did not drill for the "black gold," but he controlled it through the ownership of refineries and the manipulation of transportation of the fuel by rail and pipeline.[3] He stayed out of the boom and bust production of oil because it was "too risky."[4] And risky it was. For example, Colonel Edwin Drake himself, driller of the initial Titusville well, left the oil region in 1863 and eventually ended up penniless a few years after his historic achievement.[5] Drake was later granted a small pension from the state of Pennsylvania. But for savvy investors, it was an age where industrial expansion and profits lay ripe for the picking. In the new energy industry, there was money to be made, and those that got there first would make it. During the 1870s, the over-expansion of the petroleum search in western Pennsylvania and the new state of West Virginia was followed by a severe depression in the industry with declining prices and production. Though many oil pioneers quickly became millionaires, once the bottom fell out of the market after the Panic of 1873, bankruptcies and failures were quite common. Sabotage between oil transportation interests occurred as pipelines were destroyed by the competitive horse and wagon teamsters. Armed guards were posted during pipeline construction. Competition became so cutthroat among the producers, refiners, pipelines, and railroads, most of them were forced into combinations and alliances.

The thirty-one-year-old penny-pinching, somber-looking Baptist business-man created the Standard Oil Company in 1870. Despite Rockefeller's baron-like,

John D. Rockefeller, already vastly wealthy from the refining of oil in western Pennsylvania, initially knew little of the natural gas often found in the process of drilling oil wells. Once convinced by his lieutenants that it could be a marketable product, he urged that Standard Oil's National Transit Company pursue the business "earnestly" (courtesy Drake Well Museum, Pennsylvania Historical and Museum Commission).

monopolistic tactics, he intended to, as he put it, "bring some order out of what was rapidly becoming a state of chaos" in the Pennsylvania oil fields.[6] Standard was an "alliance of investors and companies, then systematized administration under a central organization."[7] These investors included Charles Lockhart, a Scottish immigrant who started in the oil business by buying petroleum from a salt well in 1852 and later traveling to Europe in 1860 to bring attention to oil industry. Lockhart and his partner William Frew developed a successful oil merchant and refining operation in Pittsburgh and joined the Standard alliance in 1874. Other Pennsylvania oil investors followed. Later, refining companies in West Virginia became part of the Standard organization.

Specialized committees managed Rockefeller's firm by consultation and agreement. The oil titan later wrote that this method was necessary to develop the industry:

> The chief advantages from industrial combinations are those which can be derived from a cooperation of persons and aggregation of capital. Much that one man cannot do alone two can do together, and once admit the fact that cooperation, or, what is the same thing, combination, is necessary on a small scale, the limit depends solely upon the necessities of business.[8]

Rockefeller organized a "trust" in each state of operation, holding power over the various companies his company did not legally control. By 1891, Standard itself was responsible for a quarter of the United States' total oil output.[9] But beginning with the federal Sherman Anti-Trust Act in 1890, several states led their own populist charge against Standard affiliates over the next two decades. For example, though Standard made Cleveland a great oil-refining center of the world, in 1890, the Ohio attorney general brought legal action against the petroleum powerhouse for its monopolistic position.

About the same time as the expansion in Standard's control over oil refining, several Standard leaders were curious about the mysterious, but flammable stepsister discovered with oil, and explored the natural gas possibilities in the 1880s. Standard "found a situation with natural gas it did not want, did not know what to do with, but knew that it was of great value and usefulness if it could be harnessed and utilized."[10] Many small companies formed near where natural gas was discovered, but they soon had trouble meeting the demand from their isolated local supplies. Some of Standard's leaders realized natural gas could be a valuable commodity and Rockefeller interests quickly seized the dawn of the incipient industry. Through an "encircling" movement in Appalachia, Standard first absorbed natural gas firms throughout northwestern Pennsylvania and Buffalo, and then expanded into West Virginia, Ohio, as well as the already developed market of Pittsburgh.

All the President's Men

Though Rockefeller first served as active leader of the Standard Oil Trust for the last three decades of the 1800s, by the turn of the century, the plutocrat functioned

Standard Oil's National Transit Company built this august headquarters in downtown Oil City around 1875 and directed much of Standard's natural gas activity. Recently refurbished, the edifice remains a fixture in downtown Oil City and is listed on the National Register of Historic Places (courtesy Drake Well Museum, Pennsylvania Historical and Museum Commission).

only as titular head.[11] At that time, the so-called "Standard Oil crowd" of John Dustin Archbold, Henry H. Rogers, and Rockefeller's brother, William, directed major activity in the Trust. Archbold (1848–1922), son of a clergyman, joined Rockefeller in 1875 and became a life-long friend to the millionaire. Born in Leesburg, Ohio, in a Protestant Irish family, he invested in the oil business between 1864 and 1965, and became a principle owner of the Acme Oil Company. He became president of the firm in 1875, then joined Standard.[12] While Archbold focused on oil, other Standard leaders, such as Daniel O'Day, Calvin Payne, Elizur Strong, Benjamin Brewster, and Henry Rogers, headed up operations in the natural gas industry. John D. Rockefeller, Sr., however, would be long associated with the actions of "all the president's men." The Rockefeller coalition of oil and gas entrepreneurs, or "barons" depending on one's perspective, became, in Rockefeller's words, "a most happy association of busy people."[13]

The Pipes, the Pipes Are Calling — Daniel O'Day and the Gas Pipelines

In the early 1880s, Irish native Daniel O'Day, a high-level Standard manager, kept Rockefeller abreast of things occurring in the natural gas industry.[14] At that time, Standard was already using gas in some of its refineries' boilers.[15] The invisible genie of methane, however, was still seen as a dangerous mystery and best left in its lantern. O'Day, a dapper-suited businessman with a well-trimmed moustache, deplored the waste of gas occurring in the oil fields, and assured Rockefeller that they could pipe the volatile and invisible product without mishaps. Oil writer Patrick Boyle penned, "When he [O'Day] became convinced it was a good thing, its safety and practicability demonstrated, he took it up with all the enthusiasm of his practical nature."[16] Despite his initial lack of knowledge about gas, based upon the Pittsburgh experience, Rockefeller wrote to O'Day, "I am desirous to have our National Transit Company [a pipeline firm formed in 1881 by Standard and headed by O'Day] pursue the gas business earnestly."[17] Earlier, through the South Improvement Company, Rockefeller acquired United Pipe Lines in 1877 to consolidate all oil, gas, water, and steam lines. Standard then formed the National Transit Company in 1881, headquartered in Oil City, Pa.[18] National Transit expanded into pipeline and gas producing properties by the mid–1880s, acquiring interests in numerous pipelines in the region.[19] At the height of its activity, National Transit transported most of the natural gas in the United States and 85 percent of the country's petroleum.[20]

The early oil fields attracted many Irish immigrant families, and the young O'Day was one of them.[21] Born in 1844 in Ireland, he was brought to America a year later, and his parents settled on a farm in Cattaraugus County, N.Y., near Ellicottville, then a sparsely populated town on New York's Southern Tier. O'Day left home at sixteen to work in the Buffalo rail yards and warehouses, handling freight. He moved to Titusville, Pa., in August 1865, and became involved in oil transportation by railroading. Since the expansion of the oil industry was dependent on pipelines, his first pipeline venture began in 1873 after being hired by Rockefeller's American Transfer Company, building an oil line from Emlenton to the Clarion fields, and then to Oil

City. After piping oil from the Bradford fields, he developed his interest in the natural gas business around 1884.[22]

O'Day, described as "driving, occasionally ruthless, exceedingly loyal, ... furnished the vital force which made pipeline men so closely knit that, according to legend, 'if you stuck one, they all bled.'"[23] The 1889 *History of Allegheny County* described him as "a gentleman whose wonderful administrative and executive abilities have been exerted in its service with the most brilliant results."[24] O'Day, known as a demanding "giant of a man," defended his Catholic pipeline workers from local bigotry, and made pipeline management "a profession and a science." When it came to laying pipeline throughout the rural Appalachian forest, no terrain was too tough.[25] In addition to heading Standard's National Transit, he held interests in the Snow Pump Works of Buffalo, Oil City Boiler Works, the Northwestern Ohio Natural Gas Company, as well as interests in various banks, electric lighting, street railways, and elevators at Buffalo.

Irish immigrant Daniel O'Day (1844–1906) became a leader in natural gas pipeline development after he convinced John D. Rockefeller that Standard Oil could transport the great natural gas reserves found in rural western Pennsylvania to urban markets safely and efficiently (courtesy Drake Well Museum, Pennsylvania Historical and Museum Commission).

The merger movement in the late nineteenth century affected various sectors of the American economy, especially the oil and gas industry. Rockefeller and Standard were in the forefront of consolidating the natural gas business. Though most activity was centered on oil, by 1886, Standard had spent $7 million to acquire nine natural gas companies operating in New York, Pennsylvania, and Ohio.[26] O'Day became an incorporator and board member of many of these natural gas companies formed during the 1880s including United Natural Gas Company, based in Oil City; Pennsylvania Gas Company, founded in Warren (initially as the Warren Light and Heat Company); Meadville Fuel Gas Company; Northwestern Pennsylvania Natural Gas Company in Crawford County; and Manufacturer's Gas Company in Venango County. Other natural gas firms affiliated with Rockefeller interests included Buffalo Natural Gas Fuel Company, acquired in 1886; and Oil City Fuel Supply Company, originally organized by individuals outside of Standard, but purchased by National Transit in 1885.[27] Standard gas entrepreneurs were also listed as directors of the numerous incipient natural gas firms including the Ridgway Natural Gas Company and St. Marys Natural Gas Company. By the 1890s, Rockefeller secretly oversaw natural-gas companies in sixteen localities with O'Day's help.[28] Living in New York City at the turn of the century, O'Day remained critical to the oversight of the expanding natural gas business, including sitting on the board of the newly purchased Peoples and Pittsburgh Natural Gas companies until his death in 1906.

In Natural, We Trust— Creation of a Gas Trust

Standard's monopoly on oil, and its effort to coordinate the production, piping, and marketing of natural gas, was a cause for worry among many. It was on the mind of Benjamin Brewster, one of the early Standard stockholders, who often acted to "curb the zeal" of some of the other stockholders.[29] Brewster, a 49'r who made his fortune in California in the mercantile business, and later as an investor and officer in railroads, was a chief representative of Standard's pipelines. According to historian Christopher Castaneda, "Concern about the public's belief that Standard Oil sought to monopolize the gas business, as well as general apprehension about the Gas Trust's legal status with the National Transit Company, caused Brewster to recommend in 1888 that the Trust's certificates be transferred to Standard Oil."[30]

As a result of Brewster's suggestion, National Transit thus transferred seven of the natural gas affiliates to the newly formed Natural Gas Trust, keeping interests in two small companies, the Lawrence Natural Gas Company in Pennsylvania, Mahoning Gas Fuel Company (which supplied Youngstown, Ohio, from Pennsylvania wells), and part of the North Western Ohio Natural Gas Company.[31] Standard leaders Archbold, Brewster, O'Day, and Rogers, as well as other Natural Gas Trust trustees (Joseph D. Potts, H. M. Flagler, and William T. Scheide), issued certificates to National Transit for all outstanding shares in the companies. Despite the illusion of transfer and no legal connection, National Transit had "passed merely from the right hand into the left" as many of the individuals remained as officers in both firms.[32] Rockefeller served as the largest shareholder and kept an appearance of arm's length.[33] Brewster, his mien dominated by muttonchops sideburns resembling early 1880s U.S. President Chester A. Arthur, became the first president of Oil City's UNG and retired in 1888, because "the duties are — should be — and must be absorbing." He recommended "that a younger man, anxious for work and fresh for the contest" should replace him.[34] His son, J. Benjamin Brewster, later became National Transit's chief executive officer.

Benjamin Brewster (1828–1897), first president of Oil City's United Natural Gas Company, recommended that the newly formed Natural Gas Trust stock certificates be transferred from the National Transit Company to Standard Oil (courtesy National Fuel Gas Company).

The Pennsylvania Pipelines — Calvin Payne and Company

A great period of gas pipeline activity occurred between 1886 and 1891. One of the first pipelines that crossed a state border was the nation's first long-distance metal gas pipeline built in 1886, constructed by Standard interests. The line from the gas fields of McKean County, Pa., to Buffalo (see Chapter Six), was supervised by Calvin N. Payne (1844–1926), who was brought into Standard in 1885 as a veteran pipeline expert. National Transit General Superintendent William T. Scheide, who retired in 1889, first succeeded O'Day. Then the reigns of pipeline work were taken over by Payne as O'Day's "most trusted lieutenant."[35] Born in 1844 and a native of Warren, Pa., Payne started in gas drilling at age fifteen at nearby Youngsville. One of the wells he was involved in was the first to be drilled with waterpower and steel cable. Also a former railroad conductor, Payne served as president of PGC and UNG, and was an officer or director in nearly all the original gas companies in the Oil Region. He served as early straw boss on many construction projects under the tutelage of O'Day. He was one of the strongest advocates of finding new outlets for natural gas, claiming that the commodity could expand to all industrial cities.[36] Payne was also chairman of Standard's Natural Gas Committee and became president of Hope Natural Gas Company in West Virginia when O'Day died in 1906. Payne also helped lead oil transportation subsidiaries Buckeye Pipe Line Company, Eureka Pipe Line Company, and South West Pennsylvania Pipe Line Company.

Calvin Payne (1844–1926) started in drilling projects in the oil region as a teen, as the saying went, "with his foot in the stirrup." Brought into Standard Oil as a pipeline expert, he oversaw the first long-distance gas pipeline from Pennsylvania to Buffalo, led many natural gas firms in Appalachia, and founded a gas meter manufacturing company (courtesy National Fuel Gas Company).

Payne was also involved in manufacturing gas meters (see Chapter Seven) in Beaver Falls and Erie, Pa. He also worked in developing early oil production at the turn of the century for Standard in Texas.[37] He left Standard in 1913 at age seventy, but later had investments in Texas and Oklahoma as well as beginning the Modern Tool Company in Erie.[38] Though Payne died in Erie in 1926, his legacy lived on in the natural gas region. One of Payne's sons, Frank, helped lead the American Meter Company with his Erie office at Metric Metal Works. Another son, Christy, a lawyer from Venango County, took over natural gas operations of Standard Oil (New Jersey), and became president of Peoples in Pittsburgh from 1920 to 1933. And Christy Payne's son also served as vice president of Peoples during the early 1960s.

Some other major players in Standard gas activities, based upon their names listed as incorporators of dozens of firms, included Henry W. McSweeney, William T. Scheide, John Bushnell, George Chesebro, Joseph Seep, and James B. Crawford. McSweeney, born in 1856 in Pittsburgh, came to the oil region in the 1860s, and was admitted to the bar in Venango County at age twenty-one. He became a wealthy attorney in a practice after moving to Bradford in 1879.[39] McSweeney became the solicitor for National Transit, and an officer in Hope from 1898 to 1903 and also many other incorporated Standard companies. Scheide, born in 1847, was a native of Philadelphia who came to Tidioute to enter the oil industry, and first became general manager of United Pipe Lines.[40] Bushnell, who originated from a longstanding wealthy family in the region, became secretary and controller of National Transit, and served as president of Hope from 1906 to 1908.[41] Chesebro, born in New York City in 1850, was secretary and comptroller of National Transit and a key figure in the Natural Gas Trust around the turn of the century.[42] Seep, born in 1838, went to Kentucky to enter the grain and hemp business in 1849, and then to Cincinnati in 1866 to engage in cotton trading. Seep moved to Titusville in 1869 with the firm of

Bostwick & Tilford, an oil-trading agency that was Standard's buyer of oil in the early 1870s, and joined Standard in 1871.[43] Crawford (1855–1933) was born in the oil region in Emlenton, Pa., graduated from Eastman College in Poughkeepsie, N.Y., in 1876, and then returned to the oil region working for Standard, drilling in the newly discovered Bradford oil field. He later joined the Oil City Fuel Supply Company and then became president of UNG, the first head of that firm that was a local resident.

Captain John Tonkin, a former Confederate officer in the Civil War and resident of Tidioute, Pa., in Warren County, was assistant general manager of Standard's natural gas interests until 1906.[44] Born in 1827 in eastern Pennsylvania, Tonkin moved to Tennessee in his youth, and was one of the very few early Standard executives with any college education. He enlisted in the Confederate Army, and was paroled in 1865 like other rebel soldiers. He traveled the Oil City area and located in Tidioute taking a job with the Dennis Run and New York Oil Company.[45] He joined Standard in 1887, when he took

Capt. John Tonkin, one of the very few early Standard Oil executives with any college education, was a former Confederate army officer who moved to Oil City after the Civil War and eventually became a leader in several Standard Oil–controlled natural gas firms (courtesy Dominion Resources).

up leases for the Ohio Oil Company around Lima. He helped run the Northwestern Ohio Natural Gas Company, and later Standard's Mountain State and River firms (of which he became president of in 1896). He was later vice president of Hope, and also an official of the Clarksburg Light and Heat, Commercial, UNG, Oil City Fuel Supply, Mahoning Gas and Fuel, and Lawrence gas firms.[46] Tonkin acquired oil and gas properties of his own in Tidioute and Bradford, Pa., and in Kentucky in the Central Kentucky Gas Company.

The Prince and the Pauper — Henry "Hell Hound" Rogers

Perhaps the most colorful of the Standard pioneers that dabbled in the natural gas business was the Wall Street tycoon Henry Huttleston Rogers. Rogers helped direct Standard's Natural Gas Committee, which reorganized in 1902 to direct the company's natural gas interests.[47] A native of Fairhaven, Massachusetts, Rogers clerked in a grocery store, hawked newspapers, and worked on a railroad before he and a boyhood friend came to the Pennsylvania Oil Region where they built and operated a new type of refinery close to the famous Oil Creek McClintock oil well near Rouseville from 1861 to 1867. In 1868, Rogers joined the Charles Pratt Manufacturing Company in New York and patented improvements for more accurately separating naphtha fractions from kerosene and for dividing naphtha into its component parts. Pratt (1830–1891) shipped crude by the barrel on the East River and constructed a Long Island factory. Rogers then formed an alliance with Standard during the oil depression in 1874, along with other refining interests in Pittsburgh and Philadelphia, by throwing his fortunes into Rockefeller's South Improvement Company.[48]

Rogers was an inventor, organizer, negotiator, seller, and a self-proclaimed capitalist. A sea captain's son, Rogers was said to have a "lunar dualism — dark on one side, and bright on the other."[49] Rockefeller biographer Ron Chernow wrote, "From his elegant mahogany office, decorated with small bronze bulls and bears, Rogers hatched deals by the dozen, forcing reporters to work full-time to track his machinations."[50] Another more sensitive volume portrays him as a "paladin of commerce, and an inventor of genius, although the latter gift disappeared from use as his business undertakings increased, an inspiring leader, a lion in the path of opposition but who was ordinarily the gentlest and most courteous of men."[51]

Rogers was said to become the transportation "czar of Staten Island," controlling trolleys, railroads, and ferries, but still had an interest in manufactured gas companies.[52] In 1884, he and William G. Rockefeller formed the Consolidated Gas Company of New York, merging six gaslight companies and providing manufactured gas to Brooklyn. Rogers also battled for control of Boston's Bay State Gas, which sold manufactured gas.[53] He also helped found the United Gas and Improvement Company, a Philadelphia-area utility.[54] In 1885, Rogers was elected a trustee of Standard, and in 1888, he became Standard's expert on natural gas and pipeline matters.

Rogers also led Standard's Manufacturing Committee, helping to standardize processes and products among oil plants. His "remarkable energy and tenacity of purpose" resulted in his hand in numerous Standard oil and gas activities.[55] He was the first to use natural gas engines to drive the dynamos that powered electric motors that pumped the oil wells at a cost averaging less than $20 per well per month. Called a natural leader, Rogers was elevated to vice president in 1890. By 1895, Rogers was president of seven and director of thirteen of Standard's twenty major companies. He also became a member of Standard's executive committee, a position that relieved Rockefeller of active direction of the leviathan conglomerate. Rogers also served as the second president of UNG, president of National Transit, and later president of National Fuel Gas Company.

Except for Rockefeller himself, no member of the Standard group was to make such an impact on the public mind.[56] He was "a man of electric personality and inexhaustible energy."[57] Rogers was also a man of ample generosity. He donated a high school building, free library, Masonic building, memorial church, and public park to his native Fairhaven.[58] In Titusville, Pa., he erected a $100,000 memorial to oil pioneer Colonel Drake.[59] He assisted in establishing the Oil City Hospital and the Grandview Sanatorium, one of the first refuges for tuberculosis sufferers. He created a permanent endowment fund to the Titusville and Oil City Hospitals, and built the Oil City Nurses' Home.

Henry H. Rogers, who led some of Standard Oil's natural gas operations, was a colorful figure who developed relationships with the likes of African American leader Booker T. Washington and literary great Samuel Clemens, a.k.a. Mark Twain. Standard Oil historian Allan Nevins noted, "His handsome features, careful dress, and magnetic personality made him a distinguished figure in drawing room and business conference alike." Nicknamed "Hell Hound" Rogers, he admitted to being a born gambler and started poker games on weekends when the stock market closed (courtesy National Fuel Gas Company).

Early oil historian John McLaurin wrote that Rogers had "brains, earnestness, integrity and industry" and was a "liberal patron of education and apostle of good roads."[60] Likewise, Standard writers chronicled that Rogers "well trained mind and memory inspired the value and variety of his counsel."[61] Many noted people were attracted to Roger's allure, including African American leader Booker T. Washington. Rogers greatly admired literary great Samuel Langhorne Clemens (a.k.a. Mark Twain), who with his salient white mane and bushy moustache was like in appearance. Rogers helped put the famous author's finances in order, rescuing Twain's bankrupt publishing house in 1893.[62] In response, Twain once said Rogers was "the best friend I ever had," and also, "the best man I have known."[63] The "prince and the pauper" sometimes lunched and spent time together on a yacht.[64] At Twain's urging, Rogers took over the financing of the education of the blind and deaf Helen Keller, enabling her to go to college at Radcliffe.[65]

As Standard came under attack in

the press for its monopolistic tactics in the oil realm, Rogers made an effort to tell Standard's and his own side of story. During the United States Industrial Commission's investigation into Standard, Rogers claimed that the company had a story to tell and the newspapers probably would have printed their side: "But talk is so awful cheap in these days that we have preferred to keep on sawing wood, and so we haven't had our side of the case fairly presented, perhaps," Rogers testified.[66] At Twain's arrangement, Rogers met with muckraking journalist Ida Tarbell (1857–1944) of Titusville, who was writing a history of Standard.[67] Some suggest he did it as a form of revenge against Rockefeller, but he said he wanted to make the company's case made right since Tarbell would produce the piece anyway. The two met in January 1902, and Tarbell described Rogers as "by all odds the handsomest and most distinguished figure."[68] Both growing up in the Oil Region, they shared experiences of life outside of Rouseville. Tarbell liked him, sarcastically writing that Rogers was "as fine a pirate as ever flew his flag in Wall Street."[69] Rogers met with her regularly for two years, telling her frankly how Standard influenced legislation.

Tarbell's revealing series on Standard began in *McClure's* magazine in November 1902. Rogers continued to see her cordially, but when she published how Standard's intelligence network operated by putting pressure on the small retailers, Rogers was furious and broke off the relationship.[70] Tarbell also wrote of Rogers: "He and his friends had been engaged in organizing the gas interests of the East. They had engineered stock raids which had been as disastrous to Wall Street as to gambling on Main Street."[71]

As opposition heated up against Standard's oil monopoly position, Rogers vigorously, forcibly, and directly defended Standard practices against critics, including President Theodore Roosevelt, who took the oath of office after an anarchist assassinated President McKinley at the Pan American Exposition in Buffalo in 1901. Rogers and fellow Standard captain Archbold contributed $100,000 to Roosevelt's campaign in 1904. Roosevelt ordered the money returned, but it was uncertain whether it actually was.[72] Both officials went to see the president in Washington in 1906 to dissuade him from the attack on Standard. Despite the "Gilded Age" (as coined by Roger's friend Mark Twain) lobbying tactics, it did not work. Roosevelt brought forty-five antitrust actions against the monopoly.[73]

Some called him "Hell Hound Rogers" because of his speculative adventures on Wall Street.[74] His extracurricular business activities eventually caused a feud with Rockefeller when Rogers acquired a copper mining venture and was involved in a stock purchase speculation that resulted in shareholder losses. Rockefeller finally bought him out of his Standard interest in 1907. That same year, Rogers suffered a stroke. His friend Sam Clemens stayed with him during his recovery in Bermuda. Rogers died in 1909, with an estimated estate of $41 million, though earlier estimates put it at more than $100 million.[75]

The Holding Companies

At the close of the nineteenth century, natural gas companies dotted the Appalachian countryside wherever gas wells were discovered. Expansion to other potential customers depended on three factors: first, an integrated pipeline network to link the widely scattered firms; second, a coordinated gas supply; and third, adequate financing. Standard and other utility "holding companies" addressed all three. Standard's National Transit not only controlled most natural gas pipeline transportation, but also owned the prime Appalachian gas fields and had "virtually unlimited capital" to develop them.[76] Holding companies provided the necessary funds for financing long-distance pipeline construction and local pipeline networks.[77] The federal government moved to regulate interstate commerce in 1887, and later, the final federal Hepburn (Anti-rebate) Act of 1906 required oil pipelines to be common carriers, approved as a result of complaints of monopoly practices by Standard. However, gas pipelines—though obviously recognized as interstate commerce — were not included in the legislation. So the expansion and consolidation of natural gas firms continued, and Standard's entrepreneurs met these needs in eastern Ohio, western Pennsylvania, western New York, and West Virginia. By 1911, the number of larger gas companies in which Standard had interests grew to twenty.[78] The previous independent local pipeline systems began to form an interstate circulatory system for natural gas, and by 1920, 15 percent of the natural gas in the United States crossed state lines.[79] Without this structure, industry historians Louis Stotz and Alexander Jamison wrote in the 1930s, "such natural gas systems as ... Cities Service, Columbia Gas & Electric, [Standard's] East Ohio-Hope-Peoples and others could not have been built up except through the holding companies, and many hundreds of cities and towns in the territories served by these systems would still be without gas service...."[80]

In 1882, UGI organized in Philadelphia as the first utility holding company — because it operated manufactured gas plants in various cities—in which Standard had only a fraction of an interest.[81] Around the turn of the century, New Jersey reformed its laws to permit the creation of holding companies that could own the stock of other corporations, such as Standard Oil (New Jersey). Standard interests in Buffalo and western Pennsylvania elected to put many of their Natural Gas Trust investments under one umbrella by the formation of National Fuel Gas Company, incorporated in 1902 as a holding company to own the stocks of businesses producing and selling natural gas. A total of 32,453 shares of stock issued to NFG were purchased from the trustees of the Natural Gas Trust including UNG of Oil City, Salamanca Gas Company, Buffalo Natural Gas Fuel Company, Oil City Fuel Supply Company, Commercial Natural Gas Company of Bradford, and slightly over half the interest in PGC in Warren and Provincial Gas Company, Ltd. of Bridgeburg (now Fort Erie), Ontario, Canada (later sold in the 1950s). The parent company offices were run out of New Jersey and at 26 Broadway in New York City, the same address as Standard's operations.[82] NFG, merely a paper firm to hold the securities of its subsidiaries, was part of a plan to improve and systemize management of Standard's gas interests.[83] The new firm had $6.7 million in net investment and its subsidiaries served more than 57,000 customers, mostly in Warren, Oil City, and Erie in northwestern Pennsylvania, and Buffalo and Jamestown in western New York.

Many of the names of the original NFG shareholders were prominent figures in the Standard empire, including Bushnell, Chesebro, O'Day, Payne, Rogers, Seep, Strong, and Tonkin. Other trustees of the Natural Gas Trust at the time included George Colton, Ted Towl, John McManus, James H. Snow, Sam Rogers, and J. S. McKinney. Several were members of Standard's Natural Gas Advisory Board (later known as the Natural Gas Committee), including Bushnell, O'Day, Payne, and Strong. According to one account, there is no record of the number of shares held by each individual, but most likely the trustees held the major portion. "There were no direct legal connections between this group of corporations and the gas companies within Standard Oil, but they had many stockholders in common, and some employees and officers served as links between them."[84] Rockefeller's brother, William, also served as a NFG director from 1904 to 1907.

Other turn of the century Standard leaders involved in NFG included Walter Jennings and Walter W. Richardson. Jennings, whose father was also a Standard investor and original trustee, graduated from Yale and Columbia University Law School before joining the Charles Pratt Manufacturing Co. in New York, which was also linked to Standard. Rockefeller and Pratt both gave considerable attention to developing new leaders, and, in 1889, Pratt wrote to Rockefeller recommending Jennings for a position that required independence of judgment. In 1903, Jennings was elected a Standard director and served until his death in 1933. He served as UNG's President from 1910 to 1915, succeeding Calvin Payne, and he also served as president of NFG during this period.[85] Richardson (1873–1915) began working for Standard interests at age seventeen. At thirty-seven years old, he became the youngest president of two NFG affiliates in 1910: UNG and Iroquois Natural Gas Company. He began negotiations to build additional pipelines to the newly discovered West Virginia gas fields to address the increasing demand for natural gas in the Buffalo area.

Stuart Nichols, a NFG president during the 1950s, said his company would not have been in existence unless

> far sighted men had not set up business structures which have withstood growing pains; endured through booms and depressions; expanded markets in highly competitive areas; and continued to do business at a profit after imposition of several layers of government regulation. We give credit for this foresight to John D. Rockefeller and his associates, who of course, were responsible for the founding of several of our Country's going concerns.[86]

The Keystone Companies — A Short History of Selected Northwestern Pennsylvania Natural Gas Firms

As it was discovered, much natural gas spread across western Pennsylvania on a local level before Standard's ultimate control. One of the first firms in the western Pennsylvania region was The Oil City Fuel Supply Company, created in 1881, under Pennsylvania's General Corporation Act of 1874. It was chartered to produce gas in Cranberry, Pine Grove, President, and Cornplanter townships in Venango County and its territory of distribution included Oil City and the Borough of Siverlyville. After an earlier veto by Titusville's Mayor Thomas, the city granted the firm the right to lay pipe through streets for gas in 1885.[87] Another early firm in Venango County was the Emlenton Gas Light and Fuel Company, which organized in 1882 and later became part of the Columbia system.

Soon after, the United Natural Gas Company formed in 1886 in Oil City and developed into the major natural gas supplier in northwestern Pennsylvania. Its charter authorized the firm to produce and receive natural gas and the right to supply gas to consumers in the counties of Venango, Forest, Butler, Armstrong, Clarion, Warren, Elk, and McKean. In May 1886, the directors authorized the purchase of the gas properties, including wells and equipment, owned by National Transit for $2.5 million to become part of Standard's Natural Gas Trust.[88]

UNG constructed pipelines that same year to sell natural gas to the cities of Oil City, Meadville, Sharon, and Bradford in Pennsylvania, and transmission lines were laid to the cities of Buffalo and Salamanca in New York. The firm reached agreement to supply gas to the Buffalo Natural Fuel Gas Company, another Standard firm organized in 1886.

UNG also supplied the Commercial Natural Gas Company of Bradford. Bradford lawmakers passed an ordinance in September 1885 allowing the installation of gas lines in city streets, also over the Mayor's veto.[89] In 1886, Northwestern Natural Gas Company of Meadville completed lines and that city was lighted from wells thirty-seven miles away.[90] An injunction restraining the Meadville Fuel Gas Company from laying pipe in the city was dissolved by the same state Supreme Court action that year that opened up natural gas to Pittsburgh.[91] In 1894, UNG sold leaseholds, gas wells, and gas lines to the South Buffalo gas field to the Seneca Natural Gas Company to provide gas to the South Buffalo Natural Gas Company. After becoming a subsidiary of NFG in 1902, UNG began construction of a new $100,000 headquarters at 308 Seneca Street in Oil City in 1912, down the street from the National Transit headquarters; and it opened in March 1915.

In 1892, the Oil City Fuel Supply Company consolidated with Meadville Natural Gas Company, Meadville Fuel Gas Company, Columbia Gas Light and Fuel Company, Northwestern Pennsylvania Natural Gas Company, and the Manufacturers Gas Company (Oil City). And, in 1908, UNG merged with Oil City Fuel Supply Company. Further consolidation made UNG the primary natural gas supplier and distributor in the oil and gas region of northwestern Pennsylvania. In 1913, UNG purchased the Commercial Natural Gas Company of Bradford, the Franklin Natural Gas Company (formed in 1885), and the Forest Gas Company of Tidioute.

Other smaller firms organized near well discoveries in rural northwestern Pennsylvania. In 1890, the Venango Gas Company was granted the right to lay pipe in Oil City. Gas in the Clarion, Pa., area began in 1883 with the Clarion Light and Heat Company, which, in 1891, became the Clarion and Tylersburg Gas Company, producing and distributing gas in Clarion and Forest County. The firm was renamed the Clarion Gas Company in 1902. The company borrowed money from the Pittsburgh Oil and Gas Company, and, in 1904, built a gas line from Miola, Pa., to the Ohio State line near the southwest corner of Crawford County. The firm's headquarters was once located in Pittsburgh, but moved to Oil City in 1914. Clarion later became part of UNG in 1919.[92]

Gas in Ridgway, Pa., began when a group of citizens completed a producing well on the "Willard White" well tract near Johnsonburg in 1884. The group decided to transport this gas to Ridgway where it could be sold to supply heat and light through a four-inch pipeline. The Ridgway Light and Heat Company received its charter in 1885. Additional acreage was acquired, more wells were drilled, and pipelines were extended. In 1902, the firm was merged with the Clarion River Gas Company and the consolidated corporation took the name Ridgway Light and Heat Company. This merger gave the consumers at Ridgway an adequate supply of gas.[93]

Gas service in nearby St. Marys, Pa., started in 1889 when the St. Marys Gas Company drilled wells and laid distribution lines, and extended service to Emporium. In 1928, the company reorganized as the St. Marys Natural Gas Company, and then consisted of 112 gas wells and pipelines serving the Boroughs of St. Marys, Emporium, and vicinity.[94] Nearby Johnsonburg, Pa., was originally serviced by the Consumers Gas and Heat Company.[95] Also, the Jefferson County Gas Company formed in 1902. The firm was a non-utility producing natural gas in Elk, Forest, and Jefferson counties in Pennsylvania.

Gas service in northern Pennsylvania also began that year in the natural gas fields outside Warren, Pa., south of the New York state line. In 1881, C. A. & D. Cornen drilled a wildcat well more than 1,000 feet deep in Clarendon, and hit a vein of gas. Rocks were thrown out of the borehole and "chunks the size of hen's eggs were sent up through the derrick as though shot from a cannon."[96] Investors laid a pipeline to nearby Clarendon, furnishing fuel for twenty-six oil drilling wells, three pumping wells, 125 stoves, two machine shops and two pump stations. Afterward, the Warren Light and Heat Company formed in 1881 to supply gas to the Borough of Warren and vicinity. The new company then built an eight-inch line to Clarendon in 1883. The firm purchased the properties of several small gas companies and reorganized in 1885, changing its name to Pennsylvania Gas Company (PGC).[97] Other firms in the Warren-Jamestown, N.Y., area during this period included the Jamestown Gas Company (1881), Jamestown Fuel and Light Company (1885), New York and Pennsylvania Gas Heating Company, Chautauqua Gas Company, and the Tri-County Natural Gas Company.

A *Jamestown Dispatch* account recorded the event as gas came to Jamestown in 1885: "Tonight the streets are filled with crowds watching the illumination by the gas burning from several standpipes. The roar of the flames can be heard for a long distance. The Pennsylvania Gas Company owns the line and has forty miles of gas pipe in Jamestown's streets, the gas territory and pipe line and fixtures representing over $800,000."[98]

In February 1886, PGC contracted with Standard's National Transit to lay an eight-inch pipeline from Warren to the Erie County municipality of Corry, and the City of Corry Council passed an ordinance granting PGC a franchise. Natural gas turned into the mains at Corry from the rural wells at Ludlow and required forty-one minutes to traverse the twenty-seven miles when it tapped the Warren line.[99]

Erie Gas Company, a manufactured gas firm incorporated in 1852 to provide gaslight, competed with PGC that supplied the Lake Erie shoreline city of Erie with natural gas once lines were extended east from Warren. The Erie, Pa., Common Council authorized PGC to lay and maintain pipes in the streets, avenues, and alleys in the city on March 16, 1886, after overriding an earlier veto of Mayor F. A. Mizener by a vote of 18 to 5.[100] When natural gas pressure filled the lines in Erie on November 26th of that year, thirty customers were brought into service and forty-two the following day. Oddly, the first person who actually signed up for service did not get his gas range, water heater, and room-heating grate hooked up until three days later.[101]

Though PGC was initially of Pennsylvania origin, it received the okay to do business in New York. Afterward, it progressively extended pipelines to other towns. The firm built a headquarters at 213 Second Avenue in Warren in 1926, and later remodeled and enlarged it in 1956. The headquarters was sold in 1974 by PGC's parent firm, NFG, to the United Refining Company.

Another early firm in north-central Pennsylvania was the Smethport Gas Company, originally chartered in 1874.[102] It became the Smethport Natural Gas Corporation in 1930 and consisted of sixty-seven gas wells, and pipelines and distribution plant serving Smethport in McKean County, Pa. Further west, the Mercer County Gas Company organized in 1904. Mercer did not produce gas, so the firm bought its gas from the Clarion Gas Company and supplied gas in the boroughs of Fredonia, Hadley, Jamestown, and Osgood.[103]

The Mars Natural Gas Company organized in 1913, and under its charter, it was authorized to drill for, transport, and sell petroleum, natural gas, and "other volatile substances" that included various casinghead liquids (propane, butane, etc.). In 1917, Mars sold its distribution lines to UNG and operated as a non-utility called The Mars Company. Mars purchased and developed numerous small natural gas and oil producing properties.[104] In the late 1970s, Mars was renamed Seneca Resources Corporation, now a NFG exploration and production firm.

Other firms included the North Penn Gas Company, with its affiliates Dempseytown Gas Company, and Allegany Gas Company in New York State, which provided gas to customers in Potter, Forest, McKean, Clarion, and Venango counties in Pennsylvania, including a refinery and various glass plants. Also, the T. W. Phillips Company served several thousand customers in Butler County, Pa., and, by 1913, owned more than 700 wells with more than 100,000 acres under lease. The small firm became part of the Peoples Natural Gas system in 2011.

Though hundreds of small community gas companies in the region have since been absorbed by the larger utility companies, some smaller firms still remain such as the Erie area North East Heat & Light Company and Gasco Distribution Systems, Inc., which serves Kane, Pa., and other small distribution systems in Ohio, Kentucky and Tennessee.

South to Hope, West to East Ohio — Standard's Gas Interests Expand

Over time, Standard gas interests continued their "encircling" movement to capture both natural gas supplies and subsequent markets in Appalachia. By the end of the nineteenth century, the potential markets in eastern Ohio, including Cleveland, and the expanding industrial demand in Pittsburgh put pressure on the already dwindling supply produced in the heart of the production region in Pennsylvania. The key to success lay in securing the phenomenal new natural discoveries south in West Virginia and transporting the fuel to distant markets. To accomplish this, in 1898, Standard organized the Hope Natural Gas Company to produce, gather, and transport "unused, unwanted, economical unfamiliar" gas in West Virginia through long-distance lines to the inchoate East Ohio Gas Company for the expanding industries in the Cleveland market.[105] Hope, whose stock was held by Standard's National Transit, was formed from the gas wells owned by the West Virginia Standard firm South Penn Oil Company (organized to explore for oil in West Virginia and Pennsylvania) and Carter Oil Company.

On September 17, 1898, for a fee of $61, West Virginia's secretary of state granted Standard (New Jersey) a certificate of incorporation for Hope based on $200,000 of issued stock. Though the firm began with only twelve employees based in Oil City, Pa., the familiar Standard leaders including Strong, Tonkin, McSweeney, Payne, and Robert S. Hampton were "hopeful that natural gas (an offshoot of oil production) would prove to be the wave of the future."[106] For energy hungry markets in Ohio and Pittsburgh, it was. The following year, Hope purchased eleven gas wells, and 29,904 acres of leaseholds from South Penn Oil Company. Most of the $232,000 investment was in leaseholds in Wetzel County, W.Va., bordering the southwest corner of Pennsylvania. The firm had thirty-two miles of pipeline and one customer—East Ohio.

Standard's immediate goal for West Virginia gas was the industrial Mahoning Valley, cautiously broadening slowly because other prior ventures found that gas supplies played out quickly.[107] Chosen over possible pipelines to Baltimore and Washington on the East Coast, Hope's first pipeline became known as the "Akron ten-inch," though it originated from an eight-inch line in Wetzel County, W.Va. It connected to East Ohio's ten-inch pipeline across the Ohio river, another Standard affiliated gas firm to move natural gas in interstate commerce (see Chapter Six).[108] In 1902, Hope opened its first field office in New Martinsville, W.Va., and then acquired Flaggy Meadow Gas Company (National Transit formed Flaggy Meadow in 1891 from other gas properties of South Penn and Carter Oil).[109] The original field office of Flaggy Meadow was a small shanty on a mud road at Piney, W.Va.[110] Pittsburgh's Peoples connected its lines with Hope after Standard acquired the Pew firm in 1903. In 1904, Hope, initially only a vehicle to acquire gas supplies for other Standard affiliates, began to sell and supply gas itself in towns and cities in West Virginia.[111] Hope eventually absorbed several firms that acquired and pooled gas supplies, and laid pipelines to serve customers in West Virginia and Ohio, including the Reserve Gas Company, Connecting Gas Company, Union Gas Company, and the Northwestern Natural Gas Company.[112] Hope relocated its field office in New Martinsville to the Empire Bank Building in Clarksburg in 1907. In 1910, Hope bought the Mountain State Gas Company (supplying gas to Parkersburg and Sistersville), Home Gas Company (operating a plant at Mannington), and all the West Virginia properties of Fayette County Gas Company, acquiring leaseholds totaling 1.4 million acres.[113] Ten years later, operating primarily in the northern part of West Virginia, Hope increased its gas production, stepped up purchases from other companies, increased its gas plant, and was at that time the largest gas producer in the United States.[114]

By 1928, Hope operated more than 3,257 gas wells, had fifty compressor stations, and nearly 9,000 miles of pipeline.[115] Other exchanges followed with the United Fuel, Freehold Oil and Gas Company, and a contract to supply gas needs of the Manufacturers Light and Heat Company.[116] Hope acquired Clarksburg Light and Heat Company in 1923, the Glenville Natural Gas Company, and constructed a new office at 445 West Main St. in Clarksburg.[117] Hope moved its corporate office from Pittsburgh to Clarksburg in 1940. The firm served thirty-two of West Virginia's counties as well as the Pittsburgh area with most of its gas from Appalachian sources.

After becoming a part of the Consolidated Natural Gas System in 1943, Hope later purchased gas properties of Monongahela Power Company to serve Fairmont and Morgantown, W.Va., in 1950.[118] In 1965, CNG's interstate pipeline merged with its sister company, New York State Natural Gas Corporation (New York State Natural), and was renamed Consolidated Gas Supply Corporation (later changed in 1984 to Consolidated Gas Transmission Corporation), with a total investment of $107 million.[119] By 1997, Consolidated Gas Transmission had 3,362 production wells, 1,510 storage wells, and 10,000 miles of pipeline.[120]

East Ohio began as a marketing company of Rockefeller's National Transit, incorporated on September 8, 1898, as a gas arm of Standard Oil (New Jersey), with O'Day as a principal organizer.[121] The firm's main office was in Lima, Ohio, where O'Day and some of the incorporators lived. National Transit built a ten-inch wrought iron pipeline from Pipe Creek on the Ohio River to Akron, with branches to Canton, Massillon, Dover, New Philadelphia, Uhrichsville, and Dennison. Akron — not yet the rubber-manufacturing capital of the world with a population of only 43,000 — was an uncertain market to first to take advantage of the new gas supplies. But East Ohio was granted an Akron franchise in 1898, and buried twenty-two miles of pipe in the city. After roman candles were shot into an ostentatious flambeau pipe on a downtown street, Akron residents saw natural gas burn for the first time on May 10, 1899.[122] Still, the new product in the former manufactured gas town was treated with reservation. One account stated, "Everyone wanted to wait until his neighbor had tried it out."[123]

Elizur (or E.) Strong worked the Pennsylvania oil fields and eventually became the first president of East Ohio Gas Company. He directed a long-distance pipeline from West Virginia to the Cleveland markets (courtesy Dominion Resources).

Standard investor Elizur (or E.) Strong became the first president of East Ohio, and also was on the list of incorporators (who along with Calvin Payne owned nearly all the stock) and shareholders of numerous other gas companies in the region including UNG, Peoples, Meadville Natural Gas Company, and the Northwestern Pennsylvania Natural Gas Company.[124] His headquarters was in Oil City, Pa., and he lived in nearby Saegertown.[125] Strong started working in the Pennsylvania oil fields as a driller of oil wells, and was described as a "powerful man physically, a tireless worker, a man quite without sloth in his own makeup and intolerant of sloth in others, and completely attentive to the interests of the big company for which he worked."[126] Strong directed a long-distance line across the Ohio River and eastern Ohio to Cleveland markets, and brought innovations in pipeline building, such as hinged sections allowing the construction of longer and wider pipes. One former employee described him as "the type of man with whom you did not argue nor ask questions."[127] Strong led Peoples and East Ohio until his death in 1906.

As in Pittsburgh and Buffalo, there was not unanimous support for introduction of natural gas into Cleveland. The city's progressive mayor, Tom L. Johnson, instinctively opposed private firms, and supported municipal ownership of public utilities, such as the city's streetcars.[128] However, Johnson eventually came out on the side of East Ohio. One account stated, "City council debated hotly and one councilman dramatically waved the cash he said he had been offered by East Ohio's competitors."[129] Cleveland finally received natural gas from Standard on January 1, 1903. A subsequent Cleveland mayor, Newton D. Baker, said, "it is very doubtful whether anything has ever happened in this city — any one thing — which did more for its prosperity, did more for its beauty, did more for the convenience, the comfort, the happiness and, perhaps, the health of the people who live here than the introduction of natural gas."[130] By 1904, East Ohio had 17,000 customers in Cleveland and would grow to 109,000 by 1920.[131]

The Standard interests secured the franchise despite concerns of private ownership and manufactured gas competition through the efforts of Martin B. Daly, a pioneer "market surveyor" who found natural gas market potentialities. Daly, who once worked at age eighteen as Strong's tool dresser in the early oil exploration days in Bradford, Pa., later cleared leases, constructed pipelines and pumping stations, and scouted for oil.[132] He applied gas metering as general superintendent of the Buffalo Natural Gas Fuel Company, and also introduced metering to the Standard-controlled Northwestern Ohio Gas Company, when gas from local fields supplied Toledo, competing with manufactured gas billed at a flat rate.[133] Toledo's initial gas effort was called an "expensive experiment" in municipal ownership before it was taken over by private interests. After the city bought and drilled gas wells and laid pipelines in Lucas and Wood Counties, the gas supply soon faulted and the wells produced saltwater.[134]

Daly, described in an East Ohio company history as "a man of quiet dignity and low-voiced, restrained, and persuasive in an argument against the opposition," succeeded Strong as East Ohio president in 1906, and managed significant growth for the firm until he died at his desk twenty years later. Ralph W. Gallagher, who worked in the western New York oil fields and on western Pennsylvania pipelines, succeeded him. Gallagher later became chairman of Standard (New Jersey).[135]

After its incorporation, East Ohio purchased the Mahoning Gas Fuel Company (originally founded in 1886) in 1908, and absorbed the consolidated manufactured gas firms of Cleveland Gas Light and Coke and the Peoples Gas Light Company in 1910, adding 65,000 customers. Also acquired were the Canton Gas Light Company in 1911, and the following year, the Mohican Oil and Gas Company (initially formed in 1904 and included the properties of the Ohio Union Oil and Gas Company that began in 1903). The firm built a six-story office building at East Sixth and Rockwell in Cleveland in 1916. Later purchases included the Akron Gas Company (originally incorporated in 1891) in 1921, and the Youngstown Gas Company (first formed in 1926) in 1927.[136] The Ohio Gas Company had previously served Youngstown from local sources and Mahoning, which purchased gas from Standard's Lawrence Natural Gas Company of Pennsylvania.[137]

After Peoples, East Ohio, Hope, River, and New York State Natural evolved into CNG in 1943, other area firms would become part of the East Ohio system. They included the Portage Lake Gas Company in 1945, Lake County Gas Company (incorporated in 1926) in 1955, and the Lake Shore Gas Company in 1957. Lake Shore, acquired from Associated Electric Company in 1945, also consisted of the Jefferson Gas Company purchased in 1935, North Eastern Oil & Gas Company purchased in 1931, and the Ashtabula Gas Company (founded in 1895), purchased in 1925. The Painesville Gas Department, originally incorporated as the Painesville Gas Light and Coal Company in 1861, was purchased by East Ohio in 1959. The company moved into a new downtown skyscraper headquarters in Cleveland that year and remained there until 2003 until moving to another Cleveland location. East Ohio, once the largest natural gas utility in the world, served 1.2 million customers in 400 eastern and western Ohio communities in 2003.[138]

Mountain and Bluegrass Companies — A Short History of Selected West Virginia and Kentucky Gas Firms

Besides Hope, numerous firms sprouted around the West Virginia gas and oil finds to furnish the major cities and towns, many of them having connections with Standard through National Transit, South Penn Oil, or the Forest Oil Company. The Natural Gas Company of West Virginia formed in 1885 after the first substantial gas well in the Northern Panhandle of the state at Wellsburg. Mountain State Gas Company, organized in 1892 by Standard interests, served Parkersburg from the Pleasants County field.[139] Clarksburg was served by three firms, Home Gas Company (later a Columbia affiliate), West Fork Gas Company, and Monongahela Development Company (owned by National Transit). Charleston was served by the Charleston Natural Gas Company beginning in 1893. The Fairmont and Grafton Gas Company was organized in 1894 and absorbed the Fairmont Manufactured and Natural Gas Company.[140] Gas came to Wheeling in 1896 provided by the West Virginia Natural Gas Company. Huntington and Kenova followed with gas provided by the Tri-State Natural Gas Company, importing gas from Warfield, Kentucky.[141] National Transit then organized Clarksburg Light and Heat Company in 1904 with Standard's Elizur Strong as president.[142] Other Standard-related firms doing business in West Virginia included Monongahela Development Company, Pittsburgh Natural Gas Company, Reserve Gas Company, River Gas Company, United Fuel, and New Dominion Oil and Gas Company.

These firms initially served glass factories in the tri-state area, including Pittsburgh Plate Glass, various pottery manufacturers, and later Weirton Steel. Weston City built early glass plants and carbon black factories, and the Weston Gas Company was chartered in 1893. It was purchased by Johnson W. Camden (a major pioneer in oil and gas) in 1898, and then called the Weston Natural Gas and Fuel Company. The firm was later sold to the Keener Oil and Gas Company, and eventually Hope bought it out in 1925.[143]

In 1902, the Kanawha Natural Gas and Fuel Company laid a pipeline into Charleston. The city was already served by two distributors, Charleston Natural Gas Company on the east side of the Elk River and the Kanawha Natural Gas, Light and Fuel Company on the west. The two firms were absorbed later by a third firm in the area, the United States Natural Gas Company. That company also absorbed the Triple

State Natural Gas Company and established offices at Huntington in 1905. In 1909, United Fuel took the smaller firm over, and proceeded to tie in various Ohio, West Virginia, and Kentucky communities, including Ashland, into its system. United Fuel also provided gas for the Columbia Gas and Electric Company, Ohio Fuel Supply, and along with Hope — the largest producer in West Virginia — dominated the natural gas industry within the state.[144] United Fuel, owned by both Standard and Columbia, was formed in 1903 to search for new gas supplies for Ohio markets and was largely involved in developing the natural gas fields in southern West Virginia. The firm's initial officers included gas pioneer George W. Crawford, president, H. C. Reesner, secretary and treasurer, and J. M. Gerard, general manager. In its first few years of operation, United Fuel acquired various Standard dominated firms, including the Cabin Creek Gas Company, Charleston Natural Gas Company, Devenport Oil and Gas Company, Hamilton Natural Gas Company, Kanawha Gas Company, Kanawha Natural Gas Light and Fuel Gas Company, Kanawha Water and Light Company, Southside Water and Light Company, Triple State Natural Gas Company, Union Natural Gas Company, and The United States Natural Gas Company, as well as some properties in the southern part of the state held by Hope and several smaller firms. Later, in the late 1920s and early '30s, United Fuel acquired the Ohio Fuel Oil Company, Central Kentucky Natural Gas Company, Charleston-Dunbar Natural Gas Company, and the Kentucky By-Products Coal Company.[145] By the early 1930s, United Fuel served about 60,000 customers and owned more than 1,000 gas wells and 2,500 miles of pipeline. It eventually became a wholly-owned Columbia subsidiary.

By 1963, a total of forty-six natural gas distributors served West Virginia, the largest being United Fuel, serving 178 communities; Hope, serving 167 communities, Manufacturers Light and Heat Company, Godfrey L. Cabot, Inc., and Cumberland and Allegheny Gas Company serving between thirty and fifty communities; and Carnegie Natural Gas Company, Consumers Gas Utility Company, Pittsburgh's Equitable Gas Company, and South Penn Natural Gas Company, all serving between ten and fifteen communities.[146]

Various firms served Kentucky after the industry began in the late nineteenth century. United Fuel supplied consumers in Ashland, Inez, Kinner, Catlettsburg, Warfield, Pollard, Russel, Buchanan, Louisa, and Kavanaugh from a large production of West Virginia wells to augment production from Kentucky wells. In 1922, the Warfield Natural Gas Company formed to take over United Fuel's natural gas properties in Kentucky.[147] Central Kentucky, including properties controlled by United Fuel, operated wells in Menifee and Powell counties, and imported gas from West Virginia to supply consumers in Lexington, Winchester, Mount Sterling, and Rothwell. Central Kentucky supplied gas to Cincinnati, Ohio, beginning in 1910, and Lexington, Kentucky, in 1912. United Fuel would transfer its distribution properties of Central Kentucky to Columbia Gas of Kentucky in 1958. Other firms included Union Light, Heat & Power Company, of Covington, which received some of its gas produced by Columbia in West Virginia, Monticello Gas Company, organized in 1912 to supply consumers in Monticello, and Maysville Gas Company of Maysville.[148]

Louisville Gas and Electric is a combined electric-gas utility that dates back to 1838, when Louisville Gas and Water formed to light the streets of Louisville with manufactured gas to deter crime. In 1890, the firm amended its charter to operate electric companies, and, in 1913, merged with Kentucky Heating, Louisville Gas, and Louisville Lighting, creating LG&E. In 1940, LG&E brought Kentucky gas to Louisville and mixed natural gas with manufactured gas it continued to produce.[149]

Kentucky Natural in Louisville, formed in 1933 and owned by the Missouri-Kansas Pipeline Company, extended its lines into Indiana in the early 1930s, and in 1939, acquired Universal Gas Company, which constructed a pipeline from Terre Haute to Martinsville, In., helping to convert the area to gas in 1940. Kentucky Natural became part of Texas Gas Transmission Corporation when it incorporated in 1945. Some other firms producing, transporting, or distributing natural gas in the state included Kentucky Natural Gas of Owensboro, Kentucky–West Virginia Gas Company, and Kentucky Cities Gas Company.

The Buckeye State Ventures — A Short History of Selected Ohio Gas Companies

Various gas discoveries in Ohio led to the creation of local gas firms, many later consolidated into Standard and Columbia. In 1894, the Logan Natural Gas Company laid pipes to about sixty towns in Athens, Licking, Knox, Morrow, Ashland, Seneca, Marion, Crawford, Richland, Wyandot, and Huron counties.[150] The Ashtabula Gas Company formed in 1895 from production in wells along the Lake Erie shoreline, and some gas imported from Clarion County, Pa. About 175 families heated with local natural gas by 1901. By 1923, the shallow gas wells in the region were practically exhausted, and the city considered a clause to a city ordinance requiring the company to build an artificial gas plant, but later voted to kill it.[151] The Lake Shore Gas Company organized in 1925, and bought Ashtabula along with NorthEastern Oil and Gas Company. In 1926, Lake Shore became part of the Associated Gas and Electric System before being purchased later by East Ohio.

The Ohio Cities Gas Company (Ohio Cities) organized in 1913 (originally as the Columbus Production Company) with $6 million in assets, and in six years grew to be one of the largest of the independent producing and refining companies in the country with assets of $125 million. Addressing the "failing fortunes" of the Columbus Gas & Fuel Company, which served 41,000 customers in Columbus, Ohio Cities "quietly" leased 250,000 acres of West Virginia gas lands and began an intensive drilling campaign. In a deal with the Ohio Fuel Supply Company that exchanged Ohio Cities' gas fields in the state, Ohio Cities obtained a twenty-year gas contract and took control of the Federal Gas & Fuel Company in Columbus so they would have a monopoly in the city. Ohio Cities later purchased Springfield Gas Company in 1914 and Dayton Gas Company in 1916, serving 108,000 customers between the three firms.[152] Ohio Cities was purchased by the Pure Oil Company (New Jersey) in 1917 and adopted the Pure Oil name.

The Appalachian Natural Gas Corporation engaged in production and distribution of natural gas in Ohio, West Virginia, and Kentucky. Incorporated in Delaware, it owned a controlling interest in Ohio Southern Gas Company, Wayne United Gas Company, Ohio Valley Gas Corporation, Ohio Kentucky Gas Company, and a substantial interest in Allegheny Gas Corporation. The company owned gas wells and pipelines in Ohio, West Virginia, Kentucky, and Tennessee, and maintained connections to pipelines run by Columbia Gas & Electric, Standard (New Jersey), and Standard Gas & Electric. It served the manufacturing centers of Columbus, Portsmouth, Zanesville, Newark, and Mt. Vernon in Ohio, Huntington and Charleston in West Virginia, and Ashland in Kentucky. It sold gas under long-term contracts to pipeline companies such as United Fuel.[153]

Cincinnati Gas & Electric Company provided electric and gas service to a 3,000-square-mile area of southwestern Ohio, Kentucky, and Indiana. The firm's predecessors began in 1837 when local interests obtained a charter for the Cincinnati Gas, Light & Coke Company, which used distilled coal to manufacture gas for lighting and produce coke for domestic heating from a plant built by 1843. After Cincinnati's "Light War" between manufactured gas and electric interests in the 1880s and '90s, the two energies combined and renamed the new firm CG&E.[154]

Columbia piped natural gas from West Virginia gas fields to Ohio, and in 1911, CG&E became a subsidiary of Columbia. By 1917, CG&E provided gas service to 20,000 residential customers. In the 1920s due to the consumer demand, the firm provided mixed manufactured and natural gas to many of its customers, and opened a twenty-story corporate headquarters in downtown Cincinnati. The firm separated from the Columbia system in 1944, and acquired other Columbia holdings such as Union Light, Heat & Power Company that operated in six counties in northern Kentucky.[155]

Gas on the Niagara Frontier — A Short History of Selected Western New York Gas Companies

At the turn of the twentieth century, gas companies formed all along the New York shores of Lake Erie near William Hart's first natural gas well in Fredonia. The small firms fought for franchises and market shares as they discovered additional wells. In most cases, the small companies' gas supply was soon insufficient to meet the demand. As mentioned earlier, Fredonia was the home of the first natural gas company in the United States — the Fredonia Gas Light & Water Company, incorporated in 1858. Its successor, the Fredonia Natural Gas Light Company, operated under a franchise dated in 1864, and later reorganized in 1895. The firm was acquired by the Niagara and Erie Power Company in 1910, but was unable to compete with the Frost Gas Company (formed in 1906 in Fredonia). It later sold its capital stock to W. E. Carroll, who operated the property as a private interest until 1916.[156]

In Dunkirk, N.Y., the City Council considered granting a franchise to many gas companies to spur competition. The *Dunkirk Evening Observer* wrote in 1903: "The only way to get gas at a reasonable figure is to throw the field open to all. This will invite competition and insure gas at a figure that will make it more profitable for residents to burn it than coal."[157] The Council set a maximum gas rate and wanted to see the books of prospective companies. Various investors rushed to get franchises in the Chautauqua County communities of Fredonia, Dunkirk, Silver Creek, Sheridan, and Westfield, promising to supply natural gas to local residents. Also, the nearby Mayville Oil and Gas Company formed in 1900. But the new gas entrepreneurs felt that a combination of these interconnecting firms with pipelines would improve gas service. As a result, a total of eleven companies consolidated in 1918 to form Republic

Light, Heat and Power Company, Inc., including Fredonia Natural Gas Light Company, South Shore Natural Gas & Fuel Company of Dunkirk (formed in 1904), Silver Creek Gas & Improvement Company (formed in 1903), Citizens Gas & Fuel Company of Dunkirk (founded in 1900), and Central Station Heating & Construction Co. in Fredonia (formed in 1916).

Cities Service Company, controlled by utility magnate Henry L. Doherty, owned Republic. Doherty, who started his career as an office boy with the Columbus Gas Company, was noteworthy for his work in the manufactured gas, street railway, and electric light and power industry. Doherty eventually became an organizer of utility interests by reorganization, management, and financing of public utility companies operating for many years prior throughout the Midwest. Cities joined together more than 120 companies, scattered through twenty-three states, Canada, Mexico, and Columbia.[158] In 1912, Doherty began acquiring natural gas properties. The challenge of moving natural gas from remote fields through an interconnected pipeline network made the whole Cities, created in 1910, greater than the sum of the independent parts. By 1913, Doherty's group controlled more than fifty separate utility firms in fourteen states.[159] Doherty interests also took control of Dominion Natural Gas Company in southern Ontario, Canada, which had operated gas fields since 1905, financed by Pittsburgh-area gas investors.[160] Manufactured gas was still an important part of the business until 1920, and then Doherty invested in oil. By the mid–1930s, Cities provided natural gas service to more than 300,000 customers in 280 communities.[161]

Republic managed Doherty's electric and gas assets on the Niagara Frontier. Republic supplied natural gas to Batavia and Dunkirk, and to various villages in Chautauqua, Erie, Genesee, and Ontario counties. The company also distributed manufactured gas to cities of Niagara Falls, Tonawanda, North Tonawanda, the village of Kenmore, and various other Buffalo suburbs. Republic sold both natural and mixed gas to customers and operated several facilities including western New York offices in Akron, Attica, Batavia, Clarence, Dunkirk, Fredonia, Honeoye Falls, Kenmore, Niagara Falls, Silver Creek, Tonawanda, and Westfield.

Another firm related to Doherty interests was the Penn-York Natural Gas Corporation. Organized in 1936, it was a non-utility engaged in the purchase and transmission of natural gas for resale to Republic. Penn-York also purchased gas from the New York State Natural, and transported the fuel about eighty miles for resale for its only customer — Republic. The sale included one compressor station at Angelica, N.Y., and 130 miles of transmission lines.

East of Buffalo in Batavia, N.Y., gas interests in 1891 looked to the city fathers for permission to lay lines in the city just in case natural gas would be discovered nearby.[162] The Alden-Batavia Natural Gas Company, incorporated in 1901, then brought gas to Batavia by the beginning of 1902. That company also eventually became part of Republic. Gas from the Pavilion Natural Gas Company also supplied gas to Batavia from rich gas fields in the Town of Pavilion. Later, the Brocton Gas & Fuel Company (incorporated in 1904) was purchased in 1922 by Republic. The Frost Gas Company was acquired by the Doherty interests, and, in 1922, the corporate name changed to the Northwestern New York Gas Company. Cities sold Republic to an NFG affiliate in 1953.

New York State Natural was first organized in 1913, producing and distributing

Utility magnate Henry Doherty stands atop 60 Wall Street in New York City, in front of the Cities Service logo flag. Doherty built a public utility empire throughout the United States, including gas interests along the Lake Erie shoreline in New York. Doherty, who started his career as an office boy with the Columbus Gas Company, also became a pioneer natural gas promoter for natural gas cooking (courtesy National Fuel Gas Company).

gas in Pavilion in Genesee County, N.Y. After selling its distribution property to Valley Gas Corporation, it became a pipeline supplier to affiliated and unaffiliated gas distributors in 1931. By 1934, the firm was owned by both the Columbia Gas System and Standard Oil (New Jersey), and, in 1943, by CNG. As local gas shortages erupted by 1939, the company purchased gas from West Virginia through Hope. CNG's transmission company then began selling gas to unaffiliated companies for distribution in Rochester, Syracuse, Ithaca, Cortand, Auburn, and other western New York and Pennsylvania cities.[163]

Gas service began in the City of Buffalo primarily through Standard's Buffalo Natural Gas Fuel Company. On March 15, 1886, the Buffalo Common Council, after a lengthy debate, granted the new firm a franchise by a 23 to 3 vote, ending an effort led by manufactured gas firms to keep natural gas out of the Buffalo market.[164] Later, Iroquois Natural Gas Corporation organized in 1911 as a subsidiary of NFG, and opened offices in 1913 at a new office building at 45 Church Street in downtown Buffalo. Iroquois included two major properties: Buffalo Natural Gas Fuel Company and the New York State properties of UNG. Buffalo purchased its supply of natural gas from UNG except for a limited amount for a short time from Provincial Natural Gas and Fuel Company, another NFG firm, in Canada. All these operating properties were located in the counties of Allegany, Cattaraugus, Chautauqua, and Erie, and were used in the production, transmission, and distribution of natural gas to parts of Buffalo and various villages and hamlets. The NFG affiliate was renamed Iroquois Gas Corporation in 1923 (the word "natural" removed to reflect the sale of both manufactured and natural gas). In 1956, the New York State Public Service Commission approved a merger between Republic and Iroquois, making Iroquois the largest gas utility in western New York.[165] Iroquois moved its headquarters to a new downtown Buffalo skyscraper at Lafayette Square in 1958, and after adopting its parent NFG name in 1974, based its operations there until the firm relocated its corporate headquarters to a Buffalo suburb in 2003.

Other firms on New York's Southern Tier included Empire Gas and Fuel, incorporated in 1885 by Justin Bassett and Edwin Colton Bradley as a successor to Empire Gas Company which the two brothers started in 1881 in Elmira. In 1889, they also purchased the Van Wert Gas Company at Van Wert, Ohio, and the Buckeye Gas Company in Circleville, Ohio. Empire supplied gas to boilers used in drilling oil wells in the Allegany field, the northern limit of oil exploration in the United States. Empire's first distribution system served four towns, including Allentown, Wellsville, Richburg, and Bolivar. When gaslights came to Wellsville through a 5⅝-inch line, the *Wellsville Daily Reporter* on April 14, 1882, reported that "the village received its baptism of gas light and most gloriously was it done. Night was abolished for a time and the whole length of Main Street bathed in a blaze of light."[166] Other companies taken over by Empire during the years included the Cuba Gas Company (originally formed in 1884), Mutual Gas Company of Andover (originally formed in 1889 supplying the town with gas from area wells), Manufacturers Gas Company of Wellsville, and, in 1941, the Hornell Gas Light Company (which had started gas service in 1899 and acquired the Canisteo Gas Company). These companies used local wells until the supply was exhausted and then began buying most of their gas from interstate pipelines.

The Bradleys also joined with Pittsburgh natural gas pioneers Pew and Emerson in organizing the Keystone Gas Company which supplied Olean, N.Y., and Bradford, Pa., from a very large gas well drilled nearby.[167] In 1883, Keystone entered a contract with the city of Olean to light fifty street lamps, and "to keep the same lighted from sunset to dawn … at a cost of two dollars a year for each lamp so lighted."[168] The firm bought the Consumers Gas Company in Watkins Glen in 1931, and later bought gas from the Home Gas Company of Binghampton, N.Y., a subsidiary of Columbia that ran a pipeline into eastern New York State.[169]

Producers Gas Company in Olean, N.Y., was organized in June 1891, and immediately acquired various leases and wells in Genesee Township and a transmission main and distribution system in the town of Porterville. In 1892, Producers extended its transmission mains into the town of Olean. In 1900, the company merged with the Allegany Gas Company of Friendship, N.Y., resulting in the acquisition of wells in the town of Wirt and transmission mains and distribution systems in the villages of Friendship and Belmont. In 1901, the mains extended in the town of Belfast and the Village of Angelica. A subsidiary, McKean County Gas Company, was incorporated in 1906. After local wells waned, the firm later bought gas from Godfrey L. Cabot, Inc., and in 1946, the CNG system.[170]

Located in the Finger Lakes area on the Southern Tier of New York State is Corning Natural Gas, which serves approximately 14,000 customers in fifteen townships with 385 miles of pipeline throughout an area of about 400 square miles. The investor-owned firm provides wholesale gas delivery services to NYSEG in Elmira, N.Y., and to the Village of Bath, N.Y., for the municipally-owned Bath Electric, Gas & Water System.[171]

The Columbia Gas System spread throughout the Empire State by purchasing many smaller firms and extending pipelines into areas that previously did not have gas service. Columbia grew during the 1920s and '30s, and purchased several firms in south central New York including the Keystone Gas Company serving Olean, Home Gas Company at Ceres, Binghampton Gas Works (serving manufactured gas), and Consumers Natural Gas Company around Watkins Glen. After the discovery of gas in the Tioga gas fields in north-central Pennsylvania, Columbia's investment in the Lycoming United Gas Corporation and the New York State Natural, along with Standard (New Jersey), brought natural gas to central New York, including Syracuse.[172]

Other parts of upstate New York are served by three major investor-owned, electric-gas combination utilities including Rochester Gas and Electric, Niagara Mohawk, and the New York State Electric and Gas Corporation.

RG&E's roots go back to the Rochester Gas Light Company, formed in 1848, four years after the city was fully incorporated. That firm generated manufactured gas, and the city of Rochester did not use natural gas except for the failed experiment from the West Bloomfield well in 1872. The gas light firm and three area electric firms, including Edison Electric (the first electric firm in the nation to install underground electric wiring and measure electricity through meters), consolidated in 1892 to form RG&E.[173] The city did not use pure natural gas until 1952 when supplies from the southwest became available. RG&E now serves approximately 303,000 natural gas customers in a nine-county region in its 2,700-square-mile service territory centering around the City of Rochester in upstate New York.

Niagara Mohawk predecessors trace their beginnings to the generation of hydro-electric power by George Westinghouse at Niagara Falls in the 1880s. By 1896, Buffalo streets were lighted for the first time by the energy from Niagara Falls. In 1929, three separate holding companies owning fifty-nine smaller firms came together as the Niagara Hudson Power Corporation. In the 1930s, this firm also first mixed natural gas into the manufactured gas it produced. To help finance expansion, many gas firms in the region aligned themselves with electric companies and constructed pipelines along the same power-line rights-of-way.[174] The various firms were realigned and a single operating company called Niagara Mohawk was created in 1950. The firm's gas service began from lighting a few streetlights by the Albany Gas Light Company in 1841 to providing gas service to more than 385,000 customers by the mid–1960s, mostly in a fifteen county area of central and eastern New York, including the cities of Watertown, Syracuse, Utica, Schenectady, Troy, and Albany.[175]

NYSEG changed to its current name from the Ithaca Gas & Electric Corporation in 1929, and is formed of more than 200 New York gas and electric firms.[176] Some of the larger firms included Eastern New York Electric & Gas Corporation, Elmira Water, Light & Railroad Company, Binghampton Light, Heat & Power Company, Western New York Gas & Electric Corporation, and Empire Gas & Electric Company. By 1937, the company's service area stretched over 35 percent of New York State.[177]

Breaking Up Is Hard to Do —
Standard Oil and Natural Gas

Despite the federal government's legal attack on Standard's oil operations, the company continued to acquire natural gas interests. Even before the breakup, journalist Ida Tarbell wrote at the end of her History of the Standard Oil Company, that Standard would find other industries to invest in with its wealth: "They [Standard] will be gas, and we have the Standard Oil crowd steadily acquiring the gas interests of the country."[178] Standard would later turn its interest in United Fuel, which owned gas drilling leases on 800,000 acres in West Virginia, to the Columbia Gas System, as part of a deal that gave Columbia's interest in East Ohio to Standard.[179] As mentioned earlier, Joseph Pew, who first piped gas to Pittsburgh in 1885, also became affiliated with Standard in 1903. Though reportedly not unanimous in the decision to expand into natural gas, Standard interests bought Pew's Peoples firm for $4.4 million and the Pittsburgh Natural Gas Company that year.[180] Pittsburgh, which supplied many industries in the Lawrenceville area, and Lawrence Natural Gas Company, combined with Peoples in 1908. As a result of all the acquisitions, Standard affiliates at this time produced about 14 percent of the natural gas used in the United States and conducted oil and gas operations in New York, Pennsylvania, Ohio, West Virginia, Kentucky, Ohio, and Indiana.[181] One newspaper wrote at the time, "Consumers in some of these places would be surprised to learn that they are burning Standard Oil gas."[182]

During the early twentieth century, the companies associated with Standard and other firms negotiated thousands of Appalachian leasehold agreements for the purchase of oil, gas, storage, and surface properties. Oil and gas lands were sometimes rented by the year, either at a fixed rate at the time of the lease, or graduated upon the amount of production. Since much of the potential natural gas production occurred in rural areas, many landowners granted leases to gas exploration firms at bargain rates, perhaps not realizing the wealth of potential under their farms and forests. The "rule of capture" in gas production allowed any leaseholder to withdraw as much gas as possible, even if the driller depleted the reserves in a field where other producers held leases.[183] This oil and gas tenet was based on a bizarre English law that permitted the practice of luring a wild animal from a neighbor's property to one's own property — natural gas having the power of a fugitive "animal" to migrate from one property to the next.[184] The only recourse was to go and do likewise. As a result, many Appalachian gas fields were evanescent, their contents quickly drained and much gas was wasted.[185] If one wasn't lucky enough to have gas underneath his property, a market developed for subsurface "mineral rights" from which landowners could earn revenue. Standard's prominence in acquiring oil and gas rights continued to produce apprehension among some. An editorial in the *Dunkirk Evening Observer* on August 9, 1910, warned against giving leases to UNG, due to its history with the Rockefeller empire: "The Standard Oil Co. is known both as to name and policy to every reader of this paper. It aims to own the earth and the people therof."[186] After discovery of the Taylorstown well in southwestern Pennsylvania, advice from a local minister regarding oil and gas men coming to claim leases in Washington County warned "shun these people as you would a viper for they come to deceive."[187] In addition to its oil quest that led to millions of acres in mineral rights, Standard and its descendants acquired thousands of acres of land in Pennsylvania for gas drilling through its interests in UNG and other firms.

Though it controlled more than 2,000 companies, Standard's share of the natural gas production industry was not totally dominant in Appalachia. Other entrepreneurs were drilling for gas along the Lake Erie shore. However, Standard continued to face attack for its supremacy in the petroleum industry, and, in 1906, legal challenges began that eventually led to the demise of the oil monopoly. The federal government charged that Standard "gained its dominant position not by superior efficiency, but by unfair and immoral acts— rebate-taking, local price-cutting, operation of bogus 'independents,' improper control of pipe lines," etc.[188] The U.S. Supreme Court upheld the dissolution and ordered the break-up of the Standard Oil Trust in 1911, including spinning off Standard's pipeline subsidiary, National Transit. National Transit eventually became a wholly-owned subsidiary of Pennzoil–Quaker State Company and operated its crude oil gathering and transportation operations until 1992.

The Heavy Hand — Federal Regulation of Natural Gas

Despite the disintegration of the Standard Oil petroleum empire, the natural gas industry initially escaped the heavy hand of federal regulation. According to the Standard-influenced history *Romance of American Petroleum and Gas*, it was due to Standard's Calvin Payne "...that the court early withdrew all charges against the pipe line companies and the natural gas companies, finding that they had not infringed upon any of the provisions of the Anti-Trust Law."[189] Though the oil monopoly was splintered, Standard leaders continued to maintain an interest in numerous gas firms including East Ohio, Peoples, Hope, New York State Natural, and NFG. By the 1930s, Standard supplied nearly 100 billion cubic feet of gas to 697,000 customers in 240 cities and towns.[190] But according to critics, companies like Standard and Columbia "ruthlessly drove out competitors" to their gas supply as southwestern gas was "seen as a threat to price maintenance by the integrated utilities of the Appalachian area."[191]

Regulation was left up to the states, though individual states could not control companies that were based in other states. In response to Standard's control of pipeline systems in the beginning of the new century, discussion of natural gas pipelines as common carriers went back as far as 1914, though few crossed state lines. One argument against the idea was that less than 1 percent of industrial users consumed 65 percent of the total natural gas, which was sold at "absurdly low prices" to compete with manufactured gas. Detractors of the common carrier idea said the result would greatly increase the waste of natural gas in industrial work and prevent conservation of the "premium fuel" that should be primarily for domestic consumers.[192]

The issue of interstate transportation regulation was brewing. In the case of

Pennsylvania Gas Company vs. Public Service Commission, the U.S. Supreme Court upheld a contention by New York in 1920 that interstate transactions were local in nature, and subject to state regulation.[193] However, this did not impact interstate wholesale sales, which in *Peoples Natural Gas Co. v. Public Service Commission* later in 1926, the justices said states could not regulate interstate gas sold to gas distributors, creating a "regulatory gap."[194] But federal regulation of natural gas was on the horizon. The Federal Power Commission (FPC), created in 1920 to regulate hydroelectric power, possessed some jurisdiction over transportation of natural gas across state lines, specifically common carriage of pipelines that existed on federal lands.[195]

In the first two decades of the twentieth century, most gas transportation across state lines occurred in Appalachia due to the limits of pipeline expansion. For example, 65 percent of the 150 billion cubic feet moved interstate in 1921 was produced in West Virginia and flowed to Pennsylvania and Ohio.[196] In 1925, the Mountain State shipped 110 billion cubic feet to Ohio, Pennsylvania, Kentucky, Maryland, and Virginia.[197] Huge discoveries of natural gas in the Southwest, meanwhile, were left without a significant market. However, the creation of seamless metal pipe in the 1920s, replacing brittle and difficult to weld pipe, enabled long-distance gas transportation and transformed the natural gas business from a regional industry to a potential national network. The first all-welded pipeline more than 200 miles in length (214 miles) was built from Louisiana to Beaumont, Texas, in 1925.[198] By 1934, nearly 40 percent of natural gas crossed state lines.[199]

As more energy firms crossed state borders, it was "inevitable that the federal government become involved in their regulation."[200] Large utility interests—such as Standard and Columbia—dominated the rapidly expanding natural gas industry, and sometimes prevented transportation of Southwestern gas to their service areas. For example, Columbia prevented entry of the Panhandle pipeline into the Detroit area until it gained a controlling interest in the Panhandle company.[201] But the stranglehold of the holding companies would not last. During the Great Depression, President Franklin D. Roosevelt, a proponent of public power systems, called for the elimination of various gas and electric utility holding companies due to unsound financial practices and inflated values of holdings. The anti-business attitude that existed during the Depression resulted in a plethora of sweeping legislative and regulatory initiatives including the Securities Act of 1933, Security Exchange Act of 1934, Federal Power Act (FPA) of 1935, and the Public Utility Holding Company Act (PUHCA) of 1935. PUHCA, for example, was created to prevent abuses by the "Power Trust," a loosely organized cartel of various holding companies in the United States in the 1920s and '30s that controlled the Northeast and Midwest gas markets.[202] The Federal Trade Commission (FTC) concluded there were sixteen "evils" in the industry, among which included a great waste of natural gas blown into the air because it had no market.[203] According to holding company opponents, the monopolistic firms could force independents to sell gas at their prices, control or influence banks, discriminate against competitors, levy excessive rates, garner undue profits, inflate assets, and water down stock.[204] The FTC recommended federal control of the industry. Trade associations and utility investors vigorously opposed the bill, and PUHCA was tied up in the courts until the 1940s. However, the action eventually led to massive reorganization of the utility industry.

The holding companies in question included Standard Oil (New Jersey); the Columbia system; Associated Gas & Electric (which reportedly owned 175 utility subsidiaries); Henry Doherty's Cities Service Company; Middle West Utilities; and Insull Utility Investments (which owned several hundred utility subsidiaries serving 6,000 communities).[205] These firms financed the first major long-distance pipelines to the north that helped cities, such as Chicago, to convert from manufactured gas to mixed and natural gas.[206] At the same time, the cartel of natural gas giants did their best to prevent "independent" gas interests from interfering in their markets.

PUHCA eviscerated the holding companies, as the "death sentence" restricted utilities to single, geographically compact, integrated systems, and required utilities to separate their natural gas and electric operations.[207] The SEC, in charge of enforcement of the law, required firms owning at least ten percent of the stock of a gas or electric company to divest or come under PUHCA regulation.[208] The ultimate effect was massive divestitures in the utility industry. For example, Columbia split into electric and gas firms and spun off Panhandle. Cities Service divested along geographic lines.

PUHCA also eradicated the remnants of Standard control out of the Appalachian gas firms. As late as 1939, the Rockefeller Foundation, the charitable arm of the Rockefeller fortune, still owned 412,042 shares of NFG stock — more than 21 percent of the shares of the company.[209] In 1943, PUHCA forced the Foundation to dispose of a sufficient number of shares so that it would hold less than 10 percent of such stock or be registered as a utility holding company. As a result, the Foundation sold all of its stock valued at approximately $4.95 million.[210] On October 15, 1943, Standard Oil (New Jersey) spun off Pittsburgh's Peoples, West Virginia's Hope, and Cleveland's East Ohio, along with New York State Natural and River Gas companies to its shareholders to form an independent firm called Consolidated Natural Gas Company, incorporated in Delaware. In return Standard received all of CNG's stock and then distributed it to Standard's stockholders on the basis of one share of CNG for every ten shares of Standard.[211] In the end, holding company control over interstate gas pipeline mileage fell from 80 percent to 18 percent.[212] Of the 234 holding companies registered with PUHCA in 1935, today only fourteen remain, including three gas firms.

In addition to PUHCA, Congress also passed the Natural Gas Act (NGA) of 1938, marking the entrance of the federal government into the field of regulatory control of the natural gas industry in an effort to prevent the abuse by "natural monopolies." This regulation on gas pipelines was similar in some respects to the 1935 Federal Power Act regulating electricity. There were often large disparities in the cost of residential and industrial gas rates, and charges of discriminatory pricing helped garner support for the legislation.[213] In addition, the natural gas–rival coal industry supported federal control in order to raise natural gas prices to better compete with gas and limit gas expansion.[214] In short, the NGA prevented any company from building a gas pipeline or gas compression facilities into a market already served by a gas pipeline unless the FPC first approved the construction.[215] Though the intent was to regulate pipeline rates in interstate commerce to pass the low price of wellhead gas on to the customer, it specifically exempted the wellhead price of gas, maintaining that production of gas was a local activity for the states. However, the FPC reserved the right to investigate. Since the NGA was not initially intended to regulate wellhead prices, it was generally acceptable to the industry at the time and did not face the fate of different, perhaps conflicting regulations of pipelines by multiple states. But the first challenge to the law came in 1939 when the FPC suspended a price increase by the Columbian Fuel Corporation, an independent producer, charged to the Warfield Natural Gas Company, an interstate pipeline based in Kentucky. But it was dismissed. However, later that same year, a price restriction was upheld regarding a deal between a pipeline and a producer that were part of the same firm — Billings Gas Company.[216] As more utilities transported gas across state lines, extension of the Act's vague powers in the 1940s troubled the industry. East Ohio's head, J. French Robinson — a nationally renown geologist — wrote, "It (the NGA) is a *real invitation to chaos* at a time when the industry faces the greatest potentiality for public service in its history."[217]

The new FPC also achieved a landmark regulatory action in the *FPC v. Hope* case in the early 1940s. City governments in Cleveland, Toledo, and Akron, as well as some from Pennsylvania, charged that Standard's West Virginia gas producing company, which used the firm's reproduction costs to determine rates, unfairly charged higher rates for its gas sold across state lines. After the federal regulatory agency investigated, it ordered rate reductions, cost-based regulation, and a lower rate of return for Hope's property. The case ended up in the Roosevelt reform-packed Supreme Court, which ruled against Hope in 1944.[218]

One of the major proponents of regulation of the gas industry was the coal lobby that felt that unreasonably low gas prices caused the displacement of their product. As a result, gas companies had to obtain a certificate of public convenience and necessity (a permit) to build a pipeline. For example, when the CNG's New York State Natural applied to the FPC to build a twelve-inch, high-pressure line across Pennsylvania to deliver Texas gas to its markets in 1943, "the construction was protested by representatives of the Anthracite Institute, the National Coal Association (representing most eastern bituminous coal companies), the United Mine Workers Union, and twenty-five railroads."[219] Still, the line was approved, but with delivery restrictions to industrial users. The battle with coal continued until after World War II. And the granting of interstate pipeline expansions has been regulated closely to the present day. Today, the Federal Energy Regulatory Commission (FERC), created in the late 1970s from the FPC, has comprehensive jurisdiction over interstate gas and electric operations.

The genesis of the plethora of gas companies in the Appalachian region was the countless natural gas discoveries, which until the early twentieth century were largely restricted to Ohio, West Virginia, Kentucky, Pennsylvania, New York and southern Ontario, Canada. But the blue flame was spreading. By 1912, there were 547 companies in the United States serving natural gas, including firms as far away as California.[220] But what is now produced in plenty throughout the world, was once the unique reserve of the first energy pioneers in Appalachia. These gas explorers erected a widespread industry from scratch from the ground down.

FIVE

From the Ground Down
Exploration and Production

"Eureka! [I have found it]."
— Archimedes on discovering a method to test the purity of gold,
1st century B.C.

Appalachian Wellspring

When William Hart "kicked in" or "kicked down" his seminal natural gas well in the side of a creek in Fredonia in 1821, he planted the seed of exploration that germinated throughout Appalachia. However, the serious exploration of natural gas wells would take at least another generation to bloom. In the late nineteenth and early twentieth centuries, the Appalachian region became the largest natural gas producing area in the world. But until a score of years passed after Colonel Drake struck oil in Titusville in 1859, natural gas was eschewed, and the antebellum discoveries were mostly a nuisance and an expense for those who found it.

Though natural gas was discovered in many areas during the quest for oil, only a few uses for the new fuel were found, basically due to the trouble of transporting it safely and finding a significant demand. Even producing oil was risky business. Massive oil fires in Titusville, Pa., were caused by lightning strikes in 1880, and then a devastating flood caused a widespread blaze on "Black Friday" in 1892 that took sixty lives.[1] But the danger of natural gas was more acute since it was not easily or safely contained in a barrel or tank like liquid oil. Oil industry writer George Brown lamented, "The owners of the wells were obliged to buy iron pipe to carry the gas to a safe distance from the well, where it was burned, to prevent the mischief it might do. And mischief if did do in hundreds of cases."[2] Oil drillers in Rouseville, Pa., near Oil City, struck an oil vein and huge gas pocket in April 1861 that led to a huge explosion, setting fire to the well, area buildings, and people viewing the gusher.[3] Gas fires from "blowouts" sometimes occurred from the friction of the iron tools against the side of the well bore. In April 1861, a fatal well explosion knocked several people from their feet, killing or injuring thirty people. According to petroleum author J. T. Henry's account in 1873:

> One poor wretch struggled out of the fire, believing himself to be in the hands of the evil one. His charred and naked body was speedily placed in a blanket, and he was

91

borne from the place. He lamented his supposed arrival in — —, in piercing tones of agony, which proceeded from lips burned to a cinder, and hence powerless to give proper accent to his language. He bemoaned his own fate, and calling the names of various friends warned them of his own terrible punishment. Death ensued in four hours.[4]

A group of Germans formed an association in Waterford, Pa., south of Erie, and struck gas in February 1862, throwing water twenty feet in the air. When the well's proprietor and eight others examined the well while carrying a lighted lantern close to the derrick, the vapor ignited, injuring all and killing one.[5]

Well Blowout — The striking of natural gas caused a pressure blowout, shooting natural gas, the well tools, and plumes of salt water from the well that often took days or sometimes weeks to bring under control (courtesy National Fuel Gas Company).

Over time, it became no less hazardous. In October 1887, two men died and fifteen were injured in a Pittsburgh gas explosion.[6] Two months later, five men were seriously burned on the Heuston farm in northwestern Pennsylvania at an explosion at a PGC well.[7] In addition to dangers at the well sites, attempts to pipe the fuel from local wells to residences were cumbersome and often hazardous. As a result, use of natural gas was spotty and isolated. But once a market was identified, the quest for gas was on.

Appalachian natural gas drilling in the late nineteenth and early twentieth centuries was centered in southern Ontario, western New York, western Pennsylvania, eastern Ohio, West Virginia, and eastern Kentucky. Gas drilling soon expanded outside the region to Kansas and Missouri in the early 1870s. Later, some limited fields extended into Virginia, northern Tennessee, Mississippi, and Alabama. But the largest gas supplies would be located far from Appalachia. After the turn of the century, large discoveries were found in Colorado, California, Michigan, and most significant, Oklahoma and Texas. After Appalachian wells waned, many oil and gas explorers flocked south and west in search of new discoveries. In 1919, geologist E. W. Shaw then made the first reliable estimate of U.S. gas reserves—15 trillion cubic feet. The large wells in Oklahoma, and then Texas, which led American production by 1928, easily made the Southwest the greatest producer of natural gas in the country.

Oil's Invisible Twin

Natural gas is a mixture of various hydrocarbons and nonhydrocarbons, mostly in gaseous form, including methane, ethane, and propane, with methane making up 73 to 95 percent of the total. By the time it reaches market, it is made up of about 85 percent methane (CH_4), the lightest of the hydrocarbon gases. Although other hydrocarbons used as fuel gas, such as propane (C_3H_8), release more heat energy per cubic foot than does methane, their increased weight makes them more difficult to move through a pipeline. Consequently, propane, liquefied at less than 150 psi, is contained and transported in steel tanks. Other hydrocarbons such as ethane (C_2H_6), butane (C_4H_{10}), light naphthas (mixtures of various hydrocarbons), and dozens of others, are usually obtained during the refining of petroleum or the drilling for natural gas.

Natural gas is found in the earth in "anticlines" (an upward bulge of rock layers

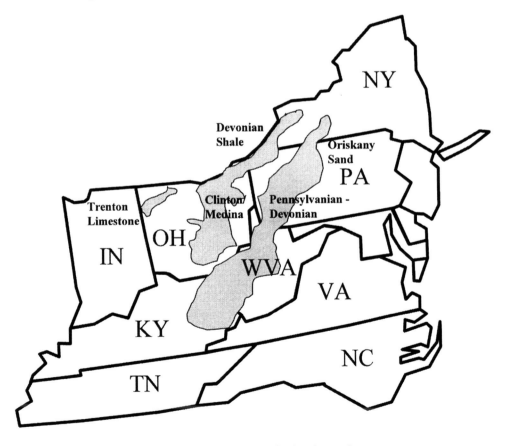

Major Appalachian gas producing formations.

that dip in the opposite direction of the crest that permit entrapment of oil and gas), "structural traps" (folds or faults in the earth's crust), "stratigraphic traps" (where a porous layer of rock is trapped between two non-porous rock layers), a combination of structural and stratigraphic traps, or sometimes in salt domes.[8] A great salt sea once existed westward from the slope of the rounded, older mountains in the Appalachian chain to what is known as the Cincinnati Arch in Ohio. The Appalachian basin deepens as it moves from western New York down toward southwestern Pennsylvania, and "source rock" contains significant deposits of fossil fuels. Therefore, anticlines and structural and stratigraphic traps in the Allegheny Plateau in the Appalachian mountains were sought after structures that held gas, oil, and water in the sandstone.

Gas is frequently mixed with oil and the gas pressure moves the oil through the strata to a well's borehole, and eventually to the surface. An 1886 article on the geology of natural gas stated that the gas and oil strata in the region were one and the same, formed from decaying vegetation. The article stated: "The first necessary condition for the presence of gas, however, is dependent upon the existence of a porous rock to serve as a reservoir to hold it."[9]

The first natural gas exploration was largely "eyeball" geology and nine out of ten wells came up dry. As mentioned previously, natural gas discoveries in Ohio, West Virginia, and Kentucky were the outgrowth of the salt industry, as saltmakers frequently, through unintentionally, hit oil or gas. Conversely, nearly all oil and gas wells in the region produced varying amounts of saltwater. In the search for natural gas, sometimes "wildcatters," independent drillers investing their own money, stumbled upon significant gas finds. In the nineteenth century, spiritualists supposedly located significant oil wells, and some petroleum explorers used a hazel or peach twig divining or "dowsing" rod—first used to hunt for minerals and buried treasure in Europe—to locate potential well sites.[10] Oil and gas "smellers" appeared from nowhere. A man from Ohio vowed that he could find gas fields by the tension in his neck muscles.[11] Heavenly inspiration was called upon as well. Despite area wells that came up dry, in 1891, in the Buffalo suburb of Lackawanna, N.Y., Catholic priest George Baker (1877?–1965) conducted eight days of Novenas to "Our Lady of Victory" to mark a potential well to fuel his parish institutions. After months of "folly," and recommendations to quit by drillers, Baker, founder of the famous Basilica in Lackawanna, persisted at his well and eventually struck gas at 1,060 feet. Land and oil speculators rushed to the area, but numerous wells drilled in the surrounding property were dry holes.[12]

Divine intervention notwithstanding, after more was learned about petroleum science, gas explorers sought potential well sites with field maps, full of geological information. As time progressed, gas producers could no longer rely on oil and gas seepages to identify potential deposits. In 1923, the U.S. Bureau of Mines, in cooperation with the Natural Gas Association, began the first of a series of scientific studies relating to geophysical exploratory methods. Over time, gas fields were identified by "plays," defined as "a group of geologically similar drilling prospects having similar source, reservoir, and trap controls of gas migration, accumulation and storage."[13] As technology and knowledge improved, geologists and geophysicists evaluated gas potential through use of well logs and sand samples. By 1970, the use of "well-logging" techniques, including radioactivity (first used in 1940) and electricity, were used to study the physical data of subsurface formations.[14] Core samples are cut out of underground rock and sand formations by a donut-shaped drill bit covered with industrial diamonds screwed onto the end of the pipe. As the bit slices a circular hole into the earth, the undisturbed "core" of rock and sand rises inside the core barrel.

Gas fields are found in "sweet spots" in the blanket sand that have porosity (tiny holes to hold gas) and permeability (an ability to allow the gas to flow through), with impermeable "cap rock" over the top to prevent migration.[15] Some of the various limestone and sandstone formations in Pennsylvania, for example, were known by the selected formal geological systems and series (listed from the deepest around 15,000 feet to the shallowest less than 100 feet) of the geological time-measured ages: Cambrian, Ordovician, Silurian, Devonian, Mississippian, and Pennsylvanian. Drillers gave symbolic names to rock formations such as Hogshooter, Cow Run, and Blue Monday. Carpet Bag sand, consisting of very hard rock, acquired its nickname because the gas driller might be fired by the contractor for not making a hole fast enough through it.[16] Other gas sands known by informal monikers assigned by drillers included Little Lime, Big Lime, Big Injun, Squaw, 100 Foot Sand, 50 Foot Sand, 30 Foot Sand, and numerous others.[17] Until deeper exploration occurred in the 1960s, most Appalachian wells, stretching from New York to Tennessee, varied in depth

Early Brine Well — Most early natural gas discoveries were found by accident in the process of drilling for brine (salt water). Wooden pump logs were used for drill pipe (courtesy National Fuel Gas Company).

from a few hundred feet to approximately 4,600 feet and had pressures as high as 800 psi. Since records were first kept, more than 40 trillion cubic feet of gas has been produced from reservoirs in more than 1,000 named fields in New York, Pennsylvania, Ohio, West Virginia, and Kentucky, as well as a few in Maryland, Virginia, and Tennessee. It is estimated that proved reserves still total 7.4 trillion cubic feet.[18]

Geology experts describe the exploration and production field as "a science and an art."[19] Geologists, often called "rockhounds" in the early years of the industry, help decide where to drill and what technology should be used. But many of the early geologists were often distrusted. Petroleum historian Paul Giddens wrote, "it was a common saying among oilmen that if they wanted to make sure of drilling a dry hole, they would employ a geologist to select a location."[20] Eventually, however, science would win out. But prior to the development of seismic (sound wave) machinery and computer data analysis, results of new wells were mixed at best. Dynamite explosions were first used to measure the speeds of sound traveling through different rock formations, which helped find the "stratigraphic traps" in gas belts where oil and gas might reside. Deeper drilling after World War II using effective surface and subsurface geology and reflection seismology yielded greater finds. Today, the use of modern "3-D" seismic technology, which allows mapping of underground gas formations, maintains a high success rate. Well drilling costs range from the thousands for shallow Appalachian wells to the millions for deep underwater wells in the Gulf of Mexico. In the young years of the industry, the investment was much lower, but the hopes just as high.

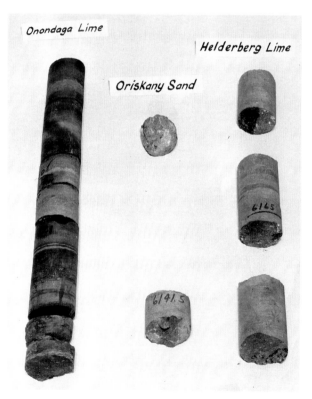

Core Samples — Natural gas was discovered in numerous geologic formations of sandstone and limestone. These well core samples enabled geologists to determine likely strata that would hold gas or oil. Pictured here are samples of Onondaga lime, Oriskany sand, and Helderberg lime (courtesy National Fuel Gas Company).

The Keystone Gassers — Selected Natural Gas Discoveries in Pennsylvania

Though manufactured gas found a significant role in urban areas, the exploration and production of natural gas in the Appalachian region held the key to success in the gas industry in its first century. Natural gas in

Pennsylvania occurs in the Appalachian geosyncline, a spoon-shaped trough 200 miles long running northeast to southwest from the New York State line to the extreme southwest corner bordering Ohio and West Virginia.[21] The heating value of natural gas diminishes from west to east in Pennsylvania, and the gas along the northern and eastern fringes of the Appalachian province consists almost entirely of methane.[22] Gas was found initially in shallow sandstone of various depths. Small wells were tapped around the region, and, in many cases, only supplied gas to an individual home or homes.[23] Once gas was found potentially useful for manufacturing as well as for residential purposes, exploration began in earnest.

Soon after the drilling of the first oil wells, large natural gas reserves were found, most of which its drillers did not know what to do with. Controlling a gas "gusher" was as easy as grabbing an invisible tiger by the tail, as the flammable vapor often ignited and led to nearly uncontrollable fires. In 1864, the so-called "Burning Well" was completed at 1,600 feet near Wilcox in Elk County, Pa. The well fire became an area spectacle, as visitors arrived to view the massive gas flare. One visitor who arrived at the site after dark described it like one would illustrate a fireworks display:

> Every seven minutes, without fail, the gas would throw the oil and water nearly twice as high as the derrick. Each time, when the flow would come, a man with a long pole, having an oiled rag on the end of it, would reach out the full length of this pole and set fire to the oil and gas. The gas would throw an eight-inch stream far up into the air. The water would form itself into a barrel shape, and the gas and oil would go straight up this round tunnel, all ablaze, entirely encircled by the water. The water would spread and fall in beautiful spray, forming all colors of the rainbow. Such a sight taking place every seven minutes cannot be described by my weak pen.[24]

Despite the threat of conflagration, more gas wells followed. The first well in the Leidy gas field in Clinton County was also drilled that year. The "East Sandy Well" drilled in an area known as "Gas City," named for its large amount of gas from area wells in Cranberry Township, Venango County, roared "like a cataract" and produced gas in 1869. It caught fire and burned for a year. Later, the well fueled oil-pumping wells, but was exhausted six years later.[25] Another "Gas City" well provided forty houses, stores, and restaurants with heat and light.[26]

On the Krouser farm four miles beyond Petersburg, near Pittsburgh, a vein of gas struck at 900 feet was of such "immense force" it lifted the drilling tools and cable, 400 feet of large well casing, dirt, stones, water, and mud out of the hole. The expelled gas sounded "like the rush of many waters," and was heard more than a mile away. One informant said the gas was enough to light two or three cities the size of Buffalo or Rochester.[27]

In Butler County, several profuse "gassers" were discovered beginning in the 1870s. After the celebrated fiery well of 1873 in Fairview, it was followed by the Harvey well in Clinton Township the following year, which struck gas in sandstone at 1,115 feet, and caught fire. One visitor described the scene: "The great mass of fine white flame, with its intense heat and brilliancy, the terrific noise of the escaping fluid, as it leaped into the atmosphere, fifteen feet wide by forty feet high, was a sight not soon to be forgotten."[28] The Burns well near St. Joe, drilled to 1,600 feet in 1875, provided gas at a pressure of 300 psi and was piped to nearby Freeport. The well remained connected until 1962, supplying gas in the community for three-quarters of a century.

A series of other powerful wells followed, pursued by many area gas companies. Later, the Pittsburgh Plate Glass Company drilled a series of wells in 1889 that included some of the largest producers in the county.[29] These included the Delmater well, a half mile from Burns, which burned one year before it was controlled. The site was originally an oil well that was drilled deeper and produced gas that was later piped to J. B. Ford Plate Glass Works below Kittanning and a large oil pumping station at Carbon Center. Butler County's largest well was opened up on the Gordon farm in Oakland Township in November 1916, and was developed by T. W. Phillips Gas & Oil Company, producing 17.5 million cubic feet per day.[30]

South of the New York State line, the Hague well, located two and a half miles east of Sheffield, near Warren, was the first commercial well in that area in 1875, though drilling began nearby a decade before. The 1,630-foot well had an original gas production sufficient to supply Sheffield with fuel for heating and illuminating purposes in 1876. The well was widely discussed by drillers because of the formation of ice near the point of gas inflow 1,350 feet below the surface.[31]

> Some have doubted this ice story, but there can be no question about it. Ice was brought up in the sand pump while drilling in mid-summer. After its completion, the well was tubed, and the tubing partly filled with water before inserting the sucker-rods. When the rods were put in, some obstruction in the tubing stopped them just about the gas vein, and they could be forced down no farther. The tubing was drawn to ascertain the cause, and several joints were found closed up solid with ice. The cold is produced, no doubt, by the sudden expansion of the gas as it enters the well from the rock, where it has been confined under a tremendous pressure.[32]

The so-called Barnesville well in the area followed in 1879.[33]

The Rodgers well was the oldest producing well in the UNG system. Lucius Rodgers, of Bradford, drilled it in 1876, southeast of Smethport. The well was left open and burned for over three years after it was drilled. Some of the drilling costs included:

- Contractor drilling $0.575 per foot
- Drilling Rig $400
- 20-hp boiler $600
- 15-hp engine on ground $260
- Casing $0.65 per foot
- 2" tubing $0.18 per foot
- 20 quarts of nitroglycerine $114.40.

When the well was tested in 1902, it still produced 100,000 cubic feet of gas per day. After cleaning in 1934, it had an open flow of more than 15,000 cubic feet per day and was still producing gas almost a century later.[34]

Two other old wells in the UNG system were the Halsey wells, drilled around 1880, which delivered gas to the Kane area in 1883. Both were in the Bradford-Kane-Elk series of wells in excess of 2,000 feet, purchased originally by Standard's United Pipeline Company.[35] Other gas drilling in northwestern Pennsylvania around this time occurred in Balltown, Shamburg, Pioneer Run, Cherry Run, Pithole, and Oil Creek in Venango County, Caldwell Creek near Titusville, Thorn Creek, Parker's Landing, and Millerstown (located in the city of Chicora) in Butler County.[36] A

2,247-foot well south of Pittsburgh in South Strabane Township struck gas in 1880, and blew in the atmosphere for a year before a six-inch line was run to the Pittsburgh area. Shortly thereafter in 1884, the Peoples Light and Heat Company drilled a well that fed nearby Washington.[37]

As mentioned earlier, the Haymaker Well was one of the most important first wells that supplied Pittsburgh and led to the creation of the Peoples and Equitable gas firms. By 1885, additional natural gas lines to Pittsburgh traveled from Murrysville, Tarentum, and Washington. Soon, many of the large white sand pools throughout western Pennsylvania were discovered. Berea sand, located in Lower Mississippian–Upper Devonian age strata, contained gas in giant fields in Pennsylvania in Leechburg in 1871, Murrysville in 1878, Greenville in 1880, and Oakford in 1885.[38] The Speechley Well, located seven miles east of Oil City, was another notable find. On April 9, 1885, English-born Captain Sam Speechley tapped a gas sand to become known as Speechley sand (also known as Bradford sand), one of the best known and most prolific gas producing horizons in the Eastern United States.[39] Despite the pessimistic advice of experienced drillers, Speechley continued to drill deeper than others had.

"How deep are you going; you will never find gas deeper," Standard's Elizur Strong supposedly said to him.

"I am going to China if I have to, to find it," was Captain Speechley's reported reply.[40] He would know if he got there, for he once traveled to the Orient on a steamer engaged in opium trading between Hong Kong and Calcutta.[41] Born in 1832 in England, Speechley entered the service of the Chinese government to help put down piracy, then a common menace in 1855 and 1856. He also operated an engineering business in Hong Kong for thirteen years before returning to western Pennsylvania.[42]

At 500 feet below the deepest previously known productive sand (Venango sand) in the area, Speechley hit gas at 1,923 feet. Later that year in July, J. B. Smithman hit a heavy gasser on the Karns farm in Pine Grove Township, one mile south of Speechley No. 1, another deep sand gas well in the area.[43] When new, the Speechley wells furnished the entire gas supply for Oil City with a ten-inch line laid by the Oil City Fuel Supply Company. A six-inch line later connected branches to Titusville and Franklin.[44] The gas producing territory was leased by Columbia Gas Company, which later consolidated into Standard's Natural Gas Trust.[45] The discovery well still produced decades later and the total field contained more than 1,000 wells.[46] The Speechley wells were largely depleted by the 1950s and well abandonments were frequent. But the famous original well continued to produce at low pressures for more than a century.

After Speechley, deeper drilling and larger discoveries ensued. In 1882, the notable McGuigan well in Washington County hit the famous Venango white sand found in the Hickory-Buffalo field in Greene and Washington counties, resulting in a volume of 30 million cubic feet per day, the largest flow of gas in the world up to that date.[47] Similarly, the Waynesburg field in Greene County was first developed from 1889 and continued to produce until 1930.[48] In 1886, drillers in Pennsylvania reached a depth of 6,000 feet.[49] The Presque Isle Natural Gas Company drilled to a depth of 4,460 feet near Lake Erie between 1887 and 1889, and penetrated the deep

Speechley Well — The original Speechley Well was drilled much deeper than previous area wells in Pennsylvania in 1885. Captain Sam Speechley, who settled on a farm in Venango County after involvement in the opium trade in the China Sea, discovered a huge natural gas pool seven miles east of Oil City. The Speechley wells then furnished the entire natural gas supply for Oil City, Titusville, and Franklin. The well is marked with a monument and was rededicated in 2000 (courtesy National Fuel Gas Company).

Trenton limestone. It had a show of gas before being abandoned without commercial production. It remained the only well to reach this geological formation in western Pennsylvania until 1941.[50]

In 1886, the first Peoples well was drilled on the Remaley Farm in Franklin Township, near the Haymaker's Murrysville well. Pew and Emerson purchased the 1,461-foot well for $75.[51] In 1893 in Washington County, Peoples found the Swagler No. 1 well; called the "largest gas well in the world" at the time, the roar from escaping vapor was heard for fifteen miles.[52]

Another significant find was discovered near the town of Jeannette, near Greensburg in Westmoreland County, at the Grapeville gas field. First struck in April 1886 by a Westmoreland and Cambria County firm, its capacity was estimated at 7 to 10 million cubic feet per day.[53] At first the supply seemed inexhaustible, and resulted in the construction of the H. Sellers McKee glass plant at Jeannette.[54] James McClurg Guffey, a nationally known oil prospector who later made significant oil and gas finds in Texas, developed the Grapeville field.[55] Guffey, born in 1842 in Sewickley Township, Westmoreland County, was a descendant of Scottish immigrants. He joined the Louisville Railroad Company at eighteen, and then his attention diverted to oil in the 1870s.[56] Guffey once drilled in Pithole, and stayed in the ephemeral oil boomtown until $30,000 homes sold for $1,000 apiece, at which point he decided to get out.[57] Guffey was a Buffalo Bill look-alike, wearing gaudy vests and pleated shirts, and a decorative broad-brimmed black hat above his long white hair. His partner John H. Galey, known as "Dr. Drill" by some Pennsylvania reporters, was "diminutive, quiet and never given to the publicity that Guffey loved." Whereas Galey "smelled" the oil, Guffey "swung the deal."[58] Guffey and Galey also investigated natural gas and oil finds in West Virginia, Kentucky, Kansas, and most significant, the first major oil gusher in Texas. Tragically, Guffey, like oil pioneer Colonel Drake before him, eventually spent the later part of his life deeply in debt.

As the century came to a close, many new gas fields were discovered throughout western Pennsylvania enabling the expansion of gas service. Natural gas was so plentiful, huge gas flares were seen all over oil country as it burned from area wells. For example, celebration of Pittsburgh's centennial in 1888 was accompanied by "giant gas jets" that lighted the Allegheny River "roaring like the noise of many waters."[59]

By 1900, though natural gas had been discovered in seventeen states, Pennsylvania reigned as the leading producer.[60] The new century led to more discoveries in the original oil and gas region such as a large find on the Cutler Farm struck in Washington County, in 1900. Pennsylvania hit its maximum gas production in 1906, producing 138 billion cubic feet.[61] By 1908, Pennsylvania had more than 8,300 producing gas wells with an annual natural gas value of $20 million, greater than the state's oil production and more than a third of the value of the entire United States natural gas production.[62]

In northern Pennsylvania, three miles from Kane at Wetmore in McKean County, the Big Keelor Well (or "great gusher") was drilled in 1906. A rumor of the discovery of the well claimed that the Keelor brothers "were quite well under the influence of liquor and as they were traveling through the woods, the one carrying the stake for marking the well tripped over a log and fell down dropping the stake. The spot where the stake landed was then chosen as the well site."[63] The 1,800-foot well in the so-called Cooper sand blew in with such force that it was impossible to manage it.[64] The *Kane Republican* reported: "When the sand was first struck a large volume of gas was struck which took several days to get under control, and about the time the drillers thought they had the well shut in, it let go with a roar that could be heard for many miles, and since that time it has shot forth millions upon millions of feet of gas." Experts at the time said it was one of the greatest gas wells ever (nearly 100 million cubic feet daily), and it attracted thousands of visitors.[65] One of the Keelors stated that he received upwards of 200 letters a day from all over the United States with schemes for shutting in the well.[66] The well blew free into the air for six weeks, was heard fourteen miles distant, and lost a "small fortune ... in the gas" before it was possible to tube and control it on November 10, 1906, with tools brought in from Pittsburgh.[67] The PGC soon bought the gas from the well.

After the shallow wells waned in the early part of the century, drilling went deeper. Peoples gas fields extended from Clarion County on the north to Ligonier in Westmoreland County on the east, West Virginia to the south, and the Ohio River on the west. In 1917, Peoples drilled the 7,248-foot R. A. Geary Well—five times the depth of the Haymaker Well—in the geological time measured Salina Age sand five miles north of McDonald in Washington County. It was not productive. Still, at the time, it was the deepest in the United States and the second deepest in the world.[68] Deep drilling continued to attempt to satisfy the great industrial demand in Pittsburgh. Looking for new supplies of gas after its shallow wells were being depleted, in 1924, Peoples hit its deepest producer at 7,756 feet at the Booth and Finn Well at McCance, in Westmoreland County, on the Chestnut Ridge anticline.[69] The well near Latrobe, Pa., was under the direction of Standard's John B. Tonkin.[70] Another was hit at 6,822 feet at the Ligonier well in Westmoreland County, and T. W. Phillips Gas and Oil Company struck a deep well that year in Indiana County at 7,002 feet.[71] After a half century of production, the value of gas produced in Pennsylvania at the point of consumption increased from $75,000 in 1882 to $50 million in 1926.[72] But the Keystone State's wells paled in comparison to other sections of the country.

For example, by 1941, the 18,300 producing wells in Pennsylvania produced the same amount of gas as only 110 wells in California.[73]

Most of the early wells drilled in western Pennsylvania, however, were shallow, and unhappy gas producers found that within a few years, the gas pressures dropped dramatically and a promising gas field was spent. For example, in McKeesport, a gas drilling boom in 1919 led to more than a thousand wells drilled in one pool. Unfortunately, all the gas reserves were drained within fifteen months—$13 million spent on drilling resulted in only $3.5 million in gas.[74] The large Foster Well struck in August 1919 at 56 million cubic feet a day declined to only 5 million cubic feet a day the next year.[75] Drilled in the so-called Speechley sand in the Long Run pool, the find resulted in the drilling of about 650 wells (many of them dry holes)

When the Big Keelor Well (a.k.a. "great gusher") was drilled in 1906 in McKean County, Pennsylvania, the initial force literally blew the well derrick away (courtesy Drake Well Museum, Pennsylvania Historical and Museum Commission).

into the 850-acre field within a year.[76] Companies were "hastily formed and stock sold by the thousands of shares to persons who were not familiar with the business and who ultimately lost their entire investment."[77] The wells were abandoned and the fittings and machinery were sold for junk. Pennsylvania Public Service Commissioner John S. Rilling deplored the "robbing of territory" by sinking of wells by an adjacent holder, telling a 1920 federal conference on conservation, "No sooner was it known that a hungry horde of exploiters, with no regard whatever for this valuable resource, but only led on by a desire to serve their selfish purposes by methods that would not bear inspection, appeared on the scene."[78] Rilling said of the massive misuse of natural gas:

> When first discovered its worth was little appreciated. Of all the great waste that has marked the destruction of our natural resources, that committed in relation to natural gas has been the most profligate. So wanton has been its waste, so marked has been the misuse and foolish production thereof, and with such extravagance has it been taken from mother earth, that its history is but a sad commentary on the intelligence of those responsible therefor.[79]

Still, a pell-mell rush ensued by companies to obtain additional lands for drilling in western Pennsylvania. Excessive drilling that led to the quick draining of gas fields was prevalent in the first half of the century. The state's first conservation law to control gas-well spacing did not become effective until 1961.[80] And since 1921, Pennsylvania has used more natural gas than it produced, becoming a major importer of the product it once pioneered.[81]

The major portion of deeper gas in Pennsylvania was found in Oriskany sandstone, a coarse, porous and permeable quartz rock of Lower Devonian Age, though the Onondaga Formation produced substantial quantities as well.[82] But Oriskany became the most important operation in the Appalachian basin after 1921, widespread in western New York, western Pennsylvania, West Virginia, and eastern Ohio.[83] A very exciting Oriskany sand gas boom in north-central Pennsylvania, and New York's Southern Tier and Finger Lakes region began in 1930, including the discovery of sixteen Oriskany gas pools in north-central Pennsylvania.[84] Developments in the Oriskany Formation "spread like wildfire" over the next decade and UNG's exploration subsidiary, Sylvania Corporation, formed in 1928, and New York State Natural were involved in the discovery of the following important Oriskany gas pools in the Potter County, Pa.–Steuben County, N.Y. region, including: Hebron in 1931, Greenville in 1932, State Line and Ellisburg (the largest single gas pool in the Oriskany Formation in the region) in 1933, Harrison in 1934, Sabinsville in 1935, West Bigham in 1936, Woodhull in 1937, Sharon Township in 1938, and Tuscarora in 1944. In addition to the Oriskany finds, by 1936, at least thirty-six wells had been drilled to the Onondaga Formation or deeper.[85]

Wharton field, located ten miles to the northwest of Leidy, Pa., was first drilled in 1933. Initially, only a small open flow was found. Godfrey L. Cabot, Inc., a significant producer of carbon black, drilled small wells there in the early 1940s.[86] Cabot produced gas from wells in various central and western New York counties, as well as Potter and Tioga counties in Pennsylvania, beginning in 1935, and transported the gas to Rochester.[87] In Pennsylvania, the Alleghany Gas Company and the Emporium Lumber Company conducted other exploration in the region.[88] Drilling picked up, and once the wells in the area were exhausted after producing 94 billion cubic feet of gas, the field was converted to storage in 1949.[89] In southwestern Pennsylvania, Summit field in Fayette County, drilled in 1937, was a combined Huntersville Chert and Oriskany sand reservoir.[90]

The first drilling along Kettle Creek in the Leidy gas field in Clinton County, Pa., occurred in 1864 and was used for domestic purposes, including a well providing enough gas for one boiler. But the first systematic drilling of shallow wells occurred between 1922 and 1923, with seventeen wells drilled, seven of which produced gas.[91] Then, in 1949, Dorcie Calhoun located his well-known well near the village of Leidy. Perhaps "on a hunch with a non-impressive rig," Calhoun hit gas in Oriskany sand in January 1950.[92] The well blew in, and was out of control, with an estimated initial open flow of 15 million cubic feet of gas per day and a rock pressure of 4,200 psi. The production was obtained in the upper one foot of the Oriskany sand at a depth of 5,660 feet.

The striking of Oriskany in the region became one of the most significant discoveries in the northern part of the Appalachian plateau province.[93] According to one account of the discovery of the Leidy gas pool, "Gas fever spread to young and old, and those who could spare it punked down their money for stocks in a number of drilling companies with optimistic plans and hopes."[94] But CNG's New York State Natural had "quietly" leased most of the Leidy pool acreage two years previous. The H. E. Finnefrock Well in February 1951 by CNG's New York State Natural in the Leidy field bore the distinction at its discovery as the largest gas well ever discovered east of the Mississippi River, and the largest Oriskany well in the nation. Drilled near a faulted zone that contributed to the cracking of the productive sandstone, the well produced at the tremendous rate of 145 million cubic feet per day and 4,200 psi. The drilling tools were ejected into the sky and when the drilling stem landed, it buried itself six feet into the ground. Another producing well nearby also blew out its drilling tools, causing a spark that started a five-day fire. Exploding a forty quart nitroglycerin charge in the well created a vacuum that extinguished the flames.[95]

The Fickle Fanny Well, drilled in the Tamarack pool of the Leidy gas field, also came with a roar in February 1952. It caught fire for a week, and "Red" Adair, the famous well firefighter from Houston, was rushed by plane to help extinguish the blaze. However, without notice, it amazingly extinguished itself.[96] Quick development of the area Oriskany pools, including Tamarack, Greenlick, and Downs, soon depleted the fields. The Greenlick pool produced 50 billion cubic feet and was converted to storage in 1961. The Tamarack and Downs pools were converted to storage in 1971 after producing 11.4 billion cubic feet.[97]

South of Leidy, Sylvania drilled a wildcat well in the wooded hills of Cameron County in central Pennsylvania and hit the Driftwood–Benezette Oriskany sand in 1951. After a new "bazooka-type" shot (a shaped explosive charge) was detonated deep in the well, gas was tapped at 5,895 feet. The initial open flow was more than 4 million cubic feet per day and the initial rock pressure was 3,825 psi. One well scout said when he saw the blow and heard the shriek of the gas, "That's good enough for me!"[98] After the successful strike, several hundred wells were drilled over a belt of land known as the "Colonel Eaton Tract" extending fifteen miles in the Benezette area.[99] It ranked as one of the largest Oriskany gas pools to that time, second only to West Virginia's Kanawha pool.

New drilling in the northwestern Pennsylvania Oriskany formations continued after World War II due to strong natural gas demand. The largest number of successful deep gas wells in Pennsylvania, 162, were drilled in Potter County in 1949, followed by seventy-seven in Tioga, and twenty-seven in Fayette, for a total of 285 producing gas wells in the state.[100] In southwestern Pennsylvania, Peoples sunk a successful deep well at the end of the 1940s at the Piper Well on Chestnut Ridge in Fayette County at 8,552 feet.[101] And in 1949, the W. R. Barton Estate No. 8 Well of the Manufacturers Light and Heat Company in Fayette County, drilled to 10,312 feet, was the deepest well of that time in the entire Appalachian region.[102] Discovery of Oriskany gas increased production from 115 billion cubic feet in 1937 to 158 billion cubic feet in 1954.[103] In addition to deep Oriskany exploration, drilling in Trenton limestone found gas in 1941 near Transfer, located between Sharpsville and Greenville in Mercer County, at 6,830 feet. In addition, a test well along the shore of Lake Erie near the Pennsylvania-Ohio line encountered the top of the Trenton Formation at 4,440 feet.[104]

Until deeper Appalachian exploration occurred around 1960, most wells varied in depth from a few hundred feet to approximately 4,600 feet. In 1959, a deep well in the Gatesburg sand was located near Albion in Erie County, Pa., at 5,910 feet, far below the Oriskany and Medina formations in the area. This discovery at nearly 6,000 feet contrasted to depths of Gatesburg finds at Oil City at 8,400 feet and Clarion at 10,600 feet. Finds like this stimulated the quest for deeper production in Pennsylvania.[105] But some of the Gatesburg fields in western Crawford County only produced for eighteen months.

In the southwestern Pennsylvania region, Peoples also struck the significant Blair gas pool at Laurel Ridge near Seven Springs in 1958. The Elk Run pool in the Frostburg field in Jefferson County, was found in 1965 by CNG, resulting in 4,000 acres of drilling land.[106] But overall, the volumes in the state were declining. Pennsylvania's natural gas

Driftwood Well — A successful wildcat well on the Eaton farm in Cameron County in 1951 set off a drilling boom in deep Oriskany sands in the Driftwood-Benezette field of central Pennsylvania (courtesy National Fuel Gas Company).

production dropped from nearly 114 billion cubic feet in 1960 to just under 74 billion cubic feet in 1972.[107] Still, Pennsylvania accounted for 28 percent of total gas deliveries of the Appalachian region in 1970.[108]

Empire Firsts — Selected Natural Gas Discoveries in Western New York

Besides natural gas flowing from Pennsylvania wells in the latter part of the nineteenth century, there was also an active search for gas sources closer to the expanding market in the growing city of Buffalo. After the Fredonia discovery, numerous shallow gas wells were drilled in the Chautauqua County shale belt from the Pennsylvania line to the eastern border of Chautauqua County, supplying farms, orchards, and vineyard owners with heat and light.[109] The Fredonia Gas Company produced about 1.1 million cubic feet of gas from these low-pressure wells later in the nineteenth century.[110] Besides the younger Upper Devonian Age shallow shales prominent along the Lake Erie shoreline, natural gas in New York comes from two primary formations, the Oriskany sands of early Devonian Age and deeper Medina sands of the older Silurian Age (the largest and longest producing formation in the state).[111] In fact, the Medina Formation is one of the most significant trends in the Appalachian basin extending from Kentucky to southwestern Ontario. Overdrilling was common and wells drilled too close together caused much waste. Many wells were plugged and abandoned as 40 to 50 percent of the 2,600 Medina wells drilled in New York by World War II were dry holes.[112] Still, the Lakeshore gas field, first tested by the Fredonia Gas and Fuel Company in 1887, but not actively developed until 1903, eventually produced 426 billion cubic feet of gas from 4,000 wells.[113]

The first gas well sunk in Erie County, near Buffalo, was at Getzville between 1858 and 1859. Following the discovery of oil in Pennsylvania in 1859, some Oil City parties secured leases in the town of Boston, and drilled a well near Patchen. They struck gas, but oil was the object and the gas was disregarded.[114] The first commercial oil well in New York, the Job Moses No. 1 well near Limestone in Cattaraugus County in 1865, also found some natural gas, though only the oil was used.[115]

Gas wells were reportedly drilled in Buffalo in 1871 for the city's use.[116] In 1872, the Buffalo Gas Light Company, a manufactured gas firm, drilled a well at their gasworks near the corner of West Genesee and Jackson streets in downtown Buffalo and struck a pocket of gas, which lasted only a short time. This firm drilled the well to see if natural gas could be utilized for illuminating purposes. The small amount discovered was used as fuel under the manufactured gas plant's boilers. The well was abandoned after the supply petered out and only caustic sulfur gas was produced.[117]

The Buffalo Cement Company began the first systematic search for gas within Buffalo in 1883. The firm sunk a well with a diamond bit drill to 451 feet within city limits, opening up the search for gas in the Medina Formation, which extended from the Niagara Falls region to New York's Southern Tier. Erie County had the largest amount of Medina fields, at first varying from 700 to 3,000 feet. This sandstone contained very little water, no oil, but ample gas production.[118] After drilling two unsatisfactory wells, a third 900-foot well in 1887 delivered a good flow of gas.

Afterward in 1889, Gerhard Lang drilled a well near his brewery at Best and Jefferson streets in Buffalo and found gas. Drilling nearby followed and the Erie County Pipe Line brought the surplus gas to dwellings in the vicinity. A firm called the East Side Fuel Company organized and was later absorbed by the Erie County Pipe Line organization. That group also drilled a well on the Canadian side of the Niagara River, after other successful wells in Canada led to more development in southern Ontario.[119] Though oil wells had existed in western Ontario near the border with the Detroit area for many years, natural gas drilling began across the border from Buffalo and Niagara Falls after entrepreneurs assumed that the same geological formations in the Appalachian basin that produced natural gas throughout Ohio, Pennsylvania, and New York also might run underneath Lake Erie to Canada. Eugene Coste — partially funded by his father Napoleon, a French-born British citizen who once did contract work on the Suez Canal — successfully drilled the first well in the region. The Coste No. 1 Well in Gosfield Township was completed on January 23, 1889, and produced 10 million cubic feet a day.[120] Soon, American entrepreneurs from the oil region crossed the border to drill wells.

After a rich supply of gas was discovered at Father Baker's well in the Lackawanna–West Seneca area in 1891, drilling accelerated in the vicinity. The following year, the South Buffalo Natural Gas Company started with backing from the Standard interests, which controlled the Buffalo Natural Gas Fuel Company "under arrangements mutually advantageous."[121] By 1895, the company drilled forty-five wells. In 1896, the Buffalo Natural Gas Fuel Company bought out the firm and all the wells, including the Canadian fields, and supplied about 9,000 customers.[122]

South of Buffalo, the Chipmonk gas field in Cattaraugus County, first drilled in 1891, provided many gassers, but the field was soon exhausted.[123] Natural gas was then found in Corfu, west of Batavia in Genesee County, in the 1890s. In 1897, a natural gas test well in Attica in Wyoming County, proved to be a gasser with an estimated 250,000 cubic feet produced per day from a depth of 1,800 feet. The *Batavia Daily News* wrote, "The pressure was so strong that it lifted the 3,000 pound drill and kept it suspended so that it was impossible to bore any further."[124] As a result, the Attica Natural Gas Water & Electric Company incorporated in 1901. Gas was also soon discovered in nearby Akron and Alden in eastern Erie County. The Genesee County Pavilion gas field, first discovered in 1906, extended thirty-five miles to the northern edges of Wyoming County and western border of Livingston County with wells 1,600 to 1,800 feet deep.[125] Despite the large Ontario County West Bloomfield well that attempted to supply Rochester with natural gas for illumination in the early 1870s, little gas was found in northern Monroe County along the shores of Lake Ontario. For example, a 3,100-foot test well drilled in 1901 in the city of Rochester was a dry hole and later called "Old Rochester."[126]

As natural gas discoveries on the shores of Lake Erie found potential markets, the scramble to obtain mineral rights for land ensued. Many entrepreneurs drilled wells and sought a receptive market. In 1912, gas was discovered in the North Collins and Collins fields in southern Erie County. Likewise, a pool of gas was developed between 1912 and 1913 in Orchard Park. A huge gasser was hit by drillers associated with Standard in 1922 on a farm in the town of Arkwright, south of Dunkirk in Chautauqua County, and yielded more than 13 million cubic feet of gas per day.[127] Numerous similar wells in the area followed. The first well drilled in the Town of Aurora occurred in 1927, and, by 1929, thirteen wells were completed at an average depth of 2,300 feet in Medina sandstone. This local production field was converted to underground storage in 1953 in a partnership between Iroquois Gas Corporation and Tennessee Gas Transmission Company.[128] New natural gas production development by Iroquois in 1929 was the largest in any year in the area since Standard's commencement of the natural gas business in the area in 1886.

Although shallow Appalachian wells were waning, there were some new discoveries. The Trenton Formation of the Ordovician Age limestone held natural gas in a formation 400 to 800 feet wide and was found in commercial quantities in the central New York counties of Oswego, Onondaga, Oneida, and Lewis.[129] Most significant, however, was the finding of Oriskany gas in 1930. The Allegheny Gas Company, a North Penn Gas Company predecessor, drilled in its L. B. Palmer No. 1 Well in Farmington Township, Tioga County, N.Y., striking an Oriskany Formation with a 20 million cubic foot open flow that blew wild for weeks.[130] The find opened one of the greatest lease campaigns in the entire region. Also that year, a large volume in Oriskany was found in the Wayne-Dundee field in Schuyler County, N.Y. The Belmont Quadrangle Drilling Corporation completed one of the largest gas wells in the region in Greenwood Township in Steuben County in 1934, hitting gas at 4,738 feet, with an initial daily production of 50 million cubic feet.[131] The discovery of gas in the overlying Tully limestone in a well near Richburg in Allegany County, may also have contributed to the attractiveness of these deeper formation possibilities. The entry of Columbia gas interests into the area encouraged new drilling that supplied natural gas expansions to central New York. The Oriskany fields and Onondaga fields of Tioga and Schyler counties represented deeper gas, compared to the shallower Upper Devonian Formation.[132] New York State Natural wells in Woodhull Township, Steuben County, resulted in 100 million cubic feet of gas withdrawn per day from the Oriskany field in 1938. The Penn-York Corporation, part of Republic Light and Heat Company, also found significant production in the so-called "State Line" Formation at depths ranging from 5,000 to 6,000 feet, and transported the gas west to Lake Erie markets. The Cunningham Gas Company initially found that formation in Oswayo Township in 1933 in a 4,879-foot well that produced 11 million cubic feet of gas a day. More discoveries followed in Alma, Willing, and Independence townships in Allegany County in the 1930s. The Oriskany sand pools were great producers, but were quickly drained. Many were later developed into storage areas due to their effective acceptance of injected gas and quick withdrawal during the winter months.

Some other gas fields included the Chemung Formation in Steuben County drilled in 1931 and Niagara Limestone in Seneca County in 1932. Producing wells during the Depression cost around $25,000 and the cost of an Oriskany dry hole was around $14,000.[133] New York's deepest well in the first half of the century — 8,625 feet — was the Roy Harrington No. 1 discovery well in the Woodhull gas field in Steuben County. First drilled by the Southwestern Development Company in 1937, it was deepened by the New Penn Development Corporation in 1943.

The Empire Gas and Fuel Company struck one of the largest wells in western New York in April 1939 in Independence Township, Allegany County, nine miles

southeast of Wellsville. The incredible pressure from the well
mud, and gas from not only the main well, but also other shallow o.
in the area. Area families were evacuated due to the fire hazard a
from Texas was flown in to control the well with cement, clay, and
pumped into it. It took twenty days to bring the "wild well" under c
that time, an estimated 600 million cubic feet of gas was wasted.[134]

In 1944, Sylvania drilled the Frazier No. 1 Well in Steuben County, a.   .
seismograph surveys. This lead to the discovery of the Tuscarora pool that ɩ   .ɩcually
became one of the most valuable storage pools in the NFG system. Drillers lost their
tools in the well at a depth of 3,802 feet, and "fished" for them for a month. Oriskany
sand gas was finally hit late that year, with an initial open flow of more than 8 million
cubic feet per day and a rock pressure of 2,040 psi. Oriskany sand gas was also found
in Allegany State Park by the Felmont Oil Corporation in southern Cattaraugus
County in 1955, in an area first drilled in the 1870s.[135]

More Onondaga exploration in Western New York and northwestern Pennsylvania began in the 1960s and '70s, beginning with the discovery of the Wyckoff field
in Steuben County, in 1967.[136]

The West Gateway— Selected Natural Gas Discoveries in Ohio

By 1850, Ohio ranked fourth in the United States in quantity and value of salt
produced and salt wells were dug with frequency.[137] Consequently, unintended gas
and oil discoveries occurred while digging for brine. Once drilling for fossil fuels in
Ohio commenced on purpose, it thrived throughout the eastern half of the state,
almost entirely in the Allegheny Plateau in shallow stratigraphic traps or limited Lake
Erie shoreline deposits. The principal underground horizons in northeastern Ohio
include various sandstones and limestones ranging from Pennsylvanian to Cambrian
Age, especially: Berea sand at depths of 500 to 2,000 feet; Oriskany sand from 2,000
to 3,500 feet; Newburg limestone from 2,400 to 3,660 feet; and Clinton sand (elsewhere known as the Medina Formation) from 2,000 to 5,300 feet.[138] Exploration
thrived in the southeast near West Virginia, which also was a major focus for oil
drilling. Though Ohio wells were usually lower in pressure than other Appalachian
wells, discoveries were plentiful.

In 1881, natural gas was discovered in Cincinnati, causing a "sensation."[139] But
the state's first significant production began in 1884 in Findlay, Hancock County, in
northwestern Ohio, struck in an Ordovician Age geologic formation known as Trenton–Black River that stretched into eastern Indiana. German physician Dr. Charles
Oesterlin, also an expert geologist, smelled a strong odor of sulphureted hydrogen
throughout many parts of the town, most prominent near a small stream on one side
of the village. Oesterlin examined a gas spring and when a lighted torch was brought
near it, an explosion occurred, but no one was injured. Perhaps intrigued by the success of natural gas in Pittsburgh, he drilled a 1,092-foot well through solid limestone
in 1884, striking gas that produced 150,000 cubic feet per day. One visitor recalled,
there was a "terrific roar like that of Niagara, or, more exactly, like the noise of escaping steam of a thousand locomotives, filled the air and made the ground tremble,

while the whole town was lighted up as though every building in it had suddenly broken into flame."[140] Findlay — whose population swelled from 6,000 to 15,000 in two years after the discovery — was illuminated in 1887 and thanks to the huge natural gas torches along the town's streets "there were no dark corners in it." There were no meters, and customers could consume as much as they wanted. And similar to a warning issued to oil pioneer Drake, one story told of man lamenting the natural gas wells because the drillers were ruining God's plan to use the flammable substance to blow up the world when the time came.[141]

The Findlay find set off a frantic gas boom in the northwestern Ohio-Indiana region that led to the drilling of more than 100,000 wells.[142] Seventeen counties in Indiana, with Muncie and Anderson at the center, produced massive amounts of natural gas in the state, much of it wasted. It was estimated that an average of 100 million cubic feet of natural gas per day was blown off into the atmosphere or burned, totaling about 15 billion cubic feet over six months.[143] "In some places night was virtually indistinguishable from day. Flambeau torches of natural gas burned wastefully along city and county roads. It became the fashion to erect arches of perforated iron pipe over roads leading into the towns, fire gas into them, and let them burn night and day."[144] But by 1902, there were only 5,820 active wells in the state.[145]

Though successes were plentiful, so were disappointments. Early in 1885 B. C. Faurot, of Lima, started drilling for gas, hoping to obtain an abundance for a strawboard factory, but struck oil instead.[146] And often in the Trenton fields in the region, sulfur-tainted oil and hydrogen sulfide gas (H_2S), the "rotten egg" smelling corrosive contaminant (a.k.a. "sour" gas), accompanied production from the wells. The fetid gas has an offensive odor and breathing excessive amounts can be fatal.[147]

In February 1886, the Karg Well at Lima was said to be heard fifteen miles away and, after igniting, its light seen as far as fifty-five miles away.[148] In the late nineteenth century, the Trenton limestone field of northwestern Ohio was also one of the largest producing fields of oil in the United States, making Ohio the nation's leading petroleum producer in 1896.[149] The Lima, Ohio–Indiana oil and gas field, however, produced not from the Appalachian geologic basin, but the Cincinnati Arch, which separates the Appalachian basin from the Michigan and Illinois basins.[150]

In spite of the waste, drilling accelerated. In 1887, natural gas was struck at 1,957 feet, near Lancaster, Fairfield County, the first in Clinton sandstone, producing 74,800 cubic feet per day. In April of that year, a large gas strike was found near Bowling Green.[151] Gas from wells in Wood County was piped to Toledo, Lucas County, where the town held a natural gas jubilee in September 1887.[152] The Clinton sand wells started a drilling boom resulting in 17,679 wells drilled in Ohio over the next forty years.[153] In 1888, the Thurston gas field was discovered between Lancaster, Fairfield County, and Newark, Licking County. The following year, gas from Clinton sand wells drilled at Newark was used in the town, and a ten-inch line was laid to the state capital at Columbus in Franklin County. In 1893, the Sugar Grove field in parts of Fairfield and Hocking counties, perhaps the richest in central Ohio, also brought gas to Columbus. And another Clinton sand area, the Homer gas field, was discovered in Knox and Licking counties, and later piped to Columbus and Zanesville in Muskingum County.[154] The Chicago Oil Company, struck a "tremendous gasser" in shale rock at only 385 feet on the Wallace farm in Washington Township, in Hancock

County, in May 1894. But the gas caught fire and burned down the derrick.[155] However, despite the copious discoveries, many of these gas producing areas, once thought to last in perpetuity, were soon spent. Ohio enacted its first conservation law in 1889, ordering that wells be shut-in within three months to prevent the waste of gas.[156]

Though Cleveland would not have large-scale natural gas deliveries until 1903, gas in the area was present fifteen years before. In 1885, a Lakewood-area florist named, appropriately, J. M. Gasser, struck gas on his property and used it for lighting and heating a greenhouse.[157] Nearly thirty years later, a short-lived gas boom resulted in numerous wells drilled in the area. In 1913, the Lakewood Gas Company formed, drilling thirty-four wells at a depth of around 2,700 feet in the Clinton sandstone, twenty-three of them producing. Some produced as much as 6 million cubic feet a day, but complaints by residents claimed that brine from the wells was ruining nearby shrubbery, and the Lakewood Council passed regulations prohibiting drilling within 100 feet of dwellings. However, the field soon diminished in 1915, and many investors lost their shirts when boom turned to bust. However, many wells continued to produce low levels of gas used for private homes, businesses, and farms for light and fuel.[158]

Though East Ohio purchased most of its supply of gas from Hope in West Virginia, it began its own gas well purchasing and drilling effort in the Buckeye State. It began with the purchase of three wells in 1906, and the firm later bought 119 wells from the Mohican Gas Company. Fields were opened in Danville in 1910, Wayne County in 1912–15, and South Park in 1916. East Ohio's largest drilling campaign from 1918 to 1919, caused by market demand increasing and the firm's supply dwindling, included Chippewa field, which later became East Ohio's first storage area in 1941. Other later gas fields included Killbuck in Holmes County in 1925, North Olmstead in 1925, Franklin Township near Clinton in 1927, Tuscarawas County in 1935, Highland Heights in Cuyahoga County in 1938, and Hinckley Township in 1939.[159] The firm increased its total of active wells to 371 by 1941.[160]

Ohio Fuel opened the Cambridge field in Guernsey County in southeastern Ohio in 1922 with the wildcat Miller No. 1 Well. The field was similar to other Oriskany Formations, and the firm completed 270 gas wells spread out over 14,000 acres.[161] The gas was used for the local glass and brick industries.[162]

Some of the major gas fields throughout Ohio included: Sugar Grove in Knox and Hocking counties, where the earliest Clinton sandstone was first drilled in 1893 and once depleted, it was converted to gas storage in 1936; Homer in Knox and Licking counties; Ashland-Lorain in Ashland, Medina, Richland, Lorain, and Wayne counties; Hinckley-Granger in Medina County, first drilled in 1928; Sharon, covering 102,080 acres in five counties in southeastern Ohio, first drilled in 1942; Canton, spanning 320,000 acres across eight counties in east-central Ohio, completed in 1945; East Canton, discovered in 1953; and North Jackson, throughout 108,000 acres in Mahoning and Trumbull counties, found by East Ohio in 1963.[163] Since the first discoveries, oil and gas production has occurred in seventy-six of Ohio's eighty-eight counties, with 268,000 wells drilled. The Buckeye state ranks fourteenth in gas wells drilled and seventeenth in production, much of it from Clinton sand with wells with depths that approach 5,000 feet.[164]

Country Roads — Selected Natural Gas
Discoveries in West Virginia

Despite the general acceptance of the Drake Titusville Well launching the quest for oil in August 1859, West Virginia historians assert that the "Little Mountain State" may have initiated the domestic petroleum industry months earlier in 1859 when the Rathbone Brothers began boring a salt well at Burning Springs Run near Little Kanawha. The area attracted deer, buffalo, and elk to lick the salt-incrusted rocks and soil. The Rathbone's slow-boring spring pole derrick struck oil at 200 feet the following year after Drake's find. However, petroleum known as "Seneca Oil," used for its medicinal properties, was discovered while searching for saltwater in the 1830s and was shipped to Pittsburgh, Baltimore, Philadelphia, New York, St. Louis, Cincinnati, and Chicago from 1848 to 1856.[165] In 1860, Burning Springs was regarded as a "health resort," and "every month many ailing persons came to drink the nauseous waters and bathe their 'jints' [sic] with the oil fluid."[166] The Rathbone well eventually produced 200 barrels a day, and a second well produced 1,200 barrels daily. By 1861, a town with several thousand sprung up near the find, and all light, including that of a hotel, was lit by natural gas produced from the site. Natural gas still flows from the well, possibly making it the oldest producing gas well in the nation (the oldest producing oil well is the McClintock well at Rouseville, Pa., near Oil City).

The Burning Springs oil field was later destroyed in nine hours by Confederate Raiders in 1863, resulting in a loss of an estimated 100,000 to 300,000 barrels of oil, the first of many oil field incursions during the Civil War, but it was later refurbished.[167] Still, the gushing oil and spewing natural gas in the hills and valleys produced millionaire oil barons who used their wealth politically to bring about statehood for West Virginia during the nation's conflict. West Virginia was admitted to the Union as the thirty-fifth state on June 20, 1863. Though most of the people sympathized with the South, the oil tycoons around Parkersburg steered the state in Lincoln's column to protect their oil investments. As a result, major oil investors became mayors, congressmen, senators, and governor.[168] And, by 1876, there were 292 wells in the state producing 900 barrels of oil daily.

Though much of the mountainous region's land was unsuited for agriculture, large discoveries of mineral deposits of natural gas were unearthed throughout the nineteenth century in West Virginia, complementing the state's ample supply of coal and oil. In 1843, a well drilled by Dickenson & Shrewsberry struck a gusher of gas at 1,000 feet in depth. According to an account by historian Dr. J. P. Hale of Charleston:

> So great was the pressure of this gas and the force with which it was vented through this bore-hole, that the auger, consisting of a heavy iron sinker, weighing some 500 pounds, and several hundred feet more of augur poles, weighing in all, perhaps 1,000 pounds was shot up out of the well like an arrow out of a crossbow. With it came a column of saltwater, which stood probably 150 feet high. The roaring of this gas and water, as they issued, could be heard under favorable conditions for several miles....[169]

Other drillers began to drill for saltwater and gas on purpose, using an ingenious method to separate the liquid from the gas. While the brine piped from the well hole fell into a holding tank, the lighter gas rose in a container known as a "hogshead," and was piped directly to the furnace that boiled the brine.[170]

After the war, drilling at the "Burning Springs" region picked up in 1866, originally for oil. John Jones drilled deeper than other efforts and struck oil with great gas pressure at 800 feet. It shot oil for five days, six inches of oil suffusing on the nearby river for ten miles and the air was "so saturated with gas that people fled from the area and no fires were allowed in the vicinity."[171] But one account recorded that a man carrying a kerosene lantern accidentally set the find ablaze.[172] As the oil boom ensued, natural gas became abundant as well. Though much was wasted, efforts to pipe it in the area helped supply ninety oil-pumping engines and the community with illumination for two years. In 1868, the Rathbone Gas Company was organized by J. W. Butters, B. Flint, W. H. H. Wheaton, I. Sannborne, Jr., and L. D. Wheaton.[173]

West Virginia gas was produced initially from shallower limestones and sandstones including Greenbrier limestone, and Big Injun, Weir, and Berea sandstones.[174] Thousands of wells from southwestern Pennsylvania to eastern Kentucky have been drilled in Big Injun sands, first discovered in 1886 at Mount Morris, Pa.[175] Weir sands were first discovered in 1911 in Kanawha County, in the Blue Creek gas field, and then later in Kentucky in such fields as Oil Springs, Ivyton, and Paint Creek.[176] Berea sand and similar sandstones, first discovered in 1859 in East Liverpool, Ohio, extended throughout in southwestern Ohio, West Virginia, and eastern Kentucky.

Still, the West Virginia oil and gas fields developed slowly, as the investment by Standard and others went primarily to Pennsylvania, since at first there was a reluctance to invest south in West Virginia.[177] But as the Mountain State's oil industry reached peak production of 16 million barrels in 1900 (surpassing Pennsylvania in 1898), natural gas production was also growing, and the state became the leading United States gas producer from 1906 to 1917. The principal companies exploring for gas were Hope, United Fuel, Carnegie, Manufacturers, Columbia and Equitable. In 1912, West Virginia produced 239 billion cubic feet of gas valued at $33.3 million, supplying the cities of Cleveland, Toledo, Cincinnati and Portsmouth in Ohio, Pittsburgh in Pennsylvania, and Covington in Kentucky.[178]

Dr. I. C. White (1848–1927), the official West Virginia state geologist who conducted the first geological survey of the state in 1898, inaugurated the science of petroleum geology in the state with his "anticlinal" theory (first conceived by geologist H. D. Rogers in 1860) that resulted in the finding of the Mannington–Dolls Run pool by a wildcat well in 1889.[179] The eminent geologist, whose theory ended up finding much natural gas, also became West Virginia's leading energy conservationist. White was born on a farm in Pennsylvania-bordering Monongalia County, W.Va. After graduating with high honors at West Virginia State University in 1867, he assisted in the second geological survey of Pennsylvania in 1875, then was elected professor of geology at West Virginia University. He was an assistant on the U.S. Geological Survey, and spent time in Russia on excursions across the empire including observing the famous Baku oil fields.[180] White's work for Jacob J. Vandergrift's Forest Oil Company in 1883 led him to study all the great gas well discoveries of Pennsylvania, which he noted were near the crowns of anticlinal folds. The theory was published in *Science* in June 1885 under the title "Geology of Natural Gas."

Though Pennsylvania State geologists attacked the model, Ohio's State Geologist Edward Orton supported it. White's prediction was tested during with the celebrated Grapeville gas field and the Hess gas field at Washington, Pa. Driller James M. Guffey also used the principles to drill in the celebrated Taylorstown oil pool in Pennsylvania in 1888–90.[181]

White also believed that West Virginia would prove even more prolific than Pennsylvania for the same reason, and Guffey was one of the first old Venango and Clarion County, Pa., operators to follow the lead, acquiring 500,000 acres of oil and gas leases in West Virginia between 1884 and 1885.[182] White's anticline existed along an imaginary line along the length of the western foothills of the Allegheny Mountains and he developed an oil field along the whole length of the Burning Springs anticline that ran not northeast and southwest like the Chestnut Ridge anticline did in Pennsylvania, but almost due north and south.[183] White was proved right regarding his prediction of the Mountain State's bounty. Oil was discovered in the Mannington field in Marion County in 1889 by several oil firms, as well as the Flaggy Meadow Gas Company.[184] The pursuit of West Virginia fossil fuels was on, led by Standard's South Penn (chartered in 1889 and later part of Pennzoil), which was among the first firms to engage actively in Monongalia, Marion, and Wetzel counties. Other companies followed including the Carter Oil Company (also later a subsidiary of Standard), Hope, Equitable, Carnegie, and the Manufacturers Light and Heat Company.[185] But development of the "deep pockets" of oil and gas locked away in the vast reservoirs in rural West Virginia required "deep financial pockets." The enormous investment required could only come from prodigious firms like Standard. And the oil and gas discoveries kept coming. The Sistersville field, the next major find around 1890, was thought to be the greatest producing oil field in the world.[186]

Immediately south across the Ohio River bordering the southwest corner of Pennsylvania, the lush West Virginia gas fields located in the deepest trough of the Appalachian basin included Marshall and Metzel counties as well as others in the West Virginia panhandle. In April 1890, the Blackshere No. 2 Well in the Mannington field struck a pocket of gas, resulting in the drillers being blown off of the derrick, and the ensuing fire destroyed the entire rig.[187] In July of that year, another big strike occurred on the Lee Sheets farm near Sistersville throwing water from the well "to a great height." The well had an estimated capacity of 3 million cubic feet of gas a day.[188]

A landmark discovery well, known as "Big Moses" in Tyler County in September 1894, was the first 100 million cubic foot well in the United States.[189] The huge well was located near Middlebourne on Indian Creek and first owned by the Victor Oil Company. The well, struck at 1,750 feet in Keener sand on a farm owned by "Moses" Spencer, blew uncontrolled for a year, initially at 575 psi. According to witnesses, the gas caused the ground to shake as if it was an earthquake.[190] One of the drillers, J. N. (Nelse) Curry, wrote in his diary on September 27, 1894: "Hells to pay at the well now—the gas broke in anew at midnight last night and she is howling worse than ever now and has got 35 psi of open pressure and we can't case her until the gas weakens."[191] Lightning struck the drilling rig two or three times and the rig burned down. The Wheeling Natural Gas Company finally brought in the gas from Big Moses in early 1895. Later the Pittsburgh and West Virginia Gas Company, and eventually

Equitable purchased the fuel. It continued to produce gas for more than seventy-five years until it was finally plugged in the 1970s.[192]

On the north-south anticline around 1900, the Blue Creek (Falling Rock) gas field was discovered in Kanawha County on a tributary of the Elk River northeast of the state capital of Charleston. Oil prospectors Guffey and Galey struck a big gasser on the Mullady farm, and it proved to be one of the largest ever tapped in the state. The pressure of the well blew the drilling tools and 500 feet of the casing out of the hole. It took several weeks to bring the well under control, while hundreds of millions of cubic feet of gas escaped into the air.[193] United Fuel, Hope, South Penn, and Elk Refining explored there and oil was discovered later in 1911.[194] In 1902, the *Buffalo Courier* reported that the West Virginia gas belt was said to be the greatest that had ever been opened, and a large pipeline — owned by Standard — was planned to Buffalo and other western New York cities.[195] Most West Virginia gas, however, eventually went to Cleveland, Cincinnati, and Pittsburgh. For example, Hope in West Virginia built a pipeline to the Pennsylvania border in 1905 to supply Peoples in Pittsburgh, while other Standard lines crossed the Ohio River to northeastern Ohio a few years before. There was even a proposal to bring the great West Virginia gas discoveries east to Baltimore, where the manufactured gas industry got its start in 1816. "Right-of-ways," strips of land approximately fifty to seventy-five feet in width that needed to be cleared to allow the stringing of pipeline, had been purchased across the Blue Ridge Mountains for the route. But East Ohio's Martin B. Daly convinced Mountain State producers that Cleveland was a better market.[196] And by the 1920s, Ohio became the largest importer of natural gas.[197] While Pennsylvania, New York, and Ohio demand for natural gas was seemingly unquenchable, West Virginia would be the only state in the region that produced more gas than it consumed. In 1910, the value of West Virginia's gas stood at $23.8 million.[198] West Virginia held the top producing position in the U.S. for fourteen years until Oklahoma displaced it.

By 1912, the average depths of wells ranged from 1,400 to 3,400 feet in Tyler County; 1,000 to 3,560 feet in Wetzel County; and 1,290 to 3,478 feet in Marion County.[199] A 1912 Federal Geological Survey claimed that there was a proven existence of deeply buried strata containing high pressure gas over many large areas in West Virginia, including Lewis, Harrison, Marion, Monongalia, and Wetzel counties. An earlier oil boom in Lewis County found huge quantities of natural gas, and "reinforced the idea that money could be made by utilizing rather than wasting the natural gas which was encountered while drilling for oil."[200] Two years later, the Survey said the most prolific fields were in Lewis, Harrison, and Ritchie counties, and showed little decline from year to year. These shallow sands in wells less than 3,000 feet in the north-central West Virginia counties of Marion, Harrison, and Lewis served as Hope's main source of supply for many years.[201] The fields were expected to be "ample for many years for its own needs as well as for the needs of the adjacent states within the limits of practical transportation."[202] The first well, Barbour County No. 998, produced gas from what would become the prolific Benson trend of the Elk play in northern West Virginia. It was drilled in 1909 in west-central Barbour County and became a favorite target of gas well drillers in the Mountain State.[203]

Because of the declining gas output in Pennsylvania, West Virginia stepped up its drilling between 1910 and 1920 and production hit its high point in 1917 with 308 billion cubic feet produced.[204] Despite the hopes of many in Appalachia, most of the easy shallow gas was discovered in the first quarter of the twentieth century. Production declined from 1917 to 1934 as the old wells fell from huge pressures of up to 1,000 psi to only 100 and 200 psi. Though West Virginia benefited from great gas exports during this period, worries about the dwindling supply led the state to consider giving its own citizens preference to the indigenous gas supply. The state passed the Steptoe bill in 1919 that prohibited interstate gas sales unless the gas was unmarketable intrastate, attempting to prevent a third straight winter of shortages that closed factories and schools as well as to stop losing businesses to Ohio.[205] The gas importing states of Ohio and Pennsylvania objected, and eventually in 1923, the U.S. Supreme Court ruled that the West Virginia policy interfered with interstate commerce.[206]

Other firms were exploring in the state by 1920, including the Ohio Cities Gas Company, United Fuel, and Columbia.[207] Drilling picked up the in 1930s and continued until 1970.[208] For new supplies, drilling had to go deeper. Hope Well No. 4190, drilled in 1918 on the Martha Goff farm in Harrison County at a depth of about 7,400 feet, was reported to be the world's deepest well at the time. It produced until 1965 and was then adapted for storage.[209] The record for deep drilling again was broken in 1919 by Hope's I. H. Lake Well near Fairmont, Marion County, drilled at 7,579 feet. But after losing the drilling tools deep in the well, it yielded no gas.[210] United Fuel completed the first commercial Oriskany sand well in Kanawha County in 1930, south of Charleston.[211]

The giant Oriskany sand gas field in the Elk-Poca region in Jackson, Putnam, and Kanawha counties was found in 1935, beginning with the Frankenberger Well, and Oriskany discoveries were found east of the older fields in 1944.[212] The deepest test well drilled for Hope was conducted by the Falcon Seaboard Drilling Company near Clarksburg, reaching 10,000 feet in 1941, and a second in 1954 dove to 13,324 feet.[213] Hope's first extreme deep test well was completed in 1955 at a depth of 13,331 feet, penetrated all sedimentary formations, but failed to result in significant production.[214] Later, other Oriskany discoveries, as well as the Newburg sand of the Upper Silurian Age in the west-central part of the state found in 1966 and Tuscarora sand at 11,000 feet in eastern Monongalia County, became the deepest target for gas drilling.[215] For example, the Bell No. 1 Well struck in March 1968 in Wirt County in Newburg sand hit gas pressure so intense it blew a million dollars worth of gas into the air every day. Famed Texas "well-tamer" Red Adair was called in to help cap the well.[216] Newburg discoveries included the Kanawha Forest field, Rocky Fork, and Cooper Creek fields. The Tuscarora Formation was first drilled in West Virginia and Pennsylvania in the 1960s, then again in the late 1970s and early 1980s.[217]

Further eastward, the first successful gas well was drilled in the state of Virginia in 1931 by the Bristol Natural Gas Corporation, a discovery well of the Early Grove field in Scott and Washington counties. Later other gas fields were established in Buchanan, Dickenson, Wise, Lee, and Russell counties.[218] Also, the first commercial gas well in Maryland was sunk in 1949 by the Cumberland & Allegheny Gas Company near Oakland.[219]

Hope Well No. 4190, drilled to a depth of 7,400 feet in Harrison County, West Virginia, became the world's deepest well in 1918. After producing gas until 1965, it was then converted to gas storage (courtesy Dominion Resources).

The Bluegrass Wells — Selected Natural Gas Discoveries in Kentucky

In Kentucky, oil and natural gas occur throughout much of the western, south-central and eastern parts of the state, in places such as Burning Springs, Oil Springs, and Oil Valley. The eastern part of the state is included in the Appalachian geological basin, producing gas from various sandstones, carbonate rock, and shale reservoirs, while the western region is part of the Cincinnati Arch.[220] On the upper Cumberland River, gas built up in such quantities beneath the sheets of the Lower Silurian limestone, that tons of rock and earth were sometimes blown out with such force the occurrences were known as "gas volcanoes."[221] Similar to other Appalachian areas, the search for salt resulted in various natural gas finds after the 1819 Martin Beatty Well in McCreary County, and the search for crude petroleum around the Civil War years resulted in more discoveries in the rugged terrain of the Cumberland Plateau. Though there were occasional wildcat booms, petroleum and gas extraction took a secondary place to coal.[222] Though the state did not become a major oil and gas producer, one firm — Ashland Oil — did achieve significant status.

In addition to the hunt for oil, the discovery of the Trenton Formation in northern Ohio and northeastern Indiana in the 1880s also encouraged deep drilling in western Kentucky. A large gas strike was reported on New Year's Day, 1884, on the property of the Tug River Coal and Salt Company, near Wakefield, Kentucky, at depth of 1,300 feet.[223] Finds included gas and oil west of Glasgow in Barren County, shale gas in Meade County, and gas in Lower Mississippian limestone near Cloverport, Breckinridge County.[224] Most natural gas was discovered in significant "paying" sands including Black lime or Beaver sand of Hart County, Caney sand in Morgan County, Big Six lime in Breathitt County, Salt sand of Magoffin County, Maxon sand in Pike, Martin, and Floyd counties, and shale gas in Floyd and Boyd counties.[225] Other gas bearing formations in Kentucky included Bradley, Big Injun, Weir, and Berea sands, and Big and Corniferous limestone.

The Ashland gas field in Boyd and Greenup counties, adjacent to Ohio and the Big Sandy River near Ashland, was one area of commercial significance for area industry. The first shallow wells were drilled there between 1880 and 1890, and beginning around 1914, the local iron and steel companies drilled, produced, and used the gas in manufacturing operations. Like many others, the field was soon depleted.[226]

The Big Sandy field, located on the Big Sandy River covering parts of Floyd, Pike, Knott, and Magoffin counties, was first discovered in 1892. Then, Louis Henry Gormley of New Castle, Pa., drilled the Howard Purchase No. 1 Well at the mouth of Salt Lick Creek, about seventy miles south of Ashland.[227] More than 80 percent of the gas from the Big Sandy field comes from black shales, where more than 10,000 wells have been drilled to date, producing more than 2.5 trillion cubic feet of gas.[228]

Eastern Kentucky provided most of the oil and gas developments around the turn of the twentieth century, including the Warfield gas field in Martin County, the Ragland oil pool in 1900, the Menifee gas field, and the Burning Fork gas wells of Magoffin County. The first well drilled for oil occurred in 1867 on the Hughes farm on Little Richland Creek, five miles from Barbourville. At 400 feet in depth, workers lost the drilling tools and abandoned the effort. Later, oil explorers Guffey and Galey drilled several wells in 1896, nine miles from Barbourville. The Clay County (a.k.a. Oneida) field, on the south fork of Kentucky River near Burning Springs, was brought in during 1898.[229] Many Kentucky fields were shallow and were quickly exhausted or limited due to low prices.

Some of the other early discoveries of gas and oil in the region included a 1,500-foot deep test well on Hutchins farm near Big Richland Creek in 1902. Also, a good gasser was struck at 2,700 feet on the William Tye farm on the Cumberland River, two miles from Barbourville. The following year wells drilled by the Barbourville & Cumberland Valley Oil Company hit pay sands with a daily output of 500,000 cubic feet. Likewise, a 1,430-foot well on the G. W. Mayhew farm on the Cumberland River hit a strong flow of gas in Big Injun sand with a daily flow of 1.5 million cubic feet.[230] The Williamsburg field in the center of Whitley County was also first drilled in 1902.

The state saw a decline in production after 1910, but there were still gas discoveries. A wildcat well in December 1916 near Anneta, one-half mile south of Leitchfield, produced an estimated 2 million cubic feet a day.[231] Still, the natural gas consumers in the state used twice as much gas as the state produced. The total value of Kentucky gas in 1912 was $497,909, while it consumed 5.1 billion cubic feet valued at more than $1 million.[232]

Most natural gas in the Bluegrass State from the Devonian black shale is produced in eastern Kentucky, especially Floyd County. Much initial exploration was commenced based on the geological work conducted in the 1880s by Major W. T. Davis of Louisville. A major well at 375 feet deep hit gas accompanied by saltwater in Meade County, producing about 750,000 cubic feet of gas a day. More drilling in the area provided Louisville with natural gas. Because of the gas shortage in the winters of 1918 and 1919, Louisville Gas and Electric came to investigate area fields, and, by 1930, 875 wells were drilled in Floyd County. The black shale also produced gas in the Ashland area.[233]

Significant natural gas was also found around the turn of century in the Menifee gas field (later Kentucky's first gas storage area), discovered in March 1904 by the New Domain Oil & Gas Company near Rothwell, Menifee County, at a depth of 450 feet in Corniferous limestone.[234] The greatest daily production there of 25 million cubic feet was reported by Central Kentucky Gas Company.[235] Other significant fields in eastern Kentucky included Win on the Johnson-Magoffin county line seven miles northeast of Salyersville, begun in 1917 by the Bed Rock Oil Company, but practically exhausted by 1936. Also, Redbush, in a hilly area of northwestern Johnson County twelve miles from Paintsville, was first discovered in 1918. The gas was purchased by United Fuel and Central Kentucky, and the Kentucky–West Virginia Gas Company, a sister firm of Pittsburgh's Equitable, which acquired approximately one million acres in eastern and central Kentucky by the 1920s. Ivyton field, in central-eastern Magoffin County on the Burning Fork River four miles southeast of Salyersville, was opened in 1919 by Bed Rock. The Louisville Gas and Electric Company and Ivyton Oil and Gas Company bought that gas until the field was essentially depleted by 1936. Grassy Creek in western Morgan County, fifty-five miles southwest of Ashland, was discovered in 1921. And Big Six in Breathitt and Wolfe counties, south of Ashland and Lexington, was first drilled in 1920 with probably the highest average original open flow (7.5 million cubic feet) of any gas pool in Kentucky. The Kentucky Cities Gas Company and Petroleum Exploration, Inc. operated it.[236]

Several fields discovered in the early 1930s included: Newcombe in southeastern Elliott County, and linked to Inland and United Fuel; Janet in the south-central part of Powell County, first produced in 1929; Canada in northeastern Pike County, principally produced by Piney Oil and Gas Company; Hazard in Perry County, with considerable acreage controlled by Kentucky–West Virginia; Himyar in Knox County; McKee in central Jackson County; North Triplett in northwestern Rowan County; and Martin in central and northern Martin County — one of the best gas-producing areas in eastern Kentucky. Gas from this area flowed through a twenty-inch pipeline of United Fuel connecting to Covington and Newport in Kentucky, and Cincinnati, Hamilton, and Dayton in Ohio.[237] The Upper Mississippian Age carbonate rocks are great producers of natural gas in West Virginia and eastern Kentucky, where a total of 6,000 wells produce from Greenbrier limestone in 183 fields in West Virginia, and 3,400 wells produce from Newman limestone in 257 fields of eastern Kentucky.[238]

By 1936, the value of natural gas at the point of consumption that was produced in Kentucky totaled $17,730,000.[239] Pike County in the far eastern part of the Bluegrass State was the leading producer of gas through 1970.[240]

Waste Not, Want Not — The Push for Natural Gas Conservation

In the early days of the gas industry, the fuel was squandered due to wells blowing into the air, excessive well drilling, leaking pipelines, failing to recover natural gas liquids, producing carbon black, and inefficient usage by consumers who received the product at little or no cost.[241] Though the new gas discoveries cut steel production costs in Pittsburgh toward the end of the nineteenth century, still more of the precious product was discarded when the factories shut down over the weekends. In fact, standpipes erected on the surrounding western Pennsylvania hilltops shined fires throughout the night to use up the excess gas.[242]

Because of low prices, wasteful control of gas supplies, and dwindling pressure, geologists sounded the clarion call for conservation. Ohio's state geologist, Edward Orton, emphasized the importance of natural gas in oil production in 1899, and decried the waste of gas.[243] West Virginia's Dr. White agreed, saying as a result of the competitive effort of local officials luring manufacturing interests to their areas, "this precious fuel has not only been used for the crudest forms of heat and power at a merely nominal price right in the midst of great beds of coal, but many towns, two or three decades ago, actually advertising free gas to all concerns, and as a standing advertisement permitted great torches of the same to burn up millions of cubic feet both day and night."[244] In addition, the vaporous energy from gas-producing oil wells was squandered. As early as 1891, West Virginia passed a law to prevent the wasting of natural gas at the wellhead, but it had little enforcement and did not prevent the routine blowing off of wells or flaring natural gas.[245] A well on Goose Creek west of the town of Petroleum, W.Va., spewed gas for seven years, set on fire occasionally with a flame two to four feet high.[246] White claimed that while the City of Wheeling, W.Va., sold the low heating value manufactured gas at $0.75 compared to other cities paying $1.50 to $2.50, natural gas companies sold their superior product at one-sixth the cost of manufactured gas. White told the Council of Governors in 1908 that people did not recognize the inherent value of natural gas and West Virginia's supply was three-fourths exhausted:

> The average business man assumed that the supply of natural gas was unlimited, and while turning a deaf ear to the geologists who always warned him that the supply would eventually fall through use and waste, he listened willingly and apparently approvingly to the fakers in science who assured him the supply of natural gas would never fail, that it was being manufactured at a rapid rate deep down in nature's vast laboratory.[247]

White's life-long battle to prevent the squandering of the state's vital resource earned him a spot on President Theodore Roosevelt's White House Conference on Conservation.[248] The president wrote White that "our resources are being consumed, wasted and destroyed at a rate which threatens them with exhaustion. It was demonstrated that the inevitable result of our present course towards these resources, if we should persist in following it, would ultimately be impoverishment of our people."[249]

Still the waste continued, at an estimated rate of 500 million cubic feet of gas daily, equal in energy to about 20,000 tons of coal a day, one-third of West Virginia's coal production.[250] In addition, the drilling of gas wells in areas of coal mining also presented safety problems. These issues would contribute to the state's creation of a Public Service Commission in West Virginia in 1913.[251] Further regulation occurred by 1930 through a well drilling and plugging statute preventing the waste of gas.[252] Casing and plugging were enacted by various states as well, starting with Pennsylvania in 1873. Conservation laws—of varying levels of effectiveness—were approved in New York in 1879, Ohio in 1883, Kentucky in 1892, and Pennsylvania in 1924.[253]

Natural gas shortages around World War I attracted federal interest in the waste of natural gas through careless production, inefficient use, and free gas offered to some industries or residences that were connected to gas wells. In Kentucky in 1918, the natural gas supply in Louisville failed. After a government study, it was revealed that 1.9 percent of the consumers (mostly industrial) were using 39.7 percent of the gas.[254] As a result in 1919, the U.S. Fuel Administration issued a federal order prohibiting the waste of natural gas by flambeaux "open flames," burning natural gas lights during the daylight hours, and using natural gas in inefficient appliances.[255] Samuel S. Wyer, the chief of Natural Gas Conservation of the U.S. Fuel Administration said that up to 35 percent of the natural gas from the field was wasted before it arrived to the consumer. Specifically, the carbon black industry wasted 50 percent more gas than was used by all the domestic consumers in West Virginia.[256] Secretary of the Interior Franklin K. Lane warned industry leaders as a result of such a wasteful policy, "the strong hand of the law, of the community itself, will come down upon any such industry."[257] Lane said ordinary good sense was lacking in making good use of the product. "We have been wasteful with natural gas—partly because it was a sort of by-product like the straw in the wheat field. We have been wasteful because we wanted to get rid of it and get the real thing that we were after, the oil; wasteful because we did not appreciate its value."[258] Newspapers railed against the waste of gas in the fields as well, and Ohio's governor issued a conservation proclamation in 1920.

As the demand for natural gas escalated in the early twentieth century, so did the need for new discoveries in Appalachian fields. Waste or not, supply could barely keep up with want. By 1917, Appalachian field gas production reached an all-time peak of 522 billion cubic feet per year. After forced and unrestrained production for the munitions needs during World War I, production declined rapidly through the 1920s and '30s, but picked up again during World War II.[259] But active wells were running dry. For example, in Allegheny County, Pa., in 1936, Peoples had more depleted wells than producing ones.[260] In response to the tightening of supply, Appalachian natural gas companies drilled deeper, though discoveries were not as plentiful as the early years. But by 1960, extension and deep drilling in the Appalachian gas area produced 439 billion cubic feet, 85 percent of its all-time high.[261]

Gas drilling was not limited to on land. Between 1910 and 1913, wells were drilled offshore in Lake Erie, including one near Selkirk, west of Welland, Ontario, which hit gas in large volume.[262] In 1958, offshore drilling was rejuvenated in the Great Lakes. New York State Natural drilled two wells in Lake Erie, one off the shore of the Ohio-Pennsylvania line, which produced some gas at 2,525 feet, but later shut-in. Another off of the Pennsylvania shore was a dry hole.[263] However, the offshore program was soon phased out. Later, the American Great Lake state governments prohibited drilling off the north coast of Lake Erie, though Canadian companies have drilled successfully in the Great Lakes since the 1950s.

But despite aggressive drilling programs, there would be limits to what explorers could find in Appalachia. And proportionally, the original gas fields paled in comparison to other areas of the nation. In 1912, the Appalachian region produced 74 percent of the nation's natural gas. By 1945, that amount was down to 10 percent, and, by 1970, it provided only 2 percent of the country's natural gas.[264] By the early 1960s, Appalachia consumed five times the amount of gas than it produced.[265]

But the future of the Appalachian natural gas industry would lie far beneath the ground in the Southwest and under the waters of the Gulf of Mexico. The first offshore field in the Gulf of Mexico was opened in 1938, launching discoveries that would extend into the twenty-first century. In 1956, CNG joined with Mississippi River Fuel Corporation in a ten-year exploration and development effort in the Louisiana area, and a decade later, the firm began a full-scale exploration effort in the Gulf Region.[266] By the 1970s, more Appalachian firms joined the hunt. CNG's G. J. Tankersley wrote in 1971, "The natural gas distributor shouldn't leave his future entirely in the hands of other people. His raw product is essential to his livelihood and he should be involved in obtaining that raw product at the source."[267]

Roughnecks, Drill Bits, Fishin' & Fracin'— Tools of the Trade

The earliest type of drilling, often used for water wells, was conducted by the ancient Chinese "spring pole" method, where a rope with a drilling tool was attached to a wooden pole, usually a long flexible ash or hickory sapling, about ten feet in length and ten inches in diameter. "Kicking down" on an attached rope stirrup bent the pole down and the natural spring moved the drilling tool up and down.[268] While the collection of oil in northwestern Pennsylvania was first conducted by scooping it out of oil springs, Colonel Drake was the first to drill through a "drive-pipe" casing in his Titusville oil well — an idea he failed to patent — to prevent cave-ins of silt and water in the well. Once drilling derricks came on the scene after Drake's Titusville well, drilling was mostly conducted by the arduous "cable-tool" method, until the turn of the twentieth century. Early derricks covered an area of twelve by sixteen feet at the bottom and rose in a pyramidal-framed structure to about forty feet high. The drive pipe, hammered into the upper end of the borehole in cable-tool drilling, extended fifteen to forty feet deep below the soil and loose rock. A block and tackle was rigged to the top of the derrick to hoist drilling tools, which weighed close to 900 pounds.[269] Drilling rigs, first constructed of wood, and later, iron and steel, eventually reached a standard eighty-one feet high to hold a "string" of tools more than fifty feet long.[270]

Rig workers—called "tool dressers"—removed, forged, heated, and tempered massive iron drill bits with a heavy sledge. An early tool dresser with the Alden-Batavia Natural Gas Company in 1908 was paid $75 a month, and worked a six-day, seventy-two-hour week. A driller and tool dresser operated gas or steam engines, and in standard drilling, used tools called bits, stems, jars, and sockets. Much of early drilling apparatus had its roots in the drilling of salt wells. The cable-tool drilling apparatus included the chisel bit, first developed by the Ruffner brothers for salt drilling through hard sandstone in West Virginia and later used by the oil industry.[271] The end of the drilling apparatus included sharpened metal drill bits. They were attached to a heavy, long stem, which added force to the bit. Another of the early tools included the salt man's "slip," later the oilman's "jar," developed by William "Billye" Morris, a driller in the Kanawha Valley in 1831.[272] Drilling jars were used to "jar" the drilling tools loose if they became lodged in the well bore. This allowed for deeper drilling. Sockets attached to the drilling jar aligned the tools vertically with the drilling cable.[273]

In cable-tool drilling, a drilling spike attached to the cable was lifted and dropped, pounding and pulverizing through almost impenetrable hard rock blow-by-blow, inch-by-inch. Drilling with cable tools took weeks or months to strike gas or oil deposits. Still, cable-tool drilling worked well in hard rock formations in the Appalachians, and was widely used until the 1950s.[274] However, the method required periodic bailing of rock cuttings out of the hole, slowing progress of the drilling. Still, much deep drilling was conducted with cable tools, though it faced problems

Kane Test Well—Appalachian natural gas companies had a hand in many major natural gas discoveries in the first half of the twentieth century. Drilling derricks, first constructed of wood, and then metal, held the cable tool drilling apparatus and rose in a pyramidal-framed structure to about forty feet high (courtesy National Fuel Gas Company).

in Marcellus shale, which occasionally contained highly explosive gas pockets that sometimes blew out the drilling tools.[275]

Appalachian wells often produce small amounts of saltwater that is removed periodically by bailing, pumping, or blowing to keep the well in condition. At first, brine was often stored ineffectively and became a source of contamination to surface streams and to shallow fresh-water aquifers.[276] The pungency of the salty gas and oil well byproduct varies from less than seawater to twenty times saltier than seawater.[277] In addition to removing the saltwater, heartbreaking and costly incidents occurred during efforts to bring in a gas well, such as losing drilling tools. Well workers would "fish" for wire, tools, or other equipment dropped or stuck at the bottom of the well by dangling up to 2,000 feet of wire cable down a six-inch hole. Fishing for tools due to broken cables or well cave-ins could last for months.

Early well drilling was a hazardous occupation at times, and drillers adopted the appellation "roughnecks." For example, in 1886, an employee of the Chartiers Valley Gas Company lost a foot and ankle and later died after a connecting pipe blew and exploded. Likewise, a sudden spew of gas in Kane field, near Halsey, Pa., exploded and hurled a well worker into the air, tearing off his clothes, causing serious injury.[278] Wells that exploded or caught fire severely burned those around the site and often were fatal. In addition, oil and gas fires were sometimes caused by lightning strikes.

Adding to the hazard of striking flammable gas, new wells were "shot" with the so-called "Robert's Torpedoes," or many imitations of the invention, first used in 1865 by Colonel E. A. L. Roberts in Titusville.[279] Roberts, born in Saratoga County, N.Y., in 1829, served in the army during the end the Mexican War in the late 1840s and also was an inventor of dental equipment, including a synthetic material for dentures. He came to the oil region along with his brother, an investor in oil wells. These tin-tubed torpedo devices were filled first with black gunpowder, and later with liquid nitroglycerine. The explosive liquid was invented by Italian chemist Ascanio Sobrero in 1846 and first successfully used by Swedish engineer Alfred Nobel, the creator of dynamite.[280] Nitroglycerine, which possessed thirteen times the explosive power of gunpowder, was detonated with a "go-devil," a device first used in Butler County, Pa., dropped to the bottom of the well. The explosion was often accompanied by an improvement of the well's production. However, the explosion of nitroglycerine, also employed to accelerate oil production, occasionally led to serious accidents. As one nineteenth century author wrote, sometimes the well shooters disappeared as completely as "Elijah and his chariot of fire."[281] In 1888, a teamster's wagon carrying 1,400 pounds of the volatile product exploded in Pleasantville, Pa., and as an account of the time phrased it, blew up the wagon and team "to atoms."[282] In 1895, a barge loaded with the explosive on its way to the oil and gas fields at Burning Springs, W.Va., accidentally detonated on the Little Kanawha River at Parkersburg, sinking a nearby steamboat, blowing out windows on shore, knocking down nearby buildings, and causing "general pandemonium ... throughout the town." Remarkably, only one person was killed.[283] In another example where things did not go as planned, sixty quarts of nitroglycerine accidentally exploded at a well site of the Alden-Batavia Natural Gas Company in New York in 1908. Fortunately, no one was injured but "all were showered with water and mud and several suffered from nervous shock."[284] The effort to stimulate wells grew with technology, which later used pressured water, acids, and other liquids to accelerate production. And, in the 1960s, the United States experimented with a twenty-nine-kiloton nuclear explosive to stimulate gas production beginning with "Project Gas Buggy" in New Mexico to free up gas locked in "tight-sands" formations.[285]

In addition to the cable-tool method, "Spudder" rigs were similar to a portable water well drilling machine in design, mounted on trailer wheels that could be torn down and set up quickly. Spudders replaced the traditional cable-tool rig for depths up to 6,000 feet.[286] The deepest cable-tool drilled well in the world was the E. C. Kesselring No. 1 Well in Chemung County, N.Y., drilled in 1953 by New York State Natural.[287] However "rotary" drilling proved to be faster. With rotary rigs, a drilling bit is attached to the end of a hollow drill pipe and powered by a direct sprocket gear drive. Rotary drilling was reportedly first used in 3000 B.C. by Egyptians boring into rock, and much later in the United

Roughnecks — Well workers known as "roughnecks" handled the drilling tools at the well. Rotary drill bits resemble large pinecones made of tough steel covered with sharp teeth and, in more recent years, diamond bits to cut through hard, brittle formations (courtesy National Fuel Gas Company).

States in Louisiana in 1838 by Ruben Drake with a very crude wooden drilling rig.[288] In the rotary method, as the borehole gets deeper, additional joints of hollow pipe are added to the drilling string. Instead of bailing, the rock cuttings are removed by pumping a special drilling fluid, often called "drilling mud," down the hole that subsequently carries the broken rock to the surface.

The Corsicana oil well in 1894 in Texas was the first use of rotary drilling for oil, using a mule to power the revolving platform to turn the drilling bit.[289] The famous Spindletop field near Beaumont, Texas, in 1901, also drilled with rotary tools, hit gas that collapsed the well. Standard's Calvin Payne of Erie, Pa., visited the sour springs at the Beaumont site, but concluded that evidence was insufficient to support the theory of oil there and not worth the financial risk to Standard.[290] But after continuing the well, pay dirt was struck, spewing a huge plume of gas and oil into the air that could be seen for miles. It became the symbol of the oil boom times in the rich Gulf Coast Area. Spindletop was also the first field discovered on a salt dome. Pittsburgh financier Andrew W. Mellon loaned $300,000 to drilling prospector James M. Guffey of Pittsburgh for the Spindletop well, which eventually led to the creation of Mellon's largest moneymaker—and major Standard competitor—Gulf Oil Corporation.[291] Only twenty miles away from Spindletop, a huge gusher struck shortly thereafter led to the creation of Texaco.[292] This and other major southern oil and natural gas finds that were thousands of miles away from Appalachia were not much use to the region's gas consumers at the time, but a half-century later, these gas supplies became critical to the Northeast.

Large discoveries such as these also established the rotary drill as a competitor to the older cable-tool rig in deep-hole drilling in Appalachia. An improvement to the "fish-tail" rotary bit, the "cone roller" bit, was invented in 1909 by Texas oil prospector Howard Hughes, Sr., founder of the Hughes Tool Company and father of the eccentric millionaire, Howard Hughes, Jr.[293] Rotary three-cone drill bits introduced in 1933 resembled large pine cones made of tough steel covered with sharp teeth, and, in more recent years, industrial diamonds, to break through hard, brittle formations. Rotary tools—first introduced in Pennsylvania and New York in 1936— solved problems of high gas pressures encountered in drilling and completing wells in deeper formations.[294] Development of state-of-the-art drilling bits and mud motors drilled a larger section of hole faster. As a result, with the help of rotary drilling over the next two decades, more gas was produced in Pennsylvania in 1954 than in any of the previous forty-nine years.[295] By 1955, rotary rigs drilled 86 percent of the wells in the United States.[296]

When drillers struck a producing or "paying sand" well, the gas blew out of the well hole, often with great force. Depending on expected gas flow, a very simple wellhead assembly is prepared or in case of an anticipated large gasser, a complicated series of valves and controls, commonly called a "Christmas Tree," is constructed to contain the gas and prevent waste. One early industry writer penned, "The roaring, hissing monster that almost bursts the gauge at the well is tamed and subjugated to the meekness of a dove by valves and gasometers, which can reduce the pressure to a single ounce."[297] Cementing around the outside of the casing in a well is done to prevent high pressure gas from escaping from underground formations except through the flow string pipe and to prevent surface water tables from dropping into the gas-bearing formations. In addition, improvements in "downhole" equipment, including photography and television cameras, allowed closely controlled drilling at extremely high temperatures, and, south in the Gulf of Mexico, automated production controls managed offshore operations from onshore.

Drilling picked up in the 1950s in part due to improvements in recovery from existing fields. Hydraulic fracturing procedures, which replaced the hazardous nitroglycerin torpedoes, accelerated production in a well. Fracturing—also called "hydrofracing" or just "fracing"—patented in 1949, was conducted by a propping agent (often sand grains or tiny glass beads) employed to increase the capacity of old wells to produce and eliminate expensive efforts to clean out a well. In 1952, Hope started using hydraulic fracturing with liquid pumped into wells by aircraft engines mounted on trucks. Using frac fluid of crude or kerosene, and later, water, the "fracing" increased a well's flow by up to ten times.[298] In some cases, shallow sand fracturing increased gas production by forty-fold.[299] Fracing wells in Ohio's Clinton sandstone improved well success ratios by 85 percent between 1951 and 1957.[300] High-pressure fluid jets pumped into the well also removed inorganic "scale" deposits from around the well bore to improve gas flow. For example, an Oriskany gas well in the Whippoorwill field in Cameron County, Pa., in 1962, was fractured by injecting 1,000 gallons of acid, 31,000 gallons of jelled water, 18,000 pounds of sand, and 800 pounds of walnut hull particles forced by pressure into the cracks keeping them from sealing. Hydraulic fracturing would become a critical technology for the shale gas wells in the 21st century and is discussed in detail in Chapter Nine.

All's Well Who Tends Well

Well tenders are critical field personnel who keep the gas flowing. In the early days of the industry, tenders turned the wells on and off as directed by gas dispatchers by telegraph, often in the middle of the night trudging through mud or knee-deep snow, then back home. Gas workers opened the control valve installed at the surface on the tubing or casing, or shut-in the well by the same procedure during periods of low use. Tenders ensured that all wells in the area were turned on full before 6 A.M. before the morning consumer demand so there would be sufficient pressure to get the gas supply to various locations. As soon as temperatures rose in the late morning, they returned and shut off the same wells so too much pressure would not build up on the system.[301] Eventually much of this work became electronic through "telemetering," and later, computer and satellite, as dispatchers dictated the flow of gas in and out of wells by remote control.

Appalachian wells took both great care and maintenance to provide the energy needed by area consumers. Tenders gauged pressures, bailed, and repaired the wells as required. Wells needed to be gauged — usually once a week — and often pressure-tested to determine if there was a problem of a restricted flow of gas. The field workers checked to see whether water leaked in a well, or gas leaked

Early well tenders employed at field locations were often kept on duty twenty-four hours a day, taking readings of pressure every half hour to reveal a line freezing off, and if so, trying to thaw it. Snowshoes were often used to hike from well to well, traveling along the lines, watching for freeze-ups (courtesy National Fuel Gas Company).

in the tubing, casing, or ground. Well bores were cleaned out and piping valves and structures painted to preserve them from inclement weather. The well tenders also functioned as the "sentinels of gas production," watching animals near the site that could interfere with operations. Even today, gathering well pipelines are regularly patrolled, leaks repaired, valves greased, rights-of-way mowed, line markers maintained, and roadways to wells cleared.[302]

Tenders dealt with rain, winter cold, summer heat, and even rattlesnakes that found a home at secluded rural well sites. The greatest problem was winter's "silent challenge"—freeze-ups that might occur inside the control values. The well workers thawed frozen lines by installing methanol injectors to prevent the formation of hydrates (water and gas ice crystals that could restrict gas flow). UNG line walkers walked twelve miles north from Crawford Station in Eldred Township in Jefferson County, Pa., to a shack near Pigeon Run, stayed overnight, and then walked back next day, no matter the weather conditions. Lucky well tenders often used their own horse for transportation, if they had one.[303]

Fill 'er Up — Propane and Natural Gasoline Extraction

The value of natural gas reserves increased by the end of the first decade of the twentieth century not only because of the growing demand for the fuel, but also because economical methods were discovered to recover its own "stepchildren," (i.e., liquid petroleum vapors in natural gas).[304] Among the gases and liquids removed from natural gas are methane (the main component of natural gas), propane, butane, and what became known as "natural gasolines" such as pentane and heptane. Natural gas usually not found with oil are the so-called "dry gases" largely made up of methane. But gas found in the same strata as oil are "wet gases" from which these other volatile vapors can be commercially extracted.[305]

Another Appalachian first for fossil fuels launched the liquefied petroleum (LP) gas industry, courtesy of Dr. Walter O. Snelling, an Allentown, Pa., inventor and scientist. Snelling first isolated and identified propane and butane, the two major components of LP gases, which are normally found trapped in pockets with either oil or natural gas.[306] About 70 percent of LP gases are "stripped" from natural gas, while the balance is produced from crude oil.[307] In a farm home near Waterford, Pa., a few miles south of Erie, LP stored in steel cylinders by Snelling first supplied heat and light to the home of John Gahring in 1912.[308] The first LP-powered automobile was developed in 1913.[309] Propane and butane could be liquefied easily by pressure, and were sold for the first time in 1916 to steel mills in the Pittsburgh area for cutting steel as a safe substitute for hydrogen and acetylene. Prior to 1928, sales of LP gases were confined primarily to the local cylinder business. But in 1930, the first tank car load of LP gas shipped from Hope's Hastings Station in West Virginia to Connecticut.[310] The propane and butane business continued to expand as the "bottled" LP gas gave rural areas access to the hotter-burning clean fuel that was widely used in agriculture.

By 1927, Phillips Petroleum, Standard, Shell Oil, Skelly Oil, and Lone Star Gas had entered the market. Bottled gas was later produced under trade names such as "Pyrofax," initially produced by Union Carbide. The first LP-gas tank cars and bulk trucks were used in the late 1920s and safety standards were developed in the 1930s. The American Gas Association started testing LP-gas appliances in 1935. By the late 1930s, the amount of LP gas sold totaled 2.8 billion gallons in the United States.[311] And later during World War II, U.S. production of LP gas tripled.[312]

Natural gasolines are petroleum vapors first known as "casinghead gas," (i.e., the gas which comes up between the casing and the tubing of an oil well and collected in the casinghead).[313] These fuels include a mixture of hydrocarbon gases, and, in some cases, liquids that are separated, processed, and refined. Natural gasoline is collected as petroleum vapors (often called the "drying of natural gas"), but when it is condensed, it becomes a liquid. Initially, these natural gas liquids were only a dangerous hazard and impediment to gas pipelines, as they

Line Walker — Appalachian natural gas wells and pipelines are inspected regularly for leaks, including in the depth of winter when line walkers once marched through the right-of-way with snowshoes. Today, helicopters help survey the lines (courtesy National Fuel Gas Company).

deteriorated the rubber couplings that joined the pipes together. The first efforts to decrease excessive condensation of natural gasolines in pipelines occurred by draining pipelines by placing drips, or pockets, at low places of pipeline systems where lines tended to be entirely plugged by accumulations of gasoline.[314] However, the substance was unwanted and wasted for there was no market for the gasoline collected. In 1870, M. L. Hall of Cleveland invented the first vapor stove to utilize the light portions of crude oil (naphtha) that was previously thrown into the rivers and streams. Eventually, compression, absorption, and refrigeration recovered the gasolines.

In 1872, Edwin C. Bell discovered that natural gasoline could be recovered by natural gas from compression.[315] The first experimental plant installed for the extraction of gasoline by the compression and cooling method was built between 1903 and 1904. The process successfully utilized about 4,000 gallons of so-called "casinghead gas," from oil wells almost in sight of the historic Drake well at Titusville, operated by Andy and William Fasenmeyer. The Tompsett Brothers in the northwestern Pennsylvania community of Tidioute conducted another operation.[316] The gas was run through coils in cold water, causing the product to condense in a barrel. As much as six gallons of gasoline was produced from a thousand cubic feet of natural gas. The experiment was followed by another effort in Mayburg, Forest County, Pa., and then several in the Bradford oil fields in 1906 as well as a larger operation in the Allegany field in Bolivar, N.Y.[317]

Long before the petroleum industry would rely on the "cracking" process that broke down hydrocarbons to make gasoline, the development of the internal combustion engine created an immediate demand for natural gasoline.[318] The removal of liquid petroleum gases in inadequate early gasoline refining was desired since automobile gasoline would quickly evaporate or "weather away," draining half the fuel in a car's tank on a hot summer day.[319] By 1920, 7 percent of the gasoline in the United States was obtained from natural gas.[320] But the market for natural gasoline accelerated with the American adoption of the family car. In fact, in 1930, several times more natural gas was processed for gasoline in the United States than was transported for use in households.[321]

In 1911, the first association of producers was formed to promote the natural gasoline industry in Pittsburgh, and the manufacturers of gas engines constructed machinery to extract the product. An absorption process, extracting natural gasoline under temperature and pressure using mineral seed oil, was known as the Saybolt Process. The method was named after Standard pioneer George Saybolt, at Hope's facilities in West Virginia in 1906. The process, an adoption of one established as early as 1875 in Scotland, was less volatile and more stable than compression process gasoline, and it would spread rapidly.[322] It involved bringing the gas in contact with a heavy absorbing oil, and later distilling the gasoline by heat.[323] Hope later filed a lawsuit to prevent Oklahoma Natural Gas Company from infringing on its patent, but the legal maneuver was unsuccessful. Consequently, the absorption process spread quickly across the United States.[324]

Most of the early plants were located in Pennsylvania and West Virginia. Outside Sistersville, W.Va., the Carter Oil Company used a process developed by W. H. Cooper, a mechanical engineer employed at the firm. The patent for the method was granted in 1911 and assigned to Standard.[325] In 1913, a devastating explosion destroyed the plant.[326] Also that year, Hope built a commercial plant at Hastings Station in Wetzel County, W.Va., extracting natural gas liquids that were marketed for various purposes.[327] For example, the extraction of ethane and butane became important feedstocks for the petrochemical industry.[328] In 1914, the industry produced 43 million gallons a year, and, by 1915, there were 414 plants producing gasoline from natural gas.[329] After a tankcar of the volatile product exploded at Ardmore, Oklahoma, in 1915, killing forty-three and injuring 500, the industry developed specifications and test methods resulting in considerably greater safety and quality.[330] The extraction of the gasoline, propane, and butane —formerly lost through evaporation — improved the usability of the natural gas for combustion and provided additional revenue for natural gas producers through the sale of the byproducts.

Natural gasolines were often blended with gasoline from petroleum refineries to improve "quick start" properties in "Hi-Test" gasoline for automobiles, especially desirable in cold weather.[331] Henry Westcott of Metric Metal Works in Erie, who authored the authoritative text of the industry —*Handbook of Natural Gas*— in 1913, also developed a method to measure natural gasoline and he later formed the American Gasoline Company.[332] In addition to Hope's efforts, the Pittsburgh group of Manufacturers Light and Heat Company (Columbia) operated seven gasoline extraction plants of its own by the 1930s when the process became big business.[333] East Ohio ran gasoline plants at Doylestown, Whitney, and Chippewa. Later, Equitable formed a subsidiary, Kentucky Hydrocarbon Company, in 1957, to process the natural gas liquids in Langley, Ky.

In New York, nine plants to extract gasoline from natural gas were opened in the Allegany County oil field between 1910 and 1920. The Bolivar Gasoline Company was the first, with forty stockholders, including six women. Success was mixed, with erratic prices, limited recovery of gasoline, and some explosions affecting the industry. UNG opened an oil absorption gasoline plant in its East Sharon field station in the Honeoye Valley in 1916. The Ebenezer Oil Company of Wellsville operated another extraction operation east of Allentown, N.Y., and laid a six-mile, two-inch gasoline line to a Wellsville refinery, where the gasoline was loaded on tank cars for shipping. The Empire Gas & Fuel Company constructed a gasoline recovery operation near Andover, N.Y., in 1918, and later, the Pennsylvania Gasoline Company built another plant under new patents in 1919. Natural gasoline production in New York reached its peak in the first half of the twentieth century in 1926 — 539,000 gallons.[334]

Another process to extract gasolines from natural gas occurred through the use of charcoal. Charcoal absorption gas masks were used to defend against poison gas attacks during the first World War. In 1918, the charcoal process of extracting gasoline

The Reno Gasoline Plant in Sistersville, West Virginia, was one of the first such facilities built using the natural gasoline "absorption" process that soon spread throughout the region (courtesy Drake Well Museum, Pennsylvania Historical and Museum Commission).

was first tried at one of the gasoline extraction plants at Lewis Run, near Bradford, Pa., operated by UNG under an arrangement with the Gasoline Recovery Company, owners of the Burrell-Oberfell Charcoal Process developed by George Oberfell, a former executive of Phillips Petroleum Company and Dr. George Burrell.[335] The light hydrocarbons came into contact with charcoal — often produced from coconut shells or peach pits — that had the properties to absorb it. The Mars Company, a non-utility subsidiary of UNG, eventually operated natural gasoline plants in Pennsylvania at Lewis Run in McKean County and Van and Pinegrove in Venango County, in addition to producing natural gas and oil. The Van natural gasoline plant, located ten miles southeast of Oil City, extracted the high Btu propane and butane by "stripping" the substances from natural gas in the Speechley sand gas field.

PGC's Roystone station, near Sheffield, Pa., and Lamont station, near Kane, would also extract, store, and load natural gasoline into either tank cars or tank trucks.[336] In addition, a LP vaporization plant in Erie, Pa., completed by PGC in 1947, vaporized butane, propane, and natural gasoline to form a gas suitable for mixture with the firm's manufactured "city gas" during periods of high demand.[337]

Natural gasoline extraction plants became plentiful in West Virginia due to the ample supplies of gas during the early part of the twentieth century. The state led in the number of plants in Appalachia with twenty-seven in 1917.[338] United Fuel formed the Virginian Gasoline and Oil Company in 1922 to run its oil and natural gasoline operations. Similarly, Hope organized the Hope Construction and Refining Company.[339] Though the number of natural gasoline plants in the United States dropped from 1,155 to 741 between 1928 and 1938, the overall capacity of the plants remained about the same.[340]

The Well's Done Run Dry

As Adolf Hitler marched his Nazi armies across eastern and western Europe during World War II, coal, oil, and synthetic fuels powered his war machine. Energy was critical to the United States as well as it entered the fray after the attack on Pearl Harbor in 1941. As the thirst for natural gas was unquenchable during the World War II years, Appalachian gas firms constantly sought to fulfill the wartime demand by additional discoveries. In 1942, out of a total of 2,600 wells in the country, more than 1,800 were drilled in the Appalachian region. From 1942 to 1945, out of 11,000 gas wells drilled, 7,000 were in Appalachia.[341] Besides the need for oil, natural gas and natural gas liquids were vital in the war effort. Natural gas output increased 55 percent, and natural gasoline production more than doubled.[342] In addition, natural gasoline products played an important role in developing high-octane gasoline for aviation, carbon black for synthetic rubber, and hydrogen for synthetic ammonia for explosives.[343] And the Appalachian region's natural gas would be critical to the winning effort, especially by fueling the steel mills in Pittsburgh and Sharon in Pennsylvania, Youngstown and Cleveland in Ohio, Wheeling in West Virginia, and Buffalo in New York. To meet the industrial need, the federal government encouraged augmenting Appalachian production by reducing well spacing limits from 1 to 640 acres to 1 to 160 acres for deep wells and 1 to 60 acres for shallow wells.[344] Before the war, the Appalachian region consumed about 18 percent of total natural gas produced, although it contained only 3 percent of nation's natural gas reserves. The shallow formations in the region's natural gas fields were near exhaustion, and deeper formations, like the Oriskany sand fields—a major source of supply before the war reached its peak in 1942—declined rapidly.[345] Appalachian utility companies expressed doubt about the future of natural gas supplies even before the war. NFG's 1940 annual report stated: "It is probable that in the more or less distant future all consumers will be furnished with mixed gas and eventually, when all natural gas reserves have been exhausted, consumers will be furnished with manufactured gas, provided gas then holds its present position in the economy of the country."[346]

For the Appalachian natural gas companies, it would take out-of-state supplies to tread water, let alone grow. But the area's depleted gas fields would be used again as storage reservoirs, another practice invented and developed by the energy pioneers in Appalachia. From its inception, the natural gas industry's main challenge was to transport its invisible energy from the bottom of the wells to the gas appliances of eager consumers that were located, in most cases, dozens, if not hundreds of miles away. To address this, it would take the genius of those in the Appalachian region to come up with a solution of how to get there, from here.

Six

Hidden Highway
Natural Gas Transmission

"He who pays the piper calls the tune."— Proverb

"the pull of the blue highway is strongest, when the open road is a beckoning, a strangeness, a place where a man can lose himself."
— William Least Heat-Moon, *Blue Highways*

In 1825, when William Hart lit the streets of Fredonia with natural gas light, the Erie Canal first channeled trade through a shallow waterway from Lake Erie at Buffalo to the Hudson in New York City. In 1869, the Transcontinental Railroad opened the American West to development, linking the continental United States from coast to coast by steel rail. By the 1880s, huge new spans such as the Brooklyn Bridge connected cities across great rivers. The telegraph initiated in the mid-nineteenth century, and later, the telephone, patented in 1876 by Scottish-American Alexander Graham Bell, led to a communication network by wire. The twentieth century beheld an interstate system for automobiles and the information "super highway" for computer age communication. In the midst of visible technological accomplishments by water, rail, steel beams, and wire, a "hidden highway" of underground long-distance pipelines quietly converted the blue flame Appalachian natural gas businesses from community Mom and Pop concerns to regional utilities, and eventually, into a critical link in the American energy resource network.

Pipelines have a long history. Besides the ancient Chinese channeling gas and brine through bamboo pipes, another early use of pipelines occurred in 525 B.C. in Arabia. Cambyses, the King of Persia, formed an alliance with the Arabians to pipe water to Persian troops in the desert in an effort to invade Egypt. The Arabians dug reservoirs to hold the water and built pipe made of ox hides and other skins.[1] In the United States, oil and gas pipelines developed before electricity and telephone systems. Only water pipes preceded the innovative energy transportation network.

The oil boomtown of Pithole was the site of the first petroleum pipeline in 1865, a two-inch diameter line that Samuel Van Syckel constructed on and below ground to a nearby railroad, five and one-half miles distant. Van Syckel was an oil buyer fed up with the high rates of the teamsters and poor area roads used to ship oil.[2] Though ridiculed in their conception, pipelines offered cost-effective competition to the railroads and the teamsters in transporting petroleum, and as John D. Rockefeller himself said later, "The expansion of the whole industry would have been retarded without this method of transportation."[3] However, when the oil fields went dry, Rockefeller admitted, pipelines were "about the most useless property imaginable."[4] Since natural gas could not be contained in a barrel and hauled above ground, there was no alternative than the development of an underground mode of travel through a hollow pipe. Expansion of the gas markets outside the locality around the gas wells would be tied to the technological development of pipelines.

As Easy as Hollowing Out a Log— The First Long-Distance Natural Gas Pipeline

The genesis of the thousands of miles of long-distance pipeline that lay underground

Early pipeline construction was backbreaking work; workers had to use picks and shovels to dig a pipeline trench. Here a pipeline gang digs a trench for a twelve-inch pipeline in northwestern Pennsylvania in 1914 (courtesy National Fuel Gas Company).

throughout the United States began with an audacious experiment in western New York that failed miserably. Since the first well in Fredonia, moving natural gas from the wellhead to end-users was a cumbersome and limited trial. In the infancy of the natural gas industry in the 1860s, the primary obstacle to expansion was inadequate pipelines.[5] Enormous gas wells were being discovered, but a writer of the period stated the gas was "a worthless asset, inasmuch as the most fanciful person could not conceive of the piping of the gas a sufficient distance to make it a marketable commodity."[6] However, Rockefeller and his pipeline lieutenant, Daniel O'Day, were "insistent that any practical project, such as the piping of gas or oil, should not be affected by distance and went about their plans with little or no encouragement."[7]

But before Rockefeller's Standard Oil and the Pittsburgh natural gas promoters of Pew, Vandergrift, and Westinghouse pioneered pipeline development, other entrepreneurs first broke ground shortly after the end of the Civil War. After two years of frustrating effort to find oil in West Bloomfield, N.Y., where oil and gas seepage was noticed, a large vein of gas was struck in a 480-foot well in Marcellus bituminous shales in the summer of 1865, expelling fifteen cubic feet of gas every second.[8] The well was located in an area between the east and west branches of Gates Creek on a farm owned by Enoch M. Beebe, only about eight miles from where French explorer La Salle noticed the Bristol Valley gas spring in 1669.[9] This spewing gas was a presage; there might also be oil below — what the investors were looking for. It took several weeks to continue drilling to the contract depth of 500 feet due to the strong gas flow.

> The stockholders were overjoyed at this evidence of success and expected every day that the flow of gas would diminish and the oil would come. After many weeks of waiting and no oil surfaced, they gave up hope and the project was abandoned. Later in the year the gas was lighted and the flames shot over the top of the 40-foot derrick and destroyed all the equipment.[10]

A dancing pavilion was erected and the well became a favorite picnic site where "young folks frolicked to the scrape of the fiddle and the strumming of the banjo in the light afforded by the strange illumination."[11] The site, known as the "Old Burning Well," soon found another use besides amusement. In 1870, some businessmen from nearby Elmira bought the well together with ten acres of land surrounding it in an attempt to provide natural gas through a wooden pipeline to Rochester as an alternative to manufactured gas in that city. The Bloomfield and Rochester Natural Gas Light Company formed on May 10, 1870, and, in the fall, work began to lay a line to the city twenty-five miles away.

Large iron pipe was rare at the time and steel pipe would not be introduced until the late 1890s, so the firm used twenty acres of cut Canadian white pine tree trunks for the pipe. Wooden pipes were also used by manufactured gas firms in Finger Lakes cities, such as Canandaigua in Ontario County in 1854, and were still in operation as late as 1929.[12] The logs were cut into lengths from two to eight feet "according to the soundness of the timber, and sorted to insure perfect wood." The logs were hollowed out and fitted together with a band of iron shrunk around it, then tarred inside and out. Dipping the end of a log in hot tar and driving it into another log formed a joint. A one-foot by three-foot hardwood stick hung by a rope from a horse above the ditch served as a battering ram. Two men drove a joint home with an average of nine blows, forming as many as 240 joints in one day.[13]

The pipeline ditch varied from three to ten feet in depth. Because the wooden logs provided little flexibility, turns were very gradual, and workers dug the trench nearly to grade. Iron gate valves, similar in design to those in use much later, were inserted in the line at frequent points. Gas flowed along with the project, and as each gate was placed, it was closed to hold back about eight psi for leak tests. The gates were not closed tight fearing that the powerful well pressure might blow up the line. Leaks were repaired by wrapping pipe joints with burlap (or in some cases, surplus woolen Civil War blankets), torn into strips, soaked in tar, and secured in place by two half rings of band iron bolted together.[14]

The innovative and labor-intensive project was a major engineering feat at the time. At first, there were few leaks and a good flow of gas at a suitable pressure was carried up to about five miles from Rochester when trouble arrived. According to

Iron gate valves were installed along the first long-distance wooden pipeline to hold back pressures. Though clumsy compared to modern gate valves, they were an early example of how to divert gas in a large pipeline to a town located along the route (courtesy National Fuel Gas Company).

one account, an inexperienced and "overzealous superintendent" in charge of the work shut one of the gate valves tight in an effort to see just how good a job was being done. Leaks sprouted everywhere and pressure could not be maintained.[15] Another story claimed by a workman stated that someone who was hostile to the project threw a pair of old overalls into the pipeline to stop flow of gas, and the heavy pressure backed up in the pipeline blew it up.[16]

But after some delay, the line continued, and, in the winter of 1872, the gas was turned into the mains in Rochester at St. Paul and East Main Streets. According to the *Rochester Union and Advertiser* in October 1871, city alderman discussed the issue of "natural gas" coming to their manufactured gas town and they favored providing some competition. The New York State Legislature granted additional powers for the new natural gas firm. Some, however, perhaps with an interest in the coal industry that fueled the manufactured supplies, did not support a merger between the new natural gas firm with the local manufactured gas company.[17] But investors behind the new venture perhaps were persuaded about the prospect of providing the natural product to customers who were paying $3.37 per thousand cubic feet for manufactured gas. Professor Lattimore, a Rochester scientist, stated, "no gas works could compete with the great chemical laboratory which mysterious nature had doubtless had here in operation since the world was young."[18] Just how much gas was ultimately delivered is not known, but those who did eventually receive the product were not enamored with it. The hotter-burning natural gas had little illuminating power and was not easily convertible with customers' manufactured gas burners. About $80,000 was spent in an effort to increase the illuminating value of the gas by passing it over heated lime and charcoal.[19] Still, complaints flooded in regarding the poor quality of the gas, the line leaking, and water and mud seeping into the line and freezing. Earlier estimates of huge deliveries did not materialize. In addition, when the gas was delivered from the well directly to the end users and not consumed, it accumulated and the pressure occasionally burst the pipes.[20] *The New York Times* reported that "the gassy bag suddenly cracked and shriveled up ... the gas escaped in such serious quantities that there was not enough left when Rochester was reached to light up a lantern."[21] The gas was soon shut off because it was considered of no value. The adventurous and risky pipeline — reportedly costing up to $1.5 million, a stately sum in those days — resulted in a near total financial loss; the entire works sold at an auction in Canandaigua, N.Y., in 1876 for $1,100.[22] Worthless stocks and bonds in the company put the Bank of Chemung, the second largest bank in Elmira, out of business.[23] Still, other gas wells in the area later helped form the Ontario Gas Company. Republic Light, Heat and Power Company unearthed portions of the wooden pipeline in the 1930s, as did Iroquois Gas Corporation in 1963. Though the bold wooden line did not work as planned, it was a harbinger for the industry.

The Iron Age

Some of William Hart's first gas pipes fueling the Barcelona Lighthouse were also hollow logs, similar to "pump logs" used in water wells.[24] Similarly, a four-inch wooden log transported gas made from crude oil in the rural Pennsylvania community of Tidioute, Pa., in 1871, and was later used to pipe natural gas from the nearby Queen producing field.[25] But the future belonged to metal; iron pipe was invented by iron moulder William Smith in 1843.[26] Nearly a decade after the first oil pipeline in western Pennsylvania in Pithole, iron pipe was first used for natural gas in 1872 when five and one-half miles of two-inch pipe joined Titusville, Pa., with the Newton wells in rural Crawford County.[27] The well fed at eighty psi and it delivered 4 million cubic feet of gas daily to 250 commercial and residential customers. Although this project succeeded, many similar metal pipes from wells to businesses or residences were attached together with screws and leaks were common. Often honey, glue, mucilage, glycerin, and other such substances were applied to the threads as a seal.

Later, Dresser couplings, developed and patented by former oil driller Solomon R. Dresser of Bradford, Pa., in 1887, joined individual pipes with a rubber fitting in pipe joints that reduced leakage. Dresser, who had developed a rubber "cap packer" to seal off water in oil wells and sold explosive "torpedoes" to stimulate oil production, used a "self-packing" coupling to join the ends of pipe. Though not the first coupling on the market (the National Tube Works in McKeesport, Pa., produced one earlier), a decade after Dresser's invention, his coupling became an industry standard. To promote his development, Dresser went to Malta, Ohio, to drill his own natural gas wells and supply a community using his new "leakproof" pipeline couplings. After one well burned to the ground after striking gas in 1891, Dresser persisted and tied his new couplings on a 5⅝-inch line to Malta, five miles from his wells. The Malta

Natural Gas Line was so successful, Dresser was welcomed to expand the line across the Muskingum River to McConnelsville, Ohio. Although his pipeline ruptured underneath the river, it was not caused by his couplings—some of which were unearthed seventy-seven years later, still sealed tight.[28]

The advent of iron and steel pipe resulted in longer lines. In 1876, a seventeen-mile, six-inch pipeline to carry natural gas was laid from Butler County to Etna, Pa., to supply an iron works.[29] The gas traversed the line in twenty minutes, at a pressure of 119 psi.[30] And, as mentioned previously, various Pittsburgh steel and glass factories were supplied in the 1880s by new iron pipelines flowing from area wells. In 1885, Rockefeller interests through the Oil City Fuel Supply Company laid an eight-inch line from Oil City to Titusville. Parts of the wrought iron line were reused seventy years later when laboratory analysis found that the pipe was amazingly still in good condition. UNG cleaned and scraped the old threaded and coupled pipe and tested welded sections under 500 psi.[31] And in 1889, Equitable fabricated a twenty-one mile long, thirty-six inch diameter pipeline from one-quarter inch steel plate, riveted together, and caulked to prevent leakage.[32]

Take the A Line — Shuffling Gas to Buffalo

In the 1880s, most of the noteworthy natural gas wells discovered were in western Pennsylvania. However, in addition to Pittsburgh, the potential market for much of this gas lay due north in the growing city of Buffalo, N.Y., the home of former Mayor, Governor, and then current President, Grover Cleveland. In 1886, Standard interests in the Buffalo Natural Gas Fuel Company, and serving under an agency agreement with UNG, brought the first natural gas service from Kane, Pa., to Buffalo through the "world's longest natural gas pipeline."[33] Though not as majestic and visually stunning as above ground engineering marvels such as the recently completed Brooklyn Bridge spanning the East River in New York City, the eighty-seven-mile, eight-inch wrought iron gas transmission line, directed by Standard's Calvin Payne and Daniel O'Day, was one of the great construction achievements of that period.

Hundreds of hired men dug the trench for the long-distance line with the technology of the era — picks, shovels, horses, and wagons. Men camped out in temporary settlements pitched along the right-of-way, sleeping in large dormitory tents and eating in large mess tents. The twelve-foot lengths of pipe were transported by railroads as close to the construction areas as possible, and then scores of horse teams rented from local farmers hauled the pipe. Each length of pipe was lowered by hand and workers wielding gigantic pipe wrenches threaded and coupled joints. The most highly adroit men on the job were "stabbers," whose job was to line up the pipe and get the joint started in a way that the threads would not be crossed. Bolts weighing more than 200 pounds hung near the bottom of the trench.[34] According to one writer, the pipeline extended "up mountains, down valleys, under rivers and around towns. Working summer and winter, the builders completed their task in time to light and heat Buffalo homes, and to roast turkey with Pennsylvania gas at their Christmas celebration in 1886."[35]

The long-distance pipeline — known as Line "A" — was paralleled by a second eight-inch, 250-pound pressure line from 1895 (using Dresser couplings for the first

Main Lines — United Natural Gas Company constructed an eighty-seven-mile wrought-iron gas transmission line (the world's longest) from Pennsylvania to Buffalo in 1886. Pictured here is a similar "main" line to Buffalo built in 1912 (courtesy National Fuel Gas Company).

time to join the pipe) through 1898, and then by a third twelve-inch line in 1903. In 1912, a fourth twenty-inch line was laid. These "main" lines (sometimes called "trunk" lines) arrived at the south Buffalo city line. Approximately thirty miles of the line was still being used by UNG sixty years later from Lewis Run, Pa., to the New York State line.

In 1973, the original eight-inch wrought iron, screw-pipe transmission line was renewed by inserting four-inch plastic pipe through the line. The new pipe was pulled through the old metal line by a modified "pig," a device that usually travels though the pipeline to root out dirt. Compared to the months of work and thousands of man-hours eighty-seven years before, a ten-man crew installed and tested 29,000 feet of pipe in five weeks using one small bulldozer, one truck, four pickups, and two tractors.[36]

The Akron Ten-Inch

The first oil pipeline in West Virginia was built in 1879, a fifteen-mile line that extended from the Volcano oil field to a Parkersburg refinery.[37] Twenty years later, and a more than a decade after Payne's natural gas pipeline to Buffalo, another early Standard interstate gas pipeline in Appalachia became known as the Hope–East Ohio

The first transmission line across the Ohio River in 1898 was known as the "Akron ten-inch" that eventually transported natural gas from the West Virginia gas fields all the way to Cleveland. Here, a "pipe jack" and a strong wooden pole were necessary to properly align the pipe for connecting (courtesy Dominion Resources).

"Akron Ten-inch." It originated from a laboriously built eight-inch screw-pipe line from wells in Wetzel County, W.Va., and connected to a ten-inch line across the Ohio River, owned by East Ohio. Crossing the river was called an engineering accomplishment of "prime magnitude."[38] Under supervision of National Transit Company officials O'Day and Strong in 1898, the pipeline concern felt confident to justify huge expenditures necessary to pipe the West Virginia gas to cities in eastern Ohio, beginning with Akron. The pipeline right-of-ways were probably adopted by Hope from the Mountain State Gas Company in 1897. Horse and wagon hauled the pipe over muddy roads, lifted by hand or winch to maneuver it into position. When necessary to adjust to the curves of the ditch, the pipe was bent by heating it in an open fire and laboriously squeezing it by a "bending gang" tightening chains attached to both ends.[39] The pipe was filled with sand to prevent buckling while heated by the crude bonfire. The pipe often became too hot and had to be chilled to prevent the pipe from stretching at the end.[40] In fact, it was common to bend pipe without machinery up until 1940, with cold bends for small diameter pipe and fire bends for larger sizes up to twelve inches. Later, pipe-bending machines were introduced, allowing increased flow and less friction through the curved pipe and reducing maintenance costs.[41]

During the Ohio construction, there were problems with leaks, washouts, blowouts, and frozen lines. But East Ohio applied Dresser couplings to its lines to prevent leaks at the joints. By 1903, a second line extended 108 miles, through eighteen-inch pipe to Cleveland. The Akron ten-inch remained in service until 1919. A third line was built in 1907, crossing at Clarington, and two others were constructed between 1912 and 1916, including a 200-mile-long, twenty-inch diameter line between West Virginia and eastern Ohio. By the 1920s, East Ohio was connected to five "trunk" lines across the state of Ohio, varying in size from fourteen to twenty inches, supplying 350,000 consumers.[42]

Elsewhere in the state, the newly formed Columbia Corporation in 1906 constructed another major line linking the great West Virginia natural gas discoveries as well as those in Kentucky, through a twenty-inch line extending 183 miles to Cincinnati, Ohio.

Manic Compression

In the beginning of the twentieth century, natural gas was still a little known fuel making up only 3.2 percent of the United States annual energy supply, and many regarded it as unreliable and transient. But the energy pioneers of Appalachia saw that if this natural resource was properly handled, it could become a useful servant. Huge gas wells were being discovered across the countryside of western Pennsylvania, Ohio, and West Virginia. That production needed to find a market and transportation network. By 1902, 68 percent of the nearly 25,000 miles of natural gas pipeline in the United States was located in Pennsylvania, Ohio, West Virginia, and New York. And the pace was quickening. Many towns and communities in the region developed independent gas systems from a gas well or two and a few miles of pipe. Expansion, however, ironically required compression.

Most gas flowed through early pipelines under the natural pressure of the well. Pressure control was maintained manually, requiring men to leave their homes to turn wells on and off. But it was soon apparent that the natural pressure would not force gas through pipelines over long distances. Necessity being the mother of invention, elaborate gas compressors built to increase the pressure of the gas — developed on the same principle as a bicycle pump — pushed the product from production regions to distribution areas. In 1880, the Bradford Gas Company, transporting gas through pipelines at Rixford, Pa., put the first natural gas compressor into operation. The duplex compressor was driven by a 580-horsepower (hp) steam engine with a compressing capacity of 5 million cubic feet a day and a discharge pressure of sixty psi.[43]

A motivating factor for compressing gas occurred after the famous Murrysville field, site of the powerful Haymaker Well, began to decline around 1890. Engineers like George Westinghouse considered storing natural gas in tanks or increasing the size of pipelines. Joseph Pew, who had purchased the original well, conceived the idea of the "gas compressor station," allowing natural gas to be moved over a large area.[44] As a result, in 1890, a natural gas compressor station was built at the Murrysville field east of Pittsburgh from Pew's idea, installing a pumping machine built by the Hall Steam Pump Company.[45]

Compressing gas into a smaller volume increased the amount of gas that could flow through a pipeline, and, by building up the pressure, it also boosted its velocity through the line. By the end of the 1800s, pressure problems and gas shortages called for a need to move gas over longer distances. Just before the turn of century, these internal combustion engines, powered by steam or natural gas, became widely available. They were mammoth thirty- to forty-foot-long compressing machines, with flywheels ten to twelve feet in diameter installed in "pumphouses" throughout the region.

Roy Stone's Station

In 1893, Pennsylvania Gas Company's (PGC) Roystone station, located about sixteen miles east of Warren, Pa., was constructed to pump gas from the Warren and Sheffield wells to faraway markets such as Corry and Erie, as well as Jamestown, N.Y. Previously the gas was "free-flowed" locally. The station — PGC's largest compressor facility at one time — burned down within two years and then was rebuilt in 1895. It suffered another tragedy with an explosion in 1903, killing some station operators. Over time, the station expanded and it operates to this day.

The station was named after "Roy Stone," a Union Civil War Captain from Prattsburg, N.Y., and later Warren, Pa. Stone was wounded at Gettysburg and later served in the Spanish American War.[46] Stone, an heir to thousands of acres of timber in the region, speculated in oil, became a partner in a tannery in Warren, and pioneered in elevated railroads, including the famous "Peg Leg" monorail in the oil fields near Bradford, Pa.[47] PGC's holdings in the Sheffield and Ludlow areas were dubbed "Roy Stone's Station," and the name stuck — though later combined to Roystone.[48] Locally produced gas came into the station at two psi and left at much higher pressures. The original compressors were steam driven with natural gas used in the boilers to generate the steam. In March 1915, the station pumped more than 700 million cubic feet of gas. As of that time, two of the engines were fired by natural gas, using only 6 percent of the gas to run the engines.[49] Natural gas-fired engines later replaced all the original steam compressors.

Roystone not only compressed local gas produced from the Ludlow and Elk County fields in its early years, but also eventually moved gas in and out of storage wells and transported interstate pipeline gas to market. Like many compressor facilities, rustic company-owned homes surrounded the station. Operators lived close to where they worked, ready to start and stop compressors as needed, instructed by telegraph from gas dispatchers at distant locations.

The Old Battleship — The First Natural Gas–Powered Compressor

UNG installed a 1,000-hp gas engine compressor in 1899 at Sergeant compressor station (Halsey field) near Mt. Jewett, Pa. According to the firm, it was the first such natural gas-powered compressor built in the United States. Sergeant compressor station, first known as Halsey station, was the oldest in the UNG system. The station was directly connected to Lamont station in 1951 and withdrew gas produced and purchased at Halsey, Clermont, and Kane fields. The huge, sonorous compressing machine still operated in the 1950s, pumping gas to customers in Pennsylvania and

Gas Compressors — Just before the turn of the century, internal combustion engines — mammoth 30- to 40-foot long machines, with flywheels 10 to 12 feet in diameter — became available to pump natural gas through pipelines over long distances. Large engine parts, including bedplates, main frames and flywheels, were hauled on eight-wheeled wagons that were pulled by 10 or 12 teams of horses and mules (courtesy National Fuel Gas Company).

north to Buffalo. This engine, designed by National Transit Pump and Machine Company, a Standard firm located at Oil City, Pa., was seventy-four-feet long, twenty-one-feet wide, with two flywheels thirteen-feet in diameter — the largest of its kind. The natural gas-driven machine operated on four cylinders, with a twenty-five-inch bore, and forty-eight-inch stroke.[50]

According to a recollection by Samuel B. Daugherty, then a draftsman in the National Transit plant, Standard's Calvin Payne (who later became UNG and PGC President) asked the new gas-driven engine designer, John S. Klein: "Wouldn't the noise be objectionable?"

"It will be the sweetest music in the world to hear," the superintendent of the National Transit Shop in Oil City replied.[51]

Horse teams and wagons transported the estimated 140-ton compressor from Oil City to the station site. Eight and ten huge horses drew special low wagons with eight-inch wide wheels. After the ground froze, several parts were skidded on sleds. Since gas compression was new technology, operators had to "learn the hard way" with an engineer and oiler on each unit to keep the wheels turning.[52] One account reflected:

Old Battleship Compressor — United Natural Gas Company installed the first 1,000-horse-power natural gas-powered compressor engine in 1899 in Mt. Jewett, Pennsylvania. Due to its massive size and shape, it was nicknamed "the old battleship" (courtesy National Fuel Gas Company).

This old engine was started originally from a dead stop position by injecting a previously prepared explosive mixture into the cylinders, and igniting. At each revolution of the engine it was given another "shot" of explosive mixture and ignited until, with luck, it continued to run smoothly. Not infrequently a crew of men would spend days getting an engine started — with the dispatchers clamoring for more gas.[53]

In 1912, UNG rebuilt the colossal compressor, nicknamed "the old battleship" due to its shape and size, with air-starting equipment, and operated it until 1958. On the day of the machine's retirement, one observer noted, "She started like a house afire and ran beautifully until the fuel was turned off; then all present watched with obsequious lament the last gasp and the final rocking of the big flywheel as if it were loathe to quit."[54]

Originally designed and built in Oil City, the Snow-Holly Works of the Worthington Pump & Machinery Corporation obtained the drawings of the original National Transit compressor and later manufactured them in Buffalo. The classic "Snow" engines, now the focus of gas and steam engine buffs, were 400-hp, four-cycle horizontal engines that used natural gas as a fuel to propel the gas through the pipelines. The Snow engines received national attention in the early twentieth century as the gas and oil pumping engines were installed in New York, Pennsylvania, Ohio, West Virginia, Kansas, Arkansas, Oklahoma, Louisiana, Texas, California, and Ontario, Canada.[55]

Gas compressor stations soon became prevalent throughout the Appalachian countryside in the early part of the century. Starting and stopping compressors became effective ways to raise and lower pressures in the lines to control flow. Over time, both improved pipeline couplings and more powerful compressors enabled higher pressures and capacity in long-distance lines.[56]

Hope and Hastings, Peoples and Brave

At the beginning of the twentieth century, the huge demand for gas in Pittsburgh and Cleveland led to the need to import gas from the newly discovered wells in the hills of West Virginia. The natural high pressure of the original wells diminished, and the gas needed assistance to travel to its final destination. Hastings station in the town of Pine Grove, in Wetzel County, W.Va., which eventually became the hub of the Hope system that transported West Virginia gas to Cleveland, was built in 1902 on a five-acre site leased yearly for $150. The company purchased the property along with 145 acres of land in 1906. The station, named after the nearly six-foot-seven-inch tall general superintendent of the company, Denny Hastings, then became the largest natural gas pumping station in the world.[57] It featured two multi-ton 4,500-hp horizontal Snow engines, the largest ever to that time to pump natural gas. The engines were loaded into wagons from the nearest railroad forty miles away, and lugged up hills and valleys over red mud roads by long lines of straining horses and men, usually working twelve hours a day, seven days a week.[58] The station pumped gas through two sixteen-inch lines thirty-five miles to the Pennsylvania state line, joining the Peoples pipeline system.[59] In 1912, the engines were separated so only half the pumping effort would be lost in case of engine trouble. Another Hastings unit was constructed in 1926 for backup. The boilers powering the units were converted

Construction of the sprawling Hastings station of Hope Natural Gas Company began in 1902. Hastings became a community of its own; it had more than sixty company-owned structures, including residential dwellings, a community hall (pictured here), a general store, a church, a post office, a hotel, and an athletic field (courtesy Dominion Resources).

to coal in 1916 because of the shortage of gas, and not changed back to gas until some-time after World War II. Hastings became a "clearinghouse" for natural gas critical to the Cleveland market. The gas pumped through the station was produced in widely separated gas fields, some production coming as far as 150 miles away. More than sixty company-owned dwellings housing the facility's workforce, including a hotel and a general store, surrounded the station. Many of the original mammoth engines remained in service for forty years until the station was rebuilt in 1946–48. In 1968, the old steam plants at Hastings were discontinued, and Hope's Lightburn and L. L. Tonkin stations conducted the "clearinghouse" responsibilities.[60]

Between 1910 and 1920, Hope experienced great growth in demand for its gas supply and began purchasing gas from other West Virginia firms. As a result, there was a corresponding need for new compression facilities, and the company doubled its gas plant distribution facilities, including the number of compressor stations, increasing from seven to twenty-seven in the ten-year span.[61] By 1925, Hope had fifty compressor stations, 8,777 miles of pipeline and 3,257 wells.[62] In the southern part of the state, United Fuel grew from one compressor station in 1914 to twenty-eight by 1928.[63]

Once Standard's National Transit purchased Peoples, work began on a large compressor station near the Pennsylvania–West Virginia state line. The company had earlier built compressor facilities in the Murrysville field, and Rural Valley and Girty in Armstrong County, Pa., as well as laying twelve-inch pipelines from its various gas fields to Pittsburgh.[64] Peoples constructed a twenty-inch line to West Virginia to

Brave Station — Peoples Natural Gas Company constructed Brave compressor station near the West Virginia border in the first decade of the twentieth century — then the largest of its kind. Teams of horses hauled the engines in on a sometimes seven-day journey from Waynesburg, Pennsylvania, seventeen miles away. The first coal-fired steam compressors were operating by 1907. Pictured here is the station as it appeared in 1950.

Davis Station — Hope Natural Gas Company's second gas compressor facility, Davis station, was constructed in the rural hills of north-central West Virginia, south of Clarksburg, in 1907 (courtesy Dominion Resources).

connect to the Hope network in 1904, as well as taking ownership of Hope's wells and pipeline connections in Greene County, Pa.[65] Brave compressor station, built on a rural site that was once an Indian burial ground, was constructed from bricks made locally with sand dug from local creek beds.[66] The company also financed a railroad to bring the coal in from area mines. At the time it was built, Brave was the largest compressor station of its kind in the world.[67] The station suffered a severe explosion in 1917 that killed six employees. However, the plant was not phased out until 1959. Additional stations came on line as Peoples expanded in the early part of the century including a gas engine plant in Clarion County. Eventually gas engines replaced smaller steam plants in Armstrong and Westmoreland counties.[68] Peoples also operated compressor stations under the names of Mt. Royal and Imperial; and later, larger stations at

Heath Station Construction — The huge multi-ton compressors for Heath station in Pennsylvania were transported across the Clarion River in 1912 and hauled over muddy roads by horse and wagon (courtesy National Fuel Gas Company).

Dice and Wall in Allegheny County; Gibson in Washington County; Baum, Belknap, Girty, Valley, and Roaring Run in Armstrong County; Truittsburg in Clarion County; and Vinco in Cambria County.[69]

Horses and Rivers — The Building of a Rural Gas Compressor Station

Compressor stations were initially built on the sites of ample gas fields to pump the gas to market. However, in most cases, these were remote locations far from the urban population. In 1912, UNG constructed a station at Millstone field on the site of a lumber mill dam (Lathrop's Mill) that impounded Callen Run near the south bank of the Clarion River in Pennsylvania. The station, first known as Cross station, named after Raymond Cross (the UNG president at the time and later executive with the Columbia Gas System), was renamed Heath station in 1938 after the township where it is located on an eighty-acre site in Jefferson County, Pa.

The facility withdrew certain gas produced and purchased by UNG from the more than 300 producing wells in Millstone field. Construction began in June 1912 with clearing and grading of the remote site. The massive compressor engines were hauled on the Tionesta Valley Railroad, but the railroad stopped well short of the construction site. Horse and wagon made up the rest of the way, including passage across the Clarion River. The teamsters lugged the huge engines over muddy roads to the area. One of the station's builders—Reuben Zimmerman—rented his horse team, "Dick and Doll," to UNG to help move the twenty-one-ton engines. Zimmerman's team was the only one of twenty that would work in water, helping to haul the first of two 400-hp Snow engines on an eight-wheeled wagon across the Clarion River. Large engine parts—bedplates, main frames, and flywheels—were hauled on wagons pulled by ten or twelve teams of horses and mules. Smaller engine parts, boxes, and crates of fittings were carried on regular freight wagons by one or two horse teams. It took twenty teams twenty-one days to move the engines to the site. Many of the men involved in the construction were former loggers, as lumber was the primary industry in the area at that time, and probably knew little about the important station they were building.[70]

The first compressors connected to wells the following January and the station began pumping. Additional foundations were constructed for two more Snow compressor units that arrived in the summer of 1915, and the group also built five dwelling houses for station operators along with a pumphouse. The remaining compressors started pumping in 1916.[71]

Field workers passed down the skills to operate the massive machines "from generation to generation." In the words of one station operator, the process involved all five senses:

> The sound of the constant rhythm like an Indian drum, yet interrupted like cannon fire when things went awry. To touch the warmth of a smooth running main bearing, only to feel a blister erupt from your finger on the next one you check. The smell of burning oil and paint if an intake valve failed to close completely. The taste of oil and brass and June bugs when the blowgun clogs trying to unplug the drams. The sight of large smoke rings from the engine exhaust on a frozen moonlit night drifting away to the stars.[72]

The six Snow gas engines installed in the 1912–16 era represented one of the oldest groups of slow speed horizontals in operation when they were taken out of service in 1995.

Other stations on the Pennsylvania countryside followed. Ormsby compressor station in McKean County, Pa., was originally constructed in 1896 as a steam plant for UNG. The Manufacturers Light & Heat Company (of the Columbia system) owned a 45 percent interest in the station and production field, but that share was later acquired by UNG. Ormsby field had thirty-five wells—many were the area's oldest wells still in operation as they were depleted in the 1950s.

Van compressor station, formerly known as Strong station (named after Standard natural gas pioneer Elizur Strong), was built between 1904 and 1905, in Venango County on a 170-acre tract of land. The plant consisted of four 500-hp gas engine units, all of which were removed about 1920. In 1910 and 1911, two additional 600-hp Snow units were installed, moved from Oil City by teams of horses. The bedplate

Heath station, near Brookville, Pennsylvania, was built in 1912 to pump gas from local wells to far-off markets. Callen Run flows past the compressor facility and is popular with anglers who venture out before the crack of dawn to the trout stream (courtesy National Fuel Gas Company).

weighed thirty tons and one flywheel was eighteen feet tall. In 1917, one additional 450-hp unit was installed, and in 1918, four additional 450-hp units were placed. The plant's function was to pump gas produced and purchased in Strong and Hampton fields to Oil City, Franklin, Meadville, Titusville, and the Sharon area.

Other UNG stations included Pinegrove compressor station, originally known as Hampton, in Venango County, built between 1907 and 1908. The station withdrew gas produced and purchased by UNG in Hampton field and fed lines supplying the Oil City, Franklin, Meadville, and Titusville areas. The original Henderson station in Venango County was constructed in 1908 and 1909. Eldred station was located in Jefferson County, Pa. It was constructed in 1910 and was originally known as Crawford station after J. W. Crawford, a UNG President.

Knox station was UNG's only primary "steam station." Built in 1925 south of Brookville, it served production and storage areas of the southern half of Jefferson County. The original plant was built in 1916 and was first known as Barnes station. Two additional steam engines were installed in 1927. At the time, gas was being conserved, and coal at $1.50 per ton was used as fuel to generate steam. A highly mechanized arrangement conveyed the coal from railroad cars to the boiler. In later years, modern natural gas engines were installed.

Between 1905 and 1906, the Clarion Gas Company built Miola compressor station, near Clarion, Pa. The St. Mary's Natural Gas Company also installed gas compressor stations at Mt. Jewett in 1904, Wellendorf in 1907, and Island Run in 1917. The Jefferson County Gas Company operated two compressor stations—Millstone and Tillotson.

East Ohio constructed numerous compression stations for gas to travel from West Virginia to Cleveland, including the 2,000-hp Howard station, near Howard, Ohio, purchased as part of the Mohican system in 1912. It was later moved near Cleveland to pump wells from the Lakewood field, and the name changed to Puritas station.[73] The huge compressing engines were also often dragged on skids, drawn by a special hook-up of eight horses over miles of dirt roads. Others followed including Berea and Shreve stations, built during World War I, Mohican station in 1922, Whitney station in 1925 purchased from Central Ohio Gas Company, and Franklin station in 1930.[74] By this time, East Ohio had thirty-seven compressing stations with a total of 52,880-hp. Construction of East Ohio's largest facility, Robinson station, south of Cleveland, began in 1943.

More Modern Compressor — As technology progressed in the 1940s, natural gas compressors became smaller but more powerful (courtesy National Fuel Gas Company).

New York State Natural, which became part of CNG in 1943, operated numerous compressor facilities for production and transmission in northcentral Pennsylvania and the Southern Tier of New York, many near original natural gas discoveries. They included Therm City near Syracuse, Boom, Harrison, Preston, Tonkin, Ithaca (later E. M. Borger), Sabinsville, Leidy (Greenlick), South Bend, Driftwood, Luther, Homecamp, Gordon, Utica, Tyler, Helvetia, Finnefrock, State Line, and Ellisburg, as well as Jeannette and Oakford, near Pittsburgh.[75]

Laying the Lines

"The stabber wants a snapper on his spread to help the spark idiot." That was pipeline parlance for "The strawboss wants a handyman to work with his crew and help the welder."[76] The workers and materials on the job are called the "spread."

Undoubtedly, early natural gas operations were crude and laborious. Pipeline ditches were dug with picks and shovels. "Swinging a pick and shoveling ten hours a day for six days a week was my introduction to the natural gas industry," said one worker who joined UNG in 1916.[77] The first ten-inch wrought iron line for the new East Ohio firm at the turn of the century was described as "men, mules and mud" as

Pipeline Camp — Gas pipeline workers camped out in temporary settlements pitched along the pipeline right-of-way, sleeping in large dormitory tents and eating in large mess tents, moving like nomads through the completion of the pipeline. These United Natural Gas Company pipeline construction workers posed for a group photograph in 1915 (courtesy National Fuel Gas Company).

"pipe crews bridged icy creeks and streams and tunneled under hills of solid rock."[78] Though usually caulked at the joints, the lines often leaked. Pipeliners swinging eight-pound hammers onto a drill shaft cleared rocks. Workers on pipelines faced the usual hazards of sore backs, cuts and bruises, as well as unusual obstacles—working in the countryside, they sometimes found rattlesnakes in their path. Trenches in a pipeline right-of-way in the 1920s were three feet deep. An early pipeliner recollected: "Each man was to dig twenty-feet a day. At the trench's end, a laborer would lay down a shovel end-to-end four times (this was twenty feet)."[79]

Nomadic bands of workers performed early pipeline jobs, following the line to completion. Men working in country areas often camped out or boarded at nearby farms. In the early part of the twentieth century, East Ohio boarded laborers at farm houses along the right-of-way paying the host families $0.25 a meal, or $5.25 for room and board for the week. Many men quit, so gas company officials were sent from the firm's Cleveland office to search area flophouses looking for potential workers.[80] Some camps in West Virginia in 1919 watched a movie once a week shown in a tent.[81]

Tong Gangs — Most early pipelines consisted of random lengths of relatively small diameter pipe, screwed together by men using tongs, a hand tool for gripping and rotating pipe, giving bands of workers the nickname "tong gangs." Screw-type fittings were still used up until the early 1950s (courtesy Drake Well Museum, Pennsylvania Historical and Museum Commission).

In 1926, construction started on nineteen miles of a PGC ten-inch line between Jamestown, N.Y., and Warren, Pa., and twenty-nine miles of twelve-inch line. A camp was set up in which men lived during the workweek outside of Russell, Pa., and later moved to Wrightsville.[82] The gas company furnished their meals and lodging, and laborers were paid $2.50 per day. Foremen and timekeepers were regular full-time workers, while temporary laborers were hired from the surrounding region, including about 300 from the Buffalo area. Many temporary laborers were paid $1.25 a day, and a good horse team and a driver hired for $3.00 to $4.00 a day. As Penn-York Natural Gas Corporation later laid a ten-inch and eight-inch line, the Town of Arcade, N.Y., became a "boom" town as a result of "pipeliners" coming in to spend their money. Also, during the construction, pipeline right-of-ways had to be secured. Though gas pipeline firms enjoyed the right of eminent domain to acquire the right to lay pipeline across private property at the going market price, often private landowners were not sympathetic to the gas company's mission. Pipeliners told of

River Dogs — The natural gas boom of the 1950s and '60s brought natural gas to communities for the first time, and required new pipelines. This twelve-inch line project crossing the Niagara River at Buffalo involved dredging the river and the burying of the pipe under the riverbed by saddling them with 1,000-pound weights called "river dogs." Scuba divers helped direct the pipeline to its correct place on the river bottom (courtesy National Fuel Gas Company).

tales of farmers who "met the right of way seeker at the door with a sawed-off shotgun, and the sheriff's department had to protect the pipeliners from irate farmers while the line was being laid."[83]

Backhoes, trench diggers, and bulldozers replaced much manual labor, making pipeline construction easier. An apparatus for lowering pipelines into trenches was designed in 1888 by Lewis A. Boore, of the Buffalo Gas Light Company.[84] Eventually, steel pipe forty-feet in length was delivered to construction sites by enormous boom trucks, with two and one-half-ton stake flat beds, five-foot pipeline racks, and a fourteen-foot boom to lower the pipes into position. Joints were electrically welded together. Welded pipe rested on skids waiting to be lowered into the ditch by powered winches. Rock shields were applied to sections of pipeline to protect them from puncture from the surrounding earth.[85] Often, larger pipeline projects involved the ambitious crossing of mountains and rivers. Water crossings presented special challenges. Transmission lines crossing rivers and creeks were sunk with the aid of large concrete clamps called "river dogs." Pipeline right-of-ways were regularly patrolled to inspect for leaks by linewalkers, the "sentinels" of the pipeline system, who trekked through the forests in summer and donned snowshoes in winter, often lodging in boarding houses along the line. Beginning in 1955, Hope began to use helicopters to patrol the hundreds of miles of pipelines snaking through the hills and valleys of Appalachia.[86]

Pipe Dreams — Interstate Pipeline Expansion

Benefiting from its geological catbird seat on top of Appalachian gas fields, consumers in western Pennsylvania, western New York, northeastern Ohio, West Virginia, and eastern Kentucky were the first to experience the value of natural gas. Northeastern cities like Philadelphia and New York depended on manufactured, or mixed gas, for well more than a century before they were finally able to obtain full natural gas supplies after World War II. However, natural gas was spreading quickly as longer pipelines spread in other areas in the United States.

But the euphoria of fruitful Appalachian natural gas wells and seemingly unlimited supply around the beginning of the twentieth century was ephemeral. Consumers eagerly desired the hotter-burning natural gas that cost them a third as much as manufactured gas. But as early as 1916, low-pressure problems and shortages were common during the winter months, as Appalachian wells could not keep up with the demand, and utilities began curtailing industrial customers.[87] Many utilities, such as southern Ontario's Provincial Natural Gas Company raised the price of gas from $0.30 to $0.40 per thousand cubic feet in 1916 and warned consumers of an impending natural gas shortage in the winter.[88] Similar shortages affected Cleveland and Pittsburgh, as well as various gas companies in Fredonia, Cuba, Warsaw, and Dunkirk in New York, and Oil City and Sharon in Pennsylvania. In response, NFG subsidiaries planned to spend up to $3 million to build pipelines up to 150 miles away from Buffalo to connect to new gas discoveries in West Virginia.[89] By 1921, it took three average gas wells to produce the same amount of gas as the one average well ten years earlier, while production costs increased six times for the same amount of gas.[90] Peoples in Pittsburgh, saying its frequent warnings about shortages were not generally "heeded," called for conservation efforts and urged the use of coal for furnaces, reserving natural gas for only cooking, hot water heating, and supplementary heating.[91]

In the 1920s and '30s, shortages continued because natural gas became so popular as a space heating fuel that it became obvious that continued growth would soon place bigger demands on Appalachian gas producing fields than they could handle.[92] A *United States Bureau of Mines Bulletin* in 1920, stated: "Natural gas is worth TWICE the average manufactured gas in heating value, *is becoming scarce, and the demand is now greater than the available supply*."[93] Though gas discoveries in Appalachia dwindled, the opening of the rich Spindletop field near Beaumont, Texas, in 1901, and other major discoveries in Louisiana and Oklahoma, held great promise. But moving the gas from distant wells to the burner tip was the main challenge. Before natural gas became widely available in the Northeast, obstacles such as limited pipeline technology, lack of capital, and the objections of competing fuel interests needed to be hurdled. Eventually, technological improvements, consumer demand, and the willingness of investors to risk their capital energized the interstate pipeline industry.

After the first gas well in Fredonia, it took engineers almost seventy years to figure out how to transport the fuel more than 100 miles. Once the first long-distance line from Pennsylvania to Buffalo was finished by UNG in 1887, other interstate lines soon followed. The first "high-pressure" project occurred in 1891, bringing gas from northern Indiana at Greentown to Chicago at 525 psi through two parallel 120-mile, eight-inch wrought iron screw-pipe lines.[94] After the Indiana fields soon dwindled, the lines were cut off. But soon after 1900, natural gas spread to industrial centers in Cincinnati, Cleveland, and Toledo, Ohio. It would take another thirty years, however, to start delivering gas as far as 300 miles away.

As technology progressed, ditching machines and gasoline-powered tractors fitted with side booms dug ditches and laid pipe.[95] Dresser couplings stopped many leaks at the pipe joints. But to move gas long distances, it would take leakproof pipe. The National Tube Works in Pittsburgh was the first company to manufacture seamless steel tubing by the rotary piercing method for the pipe industry in 1895.[96] Other seamless steel pipe with a ⅝-inch wall thickness in six-foot lengths was made experimentally in Philadelphia in 1899.[97] Oxyacetylene welding of pipe was perfected by the end of the first decade of the 1900s, acetylene welding of pipeline became popular around 1925, and electric welding was adopted around 1940.[98] In 1925, U.S. Steel in Pittsburgh developed sixteen-inch seamless pipe, twice the size of previous tubing.[99] The availability of stronger, but thinner large-diameter steel pipe reducing friction and enabling higher pressures, thus enabled transportation of gas over long distances.[100] Some of the first seamless pipelines were "sometimes facetiously called 'stove pipe' line ... very thin walled and of high tensile strength in comparison with the normal heavy steel lines previously laid."[101] The creation of pipeline firms such as the Kentucky Natural Gas Corporation and Memphis Natural Gas Corporation (both later merged into the Texas Gas Transmission Corporation in 1948), in the 1920s helped meet the need by transporting gas over longer distances.[102] In 1930, Kentucky Natural built a pipeline from across the Ohio River to Evansville, Indiana, and in 1931, the firm extended it to Terre Haute. It eventually tied into the Panhandle pipeline system.[103] In 1930, the Natural Gas Pipeline Company of America, a consortium of gas firms, including Standard Oil (New Jersey), Insull, and Cities Service,

Tractor Construction — Crudely built pipeline jobs consisted of ditches plowed by horses and, later, gasoline-powered tractors. Workers used "Mormon boards" that dumped dirt back into the ditch. On major projects, the boards were dragged by teams of mules (courtesy National Fuel Gas Company).

built the first high-pressure, thin-walled, electrically welded cross-country pipeline that brought the underutilized large natural gas finds in Texas, Oklahoma, and Kansas to Midwest cities.[104] Thanks in part to the pipeline metallurgy technological advances, by 1931, natural gas from Texas arrived in some eastern markets when construction was completed on Panhandle's line. Panhandle, initially formed in 1929 after a huge discovery of gas ten years earlier at the Panhandle field in north Texas and the Hugoton field near Liberal, Kansas, built what was then the largest natural gas transmission project in the country. Those gas fields also became the largest gas reserve in the nation. In 1936, Hope constructed an all-welded, ninety-four-mile-long, twelve-inch-diameter, high-pressure natural gas pipeline, linking its Cornwell compressor station in Clendenin, W.Va., and its Hastings station. It was the first large pipeline using the so-called "stove-pipe" method of construction, making the previous practice of inserting couplings—sleeve-type fittings used to join the pipes—on long lines unnecessary.[105]

Even seamless pipe, however, was victim to occasional leaks. Depending on the quality of the soil, metal pipes in the ground face "electrolytic" corrosion. In the early years of the industry, it was originally thought that the urine from horses seeping into the ground caused pipeline corrosion in populated areas.[106] Protective pipe coating was first developed in 1928 to guard against metallic corrosion.[107] Eventually, high-pressure seamless steel pipe was mill-coated with a heavy application of plasticized enamel, asbestos felt, and Kraft paper to protect it from rotting. Tar and asphalt was also used. "Cathodic protection" was later installed to impose a protective electrical voltage between the pipe and the soil. Burying beds of low-voltage connections and electrochemically active metals along the line applied the principle of the common battery by transmitting pipeline-decaying current to the soil. Though its principles were first described in 1824, cathodic protection was not used on a wide scale until 1930 in Louisiana.[108]

In 1961 in eastern Kentucky, United Fuel installed the first permanent aluminum pipeline, 5,700 feet of line that crossed two mountains connecting two area wells.[109] In the 1970s, plastic pipe, which does not corrode like some unprotected metal pipe can, was extensively employed for low and medium pressure gas systems, though not strong enough for long-distance, high-pressure lines. Polyethylene, a thermo-plastic first introduced commercially in England in 1939, was first manufactured into pipes in the mid–1950s.

Before being placed into service, pipelines are tested for stress and leakage, valves are tested and lubricated, and joints are checked and strengthened. Leak survey teams patrol the lines, and biologists check vegetation for color changes that can reveal leaks. Leak detection equipment was employed and refined over the years. Some

Unloading Pipe (Hope)— Twelve-inch pipe is unloaded from a railroad car to build a New York Natural Gas Corporation line in Steuben County in 1937 (courtesy Dominion Resources).

pipeline right-of-ways are easy to walk, while others wind through rocky and hilly terrain or swampland. Often, rural right-of-ways were only accessible in winter by snowmobiles.

Despite technological improvements, the road from the Gulf Coast to the Northeast was neither smooth nor cheap. The gas volume of fields in the Southwest not only created a need for advancement in pipeline technology, but also a significant investment in compression to get the gas to markets. Large compressor stations propelled gas forward through the large pipelines at hundreds of pounds of pressure. The stations—costing millions of dollars a piece—were constructed about every 100 miles along the route to market.

Since the first long wooden pipeline sprung leaks from overpressurization, safety has been a major issue in the natural gas pipeline industry. Early metal lines that were screwed together often leaked and caused many accidents. But today's pipelines must meet stringent construction standards. Lines are hydraulically tested and scraped clean, or "pigged" by a device that removes impurities such as water, sand, and dust, increasing line efficiency.[110] In the 1940s, the "pig" consisted of two rubber-tired steel discs connected by a steel axle and covered with brushes, eighteen inches in length, and weighing sixty pounds. It was forced through the line, usually by gas pressure, sometimes making a "squealing" sound, pushing everything that stood in its way.[111] X-ray technology inspects all pipeline welds. Cleaning and priming machines removed any "holidays" (flaws in the anti-corrosion pipeline coating), and a device called a "jeep" inspected the line for such imperfections.[112] The gas industry developed its own voluntary safety standards—the American Standard Code for Pressure Piping, Gas Transmission, and Distribution Piping Systems—in 1942. Later, many states made the code mandatory, and eventually, the federal government passed the Natural Gas Pipeline Safety Act in 1968.[113] As pipeline technology improved, the natural gas industry became one of the safest energy transportation networks in the world. Despite fatal injuries from pipeline accidents declining significantly since the 1980s, the few major high pressure pipeline leaks that led to fatal explosions in highly populated areas, such as the San Bruno, California, disaster in September 2010 that killed eight people, tougher federal and state pipeline regulations were on the horizon.

Movin' on Up — Gas Dispatch

As mentioned earlier in this chapter, compressor stations transport gas through high-pressure lines to distribution points as well as shuttle gas in and out of storage. Controlling the movement of gas and delivering the energy without interruption is the gas dispatcher's responsibility twenty-four hours a day, 365 days a year. A sudden drop in temperature or a line failure might affect the supply and delivery of gas. In the early years of gas transportation, the gas dispatcher would make a "calculated guess" of what he would need, then used telegraph or later, a crank-style telephone to contact the well tenders. Dispatchers at Hope in West Virginia would receive a weather forecast once a day from Pittsburgh to assist in predicting demand, but dispatchers basically flew "by the seat of their pants."[114]

Later, remote control systems were installed, and temperatures, volumes, pressures, wind speeds, barometric pressure, and other readings were compiled regularly. Dispatchers keep their finger on the pulse of the gas system by analyzing weather reports, conducting network analysis of the pipeline system, reviewing past perform-ance records, and studying various system reports to insure that pressures in the line remain adequate. Gas control workers also conduct supply studies to meet annual and peak day requirements.

Gas measurement personnel tracked gas production, transmission, storage, roy-alty, and sales through orifice and displacement meters. A method to measure large volumes of natural gas was first developed by B. C. Oliphant, later of Iroquois, in 1910. The orifice meter, a less expensive and more versatile model invented by John G. Pew (a vice president of Hope and a cousin of Peoples co-founder Joseph N. Pew), and Howell C. Cooper of Pittsburgh in 1911, worked in the same principle as a dam in a river, by restricting gas flow that created a differential pressure that is then recorded.[115] The meter consisted of a plate containing a finely calibrated opening smaller than the line in which it was installed. Development of the orifice meter was furthered by Thomas R. Weymouth, of Standard's National Transit Company, and then manufactured by Metric Meter Works in Erie, Pa. Weymouth, later a president of Buffalo's Iroquois and an executive with the Columbia Gas System, originated the

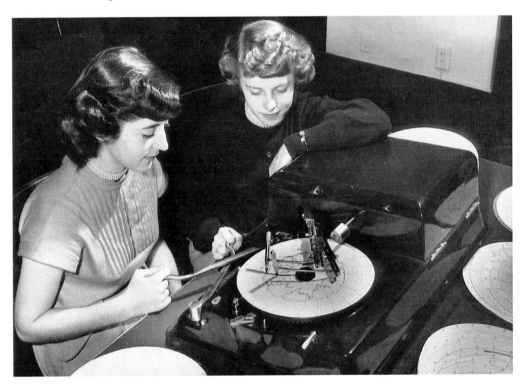

Chart Integrators — In the early days of the industry, all field meter charts and a separate chart for pressure were calculated by "hand," which required considerable time and figur-ing. In the 1930s, integrator machines enabled operators to calculate measurements quicker. Pictured here are East Ohio gas measurement employees translating charted analog data into numerical values to calculate accurate billings (courtesy Dominion Resources).

so-called "Weymouth Formula" for computing the flow of gas in long-distance pipelines.[116] Long before computers, pressure measurements from the meters were recorded on circular charts drawn with pens. The charts were then brought in from the field to be measured by office personnel.

Communication between the gas dispatchers and remote field locations was a challenge in the early days of the gas industry. Starting and stopping gas compressors and turning field wells on and off were conducted manually. Early communication consisted of the simplest Morse telegraph equipment and a single telegraph wire that connected dispatching stations along the pipeline route to company offices.[117] It was customary for key employees, some known as "lightning jerkers," to live in company-owned houses along these locations to receive messages. Telephones were called the "jerk water line."[118]

Regular telephone lines often did not run in the remote rural locations where compressor stations operated. Some companies laid their own communication poles and lines so the gas dispatching process could be improved. Telephone poles in one Pennsylvania location had to be replaced once because black bears clawed them

Gas Control — East Ohio Gas Company's Gross Farm station, a dispatching center fourteen miles south of Akron, became the center of the company's transmission system. Pictured here is the station in 1952 that regulated and measured natural gas flow. First telegraph, then telephone, helped dispatchers keep in touch with gas fields. Today gas control systems use computers and satellites to ensure the gas supply flows uninterrupted (courtesy Dominion Resources).

beyond repair. It was presumed the hungry bears could hear the bee-like humming on the telephone lines and climbed the wooden poles in search of honey.[119] Later, communication involved teletype, two-way radios, and ultimately, computers and satellites.

Despite the building of additional natural gas pipelines from gas fields to market and balancing their supply the best they could, the Appalachian natural gas companies faced the challenge of meeting peak demands without overbuilding pipeline capacity. The energy pioneers working for an NFG subsidiary came up with a novel solution to this problem — natural gas storage.

Nature's Sponge — The Pioneering of Natural Gas Storage

The geological advantages of Appalachia proved useful for drilling natural gas wells, but after a relatively short period many of those wells lost pressure and "ran dry." However, many of these same wells one day were reused for natural gas storage that would be critical in meeting the energy needs of the region's consumers.

Early gas markets were located near producing areas and required fairly uniform supplies of natural gas for industry with only minor seasonal variations. The early pipelines were short and could be economically constructed to handle the maximum demands. In time, however, even pipelines such as UNG's main lines bringing gas from Pennsylvania to Buffalo could not handle the winter peaks and additional pipelines designed to supplement the need could not be affordably built. A more practical solution was to store natural gas if it only could be contained like oil. Without it, the industry could not fulfill wintertime demand. The gas would not be saved in a metal tank like manufactured gas supplies, but rather, inside stone in the ground. The practice of moving gas from relatively inaccessible gas pools during off-peak periods to areas where it would be readily available to help meet peak demands is known as underground gas storage.[120]

There were unrecorded instances of gas storage in depleted sands to control line pressures and oil recycling operations in the early 1900s, so no one may actually know when the first storage effort began.[121] However, the first officially recognized underground gas storage experiments took place in 1915 in Welland, Ontario, Canada, on the properties of Provincial Gas Company, an NFG subsidiary. W. J. Judge, then a NFG vice president, conceived the idea several years before by an ineffective effort to dehydrate an abandoned salt mine near Cleveland by East Ohio. "After spending around $90,000 in the attempt to remove the water, the effort was abandoned with the project unsuccessful."[122] Judge then considered the idea of storing natural gas in former producing strata (i.e., old gas wells).

> He thought that water was the only factor that would interfere with such storage, provided the producing limits were fairly well defined and offset drilling did not threaten the area. He directed Provincial to condition a group of practically exhausted gas wells and pump natural gas back in the wells to provide reserves from which gas could be withdrawn to meet winter demands.[123]

Gas was injected, the pressure built up, and the following winter gas was withdrawn to meet peak requirements.[124] The gas was not metered, but pressures were recorded.

Although not too much was discovered from the experiment, it was repeated successfully the following year in a production field twenty-five miles south of Buffalo. Zoar field, located between Collins Center and Springville, N.Y., is thus recognized as the first successful underground storage pool in the United States.

In 1888, the Ohio Valley Oil Company developed the Kerr Well — the first producing well in Zoar field — on the William White Farm in Town of Collins, south of Buffalo. It was the largest producing gas well in Erie County, N.Y., at the time.[125] The production of 30 million cubic feet a day came from the Onondaga limestone or "Flint" in the Bertie and Cobleskill Formation at a depth of approximately 1,800 feet.[126] The gas pressure blew the drilling tools in the air and it vented freely for ten days. Local Springville residents in 1894 formed the Springville Natural Gas Company and supplied the village from the field. After two good wells were completed, UNG purchased them and laid connecting lines into the main lines leading to Buffalo. Between 1890 and 1910, UNG drilled twelve more wells, five of them productive. The

Zoar Field — After first experimenting with natural gas storage in Welland, Ontario, in 1915, Iroquois Natural Gas Corporation built Zoar compressor station, south of Buffalo, the following year. Zoar, a depleted natural gas field, is recognized as the first successful underground natural gas storage pool in the United States. Underground rock formations hold natural gas pressures the same way a sponge holds water. Pictured here is the station as it looked in 1957 (courtesy National Fuel Gas Company).

Parsell Well, four miles west of Zoar, once caught fire and burned for such a time it attracted thousands of people from all over western New York to the site.

By 1914, the initial rock pressure of the Zoar wells of more than 600 psi had declined to approximately 100 psi. In that year, a gas pumping station was built at Konert and Wilson roads in Collins. The field was put on suction and NFG's Iroquois pumped gas into Buffalo during the cold winter months. Two 450-hp Snow gas engine compressors purchased from the Snow-Steam Pump Works in Buffalo were installed at the site in 1914. Each compressor had a cast iron frame that weighed fourteen tons. The flywheel was transported over hilly country roads in two separate sections of seven tons each.[127]

By the spring of 1916, the rock pressure declined to fifty psi and under Judge's direction, Iroquois commenced storage experiments. During that summer, gas was metered into the field to determine whether it was possible and practical to store the fuel in depleted gas producing formations. At first, approximately 50 million cubic feet were injected into storage which then increased to more than 200 million cubic feet.[128] Later, more than 40 million cubic feet of gas a day for several days were drawn from the field during periods of extreme demand. Between 1923 and 1927, intensive drilling in Zoar increased deliverability of the storage. Iroquois drilled twenty-nine wells—twelve of them productive—making a total of twenty-three producing wells. By 1926, 250 million cubic feet were pumped in the field during the summer.

Zoar's gas storage eventually stretched some 7,000 underground acres of operated and protective leaseholds and contained more than thirty storage wells. Because of its high deliverability (800 million cubic feet per day), Zoar is saved for meeting high daily peaks in NFG's main pipeline system.

The Science of Storage

Natural gas is now commonly stored throughout the United States in reservoirs of sandstone or other rock formations located in a "stratigraphic trap." The reservoirs are not underground caverns, but "pockets" of porous rock encased by impervious caprock. Once supplies in many producing gas or oil fields became too small, their low pressure did not justify continued production. However, the reservoir rock can continue to hold gas pumped down the same wells to the same level of pressure that originally held the gas. In simple terms, a natural gas storage field is refilled by repressurization, holding gas in the porous rock the same way a sponge holds water.

According to one industry expert, storage field workers knew gas pools as they knew people:

> They had individuality, characteristics—yes, even personalities. They could be balky, cooperative, sick or healthy. The wells could even talk, for when water encroached enough to get into the well openings, there were gurglings and rumblings which told their troubles to the trained ear of their overseer as plainly as though the messages had been transmitted in hi-fi English.[129]

In the northeastern United States, almost twice as much natural gas is needed in winter than in summer. A peak winter day's needs can be fifteen times that of a summer day. Although pipeline companies can increase the pressures in their lines to deliver natural gas more rapidly, local market storages act as a "bank," important both from an operating aspect to meet peak demand and a financial benefit to gas customers. There is a price incentive for fairly uniform purchases of pipeline gas in summer and winter. Thus, summer gas is injected into storage for winter use, making it much less expensive to create storage than construct additional pipelines and purchase more peak demand gas. Additionally, the injection of pipeline gas in storage allows local producing wells to operate at a fairly steady rate all year round.

Many of the Appalachian storage fields vary from 1,000 to 3,000 feet, with some more than a half-mile below. Fields vary from small "peaking" storages from which gas is withdrawn at a very high rate on the coldest winter days, to large areas drawn on a day-to-day basis. As greater volumes of gas are injected into the established and confined spaces in the rock, the pressures increase and act as a measuring stick in determining the amount of gas in storage. When the storage is full to the original rock pressures of the field, there is no loss of gas due to its original "tight" container. Gas is injected into storage during the warmest eight months of the year, while withdrawal occurs mainly during the four cold winter months. Costs of developing storage capacity depend not only on the depth of the wells, but also the size of the reservoirs and the porosity of the strata. Large developments normally cost less per unit of capacity than small ones, and highly porous sandstone usually means lower capital investment per unit than less porous stone. Therefore, storage facilities are best when they have both a large capacity and high deliverability.

As mentioned previously, deliverability is improved by a process sometimes called "fracing," or by drilling new wells. Hydraulically fracturing well formations enables the storage area to be more effective in meeting heavier demands on the system during extreme weather conditions. Since the 1940s, fracing enhanced the storage and withdrawal of natural gas in the cracks and crevices of sandstone, making the injection and withdrawal of gas usually four or five times faster. The technique was first conducted by lowering a "perforating gun" and shooting holes in the well casing at the desired depth to provide channels for the flow of gas. A sandy-gel mixture was shot into the sandstone and the pressure increased until the sandstone cracked open and provided more avenues for gas to escape into the well bore. In many wells, approximately 30,000 pounds of large, round sand grains ("frac sand") were mixed with 12,000 gallons of water, a high-viscosity gel, and liquid nitrogen, transported at -320° F. In the 1950s, a large truck pumped acid into the well to dissolve any salt, and then the gel and sand mixture was driven down the well.

Expansion of Appalachian Storage Fields

After Zoar, the next, and larger scale, attempt at storage occurred in 1919 when Central Kentucky Natural Gas Company repressured the depleted Menifee gas field in Kentucky. Though some company officials thought it may not work, it was successful and remained a storage area until 1964.[130] In 1920, UNG developed the first Pennsylvania storage at Queen field reservoir in Warren and Forest counties. Storage developed slowly, as only six storage pools in three different states were developed by 1930, making a total of nine pools in six states and Canada, including Oklahoma in 1925, Kansas in 1927, and California in 1928. Texas would develop its first in 1933.[131]

Hope began investigating storage in 1932 near Bridgeport, W.Va., though the field was not developed until 1937 with the creation of Bridgeport station. The facility was destroyed by a tornado in June of 1944 and later rebuilt. The storage system is still in use and its capacity totaled 7.2 billion cubic feet in 1998.[132] However, the Comet reservoir developed by Equitable in 1936 was the first finished reservoir in the Mountain State with an estimated storage capacity of 5.1 billion cubic feet. Equitable would establish seven storage areas in West Virginia by 1957 (Comet in Taylor County, Skin Creek in Lewis County, Drain in Gilmer and Doddridge counties, Maple Lake in Taylor County, Logansport and Hayes in Marion County, Rhodes in Lewis County and Mobley in Wetzel County) with a total capacity of 25.3 billion cubic feet.[133] Hope first developed the first combination oil and gas storage in 1941 at its Fink Field in Lewis and Doddridge counties. Also in West Virginia, United Fuel developed eighteen storage pools by 1962. By that time, West Virginia ranked third in the number of storages behind Pennsylvania and Michigan.[134] Storage in other Appalachian areas also included the first Ohio pool in 1936.

The Manufacturers Light and Heat Company first piped an oversupply of summer gas at Cross Creek in Washington County, Pa., in 1937, to be held in reserve for cold weather delivery.[135] PGC first activated Keelor storage in McKean County, Pa., in 1939. Storage efforts by Peoples began in 1940 at Dice station in the Murrysville gas field near Pittsburgh.[136] Peoples also used storage to relieve pipeline pressure when it reached high levels. North Penn Gas Company in Pennsylvania also used storage.[137]

The Louisville Gas & Electric Company began experiments in the 1930s that led to the first major use of a water sand, a symmetrical dome flanked by large volumes of saltwater, for gas storage at the Doe Run field in Meade County, Kentucky, in 1946.[138]

By World War II, the number of storage pools in the United States increased to fifty-one in ten states. Since gas was critical to the war effort, twenty-four new pools were developed in the early 1940s. As Appalachian production waned, the U.S. Geological Survey recommended that surplus natural gas be stored in underground reserves. With the vast expansion of gas markets in post-war years, it was recognized that natural gas storage was the only viable solution to meet peak demand. The large interstate pipelines needed to work at a "high load factor" in which to operate economically, so the depleted gas production fields in the Appalachians provided a means of obtaining this goal.[139]

The war needs also led to above ground storage in a different fashion — by liquefaction. Godfrey Cabot first developed the process in 1914. To liquefy gas, it is cooled to a temperature of -260° F, shrinking it to 1/600th of its original volume where it becomes a liquid. And in 1937, H. C. Cooper, Hope's president, began a scientific investigation that led to construction of an experimental natural gas liquefaction plant at Hope's Cornwell station at Corton, W.Va., in 1940.[140] In an effort to store natural gas for war production, a liquefied natural gas (LNG) plant was also built that same year by Hope's sister firm, East Ohio, at East 62nd Street between St. Clair Ave. and the lake front in Cleveland for the winter season. Three mammoth spherical storage tanks — acting as giant thermos bottles — held 60 million cubic feet of gas. Based on the success of the plant, a fourth tank, cylindrical rather than spherical, was added. However, probably due to weak steel (in short supply during the war) and rock wool insulation instead of hard-to-obtain cork, the fourth 120 million cubic foot storage tank failed in October 1944.[141] A leaking white cloud of vaporizing gas fueled an explosion, igniting into a ball of flame that swept a twenty-block, mile-wide area, destroying seventy-nine homes and two factories. The disaster killed more than 130 persons, including seventy-three employees, and injured hundreds more, many of them immigrant Slovenians in a working-class neighborhood. Witnesses, many of whom thought they were being attacked by the Germans, saw a "huge flash" from downtown Cleveland office windows and reported that the sky appeared filled with flames and periodic huge balls of fire "bounced above the neighborhood." Others described "long fingers of flame shooting in various directions through the air" as if "spewing hot lava into the sky."[142] After Cleveland's greatest fire, the plant was abandoned, though the land houses the firm's current Cleveland headquarters. Though insignificant to the scale of the human tragedy, East Ohio lost 144 million cubic feet of natural gas in the disaster.[143]

After the war, natural gas compressor stations that dotted the region's countryside served two major purposes. First, the stations would pump out-of-region supplies

LNG Explosion — Pictured here is the aftermath of Cleveland's worst fire, which occurred in 1944 and was caused by the explosion of a leaking cylindrical liquid natural gas (LNG) tank. The explosion and fire destroyed the plant, killed 130 people, and decimated a twenty-block residential neighborhood near the shore of Lake Erie. The failed cylindrical tank was totally destroyed and the remains of one of the three original spherical LNG tanks (at right) lay in rubble. The frame of one of Cleveland's older manufactured gas holders (at left) also remained standing (courtesy Dominion Resources).

to market. Second, compressor stations injected and withdrew natural gas in storage from depleted gas fields. By 1949, the Appalachian states of Ohio, Pennsylvania, and West Virginia consumed 25 percent of the nation's residential natural gas, though they produced only 5.8 percent of the gas. During that year, 53 percent of the states' supply was withdrawn from storage fields.[144] As Appalachian fields rapidly exhausted, many production wells were converted to storage use in the 1950s and '60s. For example, by 1962, Pennsylvania had sixty-one active storage pools in stratigraphic traps in Pennsylvanian, Mississippian, Upper Devonian, and Medina strata, and in structural traps in Oriskany sand.[145]

Beginning in 1951, CNG and Texas Eastern developed a "massive undertaking" at the $40 million Oakford storage pool — one of the largest storages in the world — near Jeannette, Westmoreland County, Pa., along the eastern flank of the Grapeville anticline, to help improve gas deliverability.[146] The 13,548 acre storage, located in a producing area thirty miles south of Pittsburgh first drilled around 1887, could hold 60 billion cubic feet of gas, nearly 100 days delivery from the new interstate lines from the Southwest.[147] In the early 1950s, gas was injected into the storage by two 300-hp compressors.

Peoples, part of the CNG system, operated storage pools at various western Pennsylvania locations, including Murrysville and Mt. Royal; and later Dice and Hayden in Allegheny and Westmoreland counties; Patton, Webster, and Oakford in Westmoreland County; Colvin in Washington County; Truittsburg in Clarion County; and Rager Mountain in Cambria County. Hope constructed four additional fields — Fink, Kennedy, Racket, and Newberne — by 1965.[148] Gas from storage in the CNG system provided about half the fuel required by its customers during the coldest day of the winter.[149] Other CNG storage fields, which totaled twenty-six by 1957, included the New York State Natural–operated South Bend field, forty-five miles northeast of Pittsburgh, Sabinsville field in northern Pennsylvania, and Woodhull, in Steuben County, N.Y.[150] Leidy storage field, part of the original Leidy and Greenlick gas producing pools, spanned over 15,120 acres, and contained 95 billion cubic feet of capacity.[151] By the early 1970s, the CNG system owned thirteen storage fields with estimated capacity of more than 418 billion cubic feet of gas, the largest being Oakford and Leidy, both operated in conjunction with other gas companies.

Tucked away in the rugged Allegheny Mountains in northcentral Pennsylvania's Potter County, Pa. — self-described as "God's Country" — lay Hebron storage and Ellisburg compressor station. Just below the New York State line, the Hebron storage field, located about thirty-five miles southeast of Bradford, was developed by UNG, New York State Natural, and Tennessee in 1951. Ellisburg compressor station was built in 1963. The storage facility was jointly developed by UNG and CNG and was in partial operation in 1965. Ellisburg became one of the largest in the UNG system when completed in 1967.

Further south, about eighteen miles south of Coudersport, Pa., Wharton storage and East Fork compressor station in southwestern Potter County is accessible by vehicles only by narrow, two lane roads occasionally crossed by wandering elk. The Oriskany sand gas field there was first produced in 1947. UNG acquired the properties from Cabot in 1953. As the production in the field waned, the area was converted into high-pressure storage. In 1960, UNG obtained a storage lease with the state of

Pennsylvania for gas storage rights under 10,793 acres of State Forest land in the Wharton area. In 1961, UNG, Transcontinental Gas Pipe Line Corporation, and North Penn were involved in the development of the storage.

Rural Elk County, Pa., was the site of several storage areas including PGC's Owl's Nest storage and UNG's Boone Mountain storage, developed in 1947 at an average depth of approximately 1,250 feet. Island Run compressor station, located about four miles south of Ridgway in Elk County, stored and withdrew gas in and from Belmouth storage, which was developed in 1952.

Near the shores of Lake Erie, a depleted natural gas field first discovered in 1946 on the Mead farm immediately south of Erie, Pa., was converted to storage by PGC in 1959 to provide peak wintertime deliver assistance for Erie. During its gas production days, Summit field was one of the largest productive Oriskany sand reservoir in the state.[152] A storage field in nearby Corry, Carter Hill storage, was developed from a Medina sand field heavily produced in the 1940s.[153]

By 1960, Pennsylvania ranked first in all phases of gas storage, including maximum gas in storage, input of gas, maximum day output, total output and total capacity — 497 billion cubic feet.[154] By 1972, Pennsylvania increased its storage capacity to 574 billion cubic feet in sixty-eight storages, and Ohio and West Virginia's storages totaled 350 billion cubic feet.[155]

After Zoar, storage was developed in various depleted gas fields in Western New York. In 1937, Republic Light, Heat and Power Company began storage operations in Sheridan Storage in about thirty-six wells in the red and white Medina sandstone, located in the Town of Sheridan, Chautauqua County.[156] It was a link to the Penn-York Natural Gas Corporation's line with gas dispatched to the Dunkirk area. Home Gas Company's storages were located in Allegany County (Gilbert storage), and Schuyler, Steuben, and Yates counties (Dundee and Greenwood storages). In 1937, the Cabot producing firm built a ninety-five-mile-long, fourteen-inch line from its Pennsylvania state line compressor station to Rochester.[157] It was later taken over by the New York State Natural, which operated Woodhull storage in Steuben County.[158]

Iroquois operated the most storages in the region, most of them in southern Erie County, south of Buffalo. Collins storage, near Zoar, dates back to 1912 as a production field that was later converted to storage in 1948. The gas pool in the Medina sandstone contained more than thirty-five wells, approximately 2,900 feet in depth. Lawtons storage was formerly two smaller storage pools combined for operating reasons. There were more than thirty active wells there in the Medina sandstone at approximately 2,400 feet. Holland storage is located in Medina sandstone at approximately 2,500 feet. Conversion of the former production field to storage began in 1949. Bennington storage at the Erie/Wyoming County line was developed in 1951 from a production field that dates back to 1919. Aurora storage was developed in 1953 from a production field that was first drilled in 1927. Wells in the Medina sandstone were located at approximately 2,200 feet in depth. Derby was the smallest of the Iroquois storages, located in the Lake Shore district of the system. The gas pool was developed for storage around 1950 and contained fourteen Medina wells averaging 1,550 feet in depth. Colden storage field in Erie County was evenly co-owned and operated by Iroquois and Tennessee in the mid–1950s, and contained more than 200 wells. Storage facilities were also developed at Nashville in Chautauqua County in 1957, Perrysburg in Cattaraugus County, and Tuscarora in Steuben County.

Underground storage in the United States by 1964 totaled 253 locations in former gas fields; the largest storage capacity was located in the Appalachian states that were close to sizeable gas markets.[159] By 1979, there were 388 underground storage pools operated by eighty-five companies in twenty-six states as well as five companies in Canada, with total capacity of 7.33 trillion cubic feet. Pennsylvania had the largest storage capacity in the country to meet peak cold-weather demands of the middle–Atlantic and New England markets. Pennsylvania, Illinois, Michigan, Ohio, and West Virginia possessed more than half the total underground storage in the country. By 1988, Equitable operated fifteen storages in Pennsylvania and West Virginia.[160] Dominion Resources, Inc., which merged with CNG in 2000, operates the nation's largest underground natural gas storage system, with more than 960 billion cubic feet of storage capacity as of 2003.[161] NFG, the pioneer of the technology, owns or co-owns thirty-two storages in the region.[162] Storage continues to enable gas companies to expand their customer base, meet severe winter demand, avoid curtailments, and lower overall customer costs.

Winning Trench Warfare— *"Big Inch" by "Little Big Inch"*

As stated earlier, wartime industry requirements in the heavy steelmaking regions relied on oil and gas more than coal. Appalachian gas was critical to the steel industry in turning out planes, tanks, bullets, and bombs. Therefore, natural gas was a vital industry that needed protection. During World War II, armed guards patrolled Peoples' Chalfant station with sawed-off shotguns to protect against enemy sabotage.[163] The shortage of steel affected pipeline projects. In addition, the federal government placed restrictions on other uses of natural gas due to its precious availability. Appalachian natural gas production increased by more than half during the period to meet the demand.

Though gas was marketed poorly during the 1940s due to limited supply, gas sold for much less than its competitors, and that put increased pressure on an already strained system. The Federal Power Commission (FPC), Petroleum Administration for War (PAW), and the War Production Board (WPB) eventually worked in tandem to solve the paucity of gas in Appalachia and gas would find its way north to fill the energy need. But it was not easy. The WPB controlled interstate pipeline and distribution, and the PAW was responsible for natural gas production.[164] In Ohio, Columbus, Cleveland, Dayton, and Cincinnati nearly had supplies interrupted during the war, and the government stated that if they did lose needed supplies, the communities would have been out of service for up to two months. Army ordnance experts estimated that more than 300,000 tons of steel was lost due to gas curtailments.[165] Though steel production in the region was affected by the shortage, the "potential effect of such a loss of service on the war effort and human life was considered to have been much greater than the loss in steel production because of industrial curtailments. Residential customers were given first priority…. Only the coordinated effort of government and industry made possible the avoidance of a catastrophe."[166]

Panhandle's main transmission line traveled from the Panhandle gas field in Texas to Detroit, and further augmented supplies for the Midwest. To alleviate dwindling Appalachian supplies, the federal government approved a proposal to link the Panhandle system to the Ohio Fuel system as an emergency wartime measure. East Ohio also built a 120-mile connection in 1942 to secure access the new Panhandle supplies. Testifying before the FPC in 1943, executives from the CNG and Columbia systems (which provided about 60 percent of the natural gas in the region) said that even after the war was over, they would be unable to meet their customer's demand with purely Appalachian supplies.[167]

The tremendous gas reserves unearthed in the Southwest soon found other outlets. Because of the crushing wartime demand, the rush to build pipelines among numerous companies was on. Several investors, including Curtis B. Dall, an ex-husband of President Franklin D. Roosevelt's daughter Anna, formed Tennessee Gas Transmission Company in 1940, and proposed a twenty-inch pipeline that would bring gas from Acadia Parish, Louisiana, to Nashville, Tennessee, hoping that wartime shortages would bolster the argument for his plan. But since the project did not have financing, a proven gas supply, or a committed market, the FPC turned down the application because Section 7(c) of the NGA of 1938 permitted pipeline projects to existing markets only. In 1942, an amended and broadened NGA provision allowed for the issuance of certificates of public convenience and necessity for the extension, acquisition, construction, or operation of new natural gas pipelines. Tennessee's application lingered in front of federal regulators, and Standard's Reserve Gas Company, merged with Hope in West Virginia, proposed a competing interstate line that would transport gas supply from the 4 million acre Panhandle-Hugoton gas field in north Texas and Kansas and proceeded to obtain right-of-ways.[168] However, the new supplies were too costly, threatened coal and manufactured gas interests — including the railroads that transported the coal — and the plan was dropped.[169] But opposition from coal would not deter gas interests forever. The Standard firm sold its right-of-ways at cost in order to obtain a long-term gas purchase contract.[170]

Eventually, after Dall's and other original promoters' exodus from the Tennessee project, Tennessee secured a gas supply in Texas, and received approval over Hope in 1943 to build the first major pipeline from the Gulf Coast to the Appalachian region, the longest pipeline of its kind. The historic line crossing sixty-seven rivers and hundreds of roads extended 1,265 miles from the Gulf Coast at Driscoll, Texas, to Hope's Cornwell compressor station near Clendenin, W.Va., and began deliveries on October 31, 1944. About 300 miles of the pipe was produced at U.S. Steel's McKeesport's National Tube Works.[171] Built at a cost of $64 million, it delivered gas primarily to Columbia's United Fuel and the newly created CNG system, primarily Hope and East Ohio.[172] By the end of 1945, Tennessee delivered 73.5 billion cubic feet of gas into Appalachia.[173]

As the Appalachian gas supply window closed, the wartime need for oil ironically opened another door to future natural gas supplies for the energy hungry northeast. During the early years of the war, Nazi "wolf pack" U-boat attacks on oil tankers sailing from the Gulf Coast up the Atlantic seaboard sank more vessels than the nation could build, and the war plants in the Northeast ran seriously short of fuel. The crisis led the federal government to finance the construction of emergency oil pipelines from the Southwest to the Northeast to provide a secure supply of petroleum. The federally-owned "Big Inch" and "Little Big Inch" pipelines were initially emergency carriers of crude oil and petroleum products. The twenty-four-inch, 1,340-mile "Big Inch" crude oil pipeline connecting Longview, Texas, and Linden, New Jersey, and the Philadelphia area at Phoenixville, Pa., broke ground in 1942 and was completed in record time the following year at a cost of $78.5 million. Construction on the twenty-inch companion "Little Big Inch" oil products pipeline, stretching from Beaumont, Tx., to Linden, N.J., started in 1943, and was finished in an even faster span of time the next year.[174]

After the end of the war, a great national debate followed on what to do with the emergency "Inch" oil lines, as the War Assets Administration auctioned off the unneeded lines (the major oil companies preferred shipping by tanker). Arguments for the conversion to natural gas included the fact that great volumes of the precious fuel were flared — and thus wasted — in the Southwest much like it was in Appalachia years before. Most rules for conservation of gas were ignored, and, in 1934 in Texas and Oklahoma for example, the estimated amount of gas flared was 1.5 billion cubic feet per day.[175] Surplus gas produced in crude oil wells was essentially valueless because it could not be marketed, and would have to be stored in unfeasibly huge pressure tanks.[176] Meanwhile, the Northeast gas markets could not depend on shrinking Appalachian supplies. Unlike the cradle of the industry in Appalachia, until 1940, the large northeastern markets of Boston, New York, and Philadelphia were basically insulated from pure natural gas. Coal suppliers to the manufactured gas industry and railroad firms, which transported the coal, opposed the expansion of the natural product that would certainly steal their markets if made available.[177] Inflation and World War II also stoked coal and oil prices, and the premium natural gas fuel not only became a cleaner and more desirable fuel, but also the lowest-priced energy around. As a result, demand skyrocketed, doubling from 1939 to 1948. Serious shortages cropped up again during the winters of 1946–48, draining support for the anti–natural gas interests trying to keep pipelines from bringing gas northward. Though initial recommendations suggested that the pipelines should remain oil, Tennessee was the first to lease the lines for natural gas. The firm did not convert the original oil pumping stations, but delivered gas using only the well pressure to the hungry Appalachian natural gas markets of Ohio Fuel, East Ohio, Manufacturers, and Kentucky Natural Gas Company.[178] Later in 1947 after Tennessee's lease of the lines expired, the newly created Texas Eastern Transmission Corporation, formed by construction magnates Herman and George Brown, along with Oklahoma-born E. Holley Poe, placed the largest bid for the 2,800-mile "Inch" lines at a cost of approximately $143 million — the largest single cash transaction in the history of the gas industry to that time.[179] Poe was a former American Gas Association executive and director of the Natural Gas Division of the War Petroleum Administration who publicly favored conversion of the oil lines to natural gas. The bid was $12 million higher than the nearest second but more than $3 million lower than the government's assessed value of the property.[180] Pennsylvania, which resisted the effort due to the powerful coal and railroad firms, only permitted oil to be shipped through the lines. But the gas crisis helped push an eminent domain bill through Congress and Texas Eastern soon began selling gas to the CNG and Columbia systems, and it was the first interstate line to sell gas to its first target market: the Philadelphia area utilities, Philadelphia Electric and Philadelphia Gas Works in 1948.

The Appalachian gas utilities were among the first to supplement their gas supply with Southwest gas—due to their strategic geographical location. And the greatly increased demands for gas made it necessary to enter into long-term contracts for the purchases of large quantities of Southwest gas. Pipelines grew to sizes of thirty inches, capable of holding three-and-one-half times the capacity of sixteen-inch lines manufactured in the 1930s, and higher-tensile strength steel could hold increased gas pressures.[181] Manufacturers Light and Heat Company, a subsidiary of Columbia, began purchases in 1947 from Tennessee. Peoples entered into a twenty-year contract with Texas Eastern that year and built a $1.5 million thirty-eight-mile, fourteen-inch pipeline connection with the Big and Little Big Inch lines over mountainous terrain, three rivers, seven railroad crossings, and fifty-six highway and road connections.[182] UNG also agreed to buy gas for ten years through Columbia from Tennessee. UNG constructed seventy miles of twenty-inch line in 1947 to connect directly with the "Inch" line from a point near Ellwood City, Pa., in the northern part of Beaver County. UNG placed the project into operation by the end of the year and was able to buy at least 10 million cubic feet per day, available through the connection during 1948 from Texas Eastern at a price of approximately $0.27 per thousand cubic feet. Considerable amounts were spent to reconstruct and enlarge sections of the transmission system to handle higher pressures from the interstate sales. Completion of a UNG extension to an extended Tennessee gas pipeline occurred in the fall of 1950 and full contract volumes were purchased. CNG's New York State Natural completed a connection with the Little Big Inch line in 1947 and began purchases of 110 million cubic

Inch Line Connection — Appalachian natural gas utilities were among the first to purchase gas from the so-called "inch lines," originally built as wartime emergency oil lines. Here, workers are coating an "inch line" connection with hot tar during installation in 1947, allowing natural gas from the Southwest to address the post-war gas shortages (courtesy National Fuel Gas Company).

feet of gas a day.[183] By 1949, CNG, due to its connections with Panhandle for mid-continent gas, Texas Eastern gas through the "Inch" lines, and Hope's connection with Tennessee's line, reported that the gas supply after years of shortages was in "excellent shape."[184] The Little Big Inch pipeline was reconverted back to a carrier of refined petroleum products in 1958.[185]

The availability of Southwest gas resulted in an extraordinary expansion of natural gas customers and gas company employees after World War II. By 1950, natural gas was present in forty-six of the country's forty-eight states, with 18 million customers. That number would swell to 30 million a decade later. In 1945, the length of U.S. gas pipelines amounted to 82,000 miles. Within ten years, the hidden highways stretched more than 146,000 miles. Only temporary emergency expansions occurred during World War II, due to objections by coal and railroad interests. But after the war, the federal government was overrun by applications to build pipelines due to the expansion of natural gas demand. After Texas Eastern brought natural gas to Philadelphia in 1948, Transcontinental Gas Pipe Line Corporation (TRANSCO), of Longview, Texas, incorporated in Delaware, led by Texas attorney Claude A. Williams who had earlier had unsuccessfully bid on the "Inch" lines. TRANSCO then built a $235 million thirty-inch, 1,840-mile line — considered the world's longest single line — to supply the New York City area by 1951.[186] Consequently, the major utilities, Consolidated Edison of New York and Brooklyn Union Gas Company, converted to natural and mixed gas. Interestingly, other TRANSCO rivals besides the coal and

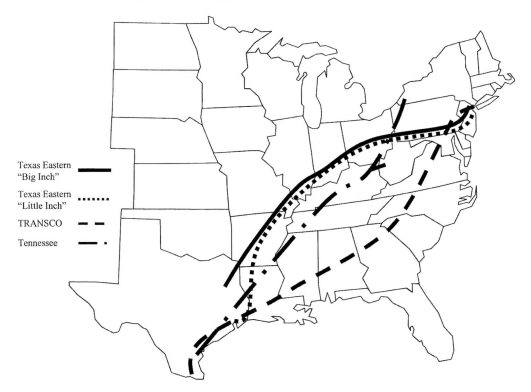

Texas Eastern "Big Inch" ——

Texas Eastern "Little Inch" ....

TRANSCO – –

Tennessee —·

Major Southwest-Appalachia pipeline routes (1951).

railroad interests included both the nascent Tennessee and Texas Eastern firms, which hoped to beat TRANSCO to the New York City market. Tennessee, unable to obtain contracts with New York City utilities, was permitted to extend its lines to serve the Buffalo market instead.[187] The federal government rejected TRANSCO's natural gas competitors, advising them to "go out and fight for business."[188]

Southwestern gas also arrived in Appalachia through the Gulf Interstate Gas Company through a thirty-inch line from Louisiana to Kentucky and West Virginia in 1954, transporting gas for Columbia companies.[189] Columbia acquired the firm in 1958, forming Columbia Gulf Transmission Company.[190]

Natural gas was provided at costs much lower than the manufactured product used in New York City for more than a century. Southwest gas moved about fifteen miles an hour and took about five days to reach New York City.[191] Gas rates in the nation's largest city were cut eighteen times in the first fourteen years, and by the early 1960s, a Brooklyn Union executive claimed "those that heated with gas doubled and accounted for more than half of Brooklyn Union's business."[192] The new interstate lines were the final nails in the coffin of the manufactured gas business in the United States as cities throughout New England eventually converted to mixed gas, and ultimately, to straight natural gas. Elsewhere in the continental United States, expansion of major interstate pipelines accelerated natural gas penetration throughout the Southeast, and mid-continent gas found its way to California.

Though the establishment of long distance interstate pipelines from the Gulf Coast to the Northeast solved the gas availability problem, demand continued to surge. Gas that was selling at the wellhead in the Southwest for $0.02 per thousand cubic feet in 1950 increased to $0.165 by 1952. Still, federal regulation through the NGA of 1938 put a damper on gas production and the industry in the Southwest returned to its wasteful ways of flaring gas.[193] The federal government soon prevented market forces by confirming its reign on prices, leading to another shortage twenty years later.

By the mid-twentieth century, the Appalachian region, which had generated its own supply of natural gas since the industry began, now became a net importer of the fuel. For example, by 1954, NFG affiliates, which once produced or purchased all of their needs through Appalachian wells, then bought supplies from five major interstate pipelines, and, by 1956, Southwest contract gas amounted to 79 percent of the system's supply.[194] By 1957, CNG purchased 72 percent of its gas supply from interstate pipeline companies, 15 percent from independent producers in Appalachia and 13 percent from its own wells.[195] Pennsylvania, which had consumed more gas than it produced since 1921, purchased 85 percent of its gas from out of state by 1960.[196] During the 1960s, pipeline companies extended their systems by utilizing stronger and larger diameter pipe. In most cases, larger diameter metal pipe was required to hold greater volumes. Pipeline diameters grew to thirty-six-, forty-two- and forty-eight-inches, and compressor stations powered by aircraft-type jet engines became commonplace.[197] By 1966, the American pipeline industry spanned 211,000 miles and the natural gas industry flew out of its humble Appalachian nest and became the sixth largest industry in the country.

The Canadian Connection

Though 85 percent of American natural gas consumption today is produced within the continental states alone, nearly all the balance now comes from the friendly neighbor to the north. Although there was oil drilling occurring in western Ontario in the second half of the nineteenth century, production of natural gas in Canada was negligible until the 1890s. In 1888, the Ontario Natural Gas Company formed by the Coste brothers midway between Kingsville and Ruthven in Essex County, opened up a 10 million-cubic foot well, the first in the productive Gosford area. In December 1894, a pipeline to Detroit was completed, and for a time gas was piped to Toledo through a disused pipeline between that city and Detroit between 1895 to 1901.[198] However, after a decline in pressure in 1900 and 1901, the exports were cut off.

Closer to Buffalo, the Provincial Gas Company organized in February 1890, following the completion of the first commercial natural gas well in Welland County, Ontario. By end of 1893, Provincial finished sixty-nine wells and acquired thirty others from Erie County (N.Y.) Natural Gas and Fuel Company. During its early years, the company laid pipelines across the Niagara River and exported most of the gas that it produced to the United States and sold it to the Buffalo Natural Gas Fuel Company. Provincial installed distribution lines in Fort Erie, Bridgeburg, Stevensville, and along the lakeshore. Later, gas was sold at wholesale to the Mutual Gas Company for distribution in Welland, Ontario. From the firm's inception, two-thirds of its capital was furnished by various investors in the United States, including some connected with Standard.

Although some natural gas initially moved into Buffalo from the southern Ontario fields in the late nineteenth century, exports to the United States from Canada were banned in the fall of 1903.[199] Provincial, then deprived of its major market in Buffalo, laid an eight-inch line to Niagara Falls, Ontario. Other gas properties in the area were purchased, including the Mutual Gas Company of Welland. However, the supply of natural gas gradually declined to such an extent that near the close of World War I, the production was insufficient to meet all demands during peak periods. It was necessary for a time to curtail sales to new customers and to restrict the extension of distribution lines. An additional pipeline was constructed across the Niagara River. In the 1920s, Provincial became a net importer of American gas. In 1924, Provincial laid two pipelines through the Niagara River — one of the river lines originally laid in 1890 was reconditioned — from Buffalo to Bridgeburg, Ontario, for transmission of gas to Canada for its consumers. Three years later, a twelve-inch line was installed on the new international Peace Bridge at Buffalo and the river lines were abandoned.

In the early 1950s, Tennessee connected with Canada's Niagara Gas Transmission, Ltd. to sell natural gas at the International Boundary for resale in Toronto and other southern Ontario communities. In 1953, Toronto's Consumers Gas Company (which had produced manufactured gas for a century), requested approval of an eighty-mile link to near Buffalo with Tennessee to add natural gas to its system. But the Niagara River–crossing proposal was denied by the Canadian government, preventing construction of a pipeline across the river chasm.[200] According to one industry official involved, it was an effort by a top Canadian politician to keep U.S. gas out of its market; by "political muscle, a bit of guile and typical resourcefulness, he simply declared the Niagara River a navigable waterway, the famous Horseshoe Falls notwithstanding."[201]

Gas flowing across the border was also an interest of NFG in the 1950s, as it explored sources of Canadian gas going south.[202] However, the government logjam prevented importation at prices that were economical. But the potential was there. In 1960, Tennessee imported Canadian gas to markets in the upper Midwest.[203] Eventually, a 2,250-mile pipeline built by Trans-Canada Pipe Lines, Ltd. in the late 1950s brought gas east into Ontario from western Canada. As Southwest interstate pipeline gas supplies declined somewhat, NFG's Iroquois contracted for sizable quantities of Canadian gas from Tennessee in 1969.

By 1972, Canada ranked third behind the United States and the Soviet Union in gas production.[204] However, Canadian imports would not receive a significant boost into the area until 1980 with the Boundary Gas Project, a joint effort of fourteen utilities, bringing a ten-year supply of Canadian gas to markets in the northeastern United States. One of the main gas import points was located at Lewiston, N.Y., near Niagara Falls, where TRANSCO and Tennessee purchased the gas.

During the 1980s, Northeast U.S. natural gas demand for heating grew rapidly as many East Coast heating customers converted to gas from oil. In addition, natural gas-fired electrical generation replaced coal, oil, and nuclear alternatives. There were billions of cubic feet of gas bottled up in western Canada looking for a market. NFG was one of six utility holding companies that applied to the FERC to import Canadian supplies.[205] NFG's Canadian import expansion connected the Niagara crossing with the firm's storage fields in the late 1980s. The twenty-four-inch Empire State Pipeline (first owned by Duke Energy and later purchased by NFG), built in the 1990s, also connected Canadian supplies at the United States/Canada border. The line ran from the Chippawa Channel of the Niagara River across western New York 157 miles to near Syracuse to help meet the increasing demand of East Coast markets. Canadian gas supplies, deregulated along with the United States, tripled between 1980 and 1999, and now make up about 14 percent of the United States' total gas supply.[206] With the discovery of massive shale gas supplies in Appalachia in the 2000s, the flow of natural gas would be reversed through the same pipelines as Canada began to import U.S. gas to meet its increased demand for clean electrical generation fuel.

Considerable Canadian gas supplies and gas flowing up from the Gulf Coast inside interstate pipelines cross at Leidy, Pa., in rural Clinton County. Leidy, first developed as a storage facility by Texas Eastern and TRANSCO in 1959, provided billions of cubic feet of winter storage service for East Coast natural gas firms.[207] It featured the intersection of major lines in the Columbia, TRANSCO, Texas Eastern, CNG, and NFG systems. Capitalizing on changes of the industry, Leidy serves as a natural gas trading center — a "hub" for major pipelines — heading to the East Coast utilities and marketers. The deregulation of the natural gas producing and pipeline industry developed new markets located at these hubs for purchasing gas, gas storage, pipeline space, and hedging gas and pipeline space in commodity exchange markets.[208]

The natural gas fields in western Pennsylvania that once provided the miracle fuel to the region are now reused as a critical link to get both southwestern United

States natural gas and western Canadian supplies to energy hungry markets on the East Coast. The pipelines that crisscross throughout the pastoral and wooded countryside of the Alleghenies, first pioneered by the natural gas entrepreneurs in the late nineteenth century, now act as a hidden highway interchange for a largely North American fuel that helps reduce U.S. overseas energy dependence.

The initial demand for natural gas in the Appalachian region was the preview of America's love affair with its "Cinderella" energy. As a result these same gas utilities were among the first to get the nation "Cookin' with Gas."

SEVEN

The Gas House Gang
Natural Gas Distribution

Tall oaks from little acorns grow.

Why not gas be the father, oil the mother and gasoline the embryo child in the reproduction of oil?

— C. R. Wattson[1]

Those Were the Days — Natural Gas Industrial Expansion

"The question most asked is 'When can I have gas?' and next, 'May we have gas to cook with?'" That statement printed in New York's *Westfield Republican* on November 14, 1906, concerning the Welch Natural Gas Company, reflects how the public first reacted to the availability of natural gas service.[2] But natural gas was appealing as a manufacturing fuel long before the turn of the twentieth century. A letter titled "Erie's Big Card" in the *Gazette* of 1870 alludes to advantages of Erie, Pa., over Pittsburgh as a location for manufacturers: "At that city [Pittsburgh], coal is convenient and cheap, but at the best it is a never-ceasing item of expense, and every year the supply will become more scarce and costly. Here our fuel [natural gas] lies right underneath our feet...."[3] The newspaper proclaimed that during the previous five years, twenty-one gas wells lit city streets, the county commissioners were thinking of drilling wells to supply government buildings, and a number of manufacturers and private citizens sunk gas wells, providing clean fuel equal to about three tons of coal per day.[4] The monopoly would not last long, as the Murrysville gas field soon supplied the iron and steel mills in Pittsburgh in the mid–1880s. The clean-burning and high-heat content qualities of natural gas attracted many industrial interests, including glass makers, iron and steel mills, and even crematories.

The economy and efficiency of natural gas, which produces a blue flame of 3,800° F, attracted the attention of major industrialists, such as Andrew Carnegie, Pittsburgh's steel magnate.[5] Carnegie's dabbling in the boom and bust oil business in the Columbia Oil Company in western Pennsylvania left a sour taste in his mouth, but he later found that natural gas was another way to cut costs at his steel mills. A November 14, 1886, issue of *Harper's Weekly* wrote: "Natural gas seems likely to make western Pennsylvania the home of such extensive manufactories and so many that its present prodigious industries will by comparison appear insignificant. It has put even bigger dreams in men's minds than the discovery of oil."[6] By 1887, a total of ninety-six rolling mills and steel mills in the area were wholly or partially using gas for fuel.[7]

The unintended discovery of natural gas led to unexpected and innovative use of the product, but sometimes it was inefficient. Drillers originally looking for oil in 1872 abandoned a gas well in Fairview, Pa., on the W. C. Campbell farm in Butler County. According to a correspondent of the *Titusville Herald*, the roar of the blowing gas and brine was equal to "the sound of Niagara," and for "a few weeks this well blew, and howled, and whistled, making night hideous and day tedious with its ceaseless 'yells,'" until the arms of science opened to receive the wasting fuel."[8] The well contractor eventually used clay to smother the flames. The gas from the 1,335-foot deep well was later used for ten years to light the streets and fuel cook stoves of nearby Petrolia, Fairview, Karns City, and Argyle, as well as powering pumps for forty area oil wells and eight pumping stations.[9] Much gas was squandered, however. At one time, sixty-three great gas torches burned in Butler County, Pa., near local oil wells,

Steel Usage — One of the first major uses of natural gas was for producing steel. Pictured here is an early twentieth century factory in Buffalo using natural gas for forging steel (courtesy National Fuel Gas Company).

which, according to one oil industry writer at the turn of the century, were "destroying one of the best servants of mankind ever known."[10] But when it could be controlled, it was utilized. In 1873, natural gas was applied as a fuel in the pottery industry in East Liverpool, Ohio, one of the first towns to use natural gas for domestic and manufacturing purposes after the first discovery of gas there in 1859. In 1874, Findlay, Ohio, was lighted by gas, and the fuel was later offered for free to local industries.[11] Natural gas flares lighted the streets at night, but since the gas was, at first, so plentiful, the lights were permitted to burn twenty-four hours a day.[12]

A major use of natural gas in the late 1800s was for glassmaking. Though glassmakers were reluctant to adopt the new fuel at first, various firms around Pittsburgh changed from coal to natural gas and it resulted in increased production and better quality.[13] More than 500 factories were built in West Virginia, especially Clarksburg, because of great quantities of silica sand to produce glass and vast reserves of natural gas for fuel.[14] But types of uses extended far beyond the making of glass, steel, and pottery in Ohio, Pennsylvania, and West Virginia — the initial focus of natural gas industrial applications.

In Parkersburg, W.Va., after the turn of the century, natural gas became a more important part of the economy, including oil and gas servicing industries and the creation of carbon black plants.[15] When many of its Pennsylvania fields declined in production, Cabot Oil & Gas Corporation moved its carbon black operations to West Virginia, drilling its first well in 1899.[16] Carbon black was a unique pigment formed by firing a natural gas flame upon a metallic surface, and was aptly called "congealed smoke." It was used for making of ink in printing and publishing in Philadelphia as early as 1864, and later in paint and automobile tire production. During World War I, it was found that using carbon black rather than zinc oxide in tires extended the life of the tire by 20 percent.[17] The carbon black industry originally concentrated in areas where there was no other natural gas demand, the gas was cheaper, and often the supply was too costly to ship to other markets. As early as 1864, a carbon black manufacturing plant was established at New Cumberland, Hancock County, W.Va., using natural gas, followed by the Hawerth and Lamb Company using a patent held by John Hawerth of Massachusetts.[18] Godfrey Lowell Cabot acquired leases in Calhoun, Wirt, and Wood counties and drilled his first well, the Mathews No. 1 in Calhoun County. Two years later, he opened a carbon black plant at Grantsville, Calhoun County, near the gas-rich Yellow field. Until 1915, it was the largest carbon black plant in the world.[19] Cabot also moved a Pennsylvania plant to Creston, southwest of Burning Springs in Wirt County, and the firm purchased another carbon black plant in Grantsville in 1910.[20] At that time, nearly all the carbon black industry was located in West Virginia, with sixteen companies in business in 1912.[21]

Natural gas later became central in the industrial contributions in World War I, as another coal and oil shortage increased natural gas demand. After the war, Iroquois' "industrial department" in the 1920s helped industry convert to and use gas. A company publication stated, "If gas is not economical for your operation, it will be frankly stated."[22] The publication claimed environmental benefits as well, saying the use of gas in place of "crude old fashioned fuels will sweep Buffalo's skys [sic] clean."[23] In Pittsburgh, natural gas remained by far the top energy choice for industry in 1928, and nearly 80 percent of consumption of Peoples' customers was burned by industry.[24]

The rubber industry used large supplies of gas, and Akron, Ohio, became the home to the Goodrich Rubber Company, Goodyear Tire & Rubber Company, and Firestone Tire & Rubber Company. Gas was used to produce automobile antifreeze compounds in the 1920s.[25] A subsidiary of Union Carbide, the Carbide and Chemical Corporation, chartered in 1920, built a large commercial plant in West Virginia in 1926 to produce synthesized chemicals from gas, including ethylene glycol that it sold under the trade name Prestone.[26] Gas also was a significant fuel to power oil field and refinery operations, and supply electric power plants and other industrial facilities.[27] Use of gas at some businesses was price sensitive. The carbon black industry, which depended on inexpensive natural gas, was hit hard by demand-produced higher prices in the mid–1920s.[28] By 1939, only Pennsylvania, Texas, and California had more than 10 percent of its industry using natural gas outside of the carbon black industry due to market considerations, labor cost differentials, and the cost of raw material, including fuel.[29] The carbon black industry reached a peak in 1948, and subsequently declined, cutting its natural gas use by 76 percent by 1965.[30]

After the lean years during the Great Depression and the scarcities and shortages during World War II, the Steel Valley economy from West Virginia to Buffalo roared with industrial development and natural gas again played a significant role. According to gas industry officials, the new Southwest pipelines transformed the often-overlooked "Cinderella" energy into the fossil fuel "glamour girl."[31] Because of its even temperature in burning, gas was also valuable in the production of steel tubing, tools and girders, metal alloys, asphalt, plastic molding for automobiles, automobile parts and tires, brass melting, porcelain enameling, metallurgy, ceramics, oil refining, cement making, ink, cereal, light bulbs, charcoal, dairy products, and dog food. By 1958, the gas industry estimated industrial use of the product covered approximately 20,000 different applications.[32] In 1949, the American steel industry alone used almost 400 billion cubic feet of gas, 45 percent more than the previous year and 10 percent more than during the height of war production in 1943.[33]

In addition to industry, gas was popular for commercial business. One of the early commercial uses of natural gas was by a crematory in Pittsburgh. In March 1886, Milton Fisher of Columbus, Ohio, was reduced to a "fine powder" by a gas incinerator in fifty minutes. One account opined, "The friends of the deceased pronounced the operation a success, but Fisher was not in shape to express his opinion."[34] However, the primary use for commercial establishments would be for preparing food. By the late 1950s, more than 90 percent of hotels and restaurants used gas for cooking.[35]

Home on the Range — Cookin' with Gas

The high penetration of natural gas appliances in many urban areas may lead one to believe that Appalachian natural gas utilities always had a monopolistic lock on their residential customers. Despite the rare use of natural gas lights, coal gas served most urban residential areas for lighting. Coal also dominated the residential space heating and cooking market in the late nineteenth century as well. In fact, there was no widespread availability of gas burning appliances until the early part of the twentieth century. However, Appalachian gas firms fought fiercely for their competitive share, first with coal, and then with oil and electricity. Therefore, gas rates had to be competitive. As the electric light bulb eroded the gas lighting market, natural gas made inroads into cooking. Shrinking supply and higher residential gas rates in the 1920s restrained the rate of growth of natural gas compared to oil and coal. But before natural gas could be applied to wide commercial use, the appliance industry needed to provide efficient products. A key process was first introduced around 1855 when German chemist Robert Wilhelm von Bunsen (1811–1899) developed the "Bunsen burner" concept of premixing gas and air prior to combustion in order to yield a high-temperature, nonluminous flame. Afterward, the development of gas appliances, many by coal-appliance manufacturers, was slow, but sure.

The first suggestion of gas for cooking dates back to 1805 by manufactured gas pioneer Frederick Winsor, but the first record of gas stoves came in 1825, a few years after William Hart's Fredonia well was supposedly used for both cooking and illumination.[36] James Sharp devised the world's first gas cooker in 1826 in Northampton, England. It was a device described as a piece of gas apparatus for cooking by enclosing a circle of gas flame with a reflecting cone in a cylinder of tin.[37] But it was not until 1851 that such equipment came into use in the U.S., and was later offered for sale in

Gas Stove Ad — Natural gas utilities marketed gas stoves as a replacement for the lighting market that was rapidly eroding in the first part of the twentieth century. Soon gas ranges would be associated with "fine cooking" (courtesy National Fuel Gas Company).

1859.[38] Another gas fire stove was introduced in 1849, also in England, which contained lumps of incombustible material heated by gas burners to resemble coal fire — similar to today's barbecue grills.[39] The first issue of the *American Gas Light Journal* in 1859 featured two advertisements for gas stoves.[40] Philadelphia's William H. Goodman and Company first offered the "Sun Dial" range, a design upon which many ranges were modeled throughout the early twentieth century.[41] Hot plates and stoves for commercial and residential purposes were produced in greater numbers by the 1880s.[42] Utilities actively promoted natural gas appliances with their sales message to homemakers that the best way to run the home was with gas. The natural gas industry conducted home service demonstrations as far back as 1879, with public lectures of gas for cooking.

Still, king coal remained omnipotent in the world of cooking stoves, its early designs popularized in the United States by Benjamin Franklin's box stove "Pennsylvania Fireplace" in 1744. But after serious promotion by gas companies, especially Henry Doherty's Cities Service, gas cooking caught on. Doherty submitted a paper to the American Gas Light Association in 1898 at its meeting in Niagara Falls, N.Y., titled "How Can We Make the Use of Gas for Cooking More Universal."[43] He became a pioneer natural gas promoter by developing fledgling natural gas appliances, sponsoring cooking demonstrations, and permitting time-payments for appliances through a customer's gas bill. The young Doherty, who managed a Madison, Wisconsin, gas firm, and later controlled a utility empire, called for a "united drive to capture the gas cooking market."[44] The merger of several gasoline stove companies, including three in Cleveland, became the American Stove Company in 1902. As the industry lost lighting customers to electricity, it began to market stoves more aggressively between 1910 and 1920.[45] Utilities such as Manufacturers in the Ohio Valley, sold "Reliable" brand gas ranges to customers.[46]

As it expanded, the gas industry became more organized. The first gas industry trade group, the Gas Light Association of America, founded in 1872, was an effort to coordinate manufactured gas practices. In 1918, the American Gas Association (A.G.A.) formed from two other organizations, the American Gas Institute and the National Commercial Gas Association, an outgrowth of a plan proposed in 1904 by Doherty. In 1927, the Natural Gas Association of America merged with A.G.A. Doherty was named head of an industry committee on "standard methods of testing fuel gas appliances" in 1903, and he recognized the need for a testing laboratory.[47] East Ohio helped get the effort off the ground with a temporary lab in 1923. A.G.A. then opened an appliance-testing laboratory in Independence, Ohio, near Cleveland, in 1927, where it helped develop standards for the industry. The "Blue Star" became the A.G.A.'s symbol of standards in 1925, guiding consumers to safer and more dependable gas appliances. Appliance manufacturers could use the symbol (a blue star in a circle) after rigorous testing of a sample appliance, backed up by a national appliance field observation program. The major emphasis was on safety, including temperature and pressure lit controls, automatic safety pilots, switches, and thermostats. The A.G.A. labs tested up to 6,000 appliances a year.

By the 1930s, natural gas ranges were associated with "fine cooking," including the radical change in design, the "Magic Chef" in 1929.[48] "Cookin' with Gas" eventually became a slogan for modern kitchens, and the gas range gradually replaced the coal stove. Specifications for gas ranges began in 1915, and as technology progressed, gas competed with electric appliances in the 1930s. The rivalry remains today. A Depression-era survey of gas customers by the Rochester Gas & Electric Company comparing gas and electric appliances found that gas ranges were considered better quality appliances, but electric ranges were cleaner and had more automatic controls and features.[49] The competitive efforts focused on cost as well. In 1941, appliance dealers in Erie, Pa., offered gas stoves at a price ranging from $31 to $109.[50]

Utilities' home services departments promoted all-gas kitchens, and offered cooking classes and baking contests. To compete with electric ranges in the 1960s, new eye-level and built-in gas ranges accented automatic lighting and controls, including color harmonics. The industry promoted a recipe book written by movie star Marlene Dietrich, in which she stated, "Every recipe I give is closely related to cooking with gas. If forced, I can cook on an electric stove, but it is not a happy union."[51] The industry promoted the "Burner with a Brain," a thermostatically-controlled top burner heat control that made every cooking utensil an automatic appliance. Other more modern developments included an indoor grilling downdraft cook top unveiled in 1980, and cool-to-the-touch burner tops.

Ashes to Ashes — Expansion of Residential Heating Markets

After gas lighting and cooking, the primary residential and commercial use for natural gas became space heating. Though not much in demand as an illuminant when first discovered, natural gas vents along pipelines were used to light many rural villages, albeit wastefully. Until the electric light eclipsed the manufactured gas industry, the artificial product was preferred for lighting. But for heat, natural gas was "unapproachable by any other fuel.... [Natural gas] does not need to be carried in and about, like coal; it makes no ashes, and consequently makes no dust, and can be regulated at will. It saves great labor to the housewife, and reduces the tug and toil of housework to a minimum."[52]

The first design of a room heater was introduced in Boston in 1859, and, in the 1860s, designs included a stove located in a home's basement under the floor to be heated. These portable "stove heaters," connected to a nearby gas cock, were usually not vented.[53] In 1884, Professor T. S. C. Lowe designed a hot air heating furnace suspended by ceiling joists. Three years later in 1887, the American Gas Furnace Company was incorporated. Since coal was the primary source for heat in the Northeast, gas furnace technology had to improve to capture this market. In the early twentieth century, experiments in house central heating were conducted using natural gas as a fuel.[54]

Natural gas was "nice fuel if you could get it." A history of Venango County, Pa., during that period asserted, "For heating houses natural gas is the greatest luxury ever bestowed on the race."[55] But the public needed to be educated on how to heat with gas. Once they were, local companies were overrun with applications. In 1914, there were five general classifications of gas heating radiators including the incandescent, reflector, gas, steam, and water radiator.[56] In 1917, the Buffalo Gas Company promoted a "Reliable Bungalow Style Gas Heater" for parts of a home not reached by the fireplace or furnace.[57] Also that year, New York City's harbor featured the world's only manufactured gas-heated battleship, with forty-three pressed-steel gas radiators.[58] Natural gas-designed boilers or furnaces were made more efficient in the 1920s so they could compete with anthracite coal.[59] Gas radiant heaters were primarily used at that time for heat in late fall and early spring before central home boilers were turned on or to heat chilly rooms that were heated by coal in the dead of winter.

Obviously, the ease of natural gas contrasted with the dirty and difficult job of shoveling coal and stoking the family furnace. Gas was a "luxury," and said to save "wear and tear of muscle and disposition, lessens the production of domestic quarrels, adds to the pleasure and satisfaction of living and carries the spring-time existence into the autumn above."[60] In 1886, 100 Buffalo civic leaders traveled to nearby Jamestown, N.Y., under the guidance of Standard's Daniel O'Day, to see what all the hubbub was about concerning this "natural" gas. The group found natural gas used for heating in

Gas Room Heater — Around the turn of the twentieth century, ornate radiant heaters were introduced, many of them made by coal stove and furnace manufacturers (courtesy National Fuel Gas Company).

private houses and manufacturing purposes and village residents were "abundantly satisfied with its use." In a statement to Buffalo's Board of Alderman on February 1, 1886, one city lawmaker said, "Where it [natural gas] has been used it has proved a great benefit to both rich and poor in the way of convenience, comfort and economy."[61] Leaving coal for home heating in its dust and ashes, natural gas was proclaimed the fuel of the future in the Appalachian region. When gas was introduced into Cleveland, a gas company foreman would approach a homeowner and say, "Do you want gas?" If the answer was "yes," and it usually was, there was no charge for running the service line.[62] A statement in a 1919 *History of Venango County, Pa.*, made the following claim: "The luxury of cheap natural gas is one of the best of nature's blessings in this happy region. It helps to make a contented people, which it is safe to say coal and ashes never did."[63]

In the early twentieth century, any community in the Appalachian region with a natural gas well and a supply of pipe was home to its own gas company. People who could be reached by natural gas lines insisted upon the form of energy that was convenient, economical, dependable, and clean. An Akron, Ohio, newspaper editorial claimed that cities like Baltimore were willing to pay far more than they did for someone providing gas for the convenience it brought: "We all remember in the past how we banked up our coal fires when we went to bed, and found it necessary to get up an hour earlier in the morning in order to shake out the ashes and renew the fire. As we stop to think about it we feel the hardship it would be if we had to do this at the present time. Gas has done away with all the trouble."[64] A pamphlet by Pittsburgh's Philadelphia Company proclaimed the labor savings of gas: "The use of gas allows people who have to rise early, at least half an hour more sleep owing to the fact that there is no delay in lighting fires. The Philadelphia Company thus contributed 5000 extra hours of sleep to its customers."[65] To help convert the thousands of potential consumers to heat with gas over coal involved convincing them of the convenience and economy of gas. Around the turn of the twentieth century, Peoples, the *Pittsburgh Leader* wrote, "virtually conducts a school of instruction in which the customers are educated to the best and most economical appliances for use."[66] The biggest obstacle to converting to gas was considered its expense. But the gas promoters had a persuasive argument.

> A fuel which carries itself into the house, which leaves no ashes to be carried out, which requires no kindling to start, which can be regulated exactly and stopped instantly, which produces no smoke to load the atmosphere, requires no labor and with proper care involves absolutely no risk, is something which the world has sought and mourned because it found it not, but has been found at last, in great abundance in natural gas.[67]

The convenience of gas over coal resulted in natural gas sales in the United States increasing from $215,000 in 1882 to $57 million in 1910.[68] By that year, natural gas had expanded to twenty-two states, though most of the customer concentration was in the Appalachian states. Because of the high population density of the region around the industrialized Ohio Valley, natural gas spread to numerous small communities. For example, in Ohio, natural gas penetration increased from 443 cities and towns in 1912 to 529 by 1917.[69]

But as local gas wells dwindled, many of these communities needed to attach to outside pipelines, and the gradual consolidation of small companies to regional utilities followed. As a result, larger gas companies continued to extend their lines to reach eager customers. For example, Iroquois built 126 miles of pipeline in Buffalo between 1924 and 1926 for new homes and to maintain pressure to existing consumers. A company publication claimed, "We find that when a person has once used gas for fuel he is extremely reluctant to change back to any other fuel."[70] What first began as a fuel for the lucky few would evolve into an expected amenity. As the *Gas Age Record* correctly prognosticated in 1923, "Today it is somewhat of a luxury. Tomorrow it will be a necessity."[71]

Gas heat was marketed as a way to replace coal to aid the "campaign for smokeless cities." Cities such as Pittsburgh, Cleveland, and Buffalo were plagued with coal dust, and smoke from imperfect combustion, which contributed to various ills. One account claimed, "The cost to Pittsburgh families for increased laundry, dry cleaning, painting and decorating, extra light and general cleaning has been estimated to average about $100 a year for each family."[72] The gas heater was proclaimed to be "healthful, the nearest approach to that of the sun itself."[73]

Pittsburgh, with its concentration of steel making, adopted the moniker the "Steel City," but regained its reputation as the "Smoky City" again by the 1940s. Motorists turned on headlights during the day and some wore surgical masks because of the industrial pollution. Conversions from coal to natural gas helped address the city's severe air quality problems. After the city created a smoke control ordinance in 1947, Peoples saw a 77 percent increase in gas heating installation in the next two years, as homeowners switched from coal.[74] In addition to growing sales in Pittsburgh, Peoples, Equitable, and Columbia expanded into new areas in western Pennsylvania as well.

Due to supply shortages, space heating on a wide scale would not be experienced until gas from the Southwest moved north after World War II. Once adequate supplies were obtained, gas utilities were flooded with an avalanche of conversions to gas heating. Large gravity warm air furnaces with fans powering hot air through numerous cylindrical ducts referred to as the "Octopus" design were common in city residential basements. The huge furnaces were often inefficient natural gas guzzlers, but not a concern since gas rates were low. In the 1950s, when natural gas was plentiful and inexpensive, heating engineers were primarily concerned with comfort and performance and had little regard for efficiency. Furnaces were oversized a minimum of 25 percent in order to provide a quick response as they had an overabundance of fresh air supply. Furnace efficiency was not an issue as the rest of the gas industry converted homes to inexpensive gas heat, saturating the market with its product. Compared to electric heat, gas provided even heating throughout the house, humidity control, and air filtration. After the price of natural gas escalated in the 1970s, gas furnace design, including high-efficiency models, improved dramatically.

As the rush to convert to gas from coal was on in the 1940s and '50s, this period became known as the "Golden Age" of natural gas. Despite new Southwest gas supplies, the flood of demand showed no sign of subsiding. Conversions to gas occurred with a flurry, and the utilities in the region expanded service to new communities previously not served by natural gas pipelines. Between 1945 and 1954, natural gas doubled its marketed production and made up 22 percent of the country's energy market.[75] For example, although 1953 was the warmest year on record in the western Pennsylvania and western New York region since 1871 when the U.S. weather bureau was started, NFG's utility heating customers grew by 31,930 that year and industrial sales jumped 18 percent.[76] By the end of the decade, 80 percent of NFG customers used gas for heating. Still, there were limits on the amount of heat conversions and new hookups utilities could add. But line extensions were well received by customers who were fortunate enough to be connected. One customer wrote to the utility: "Am surely pleased with natural gas. Something I never expected to get to heat this old-fashioned farm home of over 150 years."[77]

By the mid–1950s, the postwar American industrial economic boom was in full swing and the major industrial metropolitan areas in the United States experienced unprecedented growth. Nationally, gas sales nearly tripled by 1955 from World War II levels.[78] In Cleveland in the 1950s, 97 percent of new homes used gas for heating, 75 percent for cooking, 93 percent for water heating, 27 percent for clothes drying (double the national average), and 23 percent had gas-fired incinerators (the high saturation rate in the nation).[79] By 1966, 89 percent of homes in Pittsburgh (originally dominated by coal) were heated by natural gas, including 98 percent of new construction.[80]

Getting Into Hot Water — The Development of the Gas Water Heating Market

After space heating, water heating was another significant market to be tapped. The Romans first developed bathing through a "hypocaust," a low basement chamber where fuel was burned. It also was used for room heating. Ancient philosopher Pliny noted that Rome used only baths for medicine for 600 years.[81] Much later, gaseous saline springs in Italy were used to heat the baths of Poretta in the 1830s.[82] The first modern design of gas water heating was drawn up in 1897, though other circulating water tank types were introduced in the early 1880s.[83] The early crude water heating devices were neither efficient nor popular. The first circulating tanks had to be turned on and off manually, often causing waste when a homemaker forgot to shut off the burner.[84] Once huge gas wells were discovered in Pennsylvania, the inexpensive fuel

Water Heater Truck — For years, the basic water heater was a large, reliable tank that transformed the "Saturday night bath" into a daily hygiene habit, and gas water heaters became the second largest gas-burning appliance in the home (courtesy National Fuel Gas Company).

revolutionized the business. Automatic water heaters were developed by H. A. Tobey in 1885, J. C. Beckfield in 1895, and Edwin Ruud in 1897.[85] F. W. Robertshaw of Pittsburgh developed a mechanical device in 1899 to maintain the water temperature automatically.[86] A newspaper ad in the Buffalo Express in 1917 advertised the "Gordon Duplex Automatic Water Heater" as a "porcupine" heater that saved 25 percent on gas bills.[87] Still, development of gas water heaters suffered due to the lack of standardization and the expense of the units.[88] In the 1920s, three main types of water heaters were developed including the tank heater, the automatic storage system, and the automatic-instantaneous type. The first instantaneous gas water heater to work efficiently was first marketed in 1932.

Because of improvements in safety, free or low cost servicing by utilities, and a huge price advantage over electricity, gas hot water heat was considered a great value. Even lower cost time-of-day electric rates made life inconvenient as customers hurried to wash dishes or take showers during off-peak hours. Many homeowners, compelled to install electric heat during gas installation moratoriums during the natural gas shortage in the late 1970s, eagerly converted to gas once restrictions were later lifted.

Flash in the Pan — Alternative Natural Gas Markets

Gas got its start by turning night into day with gaslight. By the mid–1800s, manufactured gas lamps had taken over the market for oil lamps in New York City and the "Gaslight Era" was born. The new Welsbach mantle type (first invented in 1885 and its patent acquired by the Philadelphia-area firm UGI in 1887) created some hope that gas could compete with electricity for lighting. The Welsbach produced three times the illumination of open gaslights, while burning one-half as much gas.[89] It was so efficient, it was thought to be a threat to gas companies' load.[90] With the new gaslight mantle, manufactured gas interests hoped to postpone the electric onslaught and popularized a "Gaslight Era" renaissance after 1899.[91] Later, in 1907, the "fan tail" open burner gaslights were introduced. However, the progress of electricity made the soft glowing lights only a nostalgic curiosity rather than a practical application. In 1899, 75 percent of gas was used for illumination. That share was down to 21 percent twenty years later.[92] Another novelty gaslight period occurred with the abundant new supply of Southwest gas in the late 1950s, as gas utilities across the United States attempted to increase gas sales by promoting the homey feel of gaslights.

Natural gas was used successfully, and not so successfully, in other applications. Gas-"ammonia absorption type" refrigerators were introduced in 1915, but some documents cite that the appliances were first experimented with in the 1880s. The first Servel gas refrigerator was unveiled in 1925. The gas absorption type became more common in 1933, in an effort to compete with electric models that had all but eliminated the old "ice box." Unlike the electric refrigerator motors that were compression types, the initial gas models used a refrigerant (generally ammonia) absorbed in water. Gas heat was used to drive the refrigerant out of the solution into the gaseous form, creating pressure. The vapor, while under this pressure, was readily condensed to a liquid by a cooling coil of tap water. The liquid flowed into the ice chamber, the pressure was removed, and the change from liquid to gas then followed. Heat that

Gas Appliance Promotions — In the 1950s, residential marketing efforts were intense. Utilities sponsored cooking schools, kitchen planning, appliance demonstrations, home shows, model homes and home economic class programs. Home shows promoted new uses of gas, including air conditioning (courtesy National Fuel Gas Company).

was required for the change was removed from the surroundings, providing refrigeration. However, gas refrigerators had a short shelf life, as high-tech electric models dominated the market.

Gas-fired air conditioning units, first researched and tested around 1928, were introduced in the United States on a wider scale around 1937. Servel introduced the first "all-year" gas-fired air conditioner in 1948, and gas air conditioners were heavily marketed once gas supply became plentiful in the 1950s. Most of the air conditioning load was concentrated in commercial and industrial installations but there were hopes of potential residential use. Some proponents offered ludicrous pie-in-the-sky forecasts: "Whole cities will be air conditioned. Even the brief discomfort of leaving one air-conditioned building to go to another will be eliminated."[93] Despite an opportunity to increase natural gas sales, and possibly reduce the average cost of delivery to the residential customer, both residential gas refrigeration and cooling did not capture the market due to substandard performance, safety concerns, and tough electric competition.[94]

Unique and innovative uses for gas also cropped up, some for a short time period while others were more enduring. Residential "trash" incinerators were first developed in 1909, but at that time they were merely "dehydrators" that dried out materials. The first smokeless and odorless trash-burning model was developed in 1957.[95] But such residential use was largely a "flash in the pan." Gas clothes irons only had a short span of success of about a decade, eclipsed by the electric iron in 1915.[96] Driveway and sidewalk heating was tested for homes and businesses in the early 1960s. Swimming pool heating was first described in 1908, and is prevalent today.[97] The outdoor natural gas barbecue sold strongly in the 1960s and still remains popular, though propane grills are more common. Early gas-powered home clothes washing among the affluent was never popular due to the habit of "sending out the laundry," but eventually gas clothes dryers were big sellers due to their economy. "Penny-a-load" gas clothes dryers were introduced in the 1950s to compete with cheaper to purchase, but more operationally costly, electric models. Also, a gas dishwasher was introduced in 1963.[98]

An innovative concept for natural gas use forty years ago is still being experimented with today. Eastern power blackouts in the 1960s encouraged the development of fuel cells to produce electricity chemically rather than mechanically. The concept, already used in the space program, also eliminated stack pollution and water pollution discharge. Small fuel cells were the size of a conventional gas air conditioner, could be connected in a series to generate more power, and consumed one-third less fuel to generate the same electricity as any other system. Over the next few decades, several Appalachian utilities were field markets for residential, commercial, and industrial fuel cell tests.

The Clean Hanky Test — Natural Gas for Vehicles

One market for gas is potentially a serious threat to its sister fossil fuel — oil. As stated earlier, one of the major appeals of natural gas in its infancy in the 1880s was its cleanliness. Combustion of natural gas primarily produces carbon dioxide and water, with only trace amounts of other pollutant gases. Both industrial and residential customers sought gas not just for economy, but also because of its clean-burning qualities. A century later after Pittsburgh and other urban areas promoted natural gas for its environmental benefits, concern about the effects of industrial and automobile air pollution made natural gas a possible alternative fuel for vehicles. In the 1960s, buses in Zigong, China, were powered by natural gas stored in large gray bladders on the roofs. The gas bag "jiggled like Jell-O" as the bus turned corners, gradually deflating as the gas was used up.[99]

However, more practical natural gas vehicles (NGVs) are commonly used throughout the world using compressed natural gas. NGVs, which power a car through a tank of compressed natural gas, have been used since the 1940s in countries such as Italy, which had a quarter million NGVs on the road because of that nation's limited domestic oil supply. In the United States, NGVs are operated mainly by gas utilities and some mass transit and delivery fleets. An apparatus for compressing gas dates back to 1860, for use in private houses, hotels, steamboats, and railroad cars. NGVs have several advantages over gasoline including: reducing engine wear; longer lasting spark plugs; changing oil less frequently; starting engines faster in cold and hot climates; and reducing the exhaust air pollution compared to a gasoline vehicle.[100] NGVs got rolling in the Appalachian region when testing began in the 1960s and '70s, and by the '90s, utilities installed natural gas filling stations, some of them open to the public. On the federal level, the Clean Air Act amendments of 1990 set strict requirements for controlling air pollution, mandating that larger fleets in the twenty-two most polluted urban areas buy a certain percentage of clean-fuel vehicles beginning in 1998. Also, the National Energy Policy Act, passed in 1992, mandated that companies meeting specific criteria convert their fleets to alternative-fuel vehicles. Currently, natural gas powers buses and fleet vehicles in several Appalachian cities, including Pittsburgh, Cleveland, Erie, Pa., and Buffalo. A popular public relations demonstration of natural gas buses was the "clean hanky test," where a white handkerchief held over the tail pipe of a natural gas powered vehicle for several minutes revealed no black exhaust stain. But despite federal and state incentives and a slight advantage in cost with gasoline, widespread use of NGVs has not occurred due to the heavy cost of converting existing vehicles, lack of gas-dedicated vehicles, limited refueling infrastructure, and low oil prices. Interest in NGVs would be reignited in recent years due to the surplus of natural gas made available by huge shale gas discoveries in the United States.

Go Modern, Go Gas — Natural Gas Advertising

As the twentieth century progressed, gas utilities actively marketed ranges, dryers, water heaters, gaslights, gas incinerators, gas barbecue grills, fireplaces, and other gas burning equipment to residential and commercial customers. Utilities used their workforce to promote sales of gas appliances with incentive prizes and contests. Customer incentives promoted sales, including offering free holiday turkeys with the purchase of cooking appliances, sweepstakes, and raffling off natural gas appliances at home shows. As with many other products, advertising was critical in convincing the public to "Go Modern, Go Gas." A Citizens Gas & Fuel Company advertisement in the *Dunkirk Evening Observer* on June 27, 1901, declared: "By using a gas range you can cook, boil or roast and not roast or boil the cook."[101] Another ad in the same publication on March 31, 1902, read: "Now is the time and opportunity for you to get your house piped for gas. Pipe is cheap, Labor reasonable, Gas cheaper than any other illuminant, and if you are looking for light, come to the gas office and your wants will be supplied."[102] Turn of the century ads in Ohio's Ashtabula Beacon Record suggested, "On chilly nights and mornings a small gas heater will heat your room quicker, easier and cheaper than any other way. Try it and see."[103]

Industry magnate Henry Doherty actively promoted the national advertising concept in 1900.[104] The first cooperative national advertising in the industry occurred between 1912 and 1913.[105] In addition to print advertising, utilities used the new electronic media—radio—as early as 1923 to promote their products and build "good will."[106] In fact, RG&E in Rochester, N.Y., established a "radiophone" station "8XQ," as a new form of advertising.[107] In 1933, the Pittsburgh-area natural gas companies, including Peoples, Manufacturers, Equitable, and T. W. Phillips pooled their resources and ran a year-long joint advertising campaign in newspapers, radio, direct mail, and billboards to encourage consumers to "modernize" their home with gas.[108] In one advertising promotion in 1962, Peoples and other sponsors constructed a house equipped with gas appliances on the roof of the Kaufmanns department store in downtown Pittsburgh that attracted 100,000 visitors in nine weeks.[109] Perhaps the most effective marketing the gas industry conducted was by word-of-mouth. Those who did not have gas wanted it, and consequently, supply and availability could never keep up with the demand. Even without paid advertising, with the advantages of using the product — low cost, convenience, efficiency, and cleanliness — natural gas sold itself.

The immense expansion of the natural gas industry in the post-war years mirrored the changing American economy and way of life. The baby boom began, and modern appliances that added convenience to the American household symbolized the economic and technological superiority of the United States, later

"WITH AN AUTOMATIC GAS CLOTHES DRYER-I DO A LOAD LIKE THAT FOR LESS THAN 3¢..."

Gas Dryer Advertisement — In the 1950s, natural gas utilities focused on new natural gas-burning appliances, marketed to the appliance purchasing decision maker in the household — the homemaker (**courtesy National Fuel Gas Company**).

prominently promoted by Vice President Richard Nixon in his 1959 "Kitchen Debate" with Soviet premier Nikita Khrushchev at an American exhibition in Moscow. The natural gas industry, meanwhile, worked tirelessly to gain acceptance into the American home. Since many of the major appliance purchasing decisions were strongly influenced by the homemaker, that demographic was targeted heavily with advertising, cooking and baking demonstrations, "brides classes," and contests. Local gas utilities stepped up advertising efforts to meet stiff electric appliance competition. Gas utilities opened demonstration kitchens at their offices that accommodated groups for meetings and food demonstrations. As the Miss America contest achieved popularity with talent and swimsuit contests for young, unmarried women, the natural gas industry had its own version of honoring married women — Mrs. America. In the late 1950s and early '60s, the gas industry sponsored a nationwide search for the number one homemaker in the land.

The Cash Register — The Gas Meter

With thousands of miles of pipeline buried out of sight under the ground, when consumers think of gas, they usually think of the gas meter. Customers usually do not contemplate the unseen massive interlocking local distribution systems involved in distributing gas. A nondescript brick regulator station at the "City Gate" accepts high-pressure gas from larger pipelines and reduces it to medium or low pressures through valves and meters. Underground main lines flow under city streets, out of sight and out of mind. Line pressures are monitored and regulated to provide constant quality and safe delivery of the product.[110] Residential, commercial, and industrial customers connect to the mains through service lines that break off at the "curb box," and finally end at individual meters. The customer's local plumber usually provides maintenance for some underground service lines.

Despite the veiled transportation system that keeps homes warm in winter, all customers are familiar with their gas meter. Samuel Clegg, a pupil of William Murdock at his Soho Gas Works, and later an engineer with the first gas utility — the London Gas Light & Coke Company — patented a "wet" gas meter in 1815.[111] However, the meter was neither a commercial success nor was it adopted for many years. The iron wet gas meter was a metal cylinder that contained a partitioned drum half-filled with water. Gas entered the cylinder, filling the partitions, and forced the drum to rotate. The gas exited the cylinder on the opposite side and an index counted the volume of gas used.[112] Clegg also patented a "dry" meter in 1830. Samuel Hill made the first commercially produced meters in 1832 in Baltimore, beginning the Barlett-Hayward Company. These devices were frequently used for manufactured gas by 1840.[113] In 1844, Croll and Richards' patent improved the dry gas meter which became the basis for more modern meters.[114]

In 1863, standardized metering started with the formation of the American Meter Company under a fifty-year New York charter. In 1870, pre-payment meters, patented by T.S. Lacey in England, spread the use of manufactured gas. They were introduced in the United States in 1894, and by 1909, the Metric Metal Works in Erie, Pa., offered pre-payment meters for a nickel and then a quarter. Thievery of money in the meters, as well as counterfeit slugs made of metal and even ice that melted and erased the evidence of pilferage, created a few problems for the utilities using the pre-payment devices.[115] Evading the meter became another problem. An audit by the Keystone Gas Company in 1901 in Olean, N.Y., found that numerous residents ran piping around the meter or turned the meter upside down to keep the actual amount of gas from recording.[116] Meter tampering, often causing unsafe conditions, has consistently been a thorn in the side of utilities.

A flat rate for gas utility service was common in the nineteenth century, used to urge households to try the product for the first time.[117] Also, in the infancy of the industry, many meters were thought to give a false reading for natural gas, so often gas service was contracted with customers by the year based on the number of their appliances. For example, the Clarion (Pa.) Gas Company rates in 1886 were:

1st heating stove	$8.00 per year
2nd heating stove	$6.00 per year
Cook stove	$15 per year.[118]

Similarly, George Westinghouse's Philadelphia Company in 1887 charged $2.50 a month for a store in Pittsburgh and $10 a year for heating a room of fifteen square feet.[119] When gas was first introduced for manufacturing in Pittsburgh, the price, compared to coal, was very low, and was sold on unlimited contracts that led to great waste by its users. Customers left the windows open to let out the surplus heat.[120] Unlimited quantities were provided for cooking ranges for $1.00 a month, heating stoves for $0.75 a month, and lights for $0.15 per month.[121] A large country home could be heated for $75 a year, and the Duquesne Hotel in Pittsburgh was heated for $560 a year. The first increase in rates came in 1890, when they were raised 50 percent.[122] But charging by the appliance would not last. Flat rates encouraged waste, and eventually, the U.S. Department of Interior recommended banning the flat rate in 1911.[123] Natural gas firms in Appalachia, however, were ahead of the curve. Meters would address the waste and more equitably distribute utility costs.

In "the old days", customers put a quarter in the gas meter to obtain energy for their homes.

Prepayment Meter — Unlike today, when utility customers consume energy now and pay for it later, some of the first gas meters were coin operated. Customers had to pay for the product before it was used (courtesy Dominion Peoples).

More modern ways of measuring natural gas by meter occurred around 1885.[124] And in 1888, the Philadelphia Company in Pittsburgh put George Westinghouse–designed meters on all of its services, saving an estimated 60 percent on gas used.[125] The Pittsburgh Meter and Manufacturing Company later formed in 1927 from two firms (Pittsburgh and the Philadelphia Company's Equitable Meter). Boston native and industrialist Colonel Willard E. Rockwell, also known for his contributions in aviation, became president of the Equitable Meter and Manufacturing Company of Pittsburgh in 1925, and the firm became one of the largest meter production facilities in the world. In 1945, the combined firms became part of Rockwell Manufacturing Company.[126] Cast-iron-cased dry meters for high-pressure use were developed by Peoples co-founder Joseph N. Pew and William N. Milstead of the American Meter Company in 1889.[127] The Metric Meter Company, financed by Standard interests, organized in Beaver Falls, Pa., in 1888, constructing meters out of cast iron and brass.[128] That firm was organized with the help of Standard's Calvin Payne, and in 1891, Payne purchased land for an extensive three-story gas meter manufacturing plant in his wife's home town of Erie, Pa., at the corner of East 10th Street and what became known as Payne Avenue.[129] In 1895, the firm was one of four companies merged with the American Meter Company, and the renamed Metric Metal Works became one of the largest and most modern plants in Pennsylvania.[130] Metric Metal Works announced that the future of natural gas was linked to economical consumption brought on by meters: "With a meter in the house, the consumer is driven to using economical burning appliances, while the Distributor can realize at once that he has found a means to store up for future use this grandest fuel known to man."[131]

Some early meters for artificial and natural gas were made from tin. Metric Metal

Works later manufactured the spherical "Tobey" meter, designed by Toledo, Ohio, inventor Henry A. Tobey in 1892, which could withstand ninety psi. The globe-shaped Tobeys were made of cast iron, with fewer parts and simpler construction. An advertisement for the meter proclaimed: "This meter makes no noise, takes up little room, can be made either right or left hand, and with the strong brass connections furnished with each meter, can be set at an exceptionally low cost."[132]

Natural gas metering spread throughout Equitable, as well as Standard dominated companies including PGC, Peoples, Buffalo Natural Gas Fuel Company, and East Ohio. The Ironcase "A" meter was introduced in 1909, designed to hold higher pressures. Most modern meters are based on models designed in the 1920s, consisting of two diaphragms, or bellows.[133] The breathing meter's mechanical lungs, initially made of leather and later of a synthetic material, measured the fuel by inhaling gas from the mains and exhaling gas to the burner, with each breath recorded on the dials.

Meter Reader — Meter reading began with employees walking neighborhood routes with meter books. Readers persist through hot and cold weather, threatening dogs, cluttered basements, and high snow banks. By the late twentieth century, meter readers used electronic devices to take measurements and some utilities experimented with automatic meter reading devices that recorded measurements through radio waves or telephone lines (courtesy National Fuel Gas Company).

The gas company employee most familiar to the customer is the meter reader. In the early part of the 1900s, employees traveled on bicycles and made meter changes by hauling meters with a horse cart or an employee-powered pushcart. The meter man would be a common visitor to residential neighborhoods, walking down the street with a book to record measurements. Early meters located outside the home occasionally had problems in cold weather due to hydrates forming, blocking the gas flow. An early inexpensive method to unfreeze the device was by filling it with whiskey.

Because the meter readers were there to read the company's "cash register," they were not always a welcome sight in the customer's eyes. In New York City, for example, one person bred "gas dogs" leased to consumers to scare the monthly meter readers away.[134] But as meter readers would admit, most dogs didn't need special breeding to develop the talent. One of the most common injuries for readers became the dog bite, and East Ohio, for example, required their meter readers' use of "puttees," a type of leg padding to protect from attacking hounds.[135]

The Gas House Gang— Working in the Industry

The industrial age brought with it plenty of jobs, but the lords of business were not always the most benevolent of employers. Long hours, low pay, lack of health care, and exploitation of underage workers were common in the "Gilded Age" at the end of the nineteenth century. Work in the natural gas industry was not easy either, though careers in utilities proved to be more desirable than many. Standard pipeline leader Daniel O'Day claimed, "For best results, we should pay our men a little more than other people, and then the men will be anxious and earnest to do better work for us in order to retain their positions."[136] In addition, the utility industry led the way in many respects in providing attractive benefits, including life insurance in the early part of the twentieth century, and later, health benefits. A utility job, steady and secure, thus became a coveted one.

By the beginning of the twentieth century, many gas company employees still worked six days a week, twelve hours a day, and the only three holidays were Christmas, New Years, and the Fourth of July.[137] Employees were paid in cash, with a "paymaster" moving from one work "gang" to another with cash envelopes.[138] The early manufactured gas firms employed "lamp trimmers," who cleaned and replaced mantles inside gaslights of homes, stores, schools, firehouses, police stations, streetlights, and other public buildings. In case of freeze-ups in the winter, the lamp trimmer poured alcohol down the opening until it permitted the flow of gas. Some other early job titles included: water boy, stub man, laborer, messenger boy, lineman, watchman, pipe fitter, stockkeeper, caulker, auto repairman, welder, tool dresser, carpenter, switchboard operator, roustabout, well tender, bailing machine operator, oiler, gang boss, appliance installer, and salesman. Over time, work at natural gas companies often became a family affair as generations from executives to line workers were employed by the same firm. The labor union movement in the twentieth century brought with it shorter hours and more benefits, and with a few exceptions, the natural gas business enjoyed more harmonious labor relations than many other manufacturing industries.

Due to the physical nature of early natural gas operations, the industry was originally a man's world. Women would find a role initially in billing operations around 1918 when many men marched off to war overseas. East Ohio began hiring women as tellers and collectors for the first time during World War I. As with many other industries during World War II, women again replaced men, many as meter readers.[139] Throughout the history of the gas industry, men primarily filled the positions in construction and service, but women eventually became prominent in business offices. For example, at Iroquois' Buffalo commercial office in 1919, women employees amounted to only a handful. By the late 1950s, women outnumbered men in that utility's office by three to one.[140]

In the first days of the industry, local gas companies sought new franchises in many communities for permission to lay their lines. Although most work was done by hand, there was little in the way of pipeline construction, even in populated areas.

City Construction — Utility personnel once had little concern over where to lay their lines, but once many streets were paved in the 1920s, digging up a gas line became much more work (courtesy National Fuel Gas Company).

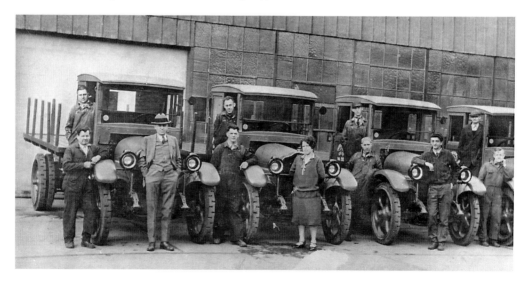

Service Vehicles — The first motor vehicles used by utilities appeared around the beginning of the twentieth century. Pictured here are United Natural Gas flatbed service trucks in 1920, which had solid tires, Presto-Lite headlights, but no heaters. In winter, candles were used to keep frost off the windshields and lanterns burned to keep the cabs warm (courtesy National Fuel Gas Company).

During early expansion, there was not much concern about digging a trench and laying a line, unless the workers had to blast through rock. But by the 1920s, a large number of city streets were paved and concrete sidewalks extended from the customer's property line to the curb. In addition, tunnels, underground conduits, telephone cables, sewers, water mains, and other obstacles made it more difficult to find suitable locations to install gas mains, causing higher costs, and more work. Vibrations caused by heavy trucks on the road required a pipe joint that would not loosen. Cast iron pipe, formed by pouring molten iron into molds, could break from vibration and shock, and the common type of lead joint was recaulked frequently. The introduction of the Dresser coupling and steel pipe, offered the strength, flexibility, and durability that were required. Later, electric pipe locators identified pipelines and other buried metallic equipment. Also, X-ray equipment determined the quality of welded pipe joints, increasing safety.

The natural gas industry first transported its pipe, compressors, and other material by horse and wagon. At the Niagara Light, Heat and Power Company in the early part of the twentieth century, the utility's distribution department consisted of one truck, two horses, a wagon, and a personal bicycle.[141] The first motor vehicles used by companies appeared in the early 1900s. The industry eventually adopted numerous vehicles dedicated to gas specific duties such as large construction, service, and appliance vans, compressor trucks, backhoes, sliding tilt bed trucks, and meter installation vehicles.

Scents and Sensibility — Gas Safety

The pungent, distinctive "rotten egg" odor of natural gas that any consumer recognizes is not natural gas at all. Coal manufactured gas had its own distinct odor, and many Appalachian natural gas wells often have a sulfurous, petroleum-like smell. But natural gas in its pure form is odorless, tasteless, and colorless. But if the transparent gas had no smell, how would anyone know if the flammable fuel was leaking? Often, you wouldn't know. A tremendous explosion from unodorized natural gas in a Texas high school in 1937 led to the worst gas industry tragedy in the twentieth century. The disaster claimed nearly 300 lives and led to calls for a standardized odorant.[142] Gas was then odorized so one of the best leak detectors — the human nose — would notice it.

The first suggestion of odorizing gas to assist in leak detection came from a meeting of the Ohio Gas Light Association in 1885.[143] The natural gas in Ohio did not possess the offensive odor of manufactured gas, which betrayed the presence of coal gas, revealing leaks and preventing accidental explosions. The unscented natural gas was regarded as "an excellence, but which may be a source of danger in its use."[144] Early attempts at odorization failed because the smell was confused with onion and garlic. Later, the city of Troy in eastern New York State was the first to require gas with a distinctive scent.[145] Beginning in 1952, an odorant called "Calodorant" was added to gas. The U.S. Bureau of Mines first experimented with another chemical — "Mercaptan" — in 1930, and this odorant later became the standard, creating an artificial, but pungent stench. It is so powerful that one quart will odorize enough gas to cook meals for 500 families for 100 years; a spilled teaspoon of the substance can stink up a city block. It is non-toxic, does not chemically react in pipelines, and burns without residue. Pipeline gas emanating from the Southwest is "scrubbed" of heavy hydrocarbons that could produce a petroleum scent, so odorometers and drip-type liquid injection odorizers are installed throughout points of the gas pipeline system.

Despite the common belief that natural gas is a volatile, dangerous substance, it is neither poisonous nor toxic. Many are surprised to learn that natural gas will not always burn. Only the proper air-gas ratio—between 4 and 14 percent natural gas mixed with air and ignited by a temperature of at least 1100° F—causes the fuel to ignite. Natural gas is lighter than air, making outdoor leaks less hazardous than petroleum spills. Unless trapped in a structure, like a building with the windows closed, the ethereal energy usually dissipates harmlessly in the atmosphere.

But before gas was properly odorized and standard safety guidelines were developed for pipelines and installation, accidents were common. In the early years of the industry, leaks from mains sometimes made their way underground into homes and businesses, some not even piped with gas. Explosions at homes and businesses were caused when unodorized natural gas collected and ignited from other flame sources. The only leak detection was a match, which often lead to disastrous consequences. Caution with gas was learned the hard way. For example, an explosion in 1890 in Greenville, Pa., blew out the front of a grocery store.[146] In May 1897, a gas explosion caused a fire at the Burial Case Manufactory in Erie, Pa., killing the watchman.[147] In Brocton, N.Y., a plumber connected pipes to a kitchen stove and went to investigate why there was no gas coming to the appliance by lighting a match in the basement. A disconnected pipe had filled the cellar with gas and an explosion followed. As witnesses reported in the *Dunkirk Evening Observer* on November 10, 1910, "Not one of them seems to be sure whether he came out the door or through the window."[148] Fortunately, the plumber was not seriously hurt. Early gas appliances without shutoff valves caused gas leaks, and consequently, in some cases, asphyxiation of its residents by displacing oxygen in the house. Escaping gas in pipeline ditches also was an ever-present deadly danger for gas company workers. For example, two men from the Chartiers Natural Gas Company were suffocated by leaking natural gas at Allegheny City, Pa., in July 1887.[149] In addition, poisonous carbon monoxide can be produced by improperly burning gas appliances.

The gas industry developed numerous safety standards, developing a permanent American Standard Code in 1927.[150] Later, more safety improvements included the use of leak detectors ranging from the Wolfe safety lamp to the Mine Safety Appliance Company's "Explosimeter," enabling gas company employees to safely check for leaks.[151] Combustible gas detectors in street patrol work check the atmosphere in manholes and other underground structures for the presence of gas that might be indicative of a leak in a nearby gas main.

Although odorant is injected into pipelines, a frequent claim by customers involves a myth about "air in the lines." As early as 1915, industry officials strove to dispel the urban legend, stating: "It is a physical impossibility to mix it in the field, and transport it with any degree of safety, because if air is put into the gas at any point excepting the "mixer," at the consumer's fixture, it would probably ignite from friction or other cause and blow up the mains."[152]

Yes, We Have No Gas — Gas Famines and Other Crises

Gas utility service is historically reliable, and with the exception of flooding, underground lines are not generally susceptible to Mother Nature, such as wind, ice, and snow that often plague electric service wires. However, keeping customers in gas was not always easy due to supply shortages. Natural gas supply shortfalls seemed to run in cycles throughout the industry's history in Appalachia as "gas famines" occurred in the 1880s, during World War I, World War II, and again in the 1970s. In Pittsburgh, there was no shortage of gas companies being created, but according to the 1889 *History of Allegheny County*, "their stock is not a favorite investment, because of the dread that the gas-supply will not be permanent."[153] Keeping gas pressure in the lines was a challenge right from the start due to pipeline failures, excessive demand, and declining wells. In December 1885, a Philadelphia Company line break cut off service to Pittsburgh steel mills. The scarcity of natural gas in Pittsburgh not only shut down industry, but also left many homeowners without gas and according to one newspaper, the "natural gas company receives few complimentary allusions."[154]

In late 1886, Franklin Natural Gas Company president Charles Mackey wrote in a telegram to the Oil City Fuel Supply Company: "Gas has been low all night and people are now complaining all over the city. We must have more gas. What is wrong?"[155] Franklin industries were later shut off, residents burned coal, and Franklin connected to Columbia Gas Light Fuel Company lines. In 1887, a break in the West Virginia Gas Company's only pipeline to Wheeling shut down all the mills, glass plants, as well as commercial stores and homes. The pipelines were later doubled and looped to prevent such occurrences.[156] In 1905, a line broke and Cleveland went without gas for two days and "people shivered in their homes."[157]

Numerous gas discoveries in western Ohio provided many communities with natural gas, but the wells quickly lost pressure. As early as 1888, the decline of gas wells in Ohio caused concern among drillers.[158] In 1886, natural gas boom in Indiana caused local officials there to lure glass manufacturers to move their plants from eastern cities to the gas towns of Indiana, offering free gas.[159] The gas was so plentiful, farmers harvested by gaslight.[160] But gas offered at no charge, uncontrolled blowing wells, and leaking lines allowed millions, if not billions, of cubic feet of the precious resource to get away. The field pressure, 325 psi in 1886, was down to 100 psi by 1900, and the state's great, but shallow, gas fields, which also initially supplied Chicago, were drained by 1907.[161] Chicago was forced to return to manufactured gas use.[162] Even in the natural gas cradle in Appalachia, shortages erupted. In 1897, the Charleston Natural Gas Company, after only three years of tapping the prolific wells in West Virginia, had concerns that its gas supply might not last.[163] There were gas "famines" reported in Buffalo as far back as 1907.[164] The World War I years were particularly difficult as cold weather and expanding gas markets led to supply squeezes. But as gas hungry consumers in Ohio conserved their energy due to the shortages, customers in West Virginia, which sat on huge gas supplies, used 50 percent more gas during this period.[165]

Major shortages reported in the World War I years continued during the postwar period. During a 1918 blizzard in Jamestown, N.Y., the manager of the local gas company said that all industrial plants were ordered to discontinue the use of gas.[166]

Natural gas demand at the time was high because of its economical appeal over man-ufactured gas, which due to the natural product's higher-heating content, was up to six times the value of artificial gas.[167] In addition, domestic gas appliances were gas guzzlers wasting 80 percent of the fuel they received.[168] As the Columbia Gas System expanded rapidly throughout western Pennsylvania and central New York, gas supply was always an issue — and the firm searched for more "reserve acreage of proven gas land large enough to provide the necessary gas to meet a constantly enlarging demand."[169] The cost of gas increased in Ohio and other areas in the early 1920s and it helped reduce consumption. Conservation became an issue due to the shrinking supply and the industry considered higher rates, restrictions on gas lighting, cutting industrial use, and rationing.[170] Although West Virginia initially attracted much industry due to enormous discoveries of cheap gas, by 1920 the supply diminished to a point that unless new supplies were secured, the state considered using the prod-uct exclusively for domestic consumers.[171]

During the Great Depression, which began with the 1929 stock market crash that reduced the Dow Jones Industrial Average by half, natural gas supplied heat for only one out of five households. Gas sales declined in many areas with American industrial production down severely. Many utilities struggled to maintain sales and continue paying dividends to their shareholders. Peoples in Pittsburgh saw their profits drop from $2.3 million to $585,000 between 1928 and 1934. By 1938, profits dwindled to $80,161.[172] Though utility rates increased with the shrinking gas supply, the utilities had little left to pay dividends. For example, in Ohio, twenty-seven util-ities operated at a loss.[173] In 1931, the average customer use of gas dropped 12.5 percent in Ohio, 11.8 percent in Pennsylvania, 6.3 percent in West Virginia, and 8.9 percent in New York.[174] Declines would continue through 1934 as natural gas prices rose, while the average worker's real income declined. Though utility common dividends were stagnant, most gas firms did not experience layoffs.

But during World War II, skyrocketing prices and shortages of coal, coke, and oil caused customers to start converting to gas heat by the tens of thousands. Various federal agencies, including the War Production Board, expressed concern about nat-ural gas supplies that were critical to war production needs in the Appalachian region, and encouraged pipelines to transport gas at full load factors, increase use of storage fields, develop curtailment schedules, and relax guidelines for new drilling.[175] But the Appalachian gas supply was dwindling and there simply was not enough product to go around.

Though oil was considered more important to gas in the war effort, federal offi-cials met with gas company leaders in 1941 and placed limitations on industrial and residential loads. Despite government war restrictions on residential gas use, people conjured "medical" exemptions to obtain gas for space heating rather than shovel coal or expose themselves to oil fumes.[176] Government restrictions and metal shortages of material made it necessary to scrape the "bottom of the barrel" for the utilities themselves to secure pipes and fittings. Gas industry representatives made personal calls to top officials of the steel industry in Washington, Pittsburgh, Youngstown, and Cleveland to ask for supplies.[177] The war tested the Appalachian natural gas indus-try to the limit as the region was the most highly industrialized section of the country. A total of 184 mills in Pittsburgh, Youngstown, Buffalo, and Wheeling, as well as

Peoples Utility Truck — Gas utilities either sold their own gas appliances or built partnerships with appliance dealers to peddle gas-consuming products. Service vehicles of various types were developed for specific jobs. Pictured here is a Peoples Natural Gas Company service truck (courtesy Dominion Peoples).

chemical, metallurgical, carbon black, and rubber plants added up to 660 war factories that used 3 million cubic feet a gas a month.[178] On New Years Day in 1945, the worst gas shortage of the war began in Appalachian region, and there was suspension of service to war producers from West Virginia to the Great Lakes.[179]

Even once hostilities overseas were over, the post-war gas demands were just as great. In 1946, 50,000 new home-heating installations were added in Cleveland, but had to be stopped in 1947 due to the gas shortage.[180] The crisis years of 1947 and 1948 "brought chills to certain Buffalo neighborhoods, and … employees were pelted with brickbats hurled from all directions" recalled NFG President Herb Clay.[181] "The price of coal and oil went up and everybody who could was putting a gas conversion burner in his furnace. We were swamped. There were shortages of steel and pipe and we couldn't get gas even if we had been able to deliver it."[182] Consumers and city and state investigators criticized the utilities for the supply shortage, but the situation was clearly beyond the local companies' control. The New York Public Service Commission in 1948 concluded, as they had seventeen years earlier, that natural gas and manufactured gas should be mixed where feasible to stretch supplies.[183] Clay said, "All of the distributing subsidiaries had to convert themselves from being primarily the suppliers of a premium heating service to upper income families to suppliers of heat for the vast majority of the local populations."[184]

In addition to contending with "famines," gas utility workers regularly battled with the elements to keep customers in service. Gas service employees responded to disruptions caused by floods, tornadoes, cold temperatures, blizzards, labor shortages, and disputes. Flooding posed not only devastating problems for community health and property, but also threatened the heart of gas utility facilities since the pipeline system lies buried in the ground. From washed out roads tearing pipelines apart to submerged customer appliances, when the rivers and creeks overflowed, service workers got busy. The first move for safety purposes was to turn off gas at meters or at the curb, remove water from mains, and make repairs and replace meters, if necessary. Once the water in the line was clear, tanks of inert gas purged the lines. After all lines were checked, service crews lit working customer appliances.

Many floods throughout the twentieth century in Appalachia caused havoc for the region's utilities. The Erie, Pa., flood in 1915 affected service for PGC and took several lives. Gas service, however, was back on the next day. A St. Patrick's Day flood in 1936 caused devastation throughout Pittsburgh and riverside communities in western Pennsylvania and Ohio, claiming more than 150 lives. Oil City, Pa., was particularly susceptible to flooding with ice jams in the Allegheny River. After a 1959 flood affected northwestern Pennsylvania, UNG President James Montgomery wrote to employees in the firm's newsletter: "Such critical occasions bring out the real difference in men ... giving a sterling account of himself and in many cases under the most trying circumstances—around-the-clock vigilance, without sleep or rest, under cold and wet conditions, and on short rations."[185] One of the widest reaching flood events in the region occurred when Hurricane Agnes ravaged the East Coast in 1972. Torrential rains overflowed rivers and streams throughout Pennsylvania and New York, resulting in millions of dollars of damage. In addition to the devastation by Agnes in western Pennsylvania and western New York, eight area utilities rallied to the aid of Pennsylvania Gas and Water Company of Wilkes-Barre, Pa., to restore service to 25,000 customers in the northeastern section of the state.[186]

Bagging a Line — In local low-pressure distribution repair, an East Ohio Gas Company utility worker "bags" a line with an inflated, round leather bag, necessary to stop of the flow of gas in the line so that the coupling can repaired (courtesy Dominion Resources).

The Lake Erie region is known for its "lake-effect" snowstorms, and those living along the lakeshore are familiar with shoulder-high snowdrifts and bitter winter temperatures. However, working in the snow and ice is a significant challenge for gas service crews when the pipeline system is buried below both snow cover and frozen ground. For example, the winter of 1962-63 was the coldest on record since 1919-20 in northwestern Pennsylvania and utilities experienced record gas sendouts as a result. Through it all, due to the diligent effort of gas employees, customers had heat. PGC president Donald Conway said, "Everyone talks about the weather but the Gas Man does something about it."[187]

Paying the Piper— The Gas Bill and the Evolution of Gas Rates

Current utility customer billing and service operations involve computerized records, electronic phone bank systems, and state of the art satellite technology. But when utility offices first opened, they probably resembled the setting of a Charles Dickens novel more than today's computer-intense operations.

In the beginning of customer relations, meter readings and bills were prepared by hand and paying the gas bill was done in person. Iroquois opened its first major office building at 45 Church Street in downtown Buffalo in 1913. Sixteen bookkeepers worked behind a teller's wicket, sitting on tall stools at four twelve-foot long desks. At first, tellers were enclosed in cages, but later the bars were lowered and eventually removed. Bookkeepers communicated with tellers through air tubes from the counter to the desk, much like modern drive-in banks. Papers were stuffed in small bullet-like containers and compressed air forced them to travel. Office workers sorted gas bill stubs from large baskets conveyed from cashiers. Customer accounting was painstakingly, but accurately recorded in four-foot wide Boston ledgers.[188] Employees addressed monthly gas bills by hand until the 1920s when billing machines were introduced.

Perhaps nothing greater draws the ire of natural gas consumers than the subject of increasing gas rates. Customers appreciate and expect safe and reliable service, but their admiration of the utility company fades rapidly when the cost of gas goes up. The first gaslight companies charged for gas by the hour and sometimes by the appliance. Then after the meter was introduced, consumers paid for the gas that was used. In 1903, utility pioneer Henry Doherty introduced the concept of "differential" rates, where a flat charge helps to cover some of the utility's high "fixed" costs.[189] A look back at the history of rates and ratemaking reveals that today's consumers are actually getting a great deal compared to many years ago.

The Fredonia Gas Light & Water Company was the nation's first natural gas corporation and charged $4.00 per thousand cubic feet for illumination in the late 1850s. In comparison, land then cost $2.00 an acre, labor $0.70 per day, tuition at the Fredonia Academy was $4.00 per term, books were priced $0.06 a piece, and a gallon of whiskey was $0.20.[190] In 1868, a Buffalo householder paid $3.75 per thousand cubic feet for low Btu manufactured gas, less a quarter discount if payment was made in bankable money within a certain time. Those costs today adjusted for inflation would be astronomical. Likewise, in 1869, a gas bill from the Niagara Falls Gas Company reveals an average cost of $4.00 per thousand cubic feet for manufactured gas. Sixty-nine years later in 1938, a bill from the Republic Light, Heat & Power Company in Niagara Falls, N.Y., charged an average cost of $0.44 per thousand cubic feet for low Btu artificial gas—89 percent less.

In Pittsburgh in 1884, the cost of natural gas supplied to the city declined from $0.40 to $0.30 per thousand cubic feet, most likely because of the huge supply and competition for business. The *American Gas Light Journal* commented at the time, "This ought to be cheap enough to satisfy anybody."[191] By the beginning of the 1900s, gas ratemaking was controversial as gas companies like the ones controlled by Standard were not in full agreement of what the invisible substance cost to extract from the fields and what its worth was to the customer. Standard leaders like Daniel O'Day and John Bushnell felt prices for natural gas were too low, while Ohio and Pennsylvania gasmen Elizur Strong and Calvin Payne, who saw new urban markets ripe for the picking, resisted increases due to competitive energies and public opinion.[192] The cost of natural gas varied widely between areas that had huge wells at their ready and cities and towns that were far from the gas fields. For example, PGC's rates in 1910 were $0.30 per thousand cubic feet for customers in Sheffield, Clarendon, and Warren, Pa., near its gas wells, and $0.32 further away in Corry and Jamestown, N.Y.[193] More significant, a natural gas customer in the large consumption state of Ohio paid more than 75 percent more for gas than in the gas-rich state of West Virginia.[194]

In the early twentieth century, it was common for customers to receive a discount if they paid their bill within a certain amount of time. Iroquois offered "discount days" on the tenth, twentieth, and thirtieth, and later discount days increased to six per month. On these days, long queues of people would line up all the way out of the utility's office into the street.[195] Many utilities required deposits by renters that ranged from five to twenty dollars depending on the size of the home.[196] These deposits came under fire during the Depression years under the New Deal administration of President Roosevelt. Still, the cost of natural gas did not increase appreciably for years.

Many industrial and residential customers were willing to pay more as long as they could get the natural product. One customer writing to the *Buffalo Courier Express* in 1916 said they were willing to pay even more than $0.35 per thousand cubic feet. "Why cannot the people who are clamoring for natural gas, every one of the 20,000, address a letter to the [New York State] public service commission, demanding that the body raise the rate, so the gas company may be able to pipe more gas into Buffalo, and serve us people who are anxiously praying for the gas?"[197] Another wrote, "If we do have to pay a little more for the gas, I know the army of waiting applicants will only be too glad."[198]

While natural gas rates remained remarkably low to the consumer, East Ohio claimed the cost of bringing in the gas increased 800 percent from 1910 to 1920.[199] Gas shortages prompted higher rates everywhere, also compounded by a large increase in federal corporate income taxes in 1916 that were eventually absorbed by the consumer. For example, East Ohio's natural gas costs jumped from $0.30 per thousand cubic feet in 1917 to $0.57 in 1925.[200] Still, the cost of natural gas increased much less than coal or oil. Despite the required investment to address gas shortages, some com-

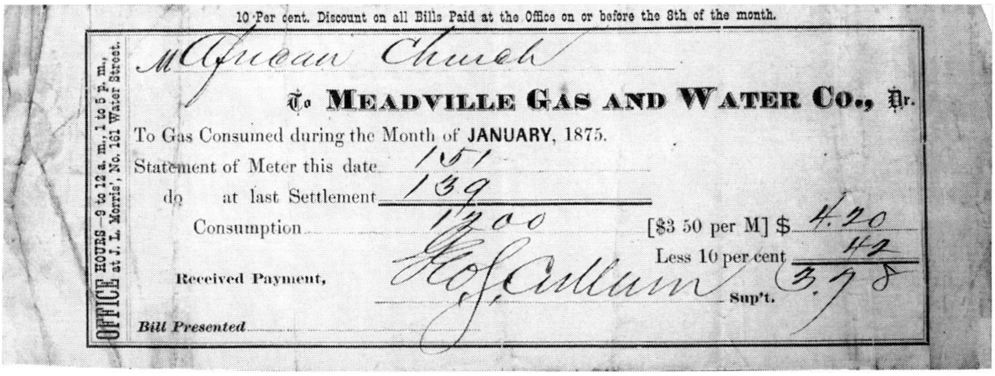

OFFICE HOURS—9 to 12 a. m., 1 to 5 p. m. at J. L. Morris', No. 161 Water Street.

10-Per cent. Discount on all Bills Paid at the Office on or before the 8th of the month.

M African Church

To **MEADVILLE GAS AND WATER CO.,** Dr.

To Gas Consumed during the Month of **JANUARY**, 1875.

Statement of Meter this date *151*

do   at last Settlement *139*

Consumption *1200*   [$3 50 per M] $ *4 20*

Less 10 per cent *42*

Received Payment,   *3 78* Sup't.

Bill Presented

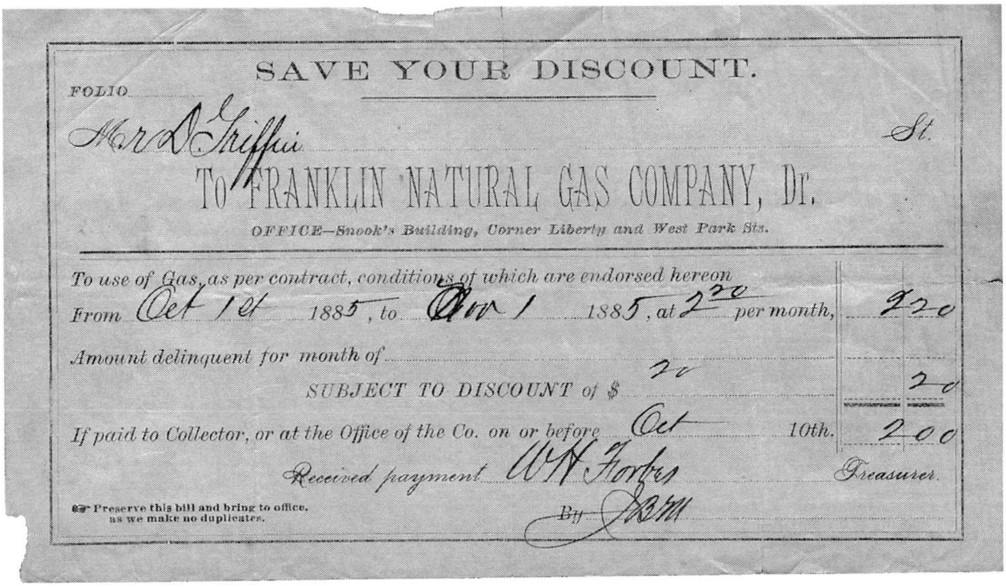

SAVE YOUR DISCOUNT.

FOLIO

Mr D Griffin   St.

To **FRANKLIN NATURAL GAS COMPANY, Dr.**

OFFICE—Snook's Building, Corner Liberty and West Park Sts.

To use of Gas, as per contract, conditions of which are endorsed hereon

From *Oct 1st* 1885, to *Nov 1* 1885, at *2 20* per month, *2 20*

Amount delinquent for month of

SUBJECT TO DISCOUNT of $ *20*   *20*

If paid to Collector, or at the Office of the Co. on or before *Oct* 10th. *2 00*

Received payment *W H Forbes*   Treasurer.

By

Preserve this bill and bring to office, as we make no duplicate.

Early Franklin/Meadville Gas Bills — In the infancy of the natural gas industry, natural gas bills were measured more by pennies than dollars. Shown here is a manufactured gas bill from the Meadville (Pa.) Gas and Water Company from 1875 and a natural gas bill from the Franklin (Pa.) Natural Gas Company in 1885 (courtesy National Fuel Gas Company).

plained that the need for new pipe was no excuse for raising rates. Critics claimed "a major portion of the increase may have been due to price setting behavior of natural gas businesses."[201] One activist newspaper in 1916 complained that Iroquois was earning over 13 percent on its stock while requesting an increase: "During the last cold spell thousands of consumers were subjected to a gas shortage that for days left firesides cheerless and cook stoves without sufficient gas pressure to boil an egg."[202] Likewise, gas consumers in Elmira, N.Y., held a "citizens indignation meeting" in 1923 on the high cost of household gas.[203]

The rate process for gas utilities that served many different municipalities was cumbersome, where local officials could, according to East Ohio president Ralph W. Gallagher in 1923, "pass an ordinance fixing the terms and conditions so drastic that a utility cannot operate at any price."[204] For example, in 1924, rates for various Pennsylvania cities per thousand cubic feet of gas ranged from $0.47 in Butler to $0.53 in Pittsburgh, $0.63 in Beaver Falls, and $0.78 in Warren and Erie.[205] Once state regulatory commissions were formed, consumer objections became high profile events. In 1918 a suit against the People's Gaslight & Coke Company in Buffalo that was opposed to an increase of cost of manufactured gas from $1.20 to $1.65 per thousand cubic feet, accused the rates of being "unjust and unreasonable, excessive, and unlawful."[206]

In a 1926 publication supplied to New York customers by Iroquois, a list of reasons for high gas bills included reminders about weather conditions, billing periods, leaky hot water faucets, usage by guests, etc. In 1926, gas was considered by the company as still "one of the least expensive things in the household budget." [207] The gas rate cost in Buffalo that year amounted to $0.70 per million Btu. This compared to much higher rates for manufactured, or mixed gas in other northern cities such as Boston ($1.90), Brooklyn ($1.90), New York ($1.70), Rochester ($1.40), and Chicago ($1.30).[208] Gas cost increases continued during the Depression years for all users, though prices increased more for residential customers. Residential prices between

Customer Office 1913 — The Iroquois Natural Gas Corporation building in downtown Buffalo in 1913 featured a large lobby with long marble-topped counters and columns, featuring bronze-grilled bank cashier teller cages and an ever-present spittoon for tobacco-chewing patrons. A *Buffalo Commercial Advertiser* newspaper said the office's "beautiful rotunda is like the nave of an ancient Grecian temple" (courtesy National Fuel Gas Company).

1930 and 1940 jumped an average of $0.68 in New York State per thousand cubic feet, $0.64 in Ohio, $0.62 in Pennsylvania, $0.49 in Kentucky, and $0.38 in West Virginia.[209]

In the coming years however, the cost of gas continued to hold a great price advantage over other fuels despite postwar inflation. During the 1940s, the average cost of gas declined, real income increased, and the quality of gas appliances improved.[210] The amount paid to producers in the field price for gas declined from eleven cents per thousand cubic feet in 1922 to a nickel in 1940.[211] After World War II, the cost of operating a gas refrigerator was still only $0.02 per day, and water heaters cost about $0.50 per person per month.[212] In 1948, the increased cost of manufactured gas supplementing natural gas supplies forced many utilities to request rate relief to compensate for past inadequate earnings. "We are unceasingly pursuing the quest for more adequate rates," wrote NFG president Leigh A. Brown in the firm's 1948 annual report.[213] CNG's president J. French Robinson stated in 1953, "Abnormally low prices imposed through regulation have created an uneconomic demand for gas service in many areas." The amount of gas that cost $2.62 in Cleveland amounted to $6.15 in Milwaukee and $8.54 in Brooklyn.[214] Likewise, gas continued to enjoy a steep advantage over other fuels. Estimates of annual costs of heating a home in Buffalo in 1956 totaled $130.22 for gas, $179.57 for fuel oil, $214.20 for anthracite coal, and $255 for coke.[215]

Overall, the cost of gas and service remained stable in the mid–1960s, but eventually inflation caused more rate cases in the latter part of the decade. Still, by 1970, residential natural gas rates had not increased significantly in Appalachia in sixty years. While the residential consumption of natural gas also remained approximately the same, since 1910 the cost per thousand cubic feet (measured in deflated 1970 dollars) had only increased 19 percent in Pennsylvania, 14 percent in New York, 24 percent in West Virginia, and actually decreased 14 percent in Ohio.[216] Rate cases would follow for all utilities in the region in the early 1970s due to higher supply costs and economic decline in rust-belt cities like Cleveland, Youngstown, Wheeling, Pittsburgh, and Buffalo. In addition, state utility gross receipts taxes imposed on gas utility bills increased with the cost of gas, compounding the problem. The teetering economy and energy shortages of the 1970s led a counter-consumer activist movement to attack the closest and most familiar targets: utilities. Public hearings on rate requests became good fodder for groups of irate senior citizens and self-appointed utility rate activists. Suddenly, after years of wearing the "White Hats" and bringing a desirable product to an eager public at an extremely low cost, all utilities were suddenly perceived by many of their customers as iniquitous corporations bent on bleeding consumers dry. Militant consumer activists picketed the homes of gas company executives in Cleveland and protesters in Buffalo hung effigies of executives in public protests.

The Regulators — The Ultimate Board of Directors

State agencies have jurisdiction over pricing by utility companies located within its state for gas and delivery service. Ratemaking for utilities has been both an art and a science, with price regulation designed to serve in the free market's stead. Due to the traditional "natural monopoly" status of utilities, much of this regulation is an essential part of insuring the safe and reliable delivery of energy to customers at the lowest possible cost. Also, gas utilities have large fixed capital costs in their pipeline systems that must be adequately funded. Therefore, government regulators are charged to balance both utility and consumer interests. But by essentially controlling the rates of return of utility and pipeline operations, the regulators function as "the ultimate board of directors" by determining what limit of profit these enterprises have the opportunity to achieve.

Early manufactured gas companies secured charters to serve in communities and were granted franchises to serve their product in an exclusive service area, and sometimes by regulated rates by the local governing body.[217] But since natural gas supply crossed community and often state lines, these approaches were not effective and some were corrupt.[218] Though some form of regulation dates back to the first manufactured gaslight company in Baltimore in 1817, modern regulation began in the early 1900s. New York's Public Service Commission formed in 1907, the first such regulatory agency in the nation. Ohio formed its Public Utility Commission in 1911. Natural gas companies in Pennsylvania have been regulated since 1913, initially by the Pennsylvania Public Service Commission. Pennsylvania public utility law was revamped in 1937 with the creation of the Public Utility Commission to regulate the rates and actions of the state's non-government public utilities. West Virginia's Public Service Commission was created in 1913 to regulate railroads, toll bridges, and ferries, and eventually expanded to natural gas and electricity. In 1920, the Kentucky legislature placed natural gas companies under the regulatory supervision of the state's Railroad Commission. These regulatory bodies granted expansions to public utility service, afforded "just and reasonable" rates for consumers, developed accounting standards, regulated the quality of natural gas, ensured safe, adequate service by utilities, and provided an opportunity for the regulated firms to earn a rate of return on their property.

In the early stages of the state commissions, the utility industry was not severely regulated, as the expansion of gas, electric, and telephone service was vastly improving the American quality of life. But as utility costs escalated, the public demanded more from its regulators. In the 1950s, the length of time it took for state regulators to adjudicate new utility rates ranged from three months to more than a year. The A.G.A. claimed the two major problems of the industry were maintenance of adequate financial rate of return and the regulatory lag of federal and state commissions.[219] As the cost of purchased gas from interstate pipelines increased in the 1950s, state regulators permitted utilities to use "Purchased Gas Cost" rate schedules or surcharges for adjustment to compensate for gas cost changes outside the utility company's control. Still, until the 1990s, virtually all of the gas sold to residential and small commercial customers was under regulated retail rates.

Another major issue in utility rate cases is fairness among customer classes. In the early years of the natural gas business, industrial customers were able to secure large gas supplies at relatively low cost by forming their own energy subsidiary and laying their own pipelines to gas fields. While the average cost of natural gas in the United States for residential customers rose from $0.38 per thousand cubic feet to

$0.62 during the 1920s, industrial costs fell from $0.17 to $0.12.[220] Correspondingly, usage among residential customers dropped while industrial use jumped 200 percent.[221] The disparity between customer classes was an issue discussed during the consideration and passage of the NGA of 1938, as critics contended that residential customers were subsidizing the industrial group.[222] Later in the century, however, state utility commissions shielded the residential class of customers, while allowing industrial rates to rise. However, residential customers had high seasonal demands, requiring high fixed costs of transmission of gas and storage, and industrial customer demand was relatively steady. Therefore, industrial customer classes often subsidized a portion of distribution costs of residential rate classes through government-approved tariffs. As competition from a deregulated environment and "self-help" wells threatened utilities' industrial sales, changes in cost distribution occurred, increasing the consumption rates for residential customers, and in some cases, creating a basic customer charge even if no gas was used.

Although regulation of "natural monopolies" seems necessary, some claim that continued federal and state regulations only add to utility rates. For example, industry researcher Paul MacAvoy asserts that utility costs could be cut 20 percent if federal and state regulation on the natural gas industry was eliminated.[223]

From Sea to Shining Sea — The Natural Gas Age

The great new gas supply from the Southwest in the 1950s not only inaugurated a new epoch in the Appalachian gas industry, but also, by 1957, spread the product to every state in the nation except Maine and Vermont.[224] Until that time, wood in the South, coal in the North, and fuel oil on the East Coast were the primary space heating sources.[225] The meteoric expansion of the market throughout the United States mirrored the brisk growth of natural gas service in the Appalachian region a half century before, increasing 84 percent. Due to the large number of gas conversions and the addition of major cities' access to natural gas between 1950 and 1960, the number of residential customers increased 337 percent in New York, 35 percent in Ohio, and 25 percent in Pennsylvania.[226] In addition, natural gas availability in the Northeast finished off the manufactured gas industry for good. New interstate pipelines converted the former "regional resource" into one of the nation's largest industries. Natural gas had come of age. After years of working in oil's shadow, by the 1950s, petroleum's long overlooked stepsister was ready to go to the energy ball.

EIGHT

Expansion, Crisis, and Recovery

*Appalachia and America
in the Late Twentieth Century*

"It is far from easy to determine whether [Nature] has proved to man a kind parent or a merciless stepmother."
— Pliny the Elder [Gaius Plinius Secundus, A.D. 23–79]

"Natural gas has a strange history — abhorred as a nuisance for many years, cherished later ... constantly undervalued in the marketplace for its virtues ... and a fugitive from justice whenever it crossed state lines."[1]
— Edgar Wesley Owen

Demand Up, Supply Down

By the mid-twentieth century, natural gas was no longer an uncommon, under-utilized fuel in the United States. Interstate pipelines broadened the gas market throughout various parts of the country, which suddenly recognized the value of the clean blue flame to which the Appalachian region did not give a second thought. In fact, according to industry researchers, natural gas was closing the gap with its dominant fossil fuel partner — oil: "Natural gas, natural gasoline, and natural gas liquids, long a stepchild of the mainstem of the industry, also loomed as both a supplement and a threat to the existing industry patterns of supply and demand."[2] Gas from the Southwest addressed the postwar supply shortage, but there seemed no limit to demand. All gas sales at Appalachian natural gas distributors were at record levels by the late 1950s, and the industry rapidly expanded to new communities. Statewide trade groups actively promoted the fuel, representing gas producers and utilities. Geologists formed the Appalachian Geological Society in 1931. The West Virginia Oil and Natural Gas Association formed in 1915 to represent industry interests, and later in 1959, the Independent Oil and Gas Association of West Virginia organized. The Kentucky Oil and Gas Association formed in eastern Kentucky in the late 1920s, representing various Bluegrass State energy firms, and merged with a similar organization in western Kentucky in 1930. The Kentucky Gas Association formed in 1967. The

Gas Flambeau — Appalachian gas companies extended service to many more rural towns and hamlets in the late 1950s and '60s. A huge flambeau was often lit during the expansion ceremonies (courtesy National Fuel Gas Company).

trade group Ohio Oil and Gas Association formed from two separate organizations representing oil and gas firms in 1947. Gas interests are now represented by the Ohio Gas Association. In 1963, Pennsylvania gas utilities formed their own association, the Pennsylvania Gas Association (an earlier group existed called the Pennsylvania Natural Gas Men's Association). It later merged with electric utilities in the 1990s into the Energy Association of Pennsylvania. New York gas utilities and pipeline companies organized the New York Gas Group in 1973, and that organization merged with the New England Gas Association (founded in 1926) to form the Northeast Gas Association in 2003. The Independent Oil and Gas Association of New York, representing gas producers, formed in 1980.

According to the *Minerals Yearbook*, growth in the Appalachian states between 1925 and 1975 kept Ohio, Pennsylvania, and New York among the highest in total natural gas customers across the United States even though natural gas usage was rapidly spreading in other areas of the country:

Year	Leading States	No. of Customers
1925	Ohio	1,094,120
	Pennsylvania	582,520

Year	Leading States	No. of Customers
	New York	222,750
	West Virginia	167,070
	Kentucky	130,780
1935	California	1,451,000
	Ohio	1,216,000
	Pennsylvania	674,000
	New York	396,000
	West Virginia	181,000
	Kentucky	166,000
1955	New York	4,155,000
	Ohio	1,896,000
	Pennsylvania	1,894,000
1975	California	6,181,000
	New York	3,810,000
	Ohio	2,559,000
	Pennsylvania	2,160,000

Source: From *Minerals Yearbook*, various years.[3]

In its first century of existence, the Appalachian natural gas industry faced the operational challenges of extending pipeline systems, marketing its new product to a public who used other energy sources, and acquiring suitable supplies to meet the rapidly escalating demand. The building of the young industry depended upon the brains and brawn of natural gas explorers, the skills and sweat of pipeline constructors, and the ingenuity of engineers. During the first half of the twentieth century, natural gas was still inexpensive in comparison to other fuels. But rough times were on the horizon. In addition to higher prices, the latter part of the twentieth century added the necessity of negotiating through the legal labyrinth of government regulation to not just thrive, but survive.

Déjà vu All Over Again — The 1970s Energy Crisis and Deregulation

As the need for the new Southwest supplies grew, new federal regulations designed to protect the consumer from excessive rates sowed the seeds of a major American natural gas shortage. A tortuous battle over deregulation began first with the production segment of the natural gas industry. In the late 1940s, there were legislative attempts to shield independent gas producers from regulation, though state regulators and cities opposed it.[4] Independent exemptions were supported by influential legislators such as chairman of the U.S. Senate Subcommittee on Interstate and Foreign Commerce and future president, Lyndon B. Johnson (D-Tx.), but President Truman, who warned of "large windfall profits" for producers, rejected one particular bill.[5] In a case involving East Ohio, the FPC ruled that a natural gas distributor selling gas that moves interstate was subject to federal control. Though the U.S. Court of Appeals ruled that East Ohio was not covered by the turbid language of the NGA of 1938, the Supreme Court in East Ohio Gas Co. v. Federal Power Commission reversed the lower court's decision.[6] Though the industry hoped for a new era of less activist FPC regulation with the election of Republican Dwight D. Eisenhower in 1952, it was not to be. The U.S. Supreme Court's 1954 Phillips Petroleum v. Wisconsin decision, which determined that Congress meant to control the price of natural gas by the NGA of 1938, led to federal wellhead price regulations on interstate natural gas, rather than relying on market forces to manage the price. The Supreme Court's interpretation of the "ambiguously worded [and] highly discretionary" law was, in the industry's view, a "tremendous expansion of the act's jurisdiction."[7] Intrastate prices (for gas bought and sold within the same state), however, were not regulated by the action. Therefore, the low price offered for interstate gas provided little incentive to drill for more supplies, but at the same time encouraged consumers to use more gas.[8] According to one gas industry official, the southwestern producers' reaction to regulation was, "I'll sit on the gas for ten years before I let the boys in Washington tell me what I can sell it for."[9] In congressional testimony, political leaders from major Appalachian cities, including Pittsburgh, Cleveland, Cincinnati, Youngstown, Buffalo, Syracuse, and Louisville supported the Court's decision, while others from Southwest producing areas opposed it.[10] A legislative attempt to deregulate the industry came close to passage in the Presidential election year of 1956 with the Harris-Fulbright natural gas bill, which provided exemption from federal regulation for independent producers of gas. Though President Eisenhower supported the concept, after reports of the attempted bribery of a U.S. Senator by the Superior Oil Company, Eisenhower vetoed the measure because it risked the integrity of the governmental process.[11] As a result, the foundation was laid for a massive natural gas shortage in the United States as below-market pricing discouraged drilling.

Soon, new supplies dwindled, while demand did not let up. In the late 1960s, CNG told federal officials it blamed the Phillips decision for its inability to secure more long-term gas supplies. By 1968, for the first time, the country's natural gas consumption was larger than the nation's gas reserves. Industry researcher Paul MacAvoy wrote that the gas industry regulations were a "welfare" policy of redistributing income to keep prices low for the consumer, and ended up hurting more than helping by restricting gas exploration.[12] The legal and political struggle between natural gas producing and consuming regions continued for two decades after the Phillips decision, culminating in the 1970s energy crisis.

By 1973, the looming energy shortage was a political football in Washington. In a speech to the annual A.G.A. convention in San Francisco in 1973, NFG Chairman and CEO Herb Clay told executives: "The nation can no longer afford the luxury of endless debate on its critical energy problems.... It wasn't so long ago that we were told that if we wanted to improve our marketing activities, we would have to learn to think like a customer. Now if we want to anticipate our problems, we will have to learn to think like a regulator or a Congressman."[13] To compound the problem, in October of that year, the Arab oil embargo hit the pot-bellied, energy-consuming United States in the gut. The price of oil escalated four-fold. Meanwhile, the Appalachian gas industry, experiencing curtailments of gas by the major interstate pipeline firms, knew that customer demand for their product far exceeded available supply coming from the Southwest. Federal- and state-mandated moratoriums on gas hookups followed, and utilities added conservation education to the responsibilities of their sales forces to temper demand.

Gas firms sought non-traditional supplies of synthetic gas from coal and oil, and imported LNG from Africa. CNG and Columbia Gas purchased LNG from ocean tankers traveling from the Hassi R'Mel fields in the Sahara desert in Algeria as well as Venezuela to help ease the gas supply crunch. Natural gas cooled to cryogenic temperatures of -260° F reduced the volume and liquefied the gas, enabling transportation across oceans through specially designed tankers.[14] CNG purchased some of the LNG at Cove Point, Maryland, on the Chesapeake Bay, at a facility operated by CNG and Columbia. U.S. natural gas companies built a total of four marine LNG terminals between 1971 and 1980. The United States received a peak receipt volume of 253 billion cubic feet of LNG in 1979, 1.3 percent of the nation's demand.[15]

Efforts to drill for domestic gas on the Atlantic Outer Continental Shelf — the subsoil and sea bed natural resources there claimed for the United States through a proclamation by President Harry Truman in 1945 — entered the early leasing phase, but citizen groups and various coastal states opposed to drilling challenged it in the courts. A federal and state moratorium on offshore drilling followed. An effort to create a synthetic fuels subsidy program lost in the U.S. House of Representatives by one vote and a natural gas deregulation bill went down by four votes. Industry leaders claimed that only the end of the federally regulated wellhead price system installed a score of years before would cure the industry's ills. The FPC Order 770 proposed

Conservation — The 1970s was a decade of natural gas shortages, rising prices, and a huge push by utilities for energy conservation by their customers to survive the crisis (courtesy National Fuel Gas Company).

to significantly increase the prices paid to gas producers in 1976 and allow annual escalations, but this was only a partial step toward deregulation. It was too little, too late.

The winter of 1976-77 was perhaps one of the most challenging that the Appalachian natural gas firms and their employees ever faced. The season was one of savage weather throughout the United States, with brutal winds and record snowfall. The cold snap was nationwide except the far West, and natural gas was diverted from the Rocky Mountain and Pacific Coast regions, saving the rest of nation from disaster. But schools and factories closed throughout the country, causing tremendous economic hardship. The nation's new president, Jimmy Carter, who had first supported gas decontrol in his campaign, reversed his position once elected. Carter declared the "moral equivalent of war" on the country's energy situation, and presented dozens of proposals to Congress, including the creation of a new Department of Energy. After much political haggling, the following year Congress passed a new energy policy to attempt to solve the natural gas shortage by augmenting supply through the Natural Gas Policy Act (NGPA) of 1978 and lessening demand by the Power Plant and Industrial Fuels Act, known as the Fuel Use Act (FUA).[16] The NGPA removed price differences between intrastate and interstate gas and provided producer incentives for hard to find deep "tight-sands" gas. The FUA discouraged use of natural gas in industrial boilers, requiring lower-priced gas to be steered to residential consumers while the higher-cost gas was directed to industry.[17] In addition, regulation of the interstate natural gas industry fell to the newly created Federal Energy Regulatory Commission (FERC), formed from the FPC.

However, 1979 was another dark one for the United States energy picture. The Iranian Revolution led to more petroleum price hikes and oil shortages, the Three Mile Island nuclear plant accident outside Harrisburg, Pa., periled the nuclear industry, and Clean Air Act requirements and mining restrictions hindered use of the United States' abundant coal supply. NFG President and CEO Louis Reif said federal leaders for the first time recognized the importance of natural gas and its role in the country's energy future. This was a "complete reversal of the governments longstanding attitude in favor of an all electric economy and its feeling that gas was a declining industry."[18] Consequently, natural gas, once again, became the "darling" of American basic energies.

The NGPA and FUA were designed to provide incentive pricing, deregulate some categories of natural gas, and restrict certain usage. The policy was a confusing mixture of twenty-six different categories of gas, including old gas, new gas, deep gas, and offshore gas, with some prices controlled, and some decontrolled. The NGPA was certainly not perfect, but it stimulated additional gas finds. The supply crisis eased a bit during the next couple of years, as both higher prices increased supply and energy conservation and an economic recession tempered demand. By 1980, the nation increased its gas reserves, and the supply problems of the 1970s were reversing.

Full deregulation in the 1980s put market forces to work. As of January 1, 1985, 60 percent of all gas sold nationally was free of price controls and another 15 percent was below ceiling prices. As a consequence of reduced consumer demand and increased supply, a gas surplus "bubble" drove prices down. Congress later passed the Natural Gas Wellhead Decontrol Act in 1989 allowing the remainder of FERC regulation of producer sales of natural gas to be eliminated gradually until full decontrol took effect in 1993. According to economist Robert Bradley, the long era of natural gas price regulation led to numerous ills, among which were higher taxpayer costs, encouragement of higher cost gas production, discouragement of conservation, gas shortages, high energy prices, and market disorder. Bradley asserted, "Neither the goal of protecting consumers or the goal of inciting producers has been achieved by price regulation and accompanying interventions."[19]

Take-or-Pay and Interstate Pipeline Deregulation

After deregulation of producer prices, the federal government then turned its sights on the second leg of the natural gas industry — interstate pipelines. The basic intent was to transform the interstate pipeline business from its job as wholesaler of natural gas (buying supplies and reselling them downstream to utilities) to merely a "transporter" of gas. Some utility markets were only served by one interstate pipeline, and there were worries that pipelines held too much market power.[20] But the biggest obstacle to interstate pipeline deregulation was the fact that most producers, pipelines, and utilities were tangled in long-term contracts for gas supplies. In order to generate the long-term supply, especially after the energy crisis in the 1970s, pipelines were saddled with "take-or-pay" contracts that required them to accept a minimum level of gas from the producers or pay for it anyway. Take-or-pay was a common element in long-term wellhead gas supply arrangements to compensate producers for providing the buyer with a stipulated delivery capability. Take-or-pay in turn converted into minimum bill requirements that utilities paid pipelines. But this caused the regulated price at the city gate to be too high to pass on to customers.[21]

Natural gas pipelines historically were not common carriers, as pipelines performed a broker function between producers and end-users. The pipeline industry sought voluntary, rather than mandatory, contract carriage on pipelines and reduction of take-or-pay contracts that burdened pipelines with costs they could not pass on to customers. The industry also wanted repeal of the FUA that restricted use of gas in large boilers. Congress eventually repealed both the FUA and "incremental pricing" of gas in 1987. Getting the pipelines out of the gas buying business, however, would result in breaking those legal contracts, the cost of which the FERC estimated to be $7 billion.[22] The question was: who would be hit with shrapnel created when the traditional pipeline structure was blown apart?

Due to an improved supply picture and lower demand, pipelines could not market the high-priced gas they had to purchase under the contracts. While the FERC allowed utilities to ultimately renege on minimum bills, it placed the pipelines on verge of financial ruin.[23] For example, Columbia Gas Transmission was forced to file for Chapter 11 bankruptcy in 1991 due to its take-or-pay liability (it would reemerge in 1995). After much regulatory involvement on the state level, most utilities and their customers shouldered part of the burden of prudently incurred take-or-pay surcharges passed on by the downstream pipelines.

The FERC issued a series of Orders (436, 451, 500, and 636) that gradually deregulated the industry. The federal actions required interstate pipeline companies to unbundle, or separate, their sales and transportation services to most customers and provide gas supply, gathering, transportation, and storage as discrete services. In the end, the FERC intended to create deregulation and competition within the industry by causing pipeline suppliers to restructure their purchase contracts. With a few exceptions, the interstate pipeline system avoided any major physical shortages or constraints in supply. The creation of a natural gas futures markets in the 1990s and complex trading on electronic bulletin boards became the order of the day as the century turned. Unfortunately, the gas "bank" and electricity accounting scandals that erupted during the rise and fall of the miscreant energy firm Enron in the early 2000s would result in a federal legislative and regulatory clampdown on how energy was traded.

Caveat Emptor — "Customer Choice" and the Future of Service

The third and final stage of deregulation has trickled down to the individual consumer. After years of being criticized as a "monopoly," the 1990s resulted in competition and choice in the utility arena, as deregulation reached the state level. Beginning in the late 1970s and early 1980s, some utilities permitted large industrial and commercial customers to transport their own purchased natural gas through utility lines. A little more than a decade later, a move was made to make the same choice available to residential customers. For example, the New York PSC approved a rate design in 1995 instructing all New York utilities to "unbundle" their services and offer market-based rates to residential customers, if appropriate. In Pennsylvania, a legislative approach required utilities to offer supplier choice. Other Appalachian states followed suit. In these choice programs, the delivery of natural gas remained the responsibility of the utility, but customers were offered a choice to buy their supply of gas directly from a producer or marketer. In addition, some local communities passed referendums allowing for municipal aggregation of gas supply. As of March 2000, twenty-three states and the District of Columbia implemented choice programs that allowed retail customers unbundled options comparable to large industrial customers.[24] Despite aggressive programs in states such as California and New York, the excitement of competition over natural gas supplies soon waned among independent suppliers as the potential for profit did not materialize. Nationwide in 2000, only 4 percent of residential customers eligible to participate in such programs chose to do so.[25] Participation in such programs for both natural gas and electricity grew steadily since.

Most Appalachian state utility commissions or legislatures implemented some type of gas supply "competition" program, with varying degrees of success. According to A.G.A. in 2000, 96 percent of gas consumed by industrial facilities could be purchased from multiple suppliers; 69 percent of all natural gas used in commercial facilities was available for purchase under a "customer choice" option; and nearly half of U.S. households with natural gas service would soon have the opportunity to purchase gas from a supplier other than the local utility. Still, since utilities did not earn a profit on the purchase price of natural gas, but only on its transportation, most states have been unable to demonstrate what residential consumers gain as a result.[26] Also, as the "customer choice" concept spread across the United States, utilities were perceived as the "supplier of last resort," which saddled them with potentially burdensome costs, including payment-troubled customers. Still, most utilities supported the concept in general for a more competitive environment.

Eat or Be Eaten — Consolidation in the Appalachian Natural Gas Industry

The 1990s brought massive consolidation throughout the United States energy industry, including natural gas companies. Both gas and electric utilities experienced a rash of mergers during the decade to "cut costs, spread expenses, and increase profits."[27] Much like a century before where Standard and other major holding companies combined local energy concerns into integrated regional networks, the modern merger movement linked together regional energy networks into Goliath-sized corporations that Rockefeller and his ilk would envy.

Takeovers in the interstate pipeline system that involved Appalachia included The Williams Companies' acquiring of TRANSCO in 1995; El Paso Corporation purchasing Tennessee, making it North America's largest pipeline system in 1994; and Duke Energy buying Texas Eastern.

Although the Columbia System was already one of the largest integrated natural gas systems in the country, in 2000 it grew even larger. NiSource and Columbia Energy Group completed a $6 billion merger, and is currently the second largest natural gas distributor in the nation. NiSource's ten distribution companies then served 3.6 million gas and electric customers primarily in nine states, including Maryland, Virginia, Indiana, Massachusetts, New Hampshire, and Maine. Columbia Gas of Ohio, headquartered in Columbus, now serves 1 million of Ohio's approximately 3 million natural gas customers, the state's largest natural gas utility. The firm's primary markets include Columbus, Toledo, Parma, Mansfield, and Springfield, but it also provides service to sixty-four of Ohio's eighty-eight counties spreading across approximately 25,400 square miles.[28] Columbia Gas of Kentucky serves 140,000 customers in the Bluegrass State, primarily in the cities of Lexington, Ashland, Winchester and Frankfort.[29] Columbia Gas of Pennsylvania, which moved its headquarters from Pittsburgh to Canonsburg, Pa., in 2004, serves 41,000 customers in the Keystone State.

Much of the CNG system (including Peoples, Hope, and East Ohio) became part of Dominion Resources (Dominion), headquartered in Richmond, Virginia, one of the nation's largest producers and transporters of electricity and gas. Dominion later sold Peoples to the private investment firm SteelRiver Infrastructure Fund North America LP in 2010 and the headquarters returned to Pittsburgh. Dominion Hope provides gas service for more than 113,000 customers in 439 communities throughout thirty-two West Virginia counties.[32] Dominion East Ohio serves 1.2 million customers in 400 eastern and western Ohio communities.[33] Elsewhere in Ohio, CG&E, now part of Cinergy after merging with Indiana's largest electric utility, PSI Energy, Inc., in 1994, serves 500,000 gas customers, primarily in Ohio.[34]

Energy East, a "super regional energy services and delivery company" that served more than 2.9 million electric and gas customers (31 percent natural gas) in 2004, controls New York utilities NYSEG and RG&E.[35] NYSEG serves approximately 250,000 natural gas customers and 830,000 electricity customers across a wide area of upstate New York.[36] RG&E provides electricity and natural gas to approximately 650,000 residents and businesses in a nine-county region centering around Rochester.[37]

In Kentucky, Louisville Gas and Electric merged with KU Energy Corporation in 1998, another Kentucky firm first formed in 1912, becoming one of the leading marketers of gas and electricity in the nation.[38] The firm, acquired by PPL Corporation of Pennsylvania in 2010, now serves around 312,000 natural gas customers in a 700 square mile service area.[39] The Atmos Energy Corporation, the largest natural gas–only distributor in the United States, acquired Western Kentucky Gas Company, and now has 3.2 million customers spread over twelve states.[40]

Other Appalachian firms, including Buffalo's NFG and Pittsburgh's Equitable, remain independent, publicly traded firms. From its original eight companies in 1902, NFG merged with or acquired certain assets of hundreds of gas companies throughout the northwestern Pennsylvania and western New York region over the next century.[41] In 1974, dissolving the near century-long names of United Natural Gas Company, Pennsylvania Gas Company, and Iroquois Gas Corporation, NFG merged the subsidiaries into one utility regulated by state governments in New York and Pennsylvania, and one interstate pipeline subsidiary regulated by the federal government.[42] In 2003, the integrated natural gas company served approximately 728,000 retail and transportation customers in western New York and northwestern Pennsylvania.[43]

Equitable Gas continued to develop its gas fields in three states and invested in its interstate pipeline system that is in relatively close proximity to major Atlantic Coast markets. Though the company's utility division was hard hit during the rollback of the steel industry in Pittsburgh in the 1980s, Equitable's exploration subsidiary expanded its oil and gas production among its extensive Appalachian fields.[44] The firm changed its name to Equitable Resources, Inc., in 1984, and changed again to EQT in 2009. As of 2011, Equitable's utility division provided natural gas distribution service to more than 275,000 customers in Pittsburgh and southwestern Pennsylvania, as well as a few areas in northern West Virginia, and conducts field line sales in eastern Kentucky.[45]

No Place Like Home— The Quest for New Appalachian Gas Supplies

Though interstate gas provides the lion's share of the supply for Appalachian gas firms today, drilling in the region's backyard is still active. Rising natural gas and oil prices, along with more improvements in drilling technology, encouraged more energy exploration in Appalachia in the late 1970s and early '80s, reversing years of decline. For example, during the 1970s energy crisis that increased the cost of gas, Pennsylvania natural gas production rose from nearly 74 billion cubic feet in 1972, to 97 billion cubic feet by 1980.[46] The flurry of drilling activity in 1980 also included 100 old-time "Spudder" cable-tool rigs operated among the modern rotary equipment in southeastern Ohio and West Virginia.[47]

By the 1970s, there was a reduction in West Virginia deep drilling productive wells in the so-called Newburg, Huntersville, Tuscarora, and Oriskany sands, although gas drilling in Cambrian Age sand reached 14,300 feet with good results. However, shallow drilling continued during that period in mostly Mississippian Big Injun sands (the most common in West Virginia), and other formations such as Devonian Shale, a rock formation of organic rich clay that William Hart drilled through to sink the first natural gas well in Fredonia, N.Y., in 1821.[48] In the late 1970s, the federal Department of Energy (DOE) and the Gas Research Institute cooperated to look for more shale gas.[49] The Upper Devonian shales contained much "dry" gas and no oil at varying depths extending from the Lake Erie shoreline in northern Ohio to West Virginia and Kentucky.[50] This gas-producing territory, which included 400,000 acres in southwestern West Virginia, 600,000 in eastern Kentucky, and lesser acreage in southern Ohio, previously did not get a lot of attention.[51] In New York State in 1978, NFG experimented with its first test of Devonian black shale from core samples with the DOE. Geologists believed the shales contained large quantities of gas, but were uncertain whether they could be extracted. The Eastern Gas Shales project evaluated reserves and worked on devising a method of stimulating rocks to yield commercial quantities. No significant production was achieved, however, due to the high cost of extraction and low natural gas prices during this period. In the early 2000s, despite another period of low prices, new technology would result in a revolution in the Appalachian shale natural gas industry (discussed in detail in Chapter Nine).

Coalbed methane, previously vented from coalmines for safety reasons, is another potential source for supplies. For example, during 1972, 8.8 billion cubic feet of gas was vented into the atmosphere from just four mines in Green and Washington counties in Pennsylvania.[52] In Wetzel County, W.Va., coalbed gas was found as early as 1905 in the Big Run field, and in 1955 in the Pine Grove field. This led to later experiments of gas recovery from coal formations.[53]

As the 1970s energy supply crisis subsided and the price of gas escalated, many industries considered drilling their own gas wells to provide their energy. Many self-help wells were sunk, affecting utility gas sales. NGPA "Tight Sands" incentive gas pricing created a massive gas drilling

1970s Gas Well — As natural gas prices increased in the 1970s, drilling in the Appalachian region picked up once again (courtesy Dominion Peoples).

boom in Ohio in the Clinton/Medina and Berea sands and Ohio shale in Appalachia.[54] Ohio's gas drilling industry peaked in 1984 before the price of gas collapsed. Despite the large price increases through the early 1980s due to the adjustment to market prices, between 1922 and 1993, the average U.S. real price for natural gas (adjusted for inflation) paid to producers only increased from $0.95 to $2.11 per thousand cubic feet.[55]

The boom and bust cycle in energy significantly turned in 1986 when both oil and gas prices dropped 40 percent. As a result, drilling in the Appalachian basin became severely depressed resulting in difficult times for the regional drilling industry for several years. By 1986, Pennsylvania had 27,600 wells, with 1,000 to 2,000 wells drilled a year, producing a total of 163 billion cubic feet of gas in 1987.[56] However, it would take more and more drilling just to keep up the pace as most wells were highly productive, but short-lived. The shallow Upper Devonian wells in the region from 500 to 5,000 feet deep produced half their capacity in the first five years of production.[57] In addition to the weak prices in the later part of the decade, changing laws and regulations regarding permitting and plugging natural gas wells (which began in Pennsylvania as far back as 1878), as well as disposing of brine collected during gas production, affected the costs borne by the drilling industry.

Another deeper drilling category that received attention was the Silurian Bass Islands trend, which produced large quantities of oil and natural gas, mostly in western New York.[58] Other efforts to find new supplies included shallow Devonian development in northwestern Pennsylvania; Medina sands in western New York, and Mississippian sands in West Virginia. The Mountain State continues to lead in Appalachian gas drilling, producing 180 billion cubic feet of gas in 2002, followed by 157 billion cubic feet in Pennsylvania, 103 billion cubic feet in Ohio, 86 billion cubic feet in Kentucky, and 36 billion cubic feet in New York.[59]

By 2002, more than 40 trillion cubic feet of gas was produced from more than 1,000 gas fields in New York, Pennsylvania, Ohio, West Virginia, Maryland, Kentucky, Virginia, and Tennessee.[60] Appalachia remained an area of potential reserves, but there was little incentive to drill despite the availability of millions of acres of gas leases throughout the Appalachian region. That changed somewhat beginning in 2001 when wellhead prices quadrupled due to high demand and low supply. Since the thousands of shallow Appalachian wells provided low productivity, traditional drilling activity targeted gas prospects in deeper formations (e.g., depths of 6,500 to 11,000 feet in the Trenton–Black River group, one of the most popular strata in the continental United States).

Despite the vast unconventional reserves in deep rock formations below Appalachia that geologists supposed held plenty of hydrocarbons, conventional wisdom concluded that without astronomically high gas prices, there was no way to economically produce them. Just a few short years into the new century, both the unheard of projections of possible reserves and the economics of extraction made "unconventional" wisdom the new school of thought. The age of natural gas shale had arrived.

NINE

Back to the Future
Appalachia and the Marcellus Shale

"This was, O stranger, once Rome's star divine,
Claudius Marcellus of an ancient line;
To fight her wars seven times her consul made,
Low in the dust her enemies he laid."
                    Marcus Claudius Marcellus (d. 208 B.C.E.)— Plutarach[1]

"Yeah, well, history is gonna change."
                    — Marty McFly (*Back to the Future*, Universal Pictures, 1985)

In the first decade of the twenty-first century, periodic natural gas price spikes pinched the pocketbooks of American consumers due to a supply/demand imbalance, exacerbated by corporate malfeasance, unrest in oil producing nations, military conflicts, severe weather, and increased demands of cleanly generated electricity. Peaking natural gas costs crippled the California electricity market in 2000 and price manipulation shenanigans led to the downfall of energy-trading chimeras such as Enron in 2001.[2] Demand-induced concerns and frantic energy trading caused natural gas wellhead prices to quadruple in early 2001 only to collapse months later. Though it did not impact prices considerably, the September 11, 2001 terrorist attacks on the United States and the wars in Iraq and Afghanistan brought uncertainty into the oil markets and the natural gas prices that tracked them. Civil and political unrest in Venezuela and Nigeria led to short-term energy price shocks.[3] Gasoline prices jumped again in 2005, the victim of Gulf Coast supply interruptions from hurricanes Katrina and Rita. Resurging economic activity and warmer-than-average summers hiking demand for gas-fired electric generation crimped natural gas stocks and resulted in roller coaster prices. The capricious cycle repeated in 2008 when oil prices surged upward. Industries such as chemical and fertilizer production, whose feedstock fuel natural gas totaled up to three-fourths of their costs, scaled back production or shut down. The two-decade long surplus bubble of natural gas in the United States seemed about to burst. And according to the U.S. Energy Information Administration (EIA), long-term gas demand was projected to accelerate by 35 percent between 2009 and 2035.[4]

Since shortly after World War II, Appalachia and most of the eastern seaboard became dependent on Gulf Coast supplies of natural gas to meet demand. However, in the 2000s, Gulf production was lagging and steady producing Appalachian wells, though still an important part of the mix, were certainly not a sufficient replacement. Bills were introduced in Congress to open up the American ocean coasts for natural gas drilling, but with offshore oil spills still fresh in the public's mind, the efforts did not gain much traction. Rep. John Peterson, a rural western Pennsylvania lawmaker and unlikely leader of natural gas offshore drilling proposals in Congress, blamed both federal bureaucracy for holding up offshore permits and the Bush Administration favoring imports of liquefied natural gas (LNG).[5] Moratoriums on gas drilling continued as well on the American side of the Great Lakes, though Canadian drillers had actively operated on their side of the international border for the previous half century, possibly siphoning U.S. gas that migrates freely in the formation under the lake's international border through the "rule of capture." With the exception of the western Gulf of Mexico, the United States remained the only major nation in the world that banned oil and gas drilling off of most of its coastline. In addition, imports from Canada, the third largest natural gas producing country in the world that addressed one-seventh of U.S. supply, seemed likely to dwindle as Canadians used more of their reserves to quench their thirst for clean-burning gas to supplant dirty coal-fired electric plants under a "cap and close" policy.[6]

As demand surged and the "peak gas" theory forecast the fading of U.S. gas supply in the Gulf of Mexico, America once again looked beyond its shores to foreign natural gas options, an ominous recurring nightmare of foreign oil dependence three decades before. The U.S. Department of Energy (DOE) listed numerous potential LNG regasification plants to accept the new supplies. The import facilities, mostly mothballed since the 1970s, geared up to receive cryogenic supplies from energy-prolific South America. The Republic of Trinidad and Tobago off the northern coast of South America provided close to half of U.S. LNG imports. Potentially, plentiful supplies were available from middle-eastern countries such as Qatar, which shared with Iran what was believed to be the largest conventional natural gas field on earth, where natural gas was produced at very low cost compared to oil. Domestic opponents to the controversial regasification plants voiced concerns over safety of such endeavors, seeing the sites as inherently dangerous and targets for terrorist attacks. But with declining domestic supply, reluctance to increase offshore exploration, and reduction of LNG transportation expenses, the formerly cost-prohibitive LNG, even from politically unstable regions of the world, looked like the only, albeit risky, bet. Despite the dismal U.S. energy forecast, foreign LNG suppliers would soon be looking toward other international customers, not America. As with many historically based assumptions about energy supply and demand in general, and natural gas in specific, the "peak gas" prognostication and U.S. supply turned out to be completely wrong.

As with oil drilling, the recovery of natural gas reserves has often been a matter of the cost of extraction versus the price of the commodity. The industry obviously picked the lowest hanging fruit first, or in this case, the shallowest sources of natural gas in the conventional sandstone and limestone geological formations. To seek additional oil and gas reserves, the drilling companies would have to go deeper offshore and on land to possibly extract the "unconventional" reserves such as "tight-sands" gas (rock formations that are not very permeable where gas cannot flow easily). These hydrocarbons are more difficult and expensive to separate from their natural location. And the lack of affordable and effective drilling technology kept certain unconventional sources imprisoned in their impermeable lock box deep in the earth.

Traditionally, the industry relied on vertical wells to reach the permeable sands, where gas pressures would run freely up the well bore and eventually through the driller's cash register with not much effort. Since its near inception, oil producers used various methods to augment output, including explosives such as nitroglycerine to stimulate well production. Beginning after World War II, the gas industry employed hydraulic fracturing (i.e., pumping high pressure water underground to break apart rock layers and injecting proppants, such as sand, into the fractures to hold them open). At the dawn of the twenty-first century, this process known commonly as "hydrofracking," or just "fracking," (also spelled "fracing" or "fraccing") along with horizontal drilling, sparked a revolution in the natural gas industry that is now a world-wide phenomenon.

Oil Well Shooting Demonstration 1959 — Long before hydraulic fracturing, oil and gas wells were stimulated by the use of nitroglycerine and other explosives to increase production of the well. This re-creation of a well "shooting" in Titusville, Pennsylvania, was shown live on NBC's *Today Show*, featuring Dave Garroway, in 1959 in celebration of the one-hundredth anniversary of Colonel Drake's first oil well (courtesy National Fuel Gas Company).

One of the hard-to-reach geologic zones known to hold natural gas supplies are abundant deep shales, isolated by impermeable rock above and below. Shallow shales like the Dunkirk/Huron black shale were the source of gas where William Hart sunk his first well in Fredonia, N.Y., in 1821. Geologically speaking, shale is the source of all natural gas, with some gas having migrated upward to porous sandstones before the shale became impermeable, and thus becoming "conventional" gas. These deep black shales, formed from bacterial, animal, and plant matter on the bottom of ancient stagnant seas, were widely geographically spread but geologically thin compared to other formations. They have been known for more than a century and drillers who struck such formations over the years with deep vertical wells often experienced "shows" (quick rushes of gas pressure) that soon died out because the gas could not travel easily through the less-than-permeable black rock. But a Texas oilman named George P. Mitchell would change all that.

Call Me Unconventional — The U.S. Shale Gale

As drilling technology advanced in the 1970s, some fossil fuel drillers began to employ "horizontal drilling" to better reach the sometimes narrow formations underground and "fracturing" had been used for decades to stimulate production. Oil driller George P. Mitchell, who began his search for petroleum in 1946 with his brother in Houston, believed that the previously untapped "unconventional" shale formations could be effectively produced with fracturing techniques. His firm, Mitchell Energy and Development, tried various methods of breaking apart shale beginning in 1981.[7] That year, the Barnett Shale, a Mississippian-age formation found at a depth ranging from 6,500 to 8,500 feet, became the first and "mother" of all shale fields in the Fort Worth basin in north-central Texas. Through the next two decades, Mitchell's company experimented with gases such as nitrogen and carbon dioxide as well as fracturing gels and propane. Finally, a combination of ordinary water and chemicals caused the shale formations to "shatter like glass."[8] Mitchell's firm merged with Devon Energy Corporation for $3.5 billion in 2002 and the company combined hydraulic fracturing technology with horizontal drilling to increase production.

Thanks to the combinations of drilling technology, shale formations that were marginally profitable to explore before would not only become economic, but it would transform the energy industry. In 1993, there were 36 permits for Barnett Shale wells using a combination of horizontal drilling and hydraulic fracturing. The number of permits increased to 961 ten years later and by 2008, there were 4,100 rigs authorized in Texas, most for gas in the shale formations. Devon became the largest producer in the Barnett Shale, which would produce 5 percent of the nation's gas supply by 2010, or a total of 1.8 trillion cubic feet. Approximately 15,000 wells were drilled in the formation by 2011.[9] Shale drilling expanded in 2004 to other formations, including the Fayetteville in Arkansas and Woodford in Arkansas and Oklahoma. Exploration in the Haynesville Shale play, located throughout eastern Texas, southwestern Arkansas, and Louisiana at depths as great as 13,000 feet, started in 2008. According to the EIA, Haynesville surpassed the Barnett as the number one natural gas producer among U.S. shale plays in 2011, with 2,100 wells exceeding production rates of 4.65 billion cubic feet per day.[10] The Eagle Ford Shale, which runs from the Mexican border to south Texas, was first drilled in the late 2000s and eventually became one of the largest oil and gas fields in the state. Thanks to these new discoveries, domestic natural gas supplies, once expected to shrink a decade before, flourished and the increased reserves along with stagnant demand cut wellhead prices in half, saving millions of dollars for American consumers.

Other named shale formations containing natural gas exist in more than half the states of the continental U.S. including: Tuscaloosa Marine in Louisiana; Brown Dense in northern Louisiana and southern Arkansas; Antrim in Michigan's Lower Peninsula; Gammon in Montana, North Dakota, and South Dakota; New Albany in Illinois, Indiana, and Kentucky; Niobrara in Wyoming and Colorado; Chattanooga in Tennessee; as well as various other shale plays in California, Arizona, New Mexico, Utah, Kansas, Mississippi, Alabama, and Maine. In Appalachia, shales such as the Upper Devonian lie under Ohio, and the Utica, which extends north under the eastern Great Lakes and into Quebec, Canada. Other shales contain large amounts of producible oil such as the Bakken Shale in North Dakota and Montana. But perhaps the most immediate strategically significant gas shale play in the eastern half of the United States lay far below the Appalachian Mountains, where the industry got its start in the early nineteenth century.

The Marcellus Shale, which contains more than half of all U.S. shale gas, was no secret to geologists for the past century, but it was another unconventional resource where gas could not be easily or inexpensively extracted. As early as the 1930s, gas explorers struck Marcellus gas in Ontario County, N.Y., south of Rochester, in a well that experienced a gas blowout when the Marcellus layer was penetrated.[11] In 1940, a month-long Marcellus blowout occurred in a well drilled near the Pennsylvania border in Whitesville, N.Y., but not much was known about the formation's overall reserves. By 2002, the U.S. Geological Survey (USGS) revealed that the unconventional brittle shale contained a potential of 2 trillion cubic feet of natural gas, but the resource could not be easily tapped.[12] That projection would be dwarfed less than a decade later as the USGS upped its projection to 84 trillion cubic feet in 2011.[13] And the gas within it was uncorked thanks to both horizontal drilling and hydraulic fracturing, unleashing the Appalachian gas genie from its geologic bottle.

The Marcellus Shale play is named after an outcrop of the rock found in 1839 southwest of Syracuse, N.Y., near the central Empire State village of Marcellus (the namesake emanating from the legendary and most highly honored Roman general who battled Hannibal). The bituminous shale Marcellus, Utica, and other shale outcrops were once erroneously thought to be the same as the coal beds found in Pennsylvania and dozens of exploratory pits were dug around central New York in the 1830s in the search for coal.[14]

The Marcellus is a very fine-grained, sedimentary, and low-density organic shale, part of the black shale succession of the Middle-Devonian-age Hamilton Group (from the geologic period spanning from 359 to 416 million years ago as determined by volcanic ash in the rock). As with other gas and oil origins, geologists generally accept that the soft rock shale layer was created by millions of years of extreme heat and pressure on microorganisms buried by mud and sediment at the deep bottom of an ancient sea that once covered eastern North America. The formation was buried due to the warping and folding and eventual erosion of the Allegheny mountains caused by a continental collision during the Taconic Orogeny (episode of mountain building or intense rock formation) during the middle Ordovician Period (about 440 million to 480 million years ago).[15]

The canoe-shaped Marcellus gas play is huge — spanning across 60 million acres in Appalachia, about 95,000 square miles according to the USGS, most of it not extensively produced. The "sweet spot" of the play is bounded at the northern edge in south-central New York State at approximately 4,000 to 5,000 feet below the surface. The prime Marcellus "fairway" (area of economic extraction) then descends in depth to about 8,500 feet as it stretches southwest through Pennsylvania, West Virginia, and eastern Ohio, as well as parts of Virginia, western Maryland, Kentucky, and Tennessee. The formation is found as far as 9,000 feet below the surface toward the west. In places where it is deeper and thicker, different levels of heat and pressure "cooked" the decomposing matter, causing carbon bonds to break down into various fossil fuels. In the southwestern portion of the play, the higher BTU reserves are more "wet" (containing natural gas liquids—propane, butane, ethane, etc.) and the northeastern part of the play contains "dry" production consisting of mostly methane. The shale is relatively porous, the tiny pores or fractures of rock holding the fossil fuel like a microscopic storage tank. But the formation is low in permeability (i.e., the ability for one substance to allow another substance to flow through it) because the pores are small and not interconnected as they are in the source of many traditional gas formations of

Marcellus Shale formation "fairway."

coarser-grained sandstone. Therefore, the shale makes it difficult for gas or water to migrate. Below and above the shale, mostly impermeable layers of rock trap the hydrocarbons in its black stone reservoir. The Marcellus is relatively thin as geologic formations go, though as much as 250 feet thick in northeastern Pennsylvania near the New York border, where much of the initial exploration would occur. But because of varying degrees of "organic richness," the thicker and shallower portions of the Marcellus are not always the most economical.[16] The shallower parts of the formation in New York State that are 25 to 100 feet thick are not as densely full of reserves as they are in Pennsylvania, West Virginia, and Ohio.

But at any depth and organic richness, the question facing gas explorers was: "Could this potential treasure trove of reserves be extracted as economically as the Southwest shales?" While other parameters play a role in economic value, a gas shale must have five properties before industry considers entering an area for leasing and later drilling. These include:

1. a suitable organic richness (known as TOC—total organic carbon);
2. thickness;
3. depth of burial;
4. thermal maturity; and
5. porosity/permeability.[17]

A sixth property also has a large impact in the economic value and the key to Appalachian success of the Marcellus: a natural fracture density, formed millions of years ago by high-pressure gas. The Marcellus has one of the finest natural fracture sets among the active gas shale plays in the U.S. and this characteristic most likely sets the Marcellus aside from the other plays.[18] These natural fractures or "joints" that hold natural gas in addition to the pores in the shale are vertical and drilling horizontally can intersect a maximum number of fractures to increase production.[19]

Home on the Range — Marcellus Kicks Down

As Southwestern gas drillers began to crack the Barnett in Texas, Range Resources, a Houston-based drilling firm actively participating in the Southwest shale areas, also had land holdings in southwestern Pennsylvania. Range's roots date back to 1976 in Appalachia with its predecessor firm Lomak Petroleum, founded and incorporated in Hartville, Ohio. The firm merged with Domain Energy Corp. in 1998, changing its name to Range Resources, and became the 15th largest publicly traded independent oil and gas company in the United States.[20] Range, which previously explored the Oriskany Sandstone and Lockport Dolomite, secured relatively inexpensive signing bonuses on leases for as little as $50 per acre. Range drilled the Renz #1 well in 2003 in southwest Pennsylvania's Washington County to test deeper formations, but the production results were disappointing.[21] However, the effort did pass through the Marcellus formation that had a brief strong show of gas. Range geologists noted the similarity between the Marcellus and the Barnett Shale including thermal maturity, reservoir pressure, thickness, porosity, and permeability, and soon recommended a "massive slickwater" hydraulic fracturing for the first major Marcellus discovery.[22] In October 2004, Range performed the first hydraulic fracture on a Marcellus well in Appalachia, which produced at a rate four times the magnitude of conventional wells. During this time, Pittsburgh-based Equitable Resources drilled producing horizontal wells in the shallower Devonian Upper Huron black shale in the Big Sandy Field of Kentucky and 20 percent of the wells flowed without stimulation.[23]

The shale test wells continued, and like the gas itself, the word leaked out quickly and after ignoring Appalachia for decades, other major natural gas exploration firms sought gas drilling rights throughout the region. With the hint of initial shale successes, the lease signing bonus figures quickly escalated to $5,000 per acre in a mad dash for drilling rights beginning in 2006 through 2008. Range hit its first gasser known as "Gulla #9" in Washington County, Pa., in 2007 and announced to investors impressive production results from five horizontal wells drilled into the Marcellus.[24]

Then, in January 2008, Penn State University issued a news release that would rock the industry, if not the world, headlined, "Unconventional natural gas reservoir could boost U.S. supply." Penn State University geologist Terry Engelder and Gary Lash, geologist and director of the State University of New York at Fredonia's Shale Research Institute, estimated that the play contained nearly 500 *trillion* cubic feet, as much as eighteen times the volume of gas contained in the Southwest Barnett Shale.[25] At current consumption rates, that would meet U.S. natural gas demand for more than 20 years. Engelder, a native of the original oil and gas region of Wellsville, N.Y., who spent time as a well-drilling roustabout as a teenager, researched shale since the 1970s. Since that initial projection, Engelder later *doubled* the calculation to 1,000 trillion cubic feet.[26] This volume of natural gas became a "game changer," estimated to surpass the BTU value of energy supplies in Saudi Arabia, and a dollar worth in the trillions. The Marcellus transformed into one of the largest unconventional natural gas reserves in the world, perhaps second only to the North Dome/South Pars gas fields, shared by Iran and Qatar in the Persian Gulf. By comparison, the largest "conventional" natural gas play in North America is the Hugoton Field of Kansas, which contains only 81 trillion cubic feet, less than one-tenth of the Marcellus amount.[27] The approximately 450,000 wells drilled in the Appalachian basin over the last 150 years produced only 47 trillion cubic feet, less than 5 percent of the estimated Marcellus reserves.[28] Because the Marcellus varies in depth, thickness, pressure, and natural fractures, it is difficult to precisely assess the level of gas contained within it. The richest amount of Marcellus gas is concentrated in the northeastern and southwestern portions of Pennsylvania, but ample quantities are located in other Appalachian states. For example, University of Maryland extension officials claimed the Marcellus Shale gas in Maryland's western Allegany County (which contains only 1 percent of overall Marcellus acreage) could be worth more than $15 billion, with an average well earning $65,000 to $524,000 a year.[29]

Though results of early Marcellus tests varied, many individual wells exceeded expectations. Two Cabot Oil & Gas Corp. gassers in Susquehanna County in northeastern Pennsylvania in 2011 were capable of producing 30 million cubic feet per day, thought to be a record for the Marcellus and enough gas to supply nearly 1,000 homes for a year. As a result, fewer than 25 landowners with the gas underneath them were sharing hundreds of thousands of dollars in monthly royalties.[30] Bradford, Tioga, and Susquehanna counties in northeastern Pennsylvania produced more than 100 billion cubic feet, accounting for more than one-third of natural gas produced by Marcellus wells in the second half of 2010.[31] Gas producers found these results more than satisfactory. Even with a depressed wellhead gas price of about $4 per thousand cubic feet (less than half what it was two years before) and drilling costs that amounted to $3 million to $4 million per well, producers like Range Resources saw an internal rate of return of 60 percent or more.[32]

These new reserves seemed to be the United States' energy ace in the hole even though the USGS pegged the technically recoverable Marcellus resources at only 84 trillion cubic feet, compared to the EIA's earlier estimate of 410 trillion cubic feet (downgraded to 141 trillion cubic feet in early 2012).[33] Different estimates were the results of different methodologies of calculation, datasets, and assumptions.[34] Earlier in 2011, the EIA Energy Outlook estimated recoverable domestic shale-gas resources in the U.S. at 827 trillion cubic feet, more than double the figure just a year before and more than 34 times the amount of gas the U.S. consumes in a year.[35] The nonprofit Potential Gas Committee (PGC), made up of volunteer natural gas industry officials, stated the U.S. possessed a total resource base of 1,898 trillion cubic feet as of year-end 2010. This was the highest resource evaluation in the PGC's 46-year history, exceeding the previous record-high assessment by 61 trillion cubic feet.[36] In addition to "proved" reserves, the PGC uses "probable," "possible," and "speculative" reserves applied to the total resource base.[37] According to the Cambridge Energy Research Associates in 2010, combining all possible and speculative domestic sources of gas, up to 3,000 trillion cubic feet of gas could be expected.[38]

Total U.S. production rose about 20 percent from 2005 to 2010 due to shale gas. This propelled the U.S. past Russia, which held the world's largest gas reserves, as the world's number one gas producer.[39] A Massachusetts Institute of Technology

(MIT) study stated that shale gas production accounted for about a fifth of the country's gas consumption in 2010.[40] The shale is no short-term resource, either. The peak production year of Marcellus may not arrive until the year 2035, when the EIA says shale could make up 46 percent of the country's supplies.[41] At the beginning of the first decade of the twenty-first century, the United States produced approximately 85 percent of its annual natural gas consumption of 22 trillion to 23 trillion cubic feet, with most of the balance coming from Canada and a small supply of overseas LNG. According to the EIA, with that domestic figure increasing, shale could provide all U.S. natural gas needs for 110 years at 2009 rates of use.[42] A good portion of the higher projections was due to the Marcellus. In Pennsylvania alone, production could grow from slightly over 327 million cubic feet per day during 2009 to more than 13 *billion* cubic feet per day by 2020.[43] An official with the Pennsylvania Department of Environmental Protection's (DEP) Bureau of Oil and Gas Management said in 2011 that combined with the huge Utica Shale formation that lay beneath the Marcellus, the state, still ranking fourth in the nation for coal production, "might be sitting on the largest gas reserves in the world."[44] Before the Marcellus, Pennsylvania imported three-fourths of its gas from other states. The Marcellus looked to not only replace those imports, but also transform the Keystone State into a net exporter to other states east, south, and west, and possibly to other nations.

Natural gas, its supplies barely keeping pace with demand a few years before, was now seen as more than just a "bridge fuel" before clean alternative fuels can be developed on an affordable mass scale. In 2011, President Barack Obama said natural gas was part of the nation's solution to wean itself from foreign oil imports, saying the potential for gas was "enormous."[45] A DOE official claimed that the new sources of natural gas could reduce the country's dependence on imported oil by providing a clean-burning automotive fuel and potentially, supplies could be exported to other countries.[46] However, the DOE and Environmental Protection Agency (EPA) focused not on production on shale gas, but rather on reviewing safety and the environmental risk management with extracting this promising, but unconventional source. Despite the euphoria of the gas rush, a *New York Times* article in June 2011 printed isolated emails of industry and regulatory officials casting doubt on the long-term economic viability of shale gas, causing some federal and state legislators to demand investigations.[47] The EIA stood by its projections, however, and the industry called the newspaper's assertions "inaccurate and misleading."[48] Resource estimates constantly change, and, if anything, history shows that the EIA is more likely to underestimate unconventional reserves rather than overestimate them. For the moment, however, once thing was clear: America was awash with gas.

You Have to Know the Territory — Shale Exploration Heads for the Appalachian Hills

As the nascent Marcellus Shale drilling industry shifted from the Southwest, oil and gas companies and their production employees followed the lease-acquiring landmen and headed for the Appalachian hills. Though there may be similarities underground in shale formations in the Southwest and Northeast, shale drillers in Appalachia knew immediately that when it came to complex industrial gas extraction, the mountainous and heavily forested topography of Pennsylvania and West Virginia were not the plains of Texas and Oklahoma. Landowners and localities unfamiliar with shale drilling, environmental worries, access challenges, and state regulatory and legislative hurdles were obstacles perhaps greater than the solid rock between the topsoil and the shale. The clash of the oil and gas regulars and the rural countryside regions created both gushers of economic hope and barrels of distrust.

Exploratory Marcellus drilling began in earnest in 2005, with much of the initial activity in Pennsylvania, where nearly three-quarters of the resources were located. Before drilling begins, however, it may take months of geologic testing, land and lease acquisition, and thorough environmental reviews. First, gas explorers seek the best comprehension of geological conditions in the area to access the potential for natural gas production. Geophysicists often

Marcellus Drilling Rig — A Marcellus horizontal drilling operation in the Pennsylvania countryside. A single Marcellus well can produce the same amount of gas as 50 to 100 traditional wells. More than 2,400 Marcellus wells had been drilled in Pennsylvania by the end of 2010 (courtesy Seneca Resources Corp.).

perform either two-or-three dimensional (2-D and 3-D) seismic testing of the underground formations. In 2-D testing, shock waves sent into the ground through seismic trucks or small charges in shallow holes reflect off rock formations to create geologic images. These are monitored by highly sensitive geophones translating the vibrations into electrical signals that are logged on a computer. Three-dimension seismic is more advanced, with 3-D imaging increasing the probability of a more accurate placement of the drilling locations.

Following preliminary geologic investigations, gas producers begin the exploration process by acquiring oil and gas leases from owners interested in leasing their land for potential exploration and drilling. Land professionals or "landmen" conduct title research in local courthouses and negotiate with landowners to develop a lease agreement. In Pennsylvania, for example, an oil and gas lease is much like a deed (and a contract subject to contract law) because it is a transfer of an interest in real estate, but below the surface.[49] County courthouses bustled with gas lease activity. For example, in Clarion County, in central Pennsylvania, lease-related documents increased 200 percent from 2009 to 2010 due to title searches for oil and gas rights.[50] Most landowners execute a standard industry lease — usually five years with extension options—provided by the gas exploration company, spelling out cash bonuses, rentals, royalties, and pooling (forming a production unit with other landowners).[51] A one-eighteenth or 12.5 percent royalty rate is the Pennsylvania state minimum, but it may be negotiated higher.[52]

Gas leases seriously altered the value of thousands of acres of farm and forest land in areas of the heaviest potential Marcellus reserves. Some property owners 10 years before the Marcellus rush signed bonuses for as little as $20 an acre, but many later received signing bonuses ranging from $2,000 to $5,000 an acre and royalty payments that totaled about 20 percent of the value of gas produced on the property. Land that was once worth $2,000 to $3,000 per acre leaped to as much as $10,000 because of Marcellus potential. In the latter part of the 2000s, thousands of acres of Appalachian land were leased for drilling, much of it in Pennsylvania, with more than 2,400 Marcellus wells drilled between 2006 to the end of 2010 in the Common-wealth.[53] Canadian-based Talisman Energy reached a contract with more than 900 Pennsylvania landowners for 32,000 acres of leased land and a $5,500-per-acre signing bonus to landowners, not including 20 percent in royalties.[54] MDS Energy Inc. of Kittanning, Pa., formed a group with about a dozen drilling companies and hundreds of landowners trying to leverage a package of 500,000 acres into a big payout from a multi-billion-dollar auction. Some landowners banded together in groups called "compacts" and attempted to reach a massive leasing deal together with 25–35,000 acres, which could increase production royalties and give them leverage in negotiation with larger drilling companies.[55]

Drilling firms usually lease the "mineral rights" of the land, not the land itself, and leases and royalties do not come without occasional contentions. Inevitably with the explosion of leasing in Appalachia, lawsuits between landowners and drillers erupted over lease extensions and other land matters. In Pennsylvania, a federal judge rejected oil and gas companies' efforts to extend leases with landowners who sued the companies because of lost time during the litigation.[56] Gas firms like ExxonMobil's XTO Energy sought to extend five-year oil and gas leases by "force majeure" on New York State's Southern Tier in 2011 because of "unpredictable and uncontrollable" state bans on hydraulic fracturing.[57] In 2011, the West Virginia Surface Owners' Rights Organization brought a lawsuit against drillers, claiming that the firms could not place additional well pads on one landowner's property in an effort to reach the reserves of a neighbor's property.[58] A group of about 25,000 Pennsylvania landowners claimed in a 2008 class-action lawsuit that Range Resources improperly calculated royalty payments on some Marcellus wells. The company denied it was wrong in the settlement, but agreed to change its methodology, and in 2011, a federal judge approved a settlement that granted the landowners about $1.3 million initially and increased their royalties by an estimated $16.6 million over five years.[59] Similarly, in Virginia, disagreements over mineral rights in recovering gas from coalbeds led to claims of millions of dollars of improper compensation against EQT Corp. and Consol Energy in 2011.[60] There is even some legal contention of what the term "mineral rights" means, as many leases do not specifically refer to natural gas, perhaps calling into question an 1882 Pennsylvania law that could potentially cause uncertainty regarding thousands of current leases. One case asking for a legal definition was appealed to the state Supreme Court.[61]

Natural gas drilling is largely regulated on the state level, with different states varying in their regulations. For example, Pennsylvania has a long history of drilling activity of thousands of wells and much state regulatory action. The Oil and Gas law of 1961 was an effort to minimize fossil fuel waste and protect property owner rights and, more recently, the Oil and Gas Act of 1984 regulated permitting, drilling, casing, bonding, operating, reporting, plugging, and site restoration for oil and gas wells.[62] The development of the Marcellus added a huge wrinkle to regulation and several Appalachian states proposed or implemented a complete overhaul of their regulatory agency structure, rules, and laws.

In Pennsylvania, once confirmation of clear title is obtained, and permitting is granted by state regulators, landowners within 1,000 feet of the proposed drill site are notified. Conventional drilling was prohibited 100 feet from streams and water bodies, wetlands, and 200 feet from buildings and water supplies, but this would be extended due to the Marcellus. Water is tested for quantity and quality prior to drilling, and other conditions around the site are documented. In order to receive a state drilling permit, drillers must prepare erosion and sediment control and stormwater management plans to protect water resources. The operator is responsible for water supply if the quality or quantity is affected, as the gas driller is "presumed to cause pollution if drilled within 6 months and 1,000 feet from water supply."[63] Marcellus wells require additional requirements for environmental protection including earth disturbance, encroachment permits, constructing structurally sound wastewater pits, impoundments and dams, water withdrawals and treatment, reuse, and disposal management plans.

Once the permitting and testing is complete, the next step is removing any timber on the site of the proposed well pad. One appeal of typical Marcellus Shale horizontal drilling is that up to ten wells can be drilled in various directions from a single well pad, reducing the overall environmental footprint of such activity to land and habitat, while producing voluminous supplies of natural gas. Horizontal drilling can protrude laterally more than a mile in some cases, providing more exposure within a formation. Some industry estimates project that six to eight horizontal wells drilled from only one well pad can produce the same volume as sixteen vertical wells.[64] Compared to some small volume shallow wells, some geologists say a single Marcellus well can produce as much as 50 to 100 traditional wells. A well pad with ten horizontal wells could potentially produce the same volume as 500 to 1,000 wells.[65]

As with many well sites in Appalachia, the old expression, "You can't get there from here," applies. Often, roads must be cut for access to the location, and the site surveyed, cleared, and leveled. The well site surface is stabilized with stone and pits are dug that may temporarily house fresh water used for the fracturing process or until other methods developed, wastewater and borehole cuttings. With large ponds, access roads, pipelines, and compressor stations, some conservationists say a single well pad could impact up to 30 acres.[66] Though typical horizontal drilling operations can take up to five acres of space, the industry emphasizes that overall land disturbance is much smaller compared to the same amount of production from traditional vertical wells.

Another contentious issue with Marcellus drilling is the concept of "forced pooling" (or the gas industry's term "fair pooling"), which is a private form of the

Marcellus Well Pad — This is a typical completed horizontal Marcellus Shale well pad featuring seven wells spaced only a dozen feet apart, spreading out horizontally once deep below ground in different directions up to a square mile, often producing 50 to 100 times the amount of natural gas than a traditional vertical well that would occupy approximately the same space. Solar-powered radio controlled pressure and flow equipment send real-time measurements to distant well control facilities (author's photograph).

government's power of eminent domain. It would permit drillers on a neighbor's leased property to horizontally drill under an unleased private owner's land even if the owner refuses to enter into a lease agreement. Allowing multiple wells from one well pad saves drilling costs and significantly reduces the environmental footprint of drilling. Additionally, the landowner would still be compensated and share in royalties, though they would not receive lease money. Specifics of pooling laws vary from state to state, but Marcellus drilling proponents want to expand the pooling provisions that can maximize the horizontal drilling effort by avoiding a fragmented patchwork of drilling pads between leased and unleased land.[67] Some landowners oppose the provision citing their right to do with the mineral rights of their land as they please, while others support expansion, fearing that without pooling, valuable gas can be siphoned from underneath their land anyway. As of 2011, there was no forced or fair pooling law in Pennsylvania, where most Marcellus activity was centered.

The Black Gold Rush — Big Gas Comes to Play

Until the 2000s, relatively small natural gas producers in Appalachia focused on conventional formations such as the Oriskany gas sand beginning in the 1950s, the deep reservoir Silurian Medina sandstone in the 1970s, and the Ordovician Trenton–Black River limestone formation in the 1990s. Many Appalachian natural gas explorers continued to plug away at traditional wells in the region, and often aided by gas marketers or brokers, found niche markets supplying large industrial customers with year-round supplies. The first Marcellus wells drilled by Range Resources and other smaller drilling firms combined with the projections of huge natural gas treasures under the Appalachian Mountains would not remain a local secret. In 2008, there were 19 firms holding leases in the play.[68] By 2011, there were several dozen energy companies prospecting for Marcellus shale gas, especially in Pennsylvania, where the lack of a severance tax and relatively hospitable regulatory environment welcomed the investment to the recession-torn Commonwealth. In West Virginia, Marcellus wells first drilled in Kanawha County in 2002 soon would be sunk in 45 of the state's 55 counties.[69] And it was no longer just regional drillers who had endured the boom and bust times of the deregulated natural gas market. As it was a century earlier with Rockefeller's Standard Oil, natural gas was now on the radar screen for "Big Oil."

Interest in the deep pockets of Marcellus would arrive from well-heeled U.S. companies in Texas, Oklahoma, California, and Colorado. For example, the privately-owned East Resources of Warrendale, Pa., founded in 1983 by Terrence M. Pegula, a 1973 Penn State University petroleum and natural gas engineer graduate, grew steadily through exploration in the Appalachian basin.[70] East Resources, created with $7,500 Pegula borrowed from his parents, was purchased by Houston-based Royal Dutch Shell PLC for $4.7 billion in 2010, giving the oil and gas giant one million acres of Marcellus Shale rights in Pennsylvania, West Virginia, and New York. The huge shale deposits attracted $9.7 billion worth of mergers and acquisitions in the first quarter of 2011 alone. In an effort to buy assets cheaply during a period of low gas commodity prices, San Ramon, Ca.–based Chevron Corp. acquired Appalachian natural gas producer Atlas Energy Inc., of Moon, Pa., for $4.3 billion.[71] The major oil and gas firm then announced it would purchase the mineral rights to 228,000 acres, primarily in Somerset County, Pa., from Chief Oil & Gas LLC of Dallas and Tug Hill Inc. for an undisclosed price.[72] After the purchase, Chief and Tug Hill maintained about 125,000 acres in the Marcellus, primarily in Bradford, Susquehanna, Tioga, Sullivan, and Wyoming counties in northern Pennsylvania.[73] Chevron operated the largest number of wells (259) in Pennsylvania by mid–2011.[74] XTO Energy, a western Pennsylvania shale gas firm, was purchased by the largest publicly traded energy company and most valuable firm in the world — ExxonMobil — for $41 billion, the company's largest single acquisition in a decade. The oil leviathan followed that purchase by buying privately held Phillips Resources and a related company, TWP Inc., for $1.69 billion in 2011, adding approximately 317,000 acres for exploration in the Marcellus.[75]

Although it is a competing fuel, coal producers would join the game as well. In 2010, Consol Energy, Inc. of Pittsburgh, acquired Richmond, Va.–based Dominion Resources Inc.'s natural gas business for $3.48 billion to diversify. Consol also acquired CNX Gas. The nation's fourth largest coal producer captured 1.46 million acres from Dominion and more than 9,000 wells, expecting to more than double production.[76] Consol's CEO J. Brett Harvey told investors the potentially lucrative Marcellus Shale play was "transformational," and a "baby" that would guarantee long-term profits, having nearly 4 trillion cubic feet of proved, probable, and possible reserves.[77] The firm later entered into a joint venture with Noble Energy of Houston.

After Range Resources got the Marcellus ball rolling, the Texas-based firm decided to abandon the Barnett Shale and cast its lot with the lucrative Appalachian basin. Range sold its Lone Star State properties for $900 million to an undisclosed company in 2011, and dedicated 86 percent of its capital budget to the Marcellus.[78] Range then had more than a million acres in southwestern and northeastern Pennsylvania and possessed between 20 and 31 trillion cubic feet of possible reserves and 239 active wells by mid–2011.

With natural gas prices at levels half what they were a few years before, well-financed firms who possessed extensive capital led the charge. Five companies, topped by Chesapeake Energy Corp., produced 69 percent of Marcellus Shale natural gas over 18 months ending in 2010, according to *Powell Shale Digest*, a trade publication. And 80 percent of that gas was found in just five counties in the northeastern and southwestern corners of the Keystone State.[79] Chesapeake acquired Columbia Natural Resources, involved in the Appalachian gas industry since the early 1900s, and had more than 7,000 wells in the Appalachia basin producing in excess of 40 billion cubic feet of gas by 2008.[80] The Oklahoma City–headquartered energy company became the largest leaseholder in the Marcellus territory with 1.5 million acres at a cost of $1.5 to $2 billion and it operated 110 wells in Pennsylvania alone by mid–2011.

Ranking second only to Chesapeake in production in Pennsylvania by mid–2011 with 185 active wells was Talisman Energy, a Canadian firm based in Calgary, Alberta, with U.S. offices in Big Flats, N.Y.[81] The firm previously was involved in the Trenton–Black River drilling program in New York and became the Empire State's largest gas producer. Talisman doubled its overall production by 2010 producing about 190 million cubic feet of gas a day. The firm had approximately 275,000 acres under lease in Bradford, Tioga, and Susquehanna counties in Pennsylvania.[82] In total, Talisman has more than 800,000 acres of rights, and an estimated 30 trillion cubic feet of reserves, though much of it in New York where it was not initially permitted to drill due to the state's temporary moratorium placed in effect in 2010. Another major U.S. player included Houston-based Cabot Oil and Gas Corp., which invested $500 million in Susquehanna County in Pennsylvania since 2006, and operated 200,000 acres in the Marcellus play. As of May 2011, the firm said it had surpassed 400 million cubic feet of natural gas production, and later had 117 active wells, ranking third in production in Pennsylvania.[83]

In addition to Canada, investment in the Marcellus flocked from global deep-pocket concerns in England, Norway, India, Russia, and Japan. British gas producer BG Group paid $950 million to buy a 50 percent interest in Dallas-based EXCO Resources for 654,000 net acres of shale gas assets, including 186,000 acres of Marcellus in Appalachia.[84] Chesapeake Energy partnered with Norwegian oil and natural gas producer Statoil ASA in Marcellus investments, where Statoil held nearly a third of Chesapeake's holdings in West Virginia's northern panhandle. By early 2011, total Chesapeake leases covered 1.8 million acres and more than 32,000 leases in West Virginia, Pennsylvania, New York, and Ohio.[85] Reliance Industries, India's largest private company, paid $392 million for a 60 percent interest in a shale gas joint venture with

U.S.-based Carrizon Oil and Gas to explore 104,400 net acres in the Pennsylvania Marcellus.[86] Atlas Energy Inc. also brokered a $1.7 billion partnership with Reliance.[87] Japan's Mitsui & Co. made a $1.4 billion investment in shale gas in Pennsylvania in 2010, taking a third share of a drilling project held by Anadarko Petroleum Corp., the largest independent oil company in the world.[88] Andarko had more than six trillion cubic feet of gas reserves over 760,000 gross acres and 41 active wells. A smaller firm, Rex Energy, based in State College, Pa., which increased its holdings 21 percent in 2010 to 60,000 acres and controlled 92,000 acres in Pennsylvania's Butler and West-moreland counties, established a joint venture in Clearfield and Centre counties with Japanese conglomerate Sumitomo.[89] Foreign buyers were involved in seven transactions of more than 50 million dollars in the first quarter of 2011 alone. The increased numbers of mergers and acquisitions in the Marcellus and other shale regions came from the well-financed players in the industry that had the capability to sustain relatively low natural gas prices during America's slow recovery from recession after 2008.

A few selected significant energy producers (in alphabetical order as of mid–2011) in the Marcellus included: [90]

AB Resources, which had 90,000 Marcellus acres in southwestern Pennsylvania and northern West Virginia that could result in 1,000 wells.

Antero Resources Corp., a Denver-based drilling firm, planned to spend the vast majority of its $559 million capital budget for 2011 for drilling and completion, leasehold acquisitions, and pipelines not in the Rockies, but in the Appalachians. Antero purchased $193 million worth of Marcellus Shale acreage from Consol Energy in 2011.[91]

Energy Corp. of America, which had investigated shale gas in Appalachia along with the DOE in the 1970s, has extensive operations and estimated reserves of one trillion cubic feet of gas in Greene County in southwestern Pennsylvania and 42 active wells.

EOG (formerly known as Enron Oil and Gas Co.) had approximately 44 active Marcellus wells in Pennsylvania and an estimated 3.3 trillion cubic feet of reserves.

EQT Corp., the Pittsburgh-based utility, pipeline, and exploration firm, whose roots date back to George Westinghouse's ventures in natural gas in the nineteenth century, was one of the largest Appalachian producers prior to the Marcellus. EQT sold 134.6 billion cubic feet of produced gas in 2010, a 34.5 increase. EQT announced that its proved reserves at the end of 2010 totaled 5.2 trillion cubic feet equivalent, up 28 percent from a year earlier.[92] EQT acquired 58,000 net acres in the Marcellus Shale in March 2010 for $280 million from a group of private investors and landowners. In total, the firm estimates it may have 20 trillion cubic feet of possible reserves and operated 49 active wells in Pennsylvania.

Pennsylvania General Energy (PGE), a Warren, Pa.-based independent firm, drilled its pioneer Marcellus Shale well in 2005 in central Pennsylvania in Elk County and later moved northeast.[93] The firm has more than a half million acres in the Marcellus area in Pennsylvania and New York and 20 active wells in Pennsylvania.

Seneca Resources, a drilling subsidiary of the century-old Standard Oil spinoff, National Fuel Gas Company (NFG), already owned thousands of acres of mineral rights in the Marcellus region. Seneca did not have to pay royalties to drill on much of the approximate one million acres of land it controls, dramatically lowering its break-even point for wells that can cost upwards of $4 million to drill.[94] The NFG subsidiary also acquired more oil and gas properties in Tioga County, Pa., from EOG Resources, Inc., for $23 million in 2010. Seneca had 43 active wells in 2011 and planned to spend more than $1 billion on drilling in Pennsylvania in 2012.[95]

Ultra Petroleum Corp., a large player in southwest Wyoming, bought into the Marcellus and had more than 260,000 net acres in Pennsylvania by the end of 2010 in five north-central counties, investing nearly $400 million, with the potential for 1,800 net drilling locations and 8 trillion cubic feet equivalent of net resource potential and 35 active wells.[96]

Williams Cos. Inc. invested into the Marcellus with Rex Energy in 2009, and acquired 42,000 net acres in northeastern Pennsylvania from a partnership between Denham Capital and Alta Resources LLC for $501 million in 2010, as well as obtaining commitments to lease 94,000 net acres in the Marcellus in Pennsylvania at an average cost of $7,000/acre. Williams operated 21 active wells in Pennsylvania.

More than 50 other smaller drilling outfits were acquiring leases and permits for wells in Pennsylvania by mid 2011. Overall in Pennsylvania, the number of Marcellus Shale well permits issued totaled 71 in 2007, 276 in 2008, 1,984 in 2009, and 3,314 in 2010 (a 67 percent increase that year alone)[97] and the state reported a 22 percent increase in shale gas production during the first half of 2011 compared with the second half of 2010.[98]

Making Straight, Sideways — The Horizontal Shale Drilling Process

The new horizontal shale drilling and hydraulic fracturing process is much more involved and expensive than traditional single, shallow vertical drilling and it would become even more complex in the Appalachian region. Although much criticized, tax credits in the oil and gas industry permitted the development of such technology. According to energy expert Daniel Yergin, author of the Pulitzer Prize–winning oil history, *The Prize*, "We wouldn't have had a shale gas revolution without an incentive in the tax code. That's what kept it going for 20 years."[99] First uses of the horizontal technique date back to the 1930s, and it was successfully employed in Pennsylvania in "slanted wells" in the mostly depleted Venango oil formation near the original Drake oil well during World War II from a bullet-shaped steel pipe horizontal drilling process combined with underground explosives. The well stimulation process was suggested by Iowa-born engineer and drilling inventor Leo Ranney (1884–1950). The ingenious Ranney, who held 3,000 patents from drilling machinery to bathtub toys, once suggested to the U.S. War Cabinet that victory over Japan in World War II could be achieved by triggering a designed earthquake set off by 12,000 pounds of explosives set two miles off the coast of the Far East island.[100] Ranney had little luck in the 20 years before the war getting attention for horizontal oil "mining" and instead designed successful horizontal water wells in London, England, and Lisbon, Spain.[101] The horizontal process was later employed in shales during the DOE-sponsored Eastern Gas

Shales Project in the 1970s, which studied the Appalachian and other basins to evaluate reserves and devise a method to stimulate rocks to achieve commercial hydrocarbon quantities.[102] In New York State, NFG experimented in 1978 with its first test of Devonian black shale from core samples with the DOE. In 1986, the DOE project with industry resulted in the first air-drilled 2,000-foot-long horizontal Devonian shale well in the Appalachian Basin.[103] There was not much overall activity during this period, however, due to suppressed natural gas prices.

The horizontal drilling process begins similar to vertical wells as a drill cuts through the surface of the earth to below the deepest aquifer containing groundwater without the use of fluids as lubricants. At this initial point, heavy steel surface pipe is inserted down the length of the drilled hole. The first and largest diameter hole or "string" is usually drilled at a shallow depth of 40 to 80 feet and is about 12 to 16 inches in diameter. A drive (or conductor) pipe is put in place to keep loose soil, sand, and gravel from caving in. Eventually, several layers of casing pipe would become industry practice to insulate groundwater supplies from leaks. The insertion of multiple levels of string lined with hard metal casing shores up the wellbore, keeping the hole open and at the same time protecting the earth and groundwater. Circulating compressed air down the drill pipe lifts the broken rock through the groundwater-protected wellbore. Multiple layers of cement (usually about 650 gallons per 1,000 feet) are pumped down the well under pressure and then forced up the outside of the steel casing from below the water table all the way to the surface isolating the well from the surrounding formation.[104] Proper cement casing installation further protects groundwater supplies by sealing the well column and preventing extracted natural gas, brine, or drilling fluids from coming into contact with freshwater zones.

Once the cement hardens on the initial string, drilling continues with metal casing extending through the vertical bore hole with the "surface string," which ranges from 7 inches to 9½ inches in diameter, drilled to about 800 feet by using a smaller bit through the conductor pipe. Before the production metal casing is installed, drillers perform logging involving an electronic sensor lowered into the hole that "reads" the bare rock density and porosity and to determine the presence of hydrocarbons.[105] Later, through the horizontal drilling phase, more casing pipe is installed, further sealing off drilling fluids and hydrocarbons from groundwater supplies. While the vertical well is still above the desired Marcellus Shale zone, the drill bit is turned sideways on a long-radius turn at a minute angle and eventually penetrates the relatively narrow formation. Each horizontal or "lateral" well, once drilled to a depth up to 9,000 feet, can then travel more than a mile sideways to reach a wide area of the thin, but valuable formation. Sophisticated downhole monitoring equipment and "geo-steering" allows drillers to adjust the angle of the hydraulic-drilled motor to keep the drill bit centered in the "sweet spot" of the formation. It takes drillers working 24 hours a day between two weeks to a month to complete all the drilling phases, often using a much in-demand rig rented for $50,000 a day. As mentioned, multiple wells only a dozen feet apart can be drilled on the same pad to offshoot into different horizontal directions to eventually cover a square mile of shale, vastly reducing the overall environmental footprint of the wells.

Romancing the Stone — The Hydraulic Fracturing Process

Once the horizontal well is drilled through the relatively thin shale formation, the next stage of the process is hydraulic fracturing, more commonly known as "fracking." This process designed to stimulate the production of oil or gas was first employed in the Hugoton field of Kansas in 1946 and by Halliburton near Duncan, Oklahoma, in 1949, in an effort to release more hydrocarbons by cracking open porous hydrocarbon-bearing rock.[106] Since that time, the process has helped augment production in more than a million wells, producing in excess of 600 trillion cubic feet of natural gas and seven billion barrels of oil.[107] The American Petroleum Institute (API) claims that 90 percent of all new wells are fractured, and without the process, the nation would lose 45 percent of domestic natural gas production and 17 percent of oil production within five years.[108] The fracturing process is one of the most expensive parts of the Marcellus process, one study finding it cost an average of $2.5 million for wells drilled in western Pennsylvania.[109] Despite the long history of this practice, fracturing shale wells became the most controversial part of natural gas extraction and that debate will be detailed later in this chapter.

Marcellus Drilling Rig at Night — Drilling a Marcellus well usually takes 24 hours a day for approximately two weeks to a month, using a drilling rig often rented for $50,000 per day at a total cost of $3 million to $4 million dollars per well (courtesy Seneca Resources Corp.).

With a similar purpose of stimulating production as was the use of nitroglycerin in oil wells in the nineteenth century, the next step in the fracturing process is inserting explosive charges through the horizontal formation. A perforation gun on a 20,000-foot electric line to the end of a lateral drill pipe is fired to punch holes through the casing and into surrounding rock. The shaped perforation charges are set off in stages. The small bullet-hole openings created from the charging process will function like holes in a lawn sprinkler as a conduit for "frack fluid," vast amounts of water, sand, and a small proportion of chemical additives pumped through the well from the surface at very high pressure.

The second stage of the fracturing process is the most intensive in labor, material, and management. Each Marcellus well will require from three to five million gallons of water

1950s Hydraulic Fracturing — Hydraulic fracturing, the injection of high-pressure water into natural gas and oil wells to stimulate production, began in the late 1940s. This scene is a typical fracturing process of a natural gas well in Pennsylvania in 1958, performed by the well services company Halliburton (courtesy National Fuel Gas Company).

during the fracturing process. According to Penn State University's Marcellus Center for Outreach and Research, gas wells drilled in the Susquehanna River Basin, which includes about half of Pennsylvania and a large portion of New York, use on average about 3.7 million gallons of water per well.[110] This compares to only about 100,000 gallons for fracking conventional wells. Water is obtained via permit from nearby streams or rivers and trucked and/or piped into the site. It takes about three months to purchase the water, truck, and run water pipelines to the well.

The "frack fluid" is generally composed of 90 percent water, 9.5 percent sand, and often less than 0.5 percent of a chemical mixture, many of the agents similar to what is used in household cleaning and cosmetic products. Drillers mix the water, sand (usually 30/50 grade), and chemicals in a "blender" and shoot the frack fluid down the well bores through powerful pump trucks at a pressure often exceeding 8,000 psi.[111] The process is conducted one stage at a time through the perforations and into the shale. The well is "perfed" and "fracked" in up to 10 to 12 stages, a heavy plug placed in the line to maintain pressure between stages.[112] Unlike vertical wells, horizontal fracking requires distinct intervals due to the difficulty in maintaining pressures sufficient to induce fractures over the significant lateral length.[113] The plugs are later drilled out.

The fracking process usually consists of four separate components including:

- an acid stage to clear cement debris in the wellbore and provide an open conduit for other frack fluids;
- a pad stage that uses "slickwater" to open the formation;
- a prop sequence stage of water combined with proppant material; and
- a flushing stage to expel the excess proppant from the wellbore, often caught in containers known as "sand traps" at the well site.[114]

As the pressurized drilling fluid fires through the holes into the formation, the pressure cracks the brittle shale, creating hairline pores allowing the natural gas contained in the formation to flow. Often the natural fracture patterns in shale will network, allowing a large volume under several acres of land to be collected from one well. Critics of the hydraulic fracturing process suggest that the "pipe bomb" pressure could open up unknown fault lines, and let fracking fluid and gas into water supplies. Geologists, however, counter that it is unlikely that frack fluid or hydrocarbons could percolate up from under thousands of feet of rock strata and enormous pressure to the aquifers. While the fluid shatters the rock, the sand grains in the mix keep the pore holes propped open, usually about one-eighth of an inch or less in width, when the fluid pressure stops. Nitrogen can also be used to aid in carrying the sand into the fractures and reclaim the water used in the process.[115] In addition to sand, companies are researching the use of other raw products that are currently part of the waste stream such as cement-based materials, recycled rock cuttings from mine waste, and flash from steel to act as proppants.[116] After fracturing, the well is "shut in" for the fractures to stabilize, and then some of the fracturing fluid returns to the surface as "flowback," discussed later in this chapter.

This approach is not much different than the fracturing process employed throughout the country for half a century to improve the deliverability of production and storage wells. However, the "frack fluid" in the shale gas extraction process and the entire concept of hydraulic fracturing would soon evolve from technical discussions in obscure industry journals to understandably concerned, but alarming and often misleading headlines throughout the world.

This Land Is Gasland— *Environmental Issues with Marcellus Shale Gas*

As the Marcellus leasing frenzy was in full swing in 2008, a New York City filmmaker named Josh Fox received a $100,000 offer to lease his family's rural northeastern Pennsylvania property for Marcellus drilling. Fox was not interested, but instead began work on an independently filmed documentary probing the environmental impact of natural gas drilling on local communities across the United States. Fox's finished product, titled *Gasland*, premiered at the Sundance Film Festival in January 2010, receiving a special jury prize, and eventually landed a broadcasted slot on the television cable network HBO. Later, the politically laden film received a nomination for cinema's coveted Oscar by the Academy of Motion Picture Arts and Sciences and four television Emmy nominations. Though *Gasland* did not win an Academy Award for Best Documentary in 2011, it did win an Emmy for Outstanding Direction for Nonfiction Programming, and it became a catalyst on which a growing opposition movement began to flare against the promising natural gas drilling effort in Appalachia, and especially hydraulic fracturing. It was not a flattering portrayal, nor, according to the drilling industry and other informed critics, an accurate or fair depiction.

The film was emotionally charged, as several neighbors of natural gas well operations throughout the United States made allegations of contaminated water wells and exposure to chemicals, demonstrated their water faucets burning from invading methane, and asserted that poorly regulated fracturing processes allegedly caused contamination of land, water, and air. Several of the film's claims were promptly debunked by the industry and various state regulators. For example, Colorado authorities stated that unlike the film's suggestions, methane contaminated water wells in that western state were not caused by drilling for thermogenic gas (created by thermal decomposition of buried organic material), but by biogenic gas (created by decomposition of organic material through fermentation such as in wetlands).[117] Another accusation suggesting that drilling led to a September 2009 fish kill in Dunkard Creek in Washington County in southwest Pennsylvania was determined by federal and state regulators to be caused by coal mine drainage.[118] The industry group "Energy In Depth" outlined various errors, exaggerations, and misstatements in the movie, including the claim that the chemicals used in fracking are secret when they are known to state regulators and often posted online.[119] Pennsylvania's environmental chief at the time, John Hanger, himself a noted environmentalist who was interviewed in the film, agreed that the natural gas industry is industrial and should be strongly regulated. Hanger, however, claimed *Gasland* presented, "a selective, distorted view of gas drilling and the energy choices America faces today."[120] The chief oil and gas geologist for the Pennsylvania Department of Conservation and Natural Resources (DCNR) later compared the film to Nazi propaganda, but later apologized.[121] Fox planned a sequel to the film in 2012.

Perhaps the most persistent allegation was Fox's premise that the hydraulic fracturing process can potentially contaminate fresh water supplies. These fears alone would lead numerous local communities, three major eastern states, a Canadian province, and European nation to temporarily ban the process of obtaining gas using the technique. Unprepared for the onslaught, the gas industry would face an uphill battle as the government, media, and public would be faced with legitimate environmental concerns, conflicting scientific evidence, and a dose of pure demagoguery.

With the tremendous pirate's treasure of hydrocarbons locked within the Marcellus, exhuming that prize would not be as easy as sinking a few cable-tool drills into the hills of Appalachia as it was more than a century before. The requirement of horizontal drilling and hydraulic fracturing would raise numerous environmental issues that are in contention as of this writing involving water supply, effect on groundwater tables, use of chemicals in the fracturing process, disposal and treatment of toxic fracturing fluid, air pollution emissions, drilling safety and accidental spills, forest fragmentation, encroachment on residential communities, road use issues, and land reclamation. Each Appalachian state approached regulation and potential

Hydraulic Fracturing — A Marcellus well site in Pennsylvania during the hydraulic fracturing process reveals the significant industrial activity necessary to obtain natural gas from deep shale formations. After the process is complete and the well is producing, only a well pad, valves, production equipment and collection tanks will remain as the site is reclaimed (courtesy Universal Well Services).

taxation of Marcellus gas extraction differently ranging from outright, if temporary, bans, to perceived red carpet encouragement for investment. In addition, the federal government is currently studying shale drilling effects for potential regulation and several bills in Congress have attempted to bring the normally state-regulated process under the aegis of the federal domain.

Land Needs

Unlike conventional gas well sites, Marcellus drilling requires about five acres of farm or forest land to be cleared and dedicated to drilling operations at an average well spacing of 40 to 160 acres per well.[122] During the process of drilling and fracking, the site's appearance is clearly an industrial one, with trucks, drilling equipment, storage facilities, and water supply or drainage ponds. Temporary housing facilities for the workers who operate 24 hours a day, seven days a week, sometimes conflict with local ordinances. The advantage of horizontal drilling, as mentioned earlier, is the capability of reducing the overall environmental impact of the well pad by drilling multiple wells from the same site. After the well is producing, the land around the well site should be reclaimed and all that remains is the "Christmas Tree" valves and the large separator tanks that capture any liquids or brine that come up through the well bore over time. Ideally, in the long run, these wells and the cleared rights of way for underground gathering pipeline should leave only the scar of any tree removal that occurred.

The impact of such drilling that is perhaps routine activity in the Southwestern oil and gas fields is a relatively new experience for many areas of Appalachia, and not always a welcome one. According to the Nature Conservancy, 10 million acres in Pennsylvania are leased for natural gas development and conservationists worry that much land will be consumed for well pads, access roads, and pipeline networks. Natural gas drilling is not the only energy source that can impact land use. The Conservancy claims that Pennsylvania could have 60,000 Marcellus natural gas wells by 2030, but by the same time it projects that 2,900 wind turbines could result in the clearing of between 38,000 to 90,000 acres of forest, where the risk of predation, changes in light and humidity levels, and the arrival of invasive species could threaten forest interior species, some globally rare.[123] A total of 3,500 acres of forest was cleared as of December 2010 for Marcellus drilling and wind turbine development. While many Marcellus wells are out of sight in heavily forested land, windmills the size of jetliners often stand prominently on the mountaintops of the Appalachians. The debate continues of how to balance the need for searching for Marcellus gas with not severely disturbing the often pristine countryside and forest in the Appalachian region.

Thirsty Wells — Water Supply for the Marcellus Drilling Process

The hydraulic fracturing process of Marcellus shale wells involves a significant amount of water — an estimated three to five million gallons per well. Most water comes from area creeks and rivers through water withdrawal management plans that need state environmental approval as well as permits from the interstate Susquehanna River Basin Commission or Delaware River Basin Commission. Though the volumes of fresh water required are seemingly significant, the industry maintains that water use is not very high compared to some other industrial processes, especially coal and nuclear power plants. New York State geologist Taury Smith said in 2011 that the average drilling complex used 8.4 million gallons of water per day in the Susquehanna River basin, compared to 20 million gallons per day for golf courses in the area.[124] Total Marcellus Shale drilling water demand from the Susquehanna River Basin reached 30 million gallons of water per day, compared to 5.9 *billion* gallons per day for power generation needs.[125] In Pennsylvania, Marcellus Shale natural gas wells use 0.2 percent of the daily statewide total water withdrawn at 1.9 million gallons per day, ranking ninth of major water uses in the state, well below electric generation power plants that use 6.43 *billion* gallons per day.[126] Estimates of increased water usage for the fracking process are less than 0.8 percent of the water drawn out of the region annually.[127]

Still, some local officials have opposed requests by drillers to withdraw water out of rivers and streams because of the potential for "negative" impact on water resources. The hot and mostly dry summer of 2011 put some Marcellus drilling areas on drought warnings and watches, though gas producers were recycling fluids or

Hydraulic Fracturing — Hydraulic fracturing a Marcellus well takes much manpower and horsepower. Three million to five million gallons of water, sand, and a small amount of chemicals are pumped down the well at very high pressures to break apart deep shale that hold natural gas, natural gas liquids, and oil (courtesy Universal Well Services).

relying on "super sources" of water such as large rivers.[128] Concern about lowered stream flows in July 2011 led the Susquehanna River Basin Commission to suspend water withdraw permits for drilling operations, golf courses, and a fish hatchery.[129] Outside of Appalachia, worries as to the possible effects of Fayetteville Shale gas development on water resources in Arkansas resulted in the USGS to begin studying water-quality and stream-flow monitoring to establish a baseline for determining trends in water quality and quantity.[130] Water supply became an issue in Texas where in 2011 the worst drought in 116 years reduced water availability in hydraulic fracturing of the Eagle Ford formation. Because of the Eagle Ford geology, it takes three to four times as much water to fracture as the Barnett Shale, requiring as much as 13 million gallons of water per well.[131]

But freshwater is not the only possible fluid source as some companies have sought purchases of wastewater, which could be major revenue generators for towns and cities. In September 2010, Dallas-based Exco Resources requested permission to draw as much as 400,000 gallons per day from treated wastewater from the sewer system in Pennsylvania's Centre County.[132] Cumberland, Maryland reached an agreement with Samson Resources of Meyersdale, Pa., which allowed the city to potentially supply up to 20,000 gallons per day of treated effluent water from its wastewater treatment plant for hydraulic fracturing.[133] The city of Clarksburg, W.Va., also considered selling its effluent water to drilling companies instead of discharging it back into the river system.[134] Seneca Resources Corp. announced that it was utilizing water from abandoned coal mines to conduct fracturing operations in Tioga County in northeastern Pennsylvania, using less freshwater and reducing existing discharge from mines to local waterways.[135] In addition, some water needs have been reduced by drillers recycling water, which is discussed later in this chapter.

The Marcellus Cocktail — What Is Frack Fluid?

"Frack fluid" is the liquid mix of water, sand, and a minute amount of chemicals needed to keep casings and drill bits from rusting, prevent deep-dwelling bacteria from clogging the drill pipe, and allow drill fluid to better penetrate the shale and enhance the flow of gas. Each fracturing job may contain different chemicals in the frack fluid mix depending on which drilling company is conducting the process, but in general in Appalachia, the mixture contains less than a dozen components, significantly fewer chemicals or combinations required compared to the shale formations in the Southwest.[136] Frack water can include surfactants (soaps to slicken the water), biocides (like chlorine used in swimming pools), scale inhibitors (like products similar to Lime Away to reduce scaling in the drill pipe), friction reducers (similar to vegetable oils), and proppants (such as sand or other small particles). Other new technology is finding less onerous fracking components. For example, the international oil and gas services company Halliburton, whose U.S. offices are based in Houston, announced creation of a new fracturing fluid that uses chemicals sourced entirely from the food industry,[137] a sample of which a company executive drank at an industry conference.[138]

The purpose of the chemicals used in frack fluid is to make the water thicker and hold the proppants in suspension, and slicker, to accelerate everything flowing through the drill pipe. Some specific chemicals (and their common uses) can include:

- hydrochloric acid (often used in swimming pool cleaners) that dissolves minerals and initiate fissures in the rock;
- sodium chloride (table salt) to allow a delayed breakdown of the gel polymer chains;
- polyacrylamide (water treatment) to minimize friction between fluid and pipe;
- ethylene glycol (anti-freeze) to prevent scale deposits in the pipe;
- sodium/potassium carbonate (washing soda, water softener) to maintain the effectiveness of other components;
- borate salts (detergents and soaps) to maintain fluid viscosity;
- glutaraldehyde (disinfectant) to eliminate bacteria in the water;
- guar gum (thickens cosmetics, baked goods, ice cream) to thicken the water to suspend the sand;
- citric acid (food additive and fruit juice) to prevent precipitation of metal oxides; and
- isopropanol (glass cleaner, antiperspirant) to increase fracture fluid viscosity.[139]

The largest public concern regarding the hydraulic fracturing process is the potential that the fluid can somehow leak into water aquifers below ground, or spill into water supplies above ground. Though the chemical "cocktail" is mostly water, the sheer volume of potentially hazardous frack fluid used and other harmful constituents that may come out of the well often alarm the public, legislative bodies, and regulators. Many have objected to the fact that the fracturing fluid formulas were secret and not regulated by the federal Safe Drinking Water Act, with an exemption passed under the 2005 U.S. Energy Policy Act. The industry maintained that the list of chemicals was not publicly withheld, but rather, the specific proprietary chemical mixtures could be kept confidential by the manufacturers of the fluid. The chemicals used in each fracturing fluid, however, must be disclosed at each drilling site, according to the Occupational Safety and Health Administration (OSHA). One congressional report issued by Democrats in the U.S. House of Representatives called for EPA protections, stating that fracking fluids contain substances identified as human carcinogens, or listed as hazardous (such as diesel fluid) under federal clean air or water laws.[140] In 2011, U.S. Senator Bob Casey (D–Pa.) introduced legislation in Congress called the Fracturing Responsibility and Awareness of Chemicals, or "FRAC Act," which would "increase disclosure and regulation of chemicals that could enter Pennsylvania's drinking water supply."[141] Even some energy company shareholders voted on disclosing the risk of fracking with 42 percent of shareholders of the energy firm Williams Cos., and 49.5 percent of stockholders of the smaller Energen Corp. supporting disclosure.[142]

Industry experts downplayed any potential threats of fracturing, but some federal officials, like Department of Interior (DOI) Secretary Ken Salazar suggested hydraulic fracturing might be the industry's "Achilles Heel."[143] However, Salazar later admitted in 2011 the claim that Americans must choose between environmental protection and the development of natural resources is a "false choice."[144] Still, federal regulators planned to issue their own revised gas production regulations.

The supposed secrecy of the fracking ingredients perhaps made the chemical concoctions more onerous than they actually are. In July 2010, Range Resources, followed by other firms, voluntarily disclosed the four fracking additives used at each well site, along with their classifications, volumes, dilution factors, and purposes. In 2011, the Ground Water Protection Council (GWPC), a national association of state ground water and underground injection agencies, and the Interstate Oil and Gas Compact Commission (IOGCC), launched the "Frac Focus Chemical Disclosure Registry" (at www.fracfocus.org) to allow companies to voluntarily disclose the content of fracturing fluids used at individual well sites.[145] A total of 44 companies disclosed chemicals used at hundreds of wells as of June 2011. That same month, Texas governor Rick Perry signed legislation that made the Lone Star State the first in the nation to require drillers to publicly reveal hydraulic fracturing fluid ingredients on a well-by-well basis. Though some of the information would be withheld because it contained trade secrets, enough disclosure was permitted as needed for regulatory study, research, and medical treatment. The industry group Marcellus Shale Coalition agreed to require all member companies to voluntarily disclose chemicals used at each well site in 2012.[146]

Regarding frack fluid contamination, the industry points to a study conducted by the EPA and another by the GWPC, which found that there have been no confirmed incidents of groundwater contamination from hydraulic fracturing.[147] The concern that frack fluid can leak from the fracture zone into aquifers is also discounted by geologists and other experts. Since the frack water is 10 times more salty than sea water and much heavier than fresh water, it is not likely to percolate up.[148] Geologists say the fluid is injected 8,000 feet deep, and if low viscosity Marcellus gas has not escaped after 275 million years, it is highly unlikely that high-viscosity frack fluid will find its way to the surface. The oil and gas division of the Pennsylvania DEP stated that every well keeps records of the extent of its fractures and no fractures have come within half a mile of an aquifer. With more than 5,000 wells drilled in Pennsylvania, though there were cases of near-the-surface methane migration (discussed later in this chapter), there was not one case where frack fluid contaminated water supplies.[149] Still, state geologists are mapping the location of the deepest water aquifers and examining the impact of hydraulic fracturing operations on groundwater supplies.[150] According to the December 9, 2011, *Wall Street Journal*, the EPA issued a controversial, industry-disputed announcement that it found chemicals likely associated with much shallower gas production practices, including fracking, in the Pavillion gas field in Wyoming, though the fracking differed from methods used in the Marcellus region, which has different geological characteristics.

Likewise, in neighboring Ohio, environmental officials said that after reviewing more than 1,000 groundwater investigations, hydraulic fracturing has not caused any groundwater contamination.[151] A report by the fracking-opponent Environmental Working Group, however, cited that the EPA concluded in 1987 that hydraulic fracturing of a 4,000-foot-deep vertical natural gas well in 1982 in Jackson County, W.Va., contaminated shallower groundwater and private wells.[152] And in 2011, the EPA launched a new investigation, expected to be complete by 2014, into the potential contamination of public water supplies by fracking. Also, states have launched their own health investigations in areas of concentrated natural gas drilling. In Pennsylvania, a state-funded study will measure baseline public health conditions to help track any future health impact from shale drilling.[153] Penn State University researchers also plan a database, funded by the National Science Foundation, which will be able to track potential impacts of Marcellus Shale activity on water quality.[154]

While hydraulic fracturing itself deep within the earth has not been scientifically identified as a risk, the chance of contamination from frack fluid is much more likely at the surface. Most of the water in a fracturing operation remains in the formation, but approximately 15 percent to 20 percent or up to 800,000 gallons of the fluid comes back to the surface as "flowback." Flowback is collected through a gas production "separator" that separates the fluid destined for disposal from the hydrocarbons coming to the surface to be piped and sold. There is concern that flowback waste can get into groundwater through poorly constructed well casings, prompting regulators to toughen up casing regulations, and the industry often added levels of casing to protect groundwater. Even drilling a water well, if not done properly, could potentially negatively affect ground water supplies.

In addition to contamination from flowback returning to the surface, there is also the threat of leaking retention ponds or spills from trucks. The spreading of salty brine wastewater from nonshale vertical wells is legally used in New York and other areas to keep dust levels down during road construction or as a de-icer in winter.[155] However, spills of high concentrations are hazardous. In July 2010, after coming into contact with fracking fluid pooling on an East Resources well, 28 cattle on a Tioga County farm were quarantined. Though it was certainly no surprise, in an experiment conducted by the U.S. Forest Service, a patch of national forest in West Virginia sprayed with salty fracking fluid suffered a quick and serious loss of vegetation.[156] Disposal of this salty, foul water has been a huge environmental concern because of total dissolved solids, or TDS, a measure of all elements dissolved in water that can include bromides, carbonates, chlorides, sulfates, nitrates, sodium, potassium, calcium, and magnesium. Relatively small spills of these substances resulted in big headlines in Appalachian newspapers.

Accidents Will Happen — Marcellus Missteps

Accidents are no strangers to well drilling, as it has been throughout its history a sometimes dangerous industrial process. In Texas, Louisiana, and other areas familiar to drilling, these mishaps are rare, but not unusual. Incidents in traditional drilling states included blowouts, claims of air pollution, methane in the drinking water, and the poisoning of cattle, apparently after the cows in the Southwest drank frack chemicals that flooded off a drill site during a storm. And in the shadow of the 2010 BP Deepwater Horizon offshore oil spill disaster in the Gulf of Mexico, news of even small oil and gas spills or fires were magnified under the media lens. As the Marcellus boom ramped up in Appalachia, a few highly publicized surface spills and well blowouts in Pennsylvania were amplified by press reports and acted as a catalyst for environmental worries. In addition to these public concerns, personal injury attorneys weighed in on the potential for "horrendous injuries" and subsequent tort litigation. As one Pittsburgh lawyer put it, "The failure scenarios are quite robust."[157]

In January 2010, 21,000 gallons of fracturing fluids spewed from a well site operated by Talisman Energy, but the liquid was contained on a well pad plastic lining.[158] Another Talisman well a year later in Pennsylvania's Tioga County suffered a blowout that sent polluted drilling wastewater and sand shooting into the air.[159] Another drilling operation in Clearfield County, operated by Houston-based EOG Resources, resulted in 35,000 gallons of frack water spewing into the air for 16 hours, some leaking into a nearby stream. In November 2010, a fracking fluid tank valve at an XTO Energy well pad in Lycoming County discharged approximately 2,400 gallons of flowback water, polluting a nearby spring and tributary.

At a Chesapeake Energy well in Washington County in southwestern Pennsylvania, a February 2011 holding tank fire damaged five condensate tanks and left three contract workers injured, one critically. A minimal amount of brine escaped and was contained in a plastic liner.[160] In response, state regulators asked drilling companies to "voluntarily" follow best practices to control highly volatile vapors.[161] In April 2011, a blowout caused by a failure of a valve flange connection resulted in fluid during the fracturing process to be discharged from the wellhead at high pressure on a Chesapeake Energy Marcellus Shale well in Bradford County in the northeastern part of the state. Thousands of gallons of fracturing fluid flowed from the site for at least half a day and Chesapeake's drilling in the state was temporarily suspended.[162] Maryland's Attorney General said he planned to sue the company for violating federal anti-pollution laws after the spill of fracturing fluid into the Susquehanna River watershed.[163] Chesapeake said it was the first valve flange failure of this magnitude in more than 15,000 wells the firm completed since its founding in 1989.[164] Pennsylvania eventually fined the drilling firm nearly $1.1 million for two incidents, one of which was the largest fine the state ever issued. A Range Resources well in Westmoreland County in November 2011 spilled more than 16,000 gallons of recycled water when an above ground water transfer line was accidentally severed, though no environmental damage was evident.[165]

A report by Pennsylvania Land Trust Association said the state identified 1,435 violations by 43 Marcellus drilling companies between January 2008 and August 2010, 952 of the violations identified as having either affected or could potentially affect the environment. However, that did not mean 1,400 spills, as one incident could cause several violations.[166] About one-third of the cases involved some type of discharge of frack water, drill pit water, drill cuttings and mud, or some other type of industrial waste. Other violations included, among others, well construction errors and erosion and sediment control. Between 2005 and February 2011, Pennsylvania imposed 89 fines against Marcellus Shale–related companies for a total of $2,106,318.[167] Still, the overall record of the industry is considered good. But as former Pennsylvania DEP head John Hanger pointed out, "there's no such thing as zero risk or zero impact drilling."[168] Over time, the best practices in the industry would modify fracturing and production techniques to help prevent any spills from escaping from the drill site through heavily lined pits, ultrasonic gas leak detectors, and various other redundant automated safety shut down procedures during production.

Mishaps were not only at well sites. In October 2010, a truck transporting frack water was forced off a road and down an embankment in Pennsylvania's Washington County, spilling much of the 4,000 gallons in the tank.[169] Another truck accident in February 2011 spilled 3,400 gallons of treated flowback water from a well drilled by Anadarko Petroleum Corp. in Swissdale, Pa., onto a highway, and another accident in Salladasburg, Pa., in December 2011 resulted in a overturned fracking fluid truck leaking its contents into a creek.[170]

In addition to the surface violations, gas drillers are considered the likely suspects of any potential problems with drinking water. In April 2011, fracking fluid from a well near Leroy Township in Bradford County spilled into a tributary of Towanda Creek in northeastern Pennsylvania, which flows to the Susquehanna River.[171] Later testing of water wells by the EPA revealed contamination; however, Chesapeake maintained the testing reflected water conditions that existed prior to the drilling.[172] In another case, 13 families in northeastern Pennsylvania sued Houston-based Southwestern Energy Co., charging that fracking fluid contaminated local groundwater in Susquehanna County. Southwestern denied any problems with their well and state environmental officials said they found no link between the well and any contamination.[173] A Pennsylvania woman blamed the health problems of her family on elevated levels of barium, iron, manganese, total dissolved solids, chlorides, and methane in her drinking well water as a result of a shale gas well drilled by Chief Oil & Gas, but the state DEP later found no connection with the well and stated the chemicals were naturally occurring.[174]

Historically, flowback is initially contained in drainage pits before disposal. Most spills can occur on the well pad itself, and some hydrogeologists claim that it will more effective to use steel tanks instead of retention ponds to contain highly corrosive salty flowback fluids and covering well pads with liners to contain spills.[175] State regulators require emergency spill plans. The ground at some wells is graded to contain larger spills into a containment pit and emergency equipment can siphon away more than 10 million gallons of water in a catastrophic spill. The development of 10-foot-high portable dams of welded steel and heavy-duty reinforced nylon/polyurethane liners that resist tearing can create an artificial lake that prevent water contamination.[176] Other industry best practices include electronic monitoring and underground drainage systems to discover leaks and keep water in catch basins, spill kits, absorbent materials, and vacuum trucks.[177] After Hurricane Irene in September 2011 swept through the northeast causing massive flooding, no evidence of spills from drilling retention ponds could be found — though as a result of flooding, rivers such as the Susquehanna in Pennsylvania contained gasoline and diesel from flooded cars and trucks, agricultural runoff, lawn chemicals, industrial waste, and human fecal matter.[178]

In addition to the contaminated salty discharge from the wells, additional concerns erupted over radiation that was present in Marcellus Shale hydraulic fracturing wastewater sampling done at wellheads. Low levels of naturally occurring radioactive material (NORM) is brought to the surface in the rock pieces of the drill cuttings and flowback, though there were concerns that the extraction process created technology-enhanced NORMS that could be hard to detect in diluted wastewater.[179] A 2010 study by a geologist at the State University of New York at Buffalo found fracking released uranium trapped in the shale that could come back to the surface. Though not thought to be a direct threat to gas drillers or the public, the concern over radioactive elements in the drinking water of millions of people in the region resulted in Pennsylvania environmental officials conducting numerous tests. They found no radioactive contaminants in the water used and produced at 12 of 14 drinking water suppliers in seven area rivers in Pennsylvania.[180] State and federal officials said testing should continue, however, and the industry group Marcellus Shale Coalition offered to assist by creating a $100,000 fund to help support water testing.[181]

"Reduce, Reuse and Recycle"— Wastewater Flowback Disposal

The rare accidental discharges of frack fluids and radiation have not been the prime concern of frack fluid disposal. Flowback water was initially addressed at treatment facilities that were properly equipped to remove the chemicals. Salty bromide concentrations in western Pennsylvania's rivers and creeks, however, put some public water suppliers in violation of federal safe drinking water standards. Although the substances are also produced by coal-fired electric plants, treatment of brine disposal water from hydraulic fracturing was thought to be a contributor. Bromides are commonly found in seawater and were once used in sedatives and headache remedies like Bromo-Seltzer before worries erupted about its toxicity. When disinfected at public treatment plants with chlorine, it facilitates formation of brominated trihalomethanes, also known as THMs, volatile organic liquid compounds linked to cancer and birth defects.[182] Penn State University research of 200 wells found some concentrations of

Gas Production Units — Gas production units, or "separators," separate the natural gas flowing from a Marcellus gas well from any liquid frack fluid also coming out of the well. The dry natural gas is piped directly into transmission lines while the fluid flows to nearby containment tanks (author's photograph).

bromide in water wells near drill sites, though bromides were not considered a hazard in a natural state.[183] In response to having detected high bromide levels in rivers in western Pennsylvania and the wastewater discharge concerns potentially affecting public drinking water sources, in May 2011, Pennsylvania requested that drillers voluntarily stop disposing wastewater at the 16 remaining municipal sewage and commercial treatment plants.[184] Though major drillers complied, later water samples in western Pennsylvania's river still showed bromide concentrations raising the possibility of other contamination sources.[185]

Pennsylvania enacted the strictest water treatment standards in the nation in August 2010, requiring treated water to meet drinking water standards before being released into the rivers. Existing treatment plant permits, however, were grandfathered. According to environmental officials, in 2009 and 2010, about 44,000 barrels of drilling waste produced by Cabot Oil and Gas were improperly sent to a treatment facility in a Philadelphia suburb and discharged into a local creek.[186] Tracking of wastewater disposal improved and Pennsylvania prosecutors cracked down on illegal dumping of flowback, charging one hauler with illegally dumping millions of gallons of Marcellus Shale wastewater, sewer sludge, and greasy restaurant slop in holes, mine shafts, and waterways from 2003 to 2009.[187] To ensure against rogue dumpers, many in the industry use global positioning devices and other wireless technology to monitor water withdrawal and disposal. Some surface contamination has been linked to road maintenance, as the brine in road salt is similar to that in flowback water.[188]

Since about one-fifth of the water pumped into the Marcellus wells comes back in flowback, the sheer volume of wastewater is a concern. In the last six months of 2010, sewage treatment plants in Pennsylvania accepted 2.7 million barrels of the flowback water, the equivalent of 116 million gallons.[189] The *New York Times* reported that an EPA lawyer called flowback "mystery liquids" since its ingredient toxins were not known and some plants were diluting, but not "treating" the waste.[190] The EPA vowed to impose its own nationwide disposal standards by 2014.[191] After concerns voiced by environmental groups and the EPA, some wastewater treatment facilities refused to accept the flowback water.[192] The small western Pennsylvania community of Licking Township was one of the first municipalities restricting disposal of wastewater from gas drilling.[193] The Buffalo (N.Y.) Sewer Authority threatened punitive action against companies that disclosed that some wastewater they hauled to a treatment facility contained flowback water.[194] In Ohio, EPA officials announced that cities could not treat the salty brine from new natural gas wells in their sewage plants and then dump it into streams. In addition, no wastewater treatment plants accept or treat fracturing fluid in West Virginia.

Legitimate disposal of wastewater was still a top concern and new private company treatment processes were developed to reduce or remove contaminants, metals, and total dissolved solids. The industry's best practices jumped on the fast track in addressing the disposal of frack fluid and other environmental issues by recycling most of the contaminated flowback water produced at the well site. Besides the obvious environmental concerns, treating wastewater was also expensive for drillers. One treatment company used a thermal distillation (evaporating water through heat to produce clean water vapor) and remove sediments.[195] Between June 2008 and May 2010, drilling companies reused about 44.1 million gallons of flowback and disposed of 21 million gallons, a recycling rate of nearly 67 percent either by directly recycling or employing mobile recycling units.[196] New portable treatment units enabling on-site treatment of wastewater reduced both costs and truck traffic.[197] For example, firms like Range Resources and Anadarko Petroleum treated wastewater at mobile plants in the field, reducing distances the wastewater was transported. In addition, other treatment firms sprouted up to remove contaminants such as sediments and metals and converted them into residual solid waste to landfills.[198]

In May 2011, the EPA asked the six largest Marcellus exploration companies to explain how and where they dispose of the flowback from drilling operations. But many firms had already been recycling most, if not all, the waste. Responding to the federal environmental agency, the six major Marcellus Shale drillers, including Chevron Appalachian, Range Resources, Chesapeake Energy, SWEPI LP (Shell), Talisman, and Cabot Oil & Gas, among others, said they treated 90 to 100 percent of their flowback water onsite and often reused it in their operations.[199] When the recycled water reached the point where it could not fracture another well, the wastewater was processed to environmental specifications by private "Zero Liquid Discharge" water treatment facilities or disposed of in federally regulated deep injection wells,

Separator Tanks — Large separator tanks collect the "flowback" of frack fluid from Marcellus gas wells. The tanks are surrounded by a sealed pit to prevent any accidental spillage from contaminating the environment around the well pad. The wastewater is then pumped into trucks for proper disposal (author's photograph).

primarily in Ohio, because Pennsylvania's geology generally does not support brine-injection wells that can absorb the liquid.[200] In June 2010, Ohio quadrupled the fees that out-of-state haulers paid to dump brine into 170 disposal wells, about half of it from Pennsylvania. Ohio accepted nearly 15 million gallons of waste in the second half of 2010 injecting it 4,000 to 9,000 feet underground into permeable sandstone trapped by an impermeable layer of rock above it.[201] If the Buckeye State's shale activity picks up, however, some officials want to ensure that its injection wells are reserved for Ohio brine.[202]

In addition to flowback disposal worries, complaints regarding the sometimes foul-smelling wastewater retainment ponds also raised the ire of drilling antagonists. To address this, companies such as Chief Oil and Gas of Dallas announced in December 2010 that it would discontinue its use of open pools for contaminated drilling water and would change to a "closed loop" process, piping flowback directly into steel containers.[203]

In addition to recycling and closed loop processes, new greener technologies are at the forefront to treat drilling fluid waste. Drilling service companies such as Baker Hughes, Inc. and Schlumberger experimented with environmentally friendly chemicals, initially developed for offshore drilling, to kill bacteria, reduce friction, and prevent mineral build-up.[204] Halliburton announced a sweeping plan to significantly reduce the environmental impact of hydraulic fracturing operations by 2013 by redesigning equipment, automating functions, using ultraviolet light to kill bacteria, and reducing the amount of fresh water required in the process.[205] The DOE National Energy Technology Laboratory experimented with an absorbent form of silica to remove impurities to clean flowback and produced water from hydraulically fractured oil and gas wells, removing more than 99 percent of oil and grease from the fluid, and more than 90 percent of benzene, toluene, ethylbenzene, and xylenes.[206]

Perhaps one potential solution to flowback waste is not to use fracturing fluids at all. Some formations can be fractured with gases rather than liquid. And in an effort to kill two birds with one stone, the New York State Energy Research and Development Authority directed a $1.5 million research effort, one of several federal DOE-supported projects, to see if whether carbon dioxide injections could replace liquid fracking, eliminating both fracking fluid and at the same time, storing power plant carbon dioxide emissions, which account for 40 percent of the greenhouse gas output, in a process called "carbon sequestration."[207] The USGS states that geologic carbon dioxide sequestration can increase oil and gas resources while preventing CO_2 release to the atmosphere.[208]

Passing Gas — Methane Migration and Natural Gas Drilling

In addition to the debate over frack fluid disposal, methane migration has become another environmental bugaboo. Possible sources of gas migration include deep-earth thermogenic gas, biogenic gas from decomposing organic matter, coal mines, sewer gas, and swamp gas. Migrating methane is not toxic and has not been found to be result of the fracking process. It does, however, present an explosion hazard if it migrates into buildings through water tables. As mentioned in Chapter One, since the times of the ancient Greeks, the pre–Revolutionary war travels of George Washington, and the first well in Fredonia, N.Y., natural gas migrated to the surface and into aquifers without direct stimulation. Methane migration cases are difficult to conclusively pinpoint. Geologists say that methane can migrate from deep shales to the surface over hundreds of millions of years through a complex system of deep fractures and faults. Some suspect that because areas of northeastern Pennsylvania do not have a history of shallow sand natural gas drilling, the methane present above the Marcellus has been a nuisance, leading to migration.[209] A state-funded Penn State University study of 200 drinking wells near Marcellus drilling sites revealed that nearly a quarter of the wells had methane contamination before drilling occurred and there was no statistical link with methane and drilling or fracking.[210]

Though methane can occasionally wander into aquifers and to the surface naturally, improperly cased and constructed wells, over pressurization, and striking shallow gas zones have been cited as culprits in several cases of migrating methane. Pennsylvania regulators issued 47 violations on 33 Marcellus wells in the first five months of 2011 for casing and cementing problems, and issued 90 violations on 64 wells in 2010. The state ordered a resident near the site of a February 2011 house explosion in Bradford, McKean County, to plug three abandoned natural gas wells (not Marcellus wells), one of which was first drilled in 1881 and later identified as a cause of the explosion.[211] An estimated 350,000 oil and gas wells have been drilled in Pennsylvania since Drake's first oil well in Titusville, and thousands remain unplugged. It is estimated that 184,000 wells were drilled before records were kept, and many were improperly plugged using tree stumps, rocks, or simply left unplugged. In Versailles, Pa., a gas well boom in 1920 led to inadequately plugged wells that later leaked gas into homes in the 1960s.[212] Newer wells are, of course, held to stricter standards. According to the Pennsylvania DEP, less than one-quarter of 1 percent of all of the wells drilled over the last 15 years had any negative impact on water wells.[213]

The EPA claimed that Range Resources may have been responsible for methane contamination of two Texas wells in 2009.[214] However, Range claimed the methane contamination did not come from its Barnett Shale wells, but from the much shallower Strawn formation, which leaked upward into an aquifer, a claim later supported by Texas regulators who absolved Range of any wrongdoing.[215] The EPA dropped its claim in 2012. In West Virginia, a property owner claimed methane contamination in a water well after Chesapeake drilled nearby gas wells, but state authorities could not isolate the source of contamination. Chesapeake said a third-party lab indicated that the methane water sample did not match the gas from its operations.[216] Outside of Buffalo, N.Y., state environmental regulators found no proof that methane gas in a Town of Collins water well was the result of area drilling (not Marcellus), but the gas is often found naturally in well water. DOE officials claimed it emanated from sewer gas from a nearby septic system.[217]

The most publicized case of methane migration during the early years of the Marcellus rush was in Dimock, in northeast Pennsylvania's Susquehanna County, where methane migration contaminated the water wells of 19 families, who later sued Cabot Oil and Gas in 2009. Cabot denied it caused the contamination and some residents in the community claimed area water contained methane since 1945.[218] Though often erroneously linked by critics to fracking, state officials said the cause was due to improper well casing. There has never been a case of contamination in the state from the actual fracking process.[219] State regulators ordered Cabot to stop drilling, provide equipment for removing methane from groundwater at 14 homes near the wells, and pay a $240,000 fine.[220] Cabot initially was ordered to fund a 12.5 mile water pipeline, but the state eventually dropped the plan in exchange for Cabot agreeing to pay $4.1 million to residents.[221] After testing and providing bottled water to residents, the firm maintained its wells were not defective and that hazardous levels of methane in water wells was naturally occurring by water wells drilled into shallow gas formations.[222] Despite some residents' objections, after remediation, state regulators eventually later proclaimed the well water was safe to drink, but the EPA also tested Dimock water supplies[223] and initial results absolved Cabot.

Methane gas was also found in seven drinking water wells near Lairdsville in eastern Lycoming County, Pa., and gas bubbling occurred in nearby Little Muncy Creek. XTO Energy, a division of ExxonMobil, operated a Marcellus well pad within about 2,300 feet of one water well. XTO suspended operations in the county, and provided the five water well owners with potable water.[224] As mentioned earlier, in Pennsylvania an oil or gas company is presumed to be responsible for any pollution if a well is drilled within 1,000 feet of a water supply if it can be shown that the contamination occurred within six months of drilling. Most drillers do a pre-drilling analysis of nearby water wells. Prior to drilling, homeowners are often surprised their wells are found to have bacteria, agricultural runoff, and sediment in water supplies and some water wells have been drilled into old coal mine pools.[225] Still, there have been other cases of methane migration cited throughout the Appalachian basin including New York, Ohio, and West Virginia.

Methane contamination was spotlighted by a 2011 Duke University study linking methane gas from deep Marcellus shales and contamination of private drinking water wells near active gas wells in northeastern Pennsylvania and New York. Researchers stated that methane, found in 85 percent of the wells, was 17 times higher on average in wells within 1,000 feet of a deep natural gas well.[226] Critics, including Pennsylvania's former environmental chief, called the report seriously flawed, citing the study's small sample size of wells in known methane detected areas such as Dimock, Pa., skewing the results, and the lack of pre-testing of wells (which researchers would later pledge to sample). State DEP investigators later probed other cases of suspected methane migration in area wells, finding no significant statistical connections between well water contamination and methane or pollutants that come up in drilling waste.[227] Still, methane migration will be at the top of the list of environmental concerns as Marcellus exploration continues.

Clearing the Air — Marcellus Production and Air Pollution

A major environmental argument for producing more natural gas is that it is the cleanest fossil fuel available, generating in combustion only a fraction of pollutants such as sulfur dioxide, nitrogen oxide, and other particulates compared to coal or oil, and significantly less carbon dioxide, a greenhouse gas, than other fossil fuels. The increased reliance on natural gas was initially embraced by many environmental groups for its earth-friendly benefits compared to coal, reflecting how the initial experience of using natural gas in nineteenth-century Pittsburgh steel mills for economic reasons resulted in the unintended but pleasant consequence of reducing the "Smoky City's" horrid air pollution. In the American Lung Association's "State of the Air 2011" report, however, the Pittsburgh area still ranked as the nation's third most polluted area for short-term particle pollution and environment groups urged the replacement of aging coal-fired power plants with natural gas electric generation as well as the conversion of garbage trucks, buses, and municipal fleets to natural gas.[228] Agreeing that the region's air quality was "unacceptably poor," the Heinz Endowments also released a report that found that industry and vehicle emissions cause environmental damage, illness, and death.[229] In 2011, the EPA's adoption of the Cross-State Air Pollution Rule, intended to reduce pollution-linked illness and mortality, brought many states into particulate compliance, except Pittsburgh-area Allegheny County, home to U.S. Steel Corp.'s Clairton Coke Works.[230]

Despite the clean-air seal of approval proudly worn by the natural gas industry, however, the production of Marcellus Shale gas did not escape counter claims that it produces its own air pollution. Many environmentalists set their sights on shale gas extraction as a source of air pollution from trucks, pump engines, fugitive methane escaping from wells, processing plants, and miasmic fumes wafting from wastewater ponds. Complaints about air quality and chemical carcinogens began during gas production in the Barnett Shale in the Forth Worth area of Texas, most notably in a community known as Dish, formerly Clark, a town with a population of 200 that changed its name in 2005 as part of a satellite television promotion that supplied every resident with 10 years of free satellite television service. Air studies by the state revealed that benzene emission, a contaminant contained in cigarette smoke, was not widespread and was either not detected or was found below levels of health concern. A 2011 study conducted by the City of Fort Worth did not reveal any significant health threats of gas production beyond setback distances.[231] Still, the Texas Commission on Environmental Quality in 2011 proposed new regulations that would require vapor-recovery systems, flares, or other emission controls on large separator tanks.[232]

Similarly, a Pennsylvania state study of air quality at Marcellus Shale wells in four north-central and southwestern Pennsylvania counties identified only low levels of volatile organic compounds, including carcinogenic benzene, toluene, and xylene, as well as carbon monoxide and nitrogen dioxide emanating from emissions from individual wells, posing no public health concerns.[233] Critics claimed this testing was only a snapshot and failed to examine the cumulative impact of the pollutants and the EPA planned long-term air quality observations.

While using natural gas to supplant coal and oil can reduce greenhouse gases such as carbon dioxide, another issue is the unintended release of methane from shale drilling. A controversial study by a Cornell University researcher suggested that greenhouse gas emissions from shale gas production over the next 20 years could actually be more than twice as high than surface-mined coal, preventing natural gas from becoming a "bridge" environmental fuel.[234] Though the estimates were roundly disputed by the industry as well as another rival Cornell study published in the same academic journal, *Climatic Change*, and called an "academic fraud" by Pennsylvania's former environmental head, the study claimed that as much as 7.9 percent of methane from the shale wells was escaping into the atmosphere by vents and leakage, resulting in a much more potent greenhouse gas (compared to carbon dioxide) released into the environment.[235] However, a Carnegie Mellon University study later found that "natural gas from the Marcellus shale has generally lower life cycle GHG emissions than coal for production of electricity in the absence of any effective carbon capture and storage processes, by 20–50 percent depending upon plant efficiencies and natural gas emissions variability."[236] In 2011, the EPA proposed new emissions standards, the first in decades, to control and reduce oil- and gas-drilling emissions from drilling, separator tanks, and compressor stations and well as using existing gas collection technologies to capture fugitive methane.[237]

Blue Highways — Transportation and Lifestyle Issues with Marcellus Drilling

Due to the high water and sand demand for fracking and fluid disposal and the need for heavy drill rigs and support equipment, the Marcellus industry found significant short-term transportation challenges including traffic congestion, deteriorated roads, emergency responses to accidents and hazardous spills, and vehicle violations. In the small town of Towanda, Pa., a hub of Marcellus activity northwest of Scranton, traffic tie-ups from hundreds of truck trips to ship water for a single well raised local ire.[238] The Lycoming County Planning Commission said Marcellus trucks and other vehicles on one particularly road led to a 348 percent increase in overall traffic.[239] Pennsylvania State Police put 250 commercial vehicles out of service during a three-day enforcement blitz in June 2010, centering on Marcellus wastewater trucks.[240] A vehicle inspection effort dubbed "Operation FracNET" in April 2011 ended with 14 drivers placed out of service, 131 trucks taken off the roads, 421 traffic citations, and 824 written warnings.[241] In West Virginia, learning from their mistakes, gas firms agreed not to run trucks during school hours and agreed to place pilot vehicles in front of larger trucks.[242]

The industry would have to post bonds to insure the protection of roads and spend hundreds of thousands to millions of dollars repairing and improving the byways it damaged. The industry-sponsored Marcellus Shale Coalition said in 2011 its member companies spent more than $411 million over the previous three years to repave, rebuild, and improve state and local roadways and infrastructure in Pennsylvania.[243] About 21 percent of the payments were made for local byways and the rest went toward state roads. Saying the industry was "more than willing" to make repairs, Pennsylvania officials claimed the industry owed as much as $35 million more for damage to low-volume secondary roads, many of which did not have sufficient structural strength for the heavy truck traffic.[244] In West Virginia, where residents complained of heavy truck traffic ruining their roads, Chesapeake Energy pledged to spend "tens of millions" of dollars to keep thoroughfares used by the company and its subcontractors in safe condition.[245] Though some localities claimed more needed to be done, others felt that after the industry's repairs, the roads had never been in such good condition.

With hundreds of out-of-town workers and equipment invading some self-described "ghost towns," the Marcellus boom resulted in both increased economic activity (to be discussed later in this chapter) and lifestyle issues in many small rural communities. Demand for housing soared, rents increased, and critics complained that locals were priced out of the community. Many hotels were full and some tourists to drilling areas had trouble finding places to stay. Increased use of public services from medical emergency responses and hospitals to police arrests for criminal activity stressed the budgets of rural farming communities. Because of the industrial and human demand, most drilling counties reported jumps in 9-1-1 calls.[246] According to news reports, some "hard working, hard drinking" rig workers "raising hell" clashed with law enforcement authorities perhaps less tolerant than in the drilling areas in the Southwest.[247] Though economic benefits came with the huge influx of employees of the gas firms, the excitement of Marcellus development proved to be a double-edged sword for formerly sleepy rural communities.

Continental Divides — From Forest Fragmentation to Earthquakes

Although Marcellus wells actually reduce the footprint of acquiring gas supplies compared to traditional drilling, the rush to develop the resources have conservationists concerned that the thousands of planned well pads in Appalachia will forever disturb the pristine forests, affecting various species' habitats and altering agricultural land into temporary industrial use. The Allegheny National Forest, established in 1923 by presidential proclamation, is home to hardwoods including black cherry, red and sugar maple, oak, ash, and hickory, and is one the smallest and most valuable in the National Forests System.[248] About one-third of the 2.1 million acres of state forests in Pennsylvania, created more than a century ago to preserve watersheds and recreation, are under lease to various drillers. The state was able to expand the park system rapidly in the 1960s and '70s with the goal of locating a park within 25 miles of every state resident while permitting about 15 percent of the mineral rights to remain in private hands.[249] In December 2009, a U.S. District Court judge ordered the U.S. Forest Service to discontinue restrictions on new oil and gas well drilling operations and follow a 30-year, court-approved procedure. The environmental group Sierra Club claimed the state is violating federal Land and Water Conservation law by permitting drilling on protected state land.[250] In 2011, however, a U.S. appeals court ruled the owners of mineral rights of the forest land did not have to wait for an environmental study before drilling.[251]

Drilling on other state-owned land created additional public debate. After an unsuccessful effort to establish a severance tax on Marcellus gas in 2010, Pennsylvania Democrat governor Ed Rendell, who first supported leasing state land, established a moratorium on further leasing. The restriction was soon lifted by his predecessor, Republican Tom Corbett, the following year. In 2010, five gas firms won bids to pay more than $128 million for the right to drill on nearly 32,000 acres in northcentral Pennsylvania public forest land.[252] As of July 2011, there were approximately 750 producing historic natural gas wells and 100 new Marcellus Shale gas wells.[253] The state Pennsylvania Fish and Boat Commission also considered leasing its land to help raise revenue for crucial repairs to dams.[254] Due to the Marcellus, revenues to the state's Oil and Gas Lease Fund jumped from $4 million to $5 million per year to $153 million in 2008.[255] In addition, a Pennsylvania state legislative report in 2011 urged that land surrounding state universities and state prisons be considered as possible drilling sites.[256] And the leasing continues, raising concerns among environmental and sportsmen groups.

West Virginia has a 1961 law prohibiting mineral extraction in public parks, but in 2011 the Supreme Court of Appeals in the Mountain State upheld the right of oil and natural gas drilling in a southern West Virginia state park created a year before the law was established. In neighboring Virginia, a draft U.S. Forest Service management plan for the 1.1 million acre George Washington National Forest would limit hydraulic fracturing on forest land.[257] Although the land should be restored with minimal visual effect after the drilling process is completed, the gaps in wooded areas still worry land preservationists.

The fragmentation of pristine forest not only gave drilling critics the shakes above ground, but also below their feet. Some earthquake scientists have identified harmless microearthquakes in the Dallas/Fort Worth area perhaps set off by hydraulic fracturing of the Barnett Shale.[258] Another non-damaging quake was registered near fracking operations across the Atlantic in Britain, leading to the stoppage of the process.[259] Some opponents of fracking fear there may be a small risk of more dangerous quakes. Earthquakes in Texas, Arkansas, and West Virginia have been associated with high-pressure waste fluid injection into disposal wells, which may have triggered the seismic events, but not hydraulic fracturing.[260] Some geologists believe that an Ohio hazardous-waste injection well was likely the cause of a series of earthquakes near Ashtabula, Ohio, from 1987 through 2001, though other experts say there is no direct correlation between earthquakes and wells.[261] Geologists investigated for links between a brine-water injection well and seven minor earthquakes in northeast Ohio in 2011, the only ones recorded with epicenters in Youngstown and the Mahoning River valley.[262] The January 1, 2012, *Wall Street Journal* reported that seismologists almost certainly believed a 2011 New Year's Eve earthquake near Youngstown, Ohio, was linked to a nearby wastewater injection well (not to fracking), which was immediately ordered by the state to shut down. The Arkansas Oil and Gas Commission banned waste injection wells in the "Natural State" in 2011 after a fault line was discovered in the area, but it was determined that seismic activity was not caused by fracking shale wells. Similarly, there is no firm link in other areas experiencing the seismic activity, such as West Virginia, that quakes were the result of hydraulic fracturing.[263] Industry spokesman scoffed at suggestions that an August 2011 earthquake near Washington, D.C., could be associated with fracking hundreds of miles away, saying that if it did, fracking also caused "the Great Depression, the Black Plague, and the break-up of the Beatles."[264] Comparing a November 2011 magnitude-5.6 earthquake that shook Oklahoma, which had the power of nearly 2,000 times that of the 1995 Oklahoma City bombing, a Stanford University geophysicist told the Associated Press that the energy released by fracking there, "is the equivalent to a gallon of milk falling off the kitchen counter."[265]

Fractured Fairy Tales to Realpolitik — Local, State, and Federal Regulation of Marcellus Production

Opponents to hydraulic fracturing throughout 2010–11 petitioned governments and staged protests in various communities from small to large in New York, Pennsylvania, and West Virginia and fracking critics took their objections to their respective state capitals in Albany, Harrisburg, and Charleston. Several college campuses showed the anti-drilling "shockumentary" *Gasland*, fueling the fire of objection to the process. A Rochester, N.Y. activist group used street theatre to protest by setting fire to symbolic glasses of polluted well water. The city's fire department noted the group was "playing with fire" as the demonstration occurred near an underground tank of explosive propane.[266] Union workers and environmental activists picketed one Pennsylvania site supporting a Marcellus Shale severance tax, but later apologized having mistakenly set up their protest where drilling was not occurring.[267] Other protesters placed bogus signs at Pennsylvania Turnpike rest stops purportedly from the state DEP suggesting that travelers test water fountains for methane with an open flame.[268]

Despite its attempts to educate the public, many in the drilling industry confess that they were unprepared for the opposition to their activities. Facing ridicule and hostile, often quasi-vulgar protests comparing the hydraulic fracturing term to an obscenity, the industry vowed that increased transparency regarding drilling, fracking, and wastewater disposal could help dispel myths and put the issues in perspective. Although the term "fracking" may have seemed innocent in the 1950s, Dave McCurdy, the head of the American Gas Association, said it became the worst possible term to use for natural gas extraction.[269] Industry groups such as the Marcellus Shale Coalition in Pennsylvania, which hired former Pennsylvania governor and Homeland Security Secretary Tom Ridge as a "strategic advisor," Independent Gas and Oil Association in New York, Ohio Petroleum Council, and the West Virginia Oil and Natural Gas Association struggled to get their message out. Television, radio, and newspaper advertisements, as well as public relations programs, were plentiful in drilling regions. Brad Gill, executive director of the Independent Oil and Gas Association of New York State, however, said, "Fear-mongering and emotion will always trump science and logic."[270] A West Virginia industry spokesperson said pro-gas drilling advertisements were meant to counter outlandish claims such as: fracking caused a farmer's calves to be born with cleft palates; fracking fluid exposure prevented a dead man's body from being cremated; and fracking could cause male children to be born homosexual.[271] A community relations effort to educate children about the gas drilling process by Talisman Energy included a coloring book featuring a cartoon "Barney-like" dinosaur, Talisman Terry, the "friendly fracosaurus." The effort was harshly criticized and lampooned by drilling opponents, who called it "propaganda" and Talisman soon extinguished the prehistoric educational tool.[272] An economist from the national oil and gas industry trade association API, admitted, "We've haven't done as effective a job as we can to explain the technology and to explain that the technology itself hasn't caused water problems but other aspects of drilling and cementing have to be done properly."[273]

Since Marcellus Shale drilling is a relatively new phenomenon, both state and federal governments have wrestled with how to regulate production and transportation, ensure environmental protection of air, water, and land resources, as well as encourage positive economic impacts of the activity and take advantage of the new wealth sprouting from under the ground. Surface discharges of water associated with shale gas drilling and storm water runoff are regulated by federal Clean Water Act regulations, underground injection of fluids from shale gas activities fall under the Safe Drinking Water Act, air emissions from engines and gas processing are regulated by Clean Air Act limits, and environmental impact of production on federal lands is analyzed through the National Environmental Policy Act (NEPA).[274] But stricter regulations would be on the horizon.

Oil and gas drilling, production, and plugging regulations have generally been left up to the states, though many environmental activists are appealing to the federal government to become more involved. As opposition groups petitioned various levels of governments, the industry responded. For example, natural gas firms in Pennsylvania spent more than $3.5 million in 2010 on lobbying regarding severance tax, drilling wastewater, and hydraulic fracturing issues before the state legislature.[275] The industry had to manage public concerns on local, state, national, and international levels.

In addition to the existing oil and gas rules, drilling is subject to numerous other land, water, and air regulations covering clean streams, conservation, hazardous waste, wildlife, highway, fish and game, erosion, sediment control, water quality and control, vehicle, safety, pipeline, permitting, and storm water management. Still, states like Pennsylvania toughened environmental regulations. As the Marcellus activity accelerated, the Pennsylvania DEP increased the number of well inspectors and instituted new standards for well construction, including casing pressure tests, cementing, monitoring by quarterly inspections, and annual reporting. The state also changed wastewater disposal laws and put in place new requirements for chemical disclosure designed to make the wells less likely to allow natural gas to escape and contaminate water supplies. Another rule mandates a 150-foot buffer from streams. Responding to objections by the Chesapeake Bay Foundation, the Pennsylvania DEP also agreed to remove its "expedited" permitting process from drilling applications located near streams with the highest water quality.[276] In 2011, the state legislature also passed a law that established spacing limitations between natural gas wells near workable coal seams. The "Marcellus Shale Advisory Commission," established in 2011 by newly-elected Pennsylvania governor Tom Corbett, and comprised of local and state government, industry, environmental, and conservation interests, presented 96 recommendations to lawmakers and regulators, most involving increased health, safety, and environmental regulations, and a fee to compensate local communities for any effects of drilling. Opposition groups such as the "Citizens Marcellus Gas Commission" composed of environment, labor, and housing organizations, responded, urging Pennsylvania officials to end the "preferred treatment" of gas firms, limit drilling to certain areas, create a drilling tax, and beef up environmental and drilling regulations.[277]

Local regulations often result in drilling companies attempting to comply with numerous different municipal laws adding costs and legal hurdles to development. The 1984 Pennsylvania Oil and Gas Act does not permit local jurisdiction to regulate or enforce laws against the Act (i.e., how drilling is conducted), but they can regulate through zoning where drilling occurs. A Pennsylvania Supreme Court ruling in 2010, *Huntley Inc. v. Borough Council of Oakmont*, affirmed the right of municipal and county officials to limit natural gas drilling to certain districts, such as agricultural, mining, or manufacturing, and exclude it from residential neighborhoods.[278] Though many financially stressed communities welcomed the expansion of Marcellus activity for its clear positive economic impact, other localities, states, and entire nations feared the environmental impact, even if their area was not in a shale-drilling region. Although there was not Marcellus activity within its jurisdiction and unlikely that drilling would occur in densely populated areas, the Pittsburgh City Council banned Marcellus drilling, becoming the first city to do so, and urged every municipality in Pennsylvania to follow its lead.[279] Several suburban Pittsburgh communities would follow with bans. A community group in nearby Murrysville, Pa., home to the storied Haymaker well that supplied Pittsburgh with natural gas in the 1880s, also pushed for a ban on drilling, eventually leading to the creation of a zoning ordinance. In January 2011, the Philadelphia City Council followed with a largely symbolic action asking for a stoppage in Marcellus development in eastern Pennsylvania and restricting Philadelphia Gas Works, the city's municipal gas utility, from purchasing Marcellus Shale supplies.[280] Fracking bans were considered or approved in numerous communities large and small throughout Appalachia from New York's Buffalo and Syracuse to West Virginia's Lewisburg and Morgantown. Voters rejected bans in two towns in

2011 but State College, Pa., approved one. Although not outright prohibition, various localities passed or considered restrictive drilling ordinances involving traffic, space, zoning and conditional use, noise levels, seismic testing, lighting, work hours, and density, occasionally resulting in legal and other retribution by gas firms. A feud between Range Resources and Mt. Pleasant Township over conditional drilling in southwest Pennsylvania's Washington County resulted in the drilling company threatening to cease all activities and economic support of businesses in the township.[281] Chesapeake Energy withdrew a $25,000 charitable contribution to a Morgantown, W.Va., farmer's market after that city banned fracking even though a court later struck down the ban.[282] The gas firm Northeast Natural Energy began fracturing operations soon after the action. Peters Township, an affluent suburb of Pittsburgh, among others, sought to put the issue of a drilling ban on the local ballot, though many were not sure it would survive court tests.[283] Some smaller communities held back on passing ordinances, or in one case in West Virginia, reversed the ban on fracking, fearing the legal fees to defend them.[284] Previously, a federal court struck down a Blaine, Pa., ordinance that enacted a ban against fossil-fuel development.[285]

For the most part, Marcellus drilling and its economic benefits were seen as a good tonic for tough economic times in Pennsylvania, but horizontal drilling and hydraulic fracturing were new and complex challenges for regulators in all states. According to the National Conference of State Legislatures, 19 states considered more than 100 bills related to hydraulic fracturing between October 2010 and July 2011.[286] In West Virginia, where there were already 59,000 active vertical wells, the state legislature appointed a special committee to study Marcellus Shale regulation and later issued emergency regulations in 2011 to protect water quantity and quality. Mountain State legislation was designed to not only regulate production and increase state well inspectors, but also to encourage natural gas use by jump-starting commercial natural gas vehicle conversion and attract "cracker" plants where butane and other derivatives are separated. To buy the legislature more time, Acting Governor Earl Ray Tomblin filed an executive order in 2011 that directed state regulators to enact additional environmental regulations governing Marcellus Shale drilling activities, including drilling applications, well inspections, land use, and water management plans.[287]

Though there was not much horizontal drilling initially in Ohio in the Marcellus play, there is anticipated production from the much deeper Utica Shale. Ohio had 44 wells drilled in the Marcellus and nine wells drilled in the Utica Shale by early 2011. Ohio Governor John Kasich stated that Marcellus and Utica Shale exploration and exploitation would be a "God send" for Ohio's economy. The Ohio Department of Natural Resources did not see the need for a shale gas drilling moratorium and felt it could ensure the safety of the public and environment by hiring additional well inspectors and implementing several changes to urban drilling laws, the first major change in 25 years. In addition, the legislature passed and the governor signed a bill that opened state parks and other lands in Ohio to oil and gas drilling, and set up a commission to oversee oil and gas leasing in the state.[288]

Further south, North Carolina's Marcellus prospects are located in Moore, Lee, and Chatham counties. Approximately 59,000 acres in the Deep River (Triassic) basin could provide a 40-year supply for the state, according to the North Carolina Geological Survey.[289] Although the state did not permit horizontal drilling and hydraulic fracturing, the state is conducting a study to be completed in 2012. About 10,000 acres were leased and pending positive results of the study, drilling, regulated by the North Carolina Department of Environment and Natural Resources, could begin by 2013.[290]

Though the Marcellus movement was largely welcomed by state officials in the historical tri-state drilling regions in Pennsylvania, West Virginia, and Ohio, hydraulic fracturing often created widespread controversy in other surrounding states. The fracking fight pitted drillers versus reluctant landowners, environmentalists, government legislatures and regulatory agencies, and, in some cases, property owners versus their neighbors. Though one public poll found that Pennsylvanians supported Marcellus drilling by a two-to-one margin,[291] another survey claimed four of five Pennsylvanians were "very" or "somewhat" concerned about fracking affecting drinking water sources. And though fewer New Yorkers were aware of the controversy, nearly nine of 10 people surveyed were concerned about fracking, though later polls showed a majority of state residents supported drilling anyway.[292] The Empire State, home to more than 14,000 active shallow wells and the site of the first commercial gas well in Fredonia, temporarily banned Marcellus activity in August 2010 pending further study. Because drilling companies focused on shale resources, conventional exploration also declined. New York natural gas production, more than half produced in the Southern Tier counties of Chemung and Steuben, dropped 20 percent in 2010 from a year prior and 29 percent since 2008, when the state produced 50.3 billion cubic feet of gas.[293] After study and much public debate, the New York Department of Environmental Conservation (DEC) agreed to allow production on 85 percent of the state's Marcellus Shale areas beginning in mid–2012, permitting drilling on private land under "rigorous and effective controls," but banning fracturing in the New York City and Syracuse watersheds, "primary aquifers," and state-owned parks, forest, and wildlife management areas.[294] The announcement was greeted with cautious optimism by drillers and contractors, though some environmental groups were still concerned about water quality protection.[295] State environmental regulators announced draft regulations for hydraulic fracturing in late 2011, attracting thousands of public comments, taking a more cautious approach than its neighbor Pennsylvania. In New York, the likely first drilling would occur where geologists say the organic richness is optimal, specifically on the state's Southern Tier counties of Broome, Tioga, and Chemung.[296]

To the east, Maryland lawmakers passed a bill that placed a moratorium on drilling in the state's western counties, and Governor Martin O'Malley later signed an executive order in June 2011 requiring the Maryland Department of the Environment and an advisory commission to complete a study to determine how to safely produce the shale gas.[297]

While New Jersey does not currently produce natural gas, the legislature approved a hydraulic fracturing ban by significant margins and sent it to the state's governor.[298] Though the Garden State was not in the Marcellus play, some northwest areas could possibly be explored in the deeper Utica Shale. New Jersey governor Chris Christie conditionally vetoed the legislation, but instead recommended a one-year moratorium.[299] In June 2010, the Delaware River Basin Commission, a multistate agency based in Trenton, N.J., declared a moratorium on drilling any gas wells in the upper Delaware River watershed, considered by an advocacy group as the nation's "most endangered" river, until it could approve new drilling regulations, eventually allowing limited drilling.[300] The agency moved to collect numerous base-line water tests.[301] New Jersey officials, also concerned about fracking wastewater contamination, supported the moratorium. The drilling industry, however, as well as Pennsylvania's environmental agency head, balked at proposed regulations that included not only water use, but also land use and industry operational standards, asserting that the Commission exceeded its legal authority.

An effort to seek a temporary ban on gas production in the Delaware watershed was declined by the Obama Administration through the Army Corps of Engineers in 2011. Still, federal legislators and regulators, and the politics that came with them, would weigh in on hydraulic fracturing via the EPA and DOE. Environmental groups wanted the federal government to step in to regulate chemical disclosure and protect air and water supplies. A 2004 EPA study frequently cited by industry found hydraulic fracturing safe, but the study involved fracking of coalbed methane wells, not shale wells, and EPA officials point out it did not involve samples on drinking water. However, responding to questions from members of the House Committee on Oversight and Government Reform in 2011, EPA Administrator Lisa Jackson admitted there was no "proven case where the fracking process itself has affected water."[302] The EPA's latest hydraulic fracturing review by 22 independent scientists studying the full life cycle of wells, including several in southwestern and northeastern Pennsylvania, and their possible effects on drinking water resources is expected to issue an interim report at the end of 2012, and a final one in 2014.[303]

Meanwhile, the DOE, DOI, and EPA assembled a group of experts to make recommendations on improving hydraulic fracturing operations. The DOE's Shale Gas Production Subcommittee submitted an general endorsement of fracking to President Obama in August 2011, stating that although the leaking of fracking fluid is "remote," it still recommended releasing more information about hydraulic fracturing activities including disclosure of all chemicals used, as well as calling for improvements in the monitoring of water usage and conditions, reducing air pollution and methane emissions, and managing short-term and cumulative impacts on communities, land use, wildlife, and ecologies.[304] In addition, another federal agency, the Securities and Exchange Commission (SEC) asked oil and gas companies to provide detailed information on fracking due to the risk companies may face related to their operations.[305]

Many Appalachian state regulators believe the states, who are closer to the drilling process and are more familiar with the local geology than their federal counterparts, should take the lead in monitoring shale gas production, though most welcome a federal database of information and research to improve production. Fracking techniques vary based on geological differences and local conditions surrounding the shale formations and therefore it is difficult to standardize a one-size-fits-all approach. A DOE shale subcommittee agreed, telling the U.S. Senate Committee on Energy and Natural Resources in 2011 that states effectively regulate the industry.[306] Supporters of federal regulation, such as the Sierra Club, claim the states are too reliant on the gas drilling industry for information and guidance and are subject to local politics. Led by the Chesapeake Bay Foundation numerous environment protection organizations petitioned the federal government in April 2011 to make a more comprehensive analysis of the cumulative impacts of natural gas drilling.[307] Based on comments submitted to the Delaware River Basin Commission, federal and state regulators remain at odds over various natural gas drilling issues from water withdrawal to wastewater disposal.[308] Despite state and industry opposition, the EPA announced in late 2011 that it would develop its own water disposal and air pollution rules by 2014.[309]

In addition to land and water use, flowback disposal, and air pollution concerns, opponents listed other actual and feared less-than-desirable effects from Marcellus activity: drilling near residential areas, hospitals, cemeteries, and daycares; loss or effect of animal habitat and songbirds; deteriorating roads; threats to archaeological sites; and tourism decline. The natural gas industry operates in the dark shadow of the negative legacy of Appalachian coal strip mining and acid mine drainage contaminating rivers and streams. Some environmentalists and outdoor groups, even if they did not oppose drilling in general, worried that the cumulative effect of many minor environmental violations could negatively affect water quality and trout stocks, forests, and wildlife.[310] Some analysts predicted that the industrial impact of drilling and its necessary infrastructure would despoil the rural agricultural landscape and viticulture in Pennsylvania and New York, affecting tourism, though one study of northwestern Pennsylvania tourism did not report such a decline after drilling.[311]

The worst nightmares of real or imagined negative environmental effects also led to bans of hydraulic fracturing in some other nations. In Canada, the Quebec Provincial government put a halt to drilling in the deep Utica Shale, pending an environmental review, causing the stocks of Calgary-based Questerre Energy and other companies with development rights in the province to lose more than 50 percent of their value.[312] A United Kingdom parliamentary committee said it found no evidence that hydraulic fracturing posed any risk to water supplies and rejected calls for a shale-gas moratorium.[313] Across the English Channel, however, the French government temporarily halted all shale oil and gas drilling activity in 2011.[314]

According to the National Regulatory Research Institute, which advises state regulators, "opponents and skeptics of fracking have not yet offered conclusive information showing serious safety and environmental problems that warrant major restrictions on shale-gas production."[315] Still, the see-saw debate of protecting and preserving the environment versus the responsible development of critical energy supplies necessary for a healthy economy may tip to one side or the other, but regulators in the future will likely attempt to straddle both positive ends to have their cake and eat it, too.

Read My Drill Bits — Taxes and the Marcellus Shale

The greatest amount of drilling activity is located in Pennsylvania due to the fact that most of the Marcellus Fairway is located in the large state and, unlike some of its neighbors, the economy-minded Keystone State did not have a severance tax on natural gas.[316] In 2010, Governor Ed Rendell fought with the state legislature to institute a natural gas severance tax, similar to what exists in many other production states, as a way to address the Commonwealth's huge budget deficit. Industry representatives from the Marcellus Shale Coalition urged a fair, competitive, and updated regulatory framework, but claimed the tax proposals would make Pennsylvania the least competitive of shale gas producing states because of other corporate taxes that already existed. No legislative agreement was reached and in 2011 Rendell's successor Tom Corbett vowed not to increase any taxes, including a natural gas severance tax,[317] though some polls showed nearly seven of 10 Pennsylvanians were in favor of one.[318]

Severance taxes, applied when oil and gas are "severed" from the ground, exist in many production states with the exceptions of Louisiana, Alaska, and Pennsylvania. West Virginia, which depends more on severance taxes as a percentage of the state budget than any other state, levied a 5 percent fee on sales of natural gas, plus an additional 4.7 cents for each thousand cubic feet produced. The tax generated only $10.5 million in state revenue in 2009.[319] Shared West Virginia state and local natural gas severance tax collections increased from $15 million in the mid 1990s to $80 million in 2008, before the recession that year and the fall in natural gas prices caused a decline in total revenues to $55 million in 2009.[320] A 2011 study by the Marshall University Center for Business and Economic Research showed that West Virginia appeared to place a higher tax burden on natural gas operators than most states, including the five surrounding Appalachian states.[321] Perhaps partially due to the tax, West Virginia drilling permits dropped from 800 in 2008 to fewer than 550 in 2009, while Pennsylvania permits skyrocketed.[322]

Tax supporters in Pennsylvania maintained that natural gas producers, many out of state, were profiting while not paying their fair share, while tax opponents said additional taxes added on to already present state corporate taxes would harm economic recovery, job growth, and deter development of needed domestic energy supplies. Drilling firm Talisman, which claimed it was spending $1 billion on capital expenses of its operations in northeastern Pennsylvania, said a severance tax would make the drilling of shale wells uneconomical.[323] Most drilling proponents, such as the Pennsylvania Oil and Gas Association (POGAM) held a "nonnegotiable" opposition to a new tax, claiming that adding a severance tax in Pennsylvania would hurt the nascent industry, especially since natural gas prices were at such historically depressed levels. Many companies drilled to hold leases because they would soon expire, not because the price was high.[324] A few drilling firms, like EQT Corp., supported a severance tax, and some legislative leaders called for a local-impact fee that would alleviate the stress on local government services impacted by drilling.[325] In 2011, Pennsylvania Governor Corbett's Marcellus Shale Advisory Commission proposed a drilling "impact fee" to mitigate the stress (e.g., traffic problems, road damage, emergency response training, etc.) in the communities where drilling occurred. Corbett relented, calling for a county-imposed fee that could reach $160,000 per well over a 10-year span to benefit communities affected by drilling, potentially raising $200 million within six years.[326] Pennsylvania approved the fee in 2012.

Without a severance tax, the Commonwealth still received revenue from shale gas activity. The Pennsylvania Department of Revenue said the drilling industry contributed $1.1 billion on corporate, sales, and employee income taxes from 2006 through the first quarter of 2011, in addition to infrastructure investments, royalty payments, and permit fees.[327] Vowing to make Pennsylvania the "Texas of the natural gas boom," Governor Corbett touted the $64 million in fiscal year 2010-11 from royalties from natural gas drilling on state-owned land, revenues that were projected to rise to $300 million by 2015-16.[328] Sales taxes collected in counties with drilling increased by more than 11 percent between 2007 and 2010, while in non-drilling counties collections declined 6 percent.[329] In Bradford County, where most of the state's drilling occurred, state sales tax collections from July 2007 to June 2010 increased by 21 percent.[330] Surrounding states also proposed similar fees.

Appalachia's Boon Leads to Boom Times

The Appalachian region is often portrayed as economically disadvantaged, from mountainous areas often associated with abject rural poverty to the north and west dotted with population-declining "rust belt" industrial centers such as Wheeling, Youngstown, Pittsburgh, and Buffalo. Could the black gold Marcellus Shale convert the region from rags to riches? One study claimed the Southwest Barnett Shale drilling added $65.4 billion dollars to the Texas economy between 2001 and 2011 and supported more than 100,000 jobs.[331] Despite the environmental opposition and regulatory demands, both enthusiastic political leaders and gas industry proponents hung their hat on the positive economic boost the sudden interest in Marcellus gas gave the Appalachian region. And unlike the boom times of the nineteenth century where fanatical oil and gas drilling resulted in ephemeral oil towns like Pithole cropping up overnight and vanishing almost as quickly, advocates suggest that the Marcellus play is mammoth and will provide direct jobs, royalty income for landowners, rising tax revenues, and beneficial ripple effects for supporting businesses for years to come.

Thanks to leasing and royalties, many Pennsylvania landowners became instant "shalionaires." Farmers once struggling to make ends meet suddenly were investing in new barns and farm equipment. Range Resources estimated that landowners received more than $5 billion in lease and royalty payments between 2002 and 2010.[332] "It's better than any milk checks we ever got," one dairy farmer told the *Pittsburgh Tribune Review* in February 2011.[333] Property values escalated in many drilling areas due to the creation of new jobs, though experts suggested some properties nearest the drilling locations may decline. In addition, some banks are concerned about offering mortgages on potential drilling sites, concerned with devaluation.[334] Conversely, the royalty revenues have resulted in many landowners retiring their mortgages. Former farming communities, plagued with high jobless rates and an exodus of residents seeking employment elsewhere, converted into thriving economic centers. The town of Canonsburg, Pa., with a population of 9,000 and known for its Fourth of July celebration, was christened as the "energy capital of the East," home to five major operators, including Range, Chesapeake Energy, and EQT. Partially due to Marcellus activity, the small eastern Pennsylvania city of Williamsport, most noted for the home of the Little League World Series, became the seventh fastest growing metropolitan area in the country and the fastest in Pennsylvania.[335]

The Pittsburgh area, once the epicenter of the corporate fossil fuel industry more than a century before, picked up activity through gas industry office relocations, expansions, and industry conferences, and political leaders hoped the major energy firms would relocate their corporate headquarters to the region. One example was Dutch Royal Shell PLC, which opened a new, 76,000-square-foot office building in Franklin Township in western Pennsylvania.[336] The federal Bureau of Labor Statistics revealed that western Pennsylvania's Washington County registered the third fastest economic growth in the nation between March 2010 and March 2011, largely a result of Marcellus drilling.[337]

According to a report by the Pennsylvania Department of Labor and Industry, the state's gas drilling activity and its support industries created 48,000 jobs from October 2009 through March 2011, raising total employment in industries connected to Marcellus shale drilling and production to more than 141,000 workers, 2 percent of total state employment.[338] Jobs in the core drilling industries grew by 11 percent, while total employment across all industries in Pennsylvania fell by 3.2 percent.[339] Employment in drilling, pipe production, pipeline construction, and gas transportation increased by almost 94 percent.[340] Unemployment rates in drilling counties dropped significantly below the state's average. Not only were there more jobs, but they paid better. Drilling and support industry salaries averaged 50 percent higher that the state's average annual wage.[341] According to the U.S. Bureau of Economic Analysis, wages and salaries paid out in Marcellus well–populated Bradford County in Pennsylvania increased by 2.5 percent from 2007 to 2009, while non-drilling areas dropped 1.5 percent.[342]

An initial criticism of the economic benefit of Marcellus jobs was that many out-of-state license plates in the drilling areas demonstrated that many of the jobs, often non-union, were being held by technically experienced oil and gas workers from the traditional drilling areas of the country in the Southwest. For example, rig crews work 12-hour shifts for two weeks and then have two weeks off, enabling many to return home, often out of state. To address job training issues, several Pennsylvania colleges and institutions created Marcellus programs from geological sciences to information technology to develop the local workforce. A Penn State Cooperative Extension study stated that it takes 420 individuals, across 150 different job types, to drill one Marcellus well.[343] The drilling and fracking process can take four to eight months, requiring 240 to 450 employees working for 37 to 59 contractors, with each well costing from $4 million to as much as $9 million.[344] The Marcellus Shale Education & Training Center stated that the total number of direct jobs needed to keep pace with the growth of the industry in Pennsylvania would range from 18,596 to 30,684 by 2014, including 9,800 to 15,900 new positions.[345]

Penn College adjusted its curriculum to the drilling industry and opened the Marcellus Shale Workforce Resource Center in partnership with the Penn State Cooperative Extension.[346] Pennsylvania College of Technology's Center for Business and Workforce Development in Williamsport opened its Marcellus Shale Education and Training Center, which included courses in welding, commercial driver's licenses, safety, forklift operation, and electronics. The Center estimated the number of full-time natural gas-related jobs in north-central Pennsylvania could more than double to between 3,200 and 5,400 positions from 2010 to 2013 and Pennsylvania's Center for Workforce Information and Analysis estimated that by 2016 those jobs might total more than 12,400.[347] In addition, Lackawanna College's Towanda center offered a program in natural gas technology with contributions from gas companies in money and equipment. The Western Area Career and Technology Center in Canonsburg, Pa., which provided adult workforce transition training, began a specialized program in Marcellus shale jobs.[348] Chesapeake Energy opened a $7 million housing and training complex in Bradford County, which included dormitories, cafeteria, laundry building, baseball field, volleyball court, horseshoe pits, and two recreation centers.[349] That firm increased its employment from 219 people to 1,032 by May 2010.[350]

An industry-sponsored Penn State economic study in 2011 stated that by 2020, the industry could create more than $20 billion in value added economic impact, generating $2 billion in state and local tax revenues and supporting more than 250,000 jobs.[351] Much of the "moving target" projections, however, depended on the pace of future drilling. Whether the assumptions of increased production due to technological advances and increased value of natural gas wellhead prices would prove true was questioned.[352] And a few job surveys claimed that although the Marcellus drilling obviously helped the state's economy, the projected increases were overinflated.

The economic echo in drilling communities in northeastern and southwestern Pennsylvania where the bulk of drilling occurred not only could be felt in local hotel, restaurant, and service industries catering to gas workers, but also would reverberate to various skilled trades such as drilling, engineering, surveying, construction, earth-moving, environmental protection, transportation, equipment maintenance, legal, and others. A 2008 Pennsylvania Economy League study estimated the total annual economic output of Marcellus drilling in the state totaled $7.1 billion. A coalition of gas drillers claimed that for every $1 invested in the Marcellus, $1.90 in economic activity is generated, what they dubbed the "Marcellus multiplier."[353] Another Penn State study revealed that one-third of northeastern Pennsylvania's Bradford County businesses and 23 percent of southwestern Pennsylvania Washington County companies reported higher sales due to drilling activity, including 100 percent of hotels and campgrounds, 50 percent of financial businesses, 35 percent of construction firms, and about 30 percent of transportation firms, and restaurants.[354] Short-line railroad activity also increased from hauling water, sand, pipe, cement, and machinery. Reading and Northern Railroad planned to add $1 million in added infrastructure due to the growth in service.[355]

Job creation and other economic activity expanded beyond Pennsylvania's borders as well. A West Virginia University study stated that Marcellus drilling created 7,600 jobs and almost $298 million in wages and benefits in the Mountain State in 2009, with gas industry employment leaping 34 percent between 2001 and 2009.[356] An economic impact study released by the Ohio Oil and Gas Energy Education Program claimed hundreds of thousands of jobs could be created and billions of dollars in tax revenue and royalty payments could be generated in Ohio as a result of gas drilling.[357] According to the Ohio Business Development Coalition, the Buckeye State seemed primed to be a key supplier of support services for the new natural gas activity much as it had for the automobile industry. U.S. Steel Corp. reportedly invested $95 million at its tube-making plant in Lorain, Ohio.[358] A new $650 million rolling mill project in economically hard hit Youngstown to construct smaller-diameter natural gas pipe was announced in 2010 by a French firm, the largest private investment announced in all of Ohio that year and perhaps the biggest in Youngstown in half a century.[359] A government report revealed the steel-oriented Ohio industry city area ranked third in the country in percentage of job growth in the year through March 2011, thanks in part to pipe making, water treatment, and oil and gas service industries serving Marcellus drilling.[360] In addition to Marcellus production effects, the drilling states hoped to attract gas-intensive manufacturing industries such as steel, chemicals, glass, and fertilizers to expand or relocate to the region because of the plentiful supply and low cost of the fuel.

Not jumping on the Marcellus bandwagon, however, could be economically costly. A study by Natural Resource Economics, conducted for the industry group API, found that while Marcellus drilling added 57,000 new jobs and $6 million in total economic value in 2009 mostly in Pennsylvania and West Virginia, continuing New York's drilling moratorium could result in lost economic output estimated up to $15 billion and lost tax revenue of up to $2 billion in that state if extended between 2011 and 2020.[361] According to a study funded by the business-backed Manhattan Institute for Policy Research, lifting the ban in New York could create $11.4 billion in economic activity and $1.4 billion in tax revenues by 2020, as well as 18,000 new jobs by 2015.[362] Even a 2011 state study by the New York DEC stated that Marcellus gas production could bring nearly 25,000 full time drilling jobs and more than 29,000 jobs in other parts of the economy, and add $31 million to $185 million a year in added state income taxes.[363] As the drilling moratorium in New York is scheduled to end in 2012, it may eventually share in the shale bounty.

The Price You Pay — Marcellus and Natural Gas Prices

"Some people have said I'm to blame for driving the price of gas down from $11 [per thousand cubic feet] to $2.50," said George P. Mitchell, who started the shale gas revolution with hydraulic fracturing, in an interview with the *Houston Chronicle.* "Well, too bad."[364]

In the mid–2000s, U.S. natural gas prices were among the highest in the world, but all natural gas prices collapsed in 2008 with the onset of a world-wide recession. Production in southwest shale regions declined as a result, but that did not dampen the pace of Marcellus activity with the rush to drill while leases were still active. Large companies investing in the Marcellus could ride out low margins, taking a long-term approach. Due to the robust supply influx of all shale gas, natural gas prices remained below the $3 per thousand cubic feet level throughout 2010–12, despite oil prices cresting over $100 per barrel for a time, essentially severing natural gas with its traditional tether to world petroleum prices. The DOE said that natural gas continued to cost less than any other home energy source. In addition, the gush in Marcellus production may help balance weather-related natural gas price spikes such as Gulf Coast hurricanes, which interrupted U.S. supply in 2004, and also insulate the U.S. from political turmoil in oil-production regions in the Middle East.

Low natural gas prices as a result of the ample Marcellus Shale supplies were much needed relief for Appalachian homeowners during an economic downturn, as well as welcome news to energy-intensive manufacturers, such as petrochemicals and fertilizer plants, devastated when natural gas prices peaked in the mid–2000s. Penn State University researchers claimed Marcellus production cut natural gas prices by 12.6 percent in Pennsylvania in 2010, saving residences and industries $633 million in energy costs.[365] UGI Utilities Inc. planned to make the Scranton/Wilkes-Barre area its first region in Pennsylvania where customers will receive all their natural gas from the Marcellus Shale by 2013.[366] According to the December 11, 2011, *Harrisburg Patriot*

News, the Pennsylvania Public Utility Commission calculated the decrease in natural gas prices saved Pennsylvania energy consumers $13 billion during the previous two years. By early 2012, thanks to a mild winter, high storage levels, suppressed economic activity, and voluminous shale gas supplies, natural gas wellhead prices were at a ten-year low. More than half of American homes use gas for heating and despite the higher-than-normal demand for natural gas, 2011 prices were still relatively low, as much as 30 percent to 40 percent lower in northern states like Illinois and Massachusetts compared to five years before.[367] One-quarter of electricity in the U.S. is natural-gas generated, so low gas prices helped keep a lid on electricity costs as well. According to the January 17, 2012, *Bloomberg Business Report*, wholesale electricity prices dropped more than 50 percent on average since 2008, 10 percent during the last quarter of 2011. The gas price decline helped those beyond Pennsylvania, especially northeastern homeowners, who have faced historically high natural gas rates being far from the production regions in the Southwest. Inflation-adjusted historically low gas prices made the investment of gas conversions from heating oil look more attractive to New England homeowners. As the oil industry did in the fields of West Virginia in the late 19th century and in the Southwest in the first half of the 20th century, the September 26, 2011, *New York Times* reported that massive flaring (and therefore, waste) of natural gas produced along with petroleum in the new prolific Bakken oil field in North Dakota was the result of low natural gas prices with no economic incentive to pipe the product to market. The National Regulatory Research Institute claimed that due to shale gas, price stability could continue for years. But it may not endure forever, as demand for natural gas is expected to grow. Recording a note of caution, a National Association of Regulatory Utility Commissioners panel concluded in 2011 that shale gas prices could double by 2015.

The Utica Club — Appalachian Shales beyond the Marcellus

While the Marcellus Shale received most of the press in Appalachia, the drill bits are not stopping there. On much of the same acreage, some drillers are finding a "triple play" of shales including the Marcellus, Utica, and Upper Devonian shales of the Huron, Cleveland, and Rhinestreet formations. The Utica Shale, an older shale formation dating 440 million to 460 million years ago and 500 feet thick in places, is found 2,000 to 7,000 feet or more below the Marcellus. However, the Utica is more widespread than the Marcellus, stretching over 170,000 square miles as far north as Lake Erie and Ontario and Quebec, Canada, extending south through eight states including New York, Pennsylvania, West Virginia, eastern Ohio, Tennessee, Virginia, and as far west as Michigan. The Utica is in an ideal geologic pressure and temperature range in western Pennsylvania and eastern Ohio at about 11,000 to 12,000 feet, extending from Titusville, home to Drake's original oil well, to Columbus, Ohio. The formation has a high BTU heating value, making it more marketable, especially for natural gas liquids.[368] And the Utica shale below the bottom of Lake Erie and Lake Ontario also leaves the potential for offshore drilling. The Utica was first drilled in Quebec by Talisman in 2008, at the Gentilly No. 1 well.[369] The "motherlode" of Canadian Utica is located near the St. Lawrence River between Montreal and Quebec City and could contain 50 trillion cubic feet of gas.[370] The estimated value of extractable natural gas from Quebec's formation is between $45 billion and $210 billion.[371] However, after vociferous outcries and threats of civil disobedience by protesters, hydraulic fracturing was suspended there until the process is proven safe to the government's satisfaction.

Though Ohio gas and oil production declined since 1984 when 15 million barrels of oil and 188 billion cubic feet of natural gas were extracted, the Utica shale has attracted much leasing in the eastern part of the state, where the formation may hold huge deposits of gas, natural gas liquids, and oil.[372] Ohio's state geologist in 2011 said a "conservative" estimate of resources in the Buckeye State could be up to 15.7 trillion cubic feet of natural gas, 21 years of the state's current consumption, and 5.5 billion barrels of oil.[373] Chesapeake Energy Corp. CEO Aubrey McClendon said the Utica Shale could be worth $500 billion, and the "biggest thing economically to hit Ohio, since maybe the plow."[374] Chesapeake Energy later entered into a $2.32 billion joint venture with Total SA, France's largest oil company, for 619,000 net acres in the natural gas liquids-rich area of the Utica Shale in Ohio.

The Utica frenzy immediately spawned numerous firms chasing leases and joint ventures. Consol Energy moved into some Utica Shale in Ohio in 2009, striking Utica reserves at 8,450 feet in Belmont County, and produced 1.5 million cubic feet of gas over a 24-hour period without hydraulic fracturing.[375] More than 1,000 leases were acquired for potential drilling in Ohio, led by Chesapeake Energy's 1.25 million acres, which concentrated on the wet gas portion of the play. Chesapeake reported positive results in 2011, one well in Harrison County producing 9.5 million cubic feet of natural gas and 1,425 barrels of natural-gas and oil liquids.[376] Other early results of oil, natural gas, and natural gas liquids in wells were "phenomenal," according to analysts.[377] Chesapeake expected to have 40 rigs operating in the Utica by the end of 2014, and believed their reserves were worth $15 to $20 billion to their shareholders. ExxonMobil announced its exploration plan in the eastern Ohio counties of Jefferson and Harrison.[378] Oil giant BP followed in 2012. Other large U.S. producers investing in the Utica include Devon Energy Corp., Anadarko Petroleum Corp., Hess Corp., and Petroleum Development Corp. and smaller firms involved included Rex Energy Corp., Gulfport Energy Corp., and Magnum Hunter Resources Corp.[379]

In Pennsylvania, Seneca Resources completed a vertical test well into the Utica shale in north-central McKean County as well as one further west in Venango County in 2011.[380] Rex Energy also completed a Utica well in Butler County north of Pittsburgh.[381] Geologists say the economic prospects are not as good in the eastern part of Pennsylvania, where hard anthracite coal is prevalent. In that region, the Utica formation is located as far as 13,000 feet below the surface (6,000 feet below the Marcellus), where the deep shale was likely "overcooked" by the earth's heat, converting the methane to carbon dioxide.[382]

In addition to the Utica and perhaps the Huron shales, producers are looking at the shallower Upper Devonian Low Thermal Maturity (also known as the Northwestern Ohio shale) covering more than 45,000 square miles in Ohio, southwestern Pennsylvania, and parts of West Virginia, New York, Kentucky, and Tennessee. Some industry officials believe the Upper Devonian may contain as much gas as the Marcellus.[383] The Rhinestreet and Geneseo shales, also located above the Marcellus, could be explored in northwest Pennsylvania with horizontal drilling and perhaps fractured with nitrogen rather than liquid frack fluid. Likewise, in the Chattanooga Shale, which stretches across East Tennessee, North Alabama, Southeast Kentucky and North Georgia, fracking operations are conducted mostly with nitrogen. The Greater Siltstone Shale also lies within the Appalachian Basin in New York, Ohio, Pennsylvania, Virginia, and West Virginia. Other non-shale formations have been tapped as well. For example, Cabot Oil & Gas in 2010 drilled a successful horizontal well through the Purcell Limestone located between two layers of Marcellus, north of Scranton, Pa., and produced an impressive 7.3 million cubic feet of gas per day over a month.[384]

Changing Horsepower Midstream — Pipeline Expansion Out of the Marcellus

When the basic arteries of the natural gas circulatory system in the hills and forests of Appalachia were first installed, it was an engineering challenge, but right-of-ways to pipe the product were secured without much fanfare with the exception of an occasional outraged farmer. In the twenty-first century, engineering, though still complex, would be only one of the industry's obstacles to blaze its expanded buried trail. Beyond expensively extracting natural gas from the deep geological shale formations, the industry had to face another hurdle: how to transport the huge volumes of gas out of Appalachia to hungry markets for distribution. Although the interstate natural gas pipeline system is considered the safest transportation network in the world,[385] recent fatal pipeline explosion and fire disasters in San Bruno, California, and others much closer in Pennsylvania, put both regulators and citizens on edge. Proposals for new pipelines and compressor stations had to persuade landowners and homeowners that these new facilities would not compromise safety or aggravate air or noise pollution.

For the previous half-century, Appalachian states imported natural gas from the Southwest and Canada to meet its needs. The Marcellus, nicknamed the "The Beast in the East" and the "Big Kahuna" of gas supply, resulted in Appalachia's cup of demand to run over, and in some cases, push out competition of future long-term pipeline contracts. The Marcellus promised to reverse the flow of gas to Appalachia to the East Coast, north to Canada, as well as westward and southward. But to accomplish that, midstream and downstream activity of constructing hundreds of miles of new gathering system lines and new interstate pipelines, storage facilities, and upgraded or new compressor stations to transport the gas had to be installed. But unlike the late nineteenth century teams of horses, wagons, and tong gangs burying lines in mostly uninhabited countryside, modern pipeline firms would have to deal with urban sprawl and numerous updated air, land, water, safety, and noise regulations to ensure construction and operation minimized its effect on homeowners, forests, farms, rivers, wildlife, and historical and recreation areas.

According to the Federal Energy Regulatory Commission (FERC), which regulates interstate pipeline activities, as of 2011 at least 15 major interstate projects involving several thousand miles of pipeline in the Northeast were proposed, most to route gas out of the Marcellus. They include projects by pipeline firms such as Columbia, Dominion, Iroquois, Millennium, NFG, Nisource, Rockies, Spectra, TETCO,

TRANSCO, UGI, and Williams. [386] These projects that are receiving intense regulatory scrutiny include interconnections with already existing interstate pipelines that must be placed to transport the fuel away from the production areas. Marcellus gas first flowed to major East Coast markets including New England, New York City, New Jersey, and Philadelphia, and projects were announced to reverse the flow and ship the bountiful supplies northward to Canada. Marcellus gas would also go south and west. Specialized pipelines would also have to be constructed for transportation of natural gas liquids extracted in western Pennsylvania, West Virginia, and Ohio. In 2010, a subsidiary of the United States' largest interstate gas pipeline firm El Paso Corp. linked with Houston-based Spectra Energy Corp. to develop a 1,100-mile Marcellus ethane pipeline system project to the Gulf Coast. A year later, the proposed $21 billion merger of another Houston firm, the energy transportation and storage company Kinder Morgan, and El Paso was expected to result in Marcellus gas flowing southward. [387] In early 2012, Enterprise Products Partners LP announced a 1,230-mile line dubbed the ATEX Express to transport Marcellus and Utica Shale ethane production to the Gulf Coast. The lack of pipeline infrastructure or "midstream" needs must be addressed to transport Marcellus gas for drilling to continue, and the FERC approved several proposals by late 2011. In addition, pipeline firms often have to construct entire gathering systems around wells. Pipeline safety of gathering lines became a major issue in Pennsylvania, the only producing state that did not regulate them, and the state sought to grant oversight of the intrastate lines to its utility commission.

Challenges to construction include mountainous and rocky terrain, wetlands, urban expansion into traditionally rural regions, and protected natural areas. Firms must seek approval by FERC and state regulators, as well as obtain permits from the U.S. Army Corps of engineers, and various fish, game, and other state and federal environmental regulatory agencies. Although the FERC normally evaluates environmental impacts of such projects, the cumulative impacts of proposed Marcellus pipelines have caught the attention of the EPA through the federal NEPA regulation. Which pipeline projects are ultimately approved will determine where the bounty of the Marcellus will travel.

Electric Landslide — New Markets for Marcellus Gas: Power, Vehicles, Liquids, Exports

While geologists were locating, drillers were drilling, and states were debating the positive and potentially negative effects of the Marcellus, the natural gas market had a different quandary on its hands. That is, what would it do with this unanticipated surge in natural gas supply? A major advantage of the Marcellus Shale play is its proximity to gas-hungry markets on the East Coast and Canada. In addition to the new clean-burning domestic energy that generated minute amounts of typical power plant pollutants and particulates, natural gas produces 30 percent less carbon dioxide emissions than oil and 45 percent less CO_2 than coal. [388] Gas is seen as an aid for electrical generation supplanting the existence of dirtier coal-fired generation plants, valuable feedstock for industries such as fertilizer, steel, and glass, a smog-free fuel for motor vehicles, and a potential export product to other nations.

Although the use of natural gas to produce electricity grew substantially since the 1990s, accounting for 920 million megawatt hours of electricity in 2009, second only to coal, many utilities worried about dependence on the fossil fuel because of its historical price instability linked with oil. Due to shale gas, however, that bond appeared broken. Increased carbon dioxide emission regulations on the coal-powered plants requiring expensive capturing technology, public reluctance to accept new nuclear generating stations (certainly in the wake of the 2011 Japan tsunami Fukushima Daiichi nuclear disaster), and the anemic growth of renewables such as government subsidized wind farms and solar generating plants, left natural gas as the only viable alternative to significantly increase electric generation capacity. The EIA maintains that regulatory pressure and costs faced by antiquated coal-powered plants will result in faster growth in natural gas-powered electrical generation due to low gas prices and relatively low capital costs.[389] An MIT study concluded that, "gas-fired power sets a competitive benchmark against which other technologies must compete in a lower carbon environment."[390] Exelon Power planned to close 1950s-era coal-fired generators in Pennsylvania in 2012 because suppressed gas prices made the coal plants no longer economical to run, and Sunbury Generation LP, planned to replace five of its six coal-fired generators in Pennsylvania with natural gas-fired turbines by 2015 due to toughening federal pollution standards.[391] Low natural gas costs also hampered development of more-expensive wind, solar, and biomass energy, as well as nuclear, and it is seen by some as a way to bridge the gap to a more secure energy and economic future.[392] The construction of two, $800 million natural gas-powered plants near Williamsport and Bradford County Pennsylvania were announced in 2011 by Moxie Energy, of Vienna, Va., which could provide electricity for up to 1.4 million people.[393] The future of the Marcellus seemed to be linked to electric generation demand, which some analysts say could double by 2020.

Using natural gas to produce electricity is cleaner and produces about half the carbon dioxide emissions than coal, but it is not the most efficient use of the fuel. The gas industry, the National Academy of Sciences, and the DOE urged Congress to revise the Energy Policy and Conservational Act's measurement of appliance energy standards to "Full Fuel Cycle Use." That is, measuring energy from its point of origin to point of use. Natural gas appliances such as furnaces in the home approach 90 percent efficiency compared to 30-percent efficiency using gas to generate electricity to then power electric appliances.[394] Some see the inefficient use of gas as a waste. Former U.S. Energy Secretary Samuel Bodman is quoted as saying using the premium fuel (natural gas) to produce electricity "is like washing dishes with a good scotch."[395]

Direct use of natural gas in vehicles, however, may trump the promise of electric cars whose charge could be generated, albeit more inefficiently, by the same natural gas. Much praise was lauded on battery-powered and pricey electric vehicles such as the Chevy Volt and Nissan Leaf that would require a greater demand on the electric grid, yet a full tank of natural gas will power a car to go twice as far as a single electric charge.[396] Though natural gas vehicles (NGVs) have been prevalent around the world for decades, they have been unable to get into high gear in the U.S., due to the lack of refilling infrastructure, paucity of investment by carmakers, and uncertainty of supply and affordability, though natural gas is now plentiful and the price as a vehicle fuel is far below gasoline. Worldwide, there are 12 million NGVs on the road. In

2009, Pakistan led all nations with 2.4 million NGVs and 3,000 fueling stations, while the U.S. only possessed 100,000, mostly fleet trucks, and 1,300 refilling stations.[397] In Brazil, NGVs make up five percent of the vehicles and consumes ten percent of the nation's overall natural gas demand.[398] Few natural gas dedicated vehicles have been produced in the U.S., with Honda offering the only off-the-line passenger vehicle.

In 2011, President Obama said domestic natural gas could help achieve a one-third reduction of imported oil over the next decade.[399] Natural gas producers vowed to create their own demand. In an effort to "help break OPEC's 38-year stranglehold on the U.S. economy," Chesapeake Energy created a $1 billion venture capital fund to invest in technologies that will replace the use of gasoline and diesel.[400] Chesapeake, among other entities, sought to install commercial vehicle stations in Pennsylvania and state legislation called for incentives for NGV development. The West Virginia legislature also adopted new tax credits to encourage the purchase of NGVs and provide credits for those looking to build alternative-fuel filling facilities. Ohio's state officials also want to explore NGVs for cars, snowplows, and other government vehicles.

Applying natural gas vehicles as a cog in the wheel of U.S. energy security has long been a piece of the "Pickens Plan," pushed by oil magnate T. Boone Pickens, which promoted wind farms to produce electricity, reserving efficient natural gas for cars and trucks. Calling the Marcellus divine intervention, Pickens said, "If we don't capitalize on natural gas, I promise you we're going to go down as the dumbest group that ever came into town."[401] Many experts believe that although it is not a perfect scenario to move to a green power economy, fuel switching as much power generation from coal to gas and as much transportation fuel from oil to gas would produce rapid and dramatic reductions in carbon dioxide emissions.[402]

Another major market for Marcellus production is the development of high BTU gas that contains natural gas liquids (ethane, butane, propane, etc.) first stripped out commercially a century before in Appalachia. These heavier hydrocarbons, amounting to 3.4 billion barrels of undiscovered, technically recoverable natural gas liquids, according to the USGS,[403] are worth more than the methane itself.[404] Drilling in "wet" plays like the Marcellus Shale to obtain the higher-priced natural gas liquids helps producers make up for low natural gas wellhead prices.[405] Propane has a strong seasonal demand and butane and pentane have identified markets. Most major "cracker" plants that produce natural gas liquid byproducts for the chemical industry are located in Texas and Louisiana, but West Virginia is hoping that the production of copious quantities of ethane during refining that can be used for a massive cracker plant to turn Marcellus gas into the widely used chemical compound ethylene, creating jobs and tax revenue.[406] Royal Dutch Shell PLC announced it would construct such a world-class facility in the region to produce ethylene, a key component used to make petrochemicals, and polyethylene, used in packaging such as milk jugs and soda bottles, adhesives, and auto parts.[407] The announcement led to a massive blitz of tax and incentive competition between Pennsylvania, Ohio, and West Virginia. Shell chose a Beaver County, Pa., site in 2012. Officials from The National Petrochemical & Refiners Association said a $3.2 billion project would boost petrochemical output in the state by $7.9 billion and mean $1.2 billion in wages to workers.[408] Dominion Resources also planned to complete a natural gas processing plant along the Ohio River in

Natrium, W.Va., by the end of 2012. Other international firms from Brazil and South Africa were also looking for potential U.S. locations for ethylene expansion.[409]

The vast quantities of gas in the Marcellus and other eastern shales also created the opportunity to export American natural gas. After years of importing Canadian gas at the border near Niagara Falls, N.Y., Marcellus gas is flowing the other way into Canada to feed that nation's demand for clean-burning electrical generation. Exports to Canada from the northeastern United States may reach a rate of up to 400 million cubic feet a day by 2020.[410] In addition, LNG facilities on the East Coast that were accepting foreign imports until the shale phenomena arrived may now have the capability to export excess U.S. capacity overseas. Richmond, Va.–based Dominion Resources Inc. applied to the DOE in 2011 to permit 1 billion cubic feet of gas per day to be exported through its Cove Point, Maryland terminal to any country with which the United States does not prohibit trade.[411]

Shales of the World

The Marcellus experience, along with other similar formations in the United States, sparked shale exploration throughout the globe. The shale frenzy was expected to increase world-wide natural gas supplies while tempering prices by removing natural gas supply strangleholds by traditional energy powers. A study sponsored by the EIA estimated that only 13 percent of shale reserves are in the United States and shale gas could supply 7 percent of the world's supply by 2030. The admitted "conservative," but uncertain, estimate totals 5,760 trillion cubic feet of technically recoverable shale gas resources in 48 shale gas basins in 32 foreign countries, compared with only 862 trillion cubic feet in the U.S.[412] The U.S. government created the Global Shale Gas Initiative in 2010 to help foreign countries seeking to extract shale gas resources do so safely and economically.[413] Shale gas exists in countries on nearly every continent including: more than two-dozen U.S. states; Quebec, Nova Scotia, British Columbia and Alberta in Canada; Mexico; Argentina in South America; England, France, Sweden, Poland, Ukraine, Hungary, and Bulgaria in Europe; Pakistan, India and China in Asia; South Africa and Morocco in Africa; and Australia.[414]

Four shale formations in northeastern British Columbia, Canada, which may have 250 trillion of cubic feet of natural gas at a value of $750 billion, have attracted investment from China and South Africa.[415] Many of the same energy firms exploring in Appalachia, such as Royal Dutch Shell, Chesapeake Energy, and Statoil, are seeking reserves in South Africa and northern African nations, where the Ghadames basin could be the biggest shale gas basin in the world.[416] The U.S. estimates Poland may have 5.3 trillion cubic meters of shale gas, which is being probed by ExxonMobil, Chevron, and other U.S. companies.[417] Royal Dutch Shell PLC plans to invest $1 billion a year on shale gas in China, where the DOE estimates unconventional reserves are 12 times higher than conventional gas reserves.[418] China's international natural gas supplies are often shipped around the world as LNG, providing critical energy supplies for countries like Japan, which possesses few natural energy resources. The first shale well in southern Australia was completed in 2011, and ConocoPhillips announced it would be the first global major corporation to explore for shale gas in the land down under.[419]

Much of the world's shale development will take cues from what happens below the hills of Appalachia, similar to what occurred during the oil and gas rush in the region during the second half of the nineteenth century, which led to later finds in the Southwest, and eventually, the Middle East. Thanks to shale discoveries, the recent doubling of current known reserves is predicted to hold down world-wide natural gas prices.[420] One 2011 study by the Baker Institute at Rice University predicted that shale gas not only can suppress prices and promote environmental advantages, but can also threaten OPEC's energy monopoly and reduce the power of gas exporters such as Russia, Iran, and Venezuela.[421] Shale gas undoubtedly has the potential to alter the world's economy, reduce worldwide greenhouse gas emissions, and upend traditional power structures among nations. According to the International Energy Agency's 2001 report, "Are We Entering the Golden Age of Natural Gas?," global natural gas resources can fulfill world demand, which would be 25 percent of all energy resources, through 2035, even at suppressed prices.[422] Whether natural gas fulfills that potential destiny, however, depends on many unforeseen factors. In any case, the last decade has seen the natural gas industry climb into a metaphorical time machine and go back to the future, returning to the rural cradle of its birth to breathe new life into a cleaner, economic, domestic, though not perfect, energy supply for the nation.

The Known and Unknown
The Natural Gas Industry in Appalachia
through Shale–Colored Glasses

"There are *known knowns*, there are things we know we know. We also know
there are *known unknowns*; that is to say we know there are some things [we
know] we do not know. But there are also *unknown unknowns*—the ones we
don't know we don't know."[1]
—Donald Rumsfeld, U.S. Secretary of Defense (comments
to reporters in 2003 regarding the Iraq War)

What is the future of the natural gas industry in Appalachia? It may be clear as
black shale. This book has mostly considered the *known knowns* of natural gas, the
history of conventional drilling, transportation, and distribution of the fuel in the
region of its birth. The Marcellus Shale has been a *known unknown* for a century, as
geologists knew it existed and long suspected it had hidden hydrocarbons, though
they were unsure how much, and uncertain how it could be freed from its natural
impermeable barrier.

At the turn of the twenty-first century, very few suspected that this *known
unknown* and unexplored formation would, thanks to new production technology,
shortly yield such an unexpected treasure trove of energy. But in the future, who can
identify the other *known unknowns* and *unknown unknowns*? Will the price of natural
gas continue to support the expensive, deep exploration into the black shales of Marcellus and Utica? How will taxes and regulation affect exploration and production?
How long will the economic hot streak continue for producing states generating jobs
and revenue? How fast will Marcellus production decline? How many new wells will
be needed to maintain production? Will there be sufficient pipeline capacity to bring
the gas out of the region to end-use markets? Will an LNG export market be developed
and make Appalachia the Persian Gulf of natural gas? Will domestic demand continue
to increase as other alternative energies such as solar, wind, biofuels, or perhaps *unknown*
energy sources are affordably developed and implemented? As the oil industry in many
regions experienced for a century and a half, will the shale boom be followed by a
bust? Will the increased use of natural gas help reduce air pollution and greenhouse
gases or create more environmental problems, some of them perhaps *unknown*?

The natural gas industry developed and matured in the hills of Appalachia, evolving into a global commercial enterprise, one of the largest businesses in the world. At the turn of the twenty-first century, its production in this region seemed minor compared to the global nature of the product. The future of the industry was thought to be located under deserts and seas in and around the Arabian Peninsula. A few short years later, the Appalachian Marcellus was seen as a several-decade-long play that not only radically changed gas markets, uses, transportation, and prices, but also promised to transform the economies of rust-belt states and perhaps the nation. But the outlook is a rosy fairy tale come true combined with a strong dose of tough reality. There are still many unanswered questions as federal and state regulators scrutinize the drilling and hydraulic fracturing process for any potential effect on the environment and health of denizens of exploration regions. The optimistic promise of gas in the reduction of pollutants and boost of jobs and tax revenues is rivaled by the pessimistic threat of land and water degradation and the delay of development of perhaps more nature-friendly alternative fuels.

Over the past half century, energy predictions for oil, gas, nuclear, and alternative fuels have been as reliable as Ouija boards in producing accurate results. Only time will tell. But one thing seems certain. The world continues to consume energy. And it will have to come from somewhere. The development of alternative fuels in the U.S. is still a wildcard. The EIA states that under current policies fossil fuels will still provide 78 percent of U.S. energy use in 2035.[2] But while coal, oil, and nuclear face huge environmental and political challenges, those in the know are betting on natural gas. A 2012 White House report titled, "Investing in America: Building an Economy That Lasts," credited the natural gas boom with fueling economic investment. Despite pressure from environmentalists over "fracking," President Barack Obama touted shale natural gas as a key ingredient to U.S. energy independence in his January 2012 State of the Union address. ExxonMobil, a company nearly synonymous with oil, now predicts that natural gas will be the fastest growing major fuel source worldwide through 2030.[3]

A Progressive Policy Institute policy memo concluded that when it comes to energy, there are no "silver bullets" or "miracle fuels," but natural gas, if exploited without endangering public health or damaging the environment, will provide a boon to the economy, reduce greenhouse gases, and address the high-energy consumption to maintain living standards around the world.[4] Still, many say natural gas is not a panacea for long-term American energy needs. But few energy sources are perfect. The negative ramifications of oil, coal, and nuclear power use are apparent. Wind power has life cycle environmental impacts from the construction of units to their effect on land and habitats. Solar power has limitations, land-use, and resource issues. Biofuels have massive land requirements. Development of hydropower is tapped out. Conservation and efficient use of energy will undoubtedly take a front row seat in the future, but there is a point of diminishing returns. Nuclear fusion, hydrogen fuel cells, tidal and ocean wave energy, and other proposed energy technologies are still more concept than reality. To twist a quote from Winston Churchill regarding the nature of democracy, "It has been said that natural gas is the worst form of energy except all the others that have been tried."

Natural gas demand continues to be robust and supplies appear limitless. The

January 24, 2012, *Wall Street Journal* reported that huge shale supplies into the marketplace caused too much of a good thing — a crash in natural gas prices, down 45 percent in one year. This led some firms like Chesapeake Energy, which emblazoned itself as "America's Champion of Natural Gas," to cut its drilling and land acquisition plans in 2012 for dry natural gas, and instead focus on the more lucrative natural gas liquids market. The largest market for gas is the desire for gas-fired electric generation, but other new uses could create even a greater demand including NGVs for fleets, commercial natural gas cooling, combined-cycle electric turbines, cogeneration of heat and electricity, and fuel cells. In addition to shale, there are still significant conventional gas reserves offshore the Atlantic and Pacific coasts and below the Rocky Mountains, and Alaska, but government bans drillings in many of these areas for environmental protection. Ironically, the environmentally conscious Canadians drill prolifically in the Great Lakes and off the Atlantic Coast. By the beginning of the 2000s, the Canadians operated more than 550 producing gas wells underneath Lake Erie, which lies between the United States and Canada.[5] There are no wells permitted on the American side and the migratory "fugitive" fuel in permeable rock formations below the lake knows no international boundaries.

To meet new demand, future technology may also create even more supplies through unconventional resources beyond shale including coalbed methane, recovery of gas through biofuels such as generating methane from landfills, and collecting gas from methane-emitting sea kelp. Perhaps the greatest amount of carbon-based fuel is contained in natural gas hydrates that lay frozen beneath the Arctic and ocean floor, though economic extraction is projected to be years away. Before future demand can be met however, the United States must untangle conflicting laws and regulations as well as cope with the costs of bringing these new sources of supply to market. Until future technology can develop an affordable energy that does not leave any environmental fingerprint, it appears that the Cinderella-fuel natural gas, once born and bred in Appalachia in the long black shadow of her fossil-fuel stepsisters coal and oil, and now reincarnated in the Marcellus Shale, is still regarded as the fairest flame of them all.

Appendix 1: Timeline

1600s	Early American settlers notice "burning springs" throughout Appalachia.
1756	Gas lighting experiments in Philadelphia.
1770	George Washington discovers burning gas springs in Appalachia.
1806	Oil and gas discovered by salt well drillers in western Virginia (now West Virginia). First drilling tools developed.
1815	Capt. Wilson reportedly discovered natural gas looking for brine in Charleston, W.Va. Wet gas meter patented by a London, England company.
1816	Gas Light Company of Baltimore becomes first manufactured-gas firm in U.S.
1818	Kentucky salt well driller Martin Beatty accidentally finds oil and natural gas.
1820	Salt well drillers discover natural gas by accident in Pittsburgh and Ohio.
1821	First commercial natural gas well drilled in Fredonia, N.Y., by William Hart.
1826	First gas cooker developed.
1830	Barcelona, N.Y., lighthouse uses natural gas. Petroleum used for medicine, light, and lubricant in West Virginia.
1831	Natural gas used by salt manufacturers in West Virginia. New drilling methods invented by William Morris in Kanawha County, W.Va.
1836	Gas used for illumination in Findlay, Ohio. Manufactured gas works begin in Cleveland and Pittsburgh.
1840	Natural gas used to evaporate brine water in Butler County, Pa.
1848	Manufactured gasworks opens in Buffalo.
1854	First deep natural gas well drilled in Erie, Pa.
1855	Robert Bunsen invents "Bunsen burner" concept.
1858	Fredonia Gas Light and Water Works Company becomes first natural gas utility in the United States.
1859	Col. Drake drills first oil well in Titusville, Pa. Oil wells follow in West Virginia and Ohio, many producing natural gas as well.
1863	First commercial gas wells drilled in Kentucky.

West Virginia becomes the 35th State of the Union, partially due to oil wealth there.

1865   Oil boomtown Pithole uses petroleum gas for lighting.
First oil pipeline built.

1867   Gas well in Oil City, Pa., supplies houses.

1868   Jarecki Manufacturing Company in Erie, Pa., becomes the first industrial user of natural gas.
Gas pumps first used for oil wells in Tidioute, Pa.

1870   Standard Oil Company formed.
Natural gas first used in Pittsburgh-area iron manufacturing.

1871   Discovery well drilled opening huge Bradford, Pa., oil and gas field.

1872   First long-distance (twenty-seven miles) wooden gas pipeline completed from West Bloomfield, N.Y., to Rochester.
First iron gas line constructed (five and one-half miles) from Newton, Pa., to Titusville.

1873   Theodore Lowe invents carbureted water gas manufacturing process.

1875   Jacob J. Vandergrift pipes natural gas in Butler County, Pa.

1878   Gas discovered at the Haymaker Well near Pittsburgh at Murrysville, Pa.
Electric light firms begin service in region.

1880   First natural gas compressor station built at Rixford, Pa.

1881   Natural gas firms begin to form throughout northwestern Pennsylvania.

1882   Thomas Edison produces electricity at power station.

1883   Natural gas supplied by first Pennsylvania-chartered natural gas company, Joseph Pew and Edward Emerson's Penn Fuel Gas Company.

1884   George Westinghouse discovers natural gas on his property, purchases Philadelphia Company to supply natural gas to Pittsburgh, develops numerous natural gas patents.
Short-lived Findlay, Ohio, and northern Indiana gas boom begins.

1885   Peoples Natural Gas Company becomes first official natural gas firm in Pennsylvania.
Speechley well drilled near Oil City, Pa.
Manufacturers Natural Gas Company (later part of Columbia) serves Pittsburgh area.
First suggestion of odorizing gas by Ohio Gas Light Association.
Gas water heater developed.

1886   United Natural Gas Company organized in Oil City, Pa.
UNG constructs 87-mile wrought iron pipeline from McKean County, Pa., to Buffalo, N.Y.
Gas also exported from Pennsylvania to West Virginia.
Gas crematory used in Pittsburgh.

1887   Dresser couplings patented, allowing construction of longer pipelines and reduced leakage.
Federal government passes Interstate Commerce Act, start of regulation interest in Standard Oil.

1888	Standard Oil forms Natural Gas Trust to hold securities of natural gas firms.
	Philadelphia Company purchases Equitable Gas interests in Pittsburgh, designs meters for gas services.
	Gas meter manufacturer Metric Metal Company forms in Beaver Falls, Pa.
1890s	Manufactured gas interests consolidate in Pittsburgh, Cleveland, and Buffalo.
	Electric and gas consolidation movement begins in many areas.
1894	Big Moses well discovered in West Virginia, first 100 million cubic foot well in the United States.
1896	Buffalo streets are lighted with electricity generated at nearby Niagara Falls, N.Y.
1898	Hope Natural Gas Company in West Virginia and East Ohio Gas Company in Ohio formed by Standard Oil interests.
	Akron "Ten-inch" line begins construction from West Virginia to Ohio.
1899	First 1,000 horsepower natural gas-powered gas compressor installed by UNG.
1901	Famous Spindletop Well drilled in Texas, leads to great Southwest discoveries of oil and gas.
1902	National Fuel Gas Company incorporated from investments in Standard's Natural Gas Trust.
1903	Natural gas delivered to Cleveland for the first time by East Ohio.
	Standard Oil interests purchase Pittsburgh's Peoples from Pew.
1903–04	First extraction of natural gasoline from natural gas by the compression and cooling method in Tidioute, Pa.
1905	George W. Crawford's Ohio Fuel Supply Company (later part of Columbia) granted a franchise in Cincinnati to serve natural gas.
1906	West Virginia surpasses Pennsylvania as largest producer of natural gas.
1907–10	Gas utility regulation begins in New York with Public Service Commission.
1909	Gas trash incinerators developed.
1911	U.S. Supreme Court breaks up Standard Oil, but firm's natural gas interests largely unaffected.
	Orifice meter invented by John G. Pew and Howell C. Cooper of Pittsburgh.
1912	Liquid propane (LP) bottled gases first supplied in Waterford, Pa.
1913	Gas utility regulation begins in Pennsylvania and West Virginia.
1915	First natural gas storage experiments in Welland, Ontario, Canada.
	Gas refrigerators introduced.
1916	First natural gas storage field in U.S. begun at Zoar Field, south of Buffalo.
1917–19	Appalachian production reaches its peak, gas shortages appear during World War I years.
1918	American Gas Association formed.
1919	UNG installs first natural gasoline recovery plant using the charcoal absorption process at Lewis Run, Pa.
	Kentucky's Menifee field becomes the second storage area in the U.S.
1920	First natural gas storage in Pennsylvania at Queen field.
	Natural gas conservation efforts begin.

1923–25   Buffalo, Cleveland, Cincinnati, Erie, and other areas build facilities to generate additional supplies of manufactured gas.

1925   East Ohio helps establish American Gas Association testing laboratories in Cleveland.

1930   Oriskany sand gas boom begins in central Pennsylvania, New York, and West Virginia.

1930s   First uses of horizontal drilling in slanted wells near Drake's first oil well in Venango oil formation.

1935   Public Utility Holding Company Act passed by Congress, eventually causes wave of holding company divestitures.

1938   Congress passes the Natural Gas Act, Federal Power Commission regulates expansion of interstate pipelines.

1942–48   Severe shortages of gas, wartime and post-war restrictions become effective, Appalachian gas fields near depletion, and underground storage facilities increase.

1943   Standard Oil (New Jersey) divests itself of Peoples, East Ohio, and Hope, which form Consolidated Natural Gas.
            Rockefeller Foundation divests itself from NFG.
            "Big Inch" crude oil pipeline begins operation.

1944   Liquefied natural gas storage tank in Cleveland fails and explodes, leading to Cleveland's greatest fire that took 130 lives.

1944–52   Appalachian companies augment gas supply from Southwest producers from "Inch" lines that are converted to gas.
            Tennessee Gas delivers Southwest gas to Appalachian markets, pipeline gas odorized.

1946   The first use of hydraulic fracturing employed in the Hugoton gas field in Kansas.

1948   The city of Philadelphia receives natural gas for the first time.

1950   Pittsburgh's Equitable separates from the Philadelphia Company.
            Another Oriskany sand boom starts in Appalachia.

1950s   Most manufactured gas operations phased out.

1952   New York City receives natural gas for the first time.
            U.S. Supreme Court Phillips Petroleum decision confirms FPC control of natural gas prices at the wellhead.

1955–68   Massive growth of customers and consumption of natural gas in Appalachia and across the United States.

1968   Appalachian companies begin receiving interstate pipeline supply curtailments.

1970s   DOE-sponsored Eastern Gas Shales Project explore possibility of extracting hydrocarbons from deep shale in Appalachia.

1973   OPEC oil embargo begins.
            Curtailments of industrial natural gas customers implemented by regional utilities.
            Appalachian companies increase local drilling and explore alternative supplies from coal, oil, and imported LNG.

1977	Cold snap and natural gas shortages close schools and factories across U.S. Natural gas customer expansion halted.
1978	Congress passes the Natural Gas Policy Act, creates Federal Energy Regulatory Commission from FPC.
1978–83	Natural gas prices escalate sharply. Utilities transport third-party gas for industry.
1982	Boundary Gas Project imports gas from Canada.
1983–85	Most gas production deregulated, surplus in market begins price decline.
1989	Natural Gas Wellhead Decontrol Act passes Congress deregulating all natural gas supplies by 1993.
1992	FERC Order 636 requires interstate pipelines to become common carriers.
1990s	Gas utilities offer residential gas supply choice programs.
1997–2004	Various Appalachian utility acquisitions and mergers into larger firms including Dominion, Energy East, and NiSource.
2004	Range Resources performs the first hydraulic fracture of a Marcellus Shale gas well in Appalachia.
2007–12	Leasing, investment, and drilling among Super Major oil and gas firms expand in Appalachia, initially in West Virginia and Pennsylvania in the Marcellus Shale, and later in the Utica Shale, mostly in eastern Ohio.

Appendix 2: Glossary

Absorption: The extraction of components from a mixture of gases when gases and liquids are brought into contact.

Adsorption: The extraction from a mixture of gases of one or more components by surface adhesion to that material with which the gases come in contact.

Air-Gas Ratio: The ratio of the air volume to the gas volume. A specified ratio of natural gas (4–14 percent) to air is necessary to achieve a desired character of combustion.

American Gas Association (AGA): The trade association representing many natural gas utilities and pipeline companies in the United States.

Anthracite Coal: Hard coal that contains few volatile hydrocarbons and burns almost without flame.

Anticline: The upward geological fold in rock strata in the earth's crust which beds or layers dip in opposite direction from the crest, forming a dome-like shape permitting possible entrapment of oil and gas.

Aquifer: A rock with both enough porosity and permeability to conduct significant volumes of water to a well or spring.

Artificial Gas— See **Manufactured Gas**

Bailer: A long, cylindrical container in cable-tool drilling used to remove water, sand, mud, or drilling cuttings from a well.

Barnett Shale: A Mississippian-age shale formation in the Fort Worth basin in north-central Texas.

Bcf: Abbreviation for billion cubic feet.

Bending Gang: A group of pipeline workers who bent pipe with the aid of chains attached to both ends of a pipe.

Billion Cubic Feet (Bcf): Gas measurement approximately equal to one trillion (1,000,000,000,000) BTUs.

Biofuel: Fuel derived from biomass such as wood, ethanol, or landfill gas.

Biogenic Gas: Methane gas produced by the decomposition of organic matter through fermentation, such as in wetlands.

Bit: The boring element attached to the bottom of the drill string used in cable tool or rotary drilling of oil and gas wells.

Bituminous Coal: Soft coal that contains volatile hydrocarbons and tarry matter and burns with a smoky, yellowish flame.

Bleed: To drain off liquid or gas, generally slowly, through a valve called a bleeder.

Blowout: Extreme pressure of a gas or oil well that results in the uncontrolled flow of gas, oil, water, or rock out of the borehole and into the atmosphere.

Borehole (Well Bore): Cylindrical hole created by the drilling for oil or gas.

Bottled Gas: Liquefied petroleum gas (LPG) contained under high pressure and stored in cylinders, often for use in rural areas where natural gas pipelines do not reach.

Brine: Salt water that often comes up the wellbore when producing oil and gas.

Broker— See **Marketer**

BTU (British Thermal Unit): A measurement for energy representing the amount of heat that is necessary to raise the temperature of 1 pound of water by 1 degree Fahrenheit.

Bunsen Burner: A gas burner in which primary air enters a tube through an adjustable opening and is combined with natural gas for combustion from an orifice at the top producing a high-temperature and nonluminious flame.

Burner, Fishtail: A tip for a gas burner that produces a wide, flat flame that is somewhat fishtail shaped.

Burner Tip: An attachment for a burner head which forms on a gas appliance. Also, a generic term that refers to the end use consumption for natural gas.

Butane (C_4H_{10}): A paraffin hydrocarbon, a gas in atmospheric conditions but is easily liquefied under pressure used in the production of rubber and as a fuel such as in cigarette lighters. It is a constituent of liquefied petroleum gas (LPG).

Bypass: Obtaining service from a new gas supplier without using the pipelines of the former supplier.

Cable Tool Drilling: One of two principal methods of drilling for gas and oil. Cable tool drilling is an older process consisting of repeatedly raising and dropping a heavy drill bit, suspended from the end of a cable, so that it punches and pulverizes its way through rock.

Canadian Gas Association (CGA): A trade organization representing all segments of the gas industry in Canada.

Candlepower: A measure of light.

Cap: A cup-shaped fitting placed on end of a pipe to seal the pipe or the action of placing the cap on a pipe. Also, to close off a gas or oil well.

Cap and Close Policy: Canadian government policy to phase out coal-fired electric generating stations and replace them with alternative fuels or natural gas burning generating stations.

Caprock: The impervious geological strata that overlay reservoir rock and holds gas or oil in a sealed reservoir.

Carbon Black: Almost pure amorphous carbon consisting of extremely fine particles used first for ink making and tire production, usually produced from gaseous or liquid hydrocarbons by controlled combustion with a restricted air supply, or by thermal decomposition.

Carbon Dioxide (CO_2): A gas produced by burning natural gas when carbon united with sufficient oxygen produces complete combustion. It is considered a greenhouse gas that is believed to exacerbate global warming.

Carbon Monoxide (CO): A poisonous, combustible gas formed by incomplete combustion of carbon or reduction of carbon dioxide.

Carbon Sequestration: The process of injecting carbon dioxide into underground rock formations to prevent the excess greenhouse gas into the atmosphere.

Carbonate Rock: A rock consisting primarily of a carbonate mineral such as calcite or dolomite, the chief minerals in limestone and dolostone, respectively.

Carbureted Water Gas: A type of manufactured gas made from coke, air, steam, and oil.

Casing: Metal tube used to line the walls of a gas well to prevent collapse of the well and to protect the surrounding earth and rock layers or aquifers from being contaminated by oil, gas, or drilling fluids.

Casing string: The entire length of all the joints of casing pipe down in a well.

Casinghead Gas: Unprocessed natural gas containing natural gasoline and other liquid hydrocarbon vapors produced from an oil well.

Cast Iron Pipe: Pipe made by pouring molten iron into molds.

Cathodic Protection: A method of preventing corrosion in natural gas pipelines that involves using electric voltage to slow or prevent corrosion.

Cementing: Pumping a liquid slurry of cement and water to various points inside or outside the well casing to seal the well to prevent leaks into aquifers.

Christmas Tree: A series of natural gas pipes and valves that sit atop a producing gas well.

City Gas— See **Manufactured Gas**

Citygate: A location at which natural gas is exchanged and pressure reduced from a high-pressure interstate gas pipeline to medium and low pressure local utility main lines.

Clean Air Act Amendments of 1990: This legislation meant to reduce airborne pollutants and curb acid rain by promoting the use of cleaner fuels in vehicles and stationary sources.

Coal Bed Methane: Methane produced from coal seams that is vented for safety reasons, but now economically recoverable in certain areas by new drilling technologies.

Coal Cake— See **Coke**

Coal Gas—See also **Manufactured Gas:** Manufactured gas made by distillation or carbonization of coal in a closed coal gas retort, coke oven, or other vessel.

Coal Oil: Kerosene.

Co-Firing: The injection of natural gas with pulverized coal or oil into the primary combustion zone of a boiler that creates a cleaner and more efficient operation.

Cogeneration: The use of a single prime fuel source in a gas turbine to generate electrical and thermal energy in order to optimize the efficiency of the fuel used.

Coke (Coal cake): A byproduct, consisting principally of carbon, produced by roasting coal to produce manufactured gas.

Combination Utility: Utility that supplies both gas and some other utility service (electricity, water, etc.).

Combined-Cycle: The utilization of waste heat from large gas turbines to generate steam for conventional steam turbines.

Commodity Charge: A charge per unit volume of gas actually delivered to the buyer.

Compacts: A group of landowners who reach a massive leasing deal with an exploration company that could increase production royalties and give them leverage in negotiation.

Compressed Gas: Gas that is held under pressure to propel it through pipelines. Also, stored gas under pressure for natural gas vehicles.

Compression: The process of compressing natural gas, reducing volume and increasing velocity during transportation in pipelines over large distances or into storage underground.

Compressor: A mechanical device for increasing the pressure of a gas, compressing its space and increasing its velocity through pipelines or into storage wells.

Compressor Station: A series of compressors to push natural gas through pipelines over a long distance, usually placed about every 100 miles of pipeline for long-haul pipelines.

Condensate: The liquid resulting when a hydrocarbon is subjected to cooling and/or pressure reduction. Also, liquid hydrocarbons condensed from gas and oil wells.

Conservation: Reduction of energy usage by weatherization of buildings through insulation or design, lowering thermostats, etc.

Core Sample: Drilling through the bore hole to collect a cylindrical sample to determine the properties of the rock strata for potential hydrocarbons.

Cost of Service: Term used in public utility regulation to mean the total number of dollars required to supply utility service.

Coupling: A sleeve-type fitting used to securely connect two pieces of pipeline to prevent leaks.

Cracking: The process that breaks down and rearranges the molecular structure of hydrocarbon chains found in wet natural gas to make natural gasolines and other products.

Crown Block: The set of pulleys at the top of the mast on a drilling rig.

Cryogenic: The science of producing very low temperatures for natural gas to produce liquefied natural gas (LNG).

Cubic Foot: A unit of measurement for volume of gas approximately equal to one hundred BTUs. It represents an area one foot long, by one foot wide, by one foot deep.

Curtailment: Restrictions of gas use, especially for industry, due to periodic shortages.

Customer Choice: Deregulation of the gas supply process enabling retail customers in monopolistic natural gas utility systems to choose their own supplier of gas.

Cuttings: A piece of rock or dirt that is brought to the surface of a drilling site as debris from the bottom of well.

Decontrol (Deregulation): The act of ending federal government control over the wellhead price of natural gas sold in interstate commerce.

Deep Gas: Gas found at depths greater than the average for a particular area; for FERC purposes, it is gas found at depths of more than 15,000 feet.

Dehydration: The process of removing liquids and moisture content from gas or other matter.

Demand: The rate at which gas is delivered to or by a natural gas system.

Demand charge: That portion of a rate for gas service which is based on the actual or estimated peak daily, hourly, or monthly usage of a customer.

Department of Energy (DOE): Main federal government agency responsible for regulating most energy sources, created in 1977.

Deregulation— See **Decontrol**

Derrick: A large load-bearing structure, first made of wood in the 19th century and later usually of bolted metal construction.

Desiccant: Any liquid or solid absorbent or adsorbent that will remove water or water vapor from a material.

Dip: The angle at which a rock formation lies in relation to a flat line at the surface that may reveal a trap of oil or gas.

Directional drilling— See **Horizontal Drilling**

Dispatching: The control of natural gas in a system involving the assignment of load to the various sources of supply.

Disposal well: A well through which water (usually salt water) is returned to subsurface formations.

Distribution: The act or process of distributing gas on the local level to consumers.

Dolomite: A type of sedimentary rock similar to limestone but containing more than 50 percent magnesium carbonate; sometimes a reservoir rock for petroleum or natural gas.

Dowsing rod: A Y-shaped wooden stick used by primitive water or gas explorers to search for likely success areas for drilling.

Drill pipe (Drive pipe): Heavy seamless tubing used to rotate the drilling bit and circulate the drilling fluid.

Drill stem: The assembly used for rotary drilling up to the drilling bit.

Drill string: A column of drill pipe with attached tools that transmits fluid and rotational power in the borehole.

Drilling: The mechanic operation of boring holes into the earth to discover fresh or salt water, oil, and natural gas.

Drilling fluid: Circulating fluid, or "muds," to force cuttings out of the wellbore and to the surface, cool the drilling bit, and to counteract downhole formation pressure. Depending on the formation, either liquids, often containing chemicals to keep the borehole clear, or gases, can be used.

Drip: A container, or segment of piping, placed at a low point in a system to collect condensate, dust or foreign material, allowing for their removal.

Drive pipe—See **Drill Pipe**

Dry Gas Production: Natural gas that contains little natural gas liquids, but rather, mostly methane.

Dry hole: A well that is unable to produce oil or gas in sufficient quantities.

Drying, Gas: Removing petroleum-like liquids from natural gas.

Dual-Fuel Capability: Ability of an energy-using facility to alternately use more than one kind of fuel.

Eagle Ford Shale: A shale formation found in south Texas.

Efficiency: Relating to heat, a percentage indicating the available BTU input to combustion equipment that is converted to useful purposes.

Electrolytic Corrosion: In a pipeline, the decomposition or destruction of the pipe wall by stray electrical currents.

Electronic Bulletin Board: In the context of the natural gas industry, an electronic service

that provides information about pipeline company rates, available capacity on lines, confirmation of delivery and so forth.

End Use: The actual purpose for which gas is used by the ultimate consumer.

Energy Information Administration (EIA): The Department of Energy (DOE) branch that
provides statistical information collection and analysis.

Energy Policy Act of 1992 — EPACT: Comprehensive energy legislation to expand natural
gas use by reforming Public Utility Holding Company Act restrictions, allowing wholesale
electric transmission access and providing incentives to developers of clean fuel vehicles.

Environmental Protection Agency (EPA): A federal agency created in 1970 to permit coordinated and effective governmental action for protection of the environment by the systematic abatement and control of pollution, through integration of research monitoring,
standard setting, and enforcement activities.

Ethane (C_2H_6): A colorless, odorless hydrocarbon gas found with natural gas.

Ethylene (C_2H_4): A colorless hydrocarbon gas of slight odor, often produced from ethane, is
a key component used to make petrochemicals, and polyethylene, used in packaging such
as milk jugs and soda bottles, adhesives, and auto parts.

Exploration: The act of searching for potential subsurface reservoirs of natural gas or oil
with the use of magnetometers, gravity meters, seismic exploration, surface mapping,
exploratory drillings, and other such methods.

Exploratory Well: A well drilled either in search of a new and as yet undiscovered accumulation of oil or gas.

Extraction Plant: A plant in which products such as propane, butane, oil, ethane, or natural
gasoline, which are initially components of the gas stream, are extracted or removed for
sale.

Fairway, Marcellus: Area of economic viability of production of natural gas in the shale formation.

Fault: A fracture in part of the earth's crust due to forces exerted on it by movement of plates,
often forming traps for oil or natural gas in the geological formations.

Fayetteville Shale: A shale formation in Arkansas.

Federal Energy Regulatory Commission (FERC): A federal agency under the Natural Gas
Act of 1978 created to replace the Federal Power Commission's (FPC) to provide interstate
regulatory functions over the electric power and natural gas transportation industries.

Federal Power Commission (FPC): The U.S. agency that regulated interstate natural gas
transportation prior to the creation of the Federal Energy Regulatory Commission (FERC)
in the late 1970s. First created in 1920 to regulate water resources, it later assumed responsibility for regulating the electric power and natural gas industries that sold or transported
electricity or gas for resale in interstate commerce.

FERC Orders 436, 451, 500, 636: Federal orders that deregulated the interstate natural gas
pipeline companies, providing a way for utilities to buy gas directly from producers and
marketing companies.

Field, Gas — See **Gas Field**

Field Pressure: The pressure of natural gas as it is found in the underground formations
from which it is produced.

Field Price: The price paid for natural gas at the wellhead or outlet of a central gathering
point in a field.

Firm Service Contract: A type of contracted service where the distributor agrees to provide
the buyer with an uninterrupted supply of gas.

Fishing: The process of retrieving drilling tools that have become dislodged and lost in the
borehole of a well.

Fitting: A metallic or plastic device such as a coupling used in joining lengths of pipe into
various piping systems.

Fixed Cost: Certain costs which in the aggregate do not vary in amount regardless of the
quantity of gas sold or transported.

Flambeau: A large natural gas flame emitting out of a stovepipe-shaped device.

Flange: A plate of material set at right angles to the surface to which it is attached and ordinarily used to fasten two sections of natural gas pipeline together.

Flaring: Burning off impurities or excess natural gas in gas and oil wells.

Flowback: Water and chemicals that come back to the surface of a well after the hydraulic fracturing process that must be safely contained, reused, or disposed of properly.

Fold: A bend in rock strata, usually in response to compressional forces.

Formation: A formation refers to either a certain layer of the earth's crust. It often refers to the area of rock where an oil or natural gas reservoir is located.

Fossil Fuels: Those fuels occurring naturally in the earth, such as natural gas, coal, or oil.

Fracking/Fracturing/Fracing/Fraccing — See **Hydraulic Fracturing**

Fracture: A break in a rock due to mechanical failure.

Fuel Cell, Natural Gas: Energy units that convert natural gas to electric power by the chemical interaction of gas and certain other metals, such as platinum or gold.

Full Fuel Cycle Use: Measuring energy from its point of origin to point of use.

Furnace: When used in a central heating system, this is a self-contained appliance for heating air by transfer of heat of combustion through metal to the air.

Gas: That state of matter which has neither independent shape nor volume. It expands to fill the entire container in which it is held. It is one of the three forms of matter, the other two being solid and liquid.

Gas, Illuminating: A gas containing relatively large amounts of unsaturated and/or heavy hydrocarbon gases and burns with a luminous flame.

Gas, Manufactured — See **Manufactured Gas**

Gas, Natural: A naturally occurring mixture of hydrocarbon and non-hydrocarbon gases found in porous geologic formations beneath the earth's surface, consisting primarily of methane.

Gas, Oil: A gas resulting from the thermal decomposition of petroleum oils.

Gas Bag: A gas-proof, inflatable bag that can be inserted in a gas pipe and inflated to seal off the flow of the gas.

Gas Bubble: An excess of natural gas deliverability relative to demand requirements at current prices.

Gas Control: A dispatching center that directs the pressures, direction, and control of natural gas through a pipeline system.

Gas Detector: A device that indicates the existence of combustible or noxious gas.

Gas Famine: A gas shortage caused by the lack of deliverability of the product.

Gas Field: A district or area from which natural gas is produced.

Gas Holder (Gasometer): A large metal receptacle used in the 19th century for storage manufactured gas from a coal plant. The tank was often telescopic in design, raising its roof as gas pressure was piped into it and falling as gas was sent out.

Gas Lease: An agreement to extract minerals from underneath a landowner's property.

Gas Research Institute (GRI): An organization sponsored by a number of U.S. gas companies to investigate new sources of supply and new uses (applications) for natural gas.

Gas Sand: The underground porous strata (sandstone, limestone, or dolomite) that contains natural gas and from which it is produced.

Gas Storage — see **Underground Gas Storage**

Gas Turbine: A prime mover in which gas, under pressure or formed by combustion, is directed against a series of turbine blades that convert into mechanical energy supplying power at the shaft.

Gas Zone: A porous, permeable formation containing natural gas under pressure.

Gasification: The process during which liquified natural gas (LNG) is returned to its vapor or gaseous state through an increase in temperature and a decrease in pressure.

Gaslight: An illuminating appliance, first fueled by manufactured gas in the 19th century.

Gasoline Plant — See **Extraction Plant**

Gasser: A "gusher" of natural gas.

Gate Valves: A valve to control the pressure of natural gas in a pipeline system.

Gathering Line: A pipeline, usually of small diameter, used in gathering gas from the field to a central point.

Geophysics: A study of subsurface geological conditions of structure or material.

Go-Devil — See **Pig, Pipeline**

Greenhouse Gas: Gases such as methane and carbon dioxide that trap heat in the atmosphere, believed by many scientists to cause a rise in global temperatures.

Haynesville Shale: A shale formation located throughout eastern Texas, southwestern Arkansas, and Louisiana.

Heat Pump: An electrical powered device that provides heat to a structure by extracting heat from outside air or through geothermal processes in the ground.

Hexane (C_6H_{14}): Any of five isomeric, volatile, liquid, paraffin hydrocarbons found in petroleum.

High BTU Gas: A term used to designate fuel gases having heating values of pipeline specification, i.e., greater than about 900 BTUs per standard cubic foot.

Hogshead: A container used to collect gas separated from saltwater coming up from a well.

Holder, Gas: A gas-tight receptacle or container in which gas is stored for future use.

Holding Companies: Firms that hold the securities of a number of other businesses.

Holidays: Flaws in anti-corrosion pipeline coating exposing the bare metal pipeline that need to be corrected before putting a pipeline in services.

Horizontal Drilling (Lateral or Directional Drilling): A drilling technology that allows producers to turn a drill bit sideways and extend boreholes horizontally to reach thin formations such as shale deposits.

Horsepower (hp): A unit of power; equivalent to 33,000 ft-lb per minute or 550 ft-lb per second (mechanical horsepower).

Hub: A market or supply area pooling/delivery where gas supply is exchanged among interstate pipelines.

Hydrates, Natural Gas: A solid material resulting from the combination of a gas with water under pressure that can restrict or stop natural gas flow in a pipeline. Also, deep underocean deposits of frozen methane.

Hydraulic Fracturing (a.k.a., Hydrofracing, Fracturing, Fracking, Fracing, or Fraccing): A method used by drillers to stimulate production to extract more natural gas from tight or nonpermeable formations (or extending the longevity of older wells) by using hydraulics (use of water and a small amount of chemicals under great pressure) to break apart the rock formations containing hydrocarbons.

Hydrocarbon: A compound that contains only hydrogen and carbon, the lightest forms being gasous (as natural gas), and with greater molecular weights liquid (oil) and the heaviest solid (coal).

Hydrogen Sulfide — See **Sour Gas**

Hydrostatic Test: A strength test of pipe filled with liquid and subject to pressure.

Illuminants: Heavy hydrocarbons in manufactured gas such as benzene that burn with a luminous flame.

Inch Lines: Emergency World War II oil transportation lines from Texas to New Jersey, later converted to natural gas in the late 1940s and early 1950s.

Incremental Pricing: A pricing mechanism established by the Natural Gas Policy Act of 1978. It is the passing through of certain costs of acquiring new gas by way of a surcharge and applying the surcharge to certain end uses by certain industrial facilities. It was repealed in 1987.

Independent Petroleum Association of America (IPAA): A trade group representing independent oil and gas producers.

Independent Producer: A non-integrated exploration and production company that receives nearly all of its revenues from production at the wellhead.

Industrial Fuel Switching: Switching from natural gas to alternate fuels such as oil by large industrial customers, primarily motivated by the relative fuel prices.

Injection Wells: Disposal wells for contaminated drilling wastewater or brine injected in deep rock formations.

Insulation: A material having a relatively high resistance to heat transfer used to contain heat in buildings to save energy.

Interconnection, System: A connection between two utility systems permitting the transfer of gas in either direction.

Interruptible Service: Contracts allow a distributing party to temporarily suspend delivery of gas to a buyer in order to meet the demands of firm service customers.

Interstate Gas: Gas transported in interstate pipelines to be sold and consumed in states other than that state in which the gas was produced.

Interstate Natural Gas Association of America (INGAA): Trade group representing the interstate pipelines.

Isobutane (C_4H_{10}): A hydrocarbon of the same chemical formula as butane but different molecular structure.

Jars: A cable drilling device attached to the drilling tool to prevent the drill bit from sticking in the bore hole and used to help free objects stuck in the hole.

Joint: The connection between two lengths of pipeline. Also, natural fractures in reservoir rock formations that can increase withdrawal of hydrocarbons.

Kerosene (Coal Oil): A hydrocarbon obtained by the distillation of oil used as a fuel for some engines, cooking, heating, and beginning in the nineteenth century, lighting.

Lamp trimmers—See **Lamplighters**

Lampblack—See **Carbon Black**

Lamplighters (Lamp trimmers): Manufactured gas workers who cleaned and replaced mantels inside gaslights of homes, stores, and streetlights.

Landfill Gas: Gas produced by aerobic and anaerobic decomposition of a landfill.

Landman (Leasehound): An exploration company employee who clears land titles and negotiates with property owners to obtain gas or oil leases.

Lateral Drilling—See **Horizontal Drilling**

Leak Detector: A device for identifying and locating a gas leak.

Leasehound—See Landman.

Limelight: The brilliant illuminant created by coal-produced gaslight treated with lime, often used in 19th century theatres.

Limestone: A sedimentary rock consisting primarily of the mineral calcite.

Linewalkers: Gas pipeline workers who patrol natural gas pipeline right-of-ways to monitor for leaks.

Liquefaction: Any process in which gas is converted from the gaseous to the liquid phase.

Liquefied Natural Gas (LNG): Natural gas that has been cooled to -260 degrees Fahrenheit where it both significantly shrinks and becomes a clear, odorless, and tasteless liquid enabling it to be transported across oceans in container ships.

Liquefied Petroleum Gas (LPG): Heavy, hot burning hydrocarbon gases such as propane and butane, separated from wet natural gas by condensation or absorption.

Liquids, Natural Gas—See **Natural Gas Liquids**

Load: The amount of gas delivered or required at any point on a system.

Local Distribution Company: A retail gas distribution (utility) company that delivers natural gas to end users.

Logging: Recording information by lowering different types of electronic measuring instruments into the wellbore and gathering and recording data of rock density and porosity to determine the presence of hydrocarbons.

Magnetometer: A device used in the exploration for hydrocarbons by measuring the intensity of the earth's magnetic field.

Main: A distribution line at a higher pressure that serves as a common source of supply for more than one service line.

Mandatory Carriage: The obligation to carry, for a fee, gas offered by another party.

Mantle: A lace-like hood or sack of some refractory material which, when placed in position over a flame, gives light by incandescence.

Manufactured Gas (Artificial, Town, or City Gas): An artificial gas first produced in the 19th century by roasting coal or oil to produce a gas suitable for illumination, but varying widely in heating content. Examples include coal gases, coke or oven gases, producer gas, blast furnace gas, blue (water) or carbureted water gas.

Marcellus Shale: A black shale formation of porous, but not very permeable rock deep under the Appalachian region being exploited with the drilling technologies of horizontal drilling and hydraulic fracturing.

Marketer (Broker): A non-regulated buyer and seller of natural gas.

Marsh Gas: Methane gas resulting from the partial decay of plants.

Mcf: An abbreviation for thousand cubic feet.

Medina Sandstone: A gas-bearing sandstone of Silurian Age.

Mercaptan: A nontoxic, nonpoisonous, but pungent organic chemical used as an odorant added to colorless, odorless natural gas to give it a "rotten egg" stench for safety reasons so it is obvious when gas is leaking from a pipeline or appliance.

Meter, Gas: A device for measuring natural gas consumption, first implemented in the late 19th century to prevent the waste of natural gas.

Meter Readers: Utility personnel who record measurements of gas usage.

Methane (CH_4): The most common and lightest in the paraffin series of hydrocarbon gases and the main component of natural gas. It is colorless and naturally odorless (odorant is added for safety reasons) and burns efficiently and cleanly compared to other fossil fuels.

Million Cubic Feet (MMCF): A volumetric measurement approximately equal to one billion BTUs.

Mineral Rights: The ownership of subsurface minerals under land or water that may be separated from the surface ownership.

Mixed Gas: Fuel gas in which natural or LP gas is mixed with manufactured gas.

MMcf: Abbreviation for one million cubic feet.

Mormon Boards: Wooden boards used to dump dirt back into a ditch once pipeline was laid in it, often dragged by teams of mules in the 19th century and later, powered equipment.

Muds, See **Drilling Fluids**

Naphtha: A loosely defined hydrocarbon between containing components of gasoline and kerosene, used in solvents and paint thinners and as a raw material for the production of synthetic natural gas.

Natural Gas — See **Gas, Natural**

Natural Gas Act of 1938: Act that resulted in the federal government's first regulation of the interstate sale or transportation of natural gas, including oversight of rates charged by interstate gas-transmission companies.

Natural Gas Liquids: The heavier hydrocarbons of propane, butanes, and pentanes (also referred to as condensate), or a combination of them that can be separated from "wet" natural gas.

Natural Gas Policy Act of 1978: One of the first efforts to deregulate the gas industry by eventually allowing the price of natural gas to be dictated by free market forces.

Natural Gas Supply Association (NGSA): A trade group representing integrated gas producers.

Natural Gas Trust: A formation of Standard Oil controlled gas companies in the late 19th century.

Natural Gas Vehicles (NGVs): Natural gas cars or trucks, usually powered by compressed natural gas, that operate much cleaner compared to gasoline transportation either as the sole fuel (dedicated NGVs) or as an option (dual-fuel NGVs).

Natural Gas Wellhead Decontrol Act of 1989: Legislation that allowed the remainder of FERC regulation of producer sales of natural gas to be eliminated gradually until full decontrol took effect in 1993.

Natural Gasoline — See also **Natural Gas Liquids:** Heavy liquid hydrocarbon gases such as pentane and heptanes stripped from wet natural gas by compression or absorption, first blended with gasoline from petroleum refineries to improve "quick start" properties in "Hi-Test" gasoline for automobiles.

Nitrogen (N_2): An odorless, colorless, generally inert gas. It comprises 79 percent of the earth's atmosphere in the free state.

Nitrogen Oxides (NOx): A pollutant emitted by the burning of fossil fuels. Natural gas produces much less of this pollutant than oil or coal.

NORM: Naturally occurring radioactive material brought to the surface in the rock pieces of the drill cuttings and flowback from wells.

Odorant: A substance (e.g., Mercaptan) giving a readily perceptible odor (e.g., rotten eggs) at low concentrations in natural gas, which in its pure state is odorless, colorless, and tasteless.

Off Peak Period: The period of time during a day, week, month or year when gas use on a particular system is not at its maximum.

Oil Shale: A convenient expression used to cover a range of materials containing organic matter which can be converted into crude shale oil and gas by heating.

Open Access: The non-discriminatory access to interstate pipeline transportation services.

Open Flow: Unrestricted volume of gas out of a well.

Organic: Materials in which carbon is a major component.

Orifice Meter: A measuring device of natural gas by differential pressure that uses an opening where the flow of gas is limited.

Oriskany Sand: A course, porous, and permeable quartz rock gas-producing sandstone of Lower Devonian Age in Appalachia.

Oxygen (O_2): A gas which forms about 21 percent by volume of the atmosphere. It is chemically very active and is necessary for combustion of gas, oil, and coal.

Paraffin: A white, tasteless, odorless, waxy substance composed of natural hydrocarbons and obtained from petroleum.

Particulates: Minute particles produced by the burning of oil or coal.

Peak Day: The 24-hour period of greatest total gas sendout by a utility.

Peak Oil or Gas Theory: The contention that oil or natural gas consumption now exceeds oil or gas production.

Peak Shaving: Using sources of energy, such as natural gas from storage, to supplement the normal amounts delivered to customers during peak-use periods.

Perforation Gun: A device for making a hole through the casing and into the producing formation of a well to provide channels for flow of gas and/or oil into the well.

Permeability: A measure of how easily a fluid can pass through a section of rock.

Petroleum: A flammable bituminous liquid that may vary from almost colorless to black, and refined to make gasoline, naphtha, or other oil products.

Phillips' Decision: Supreme Court decision in 1954 that determined that Congress could control the price of interstate natural gas, leading to federal wellhead price regulations that eventually resulted in severe shortages in the 1970s. Later legislation repealed the price controls.

Pig, Pipeline (Go Devil): A barrel-shaped device used to clean the internal surface of a pipeline with metal brushes, pushed through the line with gas pressure.

Pilot: A small flame which is utilized to ignite the gas at the main burner of a gas appliance.

Pintsch Gas: A manufactured gas made from oil used in railroad cars.

Pipe Coating: A corrosion-resistant material wrapped or applied to the outer surface of a pipeline to protect the metal from corrosion.

Pipe Tongs: A hand or power tool for gripping or rotating pipe.

Pipejack: A strong wooden pole device necessary to properly align pipeline for connection.

Pipeline: All parts of those physical facilities through which gas is moved in transportation, including pipe, valves, compressors, metering stations, and regulator stations.

Pipeline Capacity: The maximum quantity of gas that can be moved through a pipeline system at any given time based on existing service conditions such as available horsepower and pipeline diameter.

Pipeliners: Nomadic gas workers installing a pipeline.

Pitch Gas: Gas produced by pine-tar resin.

Plastic Pipe: A hollow cylinder of a plastic material used for the transportation of natural gas.

Play: A group of geologically similar drilling prospects having a similar source, reservoir, and trap controls of gas migration, accumulation, and storage.

Plugging, Well: The sealing of a well by cementing to prevent any leaks of hydrocarbons into the acquifer.

Pool — See **Reservoir**

Pooling: Landowners who form a production unit with other property owners for the purpose of leasing their mineral rights. "Forced" or "fair" pooling would permit drillers on a neighbor's leased property to horizontally drill under an unleased private owner's property even if the owner refuses to enter into a lease agreement.

Porosity: Pores or spaces between grains of sediment in sedimentary rock such as sandstone that can contain natural gas or oil. Pores holding hydrocarbons in shale rock are smaller and not as interconnected.

Powerplant and Industrial Fuel Use Act of 1978: Legislation prohibiting the use of natural gas and oil in new power plants and major fuel-burning installations. Officially repealed in May 1987.

Pressure: When expressed with reference to pipe, the force per unit area exerted by the medium in the pipe.

Producer: A natural gas company involved in exploration, drilling, and refinement of natural gas from a a well.

Propane (C_3H_8): A gaseous member of the paraffin series of hydrocarbons, easily liquefied, that is one of the components of liquefied petroleum (LP) gas often used where natural gas lines do not reach.

Proppant: Sand or other material used in the hydraulic fracturing process to hold open the fractures in shale wells so natural gas can flow through them.

Prospect: A geographical area which exploration has shown contains sedimentary rocks and structure favorable for the presence of oil or gas.

Proved Reserves — See **Reserves, Proved**

Psi: Pounds per square inch used to measure pressure in a pipeline.

Public Utility: A company performing a utility service within a specified area granted by franchise and subject to state regulation.

Public Utility (Service) Commission: A state regulatory authority charged with regulating the price of natural gas service of public utility monopolies.

PUHCA — **Public Utility Holding Company Act of 1935:** Depression-era regulations addressing the "Power Trusts" that restricted the activities of a number of public utilities, forcing them to divest from certain businesses.

Purchased Gas Costs: Costs of gas acquired by, but outside of, a local utility's control, on behalf of its customers

Purchaser: A party who buys gas from a supplier.

Purging: The act of removing any explosive mixture in a pipeline with an inert substance, such as nitrogen.

Quad: An abbreviation for a quadrillion (1,000,000,000,000,000) BTU. For natural gas, roughly equivalent to one trillion (1,000,000,000,000) cubic feet.

Radiant: An element of a burner, generally made of ceramic material that when heated by gas, radiates heat.

Radiator: A heating unit which transfers heat by radiation to objects within a visible range and by conduction to the surrounding air which, in turn, is circulated by natural convection.

Range, Gas: Cooking stove.

Rate: The unit charge or charges made to customers for natural gas.

Rate Base: The monetary amount which is used as the divisor in calculating a utility's rate of return, made up of the property used and useful in public service.

Rate Case: A proceeding before a state regulatory commission involving the rates to be charged for a public utility service, or before the Federal Energy Regulatory Commission for a pipeline.

Rate Design: The method of classifying fixed and variable costs between demand and commodity components.

Rate of Return: The ratio of total company income to a specified rate base, expressed as a percentage.

Regulator: A device that maintains a constant pressure in a pipeline.

Relief Valve: A safety device for relieving pressures in excess of the maximum allowable control pressure in a pipeline system.

Reserves, Proved: Refers to the bank of natural resources in natural reservoirs, such as natural gas or oil, which can be recovered by economic and current operating conditions. Other estimated reserved included probable, possible, and speculative reserves.

Reservoir (Pool): An underground rock stratum that forms a trap for the accumulation of oil or natural gas.

Rig: The assemblage of drilling equipment for an oil or gas well.

Right-of-Way: A strip of land, the use of which is acquired for the construction and operation of a pipeline.

River Dog: Concrete clamps placed on pipelines crossing bodies of water to sink the line to the water bottom.

Rock Shields: Protective devices to prevent pipelines from being punctured by rocks while the pipeline ditch is filled in.

Robert's Torpedoes: Devices filled with gunpowder or nitroglycerine to explode below the ground to improve a well's production.

Rockhound: Nickname for a geologist.

Rotary Drills: A modern drilling device, invented in 1909 by Howard Hughes, Sr., eventually resembling large pine cones made of tough steel covered with sharp teeth of industrial diamonds to rotate and grind through hard, brittle rock formations.

Roughneck: An oil or gas drilling worker or a general all-around worker on a drilling rig.

Roustabout: A semi-skilled oil and gas laborer who performs general work around wells.

Royalty: The amount paid to the owner of mineral-rights as payment for minerals removed, usually for gas on a percentage of the total amount removed.

Rule of Capture: The basic premise that allows a gas or oil driller from a well on his legal property to drain resources that may migrate underground from a neighbor's property.

Sandstone: A sedimentary rock consisting primarily of sand-sized particles that can serve as an effective reservoir for natural gas and oil.

SCADA — Supervisory Control and Data Acquisition: Remote controlled equipment used by gas pipeline firms to operate their gas systems by directly flow, pressure, or volumes of gas.

Screw/Threaded Pipe: Pipe sections that are threaded into one another.

Scrub: To remove certain constituents of a gas by passing it through a scrubber in which a suitable liquid absorbs or washes out the constituent.

Seamless Pipe: Rolled steel pipe without seams that enable it to hold high pressures of gas.

Sedimentary rock: A rock formed from the products of weathering.

Seismograph: A device for detecting vibrations in the earth used in prospecting for probable oil or gas bearing structures.

Sendout: Total gas produced, purchased, or withdrawn from an underground storage field within a specified time.

Separator: A piece of equipment such as gas production unit used for separating one substance from another when they are intimately mixed, such as removing oil from water, or oil from gas.

Separator Tank: Tanks located at the well site used to separate oil, gas, and water before sending each off to be processed at different locations.

Service Area: Territory in which a utility system is required or has the right to supply gas service to customers.

Service Charge: The fee charged a utility customer to recover many of the fixed costs to provide service.

Severance Tax: A tax placed on gas producers by many states on the amount of gas produced or "severed" from the ground.

Sewage Gas: A gas produced by the fermentation of sewage.

Shale: A fine-grained sedimentary rock consisting primarily of clay minerals, which is the most abundant of all sedimentary rocks.

Shale Oil: A liquid similar to conventional crude oil but obtained from oil shale.

Shooting, Well: Exploding nitroglycerine or other high explosives in a hole to shatter the rock and increase the flow of oil or gas.

Show: A supply of natural gas found while drilling into a rock formation.

Shut-In Well: A well that has been completed but is not producing. A well may be shut-in for tests, repairs, or to await construction of gathering lines.

Skunk Oil: Oil containing a high-sulfur content.

Slate: A fine-grained rock formed by the metamorphosis of clay or shale.

Smart Pig: Modern pipeline cleaning devices used to inspect pipeline interior walls for corrosion and defects, measure pipeline interior diameters, and complete other functions.

Sour Gas (Hydrogen Sulfide Gas): A poisonous, corrosive compound (hydrogen sulfide) that smells like rotten eggs found in manufactured gas made from coals or oils, or in some natural gas wells that must be removed before the natural gas is used.

Spot Market: As opposed to long-term gas purchasing contracts, this method of gas contract purchasing by the buyer and seller is of a short duration at a single volume price.

Spread: Laborers and material on a pipeline installation job.

Spring Pole Drilling: A crude, early type of drilling involving attaching a drilling tool with rope to a wooden pole, bent down with the natural spring of the limb moving the drilling tool up and down.

Spudder Rigs: Drilling equipment similar to a portable water well drilling machine in design, mounted on trailer wheels that can be torn down and set up quickly.

Stabbers: Pipeline workers whose job it was to line up the pipe to get the joint started in a way the threads would not be crossed.

Standard Oil Trust: An amalgam of smaller oil firms controlled by oil magnate John D. Rockefeller in the late 19th and early 20th centuries, eventually dismantled by a Supreme Court decision in 1911.

Stratified Trap: A structure produced by the deposition of sediments in beds or layers.

Storage — See **Underground Storage**

Strip: To remove heavier hydrocarbons from natural gas for recovery and sale.

Stripper Wells: Stripper wells are natural gas wells that produce less than 60,000 cubic feet of gas per day.

Sulfur Dioxides (SO_2): Polluting emissions produced by the burning of coal and oil which returns to earth in precipitation as "acid rain." The combustion of natural gas produces very little SO_2.

Sweet Gas: Natural gas not contaminated by impurities such as sulfur.

Sweet Spot: An area of maximum economic viability of extraction of natural gas in an underground rock formation.

Synthetic Natural Gas (SNG): Gas synthetically produced from oil in the 1970s during a period of natural gas shortages.

Take-or-Pay: The clause in a long-term pipeline gas supply contract that required a minimum quantity of gas to be paid for whether or not entire delivery was taken.

Tariff: A regulatory schedule for a gas company spelling out the terms, conditions, and rate information for types of natural gas service.

Tcf: An abbreviation for trillion cubic feet.

Telemetering: Use of an electrical or pneumatic apparatus for indicating, recording, or integrating the values of a quantity of natural gas and transmitting it to a distant point.

Therm: A unit of heating value equivalent to 100,000 British thermal units (BTU).

Thermogenic Gas: Natural gas created by thermal decomposition of buried organic material deep within the earth.

Thermostat: An automatic device triggered by temperature changes to control the gas supply and operation of a furnace or other device.

Thousand Cubic Feet (Mcf): Measurement of natural gas approximately equal to one million BTUs, often used with retail natural gas pricing.

Three-Dimensional (3-D) Seismic: Computerized images used by geologists searching for evidence of hydrocarbons to generate a detailed, three dimensional image of underground structures.

Throughput: Total of transportation volumes and tariff sales. Also, all gas volumes delivered.

Tight Sands: Gas-bearing geologic strata that holds gas too tightly for conventional extraction processes to bring it to the surface at economic rates without special stimulation.

Tobey Meter: A spherical-shaped gas meter constructed of cast iron invented in 1892 that could withstand higher pressures than earlier tin meters.

Tong Gangs: Groups of pipeline workers in the late 19th and early 20th centuries who screwed pipeline together aided by large wrenches.

Tool dressers: Rig workers who remove, forge, heat, and temper drill bits.

Town Gas— See **Manufactured Gas**

Transmission, Interstate: The network of interstate long-haul pipeline companies regulated by the federal government that transport natural gas from producing areas to end-use markets.

Transmission Company, Gas: A company which obtains nearly all of its gas operating revenues from transportation of gas for others.

Transportation: The act of moving gas from a designated receipt point to a designated delivery point as required by a contract between a pipeline company and gas supplier, or possibly a major end user.

Traps: An area of the earth's crust that has developed in such a way by folding as to hold natural gas or oil beneath the surface.

Trenton-Black River Limestone: Ordovician Age limestone formation that holds natural gas.

Trillion Cubic Feet (Tcf): A volume measurement of natural gas, approximately equivalent to one quad (one quadrillion BTU).

Unbundled Services: Unbundling, or separating, pipeline transmission, sales and storage services, along with guaranteeing "open access" to space on the pipelines for all gas shippers.

Unconventional Gas Supplies: Natural gas supplies in "tight-sands" or shale formations that are not easily extracted by conventional vertical drilling methods, often requiring horizontal drilling and hydraulic fracturing to release economical quantities of gas.

Underground Gas Storage: The use of sub-surface facilities for storing gas that has been transferred from its original location for the primary purpose of balancing loads to meet peak day requirements. In Appalachia, the facilities are usually depleted oil or gas fields.

Upper Devonian Shale: A geological formation (a.k.a. the Northwestern Ohio shale) with low permeability that underlies more than 45,000 square miles of the Appalachian Basin that can produce supplies of natural gas and oil with the use of horizontal drilling and hydraulic fracturing.

Utica Shale: An older shale formation stretching over 170,000 miles in the Appalachian region dating 440 million to 460 million years ago and found 2,000 to 7,000 feet or more below the Marcellus Shale.

Valve: A mechanical device for controlling the flow of natural gas.

Vent: An opening in an otherwise sealed tank to relieve excessive pressure. Also, the deliberate action of venting natural gas to prevent explosive mixtures from accumulating.

Viscosity: The measure of a fluid's thickness, or how well it flows.

Well Bore— See **Bore Hole**

Well Tenders: Field personnel who monitor and control gas well pressure.

Wellhead: The assembly of fittings, valves, and controls located at the surface and connected to the flow lines, tubing, and casing of the well so as to control the flow from the reservoir.

Wellhead Price: Deregulated cost of natural gas at its source.

Welsbach Mantle Lamp: A type of lamp in which the flame impinges on a knitted cup or mantle saturated with chemical compounds that are heated to incandescence to emit a bright, white light, much brighter than other gas lamps while using less fuel.

Wet Gas —See also **Natural Gas Liquids:** Natural gas that contains heavier natural gas liquid hydrocarbons such as propane, butane, ethane, etc.

Weymouth Formula: A formula for calculating gas flow in a large diameter pipeline.

Whale's Foot: Illuminating gas produced from the products of whales.

Wildcatters: Independent drillers investing their own money into well drilling.

Woodford Shale: A shale formation found in Arkansas and Oklahoma.

X-Ray Welds: A process to identify flaws in pipe welds to prevent gas leakage through the use of X-rays.

Chapter Notes

Preface to the First Edition

1. Energy Information Administration, U.S. Department of Energy, "New EIA Forecast Through 2025 Expects Growing Natural Gas Demand to Depend on New Sources of Natural Gas Supply," news release, November 20, 2002, http://usinfo.state.gov/regional/nea/text/1120oil.htm.

2. Charles A. Babcock, *Venango County Pennsylvania, Her Pioneers and People, Embracing a General History of the County* (Chicago: J. H. Beers & Company, 1919), 152. (Pennsylvania's natural gas was valued at $18,558,245 versus oil's value of $16,596,943.)

3. American Gas Association, "Questions and Answers About Natural Gas and National Energy Policy," http://www.aga.org/Content/ContentGroups/Home_Page/Limelight/Questions_and_Answers_About_Natural_Gas_and_National_Energy_Policy.htm.

One

1. M. Elizabeth Sanders, The Regulation of Natural Gas, Policy and Politics, 1938–1978 (Philadelphia: Temple University Press, 1981), 50.

2. "Natural Gas Facts," http://www.naturalgas.com/consumer/history.html.

3. John J. McLaurin, *Sketches in Crude-Oil: Some Accidents and Incidents of the Petroleum Development in all Parts of the Globe* (Harrisburg, Pa.: Published by the Author, 1896), 371.

4. Ibid.

5. Elbert C. Weaver, *The Story of Gas* (New York: American Gas Association, 1964), 4.

6. "Gas Age 75th: A Glance Backward and a Long Look Ahead, " *Gas Age*, October 2, 1958, 46–68.

7. James A. Clark, *The Chronological History of the Petroleum and Natural Gas Industries* (Houston: Clark Book Co., 1963), 3.

8. Mark Kurlansky, *Salt: A World History* (New York: Walker and Company, 2002), 26.

9. Robert K. G. Temple, *The Genius of China: 3,000 Years of Science, Discovery and Invention* (New York: Simon and Schuster, 1986).

10. Ibid.

11. Kurlansky, 26.

12. Louis Stotz and Alexander Jamison, *History of the Gas Industry* (New York: Stettiner Bros., 1938), 68.

13. U.S. Department of Energy, http://www.fe.doe.gov/education/gas_history.html.

14. Clark, 5.

15. John P. Herrick, *Empire Oil: The Story of Oil in New York State* (New York: Dodd, Mead & Company, 1949), 316.

16. Edgar Wesley Owen, *Trek of the Oil Finders: A History of Exploration for Petroleum* (Tulsa, Ok.: The American Association of Petroleum Geologists, 1975), 38.

17. Victor Lauriston, *Blue Flame of Service: A History of Union Gas Company and the Natural Gas Industry in Southwestern Ontario* (n.p.: Union Gas Company of Canada, Ltd., n.d.), 16.

18. "Many Petroleum and Natural Gas 'Firsts' Have Been Established in West Virginia," *The West Virginia Engineer*, September 1946, 10.

19. John C. Fitzpatrick, ed., *The Diaries of George Washington, 1748–1799* (New York: Houghton Mifflin, 1928), 429.

20. Weaver, 6.

21. David L. McKain and Bernard L. Allen, *Where It All Began: The Story of the People and Places Where the Oil and Gas Industry Began, West Virginia and Southeastern Ohio* (Parkersburg, W.Va.: Oil & Gas Museum, 1994), 2.

22. Eugene D. Thoenen, *History of the Oil and Gas Industry in West Virginia* (Charleston: Education Foundation, Inc., 1964), 4.

23. Harold F. Williamson and Arnold R. Daum, *The American Petroleum Industry, the Age of Illumination, 1859–1899* (Evanston, IL: Northwestern University Press, 1963), 16.

24. Stotz and Jamison, 69.

25. Thoenen, 7–8.

26. Ibid., 5.

27. Williamson and Daum, 15; and Thoenen, 6.

28. Hope Natural Gas Company, *Seventy-fifth Anniversary* (Clarksburg, W.Va.: Consolidated Gas Supply Corporation, 1973), 10 in Dominion East Ohio Collection, box 159, file folder 8, Youngstown Historical Center of Industry and Labor, Youngstown, Ohio.

29. A. R. Crum and A. S. Dugan, eds., *Romance of American Petroleum and Gas* (New York: 1911), 169.

30. Blake Malkamaki, "An Index to Early History Petroleum Sites," (adapted from an article by Jane R. Eggleston, updated September 1996), http://www.little-mountain.com/oilwell/.

31. J. T. Henry, *The Early and Later History of Petroleum with Authentic Facts in Regard to its Development in Western Pennsylvania* (Philadelphia: Jas. B. Rodgers, 1873), 23.

32. Kentucky Geological Survey, University of Kentucky, "Oil and Gas History Summary," http://www.uky.edu/KGS/emsweb/oginfo/history.html.

33. W. R. Jillson, *The First Oil Well in Kentucky* (Frankfort: Roberts Printing, 1952), http:www.uky.edu/KGS/petro/kyog02v1.htm.

34. Williamson et al., *The American Petroleum Industry, The Age of Energy Vol. 1 1865–1899* (Evanston, IL: Northwestern University Press, 1959), 90.

35. Lowell H. Harrison and James C. Klotter, *A New History of Kentucky* (Lexington, Ky.: The University Press of Kentucky, 1997), 142.

36. P.C. Boyle, ed. *The Derrick's Handbook of Petroleum* (Oil City, PA: Derrick Publishing Company, 1898), 1028–29.

37. Arthur C. McFarlan, *Geology of Kentucky* (Lexington, Ky.: The University of Kentucky, 1961), 285–86.

38. McLaurin, 372.

39. S. B. Severson, "Gas Town," *Service*, July 1945, 28.

40. *Penny Magazine*, August 26, 1837, as quoted in *Brewster Journal*, 1830, in Henry Westcott, *Handbook of Natural Gas*, 3rd edition (Erie, Pa.: Metric Metal Works, 1920); and *Fredonia Censor*, November 30, 1825, as quoted in "Gasometer, A Fredonia Landmark, Collapsed by Snow," *Fredonia Censor*, January 9, 1964.

41. *Fredonia Censor*, August 31, 1825.

42. Herrick, 321.

43. Edward Orton LL.D., "Petroleum and Natural Gas in New York," *Bulletin of New York State Museum* 6, no. 30 (November 1899).

44. Christopher J. Castaneda, *Invisible Fuel: Manufactured and Natural Gas in America, 1800–2000* (New York: Twayne Publishers, 1999), 39–40.

45. *Mueller Record*, March–April 1949, 9–11, 20.

46. Ralph Hartzel and H.P. Nagel, "From America's First Gas Well," (n.p., Republic Light Heat and Power Company, n.d.).

47. Weaver, 8.

48. "Gas Lights Return to Barcelona to End Century of Darkness," *American Gas Journal*, June 1962; and "Lighthouse at Barcelona Shines Again," *Westfield Republican*, April 11, 1962.

49. Lois Barris comp., *Death Notices 1819–1899 reported in the Fredonia Censor and a few other sources* (Fredonia, N.Y.: Chautauqua County Genealogical Society, 1991).

50. Mel Seidenberg, Lois Mulkearn and James W. Hess, comp., "Two Hundred Years of Pittsburgh History: A Chronology of Events," in Stefan Lorant, *Pittsburgh: The Story of an American City* (Lenox, MA: R. R. Donnelley & Sons Company, 1975), 542.

51. Independent Oil and Gas Association of West Virginia, "Oil and Gas History," http://www.iogawv.com/history.htm.

52. Thoenen, 6–7.

53. McKain and Allen, 8.

54. Luis Hilt, comp., "Chronology of the Natural Gas Industry," *American Gas Journal* (n.p.: E. Holley Poe & Associates, 1950).

55. McLaurin, 373.

56. Williamson and Daum, 591.

57. Westcott, 86.

58. American Gas Association, *Story of Gas: A Brief Sketch of the Manufactured and Natural Gas Industry* (New York: circa 1956), 8; and McLaurin, 375.

59. Dean Hale, ed., "Diary of an Industry, 150th Anniversary of the Gas Industry Commemorative Issue," *American Gas Journal* 193, no. 12 (October 1966), 48.

60. "Gas Wells of Pennsylvania, Ohio and New York," *The Petroleum Monthly* 2, no. 10 (October 1872), 273.

61. J. D. Sisler et al., *Contributions to Oil and Gas Geology of Western Pennsylvania* (Harrisburg, Pa.: Pennsylvania Geological Survey, 4th Series, Bulletin M 19, 1933), 73.

62. Clark, 28.

63. Columbus Group of the Columbia Gas System, *A Hand Book of Practical Information Concerning the Natural Gas Industry*, January 1934, 8; and Henry, 202–03.

64. "Gas Wells of Pennsylvania, Ohio and New York," *The Petroleum Monthly* 2, no. 10 (October 1872), 273.

65. Henry, 202; and Hale, 51.

66. *The Petroleum Monthly* 1, no. 1 (November 1870), 21.

67. J. S. Newberry, "Great Gas Blowing Wells in Ohio," *The Petroleum Monthly* 1, no. 4 (February 1871), 130–31.

68. Hale, 51.

69. "Natural Gas," *Wheeling Daily Intelligencer*, September 14, 1886, http://wheeling.weirton.lib.wv.us/history/bus/gas02.htm.

70. Thoenen, 98.

71. McKain and Allen, 173.

72. McFarlan, 286.

73. Kentucky Geological Survey, University of Kentucky, "Oil and Gas History Summary," http://www.uky.edu/KGS/emsweb/oginfo/history.html.

74. Castaneda, 4.

75. Daniel Yergin, *The Prize. The Epic Quest for Oil, Money & Power* (New York: Simon & Schuster, 1991), 19–20.

76. *The Petroleum Monthly* 1, no. 8 (June 1871), 265–66.

77. Laura G. Sanford, *History of Erie County Pennsylvania* (n.p.: Published by the Author, 1894), 265.

78. Paul H. Giddens, *The Beginnings of the Petroleum Industry Sources and Bibliography* (Harrisburg, Pa.: Pennsylvania Historical Commission, 1941), 11.

79. Boyle, 947.

80. Pennsylvania Historical and Museum Commission, "Drake Well Memorial Park, Titusville, Pa., Birthplace of the Petroleum Industry," pamphlet, 1952.

81. Giddens, 82.

82. Ibid., 82.

83. Edwin C. Bell, "Early Oil Region Oil Towns," in Crum and Dugan, 75.

84. Clark, 10.

85. Paul H. Giddens, *The American Petroleum Industry— Its Beginnings in Pennsylvania!* (New York: The Newcomen Society in North America, 1959), 8.

86. Yergin, 27.

87. Ernest C. Miller, "A List of Unusual Books and Scarce Material Related to the Early History and Development of the Petroleum Industry," Catalogue One (London: n.d.), 11.

88. *The Petroleum Monthly* 1, no. 3 (January 1871), 109.

89. James B. Garner, "A Backward Look over the Early Days of the Oil Industry," reprinted from *National Petroleum News,* October 22, 1924.

90. Yergin, 29.

91. Independent Oil and Gas Association of West Virginia, http://www.iogawv.com/history.htm.

92. McKain and Allen, 13–14.

93. Ibid., 18.

94. William Culp Darrah, *Pithole: The Vanished City: A Story of the Early Days of the Petroleum Industry* (Published by the author, 1972), 7.

95. Ernest C. Miller, *Tintypes in Oil* (Rutland, Vt.: Charles E. Tuttle Company, 1961), 39–48.

96. Clark, 35.

97. Crum and Dugan, 60.

98. Darrah, 191.

99. Ibid., 190.

100. Ibid.

101. Ibid., 29.

102. Yergin, 28.

103. Ibid., 31.

104. Ernest C. Miller, *Oily Daze at Cherry Grove* (Warren, Pa.: The Newell Press, 1942), 3–4.

105. Yergin, 32–33.

106. George H. Ashley and J. French Robinson, *Oil and Gas Fields of Pennsylvania* 1, Introduction (Harrisburg, Pa.: Pennsylvania Geological Services, 1922), 45.

107. Stotz and Jamison, 71.

108. Hilt.

109. Babcock, 151.

110. Boyle, 72.

111. *Oil and Gas Journal,* June 16, 1927; and McLaurin, 372.

112. F. L. Kellogg, "Historical Sketch of the Well and Wooden Pipe Line (1863–1872)," *Honeoye Falls Times,* May 5, 1932.

113. "Great Gas Wells Blowing in Ohio," *Titusville Morning Herald,* January 17, 1871, in Giddens, 146.

114. *The Petroleum Monthly* 2, no. 8 (August 1872), 122.

115. Henry, 208–09.

116. McLaurin, 376.

117. Hale, 51.

118. Ralph W. and Muriel E. Hidy, *Pioneering in Big Business: History of Standard Oil Company New Jersey, 1882–1911* (New York: Harper and Brothers, 1955), 172; and Ashley and Robinson, 43.

119. Castaneda, 70.

120. Joseph W. Orr, "Coal Gas Used in Oil City as Natural Product Wasted," *Oil City Derrick,* February 23, 1932.

121. McLaurin, 374.

122. Ibid.

123. Boyle, 19.

124. Ibid., 208.

125. Empire Gas and Fuel Company. Ltd., *Empire Bradley 75th Anniversary* (n.p.: Empire Gas and Fuel Company. Ltd. & Bradley Producing Corporation, 1956), 5–9.

126. Ron Chernow, *Titan: The Life of John D. Rockefeller, Sr.* (New York: Random House, 1998), 260.

127. S. J. M. Eaton, *Petroleum— A History of the Oil Region of Venango County, Pennsylvania* (Philadelphia: J. Skelly, 1860), 140.

128. Herrick, 360–62.

129. Seidenberg et al., 549.

130. Hidy and Hidy, 172.

131. "Natural Gas, Wheeling's Gas Fuel, Where it is From, From How it Comes," *Wheeling Daily Intelligencer,* September 14, 1886, http://wheeling.weirton.lib.wv.us/history/bus/GAS01.HTM.

132. Boyle, 427.

133. The Liverpool Gas Company, *Centenary Number 100,* Co-Partners' Magazine 9, no. 3 (July 1948).

134. Clark, 33.

135. McLaurin, 377.

Two

1. Oscar E. Norman, The Romance of the Gas Industry (Chicago: A. C. McClurg, 1922), 11–14.

2. The Cleveland Heater Company, *Facts Bulletin,* no. 108 (n.p.), 1948).

3. Glynnis Chantrell, ed., *The Oxford Dictionary of Word Histories* (Oxford: Oxford University Press, 2002), 227.

4. Clark, 9.

5. Stotz and Jamison, 2.

6. Westcott, 96.

7. Norman, 24–28.

8. Ibid., 29.

9. Clark, 11.

10. Ibid., 12.

11. *Gas Age,* October 2, 1958, 51.

12. Westcott, 86.

13. Norman, 30.

14. Federal Energy Administration, *The Natural Gas Story* (Washington, D.C.: Federal Energy Administration, 1975), 3.

15. Clark, 16

16. Ibid., 11.

17. Ibid., 13.

18. Norman, 43.

19. *Baltimore Gas and Electric Company* (n.p.: Publication Press, 1958), 15.

20. Ibid.

21. Castaneda, 23.

22. Clark, 23.

23. Hale, 52.

24. Norman, 71.

25. Hidy and Hidy, 738.

26. UGI Corporation, *The First 100 Years: UGI Corporation* (n.p.: 1982), 15.

27. Nevins, Allan. *John D. Rockefeller: A Study in Power* (New York: Charles Scribner's Sons, 1953), 2:52.

28. Clark, 45.

29. William T. Brannt, *Petroleum: Its history, origin, occurrence, production, physical and chemical con-*

stitution, technology, examination and uses; together with the Occurrence and Uses of Natural Gas (Philadelphia: Henry Carey Baird, 1895), 668.

30. American Gas Association, *History of the Natural Gas Industry*, A.G.A. Employee Course, (n.p., n.d.), 4.

31. Stotz and Jamison, 20–32.

32. *American Gas Light Journal* as quoted in Norman, 46.

33. Clark, 23.

34. Heritage Research, "A Brief History of the Manufactured Gas Industry in the United States," http://heritageresearch.com/manufactured_gasB.htm; and Adelheid Full, comp., *Corporate History of Dominion Natural Gas Company, Ltd. and Underlying Companies, 1854–1955* (Buffalo, N.Y.: Dominion Natural Gas Company, Ltd., April 1956), 10.

35. E. C. Brown, comp., *Brown's Directory of American Gas Companies, Gas Statistics* (Philadelphia: Progressive Age Publishing, 1887).

36. Herbert Reynolds Spencer, *Erie ... A History* (n.p.: Published by the author: 1962), 7.

37. Yergin, 23.

38. Leland D. Baldwin, *Pittsburgh: The Story of a City 1750–1865* (Pittsburgh: University of Pittsburgh Press, 1937), 207.

39. Lee Barron, *Westinghouse Centennial 1886–1986, Baltimore Divisions & Contracts Management A History* (n.p.: Barron, 1985), 18.

40. James H. Reed, "Pittsburgh and the Natural Gas Industry," *Pittsburgh and the Pittsburgh Spirit*, Addresses at the Chamber of Commerce of Pittsburgh, 1927–1928, 132.

41. Relative Numbers of Former Manufactured Gas Plants in Major American Cities, http://www/hatheway.net/05_fmgp_us.htm.

42. E. C. Brown.

43. Seidenberg et al., 552.

44. *American Gas-Light Journal* 1, no. 1, July 1 1859, (New York: John B. Murray & Bankers, no. 40).

45. Hale, 47–8.

46. *History of Erie County*, 600.

47. "Erie Gas Company," in Dominion East Ohio Collection, box 60, file folder 6, Youngstown Historical Center of Industry and Labor, Youngstown, Ohio.

48. "Yesteryear in Titusville," *Titusville Herald*, October 16, 1937 from files October 16, 1867.

49. "Looking Backwards," *Oil City Blizzard*, October 14, 1935.

50. United Natural Gas Company, *Gas Bag*, August 1963, 1–2.

51. E. C. Brown.

52. William Ganson Rose, *Cleveland: The Making of a City* (Cleveland: World Publishing, 1950), 226.

53. Ibid., 175.

54. Ibid., 231.

55. Ibid., 219–220.

56. East Ohio Gas Company, *A History of the East Ohio Gas Company, 50 Years of Service 1898–1948* (n.p., 1948), 15.

57. Ibid., 10.

58. Clark, 21.

59. "History of the Gas Company in Ashtabula," in Dominion East Ohio Collection, box 159, file folder 23, Youngstown Historical Center of Industry and Labor, Youngstown, Ohio.

60. H. Perry Smith, ed., *History of the City of Buffalo and Erie County*, 2 (Syracuse, N.Y.: D. Mason, 1884), 528; and Index to Records of Streets, Public Grounds, Waterways, Railroads, Gas Companies, Water Works, Etc., of The City of Buffalo From 1814 to 1896 (Buffalo: Bureau of Engineering, 1896).

61. Iroquois Gas Corporation, *Iroquois Historical Perspective* (n.p., 1959).

62. *Buffalo Commercial Advertiser*, November 8, 1848.

63. Ibid., May 10, 1859.

64. Richmond Hill, "Athespian Temple," (Buffalo: Courier Company, 1893).

65. "Historical article," (n.p., n.d.).

66. Buffalo Gas Light Company, "Memoranda — Gas Light in Buffalo," Report form the Office of Buffalo Gas Light Co., August 20, 1874.

67. Ibid.

68. Castaneda, 55.

69. Iroquois Gas Corporation.

70. Stotz and Jamison, 9.

71. Jenny Marsh Parker, *Rochester, A Story Historical* (Rochester, N.Y.: Scrantom, Wetmore, 1884), 371–72.

72. New York State Electric and Gas, *Tie Lines Centennial Issue, 1852–1952* (n.p., 1952), 5.

73. Clarence O. Lewis, "Niagara County History: First Electric Illumination of Falls in 1879," *Niagara Falls Gazette*, August 2, 1967.

74. New York State Electric and Gas Corporation, *Celebrating a Century of Service* (n.p., 1952).

75. Thomas Holder, *A Complete Record of Niagara Falls and Vicinage* (1882), 128.

76. "Gas," *Niagara Falls Gazette*, May 8, 1860.

77. Hale, 55.

78. Francis E. Leupp, *George Westinghouse: His Life and Achievements* (London: John Murray, 1919), 121.

79. Clark, 44.

80. *Dunkirk Evening Observer*, July 20, 1901.

81. Castaneda, 26.

82. New York State Electric and Gas, *Tie Lines*, 6.

83. Ibid.

84. *Dunkirk Evening Observer*, July 30, 1904.

85. *Dunkirk Evening Observer*, August 9, 1904.

86. Iroquois Gas Corporation.

87. Castaneda, 196.

88. History and Chronology of Manufactured Gas, Former Manufactured Gas Plants, Site and Waste Characterization. Remedial Engineering of Former Manufactured Gas plants and Other Coal-Tar Sites, http://www.hatheway.net/01_history.htm.

89. Allen W. Hatheway, "Geoenvironmental protocol for site and waste characterization of former manufactured gas plants; worldwide remediation challenge in semi-volatile organic wastes," *Engineering Geology* 64 (2002), 317–338.

90. New York State Electric and Gas, *Tie Lines*, 6.

91. Robert Silverberg, *Light for the World: Edison and the Power Industry* (New York: D. Van Nostrand, 1967), 91.

92. Jill Jonnes, *Empires of Light: Edison, Tesla, Westinghouse, and the Race to Electrify the World* (New York: Random House, 2003), 58.

93. Castaneda, 60; and Silverberg, 106.

94. Castaneda, 62.

95. Chernow, 260–61.

96. Silverberg, 108.

97. McKain and Allen, 139.

98. Thoenen, 102.

99. McKain and Allen, 173.

100. Lewis.

101. Alfred Leif, *Metering for America: 125 Years of the Gas Industry and American Meter Company* (New York: Appleton-Century Crofts, 1961), 62.

102. Nevins, 2:286.

103. S. M. Parkhill, "By the Light of Gas, the Historical Perspective," *Compressed Air Magazine*, May 1960, 19; and Hale, 64.

104. Iroquois Gas Corporation, *Iroquois Gas News*, (November 1959), 2.

105. *Statistics of the Manufactured Gas Industry For the Year 1920* (New York: American Gas Association, 1921), in Dominion East Ohio Collection, box 60, file folder 10, Youngstown Historical Center of Industry and Labor, Youngstown, Ohio.

106. Baltimore Gas and Electric Company.

107. "Gasometer, A Fredonia Landmark, Collapsed by Snow," *Fredonia Censor*, January 9, 1964.

108. Heritage Research.

109. Iroquois Gas Corporation, *The Iroquois: A Magazine for Gas Users* (n.p., 1926), 1.

110. H. Nagel to Mr. Larry Waddell, American Gas Association, March 30, 1961; and Maxon, 8.

111. Rodgers, 205.

112. "History of the Gas Company in Ashtabula."

113. American Gas Association, "Natural Gas: Cinderella to Glamour Girl," news release, April 10, 1961.

114. Albert F. Dawson, *Columbia System: A History, Columbia Gas & Electric Corporation* (New York: J. J. Little and Ives, 1937), 138–39.

115. Paula Kepos, ed., "Cincinnati Gas & Electric Company," *International Directory of Company Histories* 6 (Detroit: St. James Press, 1992), 466.

116. Richard J. Gonzalez, "Interfuel Relations Governing Natural Gas Demand and Supply," in Keith C. Brown, ed., *Regulation of the Natural Gas Producing Industry*, papers presented at a seminar conducted by Resources for the Future, Inc. in Washington, DC, October 15–17, 1970, (Baltimore: The Johns Hopkins University Press, 1972), 58.

117. East Ohio Gas Company, 36; and Philadelphia Gas Works, http://www.pgworks.com/New%20Site/CI0016a.htm.

118. National Fuel Gas Company, *1974 Annual Report*, 3.

119. National Fuel Gas Company, *Pilot Light*, June 1974.

120. Hale, 52.

Three

1. Leupp, 111.

2. Hidy and Hidy, 172.

3. Castaneda, 44.

4. Stefan Lorant, *Pittsburgh: The Story of an American City* (Lenox, MA: R. R. Donnelley & Sons, 1975), 168.

5. *History of Allegheny County, Pennsylvania* (Chicago: A. Warner, 1889), 616.

6. Seidenberg, 548.

7. *History of Allegheny County*, 620.

8. McLaurin, 376.

9. Leupp, 129–130.

10. *History of Allegheny County*, 615.

11. *New York Times*, June 23, 1885, in Hax McCullough and Mary Brignano, *The Vision and Will to Succeed: A Centennial History of the Peoples Natural Gas Company* (Pittsburgh: Peoples Natural Gas, n.d.), 14–15.

12. Robert Dale Grinder, "From Insurgency to Efficiency: The Smoke Abatement Campaign in Pittsburgh Before World War I," *The Western Pennsylvania Historical Magazine* 61, no. 3 (July 1978), 188–89.

13. Ibid., 189.

14. Castaneda, 44.

15. Hale, 52.

16. *History of Butler County, Pa.* (R. C. Brown, 1895), 290.

17. *History of Allegheny County*, 615.

18. Lorant, 150.

19. *History of Allegheny County*, 304.

20. Darrah, 36.

21. Boyle, 648.

22. *Wheeling Daily Intelligencer*, http://wheeling.weirton.lib.wv.us/history/bus/gas02.htm.

23. McCullough and Brignano, 8.

24. United Natural Gas Company, *Gas Bag*, August 1958, 18.

25. McCullough and Brignano, 8.

26. Beers, Paul B. "Reporter at Large," *Harrisburg Evening News*, March 15, 1968.

27. Seidenberg, 550.

28. McCullough and Brignano, 9.

29. Ibid., 29–31.

30. Boyle, 877.

31. Ibid.

32. McCullough and Brignano, 9.

33. *Pittsburg at the Dawn of the 20th Century, The Busiest City in the World* (Allegheny, Pa.: Pittsburg Leader, Jos. T. Colvin, circa 1901).

34. Hale, 54.

35. Castaneda, 45.

36. McCullough and Brignano, 25.

37. Hale, 54.

38. Brannt, 661.

39. Parkhill, 19.

40. Crum and Dugan, 352.

41. Pennsylvania Legislature Session of 1885, no. 32, An Act to provide for the incorporation and regulation of natural gas companies, 33.

42. Crum and Dugan, 352.

43. McCullough and Brignano, 8–10.

44. Hale, 55.

45. Leupp, 115.

46. Castaneda, 49.

47. Yergin, 92.

48. Sylvester K. Stevens, *Pennsylvania: Titan of Industry, Vol. 3* (New York: Lewis Historical Publishing, 1948), 584.

49. Stotz and Jamison, 368.

50. McCullough and Brignano, 157.

51. Ibid., 105.

52. Jonnes, 121.

53. Paul D. Cravath, "George Westinghouse the Man," in *George Westinghouse Commemoration: A*

Forum Presenting the Career and Achievements of George Westinghouse on the 90th Anniversary of his Birth (New York: American Society of Mechanical Engineers, 1937), 54.

54. Leupp, 109.
55. Jonnes, 128.
56. Parkhill, 19.
57. Barron, 17.
58. P. Reginald Belfield, from Guido Pantaleoni, "The Real Character of the Man as I Saw Him," April 1939, 5, George Westinghouse: Anecdotes and Reminiscences, vol. 3, box 1, file folder 8, George Westinghouse Museum Archives, Wilmerding, Pennsylvania, in Jonnes, 129.
59. Leupp, 113.
60. Seidenberg, 550.
61. Leupp, 119.
62. Ibid., 120.
63. Ibid., 126.
64. Ibid., 128.
65. *History of Allegheny County*, 616.
66. Jonnes, 129.
67. Barron, 17.
68. Brannt, 663.
69. Lorant, 248.
70. Leupp, 126–27.
71. Thoenen, 109.
72. Hale, 56.
73. Thoenen, 104.
74. McKain and Allen, 156.
75. Crum and Dugan, 357.
76. Jonnes, 343.
77. *Pittsburg Leader*.
78. Crum and Dugan, 357.
79. Thoenen, 109.
80. Stevens, 247.
81. *Natural Gas: A Survey of One of America's Great Public Utilities* (New York: G. E. Barrett & Co. 1927), 53.
82. Thoenen, 109.
83. Seidenberg, 560.
84. Kepos, "Equitable Resources, Inc.," 493.
85. Seidenberg, 574.
86. Thoenen, 111.
87. John H. Newell, *The Origin and Founders of the Hope Natural Gas Company* (n.p., n.d.), 12 in Dominion East Ohio Collection, box 159, file folder 74, Youngstown Historical Center of Industry and Labor, Youngstown, Ohio.
88. Dawson, 77.
89. NiSource, Columbia Pennsylvania, http://www.columbiagaspamd.com/about_us/chronology.htm.
90. Dawson, 78.
91. Ibid., 78–79.
92. Newell, 24.
93. Thoenen, 101.
94. Thomas H. Hamilton, "The Crawford Brothers and The Birth of the Natural Gas Industry," (Master's thesis, Yale University, n.p., April 23, 1984), 14–15.
95. Ibid., 22.
96. Ibid., 17.
97. Newell, 53.
98. Crum and Dugan, 358.
99. Ibid., 59–60.
100. Castaneda, 75.

101. Dawson, 14–20.
102. Castaneda, 74.
103. NiSource, Columbia Pennsylvania.
104. Dawson, 90.
105. Adele Hart, ed., "Columbia Gas System," *International Directory of Company Histories* 5 (Detroit: St. James Press, 1992), 580.
106. Christopher J. Castaneda, *Regulated Enterprise: Natural Gas Pipelines and Northeastern Markets, 1938–1954* (Columbus, OH: Ohio State University Press, 1993), 33.
107. Christopher J. Castaneda and Clarance M. Smith, *Gas Pipelines and the Emergence of America's Regulatory State: A History of the Panhandle Eastern Corporation 1928–1993* (New York: Cambridge University Press, 1996), 51
108. Hart, 580.
109. Thoenen, 338.
110. NiSource, Columbia Pennsylvania.
111. Peter Krass, *Carnegie* (New York: John Wiley & Sons, 2002), 172–176.
112. Hale, 55.
113. McKain and Allen, 195.
114. E. L. White, "Natural Gas in Findlay," *American Magazine*, December 1887, 212.
115. "Value of Natural Gas, Its Use Clarifies the Atmosphere at Pittsburg," *New York Times*, October 17, 1885, in McCullough and Brignano, 15.
116. *Pittsburg Leader*.
117. Thoenen, 97.
118. Reed, 135.

Four

1. Yergin, 103.
2. As quoted in an interview, from John Bartlett and Justin Kaplan, eds., *Bartlett's Familiar Quotations*, 16th Edition (Boston: Little Brown, 1992), 539.
3. Yergin, 39.
4. Ibid., 51.
5. Stotz and Jamison, 76.
6. John D. Rockefeller, *Random Reminiscences of Men and Events* (New York: Doubleday, Doran & Company, Inc., 1933), 82.
7. Hidy and Hidy, 1.
8. Rockefeller, 66.
9. Yergin, 53.
10. East Ohio Gas Company, 2.
11. Nevins, 2:279.
12. John W. Leonard et al., eds., *Romance of American Petroleum and Gas 2* (New York: J. J. Little & Ives, n.d.), 250.
13. Rockefeller, 89.
14. Hidy and Hidy, 172.
15. Ibid.
16. Boyle, 926.
17. Hidy and Hidy, 173.
18. Newell, 10.
19. Hidy and Hidy, 172.
20. Mary Brignano and Hax McCullough, *Spirit and Progress: The Story of the East Ohio Gas Company and the People Who Made It* (n.p.: East Ohio Gas, 1988), 17.
21. Newell, 4.

22. Boyle, 920–27.
23. Hidy and Hidy, 77.
24. *History of Allegheny County*, 303.
25. Hidy and Hidy, 77.
26. Ibid., 172.
27. Ibid., from SONJ, morgued charters and corporate records; Consolidated Accounts of Standard Oil, 174.
28. Chernow, 262.
29. Nevins, 272.
30. Castaneda, *Invisible Fuel*, 71.
31. Hidy and Hidy, 175; and East Ohio Gas Company, 9.
32. Ibid., 175.
33. Chernow, 262.
34. United Natural Gas Company, *Gas Bag,* September 1960, 3.
35. Boyle, 920–27.
36. Newell, 48.
37. Hidy and Hidy, 393.
38. Crum and Dugan, 367.
39. Boyle, 945.
40. Ibid., 946.
41. Newell, 109.
42. Crum and Dugan, 304.
43. Boyle, 930–31.
44. McCullough and Brignano, 68.
45. Newell, 35.
46. Ibid., 37–38.
47. Hidy and Hidy, 385.
48. Nevins, 2:273.
49. Ibid., 2:283.
50. Chernow, 378.
51. Crum and Dugan, 235.
52. Nevins, 2:282.
53. Ibid., 2:27.
54. Ibid., 273.
55. Boyle, 917.
56. Nevins, 2:272.
57. Ibid., 273.
58. Crum and Dugan, 251.
59. Pennsylvania Historical and Museum Commission.
60. McLaurin, 273.
61. Crum and Dugan, 252.
62. Nevins, 2:283.
63. Albert Bigelow Paine, *Mark Twain* (New York: 1912) in Nevins, 2:283.
64. Chernow, 381.
65. Yergin, 103.
66. *Pure Oil Trust vs. Standard Oil Company; United States Industrial Commission, Compiled from private and official sources by the Oil City Derrick, 1899–1900* (Oil City, Pa.: Derrick Publishing, 1901), 260.
67. Tarbell, Ida M., *All in the Day's Work: An Autobiography* (New York: Macmillian, 1939), 212.
68. Tarbell, 212.
69. Ibid., 10.
70. Yergin, 104–105.
71. Tarbell, 228.
72. Yergin, 107.
73. Ibid., 106–107.
74. Nevins, 1:272.
75. Chernow, 553.
76. J. Richard Kelso, *The Spirit of Progress: The Story of the East Ohio Gas Company and the People Who Made It* (New York: The Newcomen Society of North America, 1988), 9.
77. Edward C. Gallick, *Competition in the Natural Gas Pipeline Industry, An Economic Policy Analysis* (Wesport, Conn.: Praeger, 1993), 13.
78. Hidy and Hidy, 384.
79. John H. Herbert, *Clean Cheap Heat: The Development of Residential Markets for Natural Gas in the United States* (New York: Praeger Publishers, 1992), 19.
80. Stotz and Jamison, 293–94.
81. UGI, 8; and Hidy and Hidy, 392.
82. W. H. Locke, "Remarks by President of National Fuel Gas Company before the New York Society of Security Analysts," May 23, 1956.
83. Hidy and Hidy, 392.
84. Ibid., 383–384.
85. Hidy and Hidy, 318.
86. H. Stuart Nichols, *The Natural Gas Story from the Ground Down: The History of National Fuel Gas Company* (New York: Newcomen Society, 1963), 18.
87. Boyle, 394–95.
88. G. H. W. Sherman, *Formation and Early History of United Natural Gas Company and Consolidated Companies* (n.p.: January 1946).
89. Ibid., 400.
90. Ibid., 417.
91. Ibid.
92. W. F. Gilliland, *The Formation and Early History of United Natural Gas Company and Consolidated Companies* (n.p.: 1954), 11–14.
93. G. H. W. Sherman, *Formation and Early History of Ridgway Natural Gas Company* (n.p., January 1946).
94. Idem, *Formation and Early History of St. Marys Natural Gas Company* (n.p.: January 1946).
95. W. F. Gilliland, *The Formation and Early History of United Natural Gas Company and Consolidated Companies* (n.p.: 1954), 23.
96. *The Petroleum Age* 1, no. 4 (March 1882), 123.
97. Pennsylvania Natural Gas Company Charter, Commonwealth of Pennsylvania, January 14, 1886.
98. J. E. Henretta, "Kane & The Upper Allegheny" in *Jamestown Dispatch*, October 28, 1885, from "*Kane Leader,*" November 19, 1885.
99. Boyle.
100. An Ordinance to Authorize the Pennsylvania Gas Company to lay and maintain pipes in the streets, avenues and alleys in the City of Erie, for certain Purposes and under certain conditions herein stated, Erie, Pa., March 16, 1886.
101. "Diamond Anniversary for Pennsylvania Gas Company," *Erie Story*, November 1961.
102. Sherman, G. H. W., *Formation and Early History of Smethport Natural Gas Company* (n.p.: January 1946).
103. Idem, *Formation and Early History of Mercer County Gas Company* (n.p.: January, 1946).
104. Comet, J. A., *The Mars Company: Incorporation and History* (n.p.: May 14, 1963).
105. East Ohio Gas Company, 3.
106. CNG Transmission Corporation, Hope Gas Inc., *From Gas Lights to New Energy Heights, 1898–1998, 100 Years of Service Excellence* (Clarksburg, W.Va.: 1998), 4.

107. Newell, 11.
108. CNG Transmission Corporation, 5.
109. Newell, 10–11.
110. Ibid., 97.
111. CNG Transmission Corporation, 6.
112. Thoenen, 113.
113. CNG Transmission Corporation, 8; and Thoenen, 114.
114. Thoenen, 265.
115. CNG Transmission Corporation, 12.
116. Thoenen, 115.
117. CNG Transmission Corporation, 12.
118. Hope Natural Gas Company, 7.
119. Ibid., 8.
120. CNG Transmission Corporation, 12.
121. East Ohio Gas Company, 3.
122. Ibid., 16–17.
123. Brignano and McCullough, 18.
124. *Pennsylvania Oil Company* Minute Book, # 1, 1 and *History of United Natural Gas Company* (n.p., 1954).
125. East Ohio Gas Company, 13.
126. Ibid.
127. Ibid., 25.
128. Rose, 634.
129. Brignano and McCullough, 21.
130. "An address by M. B. Daly, President. East Ohio Gas Company," delivered before the City Club of Cleveland, December 8, 1920, 21 in Dominion East Ohio Collection, box 1, file folder 15, Youngstown Historical Center of Industry and Labor, Youngstown, Ohio.
131. Ibid., 3.
132. Ibid., 20.
133. Ibid.
134. Crum and Dugan, 42–45.
135. East Ohio Gas Company, 17.
136. The East Ohio Gas Company Corporate History Chart to June 1978, Dominion East Ohio Collection, box 159, file folder 20, Youngstown Historical Center of Industry and Labor, Youngstown, Ohio.
137. East Ohio Gas Company, 9.
138. Dominion, http://www.dom.com/about/companies/eohio/index.jsp.
139. McKain and Allen, 153.
140. Thoenen, 109.
141. Ibid., 101–02.
142. Newell, 157.
143. Ibid.
144. Thoenen, 115–117.
145. Ibid., 266–67.
146. Ibid., 348–49.
147. Ibid., 338.
148. Hill, 1268.
149. Heiney, 15.
150. "Historical Development of Natural Gas in Ohio," (n.p., n.d.) in Dominion East Ohio Collection, box 159, file folder 24, Youngstown Historical Center of Industry and Labor, Youngstown, Ohio.
151. "History of the Gas Company in Ashtabula."
152. C. A. Ward, "A Brief History of the Ohio Cities Gas Company," in Leonard et al., 265.
153. "Natural Gas The Modern Fuel," *Appalachian Gas Corporation* (n.p.: P. W. Chapman, 1930), 24.
154. Kepos, "Cincinnati Gas and Electric Company," 465.

155. Ibid., 466.
156. Hartzel and Nagel.
157. *Dunkirk Evening Observer*, September 3, 1903.
158. Leonard et al., 349.
159. Castaneda, *Invisible Fuel*, 77.
160. Lauriston, 19.
161. Stotz and Jamison, 353.
162. *Batavia Daily News*, December 17, 1891.
163. Consolidated Natural Gas Corporation, *1944 Annual Report*, 6.
164. Boyle, 417.
165. "Gas Merger of Iroquois, Republic Okd," *Buffalo Courier-Express*, November 16, 1956.
166. *Wellsville Daily Reporter*, April 14, 1882.
167. Empire-Bradley, 9.
168. Herrick, 342.
169. Ibid., 344–45.
170. Ibid., 354–56.
171. Corning Natural Gas, http://www.corning-gas.com/compprof.asp.
172. Ibid., 119.
173. Kepos, "Rochester Gas and Electric Corporation," 572.
174. Hart, "Niagara Mohawk Power Corporation," 665.
175. "1816–1966, Gas 150th Anniversary," *Gas*, January 1966, 10–11.
176. New York State Electric and Gas, *Tie Lines*, 10.
177. Kepos, "New York State Electric and Gas," 534.
178. Ida M. Tarbell, *The History of the Standard Oil Company*, briefer version edited by David M. Chalmers (New York: W. W. Norton, 1966), 212.
179. Castaneda, *Invisible Fuel*, 75.
180. McCullough and Brignano, 34.
181. Hidy and Hidy, 766.
182. Chernow, 260.
183. Sanders, 32.
184. Robert L. Bradley, Jr., *Oil, Gas & Government, The U.S. Experience* 1 (Latham, MD: Rowman & Littlefield Publishers, 1996), 61.
185. Herbert, 19.
186. *Dunkirk Evening Observer*, August 9, 1910.
187. C. R. Wattson, "Looking Backward," *Oil and Gas Man's Magazine* 12, no. 1 (Winter 1917), 21.
188. Nevins, 323.
189. Crum and Dugan, 367.
190. Stotz and Jamison, 362.
191. Sanders, 26.
192. Samuel S. Wyer, "Is It Feasible to make Common Carriers of Natural Gas Transmission Lines," reprinted from Bulletin No. 89, May 1914, (New York American Institute for Mining Engineers, 1914), 5–6.
193. Bradley, 860.
194. Ibid., 860–61.
195. Ibid., 861.
196. Sanders, 25.
197. Ibid., 28 from *Minerals Yearbook*.
198. Clark, 142.
199. Castaneda, *Invisible Fuel*, 107.
200. Sanders, 19.
201. Ibid., 26.
202. Castaneda, *Invisible Fuel*, 102.
203. Idem., *Regulated Enterprise*, 25.

204. Sanders, 33–34.

205. Federal Trade Commission, Summary Report of the Federal Trade Commission to the Senate of the United States, Doc. 92 (70th Congress, 1935) (the "FTC Report"), Vol. 72-A, 38–46 in Meyers, Kenneth R., (2003) "PUHCA Companies: Caught by Superfund," *Public Utilities Fortnightly*, April 15, 2003, 32.

206. Castaneda, *Invisible Fuel*, 91.

207. Ibid., 109–110.

208. Gallick, 13.

209. National Fuel Gas Company, Data Respecting Ownership of Capital Stock of National Fuel Gas Company, internal document, (n.p.: 1939).

210. National Fuel Gas Company, *1943 Annual Report.*

211. CNG Transmission Corporation, 17–18.

212. Gallick, 14.

213. Herbert, 2.

214. Castaneda, *Regulated Enterprise*, 29.

215. Gallick, 14.

216. Bradley, 368–69.

217. J. French Robinson, President East Ohio Gas Company, "The Natural Gas Act ... Must it become a blueprint for Chaos?" (circa 1940s) in Dominion East Ohio Collection, box 1 folder 10, Youngstown Historical Center of Industry and Labor, Youngstown, Ohio.

218. Sanders, 79–81.

219. Ibid., 53.

220. E. C. Brown.

Five

1. Mabel K. Clark, Titusville: An Illustrated History (Titusville: Titusville Area School District, 1993), 65–67.

2. George W. Brown, *Old Times in Oildom* (Oil City: Derrick Publishing, 1909), 36.

3. Paul H. Giddens, comp. and ed., *Pennsylvania Petroleum: 1750–1872, A Documentary History* (Titusville, Pa.: Commonwealth of Pa., Drake Well Memorial Park, 1947), 213.

4. Henry, in Boyle, 21.

5. Sanford, 265.

6. Boyle, 467

7. Ibid., 470.

8. W. R. Wagner and W. S. Lytle, *Geology of Pennsylvania's Oil and Gas* (Harrisburg, Pa.: Commonwealth of Pennsylvania Bureau of Topographic and Geologic Survey, 1968), 4–18.

9. Charles A. Washburner, "Geology of Natural Gas," *The Petroleum Age* 4, no. 12 (Bradford, Pa.: 1886), 1197.

10. Henry, 216.

11. Ruth Sheldon Knowles, *The Greatest Gamblers: The Epic of American Oil Exploration* (New York: McGraw-Hill Book Company, 1959), 143.

12. "Father Baker's 'Miracle' Gas Well in Use for 78 Years," *Buffalo Courier Express*, August 21, 1969, 1.

13. John B. Roen and Brian J. Walker, eds., *The Atlas of Major Appalachian Gas Plays* (n.p., The Appalachian Oil and Natural Gas Research Consortium, 1996), 1.

14. Owen, 631.

15. Maynard M. Stephens and Oscar F. Spencer, *Petroleum and Natural Gas Production* (University Park, Pa.: Pennsylvania State University, 1957), 133.

16. Hope Natural Gas Company, 11.

17. Sisler et al., 24–29.

18. Douglas G. Patchen, "Introduction to the Atlas of Major Appalachian Gas Plays," in Roen and Walker, 2.

19. National Fuel Gas Company, *Energizer*, Fall 1980, 14.

20. Giddens, 10.

21. Landes, 13.

22. Ibid., 18.

23. Sanford, 368.

24. George W. Brown, 37–38.

25. C. L. Suhr to Luke J. Scheer, Panhandle Eastern Pipe Line Company, Detroit, Michigan, October 9, 1962; and McLaurin, 375.

26. Henry, 209–10.

27. "Largest Gas Well in the Oil Regions," *The Petroleum Monthly* 2, no. 3 (March 1872), 74.

28. *History of Butler County, Pa.*, 296.

29. Ibid., 297–98.

30. Wattson, 8–9.

31. A. I. Ingham et al., *Oil and Gas Geology of the Sheffield Quadrangle, Pennsylvania* (Harrisburg, Pa.: Pennsylvania Geological Survey, 4th Series, Bulletin M 38, 1956), 4; and United Natural Gas Company, *Gas Bag*, June 1958, 10.

32. Pennsylvania Geological Survey of 1877 as quoted in "Pioneer Wells of the Gas Industry in the Appalachian Area," United Natural Gas Company, *Gas Bag*, June 1958, 10.

33. Ingham et al., 4.

34. United Natural Gas Company, *Gas Bag*, July 1958, 9.

35. Ibid., *Gas Bag*, September 1958, 8.

36. C. L. Suhr to Luke J. Scheer, Panhandle Eastern Pipe Line company, Detroit, Michigan, October 9, 1962.

37. William G. McGlade, *Oil and Gas Geology of the Amity and Claysville Quadrangle of Pennsylvania* (Harrisburg, Pa.: Pennsylvania Geological Survey, 4th Series, 1967).

38. Thomas E. Tomastik, "Lower Mississippian-Upper Devonian Berea and Equivalent Sandstones," in Roen and Walker, 56.

39. McLaurin, 374.

40. "Pioneer Wells of the Gas Industry in the Appalachian Area," *Gas Bag*, October 1958, 9–10.

41. McLaurin, 375.

42. Babcock, 579.

43. Boyle, 394.

44. *Oil & Gas Journal*, August 27, 1934.

45. Babcock, 579–80.

46. Ray Boswell, Bradley W. Thomas, R. Brandon Hussing, Timothy M. Murin, and Alan Donelson, "Upper Devonian Bradford Sandstones and Siltstones," in Roen and Walker, 70.

47. Newell, 32–33.

48. Ray Boswell, L. Robert Heim, Gregory R. Wrightstone, and Alan Donaldson, "Upper Devonian Venango Sandstones and Siltstones," in Roen and Walker, 66.

49. Hale, 55.

50. Chas. R. Fettke, *Summarized Record of Deep*

Wells in Pennsylvania, Topographic and Geologic Survey, Bulletin M 31 (Harrisburg, Pa.: Commonwealth of Pennsylvania, Department of Internal Affairs, 1950), 13.

51. McCullough and Brignano, 16.

52. Ibid., 56.

53. Boyle, 421.

54. Reed, 129.

55. McCullough and Brignano, 19.

56. Boyle, 845–56.

57. Ibid., 675.

58. Paul N. Spellman, *Spindletop Boom Days* (College Station, Tx.: Texas A&M University Press, 2001), 13.

59. McCullough and Brignano, 17.

60. Hale, 48.

61. Ashley and Robinson, 45.

62. Stotz and Jamison, 88.

63. Recollection from Mr. Charles Buhl, on July 16, 1954, oil field worker all life and driller for 30 years from Kane.

64. *Warren Evening Mirror*, September 25, 1906.

65. *Kane Republican*, September 24, 1906.

66. *Warren Evening Mirror*, Thursday, October 25, 1906.

67. Ibid., October 1, 1906.

68. Fettke, 13.

69. Kathy J. Flaherty, "Fractured Middle Devonian Huntersville Chert and Lower Devonian Oriskany Sandstone," in Roen and Walker, 103.

70. McCullough and Brignano, 69.

71. Ashley and Robinson, 44; and Fettke, 13.

72. Sisler et al., 67.

73. Commonwealth of Pennsylvania, *Pennsylvania's Mineral Heritage: The Commonwealth at the Economic Crossroads of Her Industrial Development*, Topographic and Geologic Survey (Harrisburg, Pa.: Department of Internal Affairs Bureau of Statistics, 1944), 32.

74. Dawson, 11.

75. Daly, 7.

76. Boswell et al., in Roen and Walker, 71.

77. Reed, 132.

78. Department of the Interior, *Conference on Natural Gas Conservation*, 11.

79. Ibid., 10.

80. Owen, 630.

81. Sisler et al., 67.

82. Fettke, 12.

83. Owen, 627.

84. Fettke, 13.

85. Ibid.

86. United Natural Gas Company, "Pioneer Wells of the Gas Industry in the Appalachian Area," *Gas Bag*, January 1959, 14.

87. Herrick, 374.

88. John E. Ebright, Chas. R. Fettke and Albert I. Ingham, *East Fork-Wharton Gas Field, Potter County Pennsylvania*, Topographic and Geologic Survey, Bulletin M 30 (Harrisburg: Commonwealth of Pennsylvania, Department of Internal Affairs, 1949), 4.

89. John A. Harper, "Lower Devonian Oriskany Sandstone Structural Play," in Roen and Walker, 113.

90. Flaherty, 103.

91. John R. Ebright and Albert I. Ingham, *Geology of the Leidy Gas Field and Adjacent Areas, Clinton County Pa.*, Topographic and Geologic Survey, Bulletin M 34 (Harrisburg: Commonwealth of Pennsylvania, Department of Internal Affairs, 1951), 2.

92. United Natural Gas Company, "Pioneer Wells of the Gas Industry in the Appalachian Area," *Gas Bag*, January 1959, 11.

93. Ebright and Ingham, 1.

94. John F. Skinner, *A History of New York State Natural Gas Corporation, 1913–1965* (Clarksburg, W.Va.: CNG Transmission Corporation, 1990), 11.

95. Ibid.

96. United Natural Gas Company, "Pioneer Wells of the Gas Industry in the Appalachian Area," *Gas Bag*, January 1959, 13.

97. Harper, 113–14.

98. United Natural Gas Company, "Pioneer Wells of the Gas Industry in the Appalachian Area," *Gas Bag*, February 1959, 13–14.

99. "Wells at Medix Extend Field," *Bennett's Valley News*, November 19, 1953.

100. Fettke, 15.

101. McCullough and Brignano, 104.

102. Fettke, 16.

103. Lytle, 4.

104. Herrick, 432–33.

105. United Natural Gas Company, "Pioneer Wells of the Gas Industry in the Appalachian Area," *Gas Bag*, December 1959, 7.

106. Douglas G. Patchen, "The Lower Devonian Oriskany Sandstone Combination Traps Play," in Roen and Walker, 121.

107. Governor's Energy Council, *The Pennsylvania Energy Profile, 1960–1979* (Harrisburg, Pa.: Commonwealth of Pennsylvania, 1982), 2.

108. Owen, 623.

109. Herrick, 322.

110. Robert C. Milici, "Upper Devonian Fractured Black and Gray Shales and Siltstones," in Roen and Walker, 86.

111. Kenneth K. Landes, *Petroleum Geology of the United States* (New York: Wiley-Interscience, 1970), 8.

112. Michael P. McCormac, George O. Mychkovsky, Steven T. Opritza, Ronald A. Riley, Mark E. Wolfe, Glenn E. Larsen, and Mark Baranoski, "Lower Silurian Cataract/Medina Group ('Clinton') Sandstone Play" in Roen and Walker, 156.

113. Ibid., 159.

114. James Hall, *The Structural and Economic Geology of Erie County, N.Y.* (n.p., n.d.), 346–347.

115. Herrick, 35–36.

116. Hale, 52.

117. Hall, 346–47.

118. National Fuel Gas Company, *Convenience ... Comfort ... Economy* (New York: William E. Rudge's Sons, 1955), 4.

119. Hall, 346–47.

120. Lauriston, 16.

121. Hall, 346–47.

122. Ibid.

123. Herrick, 340.

124. *Batavia Daily News*, September 9, 1897.

125. Herrick, 328.

126. Ibid, 329.

127. "Do You Remember," *Dunkirk Evening Observer*, March 25, 1965.

128. Nagel, H., "How Gas Service Came to the Village of East Aurora and the Town of Aurora," Iroquois Gas Corporation, March 1968.

129. Herrick, 329–30.

130. Skinner, 2.

131. Herrick, 332–33.

132. Fettke, 2.

133. Herrick, 336.

134. Ibid., 432–33.

135. Douglas G. Patchen, "The Lower Devonian Oriskany Sandstone Combination Traps Play," in Roen and Walker, 121–22.

136. Arthur M. Van Tyne, "Middle Devonian Ononadaga Limestone Reef Play," in Roen and Walker, 100.

137. Eugene H. Roseboom and Francis P. Weisenburger, *A History of Ohio* (Columbus: The Ohio State Archaeological and Historical Society, 1954), 122.

138. "Historical Development of Natural Gas in Ohio."

139. Clark, 55.

140. E. L. White, "Natural Gas in Findlay," *The American Magazine*, December 1887, 199.

141. Ibid., 212.

142. Owen, 125.

143. J. W. Heiney, *The Story of Indiana Gas Company, Inc.* (New York: Newcomen Society in North America, 1972), 10.

144. Ibid., 11.

145. Heiney, 11.

146. Crum and Dugan, 42.

147. Bill D. Berger and Kenneth E. Anderson, *Modern Petroleum: A Basic Primer of the Industry* (Tulsa: PennWell Books, 1981), 117.

148. Boyle, 414.

149. Ohio Oil and Gas Association, http://www.ooga.org/about/aboutindustry/background.htm.

150. Owen, 632.

151. Boyle, 452.

152. Ibid., 463.

153. McCormac et al., 159.

154. "Historical Development of Natural Gas in Ohio."

155. Boyle, 578.

156. Blakely M. Murphy, *Conservation of Oil and Gas: A Legal History, 1948* (Chicago: American Bar Association, 1949), 360.

157. E. G. Lindstrom, "Discovery of Gas—Story of Lakewood," *Cleveland Leader*, July 14, 1885, http://www.lkwdpl.org/history/naturalgas.html.

158. "Great Gas Rush of '13 Benefits Some Today," *Lakewood Sun Post*, April 24, 1975, http://www.lkwdpl.org/history/naturalgas.html.

159. "Romance of Getting the Gas," *East Ohio News*, January 1947, 4–5.

160. "East Ohio Gas Company Summary of Wells by Years," (n.p., n.d.), in Dominion East Ohio Collection, Youngstown Historical Center of Industry and Labor, Youngstown, Ohio.

161. Owen, 627.

162. Steven T. Opritza, "Lower Devonian Oriskany Sandstone Updip Permeability Pinchout," in Roen and Walker, 126–28.

163. McCormac et al., 159–61.

164. Ohio Oil and Gas Association.

165. Williamson et al., 37.

166. Howard B. Lee, *Burning Springs and Other Tales of the Little Kanawha* (Morgantown, W.Va.: West Virginia University, 1968), 14.

167. McKain and Allen, 40; and Independent Oil and Gas Association of West Virginia, "History of Natural Gas," http://www.iogawv.com/history.htm.

168. McKain and Allen, 49.

169. Ibid., 8.

170. Thoenen, 95.

171. McKain and Allen, 79.

172. Ibid.

173. Ibid., 81.

174. Landes, 24.

175. Ana G. Vargo and David L. Matchen, "Lower Mississippian Big Injun Sandstones," in Roen and Walker, 41.

176. Ibid., 46.

177. McKain and Allen, 141–142.

178. B. Hill, comp., "Natural Gas in the States of West Virginia, Pennsylvania, New York, Kentucky, Tennessee, Alabama, and Ohio," *Oil and Gas Man's Magazine* 8, no. 1 (December 1913), 1264.

179. Hope Natural Gas Company, 9.

180. Boyle, 848–849.

181. Ibid., 850.

182. Ibid.

183. Ashley and Robinson, 12.

184. McKain and Allen, 144.

185. Williamson et al., 41.

186. McKain and Allen, 147.

187. Boyle., 510

188. Ibid.

189. *Gas Age*, October 2, 1958, 58.

190. Wattson, 10.

191. McKain and Allen, 153–55.

192. Ibid., 156.

193. Williamson et al., 43.

194. McKain and Allen, 194.

195. *Dunkirk Evening Observer*, June 6, 1902.

196. Daly, 4.

197. Brignano and McCullough, 42.

198. Thoenen, 106.

199. Ibid., 107.

200. McKain and Allen, 173.

201. Hope Natural Gas Company, 13.

202. Daly, 5.

203. Alan Donaldson, Ray Boswell, Xiangdong Zou, Larry Cavallo, L. Robert Heim, and Michael Canich, "Upper Devonian Elk Sandstones and Siltstones," in Roen and Walker, 77.

204. Thoenen, 263.

205. Bradley, 859.

206. Herbert, 18.

207. Williamson et al., 41.

208. History of WV Mineral Industries—Oil and Gas, WVGES Geology, History of West Virginia Oil/Gas Industry, http://www.wvgs.wvnet.edu/www/geology/geoldvog.htm.

209. Consolidated Gas Transmission, 10.

210. Ashley and Robinson, 44.

211. Owen, 627.

212. Landes, 23.

213. Clark, 208.

214. Hope Natural Gas Company, 13.

215. Landes, 27.

216. Lee, 84–84.

217. Katharine Lee Avary, "Lower Silurian Tuscarora Sandstone Fractured Anticlinal Play," in Roen and Walker, 151.

218. Clark, 173.

219. Ibid., 228.

220. Landes, 36.

221. "Gas Wells of Pennsylvania, Ohio and New York," *The Petroleum Monthly* 2, no. 10 (October 1872), 273.

222. Harrison and Klotter, 311.

223. Boyle, 367.

224. McFarlin, 286.

225. Ibid., 288–297.

226. Willard Rouse Jillson, SC.D., *Natural Gas in Eastern Kentucky* (Louisville, Ky.: Standard Printing, 1937) 19–23.

227. Ibid., 88–89.

228. Ray Boswell, "Upper Devonian Black Shales," in Roen and Walker, 98.

229. Jillson, 166.

230. Williamson et al., 93.

231. Ibid., 96.

232. Hill, 1269.

233. McFarlin, 294.

234. M. J. Munn, *The Menifee Gas Field and the Ragland Oil Field, Kentucky* (Washington, D.C.: Government Printing Office, Bulletin 531A Department of the Interior United States Geological Survey, 1913).

235. Ibid., 3.

236. Jillson, 42–45, 64–66, 73–75, 149.

237. Ibid., 51, 55, 105, 133.

238. Richard Smosna, "Upper Mississippian Greenbrier/Newman Limestones," in Roen and Walker, 37.

239. *Kentucky, A Guide to the Bluegrass State*, compiled and written by the Federal Writers Project of the Work Projects Administration for the State of Kentucky (New York: Hastings House, 1954), 65.

240. Landes, 38.

241. Murphy, 523.

242. Newell, 62.

243. Clark, 76.

244. I. C. White, "The Rapid Exhaustion of West Virginia's Natural Gas Supply and the Best Plan for Conserving the Remainder," (n.p.: circa 1920) in Dominion East Ohio Collection, box 59, file folder 25, Youngstown Historical Center of Industry and Labor, Youngstown, Ohio.

245. Thoenen, 269.

246. Ibid., 98.

247. White.

248. Thoenen, 270.

249. Ibid., 268.

250. Ibid., 273.

251. Ibid., 282.

252. Murphy, 528.

253. Bradley 2, Appendix C: 1934–35 Chronology of State Wellhead Regulation, 1934–35.

254. *Supply and Conservation of Natural Gas in the State of Pennsylvania: Proceedings before the Public Service Commission of the Commonwealth of Pennsylvania at Pittsburgh, Pa., January 8, 1919* (Harrisburg: J. L. L. Kuhn, 1919), 14.

255. Ibid., 16.

256. Department of the Interior, *Conference on Natural Gas Conservation at the Interior Department*, Auditorium, Washington, January 15, 1920, 20–22 in Dominion East Ohio Collection, box 105, folder 2, Youngstown Historical Center of Industry and Labor, Youngstown, Ohio.

257. Department of the Interior, *Conference on Natural Gas Conservation*, 2.

258. Ibid., 4.

259. Lyon F. Terry, "The Future Life of The Natural Gas Industry," Lehman Brothers, presented before the International Oil and Gas Educational Center, March 2, 1962, 7.

260. McCullough and Brignano, 17.

261. Terry, 7.

262. Clark, 95.

263. Skinner, 21.

264. Castaneda, *Invisible Fuel*, 121.

265. Owen, 634.

266. CNG Transmission Corporation, 23; and Hope Natural Gas Company, 13.

267. G. J. Tankersley, President. East Ohio Gas Company, address before 52nd annual A.G.A. convention, New Orleans, La., October 14, 1970, 4 in Dominion East Ohio Collection, box 17, folder 1, Youngstown Historical Center of Industry and Labor, Youngstown, Ohio.

268. Henry, 249.

269. Darrah, 8.

270. Columbus Group of Columbia Gas and Electric Corporation, *An Employee Manual on the Natural Gas Business* (Cincinnati: Natural Gas Publishing Company, 1933), 13.

271. History of WV Mineral Industries—Oil and Gas, WVGES Geology, History of West Virginia Oil/Gas Industry. Adapted from an article by Jane R. Eggleston, updated Sept. 1996—page created and maintained by West Virginia Geological and Economic Survey, http://www.wvgs.wvnet.edu/www/geology/geoldvog.htm.

272. Williamson and Daum, 17.

273. Columbus Group of Columbia Gas and Electric Corporation, *A Course of Practical Information on the Natural Gas Business, Part 1* (Cincinnati: Natural Gas Publishing Company, 1933), 13–14.

274. Ron Baker, *A Primer of Oilwell Drilling* 6th Edition (Austin, Tx.: Petroleum Extension Service, The University of Texas at Austin Continuing & Extended Education, 2001), 13.

275. Owen, 630.

276. Charles W. Poth, *The Occurrence of Brine in Western Pennsylvania*, Topographic and Geologic Survey, Bulletin M 47 (Harrisburg, Pa.: Commonwealth of Pennsylvania Department of Internal Affairs, 1962), 1.

277. Ibid., 38.

278. McLaurin, 377.

279. Ernest C. Miller, *Pennsylvania's Oil Industry* (Gettysburg, Pa.: Pennsylvania Historical Association, 1959), 29.

280. Clark, 20.

281. Garner.

282. *History of Venango County Pennsylvania 1, Its Past and Present* (Chicago: Brown, Runk, 1890), 330.

283. McKain and Allen, 157.

284. *Batavia Daily News*, July 28, 1908.

285. U.S. Department of the Interior, Bureau of Mines, *Minerals Yearbook* 1972 1 Metals, Minerals,

and Fuels (Washington, D.C.: U.S. Government Printing Office, 1974), 822.

286. Stephens and Spencer, 275–76.
287. Skinner, 17.
288. Clark, 1, 19.
289. Ruth Sheldon Knowles, *The First Pictorial History of the American Oil and Gas Industry, 1859–1983* (Athens, Oh.: Ohio University Press, 1983), 21.
290. Spellman, 28.
291. Knowles, 20.
292. Ibid., 23.
293. Ibid., 28.
294. Clark, 189.
295. United Natural Gas, "Property Inspection," (n.p.), 1953.
296. Stephens and Spencer, 277.
297. McLaurin, 376.
298. Hope Natural Gas Company, 12.
299. Landes, 18.
300. Ohio Oil and Gas Association.
301. Nichols, 13.
302. United Natural Gas Company, *Gas Bag*, May 1961, 7–12.
303. Ibid.
304. Hidy and Hidy, 392.
305. George A. Burrell and Frank M. Siebert, "The Condensation of Gasoline From Natural Gas," *Oil and Gas Man's Magazine* 8, no. 9 (October 1913), 1111.
306. Ohio Propane Association, http://www.ohio-gasblueflame.com/propane/propane5.html.
307. Blue Flame and Ohio Gas, http://www.ohio-gasblueflame.com/propane/propane5.html.
308. "State Scientist Had Big Role In Helping Found Gas Industry," *Grit*, September 9, 1962.
309. Ohio Propane Association.
310. Newell, 25–27.
311. Herbert, 91.
312. Murphy, 677.
313. Columbus Group of Columbia Gas and Electric Corporation, *An Employee Manual on the Natural Gas Business*, 30.
314. Ibid., 29.
315. Zwetsch, 6.
316. George A. Burrell, Frank M. Siebert, and G. G. Oberfell, *The Condensation of Gasoline from Natural Gas* (Washington: Department of the Interior, Bureau of Mines, 1915).
317. Crum and Dugan, 219.
318. Thoenen, 239.
319. Mark J. Anton, *Suburban Propane Gas Association: The Development of a Selectively Positioned Energy Company* (New York: The Newcomen Society in North America, 1982), 7.
320. Herbert, 28.
321. Ibid., 57.
322. Harold F. Williamson et al., *The American Petroleum Industry, the Age of Energy 1899–1959* (Evanston, Ill.: Northwestern University Press, 1963), 134–35.
323. Thoenen, 249.
324. J.B. Gambrell, Jr. "Court Decision Expect to Stimulate Use of Absorption Process," (Tulsa: July 11) in Dominion East Ohio Collection, box 61, file folder 27, Youngstown Historical Center of Industry and Labor, Youngstown.

325. Newell, 25.
326. McKain and Allen, 194.
327. Hope Natural Gas Company, 4.
328. Charles F. Conaway, *The Petroleum Industry: A Nontechnical Guide* (Tulsa: PennWell Publishing, 1999), 224.
329. Babcock, 151.
330. Clark, 109, 132.
331. Harold W. Springborn, *The Natural Gas Industry* (n.p.: The American Geographical Society, 1966), 10.
332. Lief, 102.
333. Dawson, 90.
334. Herrick, 365–69.
335. H. D. Zwetsch, *A Brief History of the Natural Gas Industry* (New York: Zwetch, Heinzelmann, 1927), 7.
336. D. E. Conaway, "National Fuel Gas Company," (n.p., n.d.).
337. National Fuel Gas Company, *1947 Annual Report*, 13.
338. Thoenen, 251.
339. Ibid., 337–38.
340. Clark, 196.
341. John W. Frey and H. Chandler Ide, *A History of the Petroleum Administration for War, 1941–1945* (Washington, D.C.: United States Government Printing Office, 1946), 230.
342. Ibid., 227.
343. Knowles, 85.
344. Murphy, 677.
345. Frey and Ide, 228–29.
346. National Fuel Gas Company, *1940 Annual Report*.

Six

1. Boyle, 1027.
2. Giddens, 24.
3. Rockefeller, 85.
4. Ibid., 110.
5. Castaneda, *Invisible Fuel*, 44.
6. Nichols.
7. Ibid.
8. "Gas Wells of Pennsylvania, Ohio and New York," *The Petroleum Monthly* 2, no. 10 (October 1872), 273.
9. Herrick, 323–25.
10. Kellogg, 90–95.
11. From "Scrapbook of Amo Kreiger," (Honeoye Falls, N.Y., n.d.).
12. Herrick, 373.
13. Kellogg, 90–95.
14. Ibid.
15. Ibid.
16. Zwetsch, 6.
17. *Rochester Union and Advertiser*, October 11, 1871.
18. Herrick, 370.
19. Kellogg, 90–95.
20. "Gas Wells of Pennsylvania, Ohio and New York," *The Petroleum Monthly* 2, no. 10 (October 1872), 276.
21. "A Broken Banker: The Bloomfield Gas Well

Consumes $50,000 from Elmira," *Rochester Union and Advertiser*, May 14, 1878.

22. Herrick, 373.
23. Ibid.
24. Springborn, 7.
25. H. A. Goodman to James Montgomery, *United Natural Gas Company*, Oil City, Pa., October 1, 1956.
26. Clark, 20.
27. Hale, 51.
28. Darwin Payne, *Initiative in Energy: Dresser Industries, Inc., 1880–1978* (New York: Simon and Schuster, 1979), 59–71.
29. Hale, 52.
30. Brannt, 661.
31. *Gas Age*, July 26, 1956.
32. Clark, 65.
33. American Gas Association, "Natural Gas: Cinderella to Glamour Girl," 4.
34. Nichols, 11.
35. Ibid.
36. National Fuel Gas Company, *1973 Annual Report.*
37. Hope Natural Gas Company, 14.
38. East Ohio Gas Company, 4.
39. Hope Natural Gas Company, 15.
40. Don. E. Buckley, "Men ... Methods ... Machinery" *East Ohio Bulletin*, March 1950, 4.
41. Ibid., 3.
42. Leonard et al., 306.
43. Hilt.
44. Crum and Dugan, 352.
45. Hope Natural Gas Company, 16.
46. "Company D the Raftsmen's Guards of the Bucktails," *Warren Ledger and Warren Mail*, Warren County Historical Society, December 14, 1967.
47. Ibid.
48. Nancy Swanson, "Almost 90 Years and Still Going Strong, A Look at Roystone Station," *Valley Publishing Co.*, January 27, 1984.
49. Harold B. Bernard, "Natural-Gas Pumping Station at Roystone," *Power* 45, no. 16 (April 17, 1917), 516.
50. United Natural Gas Company, *Gas Bag*, August 1958, 1–2.
51. Memo to H. D. Clay, Exec. VP, from H. Nagel, Interview with Mr. Samuel B. Daugherty, July 1, 1958.
52. United Natural Gas Company, news release, April 30, 1958.
53. Ibid.
54. United Natural Gas Company, *Gas Bag*, August 1958, 1–2.
55. Worthington Pump & Machinery Corporation, "Gas Engines and Gas Compressors," Snow-Holly Works, (Buffalo, N.Y.: circa 1920).
56. Nichols, 15.
57. McKain and Allen, 178–79.
58. Hope Natural Gas Company, 16.
59. Thoenen, 113.
60. Hope Natural Gas Company, 19.
61. Thoenen, 265.
62. Newell, 150–51.
63. Thoenen, 266.
64. Stevens, 583.
65. Ibid.
66. McCullough and Brignano, 43.
67. Ibid., 43–45.
68. Crum and Dugan, 352.
69. McCullough and Brignano., 125–26.
70. John D. Aharrah, *The History of Heath Station*, National Fuel Gas Supply Corporation, (n.p., n.d.).
71. Ibid.
72. James R. Reinard, "Heath Station," National Fuel Gas Supply Corporation, (n.p.: April 4, 1997).
73. East Ohio Gas Company, 34.
74. Ibid., 35.
75. Skinner, 10–35.
76. United Natural Gas Company, *Gas Bag*, June 1959, 10.
77. Iroquois Gas Corporation, *Iroquois Gas News*, September 1957.
78. Brignano and McCullough, 17.
79. Bill Krellner, "Working on the pipeline," Grist from Old Mills, *St. Marys Daily Press*, November 19, 1992.
80. East Ohio Gas Company, 23.
81. Newell, 167.
82. National Fuel Gas Company, *The Pilot Light*, June 1976.
83. "History of the Gas Company in Ashtabula."
84. Hale, 69.
85. Nichols, 19.
86. Hope Natural Gas Company, 15.
87. *Dunkirk Evening Observer*, January 17, 1916.
88. "Gas Shortage Threatens," *Buffalo Express*, 1916.
89. "Company Plans Increase of Natural Gas Supply," *Buffalo Evening News*, February 18, 1916.
90. *Gas Facts*, ca 1922, 3 in Dominion East Ohio Collection, box 67, file folder 11 and 12, Youngstown Historical Center of Industry and Labor, Youngstown, Ohio.
91. The Peoples Natural Gas Company, "Natural Gas, When Its Gone What?" circa 1920, 3 in Dominion East Ohio Collection, box 68, file folder 7, Youngstown Historical Center of Industry and Labor, Youngstown, Ohio.
92. Nichols, 16.
93. "Present Natural Gas Situation," United States Bureau of Mines Bulletin, October 25, 1920, as quoted in Daly, 6.
94. Columbus Group of Columbia Gas and Electric Corporation, *An Employee Manual on the Natural Gas Business*, 34.
95. Columbia Gulf Transmission Company, *History Of Natural Gas Transmission* (n.p., 1971).
96. Seidenberg, 552.
97. Clark, 76.
98. Hope Natural Gas Company, 23.
99. Seidenberg, 560.
100. Hale, 64.
101. Nagel, 70.
102. Texas Gas Transmission Corporation, "Gas—A Century and a Half Strong," *Mcf*, Spring 1966, 20.
103. Heiney, 15.
104. Knowles, 70.
105. Hope Natural Gas Company, 4.
106. Payne, 83.
107. Hale.
108. Ibid., 46.
109. Clark, 268.
110. Berger and Anderson, 147.

111. Don E. Buckley, "First Through a New Pipe Line," *East Ohio News*, February 1947, 3.

112. Ibid., 159–60.

113. Bradley, 910.

114. Newell, 30.

115. Lief, 85–86; and Hale, 60.

116. Dawson, 120.

117. Nichols, 12.

118. Newell, 164.

119. United Natural Gas Company, *Gas Bag*, July 1961, 9.

120. Nichols, 14.

121. J. V. Goodman, Brief History of Underground Gas Storage, based on report DMC 62–41 Early History of Underground Gas Storage in the United States, American Gas Association statistical surveys (n.p.).

122. Lauriston, 95.

123. Ibid., 95.

124. Brief History of Underground Natural Gas Storage, in United Natural Gas Company, *Gas Bag*, July 1969, 5.

125. Hall, 346–47.

126. Herrick, 338.

127. Iroquois Gas Corporation, *Historical Perspective*, (n.p., n.d.).

128. W. J. Judge, President National Fuel Gas Company, letter from 26 Broadway, N.Y.C to E. B. Swanson, in "A summary of available data relating to supply and demand," 1930 Convention, American Gas Association, 420 Lexington Ave., New York in Appendix A, Underground Storage of Natural Gas, July 17, 1930.

129. Nichols, 13–14.

130. Terry, 4.

131. The Underground Storage of Gas in the United States and Canada, American Gas Association, December 31, 1982, Operating Section Report, 6.

132. Consolidated Gas Transmission, 14–15.

133. Thoenen, 343.

134. Ibid., 344.

135. Dominion, http://www.columbiagaspamd.com/about_us/chronology.htm.

136. McCullough and Brignano, 108.

137. Herbert, 82.

138. Brief History of Underground Natural Gas Storage, 6.

139. Nichols, 16.

140. Hope Natural Gas Company, 4.

141. Kelso, 14–15.

142. "A Neighborhood on Fire," *Ameriska Domovina*, September 1987.

143. Consolidated Natural Gas Corporation, *1944 Annual Report*, 11.

144. Herbert, 94.

145. William S. Lytle, *Underground Storage of Natural Gas in Pennsylvania* (Harrisburg, Pa.: Pennsylvania Geological Survey, Bulletin M 46, fourth series, 1963), 1.

146. Bufkin, 12.

147. McCullough and Brignano, 109–10.

148. Hope Natural Gas Company, 19.

149. J. French Robinson, President Consolidated Natural Gas Company, "The Cinderella Story of Natural Gas," notes form a talk prepared for delivery at the Utilities and Coal Forum, Great Lakes Regional Conference, sponsored by the Cleveland Society of Security Analysts, October 13, 1953 in Dominion East Ohio Collection, box 1, file folder 7, Youngstown Historical Center of Industry and Labor, Youngstown, Ohio.

150. Consolidated Natural Gas Corporation, *1951 Annual Report*, 19; and *1957 Annual Report*, 21.

151. Lytle, 27.

152. John A. Harper, Dana R. Kelly, and Earl H. Lin, "Petroleum — Deep Oil and Natural Gas," in Charles H. Schultz, ed., *The Geology of Pennsylvania* (Harrisburg, Pa.: Pennsylvania Geological Survey and Pittsburgh Geological Society, 1999), 509.

153. Ibid., 512.

154. Lytle, 29.

155. Minerals Yearbook, 1972, 817.

156. John R. Reeves, "Underground Storage of Natural Gas in the Medina Formations of Western New York," Republic Light, Heat and Power Company, internal document (n.p., n.d.).

157. Herrick, 374–75.

158. "Natural-gas-storage Capacity Jumps 12%," *Oil and Gas Journal* 58, no. 22 (May 30, 1960), 92.

159. Owen, 624.

160. Equitable Resources, Inc., *1988 Annual Report*.

161. Dominion Resources, Inc., *2003 Annual Report*.

162. National Fuel Gas Company, *2003 Annual Report*.

163. McCullough and Brignano, 93.

164. Murphy, 677.

165. Frey and Ide, 232.

166. Herbert, 109.

167. Castaneda, *Regulated Enterprise*, 50.

168. Idem., *Invisible Fuel*, 127.

169. Ibid., 123.

170. Hope Natural Gas Company, 4.

171. McCullough and Brignano, 95.

172. American Gas Association, "Natural Gas: Cinderella to Glamour Girl," 9.

173. Castaneda, *Regulated Enterprise*, 59.

174. Ibid.

175. Owen, 473–474.

176. C. F. Conaway, 223.

177. Castaneda, *Invisible Fuel*, 114.

178. Christopher J. Castaneda and Joseph A. Pratt, *From Texas to the East: A Strategic History of Texas Eastern Corporation* (College Station, Tx.: Texas A&M University Press, 1993), 49.

179. Hilt. Note: Both the Panhandle and Texas Eastern systems are now part of Duke Energy.

180. I. David Bufkin, *Texas Eastern Corporation, A Pioneering Spirit* (New York: Newcomen Society, 1983), 8.

181. Herbert, 91.

182. McCullough and Brignano, 103.

183. Herrick, 359.

184. Consolidated Natural Gas Corporation, *1949 Annual Report* 2.

185. Clark, 257.

186. Ibid., 234.

187. Castaneda, *Regulated Enterprise*, 128–29.

188. Ibid., 131.

189. Clark, 246.

190. Thoenen, 342–43.

191. Consolidated Edison, http://www.coned.com/about/about.asp?subframe=main.

192. Elwin S. Larson, *Brooklyn Union Gas* (New York: Newcomen Society of America, 1987), 15.

193. Bradley, 916.

194. National Fuel Gas Company, *1956 Annual Report*, 12.

195. Consolidated Natural Gas Corporation, *1957 Annual Report*, 15.

196. Lytle, 5.

197. Columbia Gulf Transmission Company.

198. Leonard et al., 68.

199. Lauriston, 95; and Judge.

200. Leonard Waverman, *Natural Gas and National Policy: A Linear Programming Model of North American Natural Gas Flows* (Toronto: University of Toronto Press, 1973), 14–15.

201. Ed Phillips, *Guts & Guile: True Tales from the Backrooms of the Pipeline Industry* (Vancouver: Douglas & McIntyre, 1990), 3.

202. "Nichols to analysts," National Fuel Gas Company, 1956.

203. Clark, 265–66.

204. *Minerals Yearbook 1972*, 819–820.

205. Kepos, "National Fuel Gas Company," 527.

206. American Gas Association.

207. Oil and Gas Journal, 1960.

208. Paul W. MacAvoy, *The Natural Gas Market, Sixty Years of Regulation and Deregulation* (New Haven, Conn.: Yale University Press, 2000), 4.

Seven

1. Wattson, 7.

2. *Westfield Republican*, November 14, 1906.

3. "Erie's Big Card," *Gazette* of 1870, in Sanford.

4. *The Petroleum Monthly* 1, no. 3 (January 1871), 109.

5. Castaneda, *Invisible Fuel*, 49–50.

6. *Harpers Weekly*, November 14, 1886 as quoted in McCullough and Brignano, 8–9.

7. Clark, 49.

8. *Titusville Herald*, September 3, 1873, in Henry, 206–07.

9. *History of Butler County, Pa.*, 296.

10. George W. Brown, 37.

11. *Gas Age*, October 2, 1958, 58.

12. Brignano and McCullough, 11–12.

13. Reed, 117.

14. West Virginia Glass, http://www.calwva.com/glassfac/glassfac.cfm.

15. McKain and Allen, 174.

16. Cabot Oil & Gas Corporation History, http://www.cabotog.com/history.html.

17. Herbert, 50.

18. Thoenen, 99, 103.

19. McKain and Allen, 157.

20. Ibid.

21. Hill, 1266.

22. Iroquois Gas Corporation, *The Iroquois*, 14.

23. Ibid., 13.

24. McCullough and Brignano, 69.

25. American Gas Association, "Automobile Antifreeze Made with Natural Gas," *Natural Gas* 11, no. 12 (December 1930), 4.

26. Williamson et al. (2), 427–28.

27. E. B. Swanson, "Natural Gas: A Summary of Available Data Relating to Supply and Demand," American Gas Association Convention, 1930, 10.

28. Sisler et al., 75.

29. "Natural Gas as a Factor in the Location of Industry," E. Holley Poe and Associates, New York, June 1946, prepared for Natural Gas Industry Committee; Federal Power Commission Natural Gas Investigation, 4.

30. Herbert, 104.

31. American Gas Association, "Natural Gas: Cinderella to Glamour Girl," 1.

32. Iroquois Gas Corporation, *Iroquois Gas News*, May 1958, 13.

33. "The Eastward March of Natural Gas: A week in the life of 1000 cubic feet from Texas to an Atlantic Coast city," *Gas Age*, 1950.

34. McLaurin, 377.

35. Iroquois Gas Corporation, "Inspection Tour, October 15 and 16, 1959."

36. Hale, 46.

37. Ibid.

38. Silverberg, 91.

39. Clark, 21.

40. Norman, 107.

41. Stotz and Jamison, 120.

42. Hale, 54.

43. Stotz and Jamison, 120–21.

44. Francis X. Welch, "A Century and a Half of Public Service," *Public Utilities Fortnightly*, reprinted from October 14, 1965, 22.

45. Herbert, 21.

46. Columbia Gas of Pennsylvania, http://www.columbiagaspamd.com/about_us/chronology.htm.

47. Clark, 83.

48. Rose, 626.

49. Herbert, 63.

50. "Glorifying Gas," 1941 Gas Service Section, *The Erie Daily Times*, February 28, 1941.

51. Iroquois Gas Corporation, *Iroquois Gas News*, December 1962.

52. *History of Allegheny County*, 620.

53. "How Man Harnessed the Ghost: The Story of Gas Heating," *Trade Winds* 5, no. 6 (February 1960), 30.

54. American Gas Association, "Chronology of America Gas Cooking, Water heating and Central House Heating," (February 1952).

55. *History of Venango County Pennsylvania*, 331.

56. *Trade Winds*, 30.

57. Advertisement, *Buffalo Express*, October 14, 1917.

58. Clark, 116.

59. Iroquois Gas Corporation, *The Iroquois*, 6.

60. McLaurin, 372.

61. *Convenience*, 16.

62. East Ohio Gas Company, 24.

63. *Venango County History 1*, 1919, 168.

64. "What natural gas has done for the City of Akron, and what precautions have been taken by the East Ohio Gas Company to protect their consumers," *Akron Times*, February 20, 1911, in Dominion East Ohio Collection, Box 57, file folder 2, Youngstown Historical Center of Industry and Labor, Youngstown, Ohio.

65. Reed, 129.

66. *Pittsburgh Leader.*

67. R. S. Thompson, "The Use of Gas or Getting the Most Out of It," *Oil and Gas Men's Magazine* 8, no. 6 (July 1913), 967.

68. Crum and Dugan, 223.

69. Herbert, 11.

70. Iroquois Gas Corporation, *The Iroquois*, 2.

71. "House Heating With Gas," *Gas Age Record*, May 5, 1923.

72. Norman, 142.

73. Ibid., 6.

74. McCullough and Brignano, 101–02.

75. Knowles, 89.

76. National Fuel Gas Company, *1953 Annual Report*, 18.

77. United Natural Gas Corporation, *Gas Bag*, January 1963, 8.

78. McCullough and Brignano, 99.

79. Brignano and McCullough, 90.

80. McCullough and Brignano, 118.

81. Norman, 109–116.

82. Owen, 5.

83. Hale, 58.

84. Stotz and Jamison, 177.

85. Ibid., 178.

86. Ibid., 179.

87. Advertisement, *Buffalo Express*, October 14, 1917.

88. Herbert, 47.

89. UGI, 22.

90. Hale, 58.

91. UGI, 21–22.

92. Williamson et al., 170–71.

93. Pennsylvania Gas Company, *Pennsylvania Gas News*, July 1965, 5.

94. Herbert, 120–22.

95. Hale, 73.

96. Welch, 22.

97. Hale, 59.

98. Ibid., 73.

99. Kurlansky, 378–79.

100. Ernest J. Oppenheimer, Ph.D., *Natural Gas the New Energy Leader*, Revised Ed. (New York: Pen & Podium, Inc., 1985), 92.

101. *Dunkirk Evening Observer,* June 27, 1901.

102. Ibid., March 31, 1902.

103. "History of the Gas Company in Ashtabula."

104. Stotz and Jamison, 274–75.

105. Ibid., 127.

106. Hale, 64.

107. Clark, 138.

108. McCullough and Brignano, 83.

109. Consolidated Natural Gas Company, *1962 Annual Report*, 7.

110. Gallick, 11.

111. Clark, 13; and Norman, 33.

112. Castaneda, *Invisible Fuel*, 25.

113. Hale, 46.

114. Clark, 20.

115. Leif, 73.

116. Herrick, 342–43.

117. Herbert, 15.

118. Clarion Gas Company bill.

119. Brignano and McCullough, 19.

120. Reed, 135.

121. Stotz and Jamison, 89

122. "The Natural Gas Industry," Taylor, Ewart and Company, November 25, 1925, no. 1, from a paper prepared Wm. B. Way, former General Secretary, Natural Gas Association of America, 2 in Dominion East Ohio Collection, box 59, file folder 38, Youngstown Historical Center of Industry and Labor, Youngstown, Ohio.

123. Herbert, 16.

124. Stotz and Jamison, 55.

125. Leif, 42.

126. Hale, 66–68.

127. McCullough and Brignano, 60.

128. Hale, 56.

129. Leif, 46.

130. Ibid., 57; and "American Meter to cut 48 jobs at Erie Plant," *Erie Times-News*, January 22, 2002.

131. Lief, 46.

132. Boyle, xxxix.

133. Ibid., 60.

134. Castaneda, *Invisible Fuel*, 53.

135. Brignano and McCullough, 64.

136. Ibid., 18.

137. Iroquois Gas Corporation, *Iroquois Historical Perspective*, (n.p., n.d.).

138. East Ohio Gas Company, 24.

139. Hale, 68.

140. Iroquois Gas Corporation, *Iroquois Gas News*, January, 1960, 2.

141. Ibid.

142. Castaneda, *Invisible Fuel*, 105–06.

143. Hilt.

144. "Gas Wells of Pennsylvania, Ohio and New York," *The Petroleum Monthly* 2, no. 10 (October 1872), 276.

145. *Trade Winds*, 30.

146. Boyle.

147. Ibid., 455.

148. *Dunkirk Evening Observer*, November 20, 1907.

149. Boyle, 460.

150. Stotz and Jamison, 163.

151. McCullough and Brignano, 112.

152. H. C. Reeser, "Natural Gas. Its Production, Transportation and Distribution," *Oil and Gas Man's Magazine* 10, no. 3 (3rd Quarter, 1915), 160.

153. *History of Allegheny County*, 616.

154. Boyle, 407.

155. "Gas shortage plagued city," *Franklin News-Herald*, August 19, 1978.

156. Newell, 33.

157. Brignano and McCullough, 22.

158. Hale, 56.

159. Crum and Dugan, 42.

160. Wattson, 11.

161. Way, 2–3.

162. Stotz and Jamison, 82.

163. Thoenen, 102.

164. *Dunkirk Evening Observer*, January 24, 1907.

165. Herbert, 22.

166. *Jamestown Post-Journal*, January 15, 1918.

167. J. H. Maxon, "Displacing Natural with Manufactured Gas," presented at the Annual Meeting of Natural Gas Association of America, Cleveland, Ohio, May 20, 21 and 22, 1919, 6.

168. Department of the Interior, *Conference on Natural Gas Conservation*, 1.

169. Dawson, 116.

170. McCullough and Brignano, 75.

171. Williamson et al. (2), 46.

172. McCullough and Brignano, 80–81.

173. "Ohioans Rapidly Learning that Natural Gas Supply Must be Properly Utilized," News Bulletin issued by the Ohio Committee on Public Utility Information, June 19, 1922, vol. 2 no. 33, 1 in Dominion East Ohio Collection, box 59, file folder 28, Youngstown Historical Center of Industry and Labor, Youngstown, Ohio.

174. Herbert, 59.

175. Castaneda, *Invisible Fuel*, 122.

176. Iroquois Gas Corporation, *Iroquois Gas News*, January 1958, 2.

177. Idem., September 1959, 2.

178. Frey and Ide, 229.

179. Ibid., 231.

180. East Ohio Gas Company, 40.

181. Bob Watson, "Profile: Herb Clay," *Buffalo Magazine* 40, no. 4.

182. Ibid.

183. Murphy, 340.

184. Herb Clay, "National Fuel Gas Company As Seen By Management," (n.p.: 1968).

185. United Natural Gas Company, *Gas Bag*, January 1959, 3.

186. Idem, December 1972, 3.

187. Pennsylvania Gas Company, *Pennsylvania Gas News*, January 1963.

188. Iroquois Gas Corporation, *Iroquois Gas News*, July 1957, 2.

189. Stotz and Jamison, 236.

190. Industry of the Week column, *Dunkirk Evening Observer*, April 1981.

191. Hale, 55.

192. Hidy and Hidy, 390.

193. Pennsylvania Gas Company History (n.p., n.d.), 25.

194. Herbert, 18.

195. Iroquois Gas Corporation, *Iroquois Gas News*, January 1959, 2.

196. Peoples Natural Gas Company, Rate Schedule, Issued Aug. 18, 1924, in Dominion East Ohio Collection, box 62, file folder 53, Youngstown Historical Center of Industry and Labor, Youngstown, Ohio.

197. Kuhn, Adam, "Wants the Gas," *Buffalo Courier Express*, February 18, 1916.

198. Newton, J. C. "One Solution," *Buffalo Evening News*, February 18, 1916.

199. Daly, 9.

200. Kelso, 12.

201. Herbert, 39.

202. "Ready to Raid Consumers," *Truth*, February 26, 1916.

203. Chemung Canal Trust Company, *125th Anniversary*, Elmira, N.Y. 1958, 12.

204. Ralph W. Gallagher, "Rates and Franchises," speech by in New York, January 17, 1923, in Dominion East Ohio Collection, box 58, file folder 53, Youngstown Historical Center of Industry and Labor, Youngstown, Ohio.

205. Rates for Various Pennsylvania cities, 1924 residential, in Dominion East Ohio Collection, box 62, file folder 33, Youngstown Historical Center of Industry and Labor, Youngstown, Ohio.

206. New York Public Service Commission, Second District, complaint by Buffalo Mayor George S. Buck, 1918, 459.

207. Iroquois Gas Corporation, *The Iroquois*, 13.

208. Ibid., 14.

209. Herbert, 67.

210. Ibid., 86.

211. McCullough and Brignano, 100.

212. O. F. Flumerfelt, "Notes covering History and Operations of Iroquois Gas Corporation for Mr. Roy Rutherford," December 18, 1946.

213. National Fuel Gas Company, *1948 Annual Report*, 8.

214. Robinson, 8.

215. "Nichols to Analysts."

216. Herbert, 161.

217. Gallick, 12.

218. Herbert, 26.

219. American Gas Association, *Gas Facts of 1958*.

220. Herbert, 37.

221. Ibid.

222. Ibid., 65.

223. MacAvoy, 120.

224. Knowles, 91.

225. Herbert, 138.

226. Ibid., 117.

Eight

1. Owen, 479.

2. Williamson et al. (2), 796.

3. U.S. Department of the Interior, Bureau of Mines, *Minerals Yearbook* (Washington: U.S. Government Printing Office, various years).

4. Bradley, 372.

5. Ibid., 375–77.

6. Ibid., 877.

7. Sanders, 11.

8. Gallick, 15.

9. Kelso, 16.

10. Sanders, 97–98.

11. Ibid., 103–104; and Bradley, 381.

12. Paul W. MacAvoy, "The Regulation-Induced Shortage of Natural Gas," in K. C. Brown, 169.

13. United Natural Gas Company, *The Gas Bag*, November 1973, 7.

14. Hope Natural Gas Company, 4.

15. History of Liquefied Natural Gas, http://www.dom/com/about/gas-transmission/covepoint/lng_history.jsp.

16. Gallick, 15.

17. Ibid., 16.

18. National Fuel Gas Company, *1978 Annual Report*, 2.

19. Bradley, 457–60, 464.

20. Gallick, 11.

21. Ibid., 17.

22. Ibid.

23. Ibid., 18.

24. MacAvoy, 100.

25. Ibid., 101.

26. Ibid., 107.

27. Edward B. Flowers, U.S. *Utility Mergers and the Restructuring of the New Global Power Industry* (Westport, Conn.: Quorum Books, 1998), 1.

28. Columbia Gas of Ohio, http://www.columbia gasohio.com/community/about.

29. Columbia Gas of Kentucky, http://www. columbiagasky.com/area.htm.

30. Dominion Resources, *2003 Annual Report*.

31. Dominion Peoples, http://www.dom.com/ about/companies/peoples/index.jsp.

32. CNG Transmission Corporation, Hope Gas, Inc.

33. Dominion East Ohio, http://www.dom.com/ about/companies/eohio/index.jsp.

34. Cinergy, http://www.cinergy.com/About_ Cinergy_Corp/Corporate_Overview/default_ corporate_fact_sheet.asp#general.

35. Energy East, http://www.energyeast.com/ aboutee.html.

36. New York State Electric and Gas, http://www. nyseg.com/nysegweb/main.nsf/Doc/profile?Open Document.

37. Energy East, http://www.energyeast.com/ company.html.

38. Flowers, 100.

39. Louisville Gas and Electric Company, http:// www.lgeenergy.com/lge/about_lge.asp.

40. Atmos Energy Corporation, http://www. atmosenergy.com/about/index.html.

41. *A Brief History of National Fuel Gas Company*, (n.p., n.d.).

42. National Fuel Gas Company, *1974 Annual Report*.

43. Idem., *2003 Annual Report*.

44. Kepos, "Equitable Resources, Inc.," 493–494.

45. Equitable Gas Company, A Brief History of Equitable Gas Company & Equitable Resources (EQT).

46. Governor's Energy Council, 2.

47. McKain and Allen, 220.

48. Dudley H. Cardwell, *Oil and Gas Fields of West Virginia* (n.p.: West Virginia Geological and Economic Survey, 1977), 2–4.

49. Robert C. Milici, "Upper Devonian Fractured Black and Gray Shales and Siltstones," in Roen and Walker, 87.

50. Ralph N. Thomas, *Devonian Shale Gas Production in Central Appalachian Area* (Lexington, Ky.: Kentucky Geological Survey, University of Kentucky College of Arts and Sciences, 1951), 2249–56.

51. Owen, 627.

52. Reginald P. Briggs and Derek B. Tatlock, "Petroleum — Guide to Undiscovered Recoverable Natural Gas Resources," in Schultz, 591.

53. Douglas G. Patchen et al., *Coalbed Gas Production, Big Run and Pine Grove Fields, Wetzel County, West Virginia* (Morgantown, W.Va.: West Virginia Geological and Economic Survey, Publication C-44, 1991), 2.

54. Ohio Oil and Gas Association.

55. Bradley 2, Appendix A: Inflation-adjusted Oil and Natural Gas Prices, 1914–17.

56. *An Energy Policy for Pennsylvania* (Harrisburg, Pa.: Pennsylvania Energy Office, 1988), 73.

57. John A. Harper, Derek B. Tatlock, and Robert T. Wolfe, Jr., "Petroleum — Shallow Oil and Natural Gas," in Charles H. Schultz, ed., *The Geology of Pennsylvania* (Harrisburg, Pa.: Pennsylvania Geological Survey and Pittsburgh Geological Society, 1999), 494.

58. Harper et al., 511.

59. Energy Information Administration, "Natural Gas Annual 2002."

60. Patchen, in Roen and Walker, 1.

Nine

1. Plutarch, *Marcellus*, written 75 A.C.E., translation by John Dryden, http://classics.mit.edu/ Plutarch/marcellu.html.

2. Federal Energy Regulatory Commission, *Price Manipulation in Western Markets*, March 26, 2003, http://www.ferc.gov/industries/electric/indus-act/ wec/enron/summary-findings.pdf.

3. Daniel Yergin, *The Quest: Energy, Security, and the Remaking of the Modern World* (New York: Penguin, 2011), 129–37.

4. Energy Information Administration, "Annual Energy Outlook (2011)," December 16, 2010, http:// www.eia.gov/neic/speeches/newell_12162010.pdf.

5. John E. Peterson, "Address to the 2011 Natural Gas History Symposium," Oil Region Alliance, Titusville, Pa., October 6, 2011.

6. Sonal Patel, "Canada to Shutter Older Coal Plants," *Power*, August 1, 2010, http://www.power-mag.com/issues/departments/global_monitor/Canada -to-Shutter-Older-Coal-Plants_2868.html.

7. "The Father of the Barnett," Jackson School of Geosciences, University of Texas at Austin, http:// www.jsg.utexas.edu/news/feats/2007/barnett/father_ of_barnett.html.

8. Andrew Maykuth, "Tapping Shale, Seeking Sustainability: A Rare Oilman," *Philadelphia Inquirer*, August 29, 2010.

9. Railroad Commission of Texas, *Newark, East (Barnett Shale) Field*, accessed May 2011, http://www. rrc.state.tx.us/data/fielddata/barnettshale.pdf.

10. Jack Z. Smith, "Haynesville Might be U.S.' Largest No. 1 Gas-Producing Shale," *Fort Worth Star Telegram*, March 21, 2011, http://www.star-telegram. com/2011/03/21/2939061/haynesville-might-be-us-largest.html.

11. Jonathan D. Silver, "The Marcellus Boom / Origins: The Story of a Professor, a Gas Driller and Wall Street," *Pittsburgh Post-Gazette*, March 20, 2011, http://www.post-gazette.com/pg/11079/1133325–503. stm, and John A. Harper and Jaime Kostelnik, "The Marcellus Shale Play in Pennsylvania," Pennsylvania Geological Survey, http://www.marcellus.psu.edu/ resources/PDFs/DCNR.pdf.

12. Derek Weber, "From Colonel Drake to the Marcellus Shale Gas Play — Transmission Developments," *Pipeline and Gas Journal*, Vol. 237, No. 3, (March 2010).

13. United States Geological Survey, "USGS Releases New Assessment of Gas Resources in the Marcellus Shale, Appalachian Basin," news release, August 23, 2011, http://www.usgs.gov/newsroom/ article.asp?ID=2893.

14. Ray Sorenson, "Natural Gas in the Pre-Drake Era," presentation to the 2011 Natural Gas History Symposium, Oil Region Alliance, Titusville, Pa., October 7, 2011.

15. "Geologic Provinces of the United States:

Appalachian Highlands Province," United States Geological Survey, http://geomaps.wr.usgs.gov/parks/province/appalach.html.

16. Governor's Marcellus Shale Advisory Commission, July 22, 2011, http://files.dep.state.pa.us/PublicParticipation/MarcellusShaleAdvisory Commission/MarcellusShaleAdvisoryPortalFiles/MSAC_Final_Report.pdf, 25.

17. Ibid., 22.

18. Ibid.

19. "Marcellus Shale–Appalachian Basin Natural Gas Play," Geology.com, http://geology.com/articles/marcellus-shale.shtml.

20. Range Resources, Company Timeline, http://www.rangeresources.com/Our-Company/Company-Timeline.aspx.

21. John A. Harper "The Marcellus Shale–An Old 'New' Gas Reservoir in Pennsylvania," Pennsylvania Geology, (Harrisburg, Pa.: 2008), 38(1).

22. Louise S. Durham, "Marcellus Gave No 'Big Play' Hints," AAPG Explorer, American Association of Petroleum Geologists, http://www.aapg.org/explorer/2010/04apr/marcellus0410.cfm.

23. Terry Engelder and Gary G. Lash, "Marcellus Shale Play's Vast Resource Potential Creating Stir in Appalachia," The American Oil and Gas Reporter (May 2008), http://www3.geosc.psu.edu/~jte2/references/link150.pdf.

24. Range Resources, Marcellus Division, http://www.rangeresources.com/Operations/Marcellus-Division.aspx.

25. Terry Engelder, "Marcellus," Fort Worth Basin Oil and Gas Magazine (August 2009), http://www.marcellus.psu.edu/resources/PDFs/marcellusengelder.pdf.

26. Jonathan D. Silver, "The Marcellus Boom / Origins: The Story of a Professor, a Gas Driller and Wall Street," Pittsburgh Post-Gazette, March 20, 2011, http://www.post-gazette.com/pg/11079/1133325–503.stm.

27. "Gregory R. Wrightstone, Marcellus Shale Facts," Energy Tribune, February 22, 2011, energytribune.com/articles.cfm/6635/Marcellus-Shale-Facts.

28. Ibid.

29. Kristin Harty Barkley, "Panelists talk pros, cons of Marcellus shale drilling," The Cumberland Times-News, March 4, 2011, http://times-news.com/local/x651391711/Panelists-talk-pros-cons-of-Marcellus-shale-drilling.

30. Michael Rubinkam, "Gushers Highlight Potential of Pa. Gas Field," Associated Press, June 26, 2011, http://www.google.com/hostednews/ap/article/ALeqM5jiDnkPwDatiCBcysSHluy2CTvCWg?docId=665b3539050d42babaaddf9438eafa91.

31. "New Production Data Shows Shale's Promise and Growth," The Times Tribune, Scranton, Pa., February 28, 2011, http://thetimes–tribune/news/new-production-data-shows-shale-s-promise-and-growth.

32. Bill Toland, "A Boom Without a Bust," Pittsburgh Post-Gazette, February 28, 2011, http://shale.sites.post-gazette.com/index.php/business/23884.

33. Ian Urbina, "Geologists Sharply Cut Estimate of Shale Gas," New York Times, August 24, 2011, http://www.nytimes.com/2011/08/25/us/25gas.html; and Erich Schwartzel, "Shale Gas Estimate

Plummets," Pittsburgh Post-Gazette, January 24, 2012, http://www.post-gazette.com/pg/12024/1205614–503.stm#ixzz1kNcaJqys.

34. Mike Orcutt, "How Much U.S. Shale Gas Is There, Really?" MIT Technology Review, August 31, 2011, http://www.technologyreview.com/energy/38463, A-1.

35. "Annual Energy Outlook (2011)." See note 4.

36. "Potential Gas Committee Reports Substantial Increase in Magnitude of U.S. Natural Gas Resource Base," Potential Gas Committee, Golden, Co., April 27, 2011, http://potentialgas.org/.

37. Christopher Helman, "How Much Gas Is There In The Marcellus Shale?" Forbes, October 11, 2011, http://www.forbes.com/sites/christopher helman/2011/10/11/how-much-gas-is-there-in-the-marcellus-shale/.

38. "Fueling North America's Energy Future," IHS Cambridge Energy Research Associates Report, 2010.

39. Energy Information Administration, "Russia," http://www.eia.gov/countries/cab.cfm?fips=RS.

40. "The Future of Natural Gas," An Interdisciplinary MIT Study, Interim Report, Massachusetts Institute of Technology, (2011), http://www.marcellus.psu.edu/resources/PDFs/MIT.

41. Ibid.

42. "Annual Energy Outlook (2011)." See note 4.

43. Pennsylvania State University, "The Economic Impacts of the Pennsylvania Marcellus Shale Natural Gas Play: An Update," (2011), http://marcellus coalition.org/wp-content/uploads/2011/07/Final-2011-PA-Marcellus-Economic-Impacts.pdf.

44. James Loewenstein, "DEP Official: Pennsylvania Might Have the World's Largest Gas Reserves, The Daily Review, Towanda, Pa., May 28, 2011, http://thedailyreview.com/news/dep-official-pennsylvania-might-have-the-world-s-largest-gas-reserves-1.1153539.

45. Bryan Walsh, "The Gas Dilemma," Time, March 31, 2011, http://www.time.com/time/health/article/0,8599,2062331,00.html.

46. Shaun Polcer, "U.S. Official Touts Potential of Shale Gas," Calgary Herald, October 20, 2010, http://www/calgaryherald.com/3698406.

47. Ian Urbina, "Lawmakers Seek Inquiry of Natural Gas Industry," New York Times, June 29, 2011, http://www.nytimes.com/2011/06/29/us/politics/29naturalgas.html.

48. Randy Ellis and Jay F. Marks, "Natural Gas Industry Strikes Back at New York Times Article," Oklahoman, June 28, 2011, http://newsok.com/natural-gas-industry-strikes-back-at-new-york-times-article/article/3580924.

49. Gas Leasing: The Marcellus Shale "Gold Rush" and its Impact on Pennsylvania, Pennsylvania Bar Institute, Mechanicsburg, Pa., PBI No. 2008–5526, 67.

50. "Clarion County Revenues Skyrocket, Thanks to Marcellus Shale Drilling Boom," The News-Herald, Franklin, Pa., January 20, 2011, A-1.

51. Gas Leasing, 69. See note 49.

52. Ibid, 107.

53. "2011 Permit and Rig Activity Report," Pennsylvania PA DEP, Bureau of Oil and Gas Management, http://www.dep.state.pa.us/dep/deputate/minres/oilgas/RIG11.htm.

54. Rachel Weaver, "Marcellus Gas Wells Generate an Amazing Bounty for Landowners," *Pittsburgh Tribune-Review*, February 27, 2011, http://www.pittsburghlive.com/x/pittsburghtrib/724939.html.

55. Tim Purko, "Uncertainty Remains as Landowners Band Together," *Pittsburgh Tribune-Review*, September 1, 2010, http://www.pittsburghlive.com/x/pittsburgtrib/business/697353.html.

56. Shannon P. Duffy, "Judge Deals Setback to Drilling Companies in Shale Case," *Pittsburgh Post-Gazette*, March 14, 2011, http://www.post-gazette.com/pg/11073/1131226-499.stm.

57. "Gas Firm Wants to Extend Southern Tier Leases," *Star Gazette*, Elmira, N.Y., July 10, 2011, http://www.pressconnects.com/article/20110710/NEWS01/107100338/Gas-firm-wants-extend-Southern-Tier-leases.

58. Ry Rivard, "Property, Mineral Rights in Conflict, Landowner Says Gas Driller Must Compensate Him for Building Facility," *Charleston Daily Mail*, Charleston, W.Va., July 5, 2011, http://www.dailymail.com/News/201107040823

59. "Judge Approves Settlement in Marcellus Shale Class-Action Suit," *Pittsburgh Tribune-Review*, March 23, 2011, http://www.pittsburghlive.com/x/pittsburghtrib/news/breaking/s_728609.html.

60. Steve Szkotak, "Lawsuits Over Va. Gas Drilling Head to Court," *The Times Leader*, Wilkes-Barre, Pa., March 14, 2011, 1.

61. Marc Levy, "Shale Gas Contracts Case Heads to Pa. High Court," Associated Press, *Pittsburgh Post-Gazette*, October 14, 2011, http://www.post-gazette.com/pg/11287/1182018-454.stm.

62. Governor's Marcellus Shale Advisory Commission, 40. See note 16.

63. *Gas Leasing*, 126. See note 49.

64. "Hydraulic Fracturing—Is It Safe? Natural Gas," *Institute for Energy Research*, May 3, 2011, http://www.instituteforenergyresearch.org/2011/05/03/hydraulic-fracturing-is-it-safe/.

65. Matthew E. Vavro, "Be Thankful for the Gas Companies," *Butler Eagle*, Butler, Pa., February 24, 2011, A-4.

66. David Thompson, "Conservancy: State Forests at Risk," *Lock Haven Express*, Lock Haven, Pa., February 17, 2011, A-1.

67. Marie C. Baca, "Forced Pooling: When Landowners Can't Say No to Drilling," *Pro Publica*, http://www.propublica.org/article/forced-pooling-when-landowners-cant-say-no-to-drilling.

68. Energy Information Administration, "Review of Emerging Resources: U.S. Shale Gas and Shale Oil Plays," July 2011, http://www.eia.gov/analysis/studies/usshalegas/pdf/usshaleplays.pdf.

69. Taylor Kuykendall, "Not Just the North: Boom to Affect All," *Register-Herald*, Beckley, W.Va., February 28, 2011, http://www.register-herald.com/todaysfrontpage/x62856646/Not-just-the-North-Boom-to-affect-all.

70. Pegula and his wife Kim in 2011 would make a commitment of the largest single financial gift in Penn State history to build a new state-of-the-art ice arena for the university. "The President's Report on the Philanthropy and Endowments 2010–11," Pennsylvania State University, 22.

71. Ben Casselman, "Chevron Bets Big on U.S. Natural Gas," *Wall Street Journal*, November 10, 2010, B-1.

72. Joe Napsha, "Shale-Related Deals in First Quarter Estimated at $9.7 Billion," *Pittsburgh Tribune-Review*, May 17, 2011, http://www.pittsburghlive.com/x/pittsburghtrib/business/s_737375.html.

73. "Chevron Buying 228,000 Acres in Marcellus Area," *Pittsburgh Post-Gazette*, May 4, 2011, http://www.post-gazette.com/pg/11124/1143985-100.stm.

74. "25 Largest Marcellus Shale Gas Producers Statewide," *Pittsburgh Business Times*, October 6, 2011, 12.

75. Michael Erman and Anna Driver, "Exclusive: Exxon Buys Two Marcellus Companies for $1.7 billion," *Reuters*, June 8, 2011, http://www.reuters.com/article/2011/06/08/us-phillips-exxon-idUSTRE75774920110608.

76. Kris Maher and Ben Casselman, "Coal Giant Consol Latest to Buy Gas," *Wall Street Journal*, March 16, 2010, B-1.

77. Erich Schwartzel, "Consol: Shale a 'Baby,'" *Pittsburgh Post-Gazette*, May 05, 2011, http://www.post-gazette.com/pg/11125/1144208-28.stm.

78. Jack Z. Smith, "Range Resources Selling Most of its Barnett Shale Holdings," *Fort Worth Star Telegram*, Fort Worth, Tx., http://www.star-telegram.com/2011/02/28/2884428/range-selling-most-of-its-barnett.html.

79. Andrew Maykuth, "Pa.'s Natural Gas Rush," *Philadelphia Inquirer*, April 3, 2011, http://articles.philly.com/2011-04-03/business/29377352_1_marcellus-formation-marcellus-shale-coalition-drilling.

80. Chesapeake Energy Corp., http://askchesapeake.aitrk1.com/Marcellus-Shale/PA/Pages/information.aspx.

81. "25 Largest Marcellus Shale Gas Producers Statewide." See note 74.

82. G. Jeffrey Aaron, "Strictly Business: Talisman Finds Success in Pa. Marcellus Shale Play," *Star Gazette*, Elmira, N.Y., September 25, 2010, http://www.stargazette.com/fdcp/?1285678260893.

83. "25 Largest Marcellus Shale Gas Producers Statewide." See note 74.

84. "FACTBOX-Key Shale Natural Gas and Oil Deals," April 5, 2011, http://www.reuters.com/article/2011/04/05/factbox-key-shale-deals-idUSN0510322320110405.

85. "Marcellus Shale Deals Far From Done," *American Agriculturist*, March 14, 2011, http://americanagriculturist.com/story.aspx/marcellus/shale/deals/far/from/done/9/47474.

86. Erika Kinetz, "Reliance Industries Buys Third US Shale Gas Stake," *Associated Press*, August 5, 2010, http://www.omaha.com/article/20100805/AP05/308059976.

87. Anya Litvak, "New International Investors Tap Into Marcellus Shale Rush," *Pittsburgh Business Times*, May 17, 2010, http://pittsburgh.bizjournals.com/pittsburgh/stories/2010/05/17/story3.html.

88. Kenneth McCallum and Jason Womack, "Mitsui Bets on U.S. Shale-Gas Project," *Wall Street Journal*, February 17, 2010, B-3.

89. Cliff White, "Dan Curay," *Centre Daily Times*, State College, Pa., February 10, 2011, http://centredaily.com/2011/02/10/2512266/dan-churay.html.

90. "25 Largest Marcellus Shale Gas Producers Statewide." See note 74. The information for this section is cited from this source unless otherwise noted.

91. Casey Jenkins, "Consol Gets $193M for Shale Land," *The Intelligencer/Wheeling News-Register*, Wheeling, W.Va., September 27, 2011, http://www.news-register.net/page/content.detail/id/559935/Consol-Ge.

92. Elwin Green, "Local Firms in Energy Sector Prove Hot Commodities, *Pittsburgh Post-Gazette*, March 22, 2011, http://www.post-gazette.com/pg/11081/1133664-334.stm.

93. Marcie Schellhammer, "Kick-Off Dinner Begins Natural Gas Expo at Pitt-Bradford," *The Bradford Era*, March 10, 2011, 1.

94. David Robinson, "National Fuel to Boost Shale Drilling," *Buffalo News*, November 6, 2010, http://www.buffalonews.com/city/communities/amherst/article243806.ece.

95. Adam Sichko , "CEO: National Fuel to spend $1B on gas drilling," *Business First*, October 7, 2011, 1.

96. Ultra Petroleum Corp., Appalachian Basin, http://www.ultrapetroleum.com/Our-Properties/Appalachian-Basin-16.html.

97. Pennsylvania Department of Environmental Protection. See note 53.

98. Laura Legere, "Marcellus Gas Production Continues Steady Growth in Pa.," *The Republican-Herald*, Pottsville, Pa., August 18, 2011, http://republicanherald.com/news/marcellus-gas-production-continues-steady-growth-in-pa-1.1190255.

99. David Wessell, "The Big Interview," *Wall Street Journal*, retrieved on February 25, 2011, http://online.wsj.com/home-page.

100. "Petrolia Man's Drilling Techniques Attracted World-Wide Attention," Publication and date unknown.

101. "Science: Oil Miner," *Time*, December 6, 1943, http://www.time.com/time/magazine/article/0,9171,850777,00.html.

102. "Governor's Marcellus Shale Advisory Commission," 18, http://files.dep.state.pa.us/PublicParticipation/MarcellusShaleAdvisoryCommission/MarcellusShaleAdvisoryPortalFiles/MSAC_Final_Report.pdf. See note 16.

103. U.S. Department of Energy, "DOE's Early Investment in Shale Gas Technology Producing Results Today," February 2, 2011, www.netl.doe.gov/publications/press/2011/11008-DOE_Shale_Gas_Research_Producing_R.html.

104. *Natural Gas Well Drilling & Development Primer*, Universal Well Services, Inc., Meadville, Pa., (2008).

105. Ibid.

106. Frac Focus, Historical Perspective, http://fracfocus.org/hydraulic-fracturing-how-it-works/history-hydraulic-fracturing.

107. Hydraulic Fracturing: Unlocking America's Natural Gas Resources, *American Petroleum Institute*, July 19, 2010, http://www.api.org/policy/exploration/hydraulicfracturing/upload/HYDRAULIC_FRACTURING_PRIMER.pdf.

108. Ibid.

109. Erich Schwartzel, "Study: Fracking Priciest for Wells," *Pittsburgh Post-Gazette*, August 31, 2011, http://www.post-gazette.com/pg/11243/1170956-28.stm.

110. "Expert Says Marcellus Drillers Reusing Two-Thirds of Water," *NGI Shale Daily*, March 23, 2011, http://shaledaily.com/news/sd20110323e.shtml?utm_source=twitterfeed&utm_medium=twitter.

111. *Natural Gas Well Drilling & Development Primer*. See note 104.

112. Pam Kasey, "A Frack Job Explained," September 9, 2010, *The State Journal*, Charleston, W.Va., http://www.statejournal.com/story.cfm?func=viewstory&storyid=85781.

113. Pennsylvania Department of Environmental Protection, "Hydraulic Fracturing Overview," http://www.dep.state.pa.us/dep/deputate/minres/oilgas/new_forms/marcellus/Reports/DEP%20Fracing%20overview.pdf.

114. Ibid.

115. *Natural Gas Well Drilling & Development Primer*. See note 104.

116. Cliff White, "PSU Professors Hope to Open Path to Successful Gas Drilling in Marcellus Shale," *Centre Daily Times*, State College, Pa., January 19, 2011, http://cnp.benfranklin.org/bftp-news/psu-professors-hope-to-open-path-to-successful-gas-drilling-in-marcellus-shale, and "Shale Prop Goes Bonkers," *Philadelphia Inquirer* in *Pittsburgh Tribune-Review*, July 1, 2011, http://www.pittsburghlive.com/x/pittsburghtrib/business/s_744738.html.

117. State of Colorado Oil and Gas Conservation Commission, Statement, www.colorado.gov/cogcc.

118. "Mike Sorghan, "Groundtruthing Academy Award Nominee 'Gasland,'" February 24, 2011, *New York Times*, http://www.nytimes.com/gwire/2011/02/24/24greenwire-groundtruthing-academy award-nominee-gasland.

119. "Debunking Gasland," June 9, 2010, *Energy InDepth*, http://www.energyindepth.org/2010/06/debunking-gasland/.

120. John Hanger, "Gasland and the Oscars," *Facts of the Day*, February 26, 2011, http://johnhanger.blogspot.com/2011/02/gasland-and-the-oscars.html.

121. Ad Crable, "Pa. Official Apologizes for Nazi Propaganda Comment Made Here," March 15, 2011, *Lancaster Online*, Lancaster, Pa., http://articles.lancasteronline.com/local/4/362603.

122. "Modern Shale Gas Development in the United States: A Primer," Ground Water Protection Council, Oklahoma City, OK, April 2009, 21, http://www.dep.state.pa.us/dep/deputate/minres/oilgas/US_Dept_Energy_Report_Shale_Gas_Primer_2009.pdf.

123. Nels Johnson, *Pennsylvania Energy Impacts Assessment, Executive Summary: Marcellus Shale Natural Gas and Wind Energy*, The Nature Conservancy, Pennsylvania Chapter, February 2011, http://www.nature.org/media/pa/tnc_energy_analysis.pdf.

124. James M. Odato, "Scientist Says the Spin Is On," *Albany Times Union*, March 14, 2011, http://www.timesunion.com/local/article/Scientist-says-the-spin-is-on-1116437.php.

125. Kent F. Perry, "Hydraulic Fracturing–A Historical and Impact Perspective," Gas Technology Institute, http://media.godashboard.com//gti/EandP_Perry_SPE_HF_Jan2011_final.pdf.

126. Governor's Marcellus Shale Advisory Commission, 66. See note 16.

127. Marianne Lavelle, "Forcing Gas Out of Rock With Water," *National Geographic*, October 17, 2010, http://news.nationalgeographic.com/news/2010/10/1 01022-energy-marcellus-shale-gas-sc.

128. Timothy Puko, "Concerns About Drought Not Slowing State's Shale Gas Drillers," *Pittsburgh Tribune-Review*, August 9, 2011, http://www.pittsburghlive.com/x/pittsburghtrib/news/s_750634.html.

129. "SRBC Suspends Aater Withdrawal Permits," *The Times Leader*, Wilkes-Barre, Pa., July 20, 2011, http://www.timesleader.com/news/ap?article ID=7358461.

130. "USGS Studying Water Resources of Fayetteville Shale," *The Sun Times*, Heber Springs, Ak., March 13, 2011, http://www.thesuntimes.com/news/x13268520/USGS-studying-water-resources-of-Fayetteville-Shale.

131. Joe Carroll, "Drought Threatens Texas Oil Boom," *Bloomberg*, June 13, 2011, http://www.bloomberg.com/news/2011-06-13/worst-drought-in-more-than-a-century-threatens-texas-oil-natural-gas-boom.html.

132. Lauren Boyer, "Marcellus Shale Industry Treated Sewer Water May Be Used at Wells," *Centre Daily Times*, State College, Pa., October 16, 2010, http://www.centredaily.com/2010/10/16/2275602/treated-sewer-water-may-be-used.html.

133. Elaine Blaisdell, "Plan in Place to Sell City Water for Natural Gas Drilling Process," *Cumberland Times-News*, March 21, 2011, http://times-news.com/local/x814643951/Plan-in-place-to-sell-city-water-for-natural-gas-drilling-process.

134. Cynthia McCloud, "Clarksburg Considers Selling Effluent Water for Fracking," *The State Journal*, Charleston, W.Va., June 16, 2011, http://statejournal.com/story.cfm?func=viewstory&storyid=101571.

135. Kathryn Klaber, "The Truth About Water Use in the Marcellus," *Lockhaven.com*, Lockhaven, Pa., http://www.lockhaven.com/page/content.detail/id/526611/The-truth-about-water-use-in-the-Marcellus.

136. Don Hopey, "How Fracking Water Is Used Is 'Green' Driven," *Pittsburgh Post-Gazette*, February 28, 2011, http://shale.sites.post-gazette.com/index.php/environment/23883.

137. Mike Soraghan, "Halliburton Announces Ecofriendly Fracking Fluid, More Disclosure," *New York Times*, November 15, 2010, http://www.nytimes.com/gwire/2010/11/15/15greenwire-halliburton-announces-econfriendly-fracking-fluid-more-disclosure.

138. "Halliburton Exec. Sips Fracking Fluid Recipe in Safety Demonstration at Industry Conference," *Washington Post*, August 22, 2011, http://www.washingtonpost.com/business/industries/halliburton-exec-sips-fracking-fluid-recipe-in-safety-demonstration-at-industry-conference/2011/08/22/gIQAVbrEXJ_print.html.

139. "Modern Shale Gas Development in the United States: A Primer," ES-3. See note 122.

140. Toxins Found In Gas Drilling Fluids, *Wall Street Journal*, April 18, 2011, A-3.

141. Jonathan D. Silver, "Bill Regulating Fracking Draws Mixed Reaction," *Pittsburgh Post-Gazette*, March 16, 2011, http://www.post-gazette.com/pg/11075/1132238-84.stm.

142. Ben Casselman and Daniel Gilbert, "'Fracking' Disclosure Is Urged," *Wall Street Journal*, May 24, 2011, B-1.

143. Elana Schor, "BUDGET: Votes Likely Tomorrow on Competing Funding Bills," *E&E Reporter*, March 8, 2011, http://www.eenews.net/pm/sample.

144. Dave Cook, "Interior Secretary: 'Fracking' Can Be Safe and Responsible," *Christian Science Monitor*, October 5, 2011, http://www.csmonitor.com/USA/Politics/monitor_breakfast/2011/1005/Interior-secretary-Fracking-can-be-safe-and-responsible-VIDEO.

145. "States Weigh Fracking Fluid Disclosure in Light of New Website, *E&E News*, April 25, 2011, http://www.eenews.net/Greenwire/2011/04/25/12.

146. "Pa. Industry Group to Disclose Drilling Chemicals," *Wall Street Journal*, October 21, 2011, http://online.wsj.com/article/AP38df81773a3c4ac7a3 5851ebd77254e4.html.

147. Ground Water Protection Council, "State Oil and Gas Regulations Designed to Protect Water Resources," May 27, 2009, http://www.gwpc.org/e-library/documents/general/State%20Oil%20and %20Gas%20Regulations%20Designed%20to%20 Protect%20Water%20Resources.pdf and Environmental Protection Agency, "Evaluation of Impacts to Underground Sources of Drinking Water by Hydraulic Fracturing," (June 2004), http://www.epa.gov/safewater/uic/pdfs/cbmstudy_attach_uic_exec_summ.pdf.

148. Donald Gilliland, "WTF: What the Frack is Hydraulic Fracturing?" *The Patriot-News*, Harrisburg, Pa., April 25, 2011, 1.

149. Nick Snow, "Pennsylvania Marcellus Rules Protect Environment, Official Says," *Oil and Gas Journal*, October 13, 2010, http//www.ogj.com/index/article-tools-template/articles/oil-gas-journal/drill.

150. Robert Swift, "State Geologists Mapping Deep Aquifers," *The Daily Review*, Towanda, Pa., April 26, 2011, http://thedailyreview.com/news/state-geologists-mapping-deep-aquifers-1.1137358.

151. "YSU Hosts Marcellus Shale Seminar," June 6, 2009, *WYTV*, http://www.wytv.com/content/news/local/story/YSU-Hosts-Marcellus-Shale-Seminar/nM5geIxW3EWFoTpyM2uT6Q.cspx.

152. Don Hopey, "D.C. Group Says 1982 Incident Shows Risk of Fracking," *Pittsburgh Post-Gazette*, August 4, 2011, http://www.post-gazette.com/pg/112 16/1165077-455.stm.

153. Laura Legere, "Cancer Institute to Conduct Shale Drilling Health Study," *The Times Tribune*, Scranton, Pa., July 8, 2011, http://thetimes-tribune.com/news/health-science/cancer-institute-to-conduct-shale-drilling-health-study-1.1172311.

154. Pennsylvania State University, "Marcellus Shale Research Network to Track Shale Region's Water Quality," news release, October 11, 2011, http://live.psu.edu/story/55665.

155. G. Jeffrey Aaron, "Wastewater from Gas Drilling Being Used for Area Road Maintenance," *Star Gazette*, Elmira, N.Y., July 20, 2011, http://www.stargazette.com/article/20110720/NEWS01/10720036 9/Wastewater-from-gas-drilling-being-used-area-road-maintenance.

156. Mireya Navarro, "Fracking Water Killed Trees, Study Finds," *New York Times*, July 12, 2011, http://green.blogs.nytimes.com/2011/07/12/fracking-water-killed-trees-study-finds.

157. Zack Needles, "Attorneys: Marcellus Shale Litigation Sure to Boom," *Pittsburgh Post-Gazette*, April 11, 2011, http://www.post-gazette.com/pg/11101/1138372–499.stm.

158. Jim Martin, "Why This Matters to Us Now," *Erie Times-News*, Erie, Pa., January 30, 2011, 7-A.

159. "Talisman Cited for Minor Gas-Well Blowout," *Bradford Era*, Bradford, Pa., January 26, 2011, A-7.

160. "DEP Investigating Feb. 23 Tank Fire in Independence Township, Washington County, PA," *Pittsburgh Post-Gazette*, March 2, 2011, http://www.post-gazette.com/pg/11061/1128965–503.stm.

161. Don Hopey, "State Asks Drillers to Use 'Best Practices' to Stem Fires," *Pittsburgh Post-Gazette*, April 2, 2011, http://www.post-gazette.com/pg/11092/1136526–503.stm.

162. Laura Olson, "State Ponders Penalties Over Drilling Site Mishap," *Pittsburgh Post-Gazette*, April 23, 2011, http://www.post-gazette.com/pg/11113/1141379–454.stm.

163. Frank D. Roylance, "Maryland Will Sue in Susquehanna Tributary 'Fracking' Spill," *The Baltimore Sun*, May 2, 2011, http://www.baltimoresun.com/features/green/bs-gr-fracking-suit-20110502,0,7352795.story.

164. Chesapeake Energy, "Chesapeake Energy To Resume Pennsylvania Well Completions," news release, May 13, 2011, http://www.chk.com/media/marcellusmediakits/pennsylvania_well_completions.pdf.

165. "DEP: No Damage From W. Pa. Drilling Water Spill," *Pressconnects.com*, November 1, 2011, http://www.pressconnects.com/article/20111101/NEWS11/111010329/DEP-No-damage-from-W-Pa-drilling-water-spill?odyssey=nav%7Chead.

166. Don Hopey, "Report: Well Drilling Violations Near 1,500 for Marcellus Shale," *Pittsburgh Post-Gazette*, August 3, 2010, http://www.post-gazette.com/pg/10215/1077192–454.stm.

167. Erich Schwartzel, "Pipeline Launches Pa. Permit and Violation Map," *Pipeline, Pittsburgh Post Gazette*, April 17, 2011, http://shale.sites.post-gazette.com/index.php/news/environment/23927.

168. Kris Maher, "More Oversight Sought for 'Fracking,'" *Wall Street Journal*, June 9, 2010, A-6.

169. Kathie O. Warco, "Fracking Truck Runs Off Road; Contents Spill," *Observer-Reporter*, Washington, Pa., October 21, 2010, http://www.observer-reporter.com/or/mostread/10–21–2010-fracking-truck-rolls.

170. "3,400 Gallons of Frack Water Spilled in Accident," *The Express*, Lockhaven, Pa., February 22, 2011, http://www.lockhaven.com/page/content.detail/id/529606/2–400-gallons-of-frack-water-spi; and "Fracking Fluid Spilled Onto Roadway in Pennsylvania Crash," Associated Press, *The Bradford Era*, December 28, 2011, p. A-9.

171. Sean D. Hamill, "Bradford County Shale Well Spews Fluids," April 21, 2011, *Pittsburgh Post-Gazette*, http://www.post-gazette.com/pg/11111/1140850–503.stm.

172. Michael Rubinkam, "EPA: Contamination in Water Wells Near Gas Blowout," *Titusville Herald*, June 25, 2011, A-1.

173. March Esch and Michael Rubinkam, "Lawsuit: Gas Drilling Fluid Ruined Pa. Water Wells," *The Buffalo News*, September 15, 2010, http://www.buffalonews.com/wire-feeds/24-hour-national-new/article191402.ece.

174. Marc Levy, "Pa. DEP Says Gas Drilling Didn't Sicken Woman," *Associated Press*, July 7, 2011, http://www.chron.com/disp/story.mpl/ap/tx/7643864.html.

175. "David Thompson, "Limiting Fracking Contamination," *Williamsport Sun Gazette*, October 18, 2011, http://www.sungazette.com/page/content.detail/id/555138/Limiting-fracking contamination.

176. Jeff Corcino, "Companies Develop Water Storage System for Gas Drilling," *The Progress*, Clearfield, Pa., April 2, 2011, http://www.theprogress-news.com/default.asp?read=26383.

177. Timothy Puko, "Pa. Requires Emergency Plans for Deep-Shale Wells; Specifics Not Spelled Out," *Pittsburgh Tribune-Review*, April 26, 2011, http://www.pittsburghlive.com/x/pittsburghtrib/news/pittsburgh/s_733986.html.

178. Donald Gilliland, "Receding Water Leaves Behind Mess of Mosquitoes, Waste and Nastiness," *The Patriot-News*, Harrisburg, Pa., September 15, 2011, http://www.pennlive.com/midstate/index.ssf/2011/09/receding_water_leaves_behind_m.html.

179. Conrad Volz, "The Devil's Details about Radioactive and Other Toxic Contaminants in Marcellus Shale Flowback Fluids," Center for Healthy Environments and Communities, March 2011.

180. Timothy Puko, "Public Water Safe from Radioactivity Throughout Region," *Pittsburgh Tribune-Review*, June 21, 2011, http://www.pittsburghlive.com/x/pittsburghtrib/news/pittsburgh/s_743117.html.

181. Don Hopey, "No Dangerous Radiation Found in Pa. Water, but EPA Urges More Radiation Checks," *Pittsburgh Post-Gazette*, March 8, 2011, http://www.post-gazette.com/pg/11067/1130460–455.stm.

182. Idem., "Bromide: A Concern in Drilling Wastewater," *Pittsburgh Post-Gazette*, March 13, 2011, http://www.post-gazette.com/pg/11072/1131660–113.stm.

183. "Study Looks at Water Quality in Private Wells Near Marcellus Drilling," Pennsylvania State University, news release, October 25, 2011, http://live.psu.edu/story/55987.

184. Don Hopey and Sean D. Hamill, "DEP asks Drillers to Stop Disposing Wastewater at Plants," *Pittsburgh Post-Gazette*, April 20, 2011, http://www.post-gazette.com/pg/11110/1140547–503–0.stm.

185. Timothy Puko, "Bromide Still High in Monongahela River, Scientists Say," *Pittsburgh Tribune-Review*, November 4, 2011, http://www.pittsburghlive.com/x/pittsburghtrib/news/pittsburgh/s_765457.html#ixzz1d2pyd0e7.

186. "Pa. Official Defends Rules on Gas Drilling Waste," *Wall Street Journal*, January 4, 2011, http://online.wsj.com/article/APfla0b0069bef43808fc2f7cde2cla7bb.html.

187. Jonathan D. Silver, "Company Accused of Illegal Dumping," *Pittsburgh Post-Gazette*, March 18, 2011, http://www.post-gazette.com/pg/11077/1132812–454.stm.

188. Josh Woods, "In DuBois ... Experts Offer Marcellus Facts," *The Progress*, Clearfield, Pa., August 7, 2010, http://theprogressnews.com/default.asp?read=23485.

189. Joe Napsha, "Private Firms Poised to Treat Wastewater," *Pittsburgh Tribune-Review*, May 19, 2011, http://www.pittsburghlive.com/x/pittsburghtrib/business/s_737873.html.

190. Ian Urbina, "Politics Seen to Limit E.P.A. as it Sets Rules for Natural Gas," *New York Times*, March 4, 2011, http://www.nytimes.com/2011/03/04/us/04gas.html.

191. Ryan Tracy, "EPA Chief Grilled on Safety of Hydraulic Fracturing," *Wall Street Journal*, March 3, 2011, online.wsj.com/article/SB1000142405274870330090457617878292959682282.html.

192. Daniel Malloy, "Some Water Treatment Plants Refuse to Take Fracking Fluid," *Pittsburgh Post-Gazette*, April 13, 201, http://www.post-gazette.com/pg/11103/1138930–84.stm.

193. Rodney L. Sherman, "Licking Township Marcellus Law Could Be First of its Kind," *Franklin News-Herald*, November 20, 2010, 3.

194. Brian Meyer, "Sewer Authority Affirms Ban on 'Frack Water,'" *The Buffalo News*, March 10, 2011, http://www.buffalonews.com/city/article363760.ece.

195. Yuliya Chernova, "In Fracking's Wake," *Wall Street Journal*, September 12, 2011, R-3.

196. "Expert Says Marcellus Drillers Reusing Two-Thirds of Water," *NGI Shale Daily*, March 23, 2011, http://shaledaily.com/news/sd20110323e.shtml.

197. Alison Griswold, "Siemens Has Developed a New Water Treatment System Designed to Handle Wastewater from Shale Drilling," *Pittsburgh Post-Gazette*, August 12, 2011, http://www.post-gazette.com/pg/11224/1166796–28.stm.

198. Andrew Maykuth, "Shale Drillers Tout Recycling as Option for Wastewater," *Philadelphia Inquirer*," March 23, 2011, http://www.philly.com/philly/news/pennsylvania/118485269.html.

199. Laura Legere, "EPA Releases Marcellus Drillers' Wastewater Plans," *The Republican-Herald*, Pottsville, Pa., July 7, 2011, http://republicanherald.com/news/epa-releases-marcellus-drillers-wastewater-plans-1.1171907.

200. Napsha. See note 187.

201. "Ohio Starts Taking Pa. Fracking Wastewater," *Times-Reporter*, Dover-New Philadelphia, Ohio, July 5, 2011, http://www.timesreporter.com/news/x230663762/Ohio-starts-taking-Pa-fracking-wastewater.

202. Spencer Hunt, "Ohio Taking in Flood of Pennsylvania's Toxic Brine for Disposal," *The Columbus Dispatch*, June 20, 2011, 1.

203. Bruce Siwy, "Gas Company Changes Drilling Process," *Daily American*, Somerset, Pa., December 6, 2010, http://www.dailyamerican.com/articles/2010/12/02/new/local/news098.prt.

204. Ben Casselman, "Firms See 'Green' in Natural-Gas Production," *Wall Street Journal*, March 30, 2010, B-7.

205. Brett Clanton, "Shale Drilling Is Going Greener," *Houston Chronicle*, December 18, 2010, http://www.chron.com/disp/story.mpl/business/energy/7345085.html.

206. Jeff McMahon, "New Material Scrubs Fracking Pollution, Energy Dept Says," May 2, 2011, http://www.netl.doe.gov/publications/press/2011/110429-Breakthrough%20Water%20Cleaning%20Technology.html.

207. Brian Nearing, "Shale Sites Studied for Emission Storage," *Albany Times Union*, August 21, 2010, http://www.timesunion.com/local/article/Shale-sites-studied-for-emission-storage-624397.

208. Mahendra K. Verma and Peter D. Warwick, (2011), "Development of an Assessment Methodology for Hydrocarbon Recovery Potential Using Carbon Dioxide and Associated Carbon Sequestration— Workshop Findings: U.S. Geological Survey Fact Sheet," 2011–3075, 2 p., http://pubs.usgs.gov/fs/2011/3075/.

209. Laura Legere, "Stray Gas Plagues NEPA Marcellus Wells," *The Times Tribune*, Scranton, Pa., July 10, 2011, http://thetimes-tribune.com/news/stray-gas-plagues-nepa-marcellus-wells-1.1173187.

210. Susan Phillips, "Study Finds Little Evidence of Water Contamination from Fracking," *State Impact, NPR*, October 25, 2011, http://stateimpact.npr.org/pennsylvania/2011/10/25/study-finds-little-evidence-of-water-contamination-from-fracking/.

211. "Pa. Orders 3 Gas Wells Near Explosion Site Plugged," *WHPT-TV*, April 8, 2011, http://www.whptv.com/news/state/story/Pa-orders-3-gas-wells-near-explosion-site-plugged/_5sFa5 — pUqT7Kjw5IWxUw.cspx, and "DEP: Since-Plugged 1881 Well Caused Bradford County House Blast," *Associated Press*, July 14, 2011, http://dailyitem.com/0100_news/x1424060645/DEP-Since-plugged-1881-well-caused-Bradford-County-house-blast.

212. Nicholas Kusnetz, "Danger in Honeycomb of Old Wells," *ProPublica*, Pittsburgh Post-Gazette, April 4, 2011, http://www.post-gazette.com/pg/11094/1136832–84.stm.

213. Gilliland, "WTF: What the Frack Is Hydraulic Fracturing?" See note 148.

214. Jack Z. Smith, "EPA E-Mail Stirs Call for Agency Documents on Range Resources Order," *Fort Worth Star Telegram*, Fort Worth, Tx., February 21, 2011, http://www.star-telegram.com/2011/02/21/2865261/epa-e-mail-stirs-call-for-agency-documents-on-range-resources-order.

215. Jack Z Smith, "Natural Gas in Parker County Water Wells not from Barnett Shale, Driller Says," *Fort Worth Star Telegram*, Fort Worth, Tx., January 18, 2011, http://www.star-telegram.com/2011/01/18/2778239/Natural-gas-in-Parker-County-water-wells-not-from-Barnett-Shale-driller-says, and Jack Z. Smith, "State Says Driller Not Responsible for Parker County Contamination," *Fort Worth Star Telegram*, March 22, 2011, http://www.star-telegram.com/2011/03/22/2942314/texas-railroad-commission-says.html.

216. Casey Junkins, "Methane Bubbling in Fish Creek," *The Intelligencer*, Wheeling, W.Va., October 17, 2010, http://www.theintelligencer.net/page/content.detail/id/547818/Methane-bubbling-in-fish-creek.

217. Stephen T. Watson, "In Collins, Effects of Gas Drilling are Debated," *Buffalo News*, October 18, 2010, http://www.buffalonews.com/city/article222843.ece.

218. Laura Legere, "Debate Over Proposed Dimock Waterline Divides Community," *The Times*

Tribune, Scranton, Pa., October 24, 2010, http://thetimes-tribune.com/news/debate-over-dimock-waterline-divides-community.

219. Tom Barnes, "Groups Rally for Marcellus Shale Gas Drilling Restrictions," *Pittsburgh Post Gazette*, September 22, 2010, http://www.post-gazette.com/pg/10265/1089281–454.stm.

220. Pennsylvania Department of Environmental Protection, "DEP Takes Aggressive Action Against Cabot Oil & Gas Corp to Enforce Environmental Laws Protect Public in Susquehanna County," news release, http://www.newsroom.dep.pa.us/newsroompublic/id=10586&typeid=1.

221. Laura Legere, "DEP Drops Dimock Waterline Plans; Cabot Agrees to Pay $4.1M to Residents," *The Times Tribune*, Scranton, Pa., December 16, 2010, http://thetimes-tribune.com/news/gas-drilling/dep-drops-dimock-waterline-plans-cabot-agrees-to-pay-$4.1M-to-residents.

222. Laura Legere, "Cabot Argues to Resume Drilling in Dimock as Tests Show Surges of Methane in Water Wells," *The Times Tribune*, Scranton, Pa., October 19, 2011, http://thetimes-tribune.com/news/gas-drilling/cabot-argues-to-resume-drilling-in-dimock-as-tests-show-surges-of-methane-in-water-wells-1.1220204.

223. Michael Rubinkam, "AP: State Regulators Will Allow Cabot to Stop Delivering Replacement Water to Dimock Residents," *Pipeline, Pittsburgh Post-Gazette*, October 19, 2011, http://shale.sites.post-gazette.com/index.php/news/environment/24135.

224. David Thompson, "5 Water Wells, Stream Contaminated by Methane," *Williamsport Sun-Gazette*, June 16, 2011, http://www.sungazette.com/page/content.detail/id/565249/5-water-wells—stream-contaminated-by-methane.html.

225. Marianne Lavelle, "A Dream Dashed by the Rush on Gas," *National Geographic News*, October 17, 2010, http//news/nationalgeographic.com/news//2010/10/101022-energy-marcellus-shale-gas-environment.

226. Don Hopey and Laura Olson, "Study Links Fouled Water, Methane," *Pittsburgh Post-Gazette*, May 10, 2011, http://www.post-gazette.com/pg/11130/1145418–113.stm.

227. "Study Looks at Water Quality in Private Wells Near Marcellus Drilling." See note 183.

228. David Templeton, "Region Gets an 'F' for Pollution," *Pittsburgh Post-Gazette*, April 27, 2011, http://www.post-gazette.com/pg/11117/1142145–113.stm.

229. David Templeton and Don Hopey, "Air Pollution Called Unacceptable," *Pittsburgh Post-Gazette*, March 10, 2011, http://www.post-gazette.com/pg/11069/1130959–113.stm.

230. David Templeton, "EPA's New Rule Will Cut Pollution," *Pittsburgh Post-Gazette*, July 8, 2011, http://www.post-gazette.com/pg/11189/1158981–454.stm.

231. Ben Casselman, "Gas Sites Spur Air Worries," *Wall Street Journal*, February 4, 2010, http://online/wsj.com/article/SB10001424052748703575004575043654062770726.html and Natural Gas Air Quality Study (Fort Worth), July 14, 2011, http://www.fortworthgov.org/uploadedFiles/Gas_Wells/ERGReport_section8.pdf.

232. Susan Schrock, "Gas Drilling's Impact on Air Quality Debated at Arlington Hearing," *Fort Worth Star Telegram*, Fort Worth, Tx., July 14, 2011, http://www.star-telegram.com/2011/07/14/3222751/gas-drillings-impact-on-air-quality.html.

233. Don Hopey, "State Study Shows No Hazard in Shale Well Air Emissions," *Pittsburgh Post-Gazette*, May 20, 2011, http://www.post-gazette.com/pg/11140/1147855–113.stm.

234. Robert W. Howart, Renee Santoro, and Anthony Ingraffea, "Methane and the Greenhouse-Gas Footprint of Natural Gas from Shale Formations," *Climatic Change*, (March 2011), http://graphics8.nytimes.com/images/blogs/greeninc/Howarth2011.pdf.

235. Tom Zeller, Jr., "Studies Say Natural Gas Has Its Own Environmental Problems," *New York Times*, April 11, 2011, http://www.nytimes.com/2011/04/12/business/energy-environment/12gas.html; and Steve Reilly, "Cornell Studies Diverge on Impact of Drilling," *Elmira Star-Gazette*, January 11, 2012, p. 5.

236. Mohan Jiang, W Michael Griffin, Chris Hendrickson, Paulina Jaramillo, Jeanne VanBriesen and Aranya Venkatesh, "Life Cycle Greenhouse Gas Emissions of Marcellus Shale Gas," *Environmental Research Letter* 6 (July-September 2011), http://iopscience.iop.org/1748–9326/6/3/034014/fulltext.

237. Don Hopey, "EPA Proposes New Emissions Rules July 29, 2011," *Pittsburgh Post-Gazette*, http://www.post-gazette.com/pg/11210/1163671–113–0.stm.

238. Steve Hargreaves, "Gas Boom Catches Community Off Guard," *CNN*, October 26, 2010, http://money.cnn.com/2010/10/07/news/economy/penn_boomtown/index.htm.

239. Mark Maroney, "Gas Drilling Leads to Congestion on Rural Roads Across Region," *Williamsport Sun-Gazette*, June 12, 2011, http://www.sungazette.com/page/content.detail/id/565101/Gas-drilling-leads-to-congestion-on-rural-roads-across-region.html.

240. PA Department of Environmental Protection, "State Enforcement Blitz Focuses on Trucks Hauling Drilling Waste Water," news release, June 23, 2010.

241. "Gas-drilling Industry has a Truck Problem," *Observer-Reporter*, Washington, Pa., April 7, 2011, http://www.observer-reporter.com/or/editorial/04–07–2011-FRACK-TRUCK-EDITORIAL.

242. Keri Brown, "Gas Industry Making Changes in Marcellus Drilling Practices," *West Virginia Public Broadcasting*, May 27, 2011, http://www.wvpubcast.org/newsarticle.aspx?id=20329.

243. Andrew Maykuth, "Study: Shale Drillers Invested $411M in Pa.," *Philadelphia Inquirer*, June 21, 2011, http://articles.philly.com/2011–06–21/news/29683935_1_shale-drillers-local-roads-state-roads.

244. Brad Bumsted and Andrew Conte, "Natural Gas Drillers' Damage to Roads Debated," *Pittsburgh Tribune-Review*, December 29, 2010, http://www.pittsburghlive.com/x/pittsburghtrib/news/regional/715701.html.

245. Casey Junkins, "Chesapeake to Spend Millions Fixing Roads," *The Intelligencer/Wheeling News-Register*, Wheeling, W.Va., July 6, 2011, http://www.theintelligencer.net/page/content.detail/id/556855/Chesapeake-to-Spend-Millions-Fixing-Roads.html, and Casey Junkins, "Traffic Upsets Dallas Residents,"

The Intelligencer / Wheeling News-Register, Wheeling, W. Va., April 21, 2011, http://www.news-register.net/page/content.detail/id/554280/Traffic-Upsets-Dallas-Residents.html.

246. Scott Detrow, "Emergency Services Stretched in Pennsylvania's Top Drilling Counties," July 11, 2011, http://stateimpact.npr.org/pennsylvania/2011/07/11/emergency-services-stretched-in-pennsylvania%E2%80%99s-top-drilling-counties/.

247. "Towns See Crime, Carousing Surge Amid Gas Boom," *Wall Street Journal*, October 26, 2011, http://online.wsj.com/article/APd45605d59dd0499fbd3851c4683c12c7.html.

248. Dave Fredley & Dave Wright, "Cooperation urged for drilling," *Erie Daily Times*, Erie, Pa., February 8, 2010, B-1.

249. Marianne Lavelle, "Parks, Forests Eyed for the Fuel Beneath," *National Geographic News*, October 17, 2010, http://news.nationalgeographic.com/news/2010/10/101022-energy-marcellus-shale-gas-parks-forests/.

250. Amy Worden and Angela Couloumbis, "Sierra Club Tells National Park Service that Pa. Is Violating Law by Allowing Gas Drilling," *Philadelphia Inquirer*, July 7, 2011, http://articles.philly.com/2011-07-07/news/29747278_1_gas-drilling-marcellus-shale-state-parks.

251. "OK to Drill in Pa. Forest, Court Rules," *United Press International*, September 22, 2011, http://www.upi.com/Business_News/Energy-Resources/2011/09/22/OK-to-drill-in-Pa-forest-court-rules/UPI-16031316686411/.

252. Marc Levy, "Five Firms Submit High Bids for Gas Drilling in Pa.," *Pittsburgh Post-Gazette*, January 13, 2010, http://www.post-gazette.com/pg/10013/1027833-100.stm.

253. Governor's Marcellus Shale Advisory Commission, 35. See note 16.

254. "Fish and Boat Commission to Sell Gas Leases," *Franklin News Herald*, Franklin, Pa., July 12, 2011, A-7.

255. Ibid.

256. Laura Olson, "Allow Gas Drilling Near Prisons and Colleges, Report Says," *Pittsburgh Post-Gazette*, October 19, 2011, http://www.post-gazette.com/pg/11292/1183221-100.stm.

257. Steve Szkotak, "George Washington National Forest Plan Would Limit Drilling, Consider Wind Energy," *Greenfield Reporter*, May 18, 2011, http://www.greenfieldreporter.com/view/story/2dfae48a12234a95b573b9b2f61db753/VA—Washington-National-Forest/.

258. Elizabeth Svoboda, "The Hard Facts About Fracking," *Popular Mechanics*, http://www.popularmechanics.com/science/energy/col-oil-gas/the-hard-facts-about-fracking.

259. "U.K. Fracking Halted After Earthquakes," *United Press International*, June 3, 2011, http://www.upi.com/Science_News/2011/06/03/UK-fracking-halted-after-earthquakes/UPI-21541307144514/.

260. Keith Johnson, "Drilling, Quakes Might be Linked," *Wall Street Journal*, March 11, 2010, A-6.

261. Spencer Hunt, "Disposal Wells a Possible Cause of Small Quakes," *The Columbus Dispatch*, March 21, 2011, http://www.dispatch.com/live/content/local_news/stories/2011/03/21/disposal-wells-a-possible-cause-of-small-quakes.html.

262. "Geologists Eye New Well After 7 Quakes in Northeast Ohio," Associated Press, *Zanesville Times Recorder*, November 1, 2011, http://www.zanesvilletimesrecorder.com/article/20111101/NEWS01/111010313.

263. Casey Junkins, "Proof Not There: Prof: Drilling, Earthquakes Not Connected," *Wheeling News-Register*, Wheeling, W.Va., April 3, 2011, http://www.news-register.net/page/content.detail/id/553713/Proof-Not-There—Prof—Drilling—Earthquakes-Not-Connected.html.

264. Donald Gilliland, "Marcellus Shale Drilling to Blame for Virginia Earthquake? No Fracking Way, Industry Officials Say," *Harrisburg Patriot News*, August 23, 2011, http://www.pennlive.com/midstate/index.ssf/2011/08/marcellus_shale_drilling_to_bl.html.

265. Jonathan Fahey and Seth Borenstein, "Experts: Okla. Quakes Too Powerful to Be Man-Made," *Associated Press*, November 7, 2011, http://hosted2.ap.org/APDEFAULT/3d281c11a96b4ad082fe88aa0db04305/Article_2011-11-07-Quake%20Drilling/id-6ce5fd8f9e1e4f85b2e1d9eaf9fb3f8d.

266. Steve Orr, "Activists Gather at Cobbs Hill to Protest Hydraulic Fracturing," *Rochester Democrat and Chronicle*, November 10, 2010, http://www.democratandchronicle.com/fdcp/?1289414103435.

267. David Hurst, "SEIU Picket Location Incorrect," *The Altoona Mirror*, May 24, 2011, http://www.altoonamirror.com/page/content.detail/id/550447/SEIU-picket-location-incorrect.html.

268. "Bogus Signs Suggest Testing Pa. Water with Fire," *The Kane Republican*, Kane, Pa., June 28, 2011, 5.

269. Ben Wolfgang, "'Fracking' Term is the Pits for Public Relations Pros," *The Washington Times*, September 20, 2011, http://www.washingtontimes.com/news/2011/sep/20/fracking-term-is-the-pits-for-public-relations-pro/.

270. Andrew Maykuth, "Strong Positions on Either Side of 'Fracking,' at EPA Hearing," *Philadelphia Inquirer*, September 14, 2010, 1.

271. George Hohmann, "Natural Gas Industry Buys Ads to Tell its Story," *Charleston Daily Mail*, Charleston, W.Va., http://dailymail.com/Business/201010191232.

272. Erich Schwartzel, "Gas Driller Halts Distribution of Coloring Book," *Pittsburgh Post-Gazette*, July 14, 2011, http://www.post-gazette.com/pg/11195/1160429-100.stm.

273. George Hofmann, "Expert Says Development of Marcellus Shale Fields Offers Huge Benefits," *Charleston Daily Mail*, Charleston, W.Va., November 9, 2010, http://www.dailymail.com/Business/201011081161.

274. "Modern Shale Gas Development in the United States: A Primer," ES 3. See note 122.

275. Robert Swift, "Natural Gas Industry Spent $3.5M on Lobbying in 2010," *The Times-Tribune*, Scranton, Pa., July 3, 2011, http://thetimes-tribune.com/news/natural-gas-industry-spent-3-5m-on-lobbying-in-2010-1.1170483.

276. Donald Gilliland, "DEP to Make Gas wells Near High Quality Streams Go Through Full Permit-

ting Process," *The Patriot-News*, Harrisburg, Pa., July 7, 2011, http://www.pennlive.com/midstate/index. ssf/2011/07/dep_to_make_gas_wells_near_hig.html.

277. Citizens Marcellus Gas Commission, "Marcellus Gas, A Citizens View," http://pennbpc.org/ sites/pennbpc.org/files/CMSC-Final-Report.pdf.

278. Elizabeth Skrapits, "Court Ruling Affirms Communities' Ability to Limit Natural Gas Drilling," *Citizens Voice.com*, Wilkes Barre, Pa., August 23, 2010, http://citizensvoice.com/news/court-ruling-affirms-communities-ability-to-limit-natural-gas-drilling.

279. Zack Needles, "Local Drilling Bans Raise Concerns, Energy Lawyers Say," *The Legal Intelligencer*, Pittsburgh Post Gazette, December 27, 2010, http://www.post-gazette.com/pg/10361/1113038–499. stm.

280. Jon Hurter, "Philadelphia Utility Asked to Avoid Marcellus Gas," *Reuters*, January 20, 2011, http://af.reuters.com/articleID=AFN1926926920110120.

281. Don Hopey," Range Resources, Mount Pleasant Township at Odds Over Well Sites," *Pittsburgh Post-Gazette*, April 6, 2011, http://www.post-gazette. com/pg/11096/1137242–454.stm.

282. "Chesapeake Energy Withdraws Morgantown Donation," *The State Journal*, Charleston, W.Va., September 1, 2011, http://www.statejournal. com/story.cfm?func=viewstory&storyid=106667.

283. Kris Maher, "New Challenges to Gas Drilling," *Wall Street Journal*, September 12, 2011, A-3.

284. Warren Scott, "Drilling Ban May Not Last Long For Wellsburg," *The Intelligencer/Wheeling News-Register*, Wheeling, W.Va., July 20, 2011, http:// www.theintelligencer.net/page/content.detail/id/557 226/Drilling-Ban-May-Not-Last-Long-For-Wellsburg.html.

285. Joe Smydo, "Pittsburgh Moves Ahead with Controversial Gas Drilling Ban," *Pittsburgh Post-Gazette*, November 10, 2010, http://www.post-gazette.com/pg/10314/1101992–53.stm.

286. Jacquelyn Pless, "Fracking Update: What States Are Doing to Insure Safe Natural Gas Extraction," *National Conference of State Legislatures*, http://www.ncsl.org/default.aspx?tabid=23224.

287. Ry Rivard, "Tomblin to Unveil Emergency Fracking Rules," *Charleston Daily Mail*, Charleston, W.Va., July 12, 2011, http://www.dailymail.com/ News/201107111188.

288. "Ohio Governor Expected to Allow Drilling in Parks," *Associated Press*, June 21, 2011, http:// www.forbes.com/feeds/ap/2011/06/21/business-us-state-park-drilling-ohio_8527526.html.

289. "Editorial: To Drill — Shale Gas Deposits Offer N.C. Energy Potential," *Fayetteville Observer*, Fayetteville, N.C., May 27, 2011, http://www.fayobserver.com/articles/2011/05/27/1097252.

290. Rose Ellen O'Connor, "North Carolina Moves Closer to Fracking," *Reuters*, June 7, 2011, http://www.reuters.com/article/2011/06/07/idUS294 056914520110607.

291. Brad Bumsted, "Poll: Pennsylvania Voters Say, 'Drill, Baby, Drill,'" *Pittsburgh Tribune-Review*, June 14, 2011, http://www.pittsburghlive.com/x/pittsburghtrib/news/breaking/s_742047.html.

292. Laura Legere, "Survey Shows Pa. Residents Concerned About Fracking," *Citizensvoice.com*, Wilkes Barre, Pa., December 22, 2010, http://citizensvoice.com/news/dirlling/survey-shows-pa-residents-concerned-about-fracking, and "New York Voters Back Fracking, Despite Concerns, Quinnipiac University Poll Finds," August 11, 2011, Quinnipiac University, news release, http://www.quinnipiac. edu/x1318.xml.

293. Steve Reilly, "Natural Gas Drilling in N.Y. Falls 20%," *Democrat and Chronicle*, Rochester, N.Y., July 19, 2011, http://www.democratandchronicle. com/article/20110719/BUSINESS/110719004/Natural-gas-drilling-N-Y-falls-20-?odyssey=mod|newswell |text|Home|s.

294. David Robinson, "Proposal Would Allow 'Fracking' in State," *The Buffalo News*, July 1, 2011, http://www.buffalonews.com/incoming/article474257.ece.

295. Mireya Navarro, "Latest Drilling Rules Draw Objections," *New York Times*, July 14, 2011 http:// www.nytimes.com/2011/07/15/science/earth/15frack. html.

296. Steve Reilly, "Drillers Target Three Counties in Southern Tier," *Binghamton Press & Sun-Bulletin*, Binghamton, N.Y., August 9, 2011, http://www. democratandchronicle.com/article/20110809/BUSINESS/108090311.

297. Darryl Fears, "Sitting Atop Huge Gas Reserve, Maryland Debates Drilling Practice Known as Fracking," *The Washington Post*, March 27, 2011, http://www.washingtonpost.com/national/sitting-atop-huge-gas-reserve-maryland-debates-drilling-practice-known-as-fracking/2011/03/22/AFDuInkB_singlePage.html.

298. Jim Efstathiou Jr., "New Jersey Lawmakers Send Christie Ban on Hydraulic Fracturing," *Bloomberg*, June 30, 2011, http://www.bloomberg.com/ news/2011–06–30/new-jersey-lawmakers-send-christie-ban-on-hydraulic-fracturing.html.

299. Sandy Bauers, "Gov. Christie Vetoes Fracking Ban, Calls for One-Year Moratorium Instead," *Philadelphia Inquirer*, August 26, 2011, http://www. philly.com/philly/health_and_science/128431568. html.

300. Andrew Maykuth, "Marcellus Shale Dispute Bubbling Up in Northeast Pennsylvania," *Philadelphia Inquirer*, July 4, 2010, 1.

301. Susan Phillips, "In Anticipation of the End of Northeast Pa.'s Drilling Moratorium, Regulators Rush to Collect Water Samples," *NPR*, October 11, 2011, http://stateimpact.npr.org/pennsylvania/2011/ 10/11/in-anticipation-of-the-end-of-northeast-pas-drilling-moratorium-regulators-rush-to-collect-water-samples/.

302. "The Facts About Fracking," *Wall Street Journal*, June 25, 2011, http://online.wsj.com/article/ SB10001424052702303936704576398462932810874. html.

303. Environmental Protection Agency, "EPA Selects Colorado, North Dakota Sites as Case Study Locations for National Hydraulic Fracturing Study," news release, June 23, 2011, http://www.epa.gov/ hydraulicfracturing.

304. "The SEAB Shale Gas Production Subcommittee Ninety-Day Report," *Pittsburgh Post-Gazette*, August 11, 2011, http://www.post-gazette.com/pg/ pdf/201108/20110811_shalereport.pdf.

305. Deborah Solomon, "SEC Bears Down on Fracking," *Wall Street Journal*, August 25, 2011, B-1.

306. Paula Dittrick, "Shale Gas Subcommittee Says States Regulate Effectively," Oil and Gas Journal, October 10, 2011, http://www.ogj.com/articles/print/volume-109/issue-41/general-interest/shale-gas-subcommittee-says.html.

307. Also signing the petition were the National Parks Conservation Association, the Appalachian Center for the Economy and the Environment, the Chesapeake Climate Action Network, the Shenandoah Valley Network, the Foundation for Pennsylvania Watersheds, Damascus Citizens for Sustainability, and Friends of the Upper Delaware River.

308. Laura Legere, "Comments on DRBC Drilling Rules Show State and Federal Agencies Divided on Oversight," *The Times Tribune*, Scranton, Pa., July 13, 2011, http://thetimes-tribune.com/news/comments-on-drbc-drilling-rules-show-state-and-federal-agencies-divided-on-oversight-1.1174736.

309. Laura Olson and David Templeton, "EPA to Control Fracking Fluids Disposal," *Pittsburgh Post-Gazette*, October 21, 2011, http://www.post-gazette.com/pg/11294/1183693–113.stm.

310. Cliff White, "Environmental impact unknown," *Centre Daily Times*, State College, Pa., February 10, 2011, State College, Pa., http://centredaily.com/2011/02/10/2512336/environmental-impact-unknown and Kevin Begos, "Sportsmen monitor gas drilling in Marcellus Shale," *Associated Press*, http://www.google.com/hostednews/ap/article/ALeqM5jZCpOSdlSNIwVU5sN5dm96EnD-OQ.

311. "Local Business Impacts of Marcellus Shale Development: The Experience in Bradford and Washington Counties, 2010," Penn State University, May 26, 2011, http://pubs.cas.psu.edu/freepubs/pdfs/ee0005.pdf.

312. Nicolas Van Praet, "Quebec Moratorium Leaves Shale Gas Drillers Staggering," *Financial Post*, June 30, 2011, http://business.financialpost.com/2011/07/01/quebec-moratorium-leaves-shale-gas-drillers-staggering/.

313. Guy Chazan, "U.K. Panel: No Water Risk from 'Fracking,'" *Wall Street Journal*, May 23, 2011, http://online.wsj.com/article/SB10001424052702304520804576341523478732238.html.

314. "French Senate Adopts Bill Banning Shale Oil, Gas Drilling," *Platts*, Houston, Tx., June 10, 2011, http://www.platts.com/RSSFeedDetailedNews/RSSFeed/NaturalGas/8984492.

315. Ken Costello, "Hydraulic Fracturing: Placing What We Know Today in Perspective," *The National Regulatory Research Institute*, October 16, 2011, 30–31, http://www.nrri.org/pubs/gas/NRRI_Hydraulic_Fracturing_Oct11–16.pdf.

316. Timothy J. Considine, "The Economic Impacts of the Marcellus Shale: Implications for New York, Pennsylvania, and West Virginia: A Report to The American Petroleum Institute," June 2010, iv, http://marcelluscoalition.org/wp-content/uploads/2010/09/API-Economic-Impacts-Marcellus-Shale.pdf.

317. Laura Olson and Tracie Mauriello, "Corbett Ignores Opinion Polls," *Pittsburgh Post-Gazette*, March 18, 2011, http://www.post-gazette.com/pg/11077/1132871–454.stm.

318. Bumsted. See note 291.

319. Sean Hamill, "Pennsylvania's Tax Level for Shale Drilling Sparks Debate," *Pittsburgh Post-Gazette*, September 27, 2010, http://www.post-gazette.com/pg/10270/1090615–454.stm.

320. "The Marcellus Money," *West Virginia MetroNews*, July 18, 2011, http://www.wvmetronews.com/news.cfm?func=displayfullstory&storyid=46620.

321. Ry Rivard, "Report Warns of State's Gas Fees Research Finds Lower Production Taxes in Most Surrounding States, Including Pennsylvania," *Charleston Daily Mail*, Charleston, W.Va., October 18, 2011, http://www.dailymail.com/News/statenews/201110170215.

322. Taylor Kuykendall, "State Lawmakers Keeping an Eye on Other States' Policies," *Register-Herald*, Beckley, W.Va., http://www.register-herald.com/todaysfrontpage/x186201530/State-lawmakers-keeping-an-eye-on-other-states-policies.

323. James Loewenstein, "Talisman: Severance Tax Would Make Drilling "Uneconomical," *Daily Review*, Towanda, Pa., September 19, 2010, http://thedailyreview.com/news/talisman-severance-tax-would-make-drilling-uneconomical.

324. Andrew Maykuth, "Rendell Signals Flexibility on Tax," *Philadelphia Inquirer*, May 2, 2010, 1.

325. Timothy Puko, "EQT Stands Firm on Shale-Drilling Tax," *Pittsburgh Tribune-Review*, May 11, 2011, http://www.pittsburghlive.com/x/pittsburghtrib/business/s_736391.html

326. Marc Levy and Kevin Begos, "Pa. Would Let Counties Set Gas Drilling Fees," *Erie Times-News*, October 4, 2011, 1.

327. Pennsylvania Department of Revenue, "Tax Payments in First Quarter of 2011 Already Surpass 2010 Totals," news release, May 1, 2011, http://www.prnewswire.com/news-releases/drilling-industry-paid-more-than-1-billion-in-pennsylvania-state-taxes-since-2006–121110909.html.

328. Kari Andren, "Gov. Tom Corbett Says Pennsylvania Gets Tens of Millions in Revenue from Marcellus Shale Without a Severance Tax," *The Patriot-News*, Harrisburg, Pa., March 29, 2011, http://www.pennlive.com/midstate/index.ssf/2011/03/gov_tom_corbett_says_pennsylva.html.

329. Penn State Cooperative Extension, "State Tax Implications of Marcellus Shale: What the Pennsylvania Data Say in 2010," http://pubs.cas.psu.edu/FreePubs/pdfs/ua468.pdf.

330. James Loewenstein, "Data Released on Economic Impacts of Marcellus Drilling in Bradford County," *The Daily Review*, Towanda, Pa., April 19, 2011, http://thedailyreview.com/news/data-released-on-economic-impacts-of-marcellus-drilling-in-bradford-county-1.1134262.

331. Jack Z. Smith "Report: Barnett Shale Added $65.4 Billion to Regional Economy in a Decade," *Fort Worth Star-Telegram*, Fort Worth, Tx., September 27, 2011, http://www.star-telegram.com/2011/09/27/3401934/report-barnett-shale-added-654.html.

332. Weaver. See note 54.

333. Ibid.

334. Ian Urbina, "Rush to Drill for Natural Gas Creates Conflicts With Mortgages," *New York Times*,

October 19, 2011, http://www.nytimes.com/2011/10/
20/us/rush-to-drill-for-gas-creates-mortgage-
conflicts.html.

335. Alyssa Murphy, "City 7th Fastest Growing in
Nation," *Sun-Gazette*, Williamsport, Pa., September
24, 2011, http://www.sungazette.com/page/content.
detail/id/568934/City-7th-fas.

336. "Shell Expands Marcellus Office," *Pittsburgh
Business Times*, http://www.bizjournals.com/pitts
burgh/print-edition/2011/04/29/shell-expands-mar
cellus-office.html.

337. Timothy Puko and Rick Wills, "Energy Sector
Fuels Jobs Surge in Western Pennsylvania," *Pittsburgh
Tribune-Review*, October 1, 2011, http://www.pitts
burghlive.com/x/pittsburghtrib/business/s_759681.
html.

338. Donald Gilliland, "Marcellus Shale Drilling
Creates 48,000 Jobs, Report Says," *The Patriot-News*,
Harrisburg, Pa., May 29, 2011, http://www.pennlive.
com/midstate/index.ssf/2011/05/marcellus_shale_
drilling_creat.html.

339. Pennsylvania Department of Labor and
Industry, Center for Workforce Information & Analysis, "Marcellus Shale Industry Snapshot Update,"
http://www.paworkstats.state.pa.us/admin/gsipub/
htmlarea/uploads/Marcellus_Shale_Snapshot_Update
_v5.pdf.

340. Joe Napsha, "Drilling Generates 48,000 Jobs,"
Pittsburgh Tribune-Review, June 3, 2011, http://www.
pittsburghlive.com/x/pittsburghtrib/business/s_7401
88.html.

341. "Marcellus Shale Industry Snapshot Update."
See note 339.

342. James Loewenstein, "Data Released on Economic Impacts of Marcellus Drilling in Bradford
County," *The Daily Review*, Towanda, Pa., April 19,
2011, http://thedailyreview.com/news/data-released-
on-economic-impacts-of-marcellus-drilling-in-
bradford-county-1.1134262.

343. Marcellus Shale Education & Training Center
(MSETC), Pennsylvania Statewide Marcellus Shale
Workforce Needs Assessment (June 2011), 7, http://
www.msetc.org/docs/StatewideWorkforceNeeds
Assessment.pdf.

344. Sean D. Hamill, "Scope of Job Creation a
Matter of Conjecture," *Pittsburgh Post-Gazette*, February 28, 2011, http://shale.sites.post-gazette.com/
index.php/business/23885.

345. "Pennsylvania Statewide Marcellus Shale
Workforce Needs Assessment." See note 343.

346. "PA workers finding a future in gas drilling,"
Ridgway Record, Ridgway, Pa., February 7, 2011, A-1.

347. Genaro C. Armas, "In north-central Pa.,
hope for more jobs from gas," *Pottstown Mercury*,
Pottstown, Pa., March 19, 2010, http://pottsmerc.
com/articles/2010/03/19/business/doc4ba39bf9304e3
025370246.prt.

348. Marianne Lavelle, "A Drive for New Jobs
Through Energy," *National Geographic News*, October 14, 2010, http://news.nationalgeographic.com/
news/2010/10/101022-energy-marcellus-shale-jobs.

349. Steve Mocarsky, "Gas Workers get to know
drill," *Times Leader*, Wilkes-Barre, Pa., November 21,
2010, 1.

350. Laura Legere, "Gas Drilling Having Substantial, and Sometimes Surprising, Economic Impact,"
Times Tribune, Scranton, Pa., April 25, 2010, http://
thetimes-tribune.com/news/business/gas-drilling-
having-substantial-and-sometimes-surprising-eco
nomic-impact.

351. Timothy J. Considine, Robert Watson, and
Seth Blumsack, "The Pennsylvania Marcellus Shale
Industry: Status, Economic Impact and Future Potential," July 20, 2011. The Pennsylvania State University College of Earth and Mineral Sciences,
Department of Engineering and Mineral Engineering, http://eidmarcellus.org/wp-content/uploads/
2011/07/Final-2011-PA-Marcellus-Economic-Im
pacts.pdf.

352. "Musing: Marcellus Impact Study Rests on
Some Shaky Assumptions," Parks Paton Hoepfl and
Brown, August 3, 2011, http://www.rigzone.com/
news/article.asp?a_id=109752.

353. Kathryn Klaber, "'Marcellus Multiplier'
Could Spark Economic Revival in Pennsylvania,"
Scranton Times, Scranton, Pa., August 7, 2010, http://
cts/vresp.com/c/?MarcellulsShaleCoalit/08899145f3/
8533e30b67/86a8d4d0b9.

354. "Local Business Impacts of Marcellus Shale
Development: The Experience in Bradford and
Washington Counties, 2010," Penn State University.

355. Patrick Sweet, "Gas Officials: Industry Will
Stimulate Local Economy," *Standard Speaker*, Hazel-
ton, Pa., June 23, 2010, http://standardspeaker.
com/news/gas-officials-industry-will-stimulate-
local-economy-1.860.

356. Vicki Smith, "WVU study: Marcellus Drilling
a Boon to Economy," *Associated Press*, January 25,
2011. http://www.pressconnects.com/article/20110
125/NEWS11/110125012/WVU-study-Marcellus-
drilling-boon-economy.

357. Ashley Rittenhouse, "Study Estimates Value
of Area's Oil, Gas Boom," *The Marietta Times*,
Marietta, Ohio, September 22, 2011, http://www.
mariettatimes.com/page/content.detail/id/538808/
Study-estimates-value-of-area-s-oil — gas-boom.
html.

358. Joe Napsha, "Lawmaker: Gas Industry Should
Be Able to Police Itself," *Pittsburgh Tribune-Review*,
May 24, 2011, http://www.pittsburghlive.com/x/
pittsburghtrib/business/s_738568.html.

359. Bill Toland, "In Youngstown, an Old Plant
Gets New Life Making Pipe for Natural Gas," *Pittsburgh Post-Gazette*, April 17, 2011, http://www.post-
gazette.com/pg/11107/1139959–503–0.stm.

360. Larry Ringler, "Report: We're No. 3 for Jobs
Finds Valley Saw Healthy Job Growth in Last Year,"
Tribune Chronicle, Warren, Ohio, April 29, 2011,
http://www.tribtoday.com/page/content.detail/id/55
6220/Report — We-re-No — 3-for-jobs.html.

361. American Petroleum Institute, "New Study
Finds Natural Gas in Marcellus Shale Region Worth
280,000 Jobs, $6 Billion in Government Revenue,"
http://www.api.org/policy/exploration/hydraulic
fracturing/upload/API%20Economic%20Impacts%
20Marcellus%20Shale.pdf.

362. Jon Campbell, "Report: Lift of Fracking Ban
Would Generate $11.4B for N.Y. by 2020," June 7,
2011, http://www.pressconnects.com/article/20110
607/NEWS10/106070361/Report-Lift-fracking-ban-
would-generate-11–4B-N-Y-by-2020.

363. Mireya Navarro, "Report Outlines Rewards

and Risks of Upstate Natural Gas Drilling," *New York Times*, September 7, 2011, http://www.nytimes.com/2011/09/08/nyregion/albany-study-shows-hydro frackings-risks-and-rewards.html.

364. Tom Fowler, "Stubborn in His Vision: Mitchell's Persistence Laid Groundwork for Shale Gas Surge," *Houston Chronicle*, November 14, 2009, http://www.chron.com/disp/story.mpl/business/energy/6720223.html.

365. Andrew Maykuth, "Penn State Report Even More Bullish on Marcellus Shale," *Philadelphia Inquirer*, July 20, 2011, http://www.philly.com/philly/news/20110720_Penn_State_report_even_more_bullish_on_Marcellus_Shale.html.

366. Elizabeth Skrapits, "UGI Says Region Will Be First to Go All-Marcellus," *The Times Tribune*, Scranton, Pa., August 22, 2011, http://thetimes-tribune.com/news/gas-drilling/ugi-says-region-will-be-first-to-go-all-marcellus-1.1191676.

367. American Gas Association, "The Positive Natural Gas Supply Situation Benefits Consumers—A Look at January, 2001," http://www.aga.org/Kc/analyses-and-statistics/studies/demand/Documents/EA1102Positive-Gas-Supply-Situation-Benefits-Consumers.pdf.

368. Kim Leonard, "Drillers Set Sights on Shale Reserve Deeper Than the Marcellus," *Pittsburgh Tribune-Review*, February 22, 2011, http://www.pittsburghlive.com/x/pittsburghtrib/news/print_724034.html.

369. "Not All Holes Are Equal," *The Montreal Gazette*, September 27, 2010, http://www.montreal-gazette.com/3583600/story.html.

370. Monique Muise, "A Guide to Quebec's Shale Gas Controversy," *The Montreal Gazette*, http://www.montrealgazette.com/story_print.html?id=3564310.

371. Nicolas Van Praet, "Quebec Moratorium Leaves Shale Gas Drillers Staggering," *Financial Post*, June 30, 2011, http://business.financialpost.com/2011/07/01/quebec-moratorium-leaves-shale-gas-drillers-staggering/.

372. Steve Bennish, "Investments Show Ohio Could Be Part of Oil Boom," *Dayton Daily News*, March 13, 2011, http://www.daytondailynews.com/news/dayton-news/investments-show-ohio-could-be-part-of-oil-boom-1106812.html.

373. Russ Zimmer, "Ohio's Shale Deposits Hold Potential for Oil, Gas, Jobs," *Zanesville Times-Recorder*, Zanesville, Ohio, April 17, 2011, http://www.zanesvilletimesrecorder.com/article/20110417/NEWS01/104170304/1002/Ohio-Legislature-OKs-Senate-Bill-5/Ohio-s-shale-deposits-hold-potential-oil-gas-jobs.

374. "McClendon Values Utica Shale at Half a Trillion Dollars, NGI Reports," *Wall Street Journal*, September 21, 2011, http://www.marketwatch.com/story/mcclendon-values-utica-shale-at-half-a-trillion-dollars-ngi-reports-2011-09-21.

375. "Consol: Utica Shale Field Worthy of Exploration," *Wall Street Journal*, November 9, 2010, http://online.wsj.com/article/AP76827f5c7ea547bbal8a9b68d20a50e5.html.

376. Chesapeake Energy, "Chesapeake Energy Corporation Discloses Initial Horizontal Well Drilling Results in Its Utica Shale Discovery and Announces Achievement of Corporate Production Milestones," news release, http://www.chk.com/News/Articles/Pages/1610725.aspx

377. "Utica Shale Wells' Gas Yield Called 'Phenomenal,'" *Bloomberg News*, September 30, 2011, http://www.pittsburghlive.com/x/pittsburghtrib/s_759423.html.

378. Dave Elias, "ExxonMobil Announces Plans to Drill in Jefferson, Harrison Counties,"*WTRF*, July 14, 2011, http://www.wtrf.com/story.cfm?func=viewstory&storyid=103310.

379. Ryan Dezember, "Utica Shale Energizes Deal Frenzy in Ohio," *Wall Street Journal*, September 27, 2011, http://online.wsj.com/article/SB10001424052970204010604576592783750697202.html.

380. David Robinson, "National Fuel Profit Rises 44% with Help from Marcellus Gas," *Buffalo News*, May 7, 2011, http://www.buffalonews.com/business/article416202.ece and Jeremy Johnson, "Utica test well being drilled in Polk," *Franklin News-Herald*, Franklin, Pa., September 9, 2011, 1.

381. "Rex Energy Drills First Utica Shale Well in W. Pa.," *Associated Press, Centre Daily Times*, State College, Pa., November 1, 2011, http://www.centredaily.com/2011/11/01/2971250/rex-energy-drills-first-utica.html#ixzz1cZfzAw00.

382. Elizabeth Skrapits, "Expert: Finding Natural Gas in Utica Shale is Unlikely; More 'Overcooked' than Marcellus," *Citizens Voice*, Wilkes Barre, Pa., May 9, 2011, http://citizensvoice.com/news/expert-finding-natural-gas-in-utica-shale-is-unlikely-more-overcooked-than-marcellus-1.1143799.

383. "Upper Devonian May Hold as Much Gas as Marcellus Shale: Range Executive," *Platts*, Houston, Tx., September 28, 2011, http://www.platts.com/RSS-FeedDetailedNews/RSSFeed/NaturalGas/6531422.

384. Andrew Maykuth, "Firms Find More Gas Beyond the Marcellus Field," *Philadelphia Inquirer*, May 23, 2010, 1.

385. U.S. Department of Transportation, Research and Innovative Technology Administration, Bureau of Transportation Statistics, "Transport Statistics by Mode," January 2011, http://www.bts.gov/publications/national_transportation_statistics/html/table_02_01.html.

386. Federal Energy Regulatory Commission, Office of Energy Projects, http://www.ferc.gov/industries/gas/gen-info/horizon-pipe.pdf.

387. Kaitlynn Riely, "Natural Gas Expansion Fuels $21B Pipeline Deal," *Pittsburgh Post-Gazette*, October 17, 2011, http://www.post-gazette.com/pg/11290/1182766-84-0.stm.

388. Energy Information Administration, "Emissions of Greenhouse Gases in the U.S," (2011), http://www.eia.doe.gov/environment/emissions/ghg_report/ghg_overview.cfm.

389. EIA Annual Outlook (2011). See note 4.

390. "The Future of Natural Gas," xiii. See note 39.

391. Clifford Krauss, "Breaking Away From Coal," *New York Times*, November 29, 2010, http://www.nytimes.com/2010/11/30/business/energy-environment/30utilities.html; and "Pa. Plant to Convert Generators from Coal to Gas," Associated Press, *The Bradford E*ra, December 29, 2011, p. 5.

392. Amy Myers Jaffe, "Shale Gas Will Rock the World," *Wall Street Journal*, May 10, 2010, R-1.

393. Alyssa Murphy, "Natural Gas Power Plants Planned Locally," July 13, 2011, *Williamsport Sun-Gazette*, Williamsport, Pa., http://www.sungazette.com/page/content.detail/id/566237/Natural-gas-power-plants-planned-locally.html.

394. Bruce Kauffmann, "Natural Gas is Efficient, Don't Let Your Energy Melt Away," *True Blue Natural Gas*, December 1, 2009, www.truebluenaturalgas.org/natural-gas-efficient-energy-melt-away.

395. Bert Kalisch, "Rethinking the Power Industry's Dash to Gas," *Power*, April 1, 2010, http://www.powermag.com/issues/departments/commentary/Rethinking-the-Power-Industrys-Dash-to-Gas_2580.html.

396. Erik Heinrich, "After an Oil Calamity, Is It Time for Natural Gas?" *Time*, June 15, 2010, http://www.time.com/time/business/article/0,8599,1995119,00.html.

397. John Deutch, "The Natural Gas Revolution," *Wall Street Journal*, July 16, 2010, A-13.

398. IEA, International Energy Agency, (2010) "The Contribution of Natural Gas Vehicles to Sustainable Transport," IEA Working Paper, OECD/IEA, Paris in "IEA, International Energy Agency, (2011), "Are We Entering the Golden Age of Natural Gas?," Paris, http://www.marcellus.psu.edu/resources/PDFs/IEA_GoldenAge.pdf, 118.

399. Dave Michaels, "Obama Endorses Pickens Plan for Natural Gas Vehicles," *Dallas News*, March 30, 2011, http://www.dallasnews.com/business/energy/20110330-obama-endorses-pickens-plan-for-natural-gas-vehicles.ece.

400. Ben Casselman, "Cheasapeake Will Invest In Uses for Natural Gas," *Wall Street Journal*, July 12, 2011, B-4.

401. Justin Juozapavicius, "Energy Magnate Pickens Defends Drilling," *Bloomberg Business Week*, April 20, 2010, http://www.businessweek.com/ap/financialnews/D9MNK6CO1.htm.

402. Matt Ridley, "The Shale Gas Shock," *Global Warming Policy Foundation*, 2011, 31, http://www.marcellus.psu.edu/resources/PDFs/shalegas_GWPF.pdf.

403. United States Geological Survey, "USGS Releases New Assessment of Gas Resources in the Marcellus Shale, Appalachian Basin."

404. Casey Junkins, "Driller: Ohio, Marshall Counties More Valuable," *The Intelligencer/Wheeling News-Register*, Wheeling, W.Va., March 31, 2011, http://www.news-register.net/page/content.detail/id/553611/Driller—Ohio—Marshall-Counties-More-Valuable.html.

405. Michael Schaal, "The Shale Gas Industry: Short Term, EIA Response to 6/17/11 New York Times inquiry on Shale Gas," Energy Information Administration, June 20, 2011, http://www.eia.gov/pressroom/releases/pdf/shale_gas.pdf.

406. "W.Va. Begins Look at Marcellus Offshoot Project," *Charleston Daily Mail*, Charleston, W.Va., May 4, 2011, http://www.dailymail.com/ap/ApTopStories/201105040874.

407. "Shell Planning Unit for Marcellus Shale Processing," *Wall Street Journal*, June 6, 2011, http://online.wsj.com/article/AP1be36f40093e4ff8899695f67b6e3a57.html.

408. Lauren Lawley Head, "Marcellus Shale Means Big Business for Chemical Industry," *Pittsburgh Business Times*, October 6, 2011, http://www.bizjournals.com/pittsburgh/blog/energy/2011/10/marcellus-shale-means-big-chemical-biz.html.

409. Andrew Maykuth, "Intriguing Possibility for Pa.'s Excess Shale Gas," *Philadelphia Inquirer*, July 3, 2011, http://articles.philly.com/2011-07-03/business/29733216_1_shale-gas-marcellus-shale-coalition-natural-gas.

410. "Tide Turns at Niagara from U.S. Imports to Marcellus Shale Exports, NGI Reports," *Wall Street Journal*, September 13, 2011, http://www.marketwatch.com/story/tide-turns-at-niagara-from-us-imports-to-marcellus-shale-exports-ngi-reports-2011-09-13.

411. Matthew Kemeny, "Virginia Firm Wants to Export Marcellus Shale's Gas," *The Patriot-News*, Harrisburg, Pa., October 9, 2011, http://www.pennlive.com/midstate/index.ssf/2011/10/virginia_firm_wants_to_export.html.

412. Annual Energy Outlook, (2011). See note 4.

413. Christina L. Madden, "Shale Gas's Fractured Hope," *Asia Times*, October 28, 2010, http://atimes.com/atimes/Global_Economy/LJ28Dj03.html.

414. Jeff Esheman and Chris Tucker, "Shale Goes Global," *Financial Journal*, August 26, 2010, http://www.ogfj.com/ogfj/en-us/index/article-tools-template.articles.oil-gas-financialjournal.special-feature-shale-goes-global.Shale-Goes-Global.html.

415. Gordon Hamilton, "B.C. Shale Gas Holds Promise of New Era in Resource Investment," *Vancouver Sun*, March 14, 2011, http://www.vancouversun.com/technology/shale+holds+promise+resource+investment/4434641/story.html.

416. Jacqueline MacKenzie, "Shale Gas Could be Game Changer for African Energy," *Business Live*, March 31, 2011, http://www.businesslive.co.za/incoming/2011/03/31/shale-gas-could-be-game-changer-for-african-energy.

417. "Poland a Shale Gas Giant?" *Warsaw Business Journal*, April 8, 2011, http://www.wbj.pl/article-54049-poland-a-shale-gas-giant.html.

418. Dinakar Sethuraman, "China's Shale Gas 12 Times Conventional Gas Reserves, EIA Says," *Business Week*, April 6, 2011, http://www.businessweek.com/news/2011-04-06/china-s-shale-gas-12-times-conventional-gas-reserves-eia-says.html.

419. Matt Chambers, "A Fracking Good Deal on Aussie Shale Gas," *The Australian*, July 14, 2011, http://www.theaustralian.com.au/business/news/a-fracking-good-deal-on-aussie-shale-gas/story-e6frg906-1226094181189.

420. Daniel Fisher, "Shale Gas Means Flat Prices Till 2020," *Forbes*, http://blogs.forbes.com/energysources/2010/09/22/shale-gas-means-flat-prices-til-2020.

421. Medlock, Kenneth B., Jaffe, Amy and Hartley, Peter, "Shale Gas and U.S. Energy Security," James A. Baker III Institute for Public Policy, Rice University, July 2011, http://www.bakerinstitute.org/publications/EF-pub-DOEShaleGas-07192011.pdf.

422. "IEA, International Energy Agency, (2011), "Are We Entering the Golden Age of Natural Gas?" Paris, http://www.marcellus.psu.edu/resources/PDFs/IEA_GoldenAge.pdf, 25.

Epilogue

1. Donald Rumsfeld, *Known and Unknown: A Memoir* (New York: Sentinel, 2011).

2. Annual Energy Outlook, (2011). See note 4.

3. "The Outlook for Energy: A View to 2030," ExxonMobil Corporation, (2010), http://www.exxonmobil.com/corporate/files/news_pub_eo_2010.pdf.

4. Roger Cooper, "Natural Gas Reconsidered," Progressive Policy Institute (July 2011).

5. Kerry O'Shea, "Environmental Review Natural Gas Production from Lake Erie," *Joint Ontario — New York Oil & Gas Conference*, Abstracts, October 24, 2002.

Selected Bibliography

American Gas Association. *History of the Natural Gas Industry.* n.p., n.d.

_____. *Story of Gas: A Brief Sketch of the Manufactured and Natural Gas Industry.* New York: circa 1956.

_____. *Story of Natural Gas Energy.* n.p., n.d.

Anton, Mark J. *Suburban Propane Gas Association: The Development of a Selectively Positioned Energy Company.* New York: The Newcomen Society in North America, 1982.

Ashley, George H., and J. French Robinson. *Oil and Gas Fields of Pennsylvania* 1, Introduction. Harrisburg: Pennsylvania Geological Services, 1922.

Babcock, Charles A. *Venango County Pennsylvania, Her Pioneers and People, Embracing a General History of the County.* Chicago: J. H. Beers, 1919.

Baker, Ron. *A Primer of Oilwell Drilling,* 6th Edition. Austin: Petroleum Extension Service, The University of Texas at Austin Continuing & Extended Education, 2001.

Baldwin, Leland D. *Pittsburgh: The Story of a City 1750–1865.* Pittsburgh: University of Pittsburgh Press, 1937.

Baltimore Gas and Electric Company. *Baltimore Gas and Electric Company.* n.p.: Publication Press, 1958.

Barron, Lee. *Westinghouse Centennial 1886–1986, Baltimore Divisions & Contracts Management: A History.* n.p.: Barron, 1985.

Berger, Bill D., and Kenneth E. Anderson. *Modern Petroleum: A Basic Primer of the Industry.* Tulsa: PennWell Books, 1981.

Boyle, P.C., ed. *The Derrick's Handbook of Petroleum.* Oil City, PA: Derrick Publishing, 1898.

Bradley, Robert L., Jr. *Oil, Gas & Government, The U.S. Experience,* 2 Vols. Latham, MD: Rowman & Littlefield, 1996.

Brannt, William T. *Petroleum: Its History, Origin, Occurrence, Production, Physical and Chemical Constitution, Technology, Examination and Uses; Together with the Occurrence and Uses of Natural Gas.* Philadelphia: Henry Carey Baird, 1895.

Brice, William R. *Myth, Legend, Reality: Edwin Laurentine Drake and the Early Oil Industry.* Chicora, Pa.: Mechling, 2009

Brignano, Mary, and Hax McCullough. *Spirit and Progress: The Story of the East Ohio Gas Company and the People Who Made It.* Cleveland: East Ohio Gas Company, 1988.

Brown, E. C., comp. *Brown's Directory of American Gas Companies.* Philadelphia: Progressive Age Publishing, 1887.

Brown, George W. *Old Times in Oildom.* Oil City: Derrick Publishing, 1909.

Brown, Keith C., ed. *Regulation of the Natural Gas Producing Industry.* Baltimore: The Johns Hopkins University Press, 1972.

Bryce, Robert. *Pipedreams: Greed, Ego and the Death of Enron.* New York: Public Affairs, 2002.

Bufkin, I. David. *Texas Eastern Corporation: A Pioneering Spirit.* New York: Newcomen Society of America, 1983.Cardwell, Dudley H. *Oil and Gas Fields of West Virginia.* n.p.: West Virginia Geological and Economic Survey, 1977.

Castaneda, Christopher, J. *Invisible Fuel: Manufactured and Natural Gas in America, 1800–2000.* New York: Twayne Publishers, 1999.

_____. *Regulated Enterprise: Natural Gas Pipelines and Northeastern Markets, 1938–1954.* Columbus: Ohio State University Press, 1993.

_____, and Joseph A. Pratt. *From Texas to the East: A Strategic History of Texas Eastern Corporation.* College Station: Texas A&M University Press, 1993.

_____, and Clarance M. Smith. *Gas Pipelines and the Emergence of America's Regulatory State: A History of the Panhandle Eastern Corporation 1928–1993.* New York: Cambridge University Press, 1996.

Chemung Canal Trust Company. *125th Anniversary*. Elmira, NY: Chemung Canal Trust Company, 1958.

Chernow, Ron. *Titan: The Life of John D. Rockefeller, Sr.* New York: Random House, 1998.

Clark, James A. *The Chronological History of the Petroleum and Natural Gas Industries*. Houston: Clark Books, 1963.

Clark, Mabel K. *Titusville: An Illustrated History*. Titusville: Titusville Area School District, 1993.

CNG Transmission Corporation, Hope Gas Inc. *From Gas Lights to New Energy Heights, 1898–1998: 100 Years of Service Excellence*. Clarksburg, WV: CNG Transmission Corporation, 1998.

Columbia Gulf Transmission Company. *History of Natural Gas Transmission*. n.p., 1971.

Columbus Group of Columbia Gas and Electric Corporation. *A Course of Practical Information on the Natural Gas Business, Part I*. Cincinnati: Natural Gas Publishing, 1933.

_____. *An Employee Manual on the Natural Gas Business*. Cincinnati: Natural Gas Publishing, 1933.

Columbus Group of the Columbia Gas System. *A Hand Book of Practical Information Concerning the Natural Gas Industry*. n.p.: Columbus Group of the Columbia Gas System, 1934.

Commonwealth of Pennsylvania. *Pennsylvania's Mineral Heritage: The Commonwealth at the Economic Crossroads of Her Industrial Development*. Topographic and Geologic Survey. Harrisburg, PA: Department of Internal Affairs Bureau of Statistics, 1944.

Conaway, Charles F. *The Petroleum Industry: A Nontechnical Guide*. Tulsa: PennWell Publishing, 1999.

Cravath, Paul D. *George Westinghouse Commemoration: A Forum Presenting the Career and Achievements of George Westinghouse on the 90th Anniversary of his Birth*. New York: American Society of Mechanical Engineers, 1937.

Crum, A. R., and A. S. Dugan, eds. *Romance of American Petroleum and Gas*. New York: Derrick Publishing, 1911.

Darrah, William Culp. *Pithole: The Vanished City: A Story of the Early Days of the Petroleum Industry*. n.p.: Published by the author, 1972.

Dawson, Albert F. *Columbia System: A History*. New York: J. J. Little and Ives, 1937.

East Ohio Gas Company. *A History of the East Ohio Gas Company: 50 Years of Service 1898–1948*. n.p.: East Ohio Gas Company, 1948.

Eaton, S. J. M. *Petroleum — A History of the Oil Region of Venango County, Pennsylvania*. Philadelphia: J. Skelly, 1860.

Ebright, John E., Chas. R. Fettke, and Albert I. Ingham. *East Fork–Wharton Gas Field, Potter County Pennsylvania*. Topographic and Geologic Survey, Bulletin M 30. Harrisburg: Commonwealth of Pennsylvania, Department of Internal Affairs, 1949.

_____, and Albert I. Ingham. *Geology of the Leidy Gas Field and Adjacent Areas, Clinton County Pa*. Topographic and Geologic Survey, Bulletin M 34. Harrisburg: Commonwealth of Pennsylvania, Department of Internal Affairs, 1951.

Empire Gas and Fuel Company Ltd. and Bradley Producing Corporation. *Empire Bradley 75th Anniversary*. n.p.: Empire Gas and Fuel Company, 1956.

An Energy Policy for Pennsylvania. Harrisburg, PA: Pennsylvania Energy Office, 1988.

Federal Energy Administration. *The Natural Gas Story*. Washington, D.C.: Federal Energy Administration, 1975.

Fettke, Chas. R. *Summarized Record of Deep Wells in Pennsylvania*, Topographic and Geological Survey, Bulletin M 31. Harrisburg: Commonwealth of Pennsylvania, Department of Internal Affairs, 1950.

Fitzpatrick, John C., ed. *The Diaries of George Washington, 1748–1799*. New York: Houghton Mifflin, 1928.

Flowers, Edward B. *U.S. Utility Mergers and the Restructuring of the New Global Power Industry*. Westport, CT: Quorum Books, 1998.

Frey, John W., and H. Chandler Ide. *A History of the Petroleum Administration for War, 1941–1945*. Washington, DC: United States Government Printing Office, 1946.

Full, Adelheid, comp. *Corporate History of Dominion Natural Gas Company, Ltd. and Underlying Companies, 1854–1955*. Buffalo, NY: Dominion Natural Gas Company, 1956.

Gallick, Edward C. *Competition in the Natural Gas Pipeline Industry: An Economic Policy Analysis*. Westport, CT: Praeger, 1993.

Giddens, Paul H. *The American Petroleum Industry — Its Beginnings in Pennsylvania!* New York: The Newcomen Society in North America, 1959.

_____. *The Beginnings of the Petroleum Industry Sources and Bibliography*. Harrisburg: Pennsylvania Historical Commission, 1941.

_____. *Pennsylvania Petroleum: 1750–1872, A Documentary History*. Titusville: Commonwealth of Pennsylvania, Drake Well Memorial Park, 1947.

Governor's Energy Council. *The Pennsylvania*

Energy Profile, 1960–1979. Harrisburg: Commonwealth of Pennsylvania, 1982.

Hall, James. *The Structural and Economic Geology of Erie County, N.Y.*, n.p., n.d.

Harrison, Lowell H., and James C. Klotter. *A New History of Kentucky*. Lexington: University Press of Kentucky, 1997.

Hart, F. Donald. *American Gas Association*. New York: Newcomen Society in North America, 1974.

Heiney, J. W. *The Story of Indiana Gas Company, Inc*. New York: Newcomen Society in North America, 1972.

Henry, J. T. *The Early and Later History of Petroleum with Authentic Facts in Regard to its Development in Western Pennsylvania*. Philadelphia: Jas. B. Rodgers, 1873.

Herbert, John H. *Clean Cheap Heat: The Development of Residential Markets for Natural Gas in the United States*. New York: Praeger, 1992.

Herrick, John P. *Empire Oil: The Story of Oil in New York State*. New York: Dodd, Mead, 1949.

Hidy, Ralph W., and Muriel E. Hidy. *Pioneering in Big Business: History of Standard Oil Company New Jersey, 1882–1911*. New York: Harper and Brothers, 1955.

History of Allegheny County, Pennsylvania. Chicago: A. Warner, 1889.

History of Venango County Pennsylvania 1, Its Past and Present. Chicago: Brown, Runk, 1890.

Holder, Thomas. *A Complete Record of Niagara Falls and Vicinage*. n.p.: 1882.

Hope Natural Gas Company, *Seventy-fifth Anniversary*, Clarksburg, WV: Consolidated Gas Supply Corporation, 1973.

Ingham, A. I., W. S. Lytle, L. S. Matteson, and R. E. Sherrill. *Oil and Gas Geology of the Sheffield Quadrangle, Pennsylvania*. Harrisburg: Pennsylvania Geological Survey, 4th Series, Bulletin M 38, 1956.

Jillson, Willard Rouse. *Natural Gas in Eastern Kentucky*. Louisville, KY: Standard Printing, 1937.

Jonnes, Jill. *Empires of Light: Edison, Tesla, Westinghouse, and the Race to Electrify the World*. New York: Random House, 2003.

Kelso, J. Richard. *The Spirit of Progress: The Story of the East Ohio Gas Company and the People Who Made It*. New York: The Newcomen Society of North America, 1988.

Kentucky: A Guide to the Bluegrass State. Compiled and written by the Federal Writers Project of the Work Projects Administration for the State of Kentucky. New York: Hastings House, 1954.

Knowles, Ruth Sheldon. *The First Pictorial History of the American Oil and Gas Industry, 1859–1983*. Athens: Ohio University Press, 1983.

_____. *The Greatest Gamblers: The Epic of American Oil Exploration*. New York: McGraw-Hill, 1959.

Krass, Peter. *Carnegie*. New York: John Wiley & Sons, 2002.

Kurlansky, Mark. *Salt: A World History*. New York: Walker and Company, 2002.

Landes, Kenneth K. *Petroleum Geology of the United States*. New York: Wiley-Interscience, 1970.

Larson, Elwin S. *Brooklyn Union Gas*. New York: Newcomen Society of North America, 1987.

Lauriston, Victor. *Blue Flame of Service: A History of Union Gas Company and the Natural Gas Industry in Southwestern Ontario*. Union Gas Company of Canada, Ltd., n.d.

Lee, Howard B. *Burning Springs and Other Tales of the Little Kanawha*. Morgantown, WV: West Virginia University, 1968.

Leif, Alfred. *Metering for America: 125 Years of the Gas Industry and American Meter Company*. New York: Appleton-Century Crofts, 1961.

Leonard, John W., D. S. Wakenight, H. L. Wood, Abel S. Dungan, Ben M. Talbott, Edwin C. Bell, Francis Lynch, R. F. Randolph, Victor Lauriston, and Chester T. Crowell, eds. *Romance of American Petroleum and Gas 2*. New York, J. J. Little & Ives, n.d.

Leupp, Francis E. *George Westinghouse: His Life and Achievements*. London: John Murray, 1919.

Lorant, Stefan. *Pittsburgh: The Story of an American City*. Lenox, MA: R. R. Donnelley & Sons, 1975.

Lytle, William S. *Underground Storage of Natural Gas in Pennsylvania*. Harrisburg: Pennsylvania Geological Survey, 4th series, Bulletin M 46, 1963.

MacAvoy, Paul W. *The Natural Gas Market: Sixty Years of Regulation and Deregulation*. New Haven, CT: Yale University Press, 2000.

McCullough, Hax, and Mary Brignano. *The Vision and Will to Succeed: A Centennial History of the Peoples Natural Gas Company*. n.p.: Peoples Natural Gas, n.d.

McFarlan, Arthur C. *Geology of Kentucky*. Lexington, KY: The University of Kentucky, 1961.

McGlade, William G. *Oil and Gas Geology of the Amity and Claysville Quadrangle of Pennsylvania*. Harrisburg: Pennsylvania Geological Survey, 4th Series, 1967.

McKain, David L., and Bernard L. Allen. *Where It All Began: The Story of the People and Places Where the Oil and Gas Industry Began, West Virginia and Southeastern Ohio*. Parkersburg, WV: Parkersburg Oil & Gas Museum, 1994.

McLaurin, John J. *Sketches in Crude-Oil: Some Accidents and Incidents of the Petroleum Development in all Parts of the Globe*. Harrisburg, PA: Published by the Author, 1896.

Miller, Ernest C. *A List of Unusual Books and Scarce Material Related to the Early History and Development of the Petroleum Industry*. Catalogue One. London: n.d.

_____. *Oily Daze at Cherry Grove*. Warren, PA: Newell Press, 1942.

_____. *Pennsylvania's Oil Industry*. Gettysburg: Pennsylvania Historical Association, 1959.

_____. *Tintypes in Oil*. Rutland, VT: Charles E. Tuttle, 1961.

Munn, M. J. *The Menifee Gas Field and the Ragland Oil Field, Kentucky*. Washington, D.C.: Government Printing Office, Department of the Interior, United States Geological Survey, Bulletin 531A, 1913.

Murphy, Blakely M., ed. *Conservation of Oil and Gas: A Legal History, 1948*. Chicago: American Bar Association, 1949.

National Fuel Gas Company. *A Brief History*. n.p., n.d.

_____. *Convenience ... Comfort ... Economy*. New York: William E. Rudge's Sons, 1955.

Natural Gas: A Survey of One of America's Great Public Utilities. New York: G. E. Barrett, 1927.

Nevins, Allan. *John D. Rockefeller: A Study in Power*. 2 Vols. New York: Charles Scribner's Sons, 1953.

New York State Electric and Gas Corporation. *Celebrating a Century of Service*. n.p.: New York State Electric and Gas Corporation, 1952.

Newell, John H. *The Origin and Founders of the Hope Natural Gas Company*. n.p., n.d.

Nichols, H. Stuart. *The Natural Gas Story from the Ground Down: The History of National Fuel Gas Company*. New York: Newcomen Society in North America, 1963.

Norman, Oscar E. *The Romance of the Gas Industry*. Chicago: A. C. McClurg, 1922.

Oppenheimer, Ernest J. *Natural Gas the New Energy Leader*, Revised Edition. New York: Pen & Podium, 1985.

Owen, Edgar Wesley. *Trek of the Oil Finders: A History of Exploration for Petroleum*. Tulsa, OK: The American Association of Petroleum Geologists, 1975.

Paine, Albert Bigelow. *Mark Twain*. New York: 1912.

Parker, Jenny Marsh. *Rochester: A Story Historical*. Rochester, NY: Scrantom, Wetmore, 1884.

Payne, Darwin. *Initiative in Energy: Dresser Industries, Inc., 1880–1978*. New York: Simon and Schuster, 1979.

Phillips, Ed. *Guts & Guile: True Tales from the Backrooms of the Pipeline Industry*. Vancouver: Douglas & McIntyre, 1990.

Pittsburgh and the Pittsburgh Spirit. Addresses at the Chamber of Commerce of Pittsburgh, 1927–1928.

Pittsburg Leader. *Pittsburg at the Dawn of the 20th Century: The Busiest City in the World*. Allegheny, PA: Jos. T. Colvin & Co. Printers, circa 1901.

Poth, Charles W. *The Occurrence of Brine in Western Pennsylvania*. Topographic and Geologic Survey, Bulletin M 47. Harrisburg: Commonwealth of Pennsylvania, Department of Internal Affairs, 1962.

Pure Oil Trust vs. Standard Oil Company; United States Industrial Commission: Compiled from Private and Official Sources by the Oil City Derrick, 1899–1900. Oil City, PA: Derrick Publishing Co., 1901.

Rockefeller, John D. *Random Reminiscences of Men and Events*. New York: Doubleday, Doran, 1933.

Roen, John B., and Brian J. Walker, eds. *The Atlas of Major Appalachian Gas Plays*. n.p.: Appalachian Oil and Natural Gas Research Consortium, 1996.

Rose, William Ganson. *Cleveland: The Making of a City*. Cleveland: World Publishing, 1950.

Roseboom, Eugene H. and Francis P. Weisenburger. *A History of Ohio*. Columbus: The Ohio State Archaeological and Historical Society, 1954.

Sanders, Elizabeth M. *The Regulation of Natural Gas: Policy and Politics, 1938–1978*. Philadelphia: Temple University Press, 1981.

Sanford, Laura G. *History of Erie County Pennsylvania*. Published by the Author, 1894.

Schultz, Charles H. ed. *The Geology of Pennsylvania*. Harrisburg: Pennsylvania Geological Survey and Pittsburgh Geological Society, 1999.

Silverberg, Robert. *Light for the World: Edison and the Power Industry*. New York: D. Van Nostrand, 1967.

Sisler, J. D., G. H. Ashley, F. T. Moyer, and W. O. Hickok. *Contributions to Oil and Gas Geology of Western Pennsylvania*. Harrisburg: Pennsylvania Geological Survey, 4th Series, Bulletin M 19, 1933.

Skinner, John F. *A History of New York State*

Natural Gas Corporation, 1913–1965. Clarksburg, WV: CNG Transmission Corporation, 1990.

Smith, H. Perry, ed. *History of the City of Buffalo and Erie County, 2.* Syracuse, NY: D. Mason, 1884.

Spellman, Paul N. *Spindletop Boom Days.* College Station: Texas A & M University Press, 2001.

Spencer, Herbert Reynolds. *Erie ... A History.* n.p.: Published by the author, 1962.

Springborn, Harold W. *The Story of Natural Gas Energy.* n.p.: American Gas Association, 1970.

Stephens, Maynard M., and Oscar F. Spencer. *Petroleum and Natural Gas Production.* University Park: Pennsylvania State University, 1957.

Stevens, Sylvester K. *Pennsylvania: Titan of Industry, 3.* New York: Lewis Historical Publishing Company, 1948.

Stotz, Louis, and Alexander Jamison. *History of the Gas Industry.* New York: Stettiner Bros., 1938.

Supply and Conservation of Natural Gas in the State of Pennsylvania: Proceedings before the Public Service Commission of the Commonwealth of Pennsylvania at Pittsburgh, Pa., January 8, 1919. Harrisburg, PA: J. L. L. Kuhn, 1919.

Tarbell, Ida M. *All In The Day's Work: An Autobiography.* New York: Macmillian, 1939.

_____. *The History of the Standard Oil Company,* briefer version edited by David M. Chalmers. New York: W. W. Norton, 1966.

Temple, Robert K. G. *The Genius of China: 3,000 Years of Science, Discovery and Invention.* New York: Simon and Schuster, 1986.

Thoenen, Eugene D. *History of the Oil and Gas Industry in West Virginia.* Charleston, WV: Education Foundation, 1964.

Thomas, Ralph N. *Devonian Shale Gas Production in Central Appalachian Area.* Lexington: Kentucky Geological Survey, University of Kentucky College of Arts and Sciences, 1951.

UGI Corporation, *The First 100 Years: UGI Corporation.* n.p.: UGI Corporation, 1982.

U.S. Department of the Interior, Bureau of Mines. *Minerals Yearbook.* Washington: U.S. Government Printing Office, various years.

Wagner, W. R., and W. S. Lytle. *Geology of Pennsylvania's Oil and Gas.* Topographic and Geologic Survey. Harrisburg: Commonwealth of Pennsylvania, 1968.

Waverman, Leonard. *Natural Gas and National Policy: A Linear Programming Model of North American Natural Gas Flows.* Toronto: University of Toronto Press, 1973.

Weaver, Elbert C. *The Story of Gas.* New York: American Gas Association, 1964.

Westcott, Henry P. *Handbook of Natural Gas,* 3rd edition. Erie, PA: Metric Metal Works, 1920.

Williamson, Harold F., and Arnold R. Daum. *The American Petroleum Industry: The Age of Illumination, 1859–1899.* Evanston, IL: Northwestern University Press, 1959.

_____, Ralph L. Andreano, Arnold R. Daum, and Gilbert C. Klose. *The American Petroleum Industry: The Age of Energy Vol. 1 1865–1899.* Evanston, IL: Northwestern University Press, 1959.

_____. *The American Petroleum Industry: The Age of Energy Vol. 2 1899–1959.* Evanston, IL: Northwestern University Press, 1963.

Yergin, Daniel. *The Prize: The Epic Quest for Oil, Money & Power.* New York: Simon & Schuster, 1991.

_____. *The Quest: Energy, Security, and the Remaking of the Modern World.* New York: Penguin, 2011.

Zwetsch, H. D. *A Brief History of the Natural Gas Industry.* New York: Zwetch, Heinzelmann, 1927.

Encyclopedias and Other Reference Works

Bartlett's Familiar Quotations. John Bartlett, and Justin Kaplan, eds. 16th Edition. Boston: Little Brown, 1992.

Glossary for the Gas Industry. American Gas Association Bureau of Statistics. New York: American Gas Association, 1967.

International Directory of Company Histories 5. V. Adele Hart, ed. Detroit: St. James Press, 1992.

International Directory of Company Histories 6. Paula Kepos, ed. Detroit: St. James Press, 1992.

Merriam-Webster's Collegiate Encyclopedia. Mark A. Stephens, ed. Springfield, MA: Merriam-Webster, 2000.

The Oxford Dictionary of Word Histories. Glynnis Chantrell, ed. Oxford: Oxford University Press, 2002.

Index